"This is a book of extraordinary richness. I found myself amused, diverted and enchanted by turn. For Tom Holland has an enviable gift for summoning up the colour, the individuals and animation of the past, without sacrificing factual integrity. He writes with a contagious conviction that history is not only a fascinating tale in itself but is a well-honed instrument with which we can understand our neighbours and our own times, maybe even ourselves. He is also a divertingly inventive writer with a wicked wit—there's something of both Gibbon and Tom Wolfe in his writing. *In the Shadow of the Sword* remains a spell-bindingly brilliant multiple portrait of the triumph of monotheism in the ancient world."

—*The Independent* (London)

"This is a handsome volume, tackling an important question from a novel perspective." —*Sunday Telegraph* (London)

"Holland tells a complex story, dotted with names and places leagues beyond the realm of popular recognition. Yet he makes it unmistakably his own. He is one of the most distinctive prose stylists writing history today, and he drags his tale by the ears, conjuring the half-vanished past with such gusto that characters and places fairly bound from the page. *In the Shadow of the Sword* may reach provocative conclusions, but it is also a work of impressive sensitivity and scholarship." —*The Telegraph* (London)

"An exhilarating read because Holland succeeds in capturing much of the excitement, strangeness and importance of a long past age. It is difficult not to be bedazzled." —*Financial Times* (London)

"An ambitious and important book. . . . His excellent book will be lauded, as it should be for doing what the best sort of books can do—examining holy cows." —*The Observer* (London)

Tom Holland

IN THE SHADOW OF THE SWORD

Historian Tom Holland is the author of the nonfiction works of history *Rubicon*, *Persian Fire*, and *The Forge of Christendom*. *Rubicon* was shortlisted for the Samuel Johnson Prize and won the 2004 Hessell-Tiltman Prize for History, and *Persian Fire* won the Anglo-Hellenic League's 2006 Runciman Award.

www.tom-holland.org

IN THE SHADOW
OF THE SWORD

*The Birth of Islam and the Rise
of the Global Arab Empire*

Tom Holland

ANCHOR BOOKS
A Division of Random House, Inc.
New York

FIRST ANCHOR BOOKS EDITION, FEBRUARY 2013

Copyright © 2012 by Tom Holland

All rights reserved. Published in the United States by Anchor Books,
a division of Random House, Inc., New York. Originally published in Great Britain
by Little, Brown, a division of Hachette U.K., London, and subsequently published
in hardcover in the United States by Doubleday, a division of
Random House, Inc., New York, in 2012.

Anchor Books and colophon are registered trademarks of Random House, Inc.

The Library of Congress has cataloged the Doubleday edition as follows:
Holland, Tom.
In the shadow of the sword : the birth of Islam and the rise of the global Arab
empire / Tom Holland.—1st U.S. ed.
p. cm.
Includes bibliographical references and index.
1. Islamic Empire—History. 2. Islam—History. I. Title.
DS36.85.H65 2012
956'.013—dc23
2012000207

Anchor ISBN: 978-0-307-47365-3

Author photograph © Sadie Holland

www.anchorbooks.com

Printed in the United States of America

To Hillos
In memoriam

Contents

Acknowledgements

This is a book that has taken me a horribly long time to complete, and opened my eyes to entire realms of complexity and fascination that I had little idea existed when I first embarked upon the project. The debts of gratitude that I owe are correspondingly immense. Firstly, to my editor, Richard Beswick; to Iain Hunt, Susan de Soissons, and everyone at Little, Brown; to Gerry Howard; to Teresa Löwe-Bahners; and to Frits van der Meij. My thanks as well to that best of agents, Patrick Walsh, and to everyone at Conville and Walsh. Whether as a pygmy standing on the shoulders of giants, or as a fool rushing in where angels fear to tread, I owe a particular due to the scholars who have helped me to negotiate a field of historical study that is, perhaps, more interestingly seeded with landmines than any other. Reza Aslan, James Carleton Paget, Patricia Crone, Vesta Curtis, Gerald Hawting, Robert Irwin, Christopher Kelly, Hugh Kennedy, Dan Madigan, Ziauddin Sardar, Guy Stroumsa and Bryan Ward-Perkins all read parts or the whole of the first draft—with responses as varied as their kindness and generosity were unfailing. I am grateful as well to Fred Donner and Robert Hoyland for allowing me to pick their brains in private conversations, and to Robin Lane Fox for stiffening my backbone at a time when I was first waking up to the full scale of the challenge I had taken on. Like an infinitely greater historian than myself, "I must profess my total ignorance of the Oriental tongues, and my gratitude to the learned interpreters, who have transfused their science into the Latin, French, and English languages." Translations from Arabic and Syriac were done for me by Salam Rassi, in whom prodigious learning goes hand in glove with remarkable patience and efficiency. Andrea Wulf, as ever, made good my lamentable lack of German. Last but not last, I must thank friends and family for putting up with five years of crazed mutterings about Hephthalites, Chalcedonians and Kharijites. Particular thanks, as ever, to Jamie Muir, for all his unstinting support, encouragement and advice; to Kevin Sim, who provided such a close and brilliant reading of the manuscript that he somehow managed to extract a film from it, and is now the person I automatically turn to whenever my desire to discuss Umayyad coinage becomes uncontrollable; and, of course, last but very much not least, to my beloved family—Sadie, Katy and Eliza.

Maps

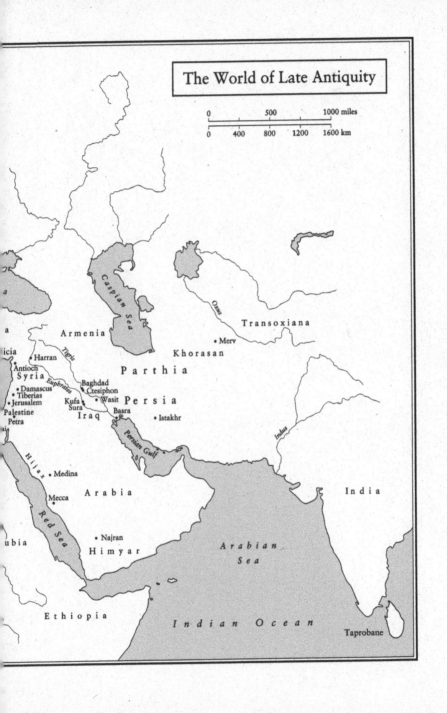

The World of Late Antiquity

0   500   1000 miles

0   400   800   1200   1600 km

Caspian Sea

Armenia

Oxus

Transoxiana

• Merv

Khorasan

icia

• Harran

Tigris

Parthia

Antioch

Syria

Euphrates

Baghdad

Ctesiphon

• Damascus

Tiberias

Kufa

Sura

• Wasit

Persia

• Jerusalem

Basra

Palestine

Iraq

• Istakhr

Petra

Indus

Persian Gulf

Hijaz

• Medina

Arabia

India

Mecca

Red Sea

ubia

• Najran

Himyar

Arabian
Sea

Ethiopia

Indian Ocean

Taprobane

Do not look for a fight with the enemy.
Beg God for peace and security. But if
you do end up facing the enemy, then
show endurance, and remember that the
gates of Paradise lie in the shadow of the
sword.

Saying of Muhammad

I

INTRODUCTION

I shall include in my narrative only those
things by which first we ourselves, then
later generations, may benefit.

Eusebius, *The History of the Church*

The degree of authority one can give to
the evangelists about the life of Christ is
relatively small. Whereas for the life of
Muhammad, we know everything more
or less. We know where he lived, what
his economic situation was, who he fell
in love with. We know a great deal about
the political circumstances and the
socio-economic circumstances of the
time.

Salman Rushdie

1

KNOWN UNKNOWNS

Between Two Worlds

Yusuf As'ar Yath'ar, an Arab king celebrated for his long hair, his piety and his utter ruthlessness, had been brought to defeat. Leaving the reek of the battlefield, he rode his blood-flecked white charger down to the very edge of the Red Sea. Behind him, he knew, Christian outliers would already be advancing against his palace—to seize his treasury, to capture his queen. Certainly, his conquerors had no cause to show him mercy. Few were more notorious among the Christians than Yusuf. Two years previously, looking to secure the south-west of Arabia for his own faith, he had captured their regional stronghold of Najran. What had happened next was a matter of shock and horror to Christians far beyond the limits of Himyar, the kingdom on the Red Sea that Yusuf had ruled, on and off, for just under a decade. The local church, with the bishop and a great multitude of his followers locked inside, had been put to the torch. A group of virgins, hurrying to join them, had hurled themselves on to the flames, crying defiantly as they did so how sweet it was to breathe in "the scent of burning priests!"[1] Another woman, "whose face no one had ever seen outside the door of her house and who had never walked during the day in the city,"[2] had torn off her headscarf, the better to reproach the king. Yusuf, in his fury, had

3

ordered her daughter and granddaughter killed before her, their blood poured down her throat, and then her own head to be sent flying.

Martyrdoms such as these, fêted though they were by the Church, could not readily be forgiven. A great army, crossing from the Christian kingdom of Ethiopia, had duly landed in Himyar. The defenders had been cornered, engaged and routed. Now, with the shallows of the Red Sea lapping at his horse's hooves, Yusuf had come to the end of the road. Not all his obedience to the laws granted to God's chosen prophet had been sufficient to save him from ruin. Slowly, he urged his horse forwards, breasting the water, until at last, weighed down by his armour, he disappeared beneath the waves. So perished Yusuf As'ar Yath'ar: the last Jewish king ever to rule in Arabia.

The collapse of the kingdom of the Himyarites in AD 525 is not, it is fair to say, one of the more celebrated episodes of ancient history. Himyar itself, despite having prospered for some six centuries until its final overthrow under Yusuf, lacks the ready brand recognition today of a Babylon, or an Athens, or a Rome. Unsurprisingly so, perhaps: for southern Arabia, then as now, was firmly peripheral to the major centres of civilisation. Even the Arabs themselves, whom the peoples of more settled lands tended to dismiss as notorious brutes—"of all the nations of the earth, the most despised and insignificant"[3]—might look askance at the presumed barbarities of the region. The Himyarites, so one Arab poet reported in shocked tones, left their women uncircumcised, "and do not think it disgusting to eat locusts."[4] Behaviour that clearly branded them as beyond the pale.

Yet, it is not only in terms of its geography that Himyar seems to lie in shadow. Similarly obscure is the period in which the death of Yusuf occurred. The sixth century AD defies precise categorisation. It seems to stand between two ages. If it looks back to the world of classical civilisation, then so also does it look forward to the world of the Crusades. Historians categorise it, and the centuries either side of it, as "late antiquity": a phrase that conveys a sense of lengthening shadows, and the Middle Ages soon to come.

For anyone accustomed to thinking of history as a succession of neatly defined and self-enclosed epochs, there is something vaguely unsettling about this. Rather like the scientist in the classic horror film *The Fly*, who ends up a mutant combination of human and insect, the world of late antiquity can seem, from our own perspective, peculiarly hybrid. Far beyond the borders of Yusuf's Himyarite kingdom, empires raised on fabulously ancient foundations still dominated the Near East and the Mediterranean, as they had done for centuries. Yet, their very age served only to highlight how profoundly they were coming to slip the moorings of their past. Take, for instance, the region immediately to the north of Arabia: the land we know today as Iraq. Here, across mudflats that had witnessed the dawn of urban civilisation, loyalty was owed to a king who was, just as his predecessor had been a whole millennium previously, a Persian. His dominions, like those of the Persian Empire that had existed a thousand years before, stretched eastwards to the frontiers of India, and deep into Central Asia. The splendours of the court over which he presided, the magnificence of its rituals, and the immodesty of his pretensions: all would have been perfectly familiar to a king of Babylon. That this was so, however, had been almost forgotten by the people of Iraq themselves. A spreading amnesia was blotting out memories that had endured for millennia. Even the Persians, far from venerating the truth about their glorious imperial heritage, had begun to obscure and distort it. The legacy of Iraq's incomparable history lived on—preserved in the Persians' fantasies of global rule and in the many glories that lent such fantasies credence—but increasingly it wore the look, not of ages departed, but of something new.

Other superpowers were less neglectful of their pasts. The great cities of the Mediterranean, built of stone and marble rather than the mud-bricks favoured by the people of Iraq, were less prone to crumbling into dust. The empire that ruled them likewise wore, in 525, a veneer of venerable indestructibility. Even to the Persians, Roman might appeared something primordial. "God so arranged things," they would occasionally acknowledge, albeit through gritted teeth, "that the whole world was lit up from the beginning by two eyes: namely, by the wise rulers of the Persian realm, and by the powerful empire of the Romans."[5] Nevertheless, the Romans themselves, although certainly never averse to flattery, knew better. Rather than believing that their empire had existed since the dawn of time, they knew perfectly well that all its greatness had evolved from nothing. To trace the course of that evolution might therefore be to fathom the secrets of its success. Even as Yusuf was vanishing into the Red Sea, plans were being laid in the Roman capital for an immense ransacking of libraries and archives, an unprecedented labour of scholarship whose goal was the preservation for all eternity of the empire's vast inheritance of laws. This was no arid, merely antiquarian project. History, no less than armies or gold, had come to function as one of the sinews of the Roman state. It offered the empire reassurance that it was precisely what it claimed to be: the model of human order. How, then, was the prestige of Caesar to be maintained, if not by a perpetual trumpeting of Rome's triumphant antiquity?

The challenge for Roman policy-makers, of course, was that the glories of the past did not necessarily provide them with a reliable guide for the future. Indisputably, the empire remained what it had been for almost a millennium: the most formidable superpower of all. Wealthier and more populous than its great Persian rival, its hold over the eastern Mediterranean, always the richer half, appeared secure. From the mountains of the Balkans to the deserts of Egypt, Caesar ruled them all. Nevertheless, it was clearly an embarrassment, to put it mildly, that what had once been the western half of Rome's empire had ceased, by 525, to be Roman at all. Over the course of the previous century, an immense swath of her holdings, like a sandcastle battered by the waves of an incoming tide, had crumbled utterly away. Britain had been lost as early as 410. Other provinces, over the succeeding decades, had followed. By the end of the century, the entire western half of the empire, even Italy, even Rome itself, had gone. In place of the venerable imperial order there was now a patchwork of independent kingdoms, all of them—with the exception of a few in western Britain—ruled by warrior elites from beyond the limits of the former empire. The relationship that existed between the natives and these "barbarian" newcomers varied from realm to realm: some, like the Britons, fought the invaders tooth and nail; others, like the Italians, were given to hailing them as though they were Caesars. Yet, in every case, the empire's collapse resulted in the forging of new identities, new values, new presumptions. These, over the long term, would lead to the establishment of a radically new political order in western Europe. Rome's abandoned provinces would never again acknowledge a single master.

Time would see both the great empires of the age—the Persian as well as the Roman—go the way of Nineveh and Tyre. Not so the states established in Rome's western provinces, some of which still commemorate in their modern names the intrusions back in late antiquity of barbarian war bands. Small wonder, then, that European historians have traditionally seen the arrival of the Franks in the land that would eventually become France, and of the Angles in the future England, as events of far greater long-term significance than the activities of any Caesar or Persian king. We know now, as their contemporaries did not, that ruin was stalking both the rival empires. A century on from the collapse of the Himyarite kingdom, and the two superpowers were staring into the abyss. That the Persian Empire would end up toppled completely while that of the Romans was left as little more than a mangled trunk, has traditionally served to mark them as dead-ends, bed-blockers, dinosaurs. How tempting it is to presume, then, that they must have perished of decrepitude and old age. The lateness of late antiquity, to those who trace in it only a calamitous arc of decline and fall, has the quality of dinner guests who refuse to get their coats once the party is over.

Except that the empires raised by the peoples of the age were not solely of this earth. Radiant though a Caesar might appear to his subjects, awesomely though his palaces and citadels might tower above the common run, and remorselessly though his array of soldiers, and bureaucrats, and tax-collectors might serve his will, yet even he was merely a mortal, in a cosmos governed by a celestial king. There was only one universal monarch—and that was God. This presumption, by the time that Yusuf was brought to bay early in the sixth century AD, was one virtually unchallenged across the entire sweep of the Near East—and it affected almost every aspect of geopolitics in the region. When Yusuf clashed with the Ethiopian invaders, far more was at stake than the petty ambitions of squabbling warlords. The interests of heaven as well had been intimately involved. Between those fighting in the Jewish cause and those in the name of Christ, the differences were so profound as to be irreconcilable. Confident though both sides were that the god they worshipped was the only god—*monos theos* in Greek—this shared conviction only rendered them all the more implacably opposed. Not just in southern Arabia, but across the entire span of the civilised world, devotion to a particular understanding of the divine had become an emotion that defined the lives of millions upon millions of people. In an age when realms might crest and fall like the spume of a wave, and even great empires totter, there was certainly no earthly power that could command such allegiance. Identity was coming to be defined, not by the kingdoms of this world, but by various conceptions of the One, the Only God: by "monotheisms."

This development signalled a transformation of human society with incalculable consequences for the future. Of all the various features of the modern world that can be traced back to antiquity—alphabets, democracy, gladiator films—none, perhaps, has been more globally influential than the establishment, for the first time in history, of various brands of monotheism as state religions. At the start of the third millennium since the birth of Christ, some three and a half billion people—over half the population of the world—identify themselves with one or other of the various religions that assumed something approaching their modern form in the 250 years either side of Yusuf's death. The period of late antiquity, then, unfamiliar though it may be in comparison to other epochs of history, is no less pregnant with relevance for that. Wherever men or women are inspired by a belief in a single god to think or to behave in a certain way, they demonstrate its abiding influence. The impact of the revolution that it witnessed still reverberates today.

It is the ambition of this book to trace the origins and the progress of that same revolution. How was it that the patterns of people's thought, over the course of only a few centuries, came to be altered so radically and so enduringly? The story is a richly human one, replete with vivid drama, extraordinary characters and often riotous colour. Yet, it is also one that imposes peculiar demands upon the historian: for much of it takes place in a dimension beyond the physical. It features kings, but also angels; warlords, but also demons. Consequently, not every event in the pages that follow can be explained purely in terms of material self-interest or political calculation. Shadowing the often brutally vivid world of mortal affairs is a dimension that is heaven-lit and damnation-haunted. Certainly, when Yusuf's contemporaries analysed his downfall, they were not naïve in their analysis. They recognised that complex issues of trade policy and the rivalries of the two distant superpowers had been lurking in the background. Yet they never doubted that the sands of Arabia had become the stage for an authentically celestial drama. The forces of heaven and hell had met and clashed. It was a matter of opinion whether Yusuf was on the side of the angels or the demons; but neither Jews nor Christians had any doubt that what had happened had derived ultimately from God. This was the core presumption of the age; and a history of late antiquity that neglects to pay due acknowledgement to it is a history that has failed.

The beliefs of the period must therefore be treated with both seriousness and empathy. Yet this does not mean that their claims should be taken wholly at face value. Back in the early fourth century, a Palestinian bishop by the name of Eusebius wrote a history of the early Church. In it, he initiated a tradition of historical enquiry that explained the past as the tracing of patterns upon time by the forefinger of God. This presumption, although stupendously influential, and not merely among Christian authors, fell out of fashion in the West several centuries ago. Whatever their personal religious convictions may be, modern historians do not generally explain past events as the workings of divine providence. All aspects of human society—even beliefs themselves—are now presumed to be products of evolution. Nor is this a uniquely modern perspective. Eusebius himself, fifteen hundred years before Darwin, had recognised in it a pernicious and peculiarly threatening heresy. Nothing was more alarming to him than the notion propagated by the enemies of his faith that it was something upstart and contingent, a mere distorted echo of more venerable traditions. His history, far from tracing changes in the doctrines and institutions of the Church, aimed to demonstrate that they had never changed in the slightest. And Christianity itself? Christianity, Eusebius presumed, had existed since the dawn of time: "For, obviously, we must regard the religion proclaimed in recent years to every nation through Christ's teaching as none other than the first, the most ancient, and the most primitive of religions."[6]

To many of us today, familiar as we are with Neanderthal burial sites and Cro-Magnon cave art, this claim does not seem obvious at all. Nevertheless, its underlying presumption—that religions have some mysterious and fundamental essence, immune to the processes of time—remains widely taken for granted. In large part, this is due to Eusebius and others like him. The great innovation of late antiquity was to fashion, out of what might otherwise have been an inchoate blur of beliefs and doctrines, individual templates for individual religions, and then to establish them as definitive. How this was accomplished is a fascinating and remarkable tale—for it touches upon the highest politics and the profoundest human emotions. The clash of great empires and the wretchedness of slaves; the shimmering of mosaics and the stench of plague pits; the clamour of teeming cities and the silence of empty deserts: all must feature. Beginning in a world recognisably ancient and ending in one medieval, it ranks as a transformation as momentous as any in history.

Yet the story is, for all that, a treacherous one to tell. Partly, this is due to the inevitable gaps and contradictions in the sources that bedevil all periods of ancient history. Take, for example, the story of Yusuf's death. There are some accounts which describe him as falling in the heat of battle, rather than riding out into the sea. More problematic still is the bias in our sources—almost all of which are Christian.* Even the chronology is a muddle, with some historians dating Yusuf's death, not to 525, but to 520. All these, it might be thought, are mere problems of detail—except that there is an additional, and much greater, complication. Any history tracing the development of rival monotheisms cannot help but use such words as "Christian" and "Jew"; and yet, as the story of Yusuf suggests, these did not necessarily mean in late antiquity what they have come to mean today. A narrative that features the persecution of veiled Christian women in Arabia by a Jewish king is clearly one set in a world at some remove from our own.

It is for this reason that the story of late antiquity is altogether stranger and more surprising than might at first appear. Indeed, it is precisely the measure of those who shaped it to such stupefying effect that they succeeded so well in veiling their own astounding creativity. In every period, of course, there are those who labour to redraft the past in the service of the present; but none, perhaps, has done it so potently, or to such enduring effect, as the historians of late antiquity. The supreme achievement of the Jewish and Christian scholars of the age was to craft a history of their respective faiths that cast themselves as its rightful and inevitable culmination, and left anything that might have served to contradict such an impression out of the story altogether. Whoever Moses might truly have been, and whether he even existed, most Jews' understanding of him today has been incalculably influenced by the rabbis of late antiquity: brilliantly

---

* We have three brief but contemporary inscriptions giving the Himyarite side of the story. Unsurprisingly, perhaps, these accuse the Christians of Najran of what today might be described as terrorism.

learned and ingenious men who devoted entire centuries of effort to demonstrating that their greatest prophet—no matter how far removed from them in time—had in fact been someone very much like themselves. Similarly, whatever Jesus might truly have believed himself to be, the Christian understanding of his mission and divinity, as taught by the vast majority of today's Churches, bears witness to the turbulent ebb and flow of late Roman politics: to the exhaustive efforts of bishops and emperors to fashion a creed that could unite all of God's people as one. The essential architecture of Judaism and Christianity, no matter how far back in time its ultimate origins may stretch, was designed in late antiquity.

Only faith—or the lack of it—can ultimately answer the great questions that lie at the heart of these religions: whether the Jews are truly God's Chosen People; and whether Jesus did in reality rise from the dead. Much the same, however, could be said of other puzzles too: how and why the Jewish belief in a single god first evolved; and what might have been the full range of doctrines in the early Church. Some of the sparks that first ignited the flames of Jewish and Christian practice can be glimpsed by the historian; but many more cannot. We see through a glass, darkly—and that glass, by and large, was fashioned by the men and women who are the protagonists of this book.

Granted, it was hardly a novel paradox that veneration of a primordial past might lead to its being masked, or even obliterated altogether. Many a wealthy patron in the ancient world flaunted his piety by erecting a colossal edifice over a modest shrine. The Jewish and Christian scholars of late antiquity, however, by the sheer force of their labours, succeeded in performing an infinitely more enduring feat of renovation. Their ultimate achievement was to craft an interpretation not only of their own various forms of monotheism but of religion itself: an interpretation that billions of people now take for granted as the supreme influence affecting both their behaviour on this earth, and the eternal destiny of their souls. It is this that makes the project of sifting through the writings of late antiquity for evidence of what might actually have happened so sensitive—and so fascinating as well.

Such a project, it goes without saying, is not one to be undertaken lightly. Nor, the complexity and ambiguity of these sources being what they are, can the story that is this book's theme be narrated without a prior explanation of how and why it is being told in the way it is.

That is why, before I embark on telling it, I pause, to tell something quite else: the making of a story.

The Greatest Story Ever Told

Winners were the favourites of heaven. Even Christians—whose god had died as a convicted criminal, nailed to a wooden cross—might succumb to this presumption. Eusebius certainly took it for granted. How could he not have done, when he had the spectacle before him of a Roman state that for centuries had been gore-streaked with Christian blood miraculously transformed into a bulwark of the Church? No need for the Caesar who had first bowed his head before Christ to wait for death to receive his due reward. Eusebius, who combined the talents of an instinctive polemicist with a profound streak of hero-worship, wrote an entire biography of the emperor, just to ram the point home. "So dear was he to God, and so blessed, so pious and so fortunate in all he undertook, that with the greatest facility he obtained authority over more nations than any who had preceded him—and yet retained his power, undisturbed, to the very close of his life."[7]

Confidence in this formula—that faith in Christ would lead to earthly glory—would take a number of knocks over the course of the succeeding centuries. Awkwardly, the more Christian the Romans became, the more their empire's frontiers seemed to contract. Theologians devised various explanations for this puzzling phenomenon—explanations which Christians, who had only to study the gospels to learn Jesus's views on the earthly and the overweening, might well find perfectly persuasive. Nevertheless, the core equation so lovingly dwelt upon by Eusebius—that worldly greatness was bestowed by God upon those who pleased Him—appeared altogether too plausible simply to be dismissed out of hand. Instead, the more the Romans found themselves locked in a desperate struggle for survival, so the more it came to be appropriated by a new and quite startlingly upstart imperial people. The identity of these same conquerors, who had not only deprived the Romans of their wealthiest provinces but had crushed the Persians underfoot altogether, could hardly have come as more of a shock to the defeated. Indeed, so unexpected was what had happened, so utterly jaw-dropping, as to appear self-evidently miraculous. What else but the hand of God could possibly explain the conquest of the world by a people previously scorned as the ultimate in savagery and backwardness: the Arabs?

Half a millennium on from the time of Eusebius, at the start of the ninth Christian century, and the close identification made by the learned between piety and worldly power still enjoyed spectacular traction. Christians themselves might have grown uncomfortable with the notion; but not so the Arabs, who rejoiced in a rampant conviction that all their astounding victories were owed directly to the favour of God. Two centuries previously, so they believed, heaven had graced their ancestors with a stream of supernatural revelations: a dispensation that trumped those of the Jews and the Christians, and had set those who subjected themselves to it upon a road to global empire. Indeed, eight hundred years after the birth of Christ, it was as "Muslims"—"those who submit to God"—that most Arabs had come to identify themselves. The vast agglomeration of territories won by the swords of their forefathers, stretching from the shores of the Atlantic to the fringes of China, served as the ultimate monument to what God had demanded of them: their submission. "Islam," they called it—shorthand for what had become, by the early ninth century, an entire civilisation.

It was not only the Arabs themselves, however, who had been

granted a rare new dignity by the coming of Islam. So too had their language. It was in Arabic, so Muslims believed, that God had climactically, and for all time, revealed His purposes to humanity. What was good enough for the Almighty, it went without saying, was good enough for mortals. By AD 800, so redeemed was Arabic from the contempt in which it had once been held that its sound had come to rank as the very music of power, and its cursives as things of pure beauty, refined to a rare and exquisite perfection by the art of its calligraphers. Among the Arabs, the written word was on the verge of becoming a mania. One scholar, when he died in 822, left behind him a library that filled a whole six hundred trunks. Another was said to have been flattened to a pulp when a tower of books collapsed on top of him while he was drunk. The story does not seem wholly implausible. One volume of Arab history, it is claimed, stretched to almost eighty thousand pages—which would have made for a crushing weight, to be sure. Clearly, then, a people who could boast of such titanic literary endeavours were far removed from an age that had scorned them as barbarians—as the Arabs themselves delighted in pointing out.

The sense of compulsion they brought to the study of their past was hardly surprising. The yearning to understand the reason for the spectacular upsurge in their fortunes, to clarify the process by which it had been brought about, and to elucidate what it revealed about the character of their god, never ceased to gnaw. Just as Eusebius, five hundred years previously, had sought answers to very similar questions in the life of a Roman emperor, so now did Ibn Hisham—a scholar originally from Iraq who by the early ninth century had settled in Egypt—likewise turn to biography in order to fathom the purposes of heaven. "*Sira,*" he termed his chosen genre: "exemplary behaviour." It was less what his subject had done that concerned Ibn Hisham than how he had done it. There was an urgent reason for this. The hero of Ibn Hisham's biography, so Muslims believed, offered the ultimate in role models. God had chosen him to serve as His mouthpiece. It was through him that the All Merciful had revealed His wishes to the

15

Arabs, and graced them with those same revelations that had then inspired them, two centuries before the time of Ibn Hisham, to erupt from their deserts and tear the world's superpowers to pieces. "We are God's helpers and the assistants of His prophet, and will fight men until they believe in God; and he who believes in God and His prophet has protected his life and property from us; and he who disbelieves we will fight in God unceasingly, and killing him will be a small matter to us."[8] This, according to Ibn Hisham, was the swaggering manifesto promoted by Arab warriors on the eve of their conquest of the world.

But who, precisely, was this "prophet?" Ibn Hisham's aim was to provide the answer. Sitting in Egypt, surrounded by the ruins of forgotten and superseded civilisations, he regarded his *sira* not merely as a biography but as a record of the most momentous revolution in history. Its subject was a man who had died only two years before the dismemberment of the Roman and Persian empires had begun: an Arab by the name of Muhammad. Aged forty, and with a moderate career as a merchant behind him, he had experienced—if Ibn Hisham were to be believed—history's most epochal mid-life crisis. Restless and dissatisfied, he had begun to roam the wilderness which stretched beyond his home town, "and not a stone or tree that he passed by but would say, 'Peace be unto you, O prophet of God.'"[9] Muhammad, understandably enough, had been left most unsettled. Voices were rarely heard in the places where he chose to wander, on his lonely quest after spiritual enlightenment. Mecca, the nearby town, stood in the depths of the Arabian desert: the ring of mountains that surrounded it, baked black by the pitilessly broiling sun, rose barren, wind-lashed and empty. Yet, it was on the slope of one of those same mountains, lying at night inside a cave, that Muhammad heard the most startling voice of all. He felt it at first as a vice tightening around his body: the grip of some terrifying supernatural entity. Next came a single command: "Recite!"* Then, as though his words were a

---

* Or perhaps "Read!" According to Ibn Hisham, the recitation appeared before Muhammad in the form of writing on a brocaded coverlet.

desperate, violent exhalation of air, Muhammad himself started to gasp out whole lines of verse:

> Recite: in the name of your Lord!
> He Who created!
> He created man from a blood clot.
> Recite! Your Lord is most bountiful.
> He taught with the pen.
> He taught man what he knew not.[10]

Muhammad was speaking, but the words were not his own. Then whose? Muhammad himself, it is said, initially suspected a *jinn*, a spirit of the deserts and winds. Perhaps this was not surprising. Mecca was, according to Ibn Hisham, a hag-ridden, demon-haunted place. Right in the centre of the city there stood a shrine built of stone and mud— the *Ka'ba*, or "Cube"—in which there squatted a whole host of fearsome gods, totems of such sinister power that men from across Arabia would gather there to pay their respects. On top of these, every household in Mecca had its own private idol: there to be rubbed against for luck before a journey. So inveterately pagan were the Meccans that they even offered sacrifices to boulders: among which were a couple of one-time lovers who had dared to have sex in the *Ka'ba*, and promptly been turned to rock. It was only natural, then, in a city so eerie, so perfumed by blood and magic, that clairvoyants should have been a common sight, rolling about in the dirt of its narrow streets, vomiting up revelations, possessed by *jinn* in the depths of their guts. So overwhelming was Muhammad's dread that he might now be suffering an identical fate that he thought to take his life. Rising to his feet, he left the cave and stumbled out into the night. Up the side of the mountain he hurried. Heading for the summit, he prepared to hurl himself from the peak, to dash himself on to the rocks.

But now the voice returned: "O Muhammad! Thou art the apostle of God and I am Gabriel." Could it really be so? Gabriel was a mighty angel, the messenger of the one God worshipped by the Jews and the

Christians, who back in ancient times—or so it was said—had revealed visions to the Prophet Daniel, and told the Virgin Mary that she was to bear a son. Looking up to the heavens, Muhammad saw the figure of a man, his "feet astride the horizon":[11] who else but the angel himself? Returning down the mountain, seeking comfort from his wife, reflecting upon the shattering trauma he had been through, Muhammad dared to contemplate a truly awesome possibility: that the voice had spoken the truth. He would not hear it again for another two years—but when at last Gabriel returned, and the silence was broken, Muhammad had no doubt that he was hearing, courtesy of the angel, the authentic words of a god. And not just any god, but the one God, the true God, the indivisible God. "There is no god but He, Creator of all things."[12]

Here, in this uncompromising assertion that there existed only a single divinity, lay the key to a starkly new vision of the universe: monotheism in the raw. With each successive revelation, Muhammad's understanding of God's oneness—and of what was owed to Him as a result—was burnished to an ever more awesome sheen. The people of Arabia—with their idols of stone, or wood, or dates mixed with rancid butter—were merely repeating what had been, since the dawn of time, humanity's greatest delusion: that the heavens and the earth were thronged with a whole teeming mob of gods. So Muhammad, ordered by his voice to "proclaim aloud"[13] God's revelations, began to preach. Again and again, he warned, mankind had succumbed to the one sin that could not be forgiven: *shirk*—the belief that God can be associated with other beings. Again and again, however, because He was all merciful, the "Lord of the Worlds"[14] had sent prophets to open the eyes of people to their folly, and summon them back to the primordial way of truth. Noah and Abraham, Moses and Jesus: all had preached the one identical message, a call for submission to God. Now, it appeared, with revelations being granted to Muhammad in ever increasing length and number, there had arisen, six centuries after Jesus, a new prophet. Indeed—the very "Seal of Prophets."[15] As the years passed and the divine continued to speak through him, so Muhammad and his growing band of followers came to realise that he was the recipient of the ultimate in messages: the definitive revelation of God.

Not that everyone concurred. "Prophecy," as Ibn Hisham would sagely observe, "is a troublesome burden. Only strong, resolute messengers can bear it by God's help and grace, because of the opposition which they meet from men in conveying God's message."[16] Which was putting it mildly. Muhammad's fellow townsmen regarded him first as a diversion; then as a provocation; and finally as a mortal danger. Particularly outraged by his uncompromising message were the members of his own tribe, "Quraysh" as they were known: a consortium of clans who had long enjoyed a peculiar respect among the scattered tribes of Arabia.[17] The prestige they enjoyed as a "People of God" reflected the lucrative role that the Quraysh had grasped for themselves as the guardians of the *Ka'ba*, and its multitude of idols: a role that Muhammad, with his wild talk of there being only a single god, seemed determined to sabotage.* The unsurprising consequence was that Mecca grew increasingly hot for the Prophet and his followers. By AD 622, twelve years after the first revelation had descended from the heavens, the threat was directly to their lives. One night, Gabriel appeared to the Prophet and warned him that the Quraysh were plotting to murder him in his bed: the time had come to leave. Following in the footsteps of his followers, many of whom had already abandoned Mecca, Muhammad obediently slipped out from the city and vanished into the night. The moment had been long anticipated: what the Prophet had now embarked upon was not some aimless flight into the wilds of the desert, but rather a meticulously planned migration—a *hijra*.

An escape that would come to be seen, in due course, as having

---

* This thesis, that Muhammad's religion was a threat to the trade of the Quraysh as guardians of the *Ka'ba*, is nowhere explicitly mentioned in Muslim tradition, but is almost universally taken for granted in modern, Western biographies of the Prophet.

transformed the entire order of time. The year in which it took place still serves Muslims, to this day, as Year One. Dates in their calendar continue to be defined as AH, or "*Anno Hegirae*: In the Year of the *Hijra*." To Ibn Hisham, the central episode of Muhammad's life was not his first revelation, but his departure from Mecca. No longer simply a preacher, he was now embarked upon a spectacular series of exploits that would see him emerge, in due course, as the leader of an entire new political order. His destination, an oasis to the north of Mecca known as Yathrib, stood in desperate need of a guiding hand. The tribes who lived there, an uneasy mixture of Jewish and Arab settlers, had long been great enthusiasts for savage feuding; but increasingly, as the violence spiralled ever more out of control, there were many weary of the perpetual bloodshed. Pressure was building in Yathrib to find a peacemaker. Someone neutral, someone trustworthy, someone authoritative. Someone, perhaps—just perhaps—with a channel direct to God. In short, between Muhammad, a prophet in need of a refuge, and Yathrib, a city in need of a prophet, there could hardly have been a more perfect fit. A match made literally in heaven, as Ibn Hisham would choose to cast it.

It is the measure of what Muhammad ultimately achieved in Yathrib that its very name would end up erased from the map. It was the fate, and the undying glory, of the oasis that had offered him sanctuary to be commemorated as "The City of the Prophet," or "*Madinat an-Nabi*"—Medina. Muhammad would spend the rest of his life there, building a society that has served as the model for Muslims ever since. Angry and clear was the reproach delivered by the Prophet to those who lived by the murderous ethics of the desert. To love gold "with a love inordinate,"[18] to steal from orphans and squander their inheritance, and to dispose of unwanted daughters by burying them alive in the sands, was, so Muhammad warned, to be bound for eternal fire. "Account is demanded of those who oppress people and commit transgression on earth, unjustly. To them there is painful torment."[19] Before the awesome infinitude of God, enthroned upon His judgement seat, even the haughtiest or most rumbustious clan chief was but the merest speck of dust. The squabbling tribes of Yathrib, overwhelmed by the floodtide of Muhammad's revelations, increasingly found their old antagonisms, and their old loyalties, dissolving amid the urgency and grandeur of his message. Yet the Prophet, even as he tamed their addiction to the more traditional pleasures of chauvinism, did not think to deny them all sense of community. On the contrary. Although Muhammad would certainly succeed in bringing peace to his oasis refuge, just as he had been invited to do, peace was hardly the limit of what he brought. Something more, very much more, was on offer to the people of Yathrib: a radically new identity, forged out of the whirling atoms of their pulverised tribal order. An identity as a single people—as the members of a single *Umma*.

"Seal of the Prophets" Muhammad may have been—but he did not disdain to found an earthly state. God continued to speak to him. His self-confidence did not dim. Obstacles in his path were swept aside or else trampled down. When the gap between rich and poor—which offended Muhammad to the core of his being—refused to narrow, he summarily outlawed usury and established an equitable taxation system. When the Jews of Yathrib, disconcerted by the transformation of their hometown into the "City of the Prophet," presumed to manoeuvre against him, they were variously expelled, enslaved or massacred. When the Quraysh, informed that Muhammad was planning to raid one of their caravans, sent a military escort out into the desert, it was met by the Prophet and his tiny band of followers beside a watering hole named Badr, and put humiliatingly to rout. Angels, "white turbans flowing behind them,"[20] shimmered in the sky above the battlefield, flashing their fiery swords, and sending Qurayshi heads flying.

Most spectacular and irrefutable sign of God's favour, however, was the transformation of Muhammad, in no more than a decade, from refugee to effective master of Arabia. He led twenty-seven campaigns in all, according to Ibn Hisham; and if occasionally there was a defeat, and if the angels, by and large, chose not to fight as they had done at Badr, but rather to serve him as a reserve, then perhaps his ultimate triumph could be considered only the more extraordinary for it. By 632, the traditional date of his death, paganism in Arabia had everywhere been put in shadow. Sweetest moment of all had been the conquest, two years previously, of Mecca itself. Riding into his hometown, Muhammad had ordered the *Ka'ba* stripped of its gods. A great bonfire had been lit. The toppled idols had been consigned to its flames. The Devil, summoning his progeny around him, had cried out in woe: "Abandon all hope that the community of Muhammad will ever revert to *shirk* after this day of theirs!"[21] Well might he have yowled. The venerable sanctuary, that pre-eminent bastion of paganism, had been brought at last to a due submission: to "*Islam*." This consecration of Mecca to the service of the One True God, however, was far from an innovation. What Muhammad had done, so he revealed to his followers, was restore the shrine to its primordial, pristine state. "God made Mecca holy the day He created heaven and earth. It is the holy of holies until the resurrection day."[22]

This assurance, even in the bleak days following Muhammad's death two years later, offered the faithful much comfort. It suggested to them that they had not been abandoned by God. Despite the loss of their Prophet, Arabia remained transfigured by the sacred still. Nor was it only Mecca, "the holy of holies," that still endured upon the face of the earth. So too did the *Umma*—and to the greater glory of all that the Prophet had taught. Over the succeeding years, the succeeding decades, the succeeding centuries, the Muslim people would serve to make of the entire world a *Ka'ba*: conquered, cleansed and sanctified. By the time that Ibn Hisham sat down to write his biography, it was not only Arabs who faced Mecca as they prayed. Strange peoples of whom the Prophet had possibly never even heard—Visigoths and Berbers, Sogdians and Parthians—could all be seen treading the sands of Arabia: pilgrims bound for the *Ka'ba*. Although Ibn Hisham himself did not touch upon this phenomenon in his *sira*, there was no shortage of other scholars eager to relate the extraordinary conquests, far beyond the limits of Arabia, that had followed the death of the Prophet. Such relish was hardly surprising. Back in the wild days of their paganism, nothing had delighted the Arabs more than a spot of loud-mouthed boasting, be it about some heroic feat of arms, some stirring deed of banditry, or some glorious humiliation forced upon a rival. Now, when they blew their own trumpets, it was all in the cause of God. From Badr to the ends of the world, the story of Islam had been one of storming military triumph. Cities infinitely greater than Mecca had been captured; peoples infinitely mightier than the Quraysh obliged to bow their necks. The scale of these victories, won in the teeth of ancient empires and venerable religions, surely furnished all the proof that anyone might need of the truth of the Prophet's claims. "This is a sign that God loves us," as one exultant Arab put it, "and is pleased with our faith, namely that He has given us dominion over all peoples and religions."[23]

And yet, all the while, there was anxiety. Even amid the wealth and splendour of a great empire, vast on a scale beyond anything that Muhammad would have imagined possible, the Muslim people could not shake off an uncomfortable sense of their own decay. A generation after Ibn Hisham had completed his biography, and the scholar who would end up crushed to death beneath his toppled books, an astounding polymath by the name of Al-Jahiz, could view the entire triumphant course of Islam's history as embodying nothing but a dying fall. There had been only the one truly golden age. Those who had heard the Prophet actually talk, who had ridden by his side, who had served him as his *Sahabah*, or "Companions": they alone could be reckoned to have practised "the authentic monotheism." Hence, of course, their astounding success. It was their generation, fresh from the burial of the Prophet, which had first embarked upon the conquest of the world—and achieved it, what was more. The men who had presided over this glorious victory charge, a sequence of leaders known as "Caliphs," or "Successors" of the Prophet, had all of them been noted intimates of Muhammad. The first, a grizzled veteran by the name of Abu Bakr, had been his companion during the perilous flight to Medina, and the father of his favourite wife; the second, Umar, had been his brother-in-law; the third, Uthman, had been married to one of his daughters. The fourth, Ali ibn Abi Talib, had rejoiced in the most splendid pedigree of all: the first male ever to convert to Islam, a step he had taken at the precocious age of nine, he was also the Prophet's cousin, before finally graduating to become, just for good measure, his son-in-law as well.* These four men had reigned for just thirty years in total, but already, by the time that Al-Jahiz was putting pen to paper, they were well on their way to being enshrined by the vast majority of Muslims as veritable paragons—*ar-Rashidun*, or "the Rightly Guided." Not, of course, that their period in power could quite compare with Muhammad's at Medina; but still, as a golden age, it came in a glorious second. "For at that time," as Al-Jahiz put it wistfully, "there was nothing in the way of offending action or scandalous innovation, no act of disobedience, envy, rancour or rivalry."[24] Islam had been pristinely Islamic still.

But after every summer there must be a winter; and after every golden age an age of iron. In 661, the era of the *Rashidun* was brought to a bloody and tragic end. The Caliph Ali was murdered. Then, two decades later, his son was cut down in battle; lips that had kissed the Prophet were prodded mockingly by a conqueror's stick. By now, a dynasty of Qurayshi despots, the Umayyads, had dug their claws deep into the Caliphate and made it their own—to the scandal of the God-fearing. The new Caliphs drank wine; they kept pet monkeys; they termed themselves, not the Prophet's Successors, but "the deputies of God." Monstrous behaviour such as this was bound to tempt the wrath of heaven; and sure enough, in 750, the Umayyads were toppled, forced to flee, and systematically hunted down by vengeful death squads. Nevertheless, the blots and stains of their near century in power were not so easily erased. No matter that the dynasty that succeeded them to the caliphal throne, the Abbasids, claimed descent from the uncle of Muhammad himself—the golden age of the *Rashidun* was not restored. Instead, no less than in the dark days that had

---

* In some traditions, he is cast as the Prophet's brother: Aaron to Muhammad's Moses.

preceded the coming of the Prophet, novelty and division seemed rife. Rival sects proliferated—and rival Caliphs too. Meanwhile, beyond the palaces in which the Successors of the Prophet dressed in silks and ate from plates of gold, the poor found themselves as oppressed as they had ever been by the arrogance of the powerful, the wealthy, the cruel. Remorselessly, the question nagged: how had it all gone wrong? And even more remorselessly: how was it best to be set right?

Two centuries on from the *hijra*, and the last man to have seen the Prophet alive was long since departed from the face of the world. Nevertheless, confronted as they were by the splintering of the times, most Muslims knew that there could be no true solution to any problem that lacked the sanction of their beloved prophet. "In the Messenger of God," the Almighty Himself had informed the faithful, "you have an excellent example to follow."[25] To sketch him was therefore to sketch the ultimate in role models: a pattern of behaviour fit to serve all mankind, and all eternity. As the years went by, and ever more biographies were written in ever more extensive detail, so the Prophet came to be ever more venerated. That his birth had been marked by incontrovertible wonders, whether the appearance of strange stars in the sky or the whisperings of *jinn* in the ears of clairvoyants, foretelling a new age to come, had been well known to Ibn Hisham; but time would radically improve on this record of miracles. Fresh evidence—wholly unsuspected by Muhammad's earliest biographers—would see him revered as a man able to foretell the future, to receive messages from camels, and palm trees, and joints of meat, and to pick up a soldier's eyeball, reinsert it, and make it work better than before. The result was one yet additional miracle: the further in time from the Prophet a biographer, the more extensive his biography was likely to be.

Not that it required a whole book to spell out a lesson from the life of Muhammad. A single anecdote, a single phrase, would do. *Hadiths*, these snatches of biographical detail were termed—and already, a bare century after the time of Ibn Hisham, they existed in their tens, perhaps their hundreds, of thousands. Anyone with a taste for lists could consult one of a number of vast compilations, arranged neatly by subject. There was barely a topic, it seemed, on which Muhammad had not opined. Should the God-fearing wish to know whether they could marry demons, or why most of the damned in hell were women, or how an orgasm during procreation would affect the appearance of the resulting child, then a *hadith* would provide the answer. Scraps from Muhammad's biography they might have been; but they were also a record, preserved for the edification of later generations, of the Prophet's entire outlook on life. What could possibly be more precious to the Muslim people than that? Taken together, as the *hadiths* increasingly were, they constituted something infinitely more significant than a mere anthology of quotations. What they embodied was a quite exceptional body of law, one that touched upon every conceivable facet of human existence and left almost nothing unregulated, almost nothing to chance: "*Sunna*," as *hadith* scholars termed it. Here, then, was yet another of the glories of the Muslim people. Not for them laws dredged up from the sump of worldly custom or invention—their laws, they proudly boasted, derived directly from heaven. It was the *Sunna*, by instructing the faithful in their duties towards the poor, and by prescribing for them with great precision how to pray, where to go on pilgrimage, what to eat, and when to fast, that had succeeded in taming the instincts of previously savage societies, and granting them a glimpse of what a civilised community of human beings might truly become. Those who lived by its tenets viewed this as an accomplishment so miraculous that they never doubted its divine origin. As one renowned *hadith*-master put it, with a triumphant show of logic, "It was brought to the Prophet by Gabriel, and Gabriel was sent from God."[26]

So it was, during the ninth and tenth Christian centuries, that episodes from the life of Muhammad came to be woven imperishably into the fabric of Muslim life. The age of the Prophet and his companions was not forgotten. Those who laboured, generation after generation, to preserve its memory never doubted the full, revolutionary implications of their undertaking. It was not enough to provide the vast mass of the faithful with codes and standards of behaviour; the appetites of the rich, and of the powerful, and of the well-fed, those whose flaunting of the dictates of social justice had so provoked the anger of the Prophet in the first place, had to be tamed as well. "No man is a believer who fills his stomach while his neighbour goes hungry."[27] Here, and in the multitude of *hadiths* like it, were maxims calculated to unsettle anyone who had grown fat on the pickings of empire. Indeed, to an elite rotten with oppression and greed, Muhammad's indignation at the inequities of human society, preserved in the record of his sayings, was bound to appear chilling in the extreme. No wonder, then, that the scholars of the Caliphate, justly suspicious of the ambitions and appetites of their rulers, should have toiled to authenticate the *hadiths*. The Muslim people could be left in no doubt about their veracity—no matter how challenging they might be. Here, for the jurists and the biographers, the historians and the religious scholars of Islam, was yet another prodigious task. The links that bound their own world to the time of the Prophet had to be certified as proven—and to the satisfaction of all.

The stakes, then, could hardly have been higher. Establish the *hadiths* as genuine, and the present would be grappled impregnably to the past. Naturally, it was essential that the struts and supports deployed for this purpose—the "*isnads*," as they were termed in Arabic—be strong enough to hold firm across the centuries. Only an unbroken succession of authorities, each traceable to the next across the generations, culminating in a personal report of the Prophet himself, could be fit for purpose. Fortunately, there was no shortage of such chains of transmission. The links of the *isnads* held true. Five hundred years on from the death of Muhammad, and it seemed to many Muslim scholars that there was barely an aspect of human life that had not, thanks to all their titanic efforts, been safely secured and fettered to some salutary *hadith*. There was now not the slightest risk that the faithful might lose sight of the Prophet's example. Just the opposite: the moorings that bound past to present could hardly have been rendered any the more secure. The *isnads*, like a tracery of filaments forged across time, seemed as infinite as they were unbreakable. Far from receding out of view, Muhammad's life had been preserved in an almost pointillist depth of detail.

Nor, of course, was that the limit of the legacy left by the Prophet to the faithful. No matter all the many wonders and prodigies increasingly attributed to him by his biographers, the Muslim people knew, deep down in their hearts, that there had been only the one transcendent miracle. "We have made the Book to descend upon you, a clear explanation for all things."[28] So God had assured Muhammad. The "Book" was, of course, the sum of all the many revelations granted to the Prophet over the course of his life; and these, written down by his followers, had then, after his death, been assembled to form a single "recitation"—a "qur'an." Quite how and by whom this great project of memorialisation had been undertaken would subsequently be much debated; but it gradually came to be accepted that the man responsible had been Uthman, the third of the Caliphs. As a result, the word of God, which had first been gasped out by the Prophet all those years before in the cave outside Mecca, was preserved in written form, to the eternal benefit of mankind: "a mercy and a remembrance to those who have faith."[29] To the Muslim people, this "recitation" was a prize beyond compare. Not a word of it, not a letter, but it was touched with the fire of God. Undimmed, undimmable, the Qur'an offered to all those who dwelt on earth something infinitely precious: nothing less than a glimpse of the radiance of heaven.

A prize such as this, it seemed to many, could only ever have existed uncreated, beyond the dimensions of time and space: for to imagine that God might somehow be distinct from His word was, of course, to commit the mortal offence of *shirk*. Quite how this insight was to be reconciled with the undoubted fact that Muhammad had received his revelations over a period of several years was a question requiring much delicate and ingenious investigation: not surprisingly, many centuries would pass before the problem was finally resolved to everyone's satisfaction. Deep waters—and only a Muslim whose entire life had borne witness to his piety, wisdom and learning could presume so much as to dip his toe into the infinitude of such an ocean. If the writing of a commentary on the Qur'an—"*tafsir*," as it was known—ranked as the most praiseworthy activity known to scholarship, then so also was it easily the most hedged about by danger. No Muslim, but he knew that "torment upon torment" awaited those who "obstructed the path to God."[30] Peril awaited the unwary student of the Qur'an at every step. The consequences of error might be fatal indeed.

And yet the challenge, over the centuries, did succeed in being met—and gloriously so. A whole ornate scaffolding of commentary, rising in ever more spreading detail, came to be constructed around the luminous core that was the Qur'an itself. One particularly notable achievement was the identification of the process by which the Prophet, step by step, had received the word of God: no simple matter, to be sure. The divine purpose, after all, had been to send a message to humanity—not to scatter clues around for the benefit of Muhammad's biographers. As a result, allusions to the life of the Prophet within the holy text were so opaque as to verge on the impenetrable. Muhammad himself, for instance, was mentioned by name a bare four times.[31] The places associated with him received only fleeting and ambiguous reference. Not even the most dramatic episodes in his career—his confrontation with the Quraysh, his flight to Medina, his purification of the *Ka'ba*—received direct corroboration. Far from providing a roadmap of the Prophet's life, the Qur'an was so dense, so allusive, so elliptical, as to require almost a roadmap itself. Fortunately for the Muslim people, however, it was precisely such a roadmap that the *tafsirs* were able to provide. Armed with these, the faithful could trace what would otherwise have been untraceable: the precise stages by which the Qur'an had been received by Muhammad. Only by reading the holy text with a commentary was it possible, for instance, to distinguish between the various revelations given in Mecca, and those given in Medina; to identify the precise verses that had followed the Battle of Badr; to recognise allusions to the Prophet's concealment in a cave during the course of the *hijra*, or to his villainous uncle, or to the domestic arrangements of his wives. Authentication, as with all the other fruits of Muslim scholarship, was provided by unimpeachable witnesses. *Isnads* stretched back resplendent to the moment of each original recitation. Proofs bristled everywhere. Immortal and uncreated the Qur'an may have been; but it had also been firmly tethered to the bedrock of the human past. God had spoken to Muhammad—and Muhammad had belonged to the world. Islam was to be regarded both as eternal, and as born of a specific moment in time, a specific place, a specific prophet.

"The believers were done a favour," so the Qur'an informed its readers, "when God sent among them a messenger, of their number, reciting to them His verses, purifying them and teaching them the Book and Wisdom, when before they had been in manifest error."[32] Here, in this ringing assertion, lay the very essence of how the Muslim people saw the origins of their faith. Origins that were to be interpreted not merely as a matter of historical record, but as indubitable and irrefutable proof of the shaping hand of God Himself.

Airy Nothings

It was hardly surprising that the great labour of fashioning the *Sunna* took Muslim scholars so long. Such was the compendious quantity of sayings attributed to the Prophet that only in the eleventh Christian century, some four hundred years after his death, could jurists plausibly claim to have bagged the lot. Even then, however, they could not relax. An even greater challenge awaited them: defining precisely what it was that God, speaking through His Prophet, had bestowed upon the Muslim people. Naturally, fathoming the purposes of an omnipotent and omniscient deity was no simple matter. As one ninth-century scholar, in a tone of awed defeatism, had put it: "Imagination does not reach Him, and thinking does not comprehend Him."[33] In the event, it would take six hundred long years of bitter and occasionally murderous argument before scholars of the *Sunna* could finally be brought to agree on the nature of the Qur'an: that it was eternal, not created, and divine, not a reflection of God.

There were certain problems altogether too critical, too sensitive, too awkward to be rushed.

Muslim theologians were not the first to wrestle with the implications of this. Long before the words of God manifested themselves in the mouth of Muhammad, Christians too had struggled to explain how a deity who transcended time and space might conceivably have descended from heaven to earth. That they identified this intrusion of the divine into the realm of the mortal with a person rather than a book had done nothing to lessen the challenge. Indeed, Christians had wrangled over the nature of Christ for quite as long as Muslim scholars would go on to debate the nature of the Qur'an. Admittedly, in the early years of the Christian faith, these arguments had hardly been such as to disturb the councils of nations; but during late antiquity, when emperors and kings started to wrestle with them too, whole empires were transformed by the arcana of such debates. Just as the civilisation of Islam would be transfigured by the musings of philosophers, so would Christendom. East and west, much of the world was destined to bear witness to what had been, perhaps, the most startling discovery of late antiquity: that pondering how God might have manifested Himself on earth could serve to transform the way entire peoples behaved and thought.

Nevertheless, while Muslims and Christians faced very similar knots, their respective attempts to unravel these set them on radically different courses. Clearly, if God were to be identified with words in a book, then those words were bound to defy all attempts at rational analysis. Even to contemplate such a project was blasphemy. Devout Muslims were no more likely to question the origins of the Qur'an than devout Christians were to start ransacking Jerusalem for the skeleton of a man with holes in his hands and feet. This was because the nearest Christian analogy to the role played in Islam by the Prophet's revelations was not the Bible but Jesus—the Son of God. The record of Christ's life, for all that it lay at the heart of the Christian faith, was not considered divine—unlike Christ Himself. Although Christians certainly believed it to be the word of God, they also knew that it had been mediated through eminently fallible mortals. Not only were there four different accounts of Christ's life in the Bible, but it contained as well a whole host of other books, written over a vast expanse of time, and positively demanding to be sifted, compared and weighed the one against the other. As a result, the contextualising of ancient texts came to be second nature to scholars of the Bible, and the skills required to attempt it hard-wired into the Christian brain. *If only this were true! Too much Western self congratulation!*

And in due course, into brains that were barely Christian at all. By the eighteenth century, the Church had long ceased to hold the monopoly on subjecting its holy texts to scholarly enquiry. The model of history promoted by Eusebius—which traced in the past the working of the purposes of God—had started to devour itself. In his massive account of the decline and fall of the Roman Empire, the English historian Edward Gibbon subjected some of the most venerated compositions of late antiquity to a pathologist's scalpel: "The only defect of these pleasing compositions is the want of truth and common sense."[34] So he dismissed, with his customary solemn sneer, the writings of one prominent saint. Yet his tone of irony was to prove a mere presentiment of the far more naked scepticism that would increasingly, from the nineteenth century onwards, see almost every tenet of the Christian faith subjected to the most merciless dissection. The shock, to a still devout European public, was seismic. In 1863, when a lapsed seminarian by the name of Ernest Renan presumed to publish a biography of Jesus that treated its subject not as a god, but as a man like any other, it was condemned in horrified terms by one critic as nothing less than a "new crucifixion of Our Lord."[35] The book promptly became a runaway bestseller. Scandalous it may have been, but the European public, it appeared, was not entirely averse to being scandalised.

Of course, it was not only the life of Christ that was being put under the microscope. Four years before the publication of Renan's tome, Charles Darwin had brought out his epochal study *On the Origin of Species*—with devastating implications for any notion that the biblical account of the Creation might somehow embody a literal truth. The genie of scepticism was now well and truly out of the bottle. Time would demonstrate that there was to be no going back, in the Christian West, on the habit of subjecting to scientific enquiry what had for millennia been regarded as the sacrosanct word of God. Throughout the nineteenth century, in the hushed and sombre libraries of German theology departments, scholars would crawl and teem over the pages of the Bible, gnawing away at the sacred text like termites. Its first five books, they demonstrated, far from having been written by Moses, as had always traditionally been taught, seemed instead to have been stitched together from multiple sources.* Not only that, but these same sources had almost certainly been written centuries after the events that they purported to describe. Moses, it appeared, had been made into a mouthpiece for laws that he might very well never have pronounced—if, that was, he had even existed in the first place. Here was an unravelling of the scriptural tapestry so destructive that even some scholars themselves began to fret over the implications. "It is to suspend the beginnings of Hebrew history," as one German theologian noted grimly, "not upon the grand creations of Moses, but upon airy nothings."[36]

Meanwhile, as scholars in Europe were busy prodding and yanking at the mighty fabric of their ancestral scriptures, their counterparts in the Islamic world had attained a whole new plateau of complacency. Back in the eighteenth century, at around the same time as Gibbon was embarking on his great history of Rome, Muslim jurists were concluding that they had at last learned every lesson to be gleaned from the example of the Prophet, and that the "gate of interpretation"[37] was therefore closed. Even Gibbon, the inveterate sceptic, had been impressed by the reams of evidence that the would-be biographer of Muhammad seemed able to draw upon. To him, and to other European scholars, the depth and detail of Muslim writings on the origins of Islam came as a revelation; nor did they ever doubt that

---

* That Moses could not possibly have been the author of the first five books of the Bible was a conclusion that had first been drawn as far back as the eleventh century, by a Jewish physician employed at a Muslim court in Spain.

Muhammad's career and character could authentically be known. "It is not the propagation but the permanency of his religion that deserves our wonder," Gibbon wrote. "[T]he same pure and perfect impression which he engraved at Mecca and Medina, is preserved, after the revolutions of twelve centuries, by the Indian, the African, and the Turkish proselytes of the Koran."[38] In comparison with the great figures of the Bible, Muhammad seemed possessed of a striking and enviable solidity. As Renan—a diligent Arabist when not putting the cat among Christian pigeons—memorably put it: "Islam was born, not amid the mystery which cradles the origins of other religions, but rather in the full light of history."[39] Ibn Hisham could not have put it any better.

Except that there was the hint, just the nagging hint, of a problem. Like the tiniest patch of dry rot, it was not, perhaps, immediately apparent; and even those who did spot it were content, in the main, to turn a blind eye. When Gibbon, in a discreet footnote, coyly acknowledged that none of the historians he had consulted for his biography of Muhammad was a writer "of the first century of the Hegira,"[40] he chose not to pursue the implications of this striking confession. A hundred years on, however, and in the wake of all the exacting criticism to which the origins of Judaism and Christianity had been subjected, the realisation was starting to dawn on certain scholars that Islam too, just perhaps, might have its own issue with its sources. The particular focus of their attentions was that vast network of struts and supports which underpinned the *Sunna*, and with it, most Muslims' understanding of their Prophet: the *hadiths*. Perhaps this was only to be expected. In an age when Jewish and Christian scholars had presumed to question the most fundamental tenets of their own faiths, those among them who turned their gaze to Islam were almost bound to raise an eyebrow at the sheer volume of sayings posthumously attributed to Muhammad. The question they asked was a simple one, but no less devastating for that: were the *hadiths* actually genuine?

Now, as it happened, a number of towering Muslim scholars had fretted over the same identical issue a full millennium before. Their researches had been exacting, and their conclusions notably severe. They had freely acknowledged that innumerable *hadiths* had been faked; that Caliphs, lawyers and heretics had invented them willy-nilly to serve their various purposes; that many *hadiths* contradicted one another. Nevertheless, Muslim scholars had insisted, there did remain gold, priceless gold, out there amid the dross. Accordingly, concerned to identify which sayings of the Prophet could be enshrined as genuine and authoritative, and which were to be junked, they had toured all the various lands of the *Umma*, collecting *hadiths* wherever they could find them, and then subjecting each and every one to the most rigorous examination. Of al-Bukhari—the most proficient and celebrated *hadith* hunter—it was said that he had collected 600,000 supposed sayings of the Prophet, and dismissed all but 7225. His collection of *hadiths*—along with those of five other great scholars—was, in effect, what constituted the *Sunna*. As a result, to question their value was to question the entire basis of Islamic law. It was also, in the ultimate reckoning, to question the truth of the portrait of the Prophet himself. The risk of heresy was palpable. Unsurprisingly, then, the vast majority of Muslims had always dreaded to take such a scandalous, such a blasphemous step.*

But this, of course, was hardly a consideration fit to rein in the exacting scepticism of the modern West. Beginning in 1890 and continuing to the present day, a succession of scholars have delivered a series of body-blows to the credibility of the *hadiths* as a record of what Muhammad himself might truly have said. Even the greatest collectors, even al-Bukhari himself, had failed to spot the clues. Heroic though all their efforts at panning for gold had undoubtedly been, yet their rigour had been largely in vain—for the ability to distinguish a

---

* Not all Muslims have accepted the authenticity of the great collections of the *Sunna*: some, back in the past, rejected them out of hand, and some, still today, have collections of their own. Other Muslims, as early as the ninth century, rejected the reliability of *hadiths* altogether, arguing—rather in the manner of modern-day Western scholars—that they were all unreliable and fabricated.

fake will invariably require a certain measure of distance, both of sympathy and time. Modern scholars have been in a position to recognise, as al-Bukhari was not, how even the most seemingly authentic *hadiths* wear a glitter that is all too often that of fool's gold. Far from bearing witness to the opinions of Muhammad, they in truth bear the unmistakable stamp of controversies that were raging two whole centuries after the *hijra*. Over and again, the Prophet had been made to serve as the mouthpiece for a whole host of rival, and often directly antagonistic, traditions. Many of these, far from deriving from Muhammad, were not even Arab in origin, but originated instead in the laws, the customs, or the superstitions of infidel peoples. What the jurists of the early Caliphate had succeeded in pulling off, by means of "a fiction perhaps unequalled in the history of human thought,"[41] was the ultimate in lawyers' tricks: a quite breathtaking show of creativity and nerve. Stitching together a whole new legal framework for the infant empire, it had become the habit of these ingenious scholars to attribute their rulings, not to their own initiative or judgement, but rather to that ultimate in authorities: the Prophet. The dry rot of fabrication, in short, was endemic throughout the *Sunna*. Joseph Schacht, a German professor schooled in the severest tradition of Teutonic textual criticism, and who in 1950 wrote a groundbreaking study of how precisely the *hadith* collections had come to be manufactured, was blunt in spelling out the implications. "We must abandon the gratuitous assumptions," he declared flatly, "that there existed originally an authentic core of information going back to the time of the Prophet."[42] In other words—as a source for the origins of Islam, the *hadiths* were worse than useless.

What about the "supports"—the "*isnads*"—that had been deployed with such care and attention to buttress the sayings of the Prophet? Their function was, of course, precisely to stamp the *hadiths* as genuine: to provide the Muslim people with tested chains of transmission, grappling hooks cast back across the tumult and upheaval of the centuries, anchors that could serve to moor them to the lifetime of the Prophet. Yet if the statements were fakes, then so too, it went without saying, were the *isnad*s. Nor was that the worst. Even supposing that a *hadith* had authentically derived from the time of Muhammad, its value to any would-be biographer of the Prophet was unlikely to be much enhanced by the fact. Context, for the historian, is all—and no Muslim scholar or lawyer who quoted the Prophet ever had the slightest interest in establishing what the original context of his sayings might authentically have been. To brandish a *hadith* was to take for granted that the advice contained within it was timeless and universal. That Muslims in the heyday of the Caliphate were living under circumstances that would have been unimaginable to Muhammad himself never so much as crossed their minds. As a result, where the *isnad*s were not being deployed to disguise a blatant fabrication, they were serving to obliterate all memory of the setting in which the Prophet's sayings had first been delivered. Rather as in an Agatha Christie novel, where it is invariably the suspect with the most ornate alibi who proves to be the murderer, so similarly, in the field of *hadith* studies, it turned out that there was no surer mark of fraud or distortion than a really exacting attention to detail. As Schacht, with the knowing disillusion of a Poirot, put it: "The more perfect the *isnad*, the later the tradition."[43] The lavish name-dropping of references, in anything affecting to cite the Prophet, was a mark, not of reliability, but of precisely the opposite.

Here, then, for anyone committed to believing that what Muslim tradition taught about the origins of Islam might actually have been the literal truth, was a most unsettling possibility. "If all *Hadith* is given up," as a noted Pakistani liberal, Fazlur Rahman, reflected a decade after Schacht's momentous study, "what remains but a yawning chasm of fourteen centuries between us and the Prophet?"[44] His tone of anguish was hardly surprising. Rahman well appreciated that it was not only the lawyers of the early Caliphate who had sought to bridge the "yawning chasm" between themselves and the age of Muhammad through the promiscuous deployment of *isnad*s. Historians had done so as well. How, for instance, had Ibn Hisham been able to substantiate his story of the spectacular contribution made by angels to Muhammad's victory at Badr? He was certainly not the first to write about it. Indeed, he positively gloried in his plagiarism, freely acknowledging that his whole book was a reworking of a biography written half a century earlier by a man named Ibn Ishaq—a child of the grandchildren of the generation of the Prophet. But that, of course, merely begs a further question: how had Ibn Ishaq obtained his own information?

"Remember when you prayed fervently to your Lord," it was written in the Qur'an, "and He answered you: 'I shall reinforce you with a thousand angels, coming in waves.'"[45] This, Muslim scholars had settled, could only have been an allusion to the Battle of Badr. Eye-witnesses too, their testimony copied by Ibn Hisham from Ibn Ishaq's book, had confirmed this verdict. "If I were in Badr today and had my sight," one of them was said to have reminisced, "I could show you the glen from which the angels emerged. I have not the slightest doubt on the point."[46] Here, then, surely, was sufficient evidence to satisfy even the most hardened sceptic? And yet, and yet . . . Both proofs relied on *isnads*. It was an *isnad* which confirmed that the verse in the Qur'an did actually refer to the victory at Badr; it was an *isnad* that confirmed the testimony of the veteran. Remove them, and there was no evidence at all. No wonder, then, that Fazlur Rahman should so have dreaded the "yawning chasm" that he saw the bleak and ravening scepticism of the West as opening up before his faith. "In the vacuity of this chasm not only must the Qur'an slip from our fingers . . . but even the very existence and integrity of the Qur'an and, indeed, the existence of the Prophet himself become an unwarranted myth."[47]

His forebodings were well founded. Over the past forty years, the reliability of what the Muslim historical tradition can tell us about the origins of Islam has indeed come under brutal and escalating attack—to the degree that many historians now doubt that it can tell us anything much of value at all. To be sure, there are still those who will recount the Battle of Badr as though it were an episode as rooted in history as, say, the Battle of Waterloo, carefully analysing Muhammad's strategy, calculating the size of his forces, and illustrating his tactics with arrows on maps.[48] Yet this, to many others, appears a spectacular misreading of the evidence, a confusion of history with something very different: literature. "Clientship and loyalty, plunder and pursuit, challenges and instances of single combat":[49] these were the themes of Ibn Hisham in his account of the Battle of Badr, just as they were similarly the themes that the Greek poet Homer, a millennium and a half earlier, had explored in his great epic of warfare, the *Iliad*. The one features angels; the other gods. Why, then, should we believe that the account of the Prophet's first great victory is any more authentic than the legend of the siege of Troy?

Certainly, it can come as a jolt to discover that, with a single exception, we have no extant descriptions of the Battle of Badr that date from before the ninth century AD. We do not even have Ibn Ishaq's original biography of Muhammad—only revisions and reworkings. As for the material on which Ibn Ishaq himself drew upon for his researches, it has long since vanished. Set against the triumphal hubbub raised by Arab historians in the ninth century, let alone the centuries that followed, the silence is deafening and perplexing. The precise state of play bears spelling out. Over the course of almost two hundred years, the Arabs, a people never noted for their reticence, and whose motivation, we are told, had been an utterly consuming sense of religious certitude, had set themselves to conquering the world—and yet in all that time, they composed not a single record of their victories, not one, that has survived into the present day. How could this possibly have been so, when even on the most barbarous fringes of civilisation, even in Britain, even in the north of England, books of history were being written during this same period, and copied, and lovingly tended? Why, when the savage Northumbrians were capable of preserving the writings of a scholar such as Bede, do we have no Muslim records from the age of Muhammad? Why not a single Arab account of his life, nor of his followers' conquests, nor of the progress of his religion, from the whole of the near two centuries that followed his death?

Even the sole exception to the rule—a tiny shred of papyrus discovered in Palestine and dated to around AD 740—serves only to compound the puzzle.[50] Reading it is like overhearing a game of Chinese whispers. Over the course of only eight lines, it provides something truly startling: a date for the Battle of Badr that is not in the holy month of Ramadan. Why should this come as a surprise? Because later Muslim scholars, writing their learned and definitive commentaries on the Qur'an, confidently identified Badr with an otherwise cryptic allusion to "the day the two armies clashed"[51]— a date that fell in Ramadan. Perhaps, then, on this one point, the scholars were wrong? Perhaps. But if so, then why should they have been right in anything else that they wrote? What if the entire account of the victory at Badr were nothing but a fiction, a dramatic just-so story, fashioned to explain allusions within the Qur'an that would otherwise have remained beyond explanation? A battle on a valley's edge won against terrifying odds; angels swooping down to strike at infidel necks; plunder seized from routed caravans: the holy text certainly alludes to all these things. Yet, aside from a single name-check, Badr itself is never mentioned.[52] There is certainly no confirmation that a great battle—such as the one described by Ibn Hisham—was ever fought there. Whatever else it may be, the Qur'an is no work of history. Startlingly, were it not for all the commentaries elucidating its mysteries, all the biographies of the Prophet, and all the sprawling collections of *hadiths*—none of which, in the form we have them, predates the beginning of the third century after the *hijra*—we would have only the barest reason to associate it with a man named Muhammad at all.

That the coming of Islam was one of the supreme revolutions of world history is evident enough. All the more devastating to realise, then, that of written evidence composed before AD 800, the only traces we possess are either the barest shreds of shreds, or else the delusory shimmering of mirages.[53] No empire can be raised amid a silence, of course; but what we chiefly hear now of the founding of the Caliphate is the merest sound and fury, tales told centuries later, and signifying, if not nothing, then very little. The voices of the Arab warriors who dismembered the ancient empires of Persia and Rome, and of their sons, and of their sons in turn—let alone of their daughters and grand-daughters—have all been silenced, utterly and for ever. Neither letters, nor speeches, nor journals, if they were ever so much as written, have survived; no hint as to what those who actually lived through the establishment of the Caliphate thought, or felt, or believed. It is as though we had no eye-witness accounts of the Protestant Reformation, or the French Revolution, or the two World Wars. No wonder, then, that a leading historian of the process by which Islam, in the ninth and tenth Christian centuries, finally came to construct an accepted past for itself, and to make sense of its rise to global power, should have lamented the "loss of the tradition's earliest layers," and pronounced it "nothing short of catastrophic."[54] Far from Islam having been born in the full light of history, its birth was shrouded in what has appeared, to an increasing number of scholars, an almost impenetrable darkness.

To be sure, there are very few scholars who would go so far as to claim that the Prophet never existed.[55] Someone by the name of Muhammad does certainly appear to have intruded upon the consciousness of his near-contemporaries. One Christian source describes "a false prophet"[56] leading the Saracens in an invasion of Palestine. This was written in AD 634—just two years after the traditional date of Muhammad's death. Another, written six years later, refers to him by name. Over the succeeding decades, a succession of priests and monks would write of an enigmatic figure whom they described variously as "the general," "the instructor" or "the king" of the Arabs. Yet these cryptic allusions—not to mention the fact that they were all made by infidels—merely highlight, once again, the total absence of any early Muslim reference to Muhammad. Only in the 690s did a Caliph finally get around to inscribing the Prophet's name on a public monument; only decades after that did the first tentative references to him start to appear in private inscriptions;[57] and only around 800, of course, did biographies come to be written of Muhammad that Muslims took care to preserve. What might have happened to earlier versions of his life we cannot know for certain; but one possibility is strongly hinted at by none other than Ibn Hisham. Much that previous generations had recorded of the Prophet, he commented sternly, was either bogus, or irrelevant, or sacrilegious. "Things which it is disgraceful to discuss; matters which would distress certain people; and such reports as I have been told are not to be accepted as trustworthy—all these things have I omitted."[58] As well he might have done. What was at stake, in Ibn Hisham's devout opinion, was not merely his status as a reputable historian, nor even his good name as a Muslim, but something infinitely more precious to him: the fate of his soul.

Here, then, at least, is *terra firma*. What we can know with absolute confidence is that by the early ninth century, the precise details of what Muhammad might have said and done some two hundred years previously had come to provide, for vast numbers of people, a roadmap that they believed led straight to heaven. God had seized personal control of human events. The world had been set upon a novel course. To doubt this conviction was to risk hellfire. Given this perspective, it is scarcely surprising that any ambition to write history or biography as we might understand it should have paled into nothingness compared to the infinitely more pressing obligation to trace in the pattern of the Prophet's life the wishes and purposes of the Almighty. That is why, in leaving the age of Ibn Hisham behind, and venturing back into the heaving ocean of uncertainty and conjecture that is the early history of Islam, today's historians can find it such a struggle to identify reliable charts. Adrift amid the shadowy vastness, what prospect of finding landfall? There is always the Qur'an, of course—and yet the holy text itself, once stripped of all its cladding, all the elaborate scaffolding of commentaries built up around it with such labour and devotion from the ninth century onwards, can seem only to add to the voyager's sense of being lost upon a darkling ocean. "It stands isolated," one scholar suggests, "like an immense rock jutting forth from a desolate sea, a stony eminence with few marks on it to suggest how or why it appeared in this watery desert."[59] Or even, most shockingly, when. After all, if the entire colossal edifice of Muslim tradition depends upon *isnads* for its veracity, and if the *isnads* cannot be trusted, then how can we know for sure that the Qur'an dates from the time of Muhammad? How can we know who compiled it, from what sources, for what motives? Can we even be sure that its origins lay in Arabia? In short, do we really know anything at all about the birth of Islam?

Scholarship, like nature, abhors a vacuum. A number of historians, over the past forty years, have responded to the eerie silence that seems to shroud the origins of Islam by rewriting them in often unsettlingly radical ways. It has been argued that the wellspring of the Qur'an lay not in Arabia but in Iraq; that it was written originally not in Arabic but Syriac, the lingua franca of the Near East at the time; that "Muhammad" was originally a title referring to Jesus.[60] By and large, when a book attempts to redraft the origins of a major world religion on quite such a jaw-dropping scale, the cover will feature a picture of the Knights Templar or the Holy Grail. A sensational argument, however, need not necessarily be an exercise in sensationalism. Far from aping Dan Brown, most of the scholars who have explored Islam's origins seem to pride themselves on making their prose as dense with obscure vocabulary, and obscurer languages, as they possibly can. As a result, their speculations have rarely impinged on the public consciousness. Despite the fact that Western interest in Islam, over the past decade or so, has soared to unprecedented heights, the mood of crisis currently convulsing the academic study of its origins has received notably little airtime. Like some shadowy monster of the seas, it only ever rarely breaks for the surface, preferring instead to lurk in the deeps.

Nor is the inherent complexity of the subject the only reason for this. Just as Darwin was physically prostrated by anxiety over how his theories might be received by his family and friends, there are many today no less nervous about causing offence to people whose whole lives are grounded in their faith. For a non-believer to claim that the Qur'an might have originated outside of Arabia, or derived from Christian hymns, or been written in Syriac, is liable to be no less shocking to Muslims than has the Muslim denial of Jesus's divinity always been to Christians. Unlike in nineteenth-century Europe, where it was disillusioned seminarians and the sons of Lutheran pastors who led the way in subjecting the origins of their ancestral religion to the full pitiless glare of historical enquiry, the contemporary Islamic world has not, it is fair to say, shown any great inclination to follow suit. No equivalent of Ernest Renan has emerged, to scandalise and titillate the Muslim faithful. The authorship of the Qur'an has not been questioned by the disillusioned offspring of imams. Those few Muslims who have sought to follow the trail originally blazed by nineteenth-century European scholars have generally opted to publish under pseudonyms—or have suffered the consequences. In the Arab world, at any rate, to doubt the traditional account of Islam's origins has been to risk death threats, prosecution for apostasy, or even defenestration.[61]

As a result, inevitably but regrettably, questioning the traditional narrative of Islam's origins remains largely what it has always been: the preserve of Western scholars. Some of these, it is true, are themselves Muslim—and one of them, a professor at the University of Münster, has proved himself such a chip off the old Teutonic scholarly block that he too, like some of his more radical infidel colleagues, has gone on record as claiming Muhammad to be a figure of myth.[62] None of which, unhappily, has done much to allay the suspicions of other Muslims that the probing of their most sacred traditions is not all some sinister conspiracy, most likely cooked up by Mossad, or perhaps the Vatican, or else American evangelicals. That the methods currently being deployed by Western scholars to place the Qur'an in its historical context were first honed upon the Bible has dented this conviction not a whit. One appalled Muslim scholar has argued that "even the crusaders' fury pales to nothing" in comparison with modern academics' "iconoclastic attack."[63] Implicit in this bellow of indignation is the presumption that non-believers have no business poking their noses into Islam's origins. As one Saudi professor sternly tells his co-religionists, "Only the writings of a practising Muslim are worthy of our attention."[64]

Taken to its logical extreme, of course, this would mean that only worshippers of Jupiter could legitimately write about the Romans, and only Odinists about the Vikings. Nevertheless, it is hardly necessary to be a Saudi theologian, or even a Muslim at all, to find something profoundly destabilising in the thesis that the stories told by Islam about its own origins might obscure as much as they reveal. The faithful, after all, are not alone in having a massive stake in the veracity of their inherited traditions. So too do plenty of non-Muslim historians. Whole centuries' worth of scholarship have been founded on the presumption that the sources for early Islam can be trusted. To this day, they continue to be recycled endlessly, whether in popular biographies of Muhammad or in academic texts.[65] It still tends to be taken for granted that they remain, for anyone wishing to construct a narrative of Islam's origins, the only real building blocks to hand. Unsurprisingly, then, over the past century—and particularly over the past few decades—many scholars of early Islam have conducted an aggressive rearguard action to save these sources from total redundancy. Despite the increasingly widespread acknowledgement among historians of the period that it is "exceedingly difficult to know much about Islamic origins,"[66] attempts to shore up the foundations continue. The building blocks fashioned by Ibn Hisham and his successors have certainly not been abandoned yet.

Paradoxically, however, these attempts to repair the damage done to the mighty edifice of Muslim tradition do more than anything else to highlight the full scale of the paradigm shift that is afflicting it. Clearly, when two scholars can devote their entire careers to studying the same languages and sources, and yet arrive at wholly contradictory conclusions, it is no longer possible to presume that there is anything remotely self-evident about the birth of Islam. Forty years ago, any querying what Muslim tradition taught about its own origins might have been dismissed as mere crankish trouble-making: one that no more merited a response from heavyweight experts than did, say, the attempt to ascribe Shakespeare's plays to Francis Bacon or the Earl of Oxford. Nowadays, it is hard to think of any other field of history so riven by disagreement as is that of early Islam. One of the world's leading Qur'anic scholars has gone so far as to speak of a "schism." "The controversy about the Qur'an," she has lamented—whether it is an authentic record of the Prophet's utterances or an anthology, stitched together from various different sources—"permeates the entire field of Qur'anic studies."[67] Yet, even to speak of "schism" may be overly optimistic. The reality, perhaps, is even messier. In truth, it can often seem—the fragmentary nature of the evidence being what it is, not to mention the complexity and sensitivity of the issues at stake—that there are as many different interpretations of Islam's origins as there are experts writing about it.[68]

All of which, in a non-specialist, can tend to inspire a peculiarly lurching sense of dizziness: the kind that might afflict someone studying a *trompe-l'oeil* in a hall of mirrors. No wonder, then, that it should sometimes feel tempting to back away from the problem altogether, to close one's eyes to it, to pretend that it does not exist. Rehash the traditional Muslim sources, and follow the path of least resistance. After all, as one prominent *hadith* scholar has cheerily admitted, the entire "*isnad* debate" is not merely "long" but "tedious." Nevertheless, as he then reminds the faint-hearted, "it is one in which scholars of Islamic origins must participate. There is no ignoring the debate in order to forge ahead with more important or more intriguing issues." To avoid it is "at best naïve and at worst negligent."[69] History, unlike faith, cannot be built upon foundations of sand.

But where is solid bedrock to be found? When I first embarked on the project of writing this book, I had no idea that locating it would prove so problematic. My initial state of ignorance being what it was, I had vaguely assumed, based on my reading of numerous biographies of the Prophet, that I would find a whole wealth of sources dating from his lifetime just waiting to be quarried. It was therefore a bit of a blow to discover that the bulk of what we have constitutes, in the memorable formulation of one historian, "a monument to the destruction rather than the preservation of the past."[70] The same questions that have been confronting scholars of early Islam for the past forty years were now staring me full in the face. How, if the underpinnings of Muslim tradition are so unstable, is it possible to write anything at all about Islam's origins? What hope, if the *isnads* and all the many writings that depend upon them are unreliable, of ever explaining the birth of one of the world's great civilisations? Can it really be the case that the lack of a story is the only story?

Fortunately, amid all the confusion and obscurity, of one thing at least we can be confident: Islam did not originate in a total vacuum. Of the world into which Muhammad was born, with its rival superpowers and its formidable array of monotheisms, we are most decidedly not ignorant. To compare the would-be universal dominions of Persia and Rome with the empire that the Caliphate became, or to trace echoes of Jewish and Christian writings in the Qur'an, is to recognise that Islam, far from spelling the end of what had gone before, seems in many ways to have been its culmination. Even the belief to which Muslims have long subscribed, that the Prophet received his revelations not by means of human agency, but courtesy of an angel, in fact hints at just how deeply rooted are the doctrines of Islam within the subsoil of the ancient Near East. From where precisely does the tradition of Muhammad's first terrifying encounter with Gabriel in a cave derive? There is no reference to it in the Qur'an; nor to the Prophet's initial agony when receiving the revelations; nor even to the hearing of any supernatural voice. Across the lands conquered by the Arabs, however, it had long been taken for granted that angels visited those particularly favoured by God—and that the experience was often agonising. Coincidence? It seems most unlikely. Rather, it surely reflects the unique circumstances of the world that the Arabs, building on the foundations laid by the Persians and the Romans, had made their own: a world in which the yearning to fathom the purposes of a single god had become universal, and Gabriel a name on everybody's lips.

All of which, to anyone pondering how a Near East divided between two venerable empires might have ended up Muslim, opens up an intriguing and suggestive line of enquiry. Is it possible that Islam, far from originating outside the mainstream of ancient civilisation, was in truth a religion in the grand tradition of Judaism and Christianity—one bred of the very marrow of late antiquity?

The Sectarian Milieu

Gabriel—or Jibril, as he is called in Arabic—is not entirely absent from the Qur'an. One verse confirms him as the agent who has been bringing down revelations into the heart of God's chosen messenger; a second, somewhat bathetically, describes him as primed to intervene in a domestic squabble between the Prophet and two of his wives.[71] Clearly, then, wherever and whenever the Qur'an may have been composed, its target audience was perfectly familiar with the most celebrated angel in the Bible. Clinching proof of this is provided by the detailed coverage given by the Prophet to what, for Christians, had always ranked as the ultimate in annunciations: Gabriel's visitation to Mary, the mother of Christ. The episode is given a notably starry role as well in the Qur'an—where it is retold not once, but twice. Mary was evidently a person much on the Prophet's mind. Not only is she the one woman in his revelations to be mentioned by name, but she features as well in a whole range of incidents quite aside from the Annunciation. Details left unrecorded by the New Testament—for instance, that she went into labour beneath a palm tree, where her son, speaking from within her womb, encouraged her to snack on a date or two—are given pride of place in the Qur'an. Gratifying evidence, so it appeared to Muslims contemptuous of the Christian scriptures, that they were far better informed about the life of Jesus than were those who, in their folly and delusion, presumed to worship him as a god.

But how had the Prophet come by these various stories? To Muslims, of course, the question was a waste of breath. Muhammad had been visited by the divine. Just as Christians believed that Mary, by giving birth to her son, had delivered what they termed the *Logos*, or the "Word,"[72] so Muhammad's followers knew that his revelations, gasped out with "the sweat dripping from his forehead,"[73] were the veritable speech of God. Muslims were no more likely to ask whether the Prophet had been influenced by the writings of other faiths than were Christians to wonder whether Mary had truly been a virgin. What the stiff-necked Jews and the obdurately blinkered Christians had failed to realise, in the opinion of the Muslim faithful, was that every single prophet mentioned in the Bible had actually been a follower of Islam. Hence the starring roles granted to so many of them, from Adam to Jesus, in the Qur'an. And to Mary too, of course. That stories of the Virgin being succoured by a friendly palm tree had actually been a Christian tradition for centuries, and seem in turn to have derived from a legend told by the pagan Greeks, was blithely ignored—as, of course, it was bound to be.[74] No Muslim scholar could possibly have countenanced a notion that the Prophet might have been in the business of filching anecdotes from infidels. The Qur'an, after all, did not derive from outside sources. Rather, it was the Jews and the Christians, by allowing their holy books to become corrupted, who had ended up with distorted, second-hand scriptures. Only in the Qur'an had the awful purity of the divine revelation been properly preserved. Every last word of it, every last syllable, every last letter, came directly from God, and from God alone.

Perhaps it was only to be expected, then—despite the profoundly ambiguous testimony of the holy text itself—that a tradition should gradually have grown up, which in due course hardened into orthodoxy, that Muhammad himself had been illiterate.* Even had the Prophet wished to curl up with an infidel book or two, in other words,

---

* Two verses, Qur'an: 7.157 and 29.48, are used to adduce the theory of Muhammad's illiteracy. 7.157 refers to him as "*ummi*": a word conventionally translated as "unlettered," but which could also mean "lacking a scripture," in the sense of being neither Jewish or Christian. Adding to the uncertainty is the fact that the Qur'an frequently refers to itself as a *kitab*, a book, while in 25.4–6, it is strongly implied that Muhammad could indeed read. Even more suggestively, Ibn Hisham has reports which imply that Muhammad could not merely read, but write.

it would have been beyond him to decipher them. Yet reassuring a reflection though this certainly provided to the faithful, it still did not rank, perhaps, as the surest evidence that the Qur'an had truly descended from the celestial heights. Even more infallible a proof was witnessed by the circumstances of Muhammad's upbringing. Mecca, after all, had been inhabited by pagans, not Jews or Christians—and it stood right in the middle of an enormous and empty desert. The ancient capitals of the Near East, which for more than four thousand years had served as the cockpits of civilisation, immense petri-dishes teeming with peoples of every conceivable faith, dense with temples, and synagogues, and churches, were a colossal distance away. Even to the borders of Palestine, where Abraham had built his tomb, and Solomon reigned, and Jesus been crucified, it was a full eight hundred miles. What likelihood, then, the Muslim faithful demanded to know, that a prophet born and raised so far from such a milieu could conceivably have been influenced by its traditions and doctrines and writings? The sheer prophylactic immensity of the desert that surrounded Mecca, impenetrable to outsiders as it was, appeared to render the answer obvious. Just as it was the blood and muscle of Mary's virgin womb that had, in the opinion of Christians, nurtured the coming into the world of the divine, so likewise, in the opinion of Muslims, was it the spreading sands of Arabia which had served to preserve the word of God, over the course of its protracted delivery, in a fit condition of untainted purity.

But the emptiness into which Islam had been born was more than physical. The void had been a spiritual one as well. Muslim scholars termed it *Jahiliyyah*—the "Age of Ignorance."[75] The Arabs, who had drunk, and stolen, and brawled, and thought nothing of burying unwanted children in the sands, nor of practising the most unspeakable sexual abominations, nor of conducting the most interminable feuds, had been lost, it appeared to their heirs, in that pitchest blackness which was the lack of knowledge of God; and this it was that had made the coming of the Prophet all the brighter, all the more dazzling and refulgent a dawn. The contrast between Islam and the age that had preceded it was as clear as that between midday and the dead of night. Yet, it was not only Arabia that had been lost in darkness. The whole world had laboured in the shadows of *jahl*—"ignorance." God, however, was great. The old order had been gloriously toppled, and a Caliphate established in its place. Everything had been brought to change. The white radiance of Islam, blazing beyond the borders of Arabia to the limits of the globe, had served to bring all humanity into a wholly new age of light.

This, however, was to redraft history in a quite stunningly radical way. Never before had the past been dismissed with such utter and imperious disdain. Even to Christians, the cycles of time redeemed by the birth of Christ had served as a preparation for the coming of the Messiah. To Muslims, however, everything that had preceded the revelations of their Prophet, all its manifold splendours and achievements, had been the merest phantom show, a *shirk*-haunted wasteland, to which Islam owed precisely nothing. The effect of this presumption was to prove incalculable. To this day, even in the West, it continues to inform the way in which the history of the Middle East is interpreted and understood. Whether in books, museums or university departments, the ancient world is invariably presumed to have ended with the coming of Muhammad. It is as though everything that had made antiquity what it was came to a sudden and crunching halt around AD 600. The inherent implausibility of this is rarely considered. Instead, at a time when most historians are profoundly suspicious of any notion that great civilisations might emerge from nowhere, owing nothing to what went before, and transforming human behaviour in the merest blinking of an eye, Islam continues to be portrayed as somehow exceptional: lightning from a clear blue sky.

Clearly, if the Qur'an did descend from heaven, then there is no problem in explaining why the stories it tells of Mary, say, should contain such palpable trace-elements of Christian folklore and classical myth. All things, after all, are possible to God. Yet even on the presumption that what Islam teaches is correct, and that the midwife of the faith was genuinely an angel, it is still pushing things to

51

imagine that the theatre of its conquests might suddenly have been conjured, over the span of a single generation, into a set from *The Arabian Nights*. Just because histories written by pious Muslims two hundred years later can serve to give us such an impression does not mean that they are right. The Near East of the Caliphate at the peak of its power and glory was decidedly not that of its foundation two centuries before. To presume otherwise is not merely to perpetuate the notion of the Arab conquests as the sudden dropping of a guillotine onto the neck of everything that preceded them, but to risk enshrining bogus tradition as historical fact. To understand the origins of Islam, and why it evolved in the way that it did, we must look far beyond the age of Ibn Hisham. We must explore the empires and religions of late antiquity.

And if we do, then the landscape through which the first Arab conquerors rode does not seem so very different from landscapes elsewhere in the one-time Roman Empire. Landscapes marked by the seismic shock of superpower collapse; by the desperate struggle of erstwhile provincials to fashion new lives, and new security, for themselves; and by the depredations of foreign invaders, speaking strange languages and adhering to peculiar creeds. What the Arab conquest of formerly Roman provinces such as Palestine and Syria served to demonstrate was that the rising tide beneath which the western half of the empire had vanished was now rolling in across its eastern possessions.

"I took from you at Herakleopolis sixty-five sheep. I repeat—sixty-five and no more, and as an acknowledgement of this fact, we have made the present confirmation."[76] This was the receipt issued by an Arab war band in 642 to the city fathers of Herakleopolis, a somnolent backwater in what only two years previously had still ranked as the Roman province of Egypt. The seamless fusion of extortion and bureaucracy contained in the document would have been nothing unfamiliar to the elites of other abandoned provinces—whether in North Africa or Spain, Italy or Gaul. The security of Rome's empire had gone—and gone for good. Compromise with barbarian overlords, in an age of Roman retreat and diminishment, had become the name of the game.

Granted, the Arabs who had come swaggering into Herakleopolis do seem to have been uniquely self-possessed. Fastidiously, they logged the date of their transaction with the city elders: in Greek, as "the thirtieth of the month of Pharmouthi of the first indiction," and in their own language, as "the year Twenty-Two." To us, with the benefit of hind-sight, it is the latter detail that leaps out. Redeemed from a provincial rubbish tip, it constitutes something truly momentous: the earliest mention on any surviving datable document of what would end up enshrined as the Muslim calendar. Clearly, then, it was something more than merely a greed for mutton that had brought the Arabs to Herakleopolis. But what? Some sense of a new beginning, of a new order, self-evidently. Yet whether their beliefs and ambitions were equivalent to what we would recognise today as Islam is altogether less clear. It is noteworthy, for instance, that the conquerors are described on the back of the receipt, not as Muslims, but as something altogether more enigmatic: *Magaritai*. What precisely this might have meant, and how it was to be linked to the unfamiliar dating system employed by the newcomers, and whether, if at all, it had been inspired by some novel understanding of God, the document does not reveal. Instead, it is the motives of those who are being screwed for livestock, the city fathers of Herakleopolis, that are the more readily transparent. How else, after all, save by attempting to patch together an accommodation with their unwanted guests, were they to salvage anything of the *status quo*? If there was much from the past that would necessarily have to be junked, then so too was there much that might be redeemed. In what had once, two centuries before, been the western half of the empire, the ghosts of Rome's vanished order still haunted the barbarian kingdoms that had been founded upon its grave. In the East as well, judging from the receipt issued at Herakleopolis, the old order did not change overnight, yielding place to new. Its legacy endured.

Of course, it was not only Roman ghosts who haunted the dominion established by the Arabs in the seventh century. In the lowlands of Mesopotamia and the uplands of Iran, there was the spectre of the empire of the Persian kings. This dominion had in turn been raised upon the foundations of still older monarchies, sediment upon sun-baked sediment: for imperialism, in the East, reached back to the dawn of time. Dimly, in the scriptures of the Jews and the Christians, this was remembered: that there had once been such things as pharaohs and great towers raised up on the banks of the Euphrates to the sky. Yet their sense of this rarely served to oppress them: for if the landscapes of Egypt and Mesopotamia could not help but bear witness to their disorientingly ancient pasts, then so also, in the East, had it become the practice of its peoples to look fixedly to the future. The Jews awaited their messiah; the Christians the return of Christ. Others too shared in what had become the common presumption of the age: that the patterns of human affairs were being traced directly by the finger of God. There were the followers of the Persian prophet Zoroaster, who saw the world as divided into warring factions of good and evil; and the Samaritans, who proclaimed in their creed how there was no god but God, and the Gnostics, who believed that it was possible for a revelation of the divine to descend via angels to chosen mortals; and all the other numerous heretics, and cultists, and sectarians that the Near East had long seemed effortlessly to breed. Prodigious the number of empires sprung from its soil might well have been—and yet not half so prodigious as the number of gods. And this was the soil, the very soil, from which were destined to sprout the pillars of the Caliphate: a dominion that proclaimed itself to be both a universal state and the instrument of heaven's purpose.

Given all this, how can it possibly make sense to explain the emergence of Islam with reference to Islam alone? That Muslim tradition attributes the origins of the Qur'an and the *Sunna* to an illiterate man living in a pagan city in the middle of a desert is a problem, not a solution. Perhaps, had the revelations of the Prophet materialised in some other period and place, then the fact that the presumptions of the late antique Near East are shot through them like letters through a stick of rock would indeed appear an authentic miracle. As it is, the distance between Mecca and the lands of the Roman and Persian empires to the north suggests a mystery of the kind that perplexed early cartographers when they mapped Africa and South America, and observed that the eastern and western coasts of the Atlantic Ocean seemed to match like the pieces of a gigantic jigsaw puzzle. Any notion that continents might have been drifting around the globe appeared too ludicrous to contemplate. Only in the 1960s, with the theory of plate tectonics, did a convincing solution finally emerge. A remarkable coincidence turned out not to have been a coincidence at all.

The close fit between the religion that came to be known as Islam and the teeming melting-pot of the late antique Near East would seem to suggest an identical conclusion. Indisputably, the order established by the Arabs in the century following the *hijra* was something novel. But originality alone does not tell the whole story. Prototype of every subsequent Islamic empire that it certainly was, the Caliphate founded in the seventh century was also something very much more: the last, the climactic, and the most enduring empire of antiquity. Such is the claim that this book aims to prove. Yet it is as well to admit, at the outset, that such a task is far from easy. Certainty, on a whole range of issues, is impossible. There can only ever be speculation. Cosmologists speak of "singularities"—warpings of time and space where the laws of physics do not apply. The puzzle of Islam's origins might be viewed in a similar way—as a black hole sucking in a great spiralling swirl of influences before casting them back out in a radically different form. The career of Muhammad, traditionally cast as the pivotal episode in the entire history of the Middle East, serves both as the climax of my narrative of the collapse of Roman and Persian power, and as the point where that narrative fragments and breaks down. Does the Qur'an really date from the Prophet's lifetime? Where, if not in Mecca, might he have lived? Why are the references to him in the early Caliphate so sparse, so enigmatic, and so late? The answers I have given to these questions are all of them unashamedly provisional—as I believe they have no choice but to be. That said, my ambition has been to sift and weigh the awesomely complex sources, to try and take account of all the many gaps and inconsistencies that exist within them, and then, albeit tentatively, to marshal them into something resembling a narrative. The context for this attempt, however, is not the traditional one, derived from the works of Muslims who lived whole centuries after Muhammad's death, but rather from those who inhabited the world into which he was born: the empire-shadowed, God-haunted world of late antiquity.

Of the full dazzling colour, variety and complexity of this age, the chronicles written by Muslim historians give barely a hint. Infidels, when they appear at all, are made to speak and act precisely as though they were Arabs.[77] Roman emperors are transformed into mirror-images of Caliphs; Jewish scholars and Christian saints become straw men, shadowy and faceless.* Fortunately, though, our understanding of the extraordinary melting-pot of imperial and religious traditions that provided the context for Islam's evolution does not depend solely on Muslim chronicles. Far from it. While seventh-century sources are threadbare to the point of non-existent, those from the preceding two centuries offer sumptuous riches. We have, for the last time, narratives composed by writers who self-consciously regarded themselves as the heirs of the great historians of classical Greece; we have collections of letters, and digests of laws, and compilations of speeches; we have a gazetteer written by a merchant, and a work of anthropology written by a barbarian, and a seeming infinitude of works of Christian piety, from histories of the Church to lives of fabulously self-mortifying saints. In fact, by the standards of other periods of ancient history, we have an almost miraculous volume of evidence—something that historians of antiquity, like magpies flocking above a cache of diamonds, have seized upon with glee. As a result, over the past few decades, the study of the period has been revolutionised. A civilisation previously dismissed as exhausted, sterile and decaying has been comprehensively

---

* It is only fair to point out that Christian historians were identically partisan. Just as infidels tended to be invisible in Muslim histories, so were pagans, back in the fourth and fifth centuries, no less invisible in histories written by Christians.

rehabilitated. What scholars emphasise now is less its decrepitude, more its energy, its exuberance, its inventiveness.

"We see in late antiquity," as one of its foremost historians has put it, "a mass of experimentation, new ways being tried and new adjustments made."[78] What emerges in the century or so after Muhammad as the religion called Islam is one consequence of this "mass of experimentation"——but there are a whole multitude of others too. The most significant of all these, of course, are Judaism and Christianity: faiths that by the time of Muhammad had taken on something like the form they wear today, but that had once themselves been swirls of beliefs and doctrines no less unformed than those professed by the Arabs in the first century of their empire. The story of how Islam came to define itself, and to invent its own past, is only part of a much broader story: one that is ultimately about how Jews, Christians and Muslims all came by their understanding of religion. No other revolution in human thought, perhaps, has done more to transform the world. No other revolution, then, it might be argued, demands more urgently to be put in proper context.

That is why a history of Islam's origins cannot be written without reference to the origins of Judaism and Christianity——and why in turn a history of the origins of Judaism and Christianity cannot be written without reference to the world that incubated them both. The vision of God to which both rabbis and bishops subscribed, and which Muhammad's followers inherited, did not emerge out of nowhere. The monotheisms that would end up established as state religions from the Atlantic to central Asia had ancient, and possibly unexpected, roots. To trace them is to cast a searchlight across the entire civilisation of late antiquity. From the dental hygiene of Zoroastrian priests to the frontier policy of Roman strategists; from fantasies about Alexander the Great in Syria to tales of buried books of spells in Iraq; from Jews who thought Christ the messiah to Christians who lived like Jews: all are pieces in the jigsaw. It would certainly make little sense to trace the course of the revolution that would climax with the forging of the Caliphate by starting with the revelations of the Muslim Prophet.

Accordingly, we begin not in Mecca, nor even in Jerusalem, but in a land that was the wellspring for two incalculably fruitful convictions: that a human empire might be global; and that the power of an all-good god might be universal.

We begin in Persia.

II

JAHILIYYA

Religion taught by a prophet or by a
preacher of the truth is the only
foundation on which to build a great and
powerful empire.

Ibn Khaldun, *A Universal History*

2

IRANSHAHR

Shah Thing

Any Persian king who doubted that he ruled the most favoured of peoples had only to stroke his chin. Whereas the creator of the universe, in His ineffable wisdom, had seen fit to give the inhabitants of more benighted regions hair that was either too curly or too straight, He had granted the men of Persia beards that embodied the "happy medium."[1] Here, in the magnificence of their personal grooming, the Persians found evidence of a far more profound pre-eminence. "Our land," they liked to point out, "lies in the midst of other lands, and our people are the most noble and illustrious of beings."[2] As with facial hair, then, so with the various attributes and qualities that made for greatness: the Persian people appeared to enjoy the best of all possible worlds.

And certainly, in the centuries that had followed Christ, the name they had carved out for themselves had been a splendid one. Their dominion had spread far beyond the limits of Persia itself: from the frontiers of Syria in the west to those of the Hindu Kush in the east; from the deserts of Arabia in the south to the mountains of Armenia in the north. Nevertheless, the very wealth and glory of such an empire could on occasion lead to anxiety as well as pride. Just as flies

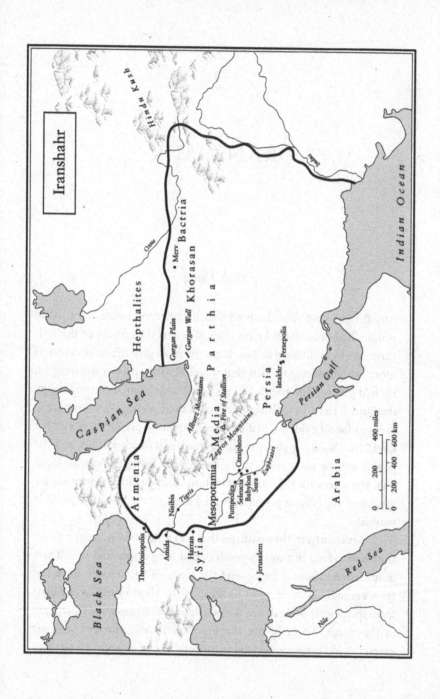

Iranshahr

were drawn to sumptuous banquets, and locusts to fields of corn, so savages were to silk and gold. The Persians, whose reputation for "courage, and boldness, and skill on the day of battle"[3] was well merited, had rarely deigned to regard such intruders as anything other than annoyances, to be swatted every so often with an almost disdainful ease; but that, over the course of the fourth Christian century, had begun to change. Rumours of war from distant frontiers had come to shadow the mood of the Persian heartlands. Victories were still being won, but against increasingly fearsome opponents. The waves crashing against the bulwarks of Persian power appeared to be growing more violent with every passing year. Whole tribes of people, whole nations, were on the move. Soon enough, and the news was darkening even further. Nomads were alarming enough; but not half so alarming as nomads with a taste for putting down roots. By the middle of the fifth Christian century, the empire of the Persians was standing eyeball to eyeball with a menacingly new order of foe: a kingdom of warrior horsemen who had parked themselves directly on its north-eastern flank.

Who were the Hephthalites, and where did they come from? No one was entirely sure. When a people such as the Persians, long settled in a much-cherished homeland, ventured to contemplate the drear immensity of the lands that stretched northwards of their empire, the origins of the savages who infested it, and of the winds that gusted though its grasses, were liable to appear to them mysteries equally without an answer. One popular theory, it was true, held that the enigmatic newcomers were Huns: the most fearsome, as they were the ugliest, of all the steppeland tribesmen. Others, however, pointed out that the Hephthalites—despite their curiously elongated skulls, their sinister taste for mullets and their contemptibly un-Persian beards— "had countenances that were almost attractive."[4] Their skin was not a sallow Hunnic yellow but, like that of the Persians themselves, fetchingly pale. Some took to calling them "White Huns": a suggestion of hybridity that emphasised precisely why the Persians found them so unsettling. These were savages who had dared to found their own monarchy, their own capital city, even their own body of laws. The Persians—who had long gloried in their own triumphant possession of those appurtenances of civilisation—could not possibly ignore such presumption. Nomads who forgot their place needed to be reminded of it—and fast. Indeed, so urgent was the problem that the Persian monarchy decided it could no longer afford to do as it had traditionally done, and delegate the patrolling of the eastern frontier to its underlings. The peril had grown too great. The time had come for the King of Persia, the *Shahanshah*, the "King of Kings" himself, to tame the Hephthalites.

So it was, during the campaigning season of AD 484, that an immense army advanced across the Gurgan Plain, an unsettled frontier zone extending east from the southernmost tip of the Caspian Sea, and which had increasingly come to mark the limits of Persian power.[5] Beyond a landscape patterned with the reassuring marks of civilisation—fields, kilns and canals—there lurked untenanted badlands. "The realm of the wolves," men called them: fit reflection of their aura of menace. As the wooded ramparts of a great chain of mountains, the Alburz, gradually receded into the distance, there came to stretch ahead of the taskforce an unbroken immensity of wild barley, and oats, and corn, rippling, so it seemed, to the limits of the world: the beginning of the steppes. Featureless as this landscape was, and lacking in anything that the Persians would have recognised as civilisation, it had repeatedly frustrated the ambitions of would-be conquerors. Yet, on this occasion, to anyone watching the great host of men, horses and elephants as they trampled down the grasses, the invaders' prospects must have appeared no less glittering than the heads of their ferociously heavy lances. A Persian army at full strength was a fearsome sight. "Everything so far as the eye can reach," as one awe-struck observer put it, "is filled with the shimmer of arms. Whole plains and hills are crowded out by mail-clad horsemen."[6] And by banners as well: since if there was one thing that a Persian warrior really adored, it was a showy flag. Every unit of cavalry possessed one, great, heavy drapes slung from crossbars, and emblazoned with flamboyant heraldic devices: stars, lions, boars. Most splendid of all, it went without saying, was the royal banner: immeasurably the largest, it was also the most sumptuously adorned. Seeing it flapping massively in the breeze, the sunlight glinting off its embroidered gold, silver and jewels, no one could have doubted who was leading the expedition into the realm of the Hephthalites.

The King of Kings, like all his royal ancestors, possessed a literally supernatural mystique. Every Persian knew it, and what was owed to it: not merely their empire, but their very freedom. Two and a half centuries previously, when their forefathers had been slaves of foreign masters, the banner of their independence had been raised by a nobleman named Ardashir—a mighty hero possessed of a mandate from the heavens. No one in the whole of Persia had been more favoured of the gods. One of Ardashir's ancestors, a man named Sasan, had officiated as the high priest of the country's holiest and most venerable temple, at Istakhr. Here, ever since ancient times, it had been the custom to present the severed heads of vanquished enemies to the great warrior goddess, Anahita, "the Strong and Immaculate." Ardashir himself had proved a worthy lieutenant of this ferocious divinity: by AD 224, he had liberated Persia from the rule of outsiders, and to such crushing effect that he had established the Persians themselves as the masters of a host of subject peoples. It was scarcely surprising, then, in the light of such a colossal achievement, that his countrymen should have distinguished about his person the eerie flickering of an aura more than human. His *farr*, the Persians termed it: the mark of his divine election. Here, no less than the empire he had founded, had been a precious heirloom. Unceasingly, as the years went by, and generation sprung from the family of Sasan succeeded generation to the throne of Persia, so had a *farr* continued to shadow each new king. Sometimes it was glimpsed in the shape of a ram; sometimes as a golden ray of light; sometimes in human form, like the sudden flitting of a figure that was no reflection across a mirror. The glamour of it all, naturally enough, helped contribute to a fearsome reputation. Even the Sasanians' enemies, people with every reason to loathe their pretensions, found it difficult not to cringe before them. "A monarchy that is proud and exceedingly powerful": so one foreign commentator described the dynasty in a tone of rueful awe. "For it is old and most intimidating, most intimidating indeed, to those who inhabit the world."[7]

Peroz, the king who had led the massive army into the Gurgan Plain, was, like all his predecessors, a descendant of Sasan. Indeed, in many ways, he was the epitome of a Sasanian: tall and handsome, in the imposing manner expected by the Persians of their royalty, and with an exceptional talent, even by the standards of his forefathers, for playing the dandy. Just as the great banner that billowed above his tent glimmered with fabulous adornments, so did the king himself: for it was his habit to sport, in addition to all his other sumptuous jewellery, "a pearl of wonderful whiteness, greatly prized on account of its extraordinary size"[8] as a stud in his ear. Foreigners may well have viewed such obsession with personal adornment as effeminate, but the Persians themselves knew better. A haughty and refined delicacy of manner; a sashaying, hip-swaying gait; a reluctance so much as to be seen in public "stepping to one side in response to a call of nature": these were the marks, in Persia, of a bold and gallant warrior.[9] Anyone who had the wherewithal was fully expected to pose and strut like a peacock. Rare was the Persian who knowingly underdressed. The gorgeous showiness of their fashion was notorious. "Most of them," it was reported of the Persian upper classes, "are so resplendent in clothes gleaming with many shimmering colours, that although they leave their robes open in front and on the sides, and let them flutter in the wind, yet from their head to their shoes no part of the body is seen uncovered."[10] Yet Peroz himself, for all his manifest talent at cutting a dash, was not defined by his sense of fashion alone. Just as significant, in the eyes of his subjects, was his palpable concern for their welfare. Vain he might have been; but he was also, in the noblest tradition of his forebears, determined to battle chaos, uphold order and propagate justice. Which was just as well: for troubles, and the efforts of Peroz to resolve them, had been a feature of his twenty-five-year reign since day one.

It had begun with a drought. Even as Peroz was being crowned, his people had been famine-stalked. The young king had responded with energy, boldness and vision. He had slashed taxes; lavished state subsidies on the poor; pressured the nobility into sharing their stockpiles of food with the hungry and desperate masses. Centuries later, this reform programme was still being commemorated in admiring tones: "Only one man ... died of hunger in the entire empire."[11] Witness, even if not literally true, to a model of famine-relief.

Next, looking to the north-east frontier, Peroz had shown himself similarly determined to fight the growing menace of the Hephthalites. More than any Sasanian before him, he had committed himself and all the resources of his empire to the great game that was the interplay of tribal rivalries in Central Asia. Merv, an ancient city midway between the Hindu Kush and the Caspian Sea, and with the potential to dominate Persia's north-eastern marches, had been transformed into a mighty bastion of royal power: massive ramparts, crowned by fired-brick towers and scored with arrow slits, were built around a vast circular citadel. Meanwhile, other strongholds, strategically situated along the frontier itself, had been founded from scratch; treasure had been lavished on fortifications, garrisons and supply depots.[12] Snaking across the fields of the Gurgan Plain, for instance, fashioned out of red brick and extending over some 150 miles, was an immense wall: the single greatest barrier ever constructed in the Near East.[13] By the time Peroz, with a quarter-century of such efforts behind him, ventured out into the steppes through the gates of the red-brick wall, it was as a general with a most formidable reputation: as "a daring and warlike man."[14]

Simultaneously, however, there was a darker side to Peroz's record. "Our kings," so the Persians liked to boast, "have never been accused of treachery"[15]—and yet this was, perhaps, to gild the lily just a bit. Even in his dealings with the White Huns, Peroz had been known to indulge in the occasional bout of collaboration. Born a younger son, he had only been able to seize the throne in the first place with Hephthalite backing. More damaging to his good name, however, had been the disastrous consequence of an earlier expedition he had led into the realm of the White Huns, eastwards of the steppelands, to the region known as Bactria, where he had found himself being ambushed in a wooded valley, surrounded, and forced to sue for terms. Predictably enough, these had proved debilitating and humiliating in equal measure: a number of key Persian strongholds had been surrendered, a crippling ransom imposed, and the *Shahanshah* himself, that god among men, obliged to prostrate himself before the boots of the Hephthalite khan.

Returning to the fray for a second time, then, Peroz was undoubtedly motivated as much by personal revenge as he was by the grander demands of geopolitics. Injured dignity required him to travel to war amid all the magnificence appropriate to the King of Kings. A teeming retinue of chefs, cooks, domestics, make-up artists and wardrobe assistants; treasury officials with chests of silver coins; even a princess or two: all had been brought to accompany their master into the anonymous immensity of the steppes. It was not only by force of arms that Peroz sought to tame the savage Hephthalites: he aimed to dazzle them as well.

Nor were the Hephthalites his only targets. Peroz faced a challenge south of the steppeland frontier as well as north of it. The lords who ruled there—in the great swath of territory that stretched between Persia and the Hephthalite kingdom—could lay claim to a heritage that was scarcely less glorious than that of the *Shahanshah* himself. Prior to the revolt of Ardashir, it was their ancestors who had ruled the empire that now ranked as Sasanian. Parthians, they called themselves; and they still cherished memories of their golden age, when the Persians and a whole host of other peoples had been kept satisfyingly under their thumb. Not that the power of the greatest Parthian families had ever truly been broken. Although, in the wake of Ardashir's famous victory of AD 224 over the Parthian king, members of the royal family had been variously exterminated or driven into exile, the warrior barons had easily weathered the change of regime. The seven great lords of Parthia acknowledged no superiors, save for the Sasanians themselves.[16] The foundations of their dominance had been cemented into place, over the course of many centuries, "by ancient law."[17] Impressively, the mightiest Parthian dynasty, the Karin, could trace a history of heroic prowess back to the very beginnings of time, when one of their forefathers had toppled a demon king, no less. Dahag, a necromancer so evil that two venomous serpents had sprouted from his shoulders and promptly started munching on the brains of babies, had ruled the world for an entire millennium—until the ancestor of the Karin, a blacksmith by the name of Kava, had led a revolt against the tyrant. Such a pedigree was a fitting measure of the pretensions of the Parthian lords—pretensions that had the backing of prodigious wealth and manpower. Indeed, it was the measure of these that the Sasanian kings, focussing their energies and attentions upon the western half of their empire, had traditionally been content to give the east a wide berth. No *Shahanshah* would ever admit it, of course, but across much of Parthia Sasanian royal authority was largely a matter of smoke and mirrors. The Karin and their fellow dynasts governed their fiefdoms less as subjects of the Persian monarchy than as partners in a sometimes uneasy confederacy. "For you are the lords each of your own province," as one of them had once declared ringingly to his fellows, "and the possessors of very great power."[18] Persian the empire may have been—but it remained, in its eastern provinces, a Parthian one as well.[19]

And here, for a *Shahanshah* with little choice but to devote his energies to combating the Hephthalites, was a most awkward complication. The urgent need to strengthen imperial defences along the north-east frontier, whether by buttressing existing cities or by raising new ones, hardly sat well with the time-honoured policy of not treading on Parthian toes. For all his swagger, Peroz was highly sensitive to this problem. While Hephthalite support had been useful in helping him claim the throne, the decisive blow had actually been struck by a Parthian warlord: Raham, of the family of Mihran. It was he who had defeated, captured and executed Peroz's elder brother and then crowned Peroz as his "protégé."[20] Twenty-five years on, the

Persian king's ambitions still rested on the support of the Parthian dynasts. Without it, he had no chance of defeating the upstart Hephthalite kingdom. Simultaneously, however, there could be no prospect of ultimate victory without marching his armies and labour-gangs directly across Parthian land. A most awkward circle to square.

But not, perhaps, wholly impossible. Peroz was subtle as well as bold; and he knew that the pen might, on occasion, be wielded alongside the sword. Even while summoning his warriors and engineers to the defence of his empire, he had also been busy mustering his minstrels, his bards and his scribes. Conscious that the days when it had been sufficient for the House of Sasan to trumpet an exclusively Persian descent were gone, Peroz had settled upon a simple but audacious expedient: he had ordered its past rewritten.

A new family tree, one more acceptable to Parthian sensibilities, more inclusive, more multicultural, was now required. So it was, obedient to their master's requirements, that scholars in the royal service had set themselves to a comprehensive upgrading of the Sasanian lineage. Fortunately, preserved in ancient texts and in the memories of priests and poets, the perfect ancestors had been waiting shimmeringly to hand. The Kayanids—like Kava, the blacksmith from whom the Karin claimed descent—were heroes from the fabulously distant past, with biographies that featured talking birds, flying chariots, fortresses raised by demons and other fantastical wonders. Unlike Kava, a mere blacksmith, however, they had all of them been graced with the *farr*— since so impeccably royal had been their dynasty that even its very name derived from the antique title of "*Kai*," or "King." This, however, was not the main reason why Peroz was suddenly so keen to claim descent from them. Rather, the true appeal of the Kayanids lay in the location of their realm—which had lain, not in Persia, but in Parthia and, northwards, into Gurgan. It was here that the Kayanid kings, the tireless guardians of their people, had made heroic stand after heroic stand, fighting in defence both of their kingdom and of their *farr*, resolute against savage enemies whose fiendish ambition it had been to

70

filch both. As Peroz advanced northwards from Parthia against the Hephthalites, he made sure to do so as the self-proclaimed heir of the Kayanids: as a king whose ultimate roots lay in the self-same lands he had come to defend.

"*Airan*," these had anciently been called: "the realm of the Aryans," or "Iran." The Persians, who traced their own origins back to this primordial north-eastern kingdom, and therefore regarded themselves as being not a whit less Aryan than the Parthians, had always been keen on the name. Long before the time of Peroz, the House of Sasan had been making great play with it in their inscriptions, their titles and all their endless bragging. They had even termed their own empire *Iranshahr*—"the Dominion of the Aryans." Now, though, under Peroz, the manufacturing of links between the Sasanian monarchy and the fabled Kayanid homeland had become an obsession. As the king gazed into a perilous and uncertain future, so had he sought to influence it by sponsoring an official systematisation of the past. Blatant fabrications had enabled Ardashir to be enshrined once and for all as what Peroz so desperately needed him to be: a descendant of the Kayanids. Meanwhile, in order to buttress the plausibility of this fraud, centuries of history were simply erased. The end result was a lineage that perfectly served the desperate needs of the time. No less than a stockpile of weapons on the great north-eastern trunk road, or a raw new fortress on the red wall beyond the Alburz Mountains, it spoke of both a crisis and an implacable determination to resolve it.

Battle-hardened pragmatist and self-appointed heir to ancient kings who had fought demons: the *Shahanshah* rode to war as both. That Peroz had resurrected the antique title of *Kai*; that he had named his eldest son "Kavad," after the first of the Kayanids; that he had stamped his coins with any number of allusions to the legendary dynasty: here were no mere idle self-indulgences. Rather, they served as potent markers of his utter seriousness of purpose. He had a dual strategy: to win the hearts and minds of his Parthian subjects even as he met the Hephthalites with an iron fist. And it seemed to be working. The decisive adventure had been launched. Peroz and his army had passed through the gates of the great red wall and headed out on to the steppes. Advancing on the nearest Hephthalite stronghold, just beyond the frontier, they had found it abandoned.[21] Clearly, the terror of the royal name had rendered the savages too terrified to stand and fight. Peroz ordered the settlement razed to the ground. Meanwhile, behind him, in Parthia, everything appeared calm. Now, all that was needed was to track down the enemy, corner them, and wipe them from the face of the earth.

Then the *Shahanshah* received the news he had been yearning to hear: the Hephthalites were ahead of him. Their outriders had been spotted, and their main army was drawing near. Peroz issued brisk orders, summoning the champions of *Iranshahr* to battle. At once, the stir of preparation spread across the camp: archers oiled and tested their bows, drivers heaved war-towers onto the backs of their elephants, and footsoldiers dusted down their wicker shields. Most urgent of all, however, was the need to ready the expedition's ultimate killers: the deadliest strike-force in the world. A one-piece helmet, "skilfully crafted to look exactly like a man's face";[22] iron plates, greaves and gloves; whips and maces, slung from the belt; a lance so long and heavy that it could be handled only if first secured to the side of a mount: these were the tools of an armoured horseman in the service of the *Shahanshah*. Barely human such a warrior might appear, when fully furnished: "a moving image wrought by a hammer."[23] Lifted up into their saddles on the shoulders of attendants, urging forward steeds that were themselves sheathed in mail and plate, forming themselves into a glittering line in the front rank of the army, the heavy cavalry of *Iranshahr* could know themselves worthy heirs of their ancestors: heroes of steel, just as the Kayanids had been.

And glancing behind them, at the slight rise where their king had stationed himself, as every *Shahanshah* did prior to a battle, they saw the ultimate reassurance of this. Now, more than ever, Peroz aimed to pose as a figure of epic. Great care had been taken to ensure that his horse was the tallest and most handsome around. Attendants stood poised by the royal mount, to ensure that it would not whinny, nor urinate, nor in any other way lower the heroic tone. The king himself, as ever, was positively ablaze with sumptuous jewellery. Meanwhile, planted behind him, where it could be seen by everyone in the ranks, there fluttered his massive standard: the *Derafsh Kaviani*, or "Flag of Kava." An expression of Sasanian power, it was also authentically, and heroically, pan-Iranian. It was no coincidence, for instance, that its name bore witness to the fabled ancestor of the Karin: for once, prior to its adornment with jewels and tassels, it had been a humble leather apron, worn, so it was said, by the demon-slaying blacksmith himself. Now, as Peroz gave the order for his cavalry to advance, it was his aim to emulate the feat of Kava: for he was looking to rout a whole army of demons.

Lumbering forwards, trotting at first, then breaking into a thunderous gallop, the heavily armoured cavalrymen aimed their lances at the more lightly armed Hephthalites. Through the dust clouds kicked up by their horses, it appeared that the enemy was clumping together in a disorganised panic. Then the Hephthalites broke, turned and streamed back across the dead centre of the plain. Raising a cry of triumph, the Persian cavalry immediately fanned out, aiming to encircle their retreating foes. They charged ever faster; the dust rose ever thicker. Arrows, hissing down through the clouds of grit, began to rattle and bounce off their armour; but the men of *Iranshahr* disdained so much as to flinch. From head to foot, their iron cladding was "proof against any missiles, and a sure defence against all wounds."[24] The arrows of contemptible nomads could do them no harm. They were, to all intents and purposes, invulnerable. Victory, surely, was theirs.

Then, suddenly, they felt their horses' hooves give way and begin to paw the air. The riders themselves flew forwards and found themselves dropping, through a nightmarish haze of dust and arrows, into the bowels of a massive ditch. Too late, the front ranks of the Persian cavalry realised that the Hephthalites had prepared for their attack with fiendish cunning. They had excavated a great trench, dug across most of the plain, which they had then covered with a thin layer of reeds and earth. They had left only the centre intact, to facilitate their own retreat; meanwhile, the pursuing Persians had blundered directly into the death-trap. "And such was the spirit of fury with which they had launched their pursuit of the enemy that those to the rear of the vanguard failed to notice the catastrophe which had over-whelmed those in the front rank. And so with horse and lance they continued to ride into the trench, and to trample down their own fel-lows, so that all were destroyed. And among the dead was Peroz himself."[25]

As to how precisely the *Shahanshah* had met his end, various accounts were given. Some said that as he crashed into the Hephthalite trench, he had torn off his own ear, and kept it clenched in his palm: for he had not wanted some savage nomad to lay claim to his famous pearl. Others said that he was left trapped in a cleft in the ground, where he died of hunger; and others yet that he had crawled away from the killing field, "only to be devoured by wild animals."[26]

Two things were certain, though. First, neither Peroz's body nor his great pearl was ever found; second, his *farr* had abandoned him for good.

Fire Starter

Only a few weary and grime-streaked Persian survivors managed to stumble back from the killing fields of Gurgan. The news that they brought with them could hardly have had more menacing implica-tions. The gore that had filled the Hephthalite trenches might as well have been the lifeblood of *Iranshahr* itself. No realm in the world could endure for long without treasure or men—and the slaughter had left the Sasanian Empire drained of both. Only a massive effort on the part of the imperial tax-collectors had enabled the expedition to ride out in the first place; now, with the flower of the empire's cavalry destroyed, there was nothing left to blunt the scythings of the Hephthalites' own horsemen. The frontier stood wide open. All the bulwarks that Peroz had laboured so hard to construct lay abandoned and tenantless. Whisperings of terror, thickening into ever more certain rumour, were soon darkening the eastern dominions of *Iranshahr*: of whole regions, where once the Kayanids had ruled, turned by the Hephthalites to shambles of blood and ash.[27]

Here, in the picking to the bone of the ancient heartlands of the Aryan people, was a fearsome challenge to the practical functioning of the entire Sasanian realm. Both its prestige and its tax base were under mortal threat. But this was not the worst. The Hephthalite flames were scorching more than fields and cities. The conflagration was also consuming structures regarded by those who had raised them as sources of a truly awesome holiness. Just as fire, in the hands of the wicked, might be used to destroy, so also, in the hands of the virtuous, might it be consecrated to the service of the heavens. This was why, studded across *Iranshahr*, there were temples that contained no statues but rather, in each one, "an altar in the middle of an enclosure, holding a large quantity of ashes, where priests keep a fire eternally burning."[28] Desecrate such an altar, so it was believed, and the order of the cosmos itself would start to totter. In the aftermath of Peroz's "overpowering and crushing defeat,"[29] as fire temples across the northern reaches of Parthia were sent crashing into ruin by the Hephthalites, there were many in *Iranshahr* who saw in the annihilation of the royal army something far more troubling, and portentous, than a mere military debacle: a darkening of the universe itself.

Yet, hope remained. The three holiest fire temples—the most luminescent and charged with power—remained inviolate. One, the "Fire of the Stallion," was enclosed within rings of towering fortifications on the summit of a hill in Media, the mountainous region that lay to the north of Persia; the second, the "Fire of the *Farr*," stood secure within Persia itself. Only the third, the *Adur Burzen-Mihr*—"Fire of Mihr is Great"—seemed at potential risk from the Hephthalites: for it lay close to the front line, in Parthia, on the ancient highway that led directly to the steppelands of the north.[30] To the devout of *Iranshahr*, however, the notion that one of their three most sacred fire temples might be despoiled, its ashes scattered, its flame extinguished, appeared almost sacrilegious in itself. To imagine such a thing was to contemplate a cosmos terminally sick.

No mortal hand had brought the three great fires into being. Rather, the Good God, Ohrmazd—the Eternal, the All-Radiant, the Supremely Wise—had lit them, "like three lights, for the watching of the world."[31] And the world had urgently needed watching. Ohrmazd, the fountainhead of all that was good and pure and right, was not the only creator god. "Truly," ran an ancient verse, "there are two primal Spirits, twins, renowned for being in conflict. In thought and word and deed, they are two: the best and the worst."[32] While Ohrmazd had brought *Asha*—"Truth and Order"—to the universe, his shadow, Ahriman, snake-haired and darkness-vomiting, had spawned their opposite: *Drug*—"the Lie." The cohorts of evil were everywhere. They ranged from nomads, such as the Hephthalites, to that most fiendish and wicked of all Ahriman's creations, the frog. In the ongoing struggle against such adversaries, mortals choosing the path of righteousness and light had long cherished the assistance that Ohrmazd sent them. Back in primordial times, the great fires had swept across the face of the earth, going wherever they were needed: one had helped in the overthrow of Dahag, the serpent-shouldered necromancer; another had assisted a Kayanid king in a particularly arduous bout of idol-smashing. Stationary though the fires had since become, they had lost not a spark of their heavenly potency. They remained what they had always been: the surest guardians of the proper ordering of the world.

Humanity too, however, had a part to play. Mortal men and women everywhere needed to commit themselves to the cause of light: to live in such a way as to render themselves branches of living flame. Fortunately, they were not without guidance from the Lord of the Universe on how best to achieve this. Many centuries earlier, a man named Zoroaster had seen a vision. Emerging from a ritual immersion in a river, into the luminous purity of a spring dawn, he found himself suddenly bathed by the infinitely purer light of Ohrmazd. Words sounded in his head: the teachings of the divine. For the first time, the Supreme Creator had revealed Himself to a mortal as He truly was: the fountainhead of all that was good. Over the succeeding years, Zoroaster witnessed many more visions. The nature of the cosmos was revealed to him, and the rituals by which he and all mortals should lead their lives. Forced into exile by the refusal of his own people to listen to his teachings, he succeeded in winning converts in a strange land. These new followers, despite all the efforts of neighbouring tribes to crush them, eventually triumphed in war; their infant religion endured and thrived. Zoroaster himself, through whom the revelations of Ohrmazd had been perfectly refracted, would be commemorated ever afterwards as the human equivalent of a sacred fire: as a divinely forged link between heaven and earth. This, in the opinion of his followers, was what it meant to be a *mathran*, a "possessor of the words of God"—a prophet.

"For Zoroaster alone has heard Our commands." So Ohrmazd Himself had pronounced. "He alone has made known Our thoughts."[33] A ringing commendation—and one that ensured that the priests who followed Zoroaster's teachings displayed a steely and unblinking concern for propriety. As they tended the sacred fires, they adhered to the regular performance of ferociously complicated rituals, knowing that each one completed would see the order of the cosmos buttressed. Yet the priests could not hope to take the fight to Ahriman unaided. Others too had to be steeled to the cosmic fight. Even the lowest slave might have a part to play. If he only performed the five daily prayers that Zoroaster had demanded of the faithful, and kept his teeth shiny clean to boot, he too could help to purge the Lie. Understandably, then, the priests of *Iranshahr* sought to keep a tight leash on the beliefs and behaviour of their countrymen. As one foreign commentator observed, "Nothing is held to be lawful or right among the Persians unless it is first ratified by a priest."[34] Without such discipline, there could be no prospect of winning the great battle for the universe.

Yet, ultimately, in the spiritual dimension as well as the earthly, one protagonist mattered more than any other: the *Shahanshah* himself. He alone could claim to have been touched by the divine. *Asha*—that supreme virtue of Ohrmazd—could not possibly be maintained without him. Nor, indeed, could the privileges and pretensions of the priesthood. Ahriman, in the malignancy of his cunning, had always been assiduous in his attempts to cultivate heresy and demon-worship. Not every corner of *Iranshahr* had been illuminated by the light of Zoroaster's teachings. While some of the Iranians' ancient gods—the Lady Anahita pre-eminent among them—had come to be ranked by the Zoroastrian priesthood as loyal lieutenants of Ohrmazd, others, so Zoroaster himself had warned, were not gods at all, but demons. Their cults, idols and adherents all needed smashing. Only the *Shahanshah*, in the final reckoning, was up to the job. If the religion of Zoroaster, instituted of Ohrmazd Himself, self-evidently existed to serve as the protector of humanity, then it was the function of kingship, in the opinion of the priesthood, to serve as "the protector of religion."[35]

A role to which the House of Sasan, over the years, had only fitfully measured up. Although many kings had certainly been piously Zoroastrian, many had not. The royal understanding of what *Asha* should be was not necessarily that of the priesthood. Religion, in the opinion of the Persian monarchy, existed to buttress the power of the throne—not the other way round. Any notion that the Zoroastrian establishment might be permitted to obtain an identity that was independent of royal control, let alone political leverage, had long been anathema to the Sasanians. Accordingly, for all that priests were often employed by the monarchy as attack-dogs, they were never let off the leash. Any hint that they might be slipping their collars had always seen them thrust firmly back into their kennels. Petted and spoiled though they might be, they were never allowed to forget who held the whip hand.

But now, amid the calamities and convulsions of the times, that was starting to change. As the Persian monarchy, battered by the onslaughts of the Hephthalites, scrabbled desperately to shore up its position, the Zoroastrian establishment seized its chance. The priests who had provided Peroz with his Kayanid ancestry were in a position to exact a considerable price for their collaboration. Not all their energies had been devoted to serving the royal interest. In their redrafted history of Persia, the priests had given themselves the role they had always dreamed of playing: that of partner, indeed twin, of the *Shahanshah*. "Born of the one womb—joined together and never to be sundered."[36] Earlier Sasanian kings would have scorned—and punished—such presumption. But Peroz did not, because he could not: his situation had grown too desperate. Rather than dismiss the pretensions of the priesthood as mere conceit, to be slapped down with disdain, he had little choice but to indulge the clergy, and then take advantage of what could be screwed out of them in return. Better a marriage of convenience than no marriage at all.

And certainly, despite the many tensions that remained between them, the monarchy and the priesthood shared similar goals. Just as it had been the ambition of Peroz to bring the antique order of the Kayanids to his tottering realm, the priests wished to enshrine the even more transcendent order of Ohrmazd within *Iranshahr*. It was only with an unwearying effort, of course, that such a campaign could ever hope to be won. Laws, long disregarded or only fitfully applied, had to be given added teeth. The guardians of light and truth had to be prepared "to smite, to smash and to overthrow the idol-temples and the disobedience that comes from the Adversary and the demons."[37] Naturally, the greatest responsibility of all still lay with the *Shahanshah*; but the Zoroastrian priesthood too, as it increasingly began to slip royal control, had set to carve out its own, independent role. Across the empire, the power of the provincial governors was being matched, and sometimes even eclipsed, by that of the *mowbeds*—the chief priests. Officially, of course, these men remained answerable to the *Shahanshah*; but already, back in the reign of Peroz's father, there had been the unmistakable glimmerings of an alternative chain of command. For the first time, there had been mention made of a *modaban mowbed*—a "chief of chief priests." Here, putting down deeper roots with each decade that passed, was an institution that could claim to embody *Asha* indeed. The word that best described it, however, was not Persian at all, but Greek. What the priests were creating, in effect, was an *ecclesia*—a "church."

And it was the ambition of this Zoroastrian Church, a prodigious and a dazzling one, to institute an order that might be truly universal: reaching backwards as well as forwards through time. It was not chaos, after all, but deception that most menaced the universe—which meant in turn that it was vital, fearsomely and urgently vital, to establish the precise truth about the life and times of Zoroaster. Yet this presented a problem. The age of the great prophet was dizzyingly remote. So remote, in fact, that the long dead language in which he had made known his revelations, although lovingly preserved upon the tongues of the learned, had descended down the ages without so much as a script. This, to the fretful leaders of the Zoroastrian Church, had become a cause of mounting anxiety. Could memory truly provide a sufficient bulwark against the corrosive effects of time? If not, then the faithful, and the whole world, were surely damned. A script was duly devised.[38] Zoroaster's revelations were entrusted, for the first time ever, to a book.

But the priests were not done with their labours yet. The process of transcribing the *mathra*—the word of God—had begged a couple of obvious questions: where and when had Zoroaster received it? Here were riddles not easily solved. There was barely a region in *Iranshahr* that had not, at some point, laid claim to the honour of having been the birthplace of the Prophet. Embarrassingly, the most ancient reports of all—dating from a time when the Persians' ancestors had themselves been nomads, living on the steppes—placed it fair and square in what was now the realm of the Hephthalites. It is impossible to know if the leaders of the Zoroastrian Church were aware of this tradition; either way, it was literally beyond the pale. Instead, with a gathering confidence and assertiveness, the *mowbeds* promoted a very different biography of their prophet. Zoroaster, they taught, had actually been born in Media around a thousand years previously, in the age of the Kayanids.* In fact, it was a Kayanid king, "mighty-speared and lordly," who had offered him asylum in the wake of his exile and had served his nascent religion as its "arm and support."[39] A veritable model of royal behaviour, in other words. Peroz, desperate for his own good reasons to identify himself with the Kayanids, had duly taken the bait. Riding to war, he had done so not merely as the heir of the dynasty as a whole, but also, and more specifically, as the heir of the Prophet's first patron. Church and state: twins indeed. Priest and king: both, it had seemed, were winners.

Except, unfortunately, that Peroz had ended up dead. A calamity, his subjects fretted, that had reflected more than simple bad luck. "No one was the cause of such losses and destruction save the divine lord of the Aryans himself."[40] This verdict, whispered increasingly across the entire span of *Iranshahr*, threatened to cripple the future of the House of Sasan. Critics condemned more than merely the royal battle tactics. Advancing towards the Gurgan Plain, the *Shahanshah* had passed the snow-capped Alburz Mountains: seat of a god named Mihr, whom it had always been peculiarly foolish to anger. The Zoroastrian priesthood ranked him—alongside Anahita—as one of the two foremost lieutenants of Ohrmazd: "sleepless and ever awake,

---

* A spider's web of misinformation that it has taken generations of scholars to untangle. For a long while, it was widely assumed that Zoroaster had lived when the Sasanian priesthood claimed that he had lived: "258 years before Alexander," or, according to our own dating system, in the early sixth century BC. Only recently has close analysis of the sacred texts served to push their likeliest date of origin very much further back, to some point between the tenth and seventeenth centuries BC. Also discounted has been the supposed Median origin of the Prophet: none of the sacred texts so much as mentions western Iran. As to whether the traditions told of Zoroaster are genuine, it is impossible at such an incalculable distance to say. "Such a choice is neither legitimate nor illegitimate: it is a mere wager" (Kellens, p. 3).

the warrior of the white horse, he who maintains and looks over all this moving world."[41] And in particular, what Mihr kept watch for was oath-breakers: those who presumed to tell lies. Possessed as he was of "a thousand ears,"[42] he was well equipped for the task. The god would certainly have tracked Peroz's original expedition against the Hephthalites, when the *Shahanshah*, ambushed and taken captive, had been obliged to bow before the boots of the khan: for Peroz had craftily timed his obeisance to coincide with the sunrise, a moment when it was required of the faithful to offer up their prayers. Even more underhand, however, had been his scorning of the treaty forced upon him by the Hephthalites; for by its terms, he had sworn with great solemnity never again to cross the frontier. An oath which, of course, he had indisputably broken. What had the destruction of Peroz and his army been, then, if not the judgement of the wrathful heavens? "For you bring down terror upon those who lie, O Mihr. You take away the strength of their arms. You take away the swiftness of their feet."[43]

The King of Kings was either the defender of Truth, or he was nothing. The miseries that had overwhelmed *Iranshahr* in the wake of Peroz's death certainly appeared to confirm the whispered notion that the House of Sasan had become agents of the Lie. Impoverishment and brutalisation were not the only spectres to haunt the realm: renewed drought compounded the miseries inflicted by the Hephthalites. As the grip of famine tightened, and the starving scrabbled after roots and withered grass amid the dust of their barren fields, ever more people started to believe that the heavenly judge was delivering his verdict on Peroz: "The villain who breaks his promise to Mihr brings death upon all the land."[44] With "the Persian treasury empty and the land ravaged by the Huns,"[45] the *farr* of Peroz's heirs was barely glimmering. Over the course of the four years that followed the disaster of Gurgan, one of his brothers was executed as a pretender to the throne, and another was deposed and blinded. Peroz's eldest son Kavad, who acceded to the throne on the back of this coup, was only just fifteen—the age at which, according to elite Persian custom, a boy was awarded a studded belt and became a man.⁴⁶ His rule could scarcely have begun in less propitious circumstances.

As to the full scale of the challenges confronting him, that could best be gauged, perhaps, by staring into the sightless eyes of his uncle. Menace was building at home as well as abroad. Not everyone in *Iranshahr* had been left impoverished by Peroz's defeat. To the great lords of Parthia, in particular, the calamities overwhelming the Persian monarchy had presented opportunity as well as peril. By the time that Kavad acceded to the throne, one of them had already moved with such boldness and swagger as to establish himself as king in all but name. Even by the standards of his forefathers, Sukhra, the head of the Karin, was quite fabulously domineering. He had also, uniquely, enjoyed an excellent war. It was under his command that the few demoralised remnants of the imperial army had managed to escape from the Gurgan front: an achievement so assiduously trumpeted that Sukhra had even presumed to cast himself as "the avenger of Peroz."⁴⁷ Amid the otherwise all-prevailing gloom, he possessed an undeniable aura of success—and exploited it to the hilt. He diverted taxes from the royal coffers into his own; he kept the warriors he had led back from Gurgan firmly under his own command. Kavad, "Lord of the Aryans" though he might be, appeared left with little save for impotence.

Between the Persian monarchy and the lords of Parthia, between the House of Sasan and the dynasties of the Karin and the Mihran, ghosts had always intruded. When Sukhra, in the pomp and glory of his magnificence, rode out beneath the great horseshoe arches of his palace, he did so at the head of warriors who seemed more like phantoms than men, conjured up from an age remoter by far than that of Ardashir, remoter even than that of Zoroaster himself. Their cloaks, their pennants, the livery of their chargers: all were green.⁴⁸ The colour was that of Mihr—the god whose anger with Peroz had turned the fields of *Iranshahr* brown. The god, if he could only be appeased, had the power to make the soil fertile and giving again. Sukhra, by invoking this conviction with such flamboyance, was not only thumbing his nose at the House of Sasan but laying claim to the most ancient and enduring of the traditions cherished by the Parthians. Not for nothing was their sacred fire named the "Fire of Mihr is Great": for in the easternmost regions of *Iranshahr*, Mihr was worshipped as he had once been by all the Aryan people, with a peculiarly single-hearted devotion. So much so, in fact, that the fervour with which the god's cult was practised across the plains and mountains of Parthia tended to leave little time for Ohrmazd Himself.[49] Just as Sukhra's green-clad private army evoked a time before the Sasanians, so, even more scandalously, did the sacred fire of Mihr serve as a reminder of beliefs that pre-dated Zoroaster. Unsurprisingly, then, the *mowbeds* had done all they could to dim its renown. Too venerable to be extinguished entirely, it had nevertheless been demoted. Mihr's fire, so the *mowbeds* had declared, was fit only for the masses: herdsmen, ploughmen, peasants. A doubly neat manoeuvre: for with it, the priests had served to cast the two remaining sacred fires—both of which lay securely within the Church's own heartlands—as the only two with authentic pedigree. That the truth was far different—that the fire temple in Persia dated back only to the time of Ardashir, and the fire in Media even later, only to the reign of Peroz himself—had ceased so much as to register.[50] It was the *mowbeds*, after all, who enjoyed the ear of the king, who commanded the resources of a spreading Church, who wrote the books. Yet still, wherever the Karin rode, their green-clad horsemen were sure to follow: serving notice that there were beliefs older than the Prophet, and still very far from dead.

Not that everyone in Parthia was necessarily convinced by Sukhra's posing as the agent of Mihr. While the Parthian dynasts had long resented Persian rule, they were far more suspicious of each other than they were of the Sasanians. Kavad, in this fractiousness, was able to distinguish a glimmering of hope. It was not only the *Shahanshah* who was affronted by the suffocating greatness of the Karin. So too was the Parthian dynasty which, decades earlier, had helped Peroz to the throne, and still regarded it as their god-given right to throw their weight around much as they pleased: the Mihran. They too, as their name suggested, regarded themselves as the favourites of Mihr; they too raised their own taxes; they too had private armies. Kavad, growing up into a full recognition of his weakness, decided that he had no choice but to turn to them for assistance. A desperate throw, and one that did little for the royal prestige, of course—but the "Lord of the Aryans" was beyond caring. To all the other miseries afflicting his people Kavad now added, as the consequence of his manoeuvre, civil war. The Mihran, wooed into making an open assault on their bitterest rivals, duly advanced against the power of Sukhra. Reaches of *Iranshahr* left untorched by the Hephthalites were now trampled down by the empire's two foremost noble families. Finally, in a climactic confrontation, it was the Karin who were overthrown. Sukhra was taken captive, and all his treasure with him. Delivered into royal hands, the great warlord was put to death.

None of which, as it turned out, improved the position of Kavad one jot. "Sukhra's wind has died away, and a wind belonging to Mihran has now started to blow":[51] centuries later, and the phrase was still proverbial. Bitterly as the gusts must have sounded in the king's ear, however, they did not sound so cruelly as they did across the blackened fields, the weed-choked roads, and the abandoned villages of his unhappy realm. War and famine were emptying the countryside. Even in the best of times, those who worked on the land had laboured under crushing burdens. All the wealth of the *Shahanshah* in his many fabulous palaces, of the dynasts in their own strongholds, and of the *mowbeds* on their fine horses, all the splendour of the aristocracy's shimmering silks, their jewels and their groaning tables, all their dancing girls, their musicians and their performing monkeys, almost everything enjoyed by the rich, in short, had been wrung from the exertions of the poor. Unsurprisingly, then, the flight of peasants from the fields had long been a cause of anxiety to the elite; and vagrants, if they were caught, could expect to be branded on their faces as rebels against Ohrmazd Himself. Increasingly, though, as misery was piled upon misery, the sheer number of people on the move started to overwhelm the authorities. Many rootless peasants headed for the cities, but many more, ganging together and brandishing cudgels and bill-hooks, took to the road and turned predator themselves. At first, they plundered their neighbours' villages and attacked travellers on the highways. Then, as they grew in number and confidence, they started to aim higher. Barely believable news began to intrude upon the councils of the great. Gangs of the despised peasantry, "like demons set at large,"[52] were moving against the nobility's granaries and estates. They had stormed palaces and divided entire treasuries among "the poor, the base and the weak."[53] Most shockingly of all, "the ignoble plebeians" were said to have passed around women captured during these assaults, handing even the perfumed wives of nobles from peasant to peasant.[54] A high-born lady streaked with the filth and the sweat of the landless: here was the ultimate image of order turned to chaos.

What did this turning of the world upon its head portend? Surely nothing less than the end of time itself. The Zoroastrian faithful had long believed that things were not eternal, and that the great struggle between Ohrmazd and Ahriman was destined to resolve itself in one final and climactic confrontation. No one, prior to Zoroaster, had ever contemplated such a notion: that mankind, rather than reproducing itself for ever, generation after endless generation, might instead be heading towards a fixed and definite end; that a terminal clash between good and evil might be approaching; that the whole universe might be weighed in the balance and judged. Such notions, doubtless, sat readily with troubled times; but the collapse of *Iranshahr* into near anarchy was not the only reason why anxiety and anticipation had risen, by the time of Kavad's reign, to an unprecedented fever pitch. No less influential, perhaps, was the date that scholars had recently assigned to Zoroaster's birth: a thousand years before the present. People had come to feel themselves living in the shadow of something truly portentous—a millennium. For decades, this had served to foster eerie whisperings: that a new prophet was destined to appear, one who would serve as the seal of all who had gone before him and would usher in, for his followers, a golden age of equality, justice and peace.[55]

The Zoroastrian establishment had found it increasingly difficult, amid the miseries of the age, to ring-fence such talk. The rumours spread; and, as they spread, they mutated and evolved. To the poor, especially, they seemed to offer a route map to a juster and happier future. The ragged armies of the dispossessed, when they seized the property of the rich, were motivated by more than mere hatred, or even hunger. Just as the *mowbeds* passionately believed themselves entrusted by Ohrmazd with the maintenance of the traditional order of things, so had the poor, no less passionately, come to believe themselves entrusted with a divine mission to bring it crashing down around their heads. Men, they declared, were created equal. It followed, then, that all good things, from food to land to women, should be held in common. The privileges of the nobility, the pretensions of the priesthood: both had to be dissolved. Such were the demands of the self-proclaimed "Adherents of Justice": the world's first communist manifesto.

How was it, in the bowels of the world's most intimidating monarchy, that such a startling movement had come into existence? Clearly, the evils and injustices of the preceding decades had done much to inspire the spirit of revolution, as too had all the many varied currents of belief abroad in *Iranshahr*, the cults and shadowy heresies that had always plagued the Zoroastrian Church. Subsequent tradition, however, would attribute the unprecedented eruption of the Adherents of Justice to the teachings of a single prophet, the messenger from Ohrmazd long foretold: a one-time priest by the name of Mazdak. Four hundred years on, and historians would still commemorate how he had ringingly "proclaimed that what God had given to man should be distributed equally, and that men had abused this in their injustice to one another."[56] Unfortunately, however, the murk that veils the lives of so many prophets from our gaze has, by and large, served to swallow up Mazdak as well. Although, in histories written a century and more after his lifetime, he is portrayed as a towering figure, no contemporary makes reference to him. Consequently, when attempting to make sense of his career, we are left with more questions than answers. Were his teachings original to him, or did he merely articulate doctrines that had been decades, even centuries, in the making? How much faith can we have in the traditional details of his biography? Did he even exist?[57]

Amid all the uncertainty, though, two facts are clear. The first is that *Iranshahr*, by the time of Kavad's reign, was teetering on the brink of a full-scale social revolution. The second is that Kavad himself, ever the opportunist, had helped to push it over the edge. Monarchs are rarely in the habit of promoting class warfare; but Kavad, "a man who for cunning and energy had no rivals,"[58] was desperately negotiating uncharted waters. His support for the revolutionaries had two aims: to ensure that his own estates were left untouched; and to foster assaults on those of the great Parthian dynasts. Yet, it is possible—even likely—that there was more to this strategy than mere cold calculation: perhaps he did genuinely look with sympathy upon the miseries and the demands of the poor. Tradition would recall that Mazdak, brought into the royal presence, had converted the *Shahanshah* to his infant faith; and tradition might conceivably be correct. Certainly, the sheer audacity of Kavad's attempt to neutralise the nobility is the best evidence we have that Mazdak did after all exist. It is hard to believe that a Sasanian would ever have identified himself with peasant insurrectionists had he not possessed an inner assurance that he was truly fulfilling the divine purpose. Cynicism fused with religiosity: such was the combination, surely, that made of Kavad a Mazdakite.

Inevitably, though, his conversion stirred up a hornets' nest. Events now began to move very fast. In 496, an alliance of nobles and *mowbeds* forced Kavad's abdication. His brother, a young boy by the name of Zamasp, was proclaimed *Shahanshah* in his place. Kavad himself was immured in the empire's most fearsome prison, the aptly named "Castle of Oblivion"—"for the name of anyone cast into its dungeons is forbidden to be mentioned ever again, with death as the penalty for anyone who speaks it."[59] Yet, to Kavad—a king so enterprising that he had toyed with communism—this was never likely to prove a terminal roadblock. Sure enough, he soon procured a complete outfit of women's clothes, gave his gaolers the slip while disguised as his own wife, and fled to the court of the Hephthalites. There, just as his father had done nearly four decades before, he secured the khan's backing and returned to *Iranshahr* at the head of a Hephthalite army. The Parthian dynasts, struggling desperately to keep their heads above the Mazdakite floodtide, found themselves powerless to help their royal cipher; Zamasp was duly toppled without a battle; blinded with burning olive oil, or else with an iron needle, he was banished into oblivion himself.

So it was, by 498, that Kavad was once again the *Shahanshah*. Nevertheless, the desperate circumstances of his realm still threatened to give the lie to that title. The empire remained racked by religious controversy, social upheaval and dynastic feuding. It was also effectively bankrupt. How, then, was Kavad to pay his Hephthalite backers for their support? A challenge, it might have been thought, fit to defeat even his ingenuity.

But Kavad was, as ever, nothing daunted. Instead, with his entire empire seemingly on the verge of implosion, he opted to go on the attack: to fix his gaze towards the setting of the sun, to cross his western border, and to take the gold he needed from there.

He would go to war with the only empire in the world that could rival his own.

The Twin Eyes of the World

Once, the predecessors of the Sasanians had ruled a dominion so vast that it had reached the shores of the Mediterranean. Egypt, Syria and even a chunk of Europe had been theirs. Memories of this golden age had grown faint, yet there were still monuments to it in Persia itself: enigmatic tombs and reliefs on cliffs of bearded kings. Most haunting of all was a great wilderness of columns, some five miles south of Istakhr: the "Place of a Hundred Pillars." Here, amid the ruins, priests would carve inscriptions—and noblemen offer sacrifices—to the spirits of the ancient kings who had built it, back in the fabulous reaches of time.

Most Persians had no doubt that these mysterious ancestors were the Kayanids. The sustained rewriting of history that occurred under Peroz had merely cemented the identification. Yet there were other traditions, very different, which endured as well. Far to the west of *Iranshahr*, the Greeks—a people to whom the Kayanids meant nothing—preserved the memory of a Persian king named Cyrus. He had been, according to their historians, "the best of all rulers,"[60] the first man ever to attempt the conquest of the world. A full half a millennium before Christ he had died—but still, among the Greeks, he was commemorated as the very model of a universal monarch. He and his successors had wielded a power more dazzling than that of any dynasty before them. One king had even sought to chain Europe to Asia by means of a bridge of boats, and to conquer Greece itself. He had failed—but only just. As a display of global reach, it had certainly proved a memorable one. Better than the Persians themselves, the Greeks knew precisely who the founders of the first world empire had been. It was not the Kayanids who had inhabited "the Place of a Hundred Pillars," but the heirs of Cyrus. Indeed, Greek historians even had their own name for the ruin: "the City of the Persians," or *Persepolis*.

It is hard to believe that the Persians themselves were wholly ignorant of this alternative history.* Anything that touched on the glory of their ancestors was bound to tickle their fancy. Sure enough, distorted echoes of what the Greeks had recorded about Cyrus and his descendants could sometimes be discerned in the fables of the Kayanids: the majesty of their rule, the vastness of their empire,

---

* The degree to which the Sasanians were aware of Cyrus and his successors is hotly debated by historians. The likelihood is that consciousness of them faded over time, for reasons largely to do with the rewriting of Iranian history in the fifth century AD. "The Place of a Hundred Pillars" does seem to be an echo of one of the original names applied to Persepolis.

even, on occasion, their names. Yet ultimately, to the Zoroastrian priests who were responsible for chronicling the past of *Iranshahr*, history such as the Greeks understood it was of only incidental significance. Far greater issues, and far greater forces, were at play. The rise and fall of earthly empires were the mere shadow-play of something infinitely more cosmic: the clash between Truth and the Lie. Nowhere, in the opinion of the Persians, better illustrated just how violently this battle had reverberated throughout the ages than the Place of a Hundred Pillars. By the time of Kavad's reign, there was a hardening consensus as to who its architect had been. Jamshid, according to fabulously ancient tradition, had been the greatest monarch of all time: ruler of the entire world, possessed of a *farr* so potent that it had kept the whole of humanity from death, the chosen one of Ohrmazd, the owner of a flying throne.* Finally, though, after a reign of a thousand years, he had aspired to become a god—and at once his *farr* had abandoned him. Cornered by Dahag, the demonic necromancer, Jamshid had been hacked to death. Darkness and evil had prevailed. Of the fallen king, and all the manifold glories of his reign, nothing had been preserved, save only the great pillared city of stone.

Takht-e Jamshid, people had begun to call the ruin—"Jamshid's Throne."† Yet, even with responsibility for its destruction firmly pinned on a brain-eating demon, the name of the true, the authentic culprit remained one fit to chill the blood of any devout Zoroastrian. Although the priests of Ohrmazd had long since forgotten what every Greek historian took for granted, that it was in fact no demon who had burned Persepolis, but rather an earthly warlord, their amnesia

---

* The stories told about Jamshid—or Yima, as he was originally known—bear testimony to centuries, and possibly millennia, of elaboration. Long before the time of Zoroaster, he was being commemorated by Iranians and Indians alike as the first man. In this primal myth, he was installed as the king of the underworld following his death.

† This is the name by which Persepolis is known in Iran to this day.

was far from total. In Persia, the name of the conqueror whose drunken arson had left the palace a smoking ruin had most certainly not been forgotten. Eight hundred years on, and the fame of Alexander the Great still blazed undiminished. To many, and not only in the West, he remained a figure of incomparable glamour: king of a once-backward Greek kingdom by the time he was twenty; master of the empire founded by Cyrus five years later; dead, having marched to the limits of the world, at the age of thirty-three. Even the Persians, whose dominion he had overthrown, were not wholly immune to the allure of his glory. At the royal court a craze was brewing for romances in which the great man, somewhat improbably, featured as the son of a Persian king. There were plenty in *Iranshahr*, however, less than thrilled by this innovation. To the Zoroastrian priesthood, in particular, any notion that the conqueror of their country might have been a hero was not merely anathema but heresy. The memories preserved by the *mowbeds* of Alexander were terrible ones: of a criminal, a vandal, accursed. "For he entered *Iranshahr* with terrible violence, war and torture, and killed the King, and destroyed and razed to the ground the court and all the kingdom."[61] Not exactly a demon, perhaps—but demonic, certainly. Even the non-existence of ancient books of Zoroastrian lore was attributed by the priests, not to the fact that they had only just come up with a script capable of recording their holy scriptures, but to Alexander's imagined taste for burning libraries. There was just a single mercy, in short: that the fiend had ended up "plunged into hell."[62]

And the evil he had done lived after him. For centuries, *Iranshahr* had been left broken and humiliated. Even Ardashir and his successors, despite their self-evident status as favourites of Ohrmazd, had found it impossible to fulfil their stated ambition—"to restore to the Persian people the complete extent of their vanished empire."[63] Long gone Alexander might be—and yet the path back to their one-time western provinces remained firmly blocked. A second superpower, no less vaunting in its pretensions than *Iranshahr* itself, had come to occupy all the lands around the Mediterranean once ruled by Cyrus.

This empire, however, was not Alexander's. Indeed, it was not even Greek. Rather, it had been won by a people whose origins lay far to the west, in an iron-jawed city by the name of Rome. More than half a millennium had passed now since the winning by the Romans of lands that had originally provided Alexander with his own first taste of global conquest: Greece and Asia Minor, Syria and Egypt. This, in itself, would have been more than sufficient to raise Persian hackles; but even more insufferable was the fact that the Romans seemed to have inherited Alexander's appetite for pushing ever further eastwards. Time and again, the emperors of "*Rum*"——the Caesars, as they were known——had attempted to topple the dominion of the Persians; and time and again, the Persians had succeeded in "annihilating their invasions."[64]

As a result, when Kavad scouted around for some heroic exploit that might demonstrate to his dubious and unhappy subjects the potency of his *farr*, he did not have far to look. Nothing, not even a wholesale slaughter of Hephthalites, could possibly rival the glory to be gleaned from humbling a Caesar. Bragging rights over the Romans offered a *Shahanshah* the ultimate in self-esteem. The House of Sasan had grasped this right from the start. Ten miles to the west of Persepolis, chiselled into a rock face where the ancient kings of Persia had once carved out their tombs, could be seen a splendid portrait of the son of Ardashir, Shapur I, crowned and imperious on his war-horse, while before him——one on bended knee, the other raising his hands in pitiful submission——two Caesars grovelled for mercy. There was more to this relief, however, than simple boasting. To defeat Rome was to defeat the successors of Alexander. It was to affirm that good would triumph over evil, that the light of Truth would ultimately banish the darkness of the Lie. To a king such as Kavad——a self-confessed heretic——this offered a tantalising opportunity. What better way of demonstrating to the fretful and suspicious Zoroastrian Church that he was truly touched by the favour of the heavens than by winning a glorious victory over the Romans, those heirs of Alexander?

And the mark of his success, as well as glory, would be loot. Such, at any rate, was Kavad's confident expectation. The land of *Rum*, as everyone knew, was quite sensationally rich. The *Shahanshah* would never have acknowledged it openly, but there was, in his decision to invade the West, just a hint of jealousy. While Rome had long served the Persians as a worthy—indeed the ultimate—foe, it had also encouraged in the House of Sasan a certain competitive sense of upward mobility. Shapur I, whose drubbings of a whole succession of Caesars had left him with an immense reservoir of prisoners, had set about exploiting the know-how of his captives with a particular gusto. Whether it was wall-paintings in the royal throne room, or a network of massive dams, or entire cities planted in the Iranian outback, his infant empire had been given a decidedly Roman makeover. Two centuries on, and the ambition of the Sasanian monarchy to emulate its western rival had diminished not a jot. A peculiarly ostentatious marker of this was Kavad's love of bathing. Here, in the opinion of many Persians, and especially the *mowbeds*, was a thoroughly shocking innovation—one that positively reeked of the Roman. This, though, for Kavad himself, was precisely the point. More, very much more, than issues of personal hygiene were at stake. To imitate Rome would be to overtake her. Truly to become wealthy required learning all the lessons of Roman greatness. Even as *Iranshahr* tottered, Kavad's fondness for a scrubdown served to signal to his people that he had his gaze fixed firmly on the future.

In the meanwhile, what could not be copied from Rome would simply have to be stolen. For more than a century, the extortion of danger money from their western neighbour had lain at the heart of the Sasanians' foreign policy. The days of beating off Roman invasions were long gone. The last serious attempt made by a Caesar to overthrow the House of Sasan had taken place back in AD 363, under the command of a would-be Alexander named Julian, and had ended with the death of the emperor himself, and the imposition upon his successor of gratifyingly humiliating peace terms. From that moment on, the Roman high command had come to accept a painful and unsettling truth: Persia could not be beaten. To continue ignoring that lesson would result only in an endless haemorrhaging of blood and gold. Cheaper, in the long run, simply to purchase coexistence. So it was, to the delight of a succession of Sasanian monarchs, that they had found themselves able to screw out of their great enemy what the Romans, with a fastidious show of delicacy, termed "subsidies," and what the Persians, amid much self-congratulatory clamour, termed "tribute." Who, for instance, had helped to fund Peroz's programme of fortifications along the northern frontier? Caesar. Who had helped to pay his ransom? Caesar. Who had contributed gold towards his final expedition? Caesar. Yet it was true as well that the annihilation of Peroz's army, and of its calamitous aftermath, had not gone unremarked in the council chambers of the West. In 501, when Kavad found himself under pressure from the Hephthalites to pay off the dues owed to them for their backing, and wrote to the emperor of the Romans, a one-time bureaucrat and notorious miser by the name of Anastasius, demanding what he euphemistically termed a "loan," Anastasius refused. Clearly, Caesar's advisers had calculated that *Iranshahr* was now a broken reed. This, for Kavad, was a most ominous development. For a century and more, the intimidating reputation of Persian arms had served to reap the House of Sasan prodigious benefit; yet now, if Kavad were to allow the ink-spotted accountants of Rome to call his bluff, not only would the Hephthalites remain unpaid, but his own prestige, and that of his entire empire, would suffer a yet further body-blow.

The *Shahanshah*, however, was hardly a man to allow a good crisis to go to waste. Peril, in his philosophy, existed solely to be turned to advantage. The Hephthalites could be recruited as mercenaries. The nobility, rather than being left to snap and tear at one another, and at the heels of the king himself, could instead be recruited to the common cause. All the seething religious antagonism that was racking Kavad's empire could be dissolved, so he trusted, upon a summons to punish the Romans. *Iranshahr* may have been bloodied, but it remained what it had always been: a state powerfully geared to war.

Not all the repeated humiliations inflicted by the Hephthalites had served to diminish the confidence felt by Kavad in his killing-machine: for the paradox was, as he well knew, that his armies were far better suited to savaging the wealthy and globe-spanning empire of Rome than they were to crushing impoverished nomads. Whatever else might be said about the Romans, they were at least civilised. They had cities that could be put under siege and armies that were not forever melting away. Above all, unlike the Hephthalites, they lay conveniently ready to hand: not lurking beyond those regions where royal authority was at its weakest, but right where the *Shahanshah* wanted them, directly on the doorstep of the land that constituted both his ultimate powerbase, and the surest guarantee of *Iranshahr*'s rank as a superpower.

"The Heart of Iran," it was called; and yet this land was not Persia, nor anywhere else inhabited by the Aryan people. Follow the trunk road that led from beyond the easternmost province of the empire—Khorasan, as it was known—and continue through Parthia and Media to the great range of mountains, the Zagros, that formed the western rampart of the plateau of Iran, and the traveller would then start to descend, through many twists and turns, to a very different world. *Eragh*, the Persians called it—the "Flat Land." The contrast with the upland regions of the empire could hardly have been more striking. Unlike Iran, where the cities planted by a succession of kings served only to emphasise the immense emptiness of the salt flats, or the deserts, or the mountains, the lowlands revealed an immense monotony of crops and brick. Whether spreading fields of barley, or smudges of brown smoke on the horizon, the tell-tale smears of urban sprawl, here were the marks of a landscape as intensively exploited as any in the world. All the gold and pearls in the imperial treasury were not as precious to the Persian monarchy as this, the truest jewel in its crown: for nowhere was more dazzlingly fecund, more blessed with fertile soil. Westwards from *Mesopotamia*, or "The Land Between the Rivers," as the Greeks called the region, there stretched nothing except for sand; but the two great rivers themselves, the fast-flowing Tigris and the sluggish Euphrates, had served between them to make what would otherwise have been fiery desert bloom.

Not unaided, however. Human muscle had been scoring the mud steppes since the dawn of time—but never had there been quite such enthusiastic sponsors of irrigation as the House of Sasan. If royal power, in the eastern provinces of *Iranshahr*, was a thing of often shimmering insubstantiality, then in the West it had always been wielded with an iron fist. Massive labour gangs, funded and controlled directly from the imperial centre, had toiled for centuries to ensure that the wealth of Mesopotamia was exploited to the full. Immense effort was required simply to ensure that the canals did not silt up, that the rivers did not flood, that all the fields and factories did not degenerate back into swamps. The Persian monarchy, though, had achieved more than merely keeping the sludge and the whining mosquitoes at bay: it had expanded the network of canals on a truly colossal scale. Most were simple irrigation channels, sliced in squares across the fields; but some, the most grandiose, were as wide and deep as the Euphrates itself. Kavad himself had commissioned the excavation of a canal that promised to be the largest that Mesopotamia had ever seen: testimony to the implacable resolve of the crown, even amid crisis and financial meltdown, not to stint on its engineering budget. Some investments were always worth the expense. Once completed, the new canal would provide fresh water for a whole new swath of Mesopotamia. Hitherto barren soil would flourish; the population would swell; cities would sprout and grow. The economy, as it had done ever since the conquest of the lowlands by the House of Sasan, would continue to boom.[65]

Only follow the money. Rare was the *Shahanshah* who had failed to sniff majesty in the scent of the Mesopotamian mud. Even Ardashir himself, the original conqueror of this land back in AD 226, had quickly abandoned any notion of trying to rule it from Istakhr, venerable hometown of his dynasty though it was. The cockpit of *Iranshahr*, from his reign onwards, had lain instead on the banks of the Tigris. Ctesiphon—a sprawling agglomeration of once-distinct towns and villages ringed by bristling walls and dominated by the towering arches of a colossal royal palace—was certainly no stranger to such a role. By establishing its capital there, the House of Sasan had consciously planted its banner amid the rubble of countless former regimes. Opposite, for instance, on the far bank of the Tigris, lay Seleucia—a city named after one of Alexander's generals. Once the haughty epitome of Greek power and self-confidence, all its streets and palaces had long since been lost to sand, and only gibbets now stood upon its walls. Ctesiphon itself, at the time of its capture by Ardashir, had been the capital of the Parthian kings. This pedigree—reinforced by the Sasanians' own lavish building projects and the prodigious growth of its population—had served to stamp this city as the undisputed capital of Asia. Unsurprisingly, then, the Romans, eager to add to the graveyard of empires, and poised menacingly as they were just three hundred miles to the north-west, had always found it an irresistible target. A near-impregnable one as well: for only once, back in 283, had a Roman emperor actually succeeded in capturing the city from the Sasanians, and even then he had promptly been struck by lightning, certain proof of the indignation of Ohrmazd. Nor was it only the heavens that stood guard over Ctesiphon. Beyond the vast ring of walls encircling the city, there stretched the immensity of the irrigation system: moat after endless moat. Back in 363, during the course of the final Roman attempt to capture Ctesiphon, even mosquitoes had been summoned to the city's defence: great clouds of them, in the wake of the deliberate cutting of the dykes by the Persians, had shadowed Julian's approach, so that "by day the light of the sun, and by night the glitter of the stars, were blotted out."[66]

Kavad faced few such impediments to his own invasion. No natural frontier, no river or chain of mountains, marked the boundary between the empires of East and West. The border itself was little more than a line drawn in the sand. Those who dwelt on either side of it spoke the same language and shared the same way of life, "so that rather than live in dread of one another," as one Roman commentator observed disapprovingly, "they inter-marry, bringing their produce to the same markets, and even shoulder the labours of farming together."[67] As a result, both the Persian and the Roman authorities were as concerned with policing their own subjects as they were with intimidating the enemy. Indeed, by the terms of a peace treaty signed more than sixty years previously, the construction of new fortresses close to the border had been banned outright. De-militarisation, however, had effectively been a Persian victory by another name: for the *Shahanshah*, unlike his Roman adversary, already commanded a great city that sat almost directly on the frontier. Nisibis was its name: once the linchpin of the entire Roman defensive system in the East, but secured for Persia back in 363, following the defeat of Julian's assault on Ctesiphon. Almost a century and a half on, and the Romans still had no rival stronghold from which to coordinate a response to any Persian invasion. For decades, as peace held between the two superpowers, this had scarcely mattered. But now, with Hephthalite mercenaries suddenly erupting across Roman territory, their hoof-beats were sounding a tattoo that generated terror hundreds of miles beyond the frontier.

Kavad's ambition stretched well beyond stripping the Roman countryside bare: he planned to seize a great city or two. Cities, after all, were where the true wealth was to be found: gold, industry and slaves. Accordingly, the *Shahanshah* did not follow the lowland roads along which rural refugees were already streaming, but headed north, through the mountains of Armenia. His first target was the city of Theodosiopolis, which he surprised, and took with ease. Then, swinging back south, he made for an even richer prize. Amida, a heavily fortified stronghold some eighty miles beyond the frontier, where its massive basalt walls lowered grimly above the upper reaches of the Tigris, had shrugged off many previous Persian attempts to capture it; nor did it promise Kavad easy pickings now. Even prior to his invasion, the city's governor had been prompted to stiffen its defences by an unprecedented array of evil portents: "locusts came, the sun was dimmed, there was earthquake, famine, and plague."[68]

There was certainly no prospect of repeating the trick that had secured Theodosiopolis, and taking Amida by surprise. Upwards of fifty thousand villagers, from all across the region, had fled the approach of the Hephthalite cavalry and taken refuge inside the city, almost doubling its population. Even though this had rendered living conditions within Amida almost unendurable, it had at least ensured there would be no shortage of people to defend its walls. Sure enough, in time, the defence of Amida would become the stuff of ringing legend. Everything the city had in its arsenal was rained down upon the besiegers: from catapult bolts to arrows; from rocks to boiling oil. Even the women and children took to the walls and hurled down stones. Meanwhile, the city's prostitutes chanted abuse at the *Shahanshah* and flashed their privates at him whenever he came into view.

After three months, though, it was Kavad who enjoyed the last laugh. A Persian detachment forced its way through a sewer that ran beneath the circuit wall and secured an inner tower. Kavad himself then stood at the base of the walls, sword drawn, to urge on the rest of his army, who raised ladders and swarmed up into Amida at last. Then, in an ecstasy of triumph and greed, they stripped the city bare. Although many of its inhabitants were taken as slaves, with the notables carefully rounded up to serve as hostages, far more were put to the sword. The streets ran with blood. Tens of thousands of bodies, when the killing was finally done, were slung beyond the city's walls. Great piles of reeking corpses, tangled and gore-smeared, provided the Persians with an intimidating trophy of their victory. Decades later, the terrible slaughter would still haunt the imaginings of all those who lived along Rome's eastern frontier.

Which, no doubt, had been precisely Kavad's aim. Although the war he had launched would soon peter out into bloody stalemate, and although Amida itself, besieged in turn by the Romans, would end up being sold back to them, albeit for a tidy profit, the *Shahanshah* could consider his war aims to have been more than met. A fearsome marker had been laid down. After long years of defeat and decay, the lord of *Iranshahr* had triumphantly demonstrated to his own subjects, and the rest of the world, that the spiral of his dynasty's decline was over. There would be no collapse. The House of Sasan had weathered the storm. Nor was that all. It remained the goal of Kavad himself, ever bold, ever ambitious, not merely to redeem the Persian monarchy from the many perils that had been beleaguering it, but to set its power upon firmer foundations than it had ever enjoyed before. Its enemies everywhere were to be hamstrung and taught their place. In 506, he duly signed a treaty with the Romans, which once again obliged Caesar to hand over a payment of gold. Some of this, of course, along with the booty of Theodosiopolis and Amida, could be used to help pay off the Hephthalites—except that even on that front there was at last some promising news. Reports were starting to be brought in by travellers from the distant-most limits of the steppes of the rise to prominence there of a whole new breed of savages: a hitherto unknown people named the Turks. It appeared that the Hephthalites themselves might be suffering from their own nomad problem. Manifold indeed were the blessings of Ohrmazd.

Meanwhile, inside *Iranshahr* itself, Kavad set about neutering other threats. Although it was his heresy that had seen him toppled in the first place, he seems not, on his return to power, to have tempered his loyalty to the teachings of Mazdak. Just the opposite, in fact. Whether prompted by conviction, or by cynicism, or by a mixture of the two, Kavad remained an enthusiastic partisan of the communist prophet. That the mighty should be humbled; that the great estates of the nobility and the clergy should be dismantled; that privilege should yield to justice: here, in these demands, was scope for reform indeed. The genius of Kavad—or perhaps his wilful blindness—was that for a long while he saw not the slightest contradiction between the two defining policies of his reign: the ring-fencing of royal power and the sponsorship of social revolution. Nothing, perhaps, better exemplified the successes that he was thereby able to obtain than the fate of the family that had threatened, at the start of his reign, to put the whole of *Iranshahr* in its shade: the Karin. Such was the scale of the onslaught launched by the Mazdakites against the power base of that haughty dynasty that it ended up shattered into pieces. The destruction of their strongholds in Media left them impotent to resist when Kavad, pressing home his advantage, forced them east, into what remained of their fiefdoms, far from the heartbeat of royal power. Revenge was sweet.

Nevertheless, the display of royal weight-throwing did still have its limits. The Karin, although certainly brought low, had been scotched, not killed. Meanwhile, their old rivals, the Mihran, continued to supply the House of Sasan with ministers and generals, just as they had ever done. Other Parthian dynasts too had positively flourished under the rule of Kavad. One prominent warlord—known to the Romans as Aspebedes—had played a leading role during the siege of Amida, and, even more lucratively, had succeeded in slipping his sister into Kavad's bed.[69] The marriage was a spectacular love-match. Although Kavad had already fathered two sons to other wives, it was his third, Khusrow, "born to him by the sister of Aspebedes, whom the father loved most of all."[70] Able, ruthless and bold: Khusrow was to prove all these things. Doubtless, then, when Kavad looked at his youngest son, it was the image of his own princely self that he saw reflected there. Nevertheless, as the years slipped by, and Khusrow grew to a strutting maturity, this naked favouritism came to threaten a major constitutional crisis. Blatantly ignoring the convention that dictated the eldest son should succeed to the throne, the *Shahanshah* began to pull all the strings he could in favour of Khusrow—even to the degree of offering bribes to Anastasius, the Roman emperor, to support his candidacy. This manoeuvring, however, rather than proving offensive to those conservative elements of the establishment that had resisted all of Kavad's attempts to undermine them, instead received their wholehearted backing: for Khusrow—unlike Kavus, his Mazdakite elder brother—was a fiercely orthodox Zoroastrian. No wonder, then, that the *mowbeds*, long put in the shade by Kavad's devotion to Mazdak, should have rallied to the younger prince's cause. No wonder, either, that the Mazdakites, contrary to all the wishes of their royal patron, should have begun to swing behind Kavus, the legal heir.

So was set the scene for the climactic crisis of Kavad's reign. By 528, the aged *Shahanshah* was backed agonisingly into a corner: forced to choose between his faith and his hopes for the future of the crown. To nominate Kavus as his successor would be to entrench Mazdakism in *Iranshahr* for good; to nominate Khusrow would be to entrust the throne to the man best qualified to consolidate royal power. In the event, Kavad opted to give free rein to his favourite son. Given the nod, Khusrow sprang into action. A formal debate was staged at Ctesiphon, at which Mazdak himself, according to the reports of the gloating *mowbeds*, was comprehensively trounced. Khusrow, in the wake of this show-trial, had the teachings of the upstart prophet formally condemned. A wave of persecutions followed, right across the empire. Massacres and confiscations rapidly drove the wretched Mazdakites underground. In Ctesiphon's royal park, so it was reported, Khusrow ordered holes to be dug and then buried his Mazdakite prisoners in them head first, so that only their legs stuck out. He then invited Mazdak himself to walk along the flower beds, inspect what had been planted there, and admire the fruit. When he did so, the prophet cried out in horror and slumped to the ground. He was then revived, hung from a tree, and used for target practice by Khusrow's archers.

Whatever the truth of this gruesome anecdote, it is certain that Kavad's willingness to abandon his faith marked a key turning point in the history of the Near East. The scope for change offered by Mazdakism had certainly not been exhausted. Potentially, as the turbulent and convulsive course of Kavad's own reign had served so potently to demonstrate, there was almost no limit to what might not be achieved by an alliance between an imperial monarchy and the revelations, if truly believed to be heaven-sent, of a prophet. As it was, however, the future of *Iranshahr* was not to be Mazdakite. In 531, Kavad died. Although Kavus, from his powerbase in the north of the empire, did attempt to seize the throne, he was speedily defeated by his younger brother, captured, and put to death. Sternly, Khusrow proclaimed the definitive end of "new customs and new ways":[71] of what had been, so he declared, a rebellion against "religion, reason, and the state."[72]

Yet, in truth, the new *Shahanshah* was set on having his cake and eating it. His enthusiasm for tradition notwithstanding, he had no intention of letting all of his father's achievements go to waste. Ancient hierarchies were to be affirmed; and yet, simultaneously, hundreds of inspectors dispatched across *Iranshahr* with licence to poke their noses into the business of anyone, including even the dynasts. The Zoroastrian priests were to be confirmed in all their rights and privileges; and yet, in a patent attempt to counter the appeal of Mazdakism, new offices created from among their ranks, focused on meeting the needs of the poor and the desperate. Four of the greatest Parthian dynasts—including a Karinid—were to be appointed to the defence of the four corners of the empire; and yet, for the first time, a standing army, beholden solely to the crown, was to be recruited and maintained. To perform such a balancing act, even for an operator as cool and iron-fisted as Khusrow, was likely to prove no easy matter. Not only the future prospects of the House of Sasan, but of *Iranshahr* itself, were likely to hang upon how he did.

Few who enjoyed the supreme privilege of being ushered into the royal presence would have doubted that Khusrow had what it took for success. "May you be immortal!" sounded the response to his every utterance; and certainly, to look upon a *Shahanshah* enthroned in all his glory was still, as it had ever been, to behold a man as close as any mortal could be to a god. His robes gleamed with jewels; his beard was dusted with gold; his face was painted like some ancient idol. Most dazzling of all was his diadem: the symbol of his *farr*. By the time of Khusrow, however, it was no longer possible for a king to wear one unsupported. Instead, as he sat on his throne, the crown had to be suspended by a chain hung from the ceiling above his head. So massive had it become, and so stupefyingly heavy the gold and jewels that adorned it, that it would otherwise have snapped his neck.

Menace, it seemed, lurked in even the most splendid show of power.

By the Rivers of Babylon

Flower-beds and fountains might have seemed an incongruous setting for mass slaughter. Nevertheless, if the stories told of the execution of Mazdak and his followers were true, they had met with their fate in a peculiarly fitting venue for an assertion of royal power. In a land such as Mesopotamia—where sand was often borne on howling winds, and where only relentless toil kept the desert from smothering the fields— there was no more precious perk of majesty than a walled and well-tended park. The ancient kings of Persia had termed such a garden a *paradaida*—a "paradise." When Khusrow dallied in arbours "fresh with the beauty of fruit trees, vines and green cypresses,"[73] or wandered past paddocks boasting "boundless numbers of ostriches, antelopes, wild asses, peacocks and pheasants,"[74] or rode with the lords and ladies of his court through his hunting grounds in pursuit of "lions and tigers of huge size,"[75] he was the heir to traditions more ancient than he knew.

Indeed, there were some among his subjects who claimed that the horticultural traditions of the region stretched all the way back to the beginning of time itself. Beyond the wall that encircled the blossom-scented air of the royal gardens, amid the immense agglomeration of settlements that sprawled for miles along the banks of the Tigris, there lived people who believed that once, shortly after the making of the heavens and the earth, all of Ctesiphon, and far beyond it, had been a paradise. "And the Lord God," it was recorded in their scriptures, "planted a garden in Eden, in the east."[76] Prior to that, under cover of a mist such as still often rose up from the Tigris, He had taken mud, and fashioned out of it, not bricks, not a city, but a man. The first man who had ever lived, in fact: "*Adam*," which meant, in the language of the people who told the story, "Earth."

The Jews, however, were not natives of Mesopotamia. Rather, they traced both their name and their origins back to a vanished kingdom— Judah—that had lain just inland from the Mediterranean Sea, some five hundred miles to the west. A fair distance, it might be thought—

and all the more so because the directest route cut across burning and near-impassable sand. However, by taking a slightly longer course, along the arc of a well-watered crescent—northwards from Mesopotamia and then curving back south—it was possible to travel from the banks of the Tigris via a succession of cities, rather than across the open desert, and arrive in Judah within a matter of months. Eleven hundred years before the time of Khusrow, this had proved sufficient to doom the tiny kingdom's independence. In 586 BC, a vast Mesopotamian army had descended upon its capital, a temple-topped city named Jerusalem, and put it to the torch. The wretched kingdom's elite had been carted off into exile. Their god—who was believed by the Jews not only to have chosen them as the objects of his especial favour, but also to have been the creator of the entire universe—seemed to have abandoned them for good.

A thousand years on, however, and it was not the Jews who had vanished from Mesopotamia, but the very memory of the conquerors who had first hauled them there in chains. Preserved in the Jewish scriptures were the visions of a man named Daniel, said to have been one of the original exiles from Jerusalem. In a dream, he had seen a tempestuous sea, out of which had emerged "four great beasts."[77] These monsters, according to an angel who interpreted the dream for the prophet, were four great kingdoms that were destined to inherit the earth, until, at the end of time, "the saints of the Most High shall receive the kingdom, and possess the kingdom for ever, for ever and ever."[78] That Daniel's vision had been a true one, and that the course of history was indeed to be interpreted as a succession of mighty empires, each one consigning its predecessor to oblivion, was more manifest in Mesopotamia, perhaps, than anywhere else on earth: for the land was an entire graveyard of abandoned capitals. Its two great rivers, rather than flowing obediently within their banks, were like restless serpents, shaking their coils with such sporadic violence that entire cities were left high and dry, or else submerged and returned to mud. The Jews of Ctesiphon, when they wandered along the banks of the Tigris, could see the shells of abandoned buildings, partly dissolved by the turbid waters: remnants of Veh-Ardashir, the first capital raised by the House of Sasan and built according to a perfectly circular plan, but which, upon an abrupt and calamitous shifting of the river's course, had been sliced in two. In turn, of course, beyond Veh-Ardashir, there loomed the sand-throttled ruins of Seleucia, its harbour choked by silt and reeds; and beyond them, some forty miles across the mud steppes, an even more battered monument to human vanity, a place that was now "nothing more than mounds and stones and decay" but once, long before, had been the greatest city in the world.[79] Abandoned by the Euphrates, emptied of its population and despoiled of its brickwork, the name of the ruin was barely to be heard now on people's lips. The Jews, however, did speak it. They had not forgotten the vanished city, nor the glamour and the terror of its reputation. They still remembered Babylon.

As well they might have done—for it was a king of Babylon who had burned their capital, enslaved their ancestors, and first embodied for the Jews that peculiar and terrifying intoxication which was the lust to rule all of mankind: "The nations drank of her wine; therefore the nations are mad."[80] Conversely, in the ruin of such a city, there had been offered to the Jews a precious reassurance: that there existed no earthly empire so great or overweening that it might not one day be dashed to pieces by their divine protector. All the convulsive rhythms of history, which over time had served to offer now one nation, and now another, the sceptre of the world, bore witness to nothing, in the final reckoning, save the purposes of the One God of the Jews. That was why, in the heartlands of Mesopotamia, it was the Jews themselves who still maintained the sacred habits of their worship, while all the temples of Babylon had "become a heap of ruins, the haunt of jackals, a horror and a hissing, without inhabitant."[81]

Only in a single city—one that lay right on the margins of the one-time Babylonian world, at the uppermost point of the Fertile Crescent's arc, just beyond the frontier with Rome—did "the ancient faith"[82] of Mesopotamia continue to flicker: for in Harran, they still worshipped the ancient gods. The landscape beyond its walls was filled with idols: strangely preserved, withered corpses, both animal and human, were wedged into fissures above mountain roads; eerie figures framed by peacock feathers and crescent moons stood guard over desert lakes. The mightiest idol of all, however, and the glory of Harran itself, was a colossal statue of the city's patron, Sin—the "Lord of the Moon." Annually, the god's worshippers would hoist him on their shoulders, carry him from his temple, parade him all around town, and then return him in triumph to his sanctuary on a barge. The rituals of this festival—the *akitu*—were of a quite staggering antiquity, and had once been practised across Mesopotamia; nor did the priests of Sin, who conducted them with a grave and sombre sense of reverence, ever forget it.[83] Yet, in truth, the same obduracy with which the people of Harran clung to their ancient cult served only to emphasise their freakishness. In Mesopotamia, the balance of power had long since swung against any notion that the moon, the sun and the stars might conceivably be deities. The Harranian idols—demonic though they often seemed to nervous visitors—were the merest flotsam, left beached by a retreating tide. The Jews, whose prophets had long foretold the doom of all gods save their own, found a particular vindication in this: "By the purple and linen that rot upon them, you will know that they are not gods; and they will finally be consumed, and be a reproach in the land."[84]

Nevertheless, for all the mingled scorn and dread with which they cast their backward stare upon the primordial traditions of Mesopotamia, the Jews had never ceased to be fascinated by them. The land that had served the first man and woman as an earthly paradise had also provided humanity with the wellsprings of its learning—a precious legacy from an otherwise vanished world. Just as the Tigris had turned all the grandeur of Veh-Ardashir to mud, a great flood had submerged the whole earth and dissolved all traces of Eden. Had a man named Noah not been given forewarning of the calamity, and built a massive ark, then life itself would have been obliterated. However, not every trace of the world before the Flood had been lost: for Noah's descendants, digging amid the mud of Mesopotamia, had stumbled across a buried cache of books.[85] These, when they were deciphered, had been found to contain the wisdom of the earliest generations of men—necromancers who had lived before the Flood. The consequence had been the reputation that had served to grace Mesopotamia ever since—not only among the Jews, but among peoples everywhere—as the land "where the true art of divination first made its appearance."[86]

Such stories reflected not only the faint aura of the sinister that had always clung to Babylonian learning, but also an ambition on the part of Jewish scholars to lay claim to its inheritance. For a thousand years and more, ever since the first deportation of the people of Judah, they had been in the habit of regarding Mesopotamia as a home away from home. Naturally, they had never entirely conquered their sense of homesickness: Jerusalem, the capital of their God-given homeland, would always represent for them the most sacred place on earth. Nevertheless, it had also long been their conviction that their ultimate origins lay not in the Holy Land but on the banks of the Euphrates. The proof of this could hardly have been a weightier one: for it was to be found in the very first book of the Tanakh, the great compendium of the holiest Jewish scriptures. There, after the stories of Adam, and of Noah, it was recorded how God, ten generations after the Flood, had spoken to a man named Abram: a native of a place called Ur. As to where precisely this mysterious city might have been, there was much dispute; but what all scholars could agree on was that it had stood somewhere in the Land of the Two Rivers.[87]

Abram had not remained in the land of his birth, though. Out of the blue, shortly after his seventy-fifth birthday, he had received a revelation from God. "Go from your country and your kindred, and your father's house, to the land that I will show you. And I will make of you a great nation, and I will bless you, and make your name great, so that you will be a blessing."[88] A tempting offer, to be sure—and one that had seen Abram duly commit to emigration. His reward had quickly followed. No sooner had Abram arrived in a land named Canaan than he had found himself being graced with a further divine revelation: an assurance that his descendants would inherit Canaan as "an everlasting possession."[89] Hence the new sobriquet that the Almighty bestowed on him: "Your name shall be Abraham; for I have made you the father of a multitude of nations."[90] And so, sure enough, it had come to pass: for Abraham had indeed ended up fathering many peoples, with the most prominent of all being the Jews. A glorious pedigree, to be sure. Much had derived from it. Abraham it was, after all, who had handed down to the Jews their sense of themselves as God's Chosen People. But he had also bequeathed them something more: the title deeds to what had once been Canaan, and now ranked as their Promised Land.

A gift that, coming from the Almighty, could only be for keeps. Here, to the half a million or so Jews settled between the Two Rivers, was a flattering assurance. As they toiled in the fields that bordered the great canals north of Ctesiphon, or squatted cross-legged beside their market stalls, or drove their pack-animals laden with merchandise through the winding and narrow streets of the sprawling capital itself, they could know that they, unlike the teeming millions who lived alongside them in Mesopotamia, were a nation set apart: for they had a homeland granted them of God. This did not mean, by and large, that they actually wished to go and live in their Promised Land. Granted, any Jew who happened to dream of barley would, so their sages had pronounced, be expected to move there straight away*—but most much preferred the idea of emigration to the reality. In truth, for many centuries now, there had been nothing to prevent the Jews from ending their exile, save only their own partiality to life in a land as fertile, cosmopolitan and prosperous as Mesopotamia. Certainly, the forced captivity imposed on them by their Babylonian masters had not

---

* Such, at any rate, was the testimony of Rabbi Zera, whose own dream of barley prompted his immediate emigration. Another anecdote described how an overly drunken celebration ended up with his throat being cut by a fellow rabbi. "The next day, this rabbi prayed on Rabbi Zera's behalf, and brought him back to life. Next year, he said to Rabbi Zera, 'Will you honour me, and come and feast with me again?' But Rabbi Zera replied, 'A miracle cannot be guaranteed.'"

endured for long. A bare four decades or so after the sack of Jerusalem, it had been the turn of Babylon herself to fall. Her captor, in 539 BC, had been none other than Cyrus of Persia, that trail-blazing exponent of global monarchy. The Jews, unsurprisingly, had hailed his achievement in rapturous terms: for not only had Cyrus humbled the hated strumpet-city of Babylon, but he had also granted them permission to return to Jerusalem, and rebuild their annihilated Temple. Yet though many had gratefully taken the Persian king up on his offer, just as many had not. Instead, they and their heirs had remained where they were, and put down such roots in the rich, thick soil of Mesopotamia that not all the savagery and swirl of great power politics, gusting across the landscape of the Near East for a millennium and more, had served to uproot them. Instead, it was upon the descendants of the Jews who had returned to the Holy Land that devastation, over the course of the centuries, had been repeatedly visited: so much so that by the early third century AD, when Ardashir and his Persians had first come clattering into Ctesiphon, it was not Jerusalem and its environs that provided the Jews with their surest heartland, but the banks of the Tigris and Euphrates.

This was a development that verged, in the circumstances, on the miraculous. Immigrants to Mesopotamia were rarely in the habit of preserving the memory of their origins for more than a couple of generations, at best. The region had long experience of serving as a melting-pot: for the rich fertility of its soil was not the only source of its prodigious wealth. Lying as it did midway between the Mediterranean Sea and the Indian Ocean, between the steppes of Central Asia and the deserts of Arabia, it was incomparably well positioned to serve as the world's clearing-house. "All that exists in it is brought there," boasted its Persian masters, "and is for our enjoyment, be it food, or drugs, or perfumes."[91] The consequence of this could be sampled with a simple stroll through Ctesiphon. Whether in the overflowing bazaars, or in the few streets large enough to cater to carts and livestock, or in the narrow alleyways through which only pedestrians could gingerly pick their way, there was not a language spoken under the sun but it could be heard somewhere in the monstrous city. Yellow-skinned men with slanted eyes, white-skinned men with straw-coloured hair, black-skinned men with flat noses: their peculiar jabberings served to season the fetid air. Yet all, over time, would prove so much mulch; for just as the streets were repeatedly being cleared of their ruts, and houses abandoned to spreading cess-pools, and whole neighbourhoods demolished to make way for new developments, so was the human fabric of Ctesiphon forever being recycled. Memories, like mud-bricks, rarely stood solid there for long. Only the Jews, it seemed, like some timeless landmark fashioned out of granite, stood proof against the process.

But how? Inimitable though their attachment to the distant homeland promised them by God certainly was, it would hardly have been sufficient in itself to prevent them from being digested into the maw of Mesopotamia. Fortunately, however, long previously, when issuing His grant of Canaan to Abraham, the Almighty had foreseen the risk. "This is my covenant which you shall keep, between me and you and your descendants after you: every male among you shall be circumcised."[92] Nor had He been content to leave things there. To a subsequent generation, so it was recorded in the Tanakh, He had issued yet further markers of the exceptional status that was theirs as the children of Abraham: never, so He had thundered, were they to eat pork, or any other meat that had not first been drained of its blood, nor were they to fashion "any likeness of anything,"[93] nor were they, on any account, to break a whole battery of other commandments, interdictions and prescriptions, which they were never to change or add to one jot. This awesome body of law was called the Torah—"Instruction"—and it gave the Jews, uniquely among the many peoples deported to Babylon, a sense that law derived ultimately, not from any mortal king, or sage, but from God alone. It was this, more than anything else, that had enabled them, throughout the long centuries of their sojourn in Mesopotamia, to preserve their identity as a nation apart. Unlike other, less privileged peoples, they had been brought by God to fathom the essence of what it meant to be human: that it lay not in any aspiration to empire, or liberty, or fame, but rather, and very simply, in being subject to a law.

Which was doubtless, for the Jews of *Iranshahr*, just as well. The House of Sasan, after all, did not look kindly upon sedition. That most Persian kings were prepared to tolerate the prickly exclusiveness of their Jewish subjects reflected their understanding that it posed their authority, not a threat, but the opposite. The bizarre distinctiveness of the Jews, in a city as teeming and inchoate as Ctesiphon, had come to the imperial bureaucracy almost as a relief: for it rendered them easier to regulate and fleece. All that was required to ensure that these peculiar aliens did not get ideas above their station, and paid their taxes obediently, was the appointment of one of their own as a tame puppet—an "exilarch." This, ever since the reign of Shapur I, had been the settled policy of the Sasanian monarchy; and it was a measure of just how smoothly it had operated that the attitude of certain kings to the Jews had even, on occasion, stretched to a lukewarm favouritism. One *Shahanshah* had gone so far as to marry the daughter of an exilarch, and sit her by his side as his queen. Unsurprisingly, then, the Jews tended to regard their Sasanian masters as a cut above other pagans. Even the Persians' notorious reluctance "to urinate in public"[94]—regarded by everyone else as a laughable foible—met with glowing approval from Jewish moralists. Such a people richly merited obedience. "For they do protect us, after all."[95]

Yet this compact, like so much else in *Iranshahr*, had started to crumble during the reign of Peroz. Not every Persian was inclined to mimic the haughty tolerance of royalty. The Zoroastrian priesthood had long viewed the Jews' obdurate refusal to acknowledge the manifest truths of Ohrmazd as a standing provocation. As what else did it brand them, so the *mowbeds* demanded to know, if not the spawn of Dahag, that brain-eating, serpent-shouldered fiend? "For it was Dahag who began the composition of the Jewish scriptures, and Dahag who was the teacher of Abraham, the high-priest of the Jews."[96] No wonder, then, as the Zoroastrian Church increasingly sought to muscle its way free of royal control, that it should also have looked to purge *Iranshahr* of such an offensively demonic minority. Already, in the reign of Peroz's father, the *mowbeds* had begun to lobby for the policy as a sure-fire way of regaining those portions of their ancient empire that had been lost for good to Alexander: "For only convert to one religion all the nations and races in your empire," they had advised the *Shahanshah*, "and the land of the Greeks will also obediently submit to your rule."[97] It was Peroz, however, eager to clutch at any straw, who had shown himself most receptive to the argument.[98] In 467, he had duly sanctioned the execution of leading members of the Jewish elite, including the exilarch. The following year, he had banned the teaching of their scriptures and the practising of their law. In 470, he had abolished the post of exilarch altogether.[99] The reversal of long-term royal policy could hardly have been any more brutal. For the first time in their millennium-long history, the Jews of Mesopotamia had suffered active persecution. Worse: they had faced abolition as a distinctive people.

Swiftly and surely, however, "the wicked Peroz"[100] had been struck down. He and all his army had been obliterated. The agonies of *Iranshahr*, so the Jews could reflect with a grim complacency, had served as the verdict of an outraged heaven. Others too, of course, had arrived at much the same conclusion; and among them had been Kavad. The clinging to a discredited policy, just because the dropping of it might offend the *mowbeds*, was hardly the new *Shahanshah*'s style; and so it was, it appears, that the ban on the teaching of the Jewish law had been quietly dropped.[101] Many Jews, eager to show their gratitude, duly rallied to his cause. In time, they came to play such a prominent role in his armies that Kavad himself, if obliged to fight on a Jewish holy day, had been known to request his adversaries for a temporary truce. Everything, it seemed, was back to normal. The balance that the Jews of Mesopotamia had always sought to strike, between obedience to their overlords and a yearning to be left alone, appeared restored to its customary equilibrium.

Except that the trauma of persecution could not so easily be forgotten. To ban Jews anywhere from studying their scriptures and their laws was, of course, to deliver them a crippling blow; and yet to ban the Jews of Mesopotamia was an act of peculiar vindictiveness. To a supreme degree, they were still, as they had ever been, a "People of the Book." Scholarship possessed the aura for them of something incomparably glorious: for in Mesopotamia, attentiveness to the word of God, such as came naturally to any Jew, had fused with a robust pride in the region's glamorous reputation for ancient wisdom, and which could be traced back to the giants who had flourished before the Flood. Tellingly, the Jewish sages who lived in the land of Abraham's birth had always taken it for granted that the favours granted to their ancestor had been his due, not simply as a man of God, but as a polymath "superior to all others in wisdom."[102] No surprise, then, that by the time that Ardashir took control of Ctesiphon, Mesopotamia should have come to boast what ranked, by the admiring assent of the Jewish people everywhere, as the two leading centres of scholarship in the world. Sura and Pumpedita lay some hundred miles apart, but were in every other way the mirror image of one another. Both stood on the western bank of the Euphrates, both were largely populated by Jews, and both gloried in the possession of a *yeshiva*, or "school," with ambitions to change the world.

It was the self-appointed mission of these two institutions, a bold and extraordinary one, to replicate on earth the very pattern of the heavens: for to understand the Torah properly, so the sages who taught in them believed, was to fathom the deepest and most hidden purposes of God. Naturally, the laws that had been given to their ancestors could never be altered; but what if there were more to them than met the untutored eye? Such was the question to which the sages of Sura and Pumpedita gave an answer quite staggering in its implications. In addition to the written Torah, so they taught, there had also been revealed a secret Torah, never recorded, but passed down instead through the ages by word of mouth, from prophet to prophet, from rabbi to rabbi, and which they in turn, in their schools beside the Euphrates, had inherited and entrusted to memory. This was the same Torah that God Himself, before embarking on the Creation, had made sure to peruse, that the angels studied ceaselessly, and that a mortal, if sufficiently learned, might use to sway demons, to change the weather, or to communicate with the dead. No wonder, then, that any sage who could legitimately lay claim to such an awesome body of wisdom should be hailed by his students as *Rabbi*—"Master." No wonder, either, that the sages of Mesopotamia, in the wake of the shock that Peroz had given them, should have realised just how precarious a thing a *yeshiva* might be, and how very easy to close down. Was it really a safe bet, some of them began to ask, to entrust a treasure as incomparably precious as the unwritten Torah solely to the memories of rabbis?

Not, of course, that they were the only sages to have fretted over such a question. It was a very similar anxiety, ironically enough, that had prompted the *mowbed*s to put the sayings of Zoroaster for the first time into writing. Now, a couple of decades or so after the death of Peroz, and the rabbis of Mesopotamia were braced for an even more gruelling project of scholarship.[103] To transcribe those revelations of God that had hitherto only existed inside their heads was certainly no simple matter. Over the course of many years, the great scholars of Sura and Pumpedita had sought to demonstrate to the Jewish people that the demands of the Torah, both written and spoken, could be applied to even the most mundane aspects of day-to-day life: that geese, for instance, should not be permitted to copulate, and that it was wrong to laugh at the overweight, and that migraines could best be cured by pouring the blood of a dead rooster over the scalp. These, and a whole multitude of teachings like them, were not, so the rabbis claimed, additions to the unchanging law of God, but rather clarifications of it; and as such were themselves a part of the Torah. They too, accordingly, would all have to be recorded. Not so much as a single ruling, not a single detail, could be omitted. So it was that the written record of the rabbis' learning, their *talmud*, was brought to testify to an apparently puzzling truth. The Torah, which the rabbis attributed to God Himself, and which they claimed had first been revealed to the Jewish people way back in the mists of time, was composed in part of their very own commentaries upon it. Not only their commentaries either. Even the size of their respective penises was held by the sages to merit detailed mention. This, to anyone untutored in the stern disciplines of rabbinical learning, might have appeared a nonsense; and yet the mysteries of God's law, it went without saying, were hardly such as could be framed by mere mortal logic. Any new insight into the Torah, provided only that it derived from a rabbi with the requisite qualifications, ranked as a revelation direct from the Almighty—no more and no less so than the written Torah itself.

The task that the rabbis of Mesopotamia had set themselves, of transcribing their *talmud*, would take entire lifetimes to complete. Such a project could hardly be hurried, after all. The sages who trod the dusty streets of Sura and Pumpedita had their gaze fixed unblinkingly upon the dimension of the eternal. The focus of their researches was the entirety of creation, nothing less. They alone, by virtue of their prodigious feats of study, had fathomed the precise configuration of the will of God—and as a consequence, so it seemed to the rabbis, of the past and the future as well. Certainly, it never crossed their minds that there might have been a time when men such as themselves had not existed. The prophets of the Tanakh, the angels, even God Himself—all were recast in their own image, as rabbis. Likewise, in their heroic struggle to identify and define every conceivable application of the Torah, the scholars of Mesopotamia had no doubt that they were shaping the order that was to come. Fortress-like though the isolation of their *yeshiva*s certainly was, yet the rabbis were all too painfully conscious of the horrors in the crumbling world beyond. Their aim, in devoting their lives to study, was not to escape such evils, but rather to purge them upon the coming of a golden age: for God had given to the Jewish people the assurance of a new and blessed era, when "all ruined cities will be rebuilt," when "the cow and the bear shall feed together," and when "death will cease in the world."[104] Only once Jews everywhere had been brought to a proper understanding of the Torah, however, would this blessed moment arrive. "If you are worthy, I will hasten it; if you are not worthy, then it will be left to arrive in its own good time."[105] Such, the rabbis explained, was the bargain that the Almighty had struck with His people. The future of the world lay in their hands.

Yet like the *mowbed*s and the Mazdakites, whose yearning for an age when justice and mercy would prevail had seen them snatching after the reins of earthly power, the rabbis were not so unworldly as to disdain the making of a similar grab. Time was clearly dragging. God Himself, as every Jew well knew, had promised his Chosen People a saviour. "The Anointed One," he would be called—the *Mashiach*, or "Messiah." With such a king at the head of the Jewish people, the world's promised redemption from suffering would have dawned— and who was to say that the convulsions of the present age did not herald its imminence? "When you see the great powers contending one with another," so it was written, "then look for the foot of the Messiah."[106] As yet, however, with not so much as a toenail in evidence, there was a desperate need for the Jewish people to be graced with an alternative leadership: one that could serve to instruct them in the obedience demanded of them by God, and thereby to speed the Messiah's arrival.

And how fortunate it was, how very fortunate, that just such a leadership should have been ready to hand. "Teaching and the mastery of a people," so a celebrated rabbi had once piously averred, "have never coincided"[107]—but that had not stopped his successors from hankering after both. Tensions between the rabbis and the exilarchate had been seething for years—and now, with the exilarch vanished from the scene, the sages of Sura and Pumpedita did not hesitate to step into the breach. Even as they continued to toil away at their transcription of the Talmud, so also, with a quite awesome display of self-assurance, were they working to impose its dictates upon the entire Jewish nation. From highest to lowest, from landowners to labourers, all were to be shaped and controlled by it. Yet the rabbis, in their determination to force through this revolution, could not, as the *mowbed*s had done, draw upon royal backing, nor, like the Mazdakites, resort to armed insurrection. Nor, if they were truly to seize the commanding heights of their society, could they confine themselves simply to administering the law courts, or liaising with imperial bureaucrats. The power that the rabbis felt called upon by God to wield was hardly to be justified in terms of bare expediency. Only the single path would ever lead them to the rule of the Jewish people. The rabbis had to offer themselves, not as functionaries, nor even as judges, but as living models of holiness.

"Whoever carries out the teachings of the sages is worthy to be named a saint."[108] Once, even in a land as respectful of learning as Mesopotamia, such a maxim would have been dismissed by many Jews as merely an ivory tower fantasy. Increasingly, however, as the leaders of the *yeshivas* responded to the convulsions of the age with an outward show of defiance and an inner display of certitude, they were gathering ever more admirers to themselves. Lacking in swords, or silks, or mail-clad horses the rabbis might have been; but they had their own markers of power, nevertheless. There were the pregnant women, eager for their unborn sons to be imbued with a spirit of sanctity and scholarship, who haunted the limits of Sura and Pumpedita. There was the widespread conviction that even a blind rabbi, should he ever be mocked, had only to turn his gaze upon the wretch who had insulted him, and the offender would immediately be reduced to "a heap of bones."[109] Above all, saturating every level of Jewish society in Mesopotamia, there was the gathering acceptance that the rabbis were justified in all their soaring claims: that the will of God could indeed only be known through the prism of their scholarship. The Torah, revealed to a grateful people in all its hitherto unsuspected complexity and detail, could now begin its proper task: that of moulding every last Jew into a rabbi.

A consummation devoutly to be wished: for then the Messiah would come, every grape would yield "thirty full measures of wine,"[110] and every woman would "bear a child on a daily basis."[111] In the meanwhile, however, prior to the dawning of this happy age, there was an additional reason, perhaps, why the rabbis of Mesopotamia could revel in the gathering pace of their winning of Jewish hearts and minds. At the beginning of time, so it was recorded in the Talmud, God had spoken to all the nations of the world, offering them each in turn the Torah; "but all had repudiated it and refused to receive it."[112] Only the ancestors of the Jews had been willing to accept the precious gift; and by doing so, they had preserved humanity from annihilation, for had the Torah only been rejected, the entire purpose of Creation would have failed. The rabbis, then, by awakening their countrymen to a profounder understanding of what was required of them by the law of God, were also working to keep the world itself upon an even keel. The more Jewish that the Jews became, in short, the better for everyone.

But what if the opposite happened? What if the Chosen People, seduced by some treacherous and plausible idolatry, should stumble, and fall, and lose their identity altogether? For centuries before the founding of the schools of Sura and Pumpedita, the Jews of Mesopotamia had managed to stand proof against the temptations of all the false gods of Babylon, and demonstrated that it needed no rabbis for them to maintain their distinctiveness. Yet over time, a new and more dangerous temptation had arisen, a teasing and honey-voiced heresy that adorned itself with the beauties of the Tanakh itself, and wore them as a whore would her paint. Across the entire span of Mesopotamia, living in the self-same villages, towns and cities in which the Jews themselves lived, there were people whose beliefs served as the most noxious mockery of everything that the rabbis taught. There was no hidden Torah, these *minim*, or heretics, claimed, beyond that which the rabbis themselves had fabricated; nor was there any need to prepare for the coming of the Messiah, for the Messiah had already come. His name, according to the *minim*, was Jesus; a man who, half a millennium previously, had been nailed by the Romans to a cross, and then risen from the dead. The reality, it went without saying, was far different. The real Jesus, so the rabbis of Mesopotamia could reveal, was in fact "the son of a harlot":[113] a failed student who had been dismissed by his rabbi for assorted sexual misdemeanours, and had then, out of pique, fallen to worshipping a brick. Far from reigning in heaven, as the *minim* laughably claimed, the truth was that he had been consigned to hell, where he would spend the rest of eternity in a plunge-bath of boiling shit.[114] God Himself, in His infinite wisdom, had foreseen the threat that Jesus would pose His Chosen People, and that was precisely why he had given them a hidden as well as written Torah: so that the *minim* would not be able to get their filthy hands on it, "and say that they were the Chosen People."[115]

Yet it remained terrifyingly the case that never, not in all their long history, had the Jewish people faced a more insidious and oppressive danger than that posed them by the worshippers of Jesus. Insidious, because the heresy was sufficiently similar to their own faith to exert a secret and terrible fascination on many of them, including even some rabbis; and oppressive because there was nowhere, it seemed, not in the whole world, that it had failed to reach. Far and wide across Mesopotamia, and Persia, and eastwards even of *Iranshahr*, the contagion had spread; but most alarming of all was its progress in the West. There, as even the Jewish subjects of the *Shahanshah* might be brought to admit, lay what was "the most important kingdom in the world: the kingdom of the Romans."[116] This kingdom it was, for half a millennium and more now, which had exercised the mastery of Jerusalem and the Promised Land; and many had been the sufferings, in all that time, that it had inflicted upon the Jewish people. Now, however, five hundred years after the birth of Jesus, the Jews had a fresh reason to dread the power and the might of Rome. The Caesars, who had once, like the kings of Babylon, raised temples to a whole infinitude of demons, had since set to closing them down—but only to replace them with a cult that was, if anything, even worse. To what had the Roman people chosen to devote themselves, if not to the most menacing false idol of all? *Christos*, they called him—which meant, in Greek, "Messiah."

Yes—in the palace of Caesar, it was now none other than Jesus who was worshipped. The Jews were no longer alone in believing themselves a people chosen of a single god. The Romans too, those lords of a dominion even richer and more intimidating than that of the

121

Persians, had recently come to enshrine as the pulsing heartbeat of their empire a conviction that Jesus did indeed reign in heaven. The roots of this assurance, however, were of a very great antiquity: older than the written Talmud, older even than Jesus himself. That the Romans had been converted to a belief in Christ was true enough; but true as well was the fact that belief in Christ, across much of the world, had taken on a colouring that was more than a little Roman.

One empire, one god: an entire millennium's worth of history had served to make them seem a natural fit.

3

NEW ROME

Shored Against Ruin

The Romans, although hardly a people given to false modesty, were sternly conscious of what their greatness owed to the realm of the supernatural. The sheer scale of their achievements made it hard for them not to be. A hint of the unearthly had always shadowed the parabola of Rome's rise to global rule. Back when the city was founded, seven and a half centuries before the birth of Christ, it had ranked as little more than an encampment of peasants and cattle rustlers, scattered unpromisingly over seven hills in an obscure corner of Italy. A thousand years later, however, as the House of Sasan was making its own first pitch for world empire, Rome's dominion had come to extend from the icy northern ocean to the sands of Africa. How on earth had it happened that a single city sat enthroned as the mistress of the world? The Romans themselves, for much of their history, had never doubted the answer. If the heavens had favoured them, then this could only be because they were the most god-fearing of peoples. "We stand powerful as much by our piety as by our force of arms."[1]

Yet, the Romans, despite enjoying the evident backing of the gods, had never quite been able to escape the faint gnawings of an inferiority

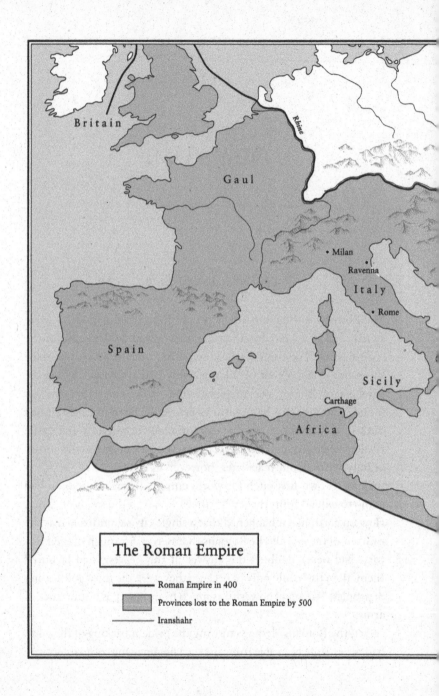

The Roman Empire

——— Roman Empire in 400

▨ Provinces lost to the Roman Empire by 500

——— Iranshahr

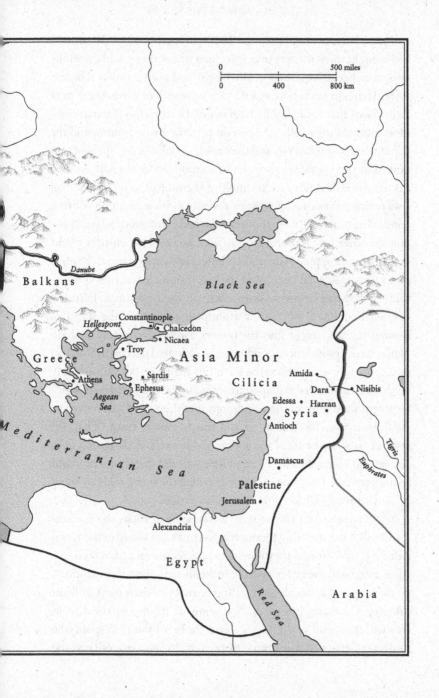

complex. If their conquests in the West—in Spain, Gaul and Britain—had brought them mastery over tribesmen whom they could cheerfully dismiss as barbarians, then in the East it had been a rather different story. There, in lands once ruled by Cyrus and Alexander, there were civilisations that could hardly help but make them feel like parvenus. Most intimidating of all—the inventors of the Doric column and the hypotenuse, of philosophy and the cookery book—were a people who ranked as the veritable cynosures of sophistication: the Greeks. The Romans, who did not care to think of themselves as provincial, had always flinched from confessing too openly to their resulting cultural cringe. They, after all, were the ones who had conquered the Greeks—not the other way round. This was why, however much they might enjoy name-dropping Plato in their letters and conversation, they had never forgotten what they owed to their own ancestral rites and customs, which had helped to bring them all their greatness. Even the Greeks themselves, when they attempted to fathom the secret of Roman success, might find themselves agreeing with this analysis. "Their state," pronounced Posidonius, a celebrated polymath who had died some fifty years before the birth of Christ, "is founded not only upon their manpower, but upon their traditional way of doing things."[2] So potent were some of these traditions that they could barely even be put into words. Too much, far too much, was at stake. What, for instance, was the name of the god or goddess whose charge it was to protect and keep watch over Rome? Reveal it, and the whole city might be undermined. Only one man had ever had the nerve to do so—and he, unsurprisingly, had come at once "to a sticky end."[3]

Yet, even when it came to state secrets such as these, the Romans could still not quite bring themselves to trust exclusively to their own cults. If it were true, as they tended to take for granted, that the most efficacious traditions were also the most ancient, then there could be no denying, yet again, the infuriating primacy of their most brilliant subjects. Centuries before the founding of Rome, so the Greeks claimed, there had stood on the Asian shores of the Hellespont, the straits that separated Asia from Europe, a city by the name of Troy; and this city, within its walls, had sheltered a most potent talisman. It portrayed Pallas Athena, the virgin goddess who, way back in the mists of time, had dropped it from the heavens, and given it her name: the Palladium. So long as the Trojans kept guard over this statue, so the story went, their city would stand impregnable—which was why, when an army of Greeks laid siege to Troy, they had found it impossible to break through the city's walls for ten long and terrible years. Finally, though, their spies had managed to steal the Palladium—whereupon Troy had promptly fallen, and been razed utterly to the ground. And the Palladium? Its fate had been much disputed. Any number of Greek cities had claimed to be its final resting place—as well they might have done, since the Palladium was not merely a priceless status symbol but the ultimate in security guarantees. Yet in truth, as time would more than demonstrate, there was only the one city that could convincingly claim to have been endowed with its awesome power. As the Greek world was increasingly put in the shade by the rising power of Rome, so the conquerors had set to appropriating the past of the conquered as well as their lands.[4] The origins of the Roman people, it had come to be asserted, lay not in Italy at all, but far to the east—in Troy. Romulus, the wolf-raised founder of Rome and its first king, had himself, so it was claimed, been descended from Aeneas, a Trojan prince. With the help of the gods, this Aeneas had escaped the sack of his city and sailed to Italy to make a new beginning. Nor was that all. Somehow—although by what precise means, no one could entirely agree—the Palladium had ended up in Rome. The future would be secure for as long as it remained there, carefully preserved in the Forum—the venerable and monument-crowded public space that had always served as the heart of the city. Link to a past immeasurably vaster and more ancient than the Romans' own, the Palladium was also something very much more: "a pledge from Fate that the empire would never fall."[5]

In AD 248, a couple of decades after the House of Sasan had seized the mastery of *Iranshahr*, the Roman people celebrated their millennium. A thousand years on from the founding by Romulus of the city to which he had given his name, however, and it was not only those who actually lived in Rome who could glory in the name of "Roman." Thirty-six years earlier, each and every free man in the empire had been granted citizenship: an enfranchisement dismissed sourly by some as an underhand attempt to broaden the tax base, but which could also plausibly be viewed in a nobler light. The Romans, despite the brutal and ravening quality of their ascent to greatness, had always sheltered, at the back of their minds, the vague but gratifying conviction that their conquest of the world had been for the world's own good. No one had expressed this more stirringly than a poet named Virgil. Back in the first flush of Rome's global rule, he had written the *Aeneid*, a sweeping epic in which the Romans were ringingly admonished never to forget their god-given duty: "to impose the works and ways of peace, to spare the vanquished and to overthrow the haughty by means of war."[6] A mission statement calculated to delight the Romans themselves, of course; yet also with a resonance that was more than merely Roman. Virgil's epic, as its title suggested, told the story of Aeneas; and while it certainly looked forward to the age when the descendants of the Trojan prince would rule the world, it looked back as well, to a heritage that derived from the East. Nor was it only Roman poets who bought into the seemingly implausible notion that an empire won amid slaughter and exploitation might embody a brotherhood of man: so too did Greek philosophers. Posidonius, a near contemporary of Virgil, had been the first of many to suggest that Rome's dominion might be nothing less than an earthly reflection of the order of the cosmos. This notion, by the time of the Roman millennium, had come almost to be taken for granted. Rome had indeed, for a period of some two centuries, imposed "the works and ways of peace." Never in recorded history had so many people lived for so long without experience of war. Given this, it was hardly surprising that distant provincials had become proud to call themselves "Roman" and hymned the world's capital in gratitude. "Everywhere, you have made citizens of those who rank as the noblest, most accomplished and powerful of peoples . . . All the world has been adorned by you as a pleasure garden."[7]

Except that increasingly, by the time of Rome's millennium, there were weeds in the garden, and brambles. The order that for so long had kept it flourishing had slumped into disrepair. Repeatedly, over the preceding half-century, soldiers' boots had trampled down its blooms. The decade immediately preceding the millennium had been particularly brutal. Rival generals had butchered one another with a wearying degree of savagery. The Roman people, standing in the shadow of the millennium, were perfectly entitled to shiver. They knew full well the ghosts that were being roused. A talent for imposing order was not their only inheritance from the distant past. So too was civil bloodshed. Romulus, the founder of Rome, had murdered his own twin brother. The line of kings that succeeded him had then been ended by a *coup d'état*, and the monarchy abolished. The republic that replaced it, and which had gone on to conquer the world, had itself, some four and a half centuries on from its establishment, collapsed amid murderous violence. The ambitions of rival generals—*imperatores*—had made the whole world to bleed. Many at the time had thought Rome herself doomed; and perhaps she would have been, had not a particularly ruthless "*imperator*" by the name of Caesar planted the banner of autocracy atop the corpse-littered rubble of the republic, and founded a second monarchy. *Augustus*, he called himself—the "Divinely Favoured One." An immodest title—but well merited. Indeed, it was the measure of his success that the word *imperator* itself evolved, over the course of his reign, to mean something much more than "general": what we, in an echo of the original Latin, now term "emperor." Virgil, who began his great epic at least in part due to the promptings of Augustus, hailed his patron as a man fated to "bring back the Age of Gold"[8]—and an age of gold, by and large, was precisely what the world had been given. True, there had been the odd lunatic emperor: Nero, for instance, half a century on from the death of Augustus, was remembered with horror by the Roman people as a man who had killed his mother, married a eunuch, and burned down half of Rome. Yet even the civil war that followed his suicide lasted barely a year; and for 150 years after his death, the empire had enjoyed a golden age. All the more alarming for the Romans, then, as the millennium was ushered in amid the scrabbling after power by would-be Caesars, to imagine that gold might be reverting to iron, and evolution going into reverse: that emperors might once again come to rank as nothing more than rival warlords.

But this was not the only shadow darkening the millennial celebrations. Trouble was brewing beyond the frontiers of the empire as well as within them. In Virgil's great poem, the Roman people had been promised a "dominion without limit";[9] but the truth was, as their strategists were perfectly well aware, that there were limits to everything. Just as there lay beyond the bulwarks of *Iranshahr* a terrifying immensity of nomad-infested grasslands, so likewise, beyond the northern reaches of Rome's empire, there stretched a whole wilderness of bogs and forests: one that seemed positively to seethe with barbarians. The conundrum of how best to ward off these savages was one that had been perplexing the Roman high command for centuries. Too backward to be worth the effort of conquering, they were simultaneously too menacing simply to be left to run amok. A knotty problem—and one that had required an appropriately deft-fingered response. Roman frontier policy took many forms. Watchful defence on the part of the legions was punctuated by bursts of pulverising aggression. Submissive tribes could expect to be rewarded with grants of gold; defiant tribes with slaughter and ruin. On occasion, the Roman military also turned the barbarians' seemingly inexhaustible relish for fighting to its own advantage by employing whole groupings of them—*foederati*—alongside the legions. Rome's aim, of course, was quite simple: to maintain a crushing superiority. In this, for most of the long period of peace ushered in by Augustus, she had been resoundingly successful. Increasingly, though, along the entire northern frontier, there were alarming signs that the balance of power might be shifting. Raids across the Rhine had been going on for decades. Further east, across the Danube, a people called the Goths had recently launched even more brutal incursions. In the year of the millennium itself, they torched whole swaths of the Balkans. All this had come as a most unpleasant surprise to the Roman authorities. It seemed scarcely believable that warlords right on the doorstep of the empire were capable of planning, leading and executing such devastation. Barbarians were simply not meant to be capable of organising themselves on such a scale. Patently, however, what had once been scattered tribal groupings were now starting to cohere into something more. Their leaders, it seemed, freighted with Roman subsidies and plunder, had been deploying this treasure to broaden their own horizons. The richer in gold they were, the more weight they had to throw around. War bands that had once numbered hundreds might now very well number thousands. This, while hardly muscle on an imperial scale, did mean that barbarian kings were increasingly packing a heavy punch. They had become, in short, just that little bit more Roman.

Which did not, of course, make them any the less contemptible. In fact, if anything, the clod-hopping of the Goths deep into the heartlands of the empire only confirmed the Romans in their scorn. The true, the ultimate shock to their complacency did not come from the North, but from the East. Rome was not yet, as she celebrated her millennium, prepared to acknowledge Persia as an equal. Nevertheless, barely two decades after Ardashir had seized the throne, she had been given a foretaste of what was to come. Shapur I, Ardashir's son, had already expelled the Romans from Mesopotamia for good. The imperial high command, in a desperate attempt to preserve the remainder of Rome's provinces in the East, had been obliged to denude the Rhine and the Danube of troops. Then, in 244, with the emperor himself on campaign in the East, there was yet another coup. The new Caesar, a hard-bitten warrior named Philip, was frantic to return from the front to Rome to shore up his position. He duly sued for peace. The truce, when it was agreed, came at monstrous cost—and Shapur made sure that the whole world knew it. It was Philip who would be portrayed on the cliff face just west of Persepolis grovelling before the triumphant *Shahanshah*. It was Philip as well, four years later, in the April of 248, who enjoyed the supreme honour of presiding over Rome's millennium celebrations.

A few months later, in 249, he was dead: killed in battle by a rival Caesar named Decius. Two years on, Decius himself was hacked to pieces by a Goth war band. A decade after that, the dignity of the imperial throne reached its nadir, when Shapur captured the latest emperor, Valerian, and used him from that moment on as his mounting block. For the Persians, a living, breathing Caesar was the ultimate in trophies; and they duly made sure to record Valerian's humiliation alongside Philip's on the cliff face just west of Persepolis. Even death did not bring an end to the humbling of the wretched emperor: his skin, flayed from his body after his death and dyed a lurid red, was lovingly preserved in a temple as one of the supreme treasures of the House of Sasan.[10]

For the Romans, however, even worse was to come. More than the dignity of the imperial title was in meltdown by now. Events were slipping terrifyingly out of control. The more unstable the situation became, the more rival warlords were tempted to snatch after the ultimate prize. The more that happened, the more the eastern provinces were left exposed. The more that the Roman high command then moved troops to stabilise the front with Persia, the more it left the northern frontier open to the barbarians there. The more that the Goths and assorted other savage people then broke through to the rich, soft lands of the south, the more unstable conditions became. How to break this vicious circle? The dominion of the Roman people, it appeared, was locked into a death spiral.

Yet, the empire did not, in the end, succumb. Instead, against all odds, and through a supreme and grinding effort of will, a new generation of emperors hauled it back from the brink. Grim, implacable and pitiless men, they forced upon their subjects a revolution no less far-reaching than the one presided over by Augustus. That "taxes are the sinews of the state"[11] had long been a Roman maxim. Recently, though, amid the agonies of the age, those same sinews had atrophied. Warfare and anarchy had made it increasingly difficult to raise revenue. The authorities, in their desperation, had debased the coinage—but that had merely led inflation to gallop out of control.

Rome had faced financial as well as military ruin. The surgery, however, when it finally came, was to prove brutally effective. To the iron-fisted warlords who now stood at the head of the empire, it appeared self-evident that only a massively enlarged military apparatus could hope to maintain the integrity of the frontiers—and that only a massively enlarged fiscal apparatus could hope to pay for it. Accordingly, over the course of a few decades, the number of soldiers and bureaucrats was multiplied by an astounding factor. The state that emerged from these reforms was to prove the most formidably governed that the Mediterranean had ever seen. Nowhere before had there existed a bureaucracy quite so complex and domineering; and nowhere before had there existed a military funded on quite so massive a scale. The light-touch autocracy established by Augustus had been transformed into something infinitely more heavy-handed: centralised, intrusive and absolute. It was a form of government that still retained the name of Roman; and yet there was a sense as well in which it marked a revolutionary change. So much so, in fact, that the new regime had gone so far as to found a second Rome.

Byzantium, this new capital had originally been called. It stood on the western shore of the Bosphorus, a narrow strait that served—like the Hellespont some one hundred miles to the south-west—to separate Europe from Asia. Greek settlers had founded the city many centuries earlier—but despite the fact that it occupied a magnificently defensible site on the tip of a promontory, surrounded on one side by sea, and on the other by an estuary named the Golden Horn, its growth had always been limited by a seemingly fatal lack of drinking water. Such a drawback, however, was hardly the kind to put off a Roman autocrat; and sure enough, in AD 324, there had arrived in Byzantium a Caesar fully determined to found on its site "another Rome."[12] The name of this emperor was Constantine—a man who stood supreme as the very embodiment of the new imperial order. Born in the Balkans, proclaimed emperor in Britain, he had spent his life criss-crossing the empire, patching it back together in the teeth of a host of rivals, all of whom he had systematically hunted down and eliminated. Although he had won the decisive victory of his reign just outside the walls of Rome, Constantine had no particular ties of loyalty to the ancient capital. What he did have, however, was an unblinking appreciation of the empire's defensive needs: of just how imperative it was to coordinate the eastern and northern fronts. Byzantium, midway between the Euphrates and the Rhine, could not have been more ideally suited to his purposes. A whole new foundation was accordingly planted on its site. A massive grid of monuments, squares and streets began to spread westwards along the course of the promontory, obliterating entire reaches of the original city as it went. Even its name was swallowed up. Although the people who lived on the site would continue to call themselves Byzantines, Byzantium itself had ceased to exist. On 11 May 330, amid a triumphant blaze of immodesty, its founder formally inaugurated it as the "City of Constantine": Constantinople.

Initially, of course, the inhabitants of the original Rome could hardly help but find the pretensions of this arriviste settlement faintly risible. Everyone knew that a city without an ancient pedigree barely ranked as a city at all. Rapidly though the population of Constantinople was soon growing, far more rapidly even than its founder had anticipated, so that in only a few decades it was bursting the landward walls he had built for the city, yet there still lurked, among those who lived there, a queasy consciousness of their own status as upstarts. Numerous efforts were made to counter this. Constantine himself—determined to purloin for his foundation the heritage that it so glaringly lacked—had stripped the Greek world bare of all its greatest treasures. The public spaces of Constantinople, adorned with famous trophies and statuary, "brazen statues of the most exquisite workmanship,"[13] had come to rank as the world's most stupefying museum. The city had even taken on the ultimate challenge: going toe to toe with Rome herself. Topographers, with a show of considerable creativity, had succeeded in establishing that Constantinople, just like her venerable predecessor, boasted seven hills. Architects had designed for her all the appurtenances of a cutting-edge imperial capital: palaces, forums, baths. Engineers had provided her with the aqueducts and harbours that any city with an ambition to equal Rome would require, if its inhabitants were to be kept watered and fed. Most strikingly of all, perhaps, Constantinople had been endowed with an ornament hitherto unique to Rome: an assembly of the great and good by the name of the Senate. This was the body, back in the distant past, long before the time of Augustus and the forging of his autocracy, that had guided Rome to the mastery of the world. It constituted a living link with the most primordial days of the empire. Now, the establishment of a Senate in Constantinople, and a Senate House, gave to the city a touch, however faint, of the long-vanished republic. It helped to put flesh on the bones of its proud claim to be the Second Rome.

And as time passed, and the city continued to increase in scale and self-confidence, so she came to appropriate for herself an even more sensational ancestry. Two hundred years on from the founding of Constantinople, and it had become widely believed that Constantine's original plan had been to establish his new capital on the site, not of Byzantium at all, but of Troy.[14] This, of course, would have been to identify it with origins even more ancient than Rome herself; nor, despite the fact that the plan had self-evidently failed to come to fruition, did this prevent Constantinople herself from laying claim to the hoary mystique of the Trojan name. There stood, for instance, in the middle of a circular forum built by Constantine, a porphyry column; and on this column there stood an image of the city's founder, crowned as though by the sun, with seven glittering rays. Constantine himself was said to have brought the stone for the column from Troy.[15] Yet the most valuable relic of all to have been redeemed from the mists of the Trojan past, and the one that boded best for the future of the city, was not even on public display. Buried deep beneath the base of the column, so it was believed, lay an antique wooden statue: the Palladium itself. The story went that Constantine "had secretly taken it away from Rome, and placed it in his forum":[16] an ultimate trumping of the ancient capital's snobbery.

In truth, though, two centuries on from the re-founding of their city, the Byzantines could scarcely care less for what the people of Rome might think of them. Their conviction that the Palladium lay buried beneath Constantine's column reflected something far more profound than merely a relish for one-upmanship. Much had changed. The same decades that had brought such suffering to *Iranshahr* at the hands of the Hephthalites had witnessed, in the western half of Rome's empire, an even more calamitous intrusion of barbarians. Rome herself, the city which for so long had stood buttressed by the favour of the heavens, had been trampled underfoot. The whole of Italy had been subjected to the rule of a Gothic king. Other provinces, too—from Africa to Gaul—had slipped from imperial control, as the one-time *foederati*, roaming seemingly at will across the shattered landscape of the Roman west, had seized control of its commanding heights. Only the eastern half of the empire—the half ruled from Constantinople—had stood proof against this headlong slide towards disintegration. With Rome herself reduced to the humiliating status of a provincial city ruled by a barbarian warlord, there remained just the one capital left standing. The right of Constantinople to the title of the mistress of the Roman world was now beyond all dispute. Why, then, that being so, should anyone seriously have doubted that the Palladium had indeed been brought there from Rome?

True, there were many in the eastern half of the empire who dreaded that their own doom was brewing, too. It seemed to pessimists that their dominion had become something terminally "shrunken, barbarised, and ruined."[17] Yet the truth was that the Roman state, even as these cries of despair went up, was very far from finished. The labour of surgery performed on the empire by Constantine, for all that it had ultimately proved inadequate to the preservation of its authority in the West, still gave to the emperors of the East a stately and a domineering tread. Certainly, in Ctesiphon, at the court of their pre-eminent rivals, no one ever thought to deny the continuing might of the Caesars. For all the success that Kavad had enjoyed in pillaging the empire's eastern frontier, and in extorting renewed payments of danger money, the Romans too had enjoyed some triumphs of their own. In 504, for instance, one of their armies had gained a measure of revenge for the rape of Amida by sweeping deep into Mesopotamia, looting and slaving as it went, while in its wake a specially appointed death squad left not a single house standing. Even more tellingly, the Romans had capitalised upon the period of hostilities with Persia to remedy their previous lack of a forward command post. In 505, the Emperor Anastasius purchased a small estate named Dara, located just ten miles from the great Persian border stronghold of Nisibis. Barely a year later, by the time that a temporary truce was signed, a massive complex of walls and watch-towers had come to loom over the fields, where previously nothing but a village had stood. It was, as the howls of protest from Ctesiphon bore witness, an initiative fit to appal Persian strategists. The entire balance of power in the region had been transformed. The Roman frontier was now decisively re-militarised. Even Kavad, towards the end of his reign, had been brought to accept the implications. In 522, the old war-horse dispatched an embassy from Nisibis with a letter for the emperor. In it, he floated a startling proposition: "that you make my son Khusrow, who is the heir to my throne, your adopted son."[18] In part, the offer was a blatant attempt to forestall any meddling by Constantinople in the succession crisis that was even then brewing in *Iranshahr*; but it also signalled just how brightly Roman prestige had come to blaze again. Sure enough, a few months later, another Persian embassy made its way to Constantinople with instructions to negotiate an enduring peace. No *Shahanshah*, it went without saying, would ever have pressed for détente with an enemy that he regarded as contemptible. The Palladium, it seemed, was working its magic still.

And certainly, even to a diplomat familiar with the scale and splendour of Ctesiphon, the capital of the rival superpower would have appeared touched by an almost supernatural quality of majesty. To approach Constantinople was to be dazzled by the most awesome cityscape in the world. So rapidly had it grown that the proud and ancient city of Chalcedon, on the Asian side of the Bosphorus, now

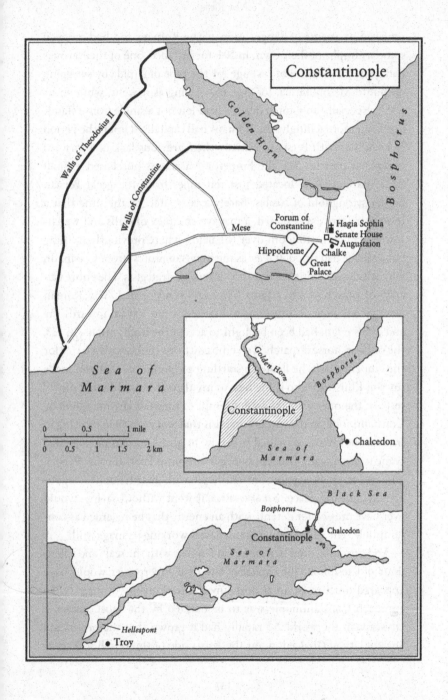

served merely as its gateway. The Persian ambassadors—boarding a ship in Chalcedon's harbour and negotiating the waters that surrounded Constantinople "like a garland"[19]—would have found marks of urban sprawl wherever they looked: for the conurbation, spreading in a ribbon along the European coastline, had long since broken through even the outermost ring of walls. Inevitably, though, it was to what lay within those hulking fortifications that the visitor's gaze was drawn: for it was there that human effort and ingenuity had most astoundingly enhanced the already stunning setting. Along the waterfront, once a bleak wilderness of mud and reeds, everything now proclaimed the voracious appetites of the capital: a three-and-a-half-mile stretch of harbours and warehouses, granaries and wharfs. Beyond them, packed so tightly together that visitors would often find themselves "cramped and walking in danger because of the great number of men and animals,"[20] there spread the homes of the city's almost half a million inhabitants: a concentration of people vaster even than Ctesiphon. Nevertheless, as the Persian ambassadors neared their destination, the skyline of Constantinople would have conveyed to them an impression, not of seething clamour, but rather of order, monumentality and space. Along the spine of the promontory, the smog bred of countless furnaces and hearths, and which hung in a pall over the lower reaches of the great conurbation, diminished upon the sea breezes, to reveal the hills that originally, before the arrival of Constantine upon them, had constituted the upper reaches of Byzantium, and now provided the New Rome, and the Roman Empire itself, with its mighty heart.

The ambassadors, once they had disembarked and made their way up from the Golden Horn, would have approached these hills along a broad, sumptuously porticoed road: the *Mese*—"Middle Street." Ahead, framed by colossal arches and gateways, stretched a succession of marmoreal open spaces. It was in the first of these, at the foot of a column pointedly adorned with depictions of Roman military triumphs, that the ambassadors would have been officially welcomed to the city; it was in the second, the circular forum built by Constantine, that the Palladium supposedly lay buried. It was not this forum, however, but a third, the square known as the Augustaion, that most magnificently embodied the capital's pretensions. On its eastern flank stood the Senate House;* to the south, adorning a massive bath-house, was the city's finest collection of antique statuary; to the west, marking the termination of the *Mese*, a domed and double-arched mass of brick and marble named the Golden Milestone. This was the monument from which imperial cartographers measured the distance to every known location: for just as the sun, and the moon, and the stars revolved around the earth, so too, it pleased the Romans to imagine, did all kingdoms revolve around Constantinople. She stood, in their confident opinion, upon the axis of the world. She was, quite simply, the "Queen of Cities."

Which explained why, in the final reckoning, the peace mission of the Persian ambassadors was doomed to fail. Just as the House of Sasan, upon the faintest scent of Roman weakness, was bound to return to the attack, so too did the Caesars, despite all the many calamities that had afflicted their empire, shrink from any public acknowledgement that their rule might be less than universal. Victory, eternal victory, was still what it had been to Virgil: their destiny and their due. Even at moments of terrible peril, when there would inevitably seem something shrill about this assertion, the sublime conviction with which it was made remained undiminished. To rule as the heir of Augustus and Constantine was to believe oneself entrusted by the heavens with the very reins of earthly power. The brute fact that there were kingdoms that did not acknowledge the supremacy of the Roman people could not, of course, be ignored; but it was possible, enthroned in a capital such as Constantinople, to ignore the implications. The city remained, in the opinion of the Caesars, the authentic cockpit of global affairs.

---

* Constantinople actually had two Senate Houses: the original stood on the edge of Constantine's forum, but the one in the Augustaion had largely superseded it by the sixth century.

This was a presumption only boosted by their own domestic circumstances. Set in the south-eastern corner of the Augustaion, between the Senate House and the marble crowd of ancient statues, there towered two bronze gates, or the "Chalke," as they were known; and beyond them, stupefyingly immense, there stretched a labyrinthine complex so incomparable that it ranked, in the opinion of those privileged enough to penetrate it, as "another heaven."[21] Originally, the palace of the Caesars had been built in a severe and militarised manner, appropriate to its founder's seriousness of purpose: for it had been modelled on the square plan of an army camp. Traces of the soldier's sensibility that Constantine had brought to his refashioning of Rome's empire were still to be seen in the corridors of power: in the sword belts worn by even quite junior officials; in the swagger sticks wielded by senior ministers; in the golds, purples and flaming reds that had always signified superior rank in the Roman army. Just because the emperor's bureaucrats dressed up like soldiers, however, did not mean that they were soldiers. The legion into which they were enrolled when they joined the civil service did not actually exist. Similarly, the sharp angles of Constantine's original palace had long since been swallowed up by extensions, so immense and sprawling in scale that for every new one being built, another would lie decaying and forgotten. Just as the language and rituals employed by the imperial bureaucracy were designed to be as incomprehensible to outsiders as possible, so might it take a lifetime to feel fully at home inside the great warren of the palace. There were gardens and judicial tribunals, pavilions and reception halls, banqueting chambers, secretariats, and even an indoor riding school. Sun-dappled terraces raised on brick stilts teetered over the breaking waves far below, while deep underground there stretched sepulchral store-rooms, kitchens and massive cisterns. The sheer vastness of it all made it seem a world unto itself. A man ensconced as the lord of such a palace might well feel that there was very little he could not do.

Perhaps it was no surprise, then, that supreme power, in the empire of the Romans, had come to wear a civilian face. The age of

Constantine, when an emperor was expected to live and die by the sword, was long past. The surest measure of what had been achieved back in that wrenching period of upheaval was precisely that it was now bureaucrats, and not soldiers, who ran the show. The warrior kings of *Iranshahr* found no equivalent in Constantinople. Rare now was the Caesar who rode out to war. An emperor best kept his grip upon the Roman state, not at the head of an army, but in a council chamber. In fact, it was perfectly possible for an emperor to have begun his career as a civil servant himself. Anastasius, whose niggardly bean-counting had so antagonised Kavad, had originally been a senior functionary in the imperial secretariat. Admirers who sought to praise him in heroic terms found themselves reduced to hailing his baldness: "his forehead gleams like silver."[22] By the time of his death in 518, he had managed to accumulate an astounding reserve of some 320,000 pounds of gold: an achievement worth any number of victories on the battlefield.

Admittedly, the man who succeeded Anastasius as emperor had been the exception who proved the rule. Justin was a peasant who had trudged from the wilds of the Balkans to join the imperial guard in Constantinople, and his subsequent rise through the ranks was a story that provoked sneers and eulogies in equal measure. While the smooth bureaucrats of the secretariat could scarce forbear to cringe at their master's lack of education, there were others who saw in his ascent to the purple a striking demonstration that anyone, even a boor from the frontier, could reach the summit of the Roman world. Nor was Justin himself so naïve as to imagine that a man of his background, in an environment where the pen was so much mightier than the sword, could conceivably rule without a literate colleague. Fortunately for him, the perfect candidate was ready at hand—one who was literate with a vengeance. Justinian, the emperor's nephew and adopted son, was a man so perfectionist, so determined to lay his hands upon every possible lever of power, that the same officials who sneered at Justin for his backwardness found themselves appalled by the resolve of his young colleague to "write almost everything himself."[23] Justinian, a man of such restless energy that he famously never slept, would have had it no other way. His tirelessness was rivalled only by the soaring scale of his ambition. More than anyone before him, Justinian had recognised in the immense apparatus of state control that had its hub in the imperial palace a truly awesome opportunity. It was his aim, once he had only secured the succession to his uncle, not merely "to watch over the empire of the Romans, but, so far as was possible, to remake it."[24] Bureaucracy, in Justinian's vision, was to become a mechanism for transforming the world.

Small wonder, then, that the proposal brought by the Persian ambassadors, that Justin should adopt Khusrow as his son, should have been given short shrift. Blame for the breakdown in negotiations was pinned adroitly on a functionary; but it was clear enough whose conceit this best served. Justinian, his eyes already set firmly on the main prize, had not the slightest interest in permitting anyone, let alone a barbarian such as Khusrow, to rank as his brother. It was not merely his right, so he believed, but his duty as Justin's heir to stand inflexibly on his dignity. Sure enough, in 527, when he duly ascended to the throne upon his uncle's death, he did not hesitate to promote himself as a man who was set infinitely apart from the common run— heaven-appointed for the achievement of prodigious things. As such, so it seemed to him, he was owed the respect and awe that was owed to the Roman state itself. Even the Senate, that living embodiment of the venerable traditions of the republic, was obliged to display its subordination in as pointed and flamboyant a way as possible. Previously, whenever a senator had entered the imperial presence, he had simply crooked his right knee. Now, under Justinian's more exacting code of etiquette, he was expected to fall flat on his face, stretch out his hands and feet as far as he could, and humbly kiss the emperor's slipper.[25] Under such a regime, the Romans' proud habit of referring to themselves as "citizens"—a tradition that reached back to the primordial days of the republic—fell increasingly into abeyance. Their new title, if a good deal less glorious, was certainly more accurate. When Justinian spoke to his people, he addressed them, quite simply, as "subjects."

Understandably, among the more independent-minded members of the Roman elite, there was a good deal of grumbling about this. Abuse, whispered behind the emperor's purple-robed back, could reach feverish heights. "It seemed as if nature had removed every tendency to evil from the rest of mankind and deposited it in the soul of this man": such was the considered verdict of one critic.[26] Justinian, despite the paranoia to which he was gnawingly prone, was nevertheless haughtily contemptuous of such mutterings. Convinced of both the scale of the challenges he faced and his unique aptitude for tackling them, he had no intention of moderating his style a jot. More than any emperor since Constantine, he believed himself charged with a mission to redeem the world. To his critics, of course, this was nothing but the rankest hypocrisy; and yet even they, reluctant to believe that Justinian might actually be sincere, were forced to acknowledge his rare genius as an actor: "For he had a marvellous ability to conceal his real opinion, and was even able to shed tears, not from joy or sorrow, but contriving them for the occasion according to the moment."[27] Others were less harsh in their judgement of Justinian. There were many, throughout the reaches of the imperial bureaucracy, who found themselves invigorated rather than threatened by their emperor's ambition, and identified profoundly with his goals. When they looked about them at the state of things, they saw, just as their master did, a broken and spavined order in desperate need of mending. When they heard Justinian declare, with a simple solemnity, "Our subjects are our constant care,"[28] they did not doubt him. When they listened to reports of how he would sit up late, scribbling, forever scribbling, to the burning of his midnight oil, they could admire him for sharing in their own deepest fantasy: that the world might indeed be refashioned upon the scratching of a pen.

"In the whirlpool and turmoil that we now experience, our affairs need the governing wisdom that comes from laws."[29] Any *mowbed* or rabbi would have concurred. That the written word might serve to alter the way in which entire peoples saw the world was fast becoming the guiding principle of the age. Justinian was certainly not alone in

The angel Gabriel speaks to Muhammad. According to Muslim tradition, the sum of the revelations granted to the Prophet were assembled after his death to form a single "recitation" – a "*qur'an.*" Where, when and how the Qur'an was actually compiled are all hotly contested questions in contemporary academic circles. (Bildarchiv Steffens/Bridgeman Art Library)

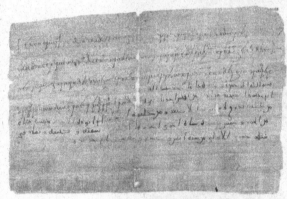

A receipt for 65 sheep, issued in AD 642 by an Arab war band to officials in a city on the Nile. It is written in Arabic as well as Greek, and contains a mention of "the year Twenty-Two": the oldest surviving mention of what would end up enshrined as the Muslim calendar.

Peroz hunting. Martial prowess, flamboyant clothing and an aptitude for slaughtering animals: the ideal attributes of a Persian King of Kings. (akg-images/De Agostini Picture Library)

The site of the "Fire of the Stallion," in the mountains of northern Iran. The temple that enclosed it was probably built in the reign of Peroz – although it took only a couple of generations for Zoroastrians to locate its origins back in the mists of time. (Paul Rudkin)

The throne room of the royal palace at Ctesiphon: all that remains of what was once the vast capital of *Iranshahr*. (The Print Collector/HIP/Topfoto.co.uk)

Iranshahr triumphant. One Caesar – Philip – bends the knee before a mounted Shapur I, while a second – Valerian – is taken captive by the wrist. Victory over Rome was always regarded by the Sasanians themselves as the supreme measure of their imperial prowess. (Tom Holland)

The Ark of the Law, from a sixth-century synagogue in the Roman province of Palestine. The most celebrated of the schools devoted to the study of the Jewish Law were located, not in the Promised Land itself, but in Mesopotamia.
(Zev Radovan/Bridgeman Art Library)

A view from beyond the Golden Horn of what, in ancient times, was the Greek city of Byzantium. It was here, in AD 324, that the emperor Constantine arrived to found a new capital. With becoming modesty, he christened it "The City of Constantine": Constantinople. The waters around the city, it was said, adorned it "like a garland."
(Tom Holland)

A column raised by Constantine to mark the inauguration of his city. Originally, it was surmounted by a statue of the Emperor, crowned as though by the sun, with seven glittering rays. Beneath its base was believed to lie the "Palladium": a talisman that had supposedly been brought, via Rome, from the sack of Troy. (Tom Holland)

A tiny surviving fragment of what for centuries was the hub of Roman power: the palace of the Caesars in Constantinople. Those privileged to enter the vast complex of halls, secretariats and gardens hailed it as "another heaven." (Tom Holland)

The emperor Justinian. "He was entrusted by God with this commission: to watch over the whole Roman Empire and, so far as was possible, to remake it." (Byzantine School [sixth century], San Vitale, Ravenna/ Giraudon/Bridgeman Art Library)

Emperor and crowds at the Hippodrome. The passions roused by chariot-racing were violent in the extreme – and in January 532, they exploded into an orgy of looting and savagery that briefly threatened Justinian's entire regime. (Tom Holland)

Christ the Good Shepherd, painted in a catacomb in Rome in the late second or early third century AD. An image drawn from a Gospel is combined with the smooth cheeks and skimpy tunic of a Greek god. (De Agostini Picture Library/ G. Cargagna/Bridgeman Art Library)

Debates about the relationship between God the Father and God the Son convulsed the Christian world for centuries. This mosaic, illustrating the baptism of Jesus, was commissioned by a follower of Arius, who taught that the Father had preceded the Son. The doctrine was condemned as heretical at the great Church Council of Nicaea, summoned by Constantine in 325. (Giraudon/ Bridgeman Art Library)

In the Near East, Jews and Christians tended to be far more familiar with one another's beliefs than their respective leaders cared to acknowledge. This bowl was inscribed by someone who had looked to play safe by invoking both the God of the Jews – "I-Am-That-I-Am" – and the Christian Trinity.

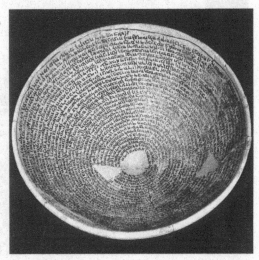

The conversion of Constantine to Christianity saw the old religious order of the empire spectacularly superseded. Here, in a cistern below Constantinople, the positioning of a toppled pagan sculpture symbolises an entire world turned upside down. (Tom Holland)

The Empress Theodora: reformed whore and Monophysite saint. (The Art Archive/ Collection Dagli Orti)

Like a phoenix from the ashes, Justinian's great cathedral of Hagia Sophia rose from the smouldering ruins left by three days of terrible rioting in Constantinople. So vast was its dome that it seemed to stupefied contemporaries "like the very firmament that rests upon the air." (Tom Holland)

The twin founders of Constantinople: Constantine stands on the left-hand side of the Virgin, and Justinian – holding the Hagia Sophia – on the right. (Tom Holland)

Caves in the Judaean desert: the haunt of Christian hermits. (Tom Holland)

A mosaic at Saint Catherine's monastery, at the foot of a mountain that was identified in the fourth century as Sinai, where Moses had received the Ten Commandments. In this image, the standing figure on the left is Moses himself: the great prophet of the Jews, recast as a Christian prophet. (Tom Holland)

Christian Jerusalem. From a mosaic in the floor of a church in Madaba, on the eastern side of the Dead Sea. (Tom Holland)

Mount Gerizim. The holiest place in the world, according to the Samaritans. (www.bibleplaces.com)

Mamre, as shown on the Madaba map. The church built by Constantine is shown to the left of the oak of Abraham. (Tom Holland)

believing that authority could most profitably be derived from books. Nevertheless, as befitted the man he was, both a Roman and a Caesar, he was able to draw upon resources that far outscaled those available to the scholars of *Iranshahr*. The imperial palace's archives were filled to bursting with documents. Whether contained in the finest ivory and written in silver ink, or simply scrawled on rough parchment and wood, they bore witness to an entire millennium of written laws. The Roman people, right from the earliest days of the republic, had always been intensely proud of their legal system. What were those of other peoples, they demanded, if not "ridiculous" in comparison?[30] It needed no stories of fantastical law-givers, such as the Greeks were forever spouting, to explain how the "*Ius*," the "Law" of Rome, had come into being, since it was so patently the product of long centuries of human effort. Whether couched as decrees of the Senate, as the rulings of private jurists, or as entire codes assembled by previous emperors, it could afford the Roman people a sense of living communion with their incomparable past. Its existence, just like that of the empire itself, bore witness to the majestic workings of time.

Yet the *Ius*, for all that, represented a problem as well as a solution. If it was true, as Justinian ringingly declared, that "what medicine is to disease, so laws are to public affairs,"[31] then there was much that first needed to be done before the emperor's prescription could be applied to the sickening world. The sheer scale and antiquity of the Roman people's achievements in the field of law had resulted in a legacy that was intimidatingly chequered. Justinian, however, was hardly the man to duck such a challenge. His first step, only a few months into his reign, was the appointment of a commission to harmonise the various unwieldy collections of laws issued by previous emperors; then, a year and a half later, he charged a second commission with the even more daunting task of collating the entire stupendous body of private writings on Roman law. Complete constitutions had to be revised; almost two thousand individual books called in and minutely sifted; tens of thousands of excerpts made. The resulting codification, achieved in record time, was so staggering an achievement that it appeared to many something more than human. Justinian himself presented it proudly as a process of restoration; but there was something about it as well of a revolution. "We have by means of old laws not only brought matters into a better condition, but we have also promulgated new laws."[32] The emperor saw no need to conceal the fact. He was himself, so he declared, *nomos empsychos*—the "living law." Here, in this self-promotion, was the ultimate refinement of what whole generations of emperors had been working to achieve.[33] Henceforward, the rules by which the Roman people lived and were bound were to have just the single fountainhead: the emperor himself, enthroned in his palatial citadel. No wonder, then, that Justinian should have sought, not merely to impose his stamp upon the long centuries of Roman legal achievement, but also to prescribe where and how that achievement should be taught. Private law schools were definitively banned. No teachers were to be licensed, save for those directly sanctioned by the state. Now, more than ever, the whole world was to be administered from the centre: from the palace of Constantinople.

Yet this presumption begged in turn an awkward question. Well-muscled though the machinery of imperial government undoubtedly appeared to be, was it possible, nevertheless, that an excessive faith might have been put in its reach and potency? The mere existence of a law, after all, did not guarantee that it would be obeyed. The world beyond Constantinople was an infinite and a seething place; and even the capital itself, "the all golden city,"[34] was perhaps less glittering, and less amenable to Justinian's purposes, than he cared to admit. Certainly, immured behind the great bronze gates of his palace, he could have little appreciation of what festered beyond the marble-paved thoroughfares of the great metropolis, in the dark and squalid slums where no emperor would ever dream of muddying his dainty slippers. The imperial elite had long taken for granted that the masses were far too stinking and fractious to be permitted near the well-springs of power. More than a century earlier, a massive programme of clearances had swept anything that was not marble and expensive from the vicinity of the palace: "for the imperial residence," it was fastidiously explained, "requires extensive grounds hidden from all the world, so that within its precincts there shall be a place to dwell exclusively for those who have been selected for the due requirements of our majesty and for the government of the state."[35]

Yet, just as the Romans, despite half a millennium of autocracy, still referred to their realm as a *res publica*, or "republic," so likewise, even in the Constantinople of Justinian, was there one ineradicable monument to the vanished age when everyone had ranked as a citizen. Back in Rome, chariot-racing had been as much a political as a sporting experience: for even the mightiest ruler had dreaded the howls and abuse of the crowds in the Circus Maximus, the city's oldest and largest public space. Constantinople, as befitted the New Rome, had come to possess a no less magnificent arena for its chariot races: the Hippodrome. The most venerable monument to have survived Constantine's flattening of the original Byzantium, it had been beautified with antique statues and obelisks, and enlarged so colossally that it had overrun the hill on which it stood. Supported along its entire southern end by massive brick struts, and boasting forty tiers of seating, it had no rival as the city's theatre of dreams. It was certainly a venue for more than sport. The imperial government, on those irregular occasions when it wished to publicise a policy, would do so in the Hippodrome. Whether it was the emperor's ritual trampling of a defeated barbarian king, or the parading of a usurper's head, or even the ceremonial burning of tax registers, spectacle was all. Justinian himself, on his accession to the throne, had made sure to stage his investiture before the crowds of the Hippodrome. Emerging from his palace down a winding staircase and into a spacious, open-air marble box, he had been greeted by the cheers of some sixty thousand of his subjects, the noise of their acclamations an almost physical blast against his face. Nevertheless, if there was indisputably advantage to be gained by an emperor from exposing himself to the crowds in this manner, there was also potential danger. The passions that the Hippodrome was capable of inspiring in the Byzantines were violent—and often literally so. For a long while now, rival teams of charioteers had been supported by rival gangs of racing fans, whose taste for fighting one another in the streets—and for menacing innocent passers-by—had draped a pall of intimidation across the entire city. Here, then, in the emperor's own backyard, right on the doorstep of his government, was precisely the order of crisis that his great pro-gramme of legal reform was intended to resolve.

And Justinian knew it. In the years prior to his accession, he had exploited the gangsterdom associated with the Hippodrome for his own ends. The most brutal racing faction of all, whose members deliberately aped the Hephthalites' aura of menace by shaving the fronts of their scalps and "allowing the hair behind to hang down in a disorderly mess,"[36] had been sponsored by the heir-apparent, and deployed on the streets of the capital as paramilitaries. Once on the throne, however, Justinian had come to regard the continued employment of hooligans with mullets as incompatible with the imperial dignity. Gang warfare in the Hippodrome was henceforward to be suppressed without fear or favour. Yet, even as Justinian himself affected a stern neutrality between the rival factions, other, less scrupulous members of the elite remained eager to sponsor their thuggery. Senators, in particular, while far too cautious to challenge the emperor's reform programme openly, had no compunction about stirring up trouble behind his back. The Hippodrome, despite all Justinian's efforts to dampen it, remained a tinderbox.

Then finally, on 14 January 532, even as the emperor's law com-missioners were scribbling away furiously in the palace next door, it exploded. Three days earlier, two rival gang-members had been tem-porarily spared execution when the gallows had snapped. Now, in the face of Justinian's refusal to confirm their reprieve, the two factions forged an unexpected alliance, combined their forces and sprung their comrades from the city jail. Intoxicated by their own daring, and per-haps encouraged by whispering senators, the gangs then went on a collective rampage. Looters fanned out across the most exclusive quar-ter in the world. Anything that could not be stolen was trashed or burned. The damage was something prodigious. Over the course of the succeeding days, many of the city's most beautiful and venerable monuments were burned to the ground. From the Augustaion to Constantine's forum, the whole of the *Mese* was reduced to smoking rubble. Justinian, holed up in his palace, attempted to stave off total disaster by means of increasingly frantic expedients. First, he dismissed some of his more notoriously venal ministers; next, he tried to bribe the faction leaders; then, he contemplated flight. Finally, screwing his courage to the sticking place, he resolved to dowse the flames of anarchy with blood—gallons of it. Squadrons of crack troops were marched through the smouldering ruins of the city, and stationed at opposite ends of the Hippodrome, where a raging but largely unarmed mob was amusing itself by calling for Justinian to be deposed. The order to attack was given; the troops advanced; the crowd was systematically hacked and trampled underfoot. Less a battle than a calculated atrocity, the massacre left the arena piled high with corpses. The death toll, so it was claimed, approached fifty thousand people.[37] If true, then one-tenth of the city's population had been wiped out in a single day.

Justinian was now secure. The crisis turned out to have buttressed his mastery for good. Less than a couple of years later, in December 533, the commissioners whose work had so nearly been aborted by the riots delivered the second of their great law revisions: what they termed the Digest. No one, of course, thought to oppose it. The decimation of the Byzantines in the Hippodrome had made sure of that. In truth, however, the lesson taught the Roman people by the unleashing in their capital of such carnage was a primordial one. The first to demonstrate it, after all, had been Romulus himself, that fratricidal founder of the original Rome, whose twin brother, jealous and embittered, had presumed to challenge his authority by jumping over the unfinished wall of his infant city: an unforgivable and capital offence. Again and again, throughout the long and bloody course of their history, the Romans had served to prove the truth of the moral. Power without the sanction of violence barely ranked as power at all.

Yet Justinian himself, for all the savagery he had unleashed, did not care to dwell too closely upon the brute reality of what had taken place beyond his palace. Just as Virgil, back in the balmiest days of Roman power, had piously attributed the forging of the empire to the favour of the gods as well as to the swords of the legions, so similarly was it important for Justinian, in the midst of all his labours for the improvement of the world, to demonstrate that he had right as well as might on his side. Fortunately for his purposes, there lay, in the wake of the riots, the perfect stage to hand. The centre of Constantinople had been left gutted. "The city was a series of blackened, blasted hills, like the reaches of a volcano, uninhabitable because of dust, smoke, and the foul stench of building materials reduced to ashes."[38] Among the many treasures destroyed in the inferno had been the Senate House and all the antique statues with which Constantine had long previously adorned the bath-house. Their loss had obliterated precious links with what was, by now, a very distant past. Yet, in truth, Justinian was pleased to see them gone. The Senate House had always loomed too large over the Augustaion for his tastes: its replacement, so he decreed, was to be built on a much smaller scale. Similarly, great works of art although the statues might have been, they had represented—to Justinian's mind—not gods, but demons. Much that had once been taken for granted by the Roman people was now dismissed by them as dangerous superstition. The entire notion of the supernatural order of things celebrated by Virgil had long since been junked as a diabolical fantasy. Even the Palladium, secure and unharmed though it still lay beneath Constantine's column, had been largely forgotten—with those who did preserve a memory of the statue likelier to regard it as an object of necromancy than a talisman.

The monuments that Justinian aimed to found upon the rubble of the old would be raised to the glory, not of the traditional gods of the Roman people, but of something very different: a single, omnipotent god. A god from whom everything to which Justinian laid claim, whether the governance of the world or "the power to make laws,"[39] directly flowed. A god who reigned eternal in the heavens—and yet who had been born a man back in the reign of Augustus, and put to death upon a Roman cross.

Justinian, rebuilding Constantinople, would stamp the city definitively, once and for all, as a Christian capital.

Joined at the Hip

Huge buildings spelled greatness. The Caesars had always appreciated this. Like the issuing of laws, the humbling of barbarians and the wearing of purple, the construction of towering monuments was very much part of what the Roman people expected of an emperor. Nor was Justinian minded to let them down. Even before the destruction of large swaths of Constantinople provided him with the perfect opportunity to rebuild the city to his own exalted tastes, he had displayed his relish for the empire's grand tradition of architectural swagger. The initial focus of his energies, however, had lain not in the capital but far away, on the eastern frontier.

Here, in 530, the Persians had responded to the latest breakdown of peace talks in time-honoured fashion—by making a land grab. The object of their campaign had been that particular bugbear of their high command, Dara. Directly in front of the walls of the fortress, a Roman army, led by a brilliant young general named Belisarius, had met the Persians and put them to flight. "Such an event was one which had not happened for a very long while."[40] Nevertheless, it had been a close-run thing: Dara's fortifications, jerry-built at immense speed, would not have withstood a concentrated siege. "And because the emperor Justinian perceived that the Persians, so far as it lay in their power, would never permit this outpost of the Romans, which was such a menace to them, to continue standing there, but were bound to persist in attacking it with all their might,"[41] he had ordered a massive rebuilding programme.[42] Dara was made to bristle. It was designed to be—and to appear—impregnable. Any passing barbarians were to look on it and despair. The emperor, aiming to ram the point home, even graced Dara with a new name: "Justiniana New Town." Here, in the hulking silhouette of its ramparts, was the manifestation of a ruler with the world in his hands.

Or so he liked to think. In fact, the message conveyed by the militarisation of the frontier was altogether more ambiguous than Justinian might have wished. The rival pretensions of Dara and Nisibis, frowning at each other across the Mesopotamian flat-lands, could easily seem to make a mockery of both. "The nations are like a drop from the bucket, and are accounted as the dust on the scales."[43] So it was written in the Tanakh. The Jews, lacking any empire of their own, treasured a distinctive perspective on international affairs. It reassured them that the great kingdoms of the world, despite all their clamour and posturing, were accounted by God "as less than nothing and emptiness."[44] They knew that the true division of the world was not the one proclaimed by the battlements of Dara, between Roman and barbarian, but something quite else: between those who lived in the manner ordained by the Almighty and those who did not.

Given this, who was to say that the scattering of the Jews far beyond the limits of their ancestral homeland was not all part of the heavenly plan? "By your descendants," God had told Abraham, "shall all the nations of the earth bless themselves."[45] This assurance had long prompted many Jews to ponder the immense distances that separated them from the Promised Land, and to arrive at a daring conclusion. As one rabbi, back in the time of Constantine, had put it with forthright conviction, "The Holy One, blessed be He, exiled us among the nations in order that converts might swell our ranks."[46] This, it might have been thought, was rather to contradict the emphasis that the Almighty had placed on the significance of Abraham's bloodline; but it was also to assert that "Jewishness," in the final reckoning, was determined less by blood than by obedience to the demands of the Torah. Accept that, and the Jews did certainly appear well placed to reshape the world. Mesopotamia was certainly far from being their only home away from home. Few were the points of the compass where they were not to be found. They had become, in a sense, more truly universal than any empire. Rather like the Greeks, they ranked not merely as a people but as the agents of a culture, of an entire way of understanding, interpreting and refashioning the world. The awesome power of their ferociously demanding God, the staggering antiquity of their laws, and the glamour of what seemed to many less a faith than a private members' club: all had combined to make the Jews objects of rare fascination to those among whom they lived. Unsurprisingly, then, there was a venerable tradition of their admirers becoming "proselytes"—"which is to say, people who have been made into Jews."[47] In Rome, the imperial authorities had been fretting about such conversions since the time of the republic. A whole succession of emperors had sought to regulate what they saw as a palpable and growing menace. A century and a half before Constantine, the circumcision of converts had been declared equivalent to castration: a crime that would see the perpetrator exiled to a desert island. Faint consolation to the Jews themselves though it might have been, there was testimony here to their faith's profound appeal. The superstitions of conquered people were rarely honoured by the Roman elite with such hostility. The resentment and indignation of the rulers of the world were nothing if not a form of tribute.

But how, precisely, was a Jew to be defined? It was to answer this question, of course, that the rabbis of Mesopotamia, back in the time of Ardashir, had founded the famous *yeshivas* of Sura and Pumpedita, and embarked upon the great project of research that would culminate in their transcription of the Talmud. Mesopotamia, however, was not the world. No matter what the rabbis themselves might care to think, most Jews were largely oblivious to their existence. For the first few centuries after the founding of the *yeshivas*, the scholars who taught in them were more interested in ensuring that they were listened to in their own backyard than in establishing a global voice. Across the eastern reaches of *Iranshahr* itself, in much of the Roman world, and in the deserts and mountains that lay beyond the reach of both empires, rabbis were signally lacking. Authority lay instead with the leaders of what had come to be known as "synagogues." These were communal meeting places where the Torah was studied and debated, and where Jewishness—*Ioudaismos*, in Greek—was rarely a given. Different communities, and different individuals, tended to define it much as they pleased. Often, it might seem as though the definition of a Jew was simply someone who described himself as such. Consequently, the boundary that demarcated Jews from non-Jews—"Gentiles," as they were called—was never entirely stable. One Jew might take the high road that led to Persepolis and there, on the lintels of that Zoroastrian holy place, carve a summons to the people of *Iranshahr* to join his faith;[48] another, panic-stricken at the thought of falling for the insidious attractions of foreign women, and thereby jeopardising the purity of Abraham's bloodline, might try and avoid so much as stealing a glance at a Gentile. Even the rabbis, despite their burning ambition to distinguish themselves and their people as rigidly as possible from the world beyond, found it impossible to agree on who precisely qualified as a Jew. Some argued that proselytes were fully Jewish. Others maintained that they were "as injurious as sores."[49] Neither side found it possible to establish a definitive answer. They had no option, so it seemed to the rabbis, save to agree to disagree.*

Except that there did exist another option. Long before the founding of the great rabbinical schools of Mesopotamia, in an era so distant that even the title of "rabbi" itself had only tentatively begun to be employed, a small group of Jews had made a spectacular announcement: that a notorious troublemaker by the name of Jesus, recently crucified and supposedly risen from the dead, was none other than the "Christ." More than that, indeed—that this same Jesus was also, in some mysterious manner, the Son of God Himself. These Christians—as they soon came to be known—had not initially thought of themselves as any the less Jewish for holding these startling beliefs. Nor

---

* One point on which all rabbis could agree was that the Amalekites, a people personally condemned to destruction by God Himself, could never become proselytes. By the time this ruling was formulated, however, no one had any idea where the Amalekites were to be found, or even if they still existed.

had it ever crossed the minds of most of them that the Torah, that incomparable framework for living granted to His Chosen People by the Almighty Himself, might conceivably have been rendered redundant. Yet there were some, pushing the implications of their new beliefs to radical limits, who had soon arrived at precisely such a conclusion.

A few decades on from Jesus's crucifixion, a group of Christians in Asia Minor received a letter that positively seethed with scandalous notions. Its author, a one-time student of the Torah called Paul, was the most spectacular rebel that the famously prescriptive Jewish educational system had ever bred. "There is neither Jew nor Greek, there is neither slave nor free, there is neither male nor female; for you are all one in Christ Jesus."[50] In this revolutionary proclamation, Paul deftly cut what had always been, for Jewish scholars, the ultimate Gordian knot. No need, so Paul announced with a flourish, to pick at the problem one moment more. Whereas once it had been the Torah which gave to the Chosen People their roadmap to the purposes of God, now, with the coming of Christ, the need for such a Law was gone. The whole question of what it was that made for a Jew had been dissolved into irrelevance. No longer was there any obligation to follow the Torah's rulings, to be bound by its strictures, to attend to all its endless finger-wagging: "Now that faith has come, we are no longer under a custodian; for in Christ Jesus you are all sons of God, through faith."[51] The Gentiles too, so Paul had concluded, were heirs to the promise made by God to Abraham. No longer were the Chosen People defined by a lineage of blood, or by adherence to a law, but by the knowledge and love of Christ. Nations everywhere, in short, might now be ranked as the children of Abraham. All it needed was for the entire world to end up Christian.

Which, as mission statements went, could certainly not be faulted for any lack of chutzpah. Paul's ambitions were quite as groundbreaking as they were global. Cults, and the divinities they celebrated, had hitherto invariably been local: attached to specific places, attached to particular peoples. Any suggestion that they might be something more, that they might be universal, was liable to strike most people as either offensive, or ludicrous, or both. Nevertheless, Paul had indeed breathed in something of the authentic spirit of the age. Enthusiasm for a brotherhood of man was increasingly in the air. Posidonius, after all, a whole century before Paul, had trusted that it would emerge as one of the fruits of Roman rule. Why, then, in a world dominated by the pretensions of would-be universal empires, should the pretensions of a would-be universal faith not find a ready audience? Sure enough, in the decades and centuries following Jesus' crucifixion, the Christian mission to the Gentiles began to thrive. Cells planted in the time of Paul steadily renewed and replicated themselves. Across lands ruled from Ctesiphon, across lands ruled from Rome, they grew, and flourished, and spread. In each one, men and women from every conceivable background, class and race would meet as equals, in a shared room, before the gaze of a severe but loving God. Equals, because all of them—the senator no less than the kitchen-maid, the Greek no less than the Briton, the philosopher no less than the whore—might be sucked down into the glutinous bog of sin; equals, because all of them, thanks to the death of Christ upon the cross, had been rendered capable of winning salvation for themselves. Never before had there been preached a message of personal responsibility quite so radical, so democratic, or so potentially wide-reaching in its appeal. Christian thinkers, in their struggle to define the principles of their faith, were engaged in a project no less well-suited to the times for being so palpably quixotic: the fathoming of the purposes of God in an ever more globalised world.

In this respect, of course, they were not so far different from the rabbis of Mesopotamia. Their methods were similar, too: for Christian sages also drew for their ultimate inspiration upon the inheritance of Jewish scripture. However, whereas the rabbis identified the Torah as something ageless and unchanging, Gentile Christians viewed it—and the Tanakh generally—merely as an "Old Testament": a cloud-dimmed glimpse of the Eternal Light that was Jesus Christ. This perspective, of course, begged an obvious question: what should a "New Testament" be?[52] Already, in the century that followed

Christ's crucifixion, scholars had begun to compile collections of writings that could provide an answer. Paul's letters were the first to be anthologised, and then various *euangelia*, or "gospels"—biographies of Christ. Just like the rabbis of Sura and Pumpedita, the Christians who compiled these texts believed that it had been given to them to meditate upon the single most earth-shattering event in human history: an intrusion of the divine into the fallen world so cosmic in its implications that the entire order of the universe revolved around it. The surest fruit of this intrusion, however, was not a body of law, as the rabbis believed, but rather the knowledge in the soul of an individual believer that Jesus was truly the Lord. "I am the way, and the truth, and the life." So Christ, according to one of the gospels, had declared. "No one comes to the Father, but by me."[53]

A ringing statement—but ambiguous all the same. It was given to few Christians to claim, as Paul himself had done, a personal vision of the risen Christ. How, then, in the absence of such direct communications, were the faithful to know what, precisely, "the way" might be? Jesus himself, when commanding his followers to "make disciples of all nations," had instructed them to do so "in the name of the Father and of the Son and of the Holy Spirit."[54] Here, however, was only further ambiguity—for who, or what, was "the Holy Spirit"? The answer to this question, one that many generations of Christian sages would labour at providing, did not come easily: for it touched upon the ineffable mystery that was the identity of God Himself. How fortunate it was, then, for the less intellectually inclined among the faithful, that the Holy Spirit might be experienced without necessarily being comprehended. Whether imagined as a dove, or as fire, or as a sound "from heaven like the rush of a mighty wind,"[55] it was, so Christians believed, the very breath of the divine upon the world. Whenever they felt themselves moved by the rapture of faith, a flickering-like ecstasy about their souls, then they could know themselves possessed by the Spirit. Not, however, that the evidence of its workings was confined to their inner lives. The Spirit was to be traced as well in the unity that it brought to the Christian people everywhere. No matter where these men and women might live, no matter what their status, they had all shared a single ceremony of initiation: an immersion in water that they termed "baptism." "For by one Spirit we were all baptised into one body—Jews or Greeks, slaves or free—and all were made to drink of one Spirit."[56] Without it, there could be no unity, no shared *Ecclesia*—no Church.

Which meant in turn that Christians everywhere could throw themselves into the business of constructing a globe-spanning bureaucracy and feel that they were thereby serving the purposes of their Lord. A relish for firing off letters was yet another way in which Paul had blazed a trail. Long-distance communications were cherished by the faithful throughout the Roman and the Iranian worlds as the lifeblood of the Church. The most trivial, as well as the most transcendent, topics were vigorously debated by Christians across the entire sweep of the rival empires. Not even a Caesar, not even a *Shahanshah*, could boast a perspective to match. Christians, well aware of this, positively gloried in the fact: "Any country can be their homeland—and yet their homeland, wheresoever it may be, is to them a foreign place."[57] There seemed no limit to the expanding scope of their identity.

Yet it was not only by thinking on a global scale that the Christian Church had succeeded in fashioning itself, over the course of barely a few centuries, into the most formidable non-governmental organisation that the world had ever seen. It operated locally as well. Little more than a generation after Jesus's crucifixion, Christians had already grown obsessed with the need for disciplined book-keeping. The paperwork of each individual church had duly been entrusted to an official chosen by the local congregation to serve as an "overseer," or "*episcopos*": a "bishop." Soon enough, however, and these same bureaucrats had begun soaringly to outgrow their origins as mere functionaries. Three centuries on, and it had become the entitlement of a bishop to rule almost as a monarch over the congregation that selected him. He it was who would act as spokesman for local Christians in their dealings with the broader Church; move to resolve their problems and defend them in times of crisis; define for them their beliefs, and prescribe for them the texts they should read, and answer for them before God. "It is manifest that we should look upon the bishop even as we would look upon the Lord Himself—standing, as he does, before the Lord."[58]

Here, then, was authority such as even a Roman or a Persian aristocrat might appreciate. Although bishops tended to shun the silks and jewels beloved of the upper classes, the coarse wool of their robes could not disguise the fact that they too, like any great magnate, dealt ultimately in patronage. "If you would be perfect, go, sell what you possess and give to the poor."[59] This injunction of Christ's, while not always followed to the letter, had nevertheless inspired among Christians a tradition of charity that was capable of providing bishops, the men who administered its fruits, with immense reserves of largesse. In city after city, the Church had come to constitute not merely a state within a state but something altogether more exceptional: a welfare state. In a world where there were few safety nets for the destitute, or the widowed, or the sick, this might serve to endow the local bishop with an often brilliant aura of holiness—and holiness, to the Christian people, spelled power. Much, in turn, was bound to flow from this. With power, a bishop could impose discipline upon his flock; and with discipline, the Church could maintain itself as something truly universal—as "catholic." Three centuries on from the lifetime of Christ, and there was nothing that would have borne a surer witness to the glory of His triumph over death, and to the workings of the Holy Spirit, than a Christian people who stood as one.

Certainly, as their propagandists never tired of pointing out, there was nothing in all the bewildering kaleidoscope of idolatrous cults that could remotely compare with the sense of common identity that most Christians did authentically share. That did not mean, however, that the Christian people enjoyed a perfect unity. Far from it. The world remained a realm of sin, and the body of the Church, as that of Christ had been upon the cross, was racked and twisted by the tortures inflicted upon it by the wicked. Not everyone who laid claim to the name of Christian was necessarily willing to acknowledge the authority of a bishop. "Beware of false prophets," Christ Himself had warned, "who come to you in sheep's clothing but inwardly are ravening wolves."[60] Food for thought—for how to tell a sheep from a wolf disguised inside a fleece? Writing in Carthage, a famous and wealthy city in North Africa, a Christian philosopher by the name of Tertullian had proffered some helpful advice: "It is the sources and the originals of the faith which must be accounted the truth."[61] Nothing was to be reckoned authentically Christian, in other words, that could not be traced, generation back through generation, to the time of Christ Himself, and of His first followers, the apostles. If this was true for doctrine, Tertullian argued, then so also was it true for priests. Any bishop who stood in a line of succession from one of the original apostles served as the heir of a Christian who had been blessed by the hands of the Son of God. What better pedigree than that? "For, undoubtedly, it preserves what the churches received from the apostles, the apostles from Christ, and Christ from God."[62]

A clinching display of logic, it might have been thought—except that other Christians too could play the same game. Formidable and peerless though the organisation of the self-proclaimed "catholic" Church might be, it was not alone in looking back to the primal origins of the faith to sanction its doctrines. Indeed, there was a sense in which the very efforts of its servants to carve a straight path through all the wilds of potential belief—an "orthodoxy"—served only to open up alternative routes. The existence of a linked network of bishoprics across the span of the known world reflected an understanding of Christ's teachings that had been shaped, above all, by Paul: an understanding that viewed the Church as a body universal, defined by faith rather than law, and ablaze with "the power of the Holy Spirit."[63] All these presumptions, however, might readily be challenged. Why, for instance, should the Church not remain what it had been back in the very earliest days of its existence: a pure body of the elect, small to be sure, but untainted by the outside world? And how was it, if the Torah were a matter of sublime irrelevance, as Paul had taught, that Christ Himself had so emphatically stated the exact opposite: "till heaven and earth pass away, not an iota, not a dot, will pass from the law until all is accomplished".[64]

Even this, however, was not to touch upon the profoundest, the most dizzying, the most perplexing question of all: what precisely was the relationship of the Holy Spirit to Christ, and of Christ, the Son of God, to His Heavenly Father? Once again, it was Tertullian—never one to shirk a challenge—who provided the most widely accepted answer. God, he explained, was Three: Father, Son and Spirit. Likewise, these three aspects of the divinity—the creator, the redeemer and the inspirer—were One. A paradox, of course—but one that Tertullian, who had not been expensively schooled in the subtleties of Greek philosophy for nothing, saw as expressive of the very essence of the divine. God, who was Three in One, and One in Three, was best thought of, he explained, as a *Trinitas*—a "Trinity."

Yet even Tertullian, despite the triumphant swagger with which he had made his case, had been under no illusion that he had proved it: "The mystery stays guarded."[65] Which was putting it mildly. Any number of slippery issues still remained to be pinned down. If God were truly One, for instance, did that mean the Son was not, as His title implied, subordinate to the Father but in every way His equal? The tendency in orthodox circles was increasingly to answer "yes"; but the fact that this implied a Son who was no less eternal than His own parent, an apparent illogicality that had worried Tertullian himself, ensured that there were plenty of Christians who scorned to agree. This, of course, in a Church where there were few means of enforcing a specific orthodoxy other than by exhortation and argument, they were perfectly at liberty to do; and it ensured that the spectrum of Christian beliefs held by the Christian people, rather than narrowing as time went on, came instead to embody a quite bewildering range of shades. It was all very well for the likes of Tertullian to argue that an impregnable mystery lay at the heart of the faith; but there were many Christians who found it difficult to leave the matter simply at that. Too much was at stake. The irreducible message of the Christian faith—that God, through the agency of Jesus, had somehow intruded into the mortal fabric of human flesh—raised as many questions as it answered, not only about the essence of the divine but about who precisely Jesus might have been. Equally God and equally man: such, three hundred years after the crucifixion, had come to be the favoured orthodoxy among the leaders of the Church. But it was not the only one. There were some Christians who argued that Jesus had been completely divine, with not a trace of the human about him. There were others who claimed that his body had provided a mortal shell for the heavenly Spirit, which was presumed to have descended upon him during his baptism, and abandoned him before he died on the cross. There were still others who insisted that Jesus had been the adopted Son of God—flesh and blood, like any other man, but no less the Christ for that. Not a permutation of beliefs, in short, but some group of Christians, somewhere, might choose to subscribe to it.

And it was precisely this range of opinion—*hairesis*, in Greek—that drove those who wished to affirm a single orthodoxy to distraction.* Of course, every Christian sect liked to imagine that its own understanding of Christ constituted the way, the truth, the life; but it was the self-proclaimed "catholic" Church, by virtue of its sheer scale, which had the most weight to throw around. The most to lose as well if it did not. Painstakingly, over the course of the centuries, it had set itself to the formidable task of clearing any number of doctrinal booby-traps from the feet of the faithful. Understandably, then, its scholars and leaders had little patience for those who would sabotage such a project. Christians who rejected the Church's authority were increasingly viewed not as fellow travellers but rather as souls lost upon crooked paths, agents of error who had wilfully chosen to abandon the one, true road of orthodoxy—as "heretics." Nothing they touched so sacred or so precious, but they would attempt to sabotage it. "For their behaviour is exactly like that of someone who, when an exquisite mosaic of a king has been fashioned by a great artist out of

---

* Among non-Christians, "*hairesis*" had come to signify a school of philosophical thought.

162

rare stones, takes the mosaic completely to pieces, and rearranges the jewels, and puts them back together to make the image of a dog or a fox—and a poorly executed one at that."[66]

Such bitterness was hardly surprising. The efforts made by generations of Christian scholars to establish the truth of what Christ might have said and done had indeed been as punctilious as those of any master-mosaicist. Only the most finely calibrated measuring-rod— a *canon*, in Greek—had been deployed for the purpose. Just as was required by the most exacting standards of the historians of the day, no gospel had been passed as "canonical" that could not be shown, to the satisfaction of catholic scholars, to derive from the authentic evidence of eyewitnesses to the events described.[67] Increasingly, only four such gospels—two attributed to disciples of Jesus; one to a disciple of Simon Peter, the chief of the apostles; and one to an associate of Paul— had come to be regarded as measuring up. Yet still, a hundred, two hundred, even three hundred years after the crucifixion, biographies of Christ continued to be cranked out. Of course, gospels such as these, composed at such a remove of time, could hardly have any great claims to biographical accuracy; but biographical accuracy, to those who composed them, was hardly the point. For many writers, the motivation might be as simple as a desire to entertain, by telling fabulous stories, and filling in some obvious gaps. What kind of games, for instance, had the infant Saviour enjoyed while playing with His friends? A host of gospels had not hesitated to provide the answer.[68] Christ's favourite stunt as a child, so it was revealed, had been to make clay birds, breathe on the sculptures, and then bring them to life. Not, perhaps, quite as edifying an anecdote as those to be found in the four canonical gospels—but innocent enough, certainly. Other adjustments to Christ's biography, however, might be altogether more momentous in their implications. Some, indeed, might strike directly at the heart of Christian orthodoxy.

When, for instance, a Christian named Basilides wished to demonstrate that Jesus had not died upon the cross, he made good the complete lack of evidence for this novel theory in the canonical gospels through a simple expedient: he wrote a whole new gospel of his own.[69] The story of the crucifixion, in Basilides's reworking of it, contained a hitherto unsuspected twist. Christ, as He was carrying His cross through the streets of Jerusalem, had magically swapped bodies with Simon of Cyrene, a man who had come to His assistance. As a result, it was the unfortunate Simon who had been crucified. Christ Himself, meanwhile, watching from a safe distance, had stood "roaring with laughter."[70]

But how precisely had Basilides come by this startling revelation? No less than his adversaries, he had perfectly appreciated the vital importance of pedigree. A gospel was nothing unless it could be traced back to a heavyweight informant. This was why, in offering to the world his account of the crucifixion, Basilides had made sure to attribute it to the classiest, the most impeccable source he could find: Simon Peter himself. Critics of Basilides, however, snorted at this claim as grotesque. Any notion that details of Christ's life and teachings might have been kept secret from his mass of followers and passed down only among a privileged few, was dismissed by them out of hand. The claims of Basilides to a privileged *gnosis*, or "knowledge"—one supposedly denied to less enlightened Christians—was dismissed by his orthodox opponents as the merest braggadocio. After all, as they never tired of pointing out, he was only one of a swarming, buzzing crowd. There were any number of "Gnostics," all with their own pretensions, all with their own scriptures. "The Church has four gospels, but the heretics have many."[71] That being so, how could any of them be trusted? All were clearly fabrications. None could plausibly be attributed to an apostle. Certainly, Basilides's laughable insistence that his gospel derived from a succession of whispered reminiscences, passed down from generation to generation and never even once put into writing, was precisely what served to brand it a fraud: "For it is evident that the perfect truth of the Church derives from its high antiquity; and that all these many heresies, being more recent in time, and subsequent to the truth, are nothing but recent concoctions, manufactured from the truth."[72]

Except, of course, that any rabbi, contemplating the pretensions of the Gentile Church, might well have made an identical point. The Tanakh, after all, long pre-dated even the earliest gospel. Christian thinkers, as they struggled to establish the parameters of their faith, were often rendered profoundly uncomfortable by this reflection. So much so, in fact, that one of them, a bishop's son by the name of Marcion, was brought by it to take the ultimate step, and deny that he owed anything to the Jews at all. Rather than acknowledge the umbilical cord that linked the gospels to the Old Testament, he simply cut right through it. Christ, so he taught, shared nothing, absolutely nothing, with the Jewish god. One preached love and mercy and occupied the upper storeys of heaven; the other issued endless laws, punished all those who did not obey them, and smouldered away in the lower reaches of the sky. Some Christians, struck by the awful logic of this, were sufficiently convinced by Marcion's teaching to establish a whole new church; others, the majority, shrank from it in horror. All of them, though, as they wrestled with the question of who or what Christ might have been, were wrestling as well with the issue of what their relationship to the Jewish past should properly be. If Jesus were truly the Messiah, then the failure of God's Chosen People to recognise that fact could rank only as a monstrous embarrassment. Self-evidently, however, the blame for such a scandal had to lie not with Christ but with the Jews themselves. Increasingly, then, the claim of the Gentile Church to embody the fulfilment of the Jewish scriptures required it to scorn the rival claims of the synagogues as thunderously as possible: "For I declare that they of the seed of Abraham who follow the Law, and do not come to believe in Christ before they die, will not be saved."[73] The Torah was a dung-heap; its students pickers after trash; all its great array of dictates a mere monument to desiccation. Never before had there been an attempt at disinheritance on quite so audacious a scale.

The rabbis, rather than dignify the Gentiles who would rob them of their patrimony with a direct rebuttal, opted instead to hold their noses and maintain a dismissive hauteur. "Let a man always flee," as one of them sniffed, "from what is repellent."[74] Nevertheless, even in their mightiest strongholds, even in the *yeshivas*, a rising tide was lapping at their feet. The danger signs had long been there to see. Christians were hardly a novelty in Mesopotamia. Indeed, they had originally arrived on its borders around the same time as the first emergence there of the rabbis themselves. Though Paul, back in the age of the apostles, had travelled westwards—to the cities of the Greek world, and to Rome—other missionaries had soon begun to turn their gaze towards the rising sun. The roads of the Fertile Crescent, after all, were quite as open as the sea-lanes of the Mediterranean. Already, by the time of the founding of the Mesopotamian *yeshivas*, in the early third century AD, there had come to exist, a mere two weeks' journey north of Sura and Pumpedita, a formidable stronghold of Christian sages—and one that lost nothing in comparison to the schools of the rabbis.

Like Harran, its immediate neighbour, Edessa lay on the fault-line between the rival empires of Rome and Persia; but unlike Harran, which positively revelled in her idolatrous reputation, Edessa was famed among Christians everywhere as the "Blessed City." Christ Himself, so it was said, had penned a missive to one of her kings. The very document itself was still to be found in the city's archives: sure proof against scepticism. Nor was that all. Edessa laid claim to an even more sensational souvenir of Christ's correspondence: His only known self-portrait, painted and sent by Him, so it was said, in response to a royal fan-letter. No wonder, given these indubitable marks of divine favour, that Christians should have believed that Edessa was destined never to fall. Certainly, the protective sympathy extended by her rulers towards the Church had enabled the city to become a veritable hot-house of Christian scholarship. The hymns, and the prayers, and the translations written there would serve to make Syriac, the language spoken by the Edessans, the lingua franca of the entire Christian Near East.

As the rabbis hunkered down inside their own schools, the influence of Edessa was already palpable in the streets that stretched beyond their walls. All very well for the rabbis to meet this challenge with an icy show of silence—but that hardly served to make it go away. A Christian, after all, was likely to have none of the compunctions about converting a Jew that a Jew might have about converting a Christian. Increasingly, in the competition between the two faiths for proselytes, it was clear which one was winning.

Yet mortal though the enmity between the rabbis and the leaders of the Gentile Church had certainly become, it was haunted by paradox. Relations between these two implacable rivals were shaped by a truth that neither could possibly acknowledge: both, in their struggle to define themselves, had need of the other. The more that Christians scorned the Jews as a people unchanged from what they had ever been, clinging blindly and obdurately to the wreckage of a superseded faith, so the more, ironically enough, did it serve to burnish the rabbis' self-image. Here, from their bitterest opponents, was confirmation of their own most prized conceits: that they were the guardians of a timeless law; that there was no hint of novelty attached to their current project; and that the ancient prophets—Daniel, Abraham, Adam—had all been rabbis exactly like themselves. Christians, however, were not the only ones to have given their foes an involuntary boost. The rabbis, by refusing to engage in open combat with the Christian heretics, were effectively declaring that the *minim* no longer ranked as even faintly Jewish—and not to rank as Jewish was, of course, to a rabbi, a truly terrible fate. This, however, was not at all how the *minim* themselves saw things. The only effect of Jewish scorn on a Gentile bishop was to boost his self-confidence, and flatter his pretensions. "Do not marvel," Christ had declared, "that I said to you, 'You must be born anew.'"[75] To the Gentile Church, the sense of itself as a daughter sprung from the womb of a withered and unregenerate mother had become a precious conceit. Just as the rabbis had every interest in dismissing Christians as bastard and unwanted spawn, so did Christians have no less an interest in casting the faith of their Jewish contemporaries as the failed parent of their own. Both, though, were wrong. The relationship between the rival faiths, that of the rabbis and the bishops, was not one of parent and child. Rather, it was one of siblings: rival twins, doomed like Romulus and Remus to mutual hatred, yet bred all the same of the identical womb.[76]

And there were still places, to the disgust of both rabbis and bishops, where a strong sense of this endured. Three centuries on from the supposed arrival in Edessa of Christ's letter, and there were few better spots from where to gauge the potentially infinite variety of human belief than "the Blessed City." To stand on its citadel and gaze around at the horizon was, for a Christian sage, to be conscious of just how various was God's creation. To the east was the empire of the Persians; to the west, that of the Romans. On the margins of the first, in Khorasan, it was the habit of "a single man to take many wives"; on the margins of the second, in Britain, "many men together take a single wife."[77] The glory of the Christian faith, so it seemed to the scholars of Edessa, was that it provided all of humanity with a means of transcending such differences of custom: of giving people, no matter where they lived, one common identity as the children of Abraham. Yet what was the Christian faith? To lower the gaze from the distant horizon, to look down into the teeming warren of Edessa's streets, was to doubt that there could be any single answer. There were some Christians walking the city who followed the doctrines of Marcion, and others who denied that Christ had suffered on the cross, and others yet who believed that the four earliest gospels should be read in the form of a single digest. To be sure, there was no lack of Christians either who were proud to account themselves members of a worldwide, orthodox Church—and yet their traditions were no less fiercely local for that. In every Christian community, not just Edessa, the cast of what people believed, and how they behaved, might be influenced by much more than their bishop. The festivals that were held in a city's streets, the languages that were spoken in its markets, and the stories that were shared around its evening fires: all might serve to influence the character of its Church. This was why, in Edessa and in cities across Mesopotamia, it mattered a very great deal that the Jews were people of flesh and blood, and not mere faceless bogeys.

They might be neighbours, colleagues—even friends.[78] The Christians of the East, almost without realising it, bore the unmistakable stamp of this. Certainly, to visitors from other Churches, they were liable to appear quite disconcertingly Jewish.

In Mesopotamia, for instance, Christians still refused to eat meat that had not first been drained of all its blood, exactly as prescribed by the Torah.[79] They celebrated the resurrection of Christ on a date arrived at by a specifically Jewish method of calculation.[80] Even the title by which they habitually addressed their priests—*rabban*—sounded similar to, and had the same meaning as, rabbi. Granted, none of this implied any sense of kinship between Jewish and Christian leaders. Quite the contrary: the rabbis' and priests' consciousness of what they shared only made them all the more determined to draw rigid dividing-lines between their two faiths. Yet, in reality, those dividing-lines were often blurred. In Edessa, for instance, the mutual obsession of Jewish and Christian scholars with one another's labours bore a particularly spectacular fruit: for the first translation of the Old Testament into Syriac was most likely made, not by Christians at all, but by Jews, who then subsequently converted and made a gift of their work to the Church.[81] Yet in truth, to many Jews, it was not always apparent that an acceptance of Jesus as the Messiah did necessarily require them to stop being Jewish. Likewise, among the ranks of Christians, there were many who persisted in obeying the Torah and who regarded Paul, not as a saint, but rather as "a renegade from the Law"[82]—the heretic of heretics. Some, indeed, saw no contradiction in hedging their bets even more comprehensively by invoking both the One God of the Jews and the Trinity of the Christians simultaneously. "By the name of I-Am-That-I-Am, the Lord of Hosts," as one particularly all-inclusive curse ran, "and by the name of Jesus, who conquered the height and the depth by his cross, and by the name of his exalted father, and by the name of the holy spirits forever and in eternity . . ."[83] Well, then, might those who sought to patrol the dividing-line between the two faiths have been appalled. "It is monstrous to talk of Jesus Christ, and yet to behave as a Jew."[84] This assertion had been made by a celebrated saint of the early Church, Ignatius, a man sup-posedly appointed bishop of the great Syrian city of Antioch by Simon Peter himself; and yet it might just as well have been made by a rabbi. Jewish and Christian leaders alike, both had the same frontier policy: to create a no-man's land. Both were equally threatened by an open, porous border.

Not, of course, that to plug one was necessarily a simple task. Those who lived in the Fertile Crescent could appreciate this better than most. The line that separated the empires of Persia and Rome did not, after all, follow the course of a natural barrier. Instead, it wound across featureless landscape, and divided peoples who more properly belonged together. Only with muscle, and resolve, and ceaseless effort could such a boundary possibly hope to be maintained. That Edessa, which in AD 216 had been formally annexed by Rome, would still remain, three centuries on, a possession of the Roman Empire, bore witness enough to the ability of the Caesars to hold a line.[85] Though Kavad, in 503, would put the city under siege, Edessa would not, unlike Amida, fall. Justinian's great building programme at Dara, a hundred miles to the east, would serve only to hammer home the point. It took might to maintain a border. Might such as only the master of a mighty empire could command.

Two centuries and more before the time of Justinian, however, nei-ther rabbi nor bishop wielded any such power. Great though the moral authority of both had become among the communities which they claimed to lead, it certainly did not extend to the building of watchtowers, to the manning of a frontier. Jews and Christians, though conscious of themselves as peoples with distinct identities, remained unclear where precisely the border between them lay. Jewish Christians and Christian Jews could still mill across it pretty much as they pleased.

Only a man who could lend to the rabbis or the bishops the full awesome power of a *Shahanshah*, or perhaps a Caesar, could hope to alter that.

But such a prospect, in AD 300, seemed scarcely imaginable.

Forging a New Heaven

To the rabbis, the notion that a Gentile king might end up a Jew was not inherently a ludicrous one. Nero himself, so it was confidently asserted in the Talmud, had been brought to repent of all his viciousness and become a proselyte. Even more startlingly, one of his descendants was supposed to have been a rabbi—and a particularly celebrated one at that.[86] The inherent implausibility of all this did not bother the rabbis themselves a jot. Rather, it served, in their opinion, only to render the miracle of Nero's conversion the more astounding and edifying. After all, if even a notorious Caesar could be brought to follow the Torah, then who was to say what powerful Gentiles might become proselytes in the future?

Christians too, when they surveyed the kingdoms of the world, lived in hope. Memories of how Jesus had communicated with the King of Edessa were cherished precisely because they seemed to suggest that even great monarchs might be touched by the Holy Spirit. Clinching proof of this arrived in AD 301, when a Parthian king named Tiridates III, lord of the ruggedly mountainous and inaccessible land of Armenia, midway between the Roman and Persian empires, accepted Christ as his lord. Not only that, but he promptly ordered his subjects to follow suit. Since the Armenians had hitherto been devout worshippers of Mihr, this raised a good few eyebrows across *Iranshahr*, where the Zoroastrian priesthood, ever suspicious of interlopers, had already marked down the "*Krestayne*" as purveyors of witchcraft. There was, however, in this accusation, more than a hint of a grudging compliment. Not even their bitterest enemies could deny the Christians a quite spectacular success rate when it came to healing the sick. Rabbis, fully alert to what they regarded as the sinister potency of Christ's name, urged invalids to guard against it, no matter what. The salutary tale was told of one rabbi who discovered, heartbreakingly, that his dying grandson had been restored to health by a magician's whispering of the name of Jesus over the sickbed—and thereby been denied any prospect of eternal life.[87] Christians themselves, of course, furiously rejected any suggestion that their powers of healing might owe anything to necromancy. Rather, the ability of their holy men and women to work miracles, to cast out malevolent spirits and even to defy the laws of nature, was due, in their devout opinion, to the precise opposite: a power derived from heaven. The quite unanticipated acquisition of their first royal convert powerfully confirmed them in this view: for Tiridates had been brought to baptism after being cured of possession by demons. Only the name of Christ had been able to work the exorcism. Only the name of Christ had been able to convince the king that he was not, in fact, a wild boar. No wonder, then, knowing this, that Christians should eagerly have scanned the *Shahanshah* too for signs of lunacy, or any other ailment, and dared to dream.

Yet the challenge they faced remained a fearsome one. Not even the most proficient exorcist among them could doubt the menace and malignancy of their adversaries. Spirits flung down from heaven at the beginning of time still stalked the earth, hunting human prey; nor had Christ's triumph over them on the cross wholly broken their grip on the empires of the world. The Persians, in their ignorance and folly, still worshipped fire; while in the teeming cities of the Romans, there was barely a square that did not stand filthy with the smoke of sacrifices paid to idols, and with the perfumes of incense burned in their honour. Christians did not deny that idols, images such as the Palladium, might be possessed of an authentically supernatural power; nor did they doubt that the spirits worshipped as gods by idolators truly existed. But to honour them, no matter how ancient the rites might be and no matter how passionately the Roman people might believe them essential to the maintenance of their empire, was akin to feeding the blood-lust of a vampire. An idol might be the loveliest in the world—and yet how did all its beauty serve it, if not as paint on the scabs of a whore?

Paul himself, arriving in Ephesus, a wealthy city on the Aegean coast of Asia Minor, had risked a lynching to press home the point: that "gods made with hands are not gods."[88] A bold thesis to push in Ephesus, of all places: for there stood in the city a temple so beautiful that it ranked as one of the seven wonders of the world. Artemis, the goddess enthroned amid its dazzling gold and marble, was a deity no less virginal or powerful than Pallas Athena—but Paul had been nothing daunted. True to form, he had refused point blank, even in the shadow of one of the holiest places in the entire empire, to make allowances for the sensitivities of those who worshipped there, or to compromise in the slightest with their convictions. As a result, not surprisingly, he had provoked a riot and almost been torn to pieces. A few years later, his continued refusal to renounce Christ had resulted in his execution by Nero in Rome.[89] Peter, and many other apostles, had perished in the same wave of judicial murders. Thereafter, over succeeding generations, many other Christians, prosecuted by the imperial authorities for insulting the gods who had supposedly made Rome great, had likewise opted to pay the ultimate price—and joyously so. After all, by doing so, they could share in the suffering of their Saviour. To be baptised anew in one's own blood was to be cleansed of every last taint of sin. The souls of those who died for Christ, ascending from the reek and shambles of the killing ground, were assured of eternal life. Nor was that the limit of their rewards—for the more spectacular their sufferings, so the more did they draw attention to the glory of Christ and His earthly Church. Each one perished as a "witness"—*martyr*, in Greek.

A point, unfortunately, entirely lost on the majority of their audience. Nothing quite like the relish of Christians for dying in the cause of their God had ever been witnessed before. When martyrs were made "to run the gauntlet of whips, or to be savaged by wild beasts, or to be roasted in iron chairs, so that they were suffocated by the reek of their own flesh as it cooked,"[90] the watching crowds were rarely impressed. Why should they be? A god best displayed his power by protecting those who worshipped him, not by demanding their deaths. The Romans knew this better than anyone. Because they had known how to bind themselves—*religare*, in Latin—to the gods, by offering them their due of sacrifices and respect, the gods had in turn bound themselves to the Roman people, and granted them all their greatness. It was this same bond—this *"religio,"* as the Romans termed it—that the superstition of the Christians appeared so grievously to threaten.[91] The martyrs' obduracy in the face of death struck the vast majority of their contemporaries as neither admirable nor heroic but as a sickness—the mark of deviant minds. It was also why, amid the agonies of Rome's near collapse in the third century, the imperial authorities turned on the Christians with an escalating ferocity, in an attempt to appease the self-evidently angry gods, and purge the empire once and for all of the enemy within. "For it was our aim," as one emperor put it, "to set everything right in accordance with the ancient laws and public discipline of the Roman people, and to ensure that the Christians too, who had abandoned the way of life of their ancestors, be returned to sanity."[92]

As wave after wave of persecution broke across the cities of the Roman Empire, both sides alike knew that much was at stake. War was being waged for control of the heavens themselves. It was not the fortitude of individual Christians, as their limbs were broken, as their flesh was made to melt, as their bodies were torn to pieces by wild beasts, that was being put to the test. Rather, it was the might and the potency of their god. By their deaths, so the martyrs believed, they were serving as the shock troops of the Holy Spirit. More and more, across the entire span of the fallen world, it was the breath of the divine that was being felt. In the bones and bloodied remains of the martyrs themselves—relics endowed with a terrifying holiness. In the miserable fates of those emperors who had presumed to persecute them: Decius, cut down by the Goths; Valerian, serving as a Persian king's mounting block. In the routing, in their mightiest strongholds, of even the most ancient and powerful demonic spirits. Any Christian martyred in Ephesus, for instance, within sight of the great temple of Artemis, won a particularly glorious victory. Every drop of Christian blood spilled in the arena served as a fresh exorcism. The filth and stench of idolatry was being purged by the cleansing power of Christ. Inexorably, the claws of Artemis, that malignant demon, were being prised from the city.

There were some Christians in Ephesus, however, who were not called to die for their faith. For them, God had other plans. In 250, when the Emperor Decius launched the first full-scale persecution of the Church, seven young Christians sought to escape arrest by hiding in a cave near the city.* There, so we are told, they were cornered, and sentenced to a living death. The entrance to the cave was bricked up. The seven young Ephesians, huddling together in their misery, fell asleep. Their slumbers, despite the wretchedness of their circumstances, proved deep and untroubled. Then, abruptly, the stones blocking off the mouth of the cave began to be moved. A shaft of light pierced the darkness. The seven sleepers awoke. Stumbling to the mouth of the cave, they found that labourers, seemingly oblivious to the wall's original purpose, were shifting the stones. Even more strangely, the stones themselves were covered with bushes and weeds. Deeply puzzled, the seven young Christians decided to send one of their number down into the city to reconnoitre the situation. As the young man approached the outskirts, his perplexity deepened into utter bewilderment. The city appeared utterly transformed. No sacrificial smoke, no clouds of incense, rose from its walls; in the market place, temples had vanished, as though into thin air; on public buildings, all mentions of Artemis had been systematically chiselled out, while on a statue of Augustus, carved into the emperor's forehead, was a cross. Rubbing his eyes in disbelief, the young man continued to the crossroads right in the centre of town, where a colossal idol of Artemis had always stood, as witness to her guardianship over the city. But even that was gone. In its place there now towered a giant cross, set there, according to an inscription, as "a sign of truth."[93] Self-evidently, something awesome, something quite beyond comprehension, had taken place.

---

* According to the Syriac writer Jacob of Serugh, there were actually eight sleepers: one who served as spokesman for the group, and seven others. Almost all other Christian sources, however, set the number at seven. The debate is pursued further in the pages of the Qur'an: "Only a few have real knowledge about them," God admonishes, "so do not argue" (18.22).

Only when the young man tried to buy bread with a coin bearing the head of Decius did he learn the full, astounding truth of what had happened. He and his six companions had been asleep for rather longer than the few hours they had initially presumed. A good deal longer, in fact. Two centuries in all the young men had been walled up inside the cave. The Almighty, observing "the faith of the blessed lambs," had stationed an angel at the entrance, "a watcher, to be the guardian of their limbs."[94] But not even the discovery that they were over two hundred years old could compare for impact with the sheer jaw-dropping scale of the transformation that had overtaken Ephesus, and the world beyond the city's walls. Back in the time of Decius, fleeing the agents of persecution, they would all of them, no doubt, have recalled the terrifying vision of Daniel: of how four beasts, which were the four great empires of the world, ruling in succession over mankind, had emerged from a raging sea. And they would have remembered as well that the fourth beast was the deadliest of all: "terrible and dreadful and exceedingly strong; and it had great iron teeth; it devoured and broke in pieces, and stamped the residue with its feet."[95] Sitting in the darkness of the cave before falling asleep, the seven young Christians would surely have had no doubt as to the identity of this beast; nor that what Daniel had been shown, in the vision of its terrifying depredations, was a prophecy of the persecution of the Church. After all, they themselves had witnessed the full horror of its savagery: "its teeth of iron and claws of bronze."[96]

Yet, Daniel had seen as well that the beast would ultimately be destroyed. And so it had proved. An empire once filthy with the pollution of idolatry, and beslathered with the blood of saints, had been transformed into something that no Christian back in the time of Decius would ever have imagined it becoming: the very mirror-image of the City of God. In AD 312—sixty-two years after the entombment of the seven sleepers and less than a decade after Rome's persecution of the Church had attained a veritable peak of savagery—the miracle of miracles had occurred: Constantine, midway through his project of uniting the empire under his sole rule, had been granted a vision of a cross in the sky. A mysterious voice had commanded, "By this sign, conquer."[97] Constantine, convinced that it was Christ Himself who had spoken to him, had done as instructed—and duly conquered. A century and a half later, the promise of victory in Daniel's vision had been spectacularly fulfilled: "And as I looked, the beast was slain, and its body destroyed and given over to be burned with fire."[98] Proof of this, should the seven sleepers need it, was provided by what had once been the greatest building in the Greek world. Long since abandoned to rising swamps, the temple of Artemis was now nothing but a carcass: its blackened columns had toppled into the mud; its shattered silhouette was barely visible through marsh-fumes and clouds of insects; its body, if not yet destroyed, was certainly decayed beyond redemption. The fires that Daniel had predicted would consume the beast blazed now directly on its steps, as lime-burners fed the temple's shattered marble into their kilns. Aside from these labourers' huts, crudely erected on the margins of the colossal wreck, there were few other marks of human habitation. People rarely visited a place so accursed. Now, in Ephesus, it was churches which dominated the commanding heights, and Christians who held the reins of power. Only occasionally would the few men and women who remained true to the worship of the ancient goddess approach her ruined temple, scrape the silt from its toppled altars, and offer a clandestine sacrifice.

"The giving of divine honours to tombs and pestiferous ashes."[99] So one Christian contemptuously dismissed the practice. Here, amplified across the centuries, was an authentic echo of the primal and magnificent scorn of Paul. As in the earliest days of the Church, so now, in the hour of its great triumph, it never crossed the minds of most Christians that those who clung to the love of gods other than Christ might conceivably have reasons for doing so aside from mere malignancy or backwardness. No other interpretation was necessary. Two centuries on from the reign of Decius, and the attitude felt by Christians towards their one-time persecutors was no longer one of dread, but rather of haughty and splendid disdain. The word they increasingly used to describe those who spurned baptism was *pagani*—"civilians."* This, of course, was to cast the Church itself as a heroic band of warriors, soldiers of Christ engaged in a mighty battle against the demons of hell; but it also served, very effectively, to imply that "pagans," no matter the fabulous range and variety of their cults, their observances, and their gods, were all, in the sordid depths of their souls, essentially the same. The notion that there existed such a thing as "paganism" gave to Christians what any great army of conquest marching into enemy territory, trusting to its size and its superior fire-power, will always looks to find: a single body of adversaries that could be pinned down, brought to battle, and given a decisive knock-out blow.

A strategy which, as it so happened, had always been the hall-mark of the Roman way of making war. Shortly after news of the miracle of the seven sleepers had arrived in Constantinople, the emperor himself—the "*imperator*"—is said to have travelled to their cave, where they gave him his blessing, then piously expired. Theodosius II, the fortunate recipient of the sleepers' benedictions, might initially have seemed an improbable heir to the grand traditions of Roman martial prowess. For all that his grandfather and namesake had been very much a warrior emperor of the old school, the younger Theodosius rarely left the gilded confines of his capital. His most tangible contribution to military policy had been purely defensive: girding the land flank of Constantinople, just over half a mile beyond Constantine's original wall, with a truly massive line of fortifications. This did not mean, however, that Theodosius gave no thought to the prosecution of war against the enemies of the Roman people. On the contrary: he devoted himself to it daily. The true battles were to be won, not from the saddle of a war-horse, but in churches and chapels. As Theodosius himself put

---

* Or possibly "rustic." The precise meaning of the word has long been debated, but there is a general consensus now that it relates to the sense that Christians had of themselves as *milites Christi*—"soldiers of Christ." The term was first used by Tertullian, but it was only after the conversion of Constantine that it began to appear on Christian inscriptions.

it in a solemn decree, "We are aware that Our State is sustained more by proper worship than by official duties, and physical toil and sweat."[100] The literal truth of this pronouncement had been vividly demonstrated during the reign of his father, when a fiery and sulphurous cloud, self-evidently of divine origin, had descended upon Constantinople. Only the prayers of the emperor himself had succeeded in dispersing it, and thereby preserving the capital from the wrath of God. Understandably, given the evidence of such miracles, Theodosius had grown up quite exceptionally devout. He fasted, he sang psalms, he averted his eyes from all temptations. His prayers, in consequence, had come to attain a rare and much valued potency. Four long decades he had reigned— and throughout that time, even as barbarian depredations had shaken the western half of the empire to the point of ruin, the provinces ruled from Constantinople, despite the odd alarm, had stood firm. Proof, if any were needed, of just what might be achieved by an emperor, if only the heavens could be won to his side.

Plus ça change indeed. For all the revolution that Constantine had initiated in the affairs of the empire, the instincts of the imperial elite, amid all the toppling of the ancient gods from their thrones, had altered, in truth, barely at all. Glory, eternal glory, remained what it had ever been: the due of the Roman people. Idols might have been smashed, and temples gutted—but not that basic, guiding presumption. What, after all, when Christ first spoke to Constantine, had He promised the emperor, if not victory, plain and simple? Constantine himself, later in life, would recall the experience of his conversion as a single moment of transcendent and soul-wrenching rapture; and yet, in truth, his spiritual journey had been altogether more protracted, perhaps, than such a memory allowed. Long before his vision of Christ, before he was even emperor, Constantine had been casting around for a divinity sufficiently powerful to sustain the formidable scope of his ambitions. It had been necessary for such a god, his own quite stunning lack of modesty being what it was, to be one of such might, potency, and magnificence as to reign, in effect, alone. At various stages in his career, Constantine had imagined that this supreme god might be

Apollo—the twin brother of Artemis—or perhaps the Sun. In the end, however, it was Christ who had passed the audition. Constantine had called on the One God "with earnest prayer and supplications that He would reveal to him who He was"[101]—and a cross of light had duly appeared in the sky. From that moment on, the emperor had not fought a single battle without first retiring to his tent to pray—"and always, after a short while, he was honoured with a manifestation of the Divine Presence."[102] Nobody, given the startling scale of Constantine's achievements, could possibly doubt the truth of this. Who were his heirs to forget it? To rule in the great city founded by Constantine was to appreciate just what was owed by the Roman people to the favour of Christ. It was to know that they were protected by a guardian of literally incomparable power. It was to rejoice in the certainty that the empire, even amid all the convulsions and upheavals of the age, rested upon foundations of a truly adamantine solidity: those same foundations that were the proper knowledge of God.

Except that here was begged an obvious question: what precisely was the proper knowledge of God? The answer to this was not, of course, remotely as self-evident as Christians had always yearned for it to be. Back in the first century of the Church, Ignatius, the great Bishop of Antioch, had coined a most suggestive word, expressive of his desperate longing for there to exist a coherent and universally accepted framework of Christian belief: *Christianismos*.[103] Two centuries on, however, and although there certainly existed an immense array of Christians, what did not exist was any consensus among them as to what *Christianismos*— "Christianity"—might actually be. The concept had proved a chimera. When Constantine, fresh from communing with the Almighty, had turned for assistance with his great labours to the supposedly "catholic" Church, he had found to his consternation that he was dealing, not with a single, monolithic organisation, but rather with an uneasy coalition of often bitterly antagonistic constituencies. To be sure, many of the tensions afflicting the various churches of his empire reflected jockeying for worldly position among ambitious bishops—but not all of them, by any means. The great kaleidoscope of Christian faith, formed as it had ever been of a bewildering array of beliefs and practices, was still in its customary state of flux. Not even the miraculous conversion of an emperor had served to distract Christian intellectuals from their favourite pastime: obsessing over the nature of God.

Throughout the early 320s, as Constantine was busy crushing the last remnants of opposition to his rule and drawing up plans for his new capital, the Church had been tearing itself to pieces over that veritable mystery of mysteries: the identity of Christ Himself. In 318, an austere and impeccably learned priest by the name of Arius had ripped open an old wound by arguing—with seemingly impeccable logic but against the authority of his own bishop—that God must have preceded His Son. Tertullian, of course, had made the same identical point; but decades of persecution had decisively altered the terms of the debate. As Arius's opponents were all too uncomfortably aware, any hint that the Son might be a secondary god, inferior to the Father, risked something truly monstrous: a blurring of what divided Christians from their pagan adversaries. If God were anything less than One, after all, why not go the whole hog and fall to worshipping Athena or Artemis? Inevitably, then, Arius's teachings provoked outrage: outrage which in turn only encouraged Arius and his supporters to dig in their heels all the more. The result was deadlock. Yet again, it seemed that Christians were utterly incapable of reaching consensus on even the most fundamental points of their belief. There existed not one but a multiplicity of Christianities.

But this was to reckon without a powerful new factor in the equation. To Constantine, the squabbling among the leaders of the Church was, quite simply, intolerable. Self-evidently, God had appeared to him and granted him victory because it was the divine will that Rome's empire be set on a new and heavenly footing. Who were Arius and his opponents, then, Constantine wished to know, to undermine his mission with their "subtle disputations on questions of little or no significance"?[104] After the failure of an initial attempt to restore harmony by knocking the two sides' heads together, Constantine moved with his customary decisiveness. Briskly, in 325, he summoned bishops from across the empire, and from *Iranshahr* too, to something wholly unprecedented: an *oecumenical*, or "worldwide," council. The venue chosen for this historic event, ostensibly because of its pleasant climate but in reality because of its location just south of Constantinople, was the city of Nicaea. Here, materialising in a blaze of gold and purple, "like some heavenly messenger of God,"[105] the emperor left the assembled bishops in no doubt as to what he wanted: an agreed and readily comprehensible definition of *Christianismos*. The bishops, suitably overawed, scrambled to obey. The followers of Arius, who constituted a decided minority in the council, found their protests being brutally sidelined. The Son, it was agreed, was "of one Being with the Father." Furthermore, He had been both God and man in equal proportions: "one Lord, Jesus Christ." Finally, just for good measure, the bishops made sure to add a mention of the Holy Spirit in their mutually agreed statement of belief. From now on, there was to be no more debate: God was definitively a Trinity.

It was not only Arius's followers who were branded heretical as a result of this momentous decision: so too were a host of other Christian sects and factions. Like the ancient street-plan of Byzantium, even then vanishing beneath the imperious grid of Constantinople, the venerable sprawl of their beliefs was put on notice of obliteration. The presence at the great council of bishops from throughout the Christian world—not to mention the faintly menacing figure of Constantine himself—had given its deliberations an unprecedented degree of heft. In the wake of Nicaea, the Church found itself possessed, for the very first time, of a creed that it could plausibly promote as "catholic"—as universal. The dream of Ignatius—that there might be such a thing as "Christianity"—appeared suddenly and dazzlingly fulfilled.

True, the show of unity quickly fractured. A bare few months after the bishops had gone their separate ways, and a whole slew of them began to backslide. While Arius himself, if the gleeful reports of his enemies were to be trusted, was soon brought to an aptly salutary end, voiding his guts in a back alley amid a quite spectacular explosion of shit, there were many, to the frustration of the orthodox, who failed to draw the obvious moral from this. Far and wide the ordure of the arch heretic's teachings had been splattered: even beyond the borders of the empire, where the Goths, although brought to Christ, had also been brought to believe with Arius, and against the creed formulated at Nicaea, that He was subordinate to the Father. Deviancy such as this, perhaps, was only to be expected from barbarians—but plenty of others had no such excuse. Many bishops, scorning what they had agreed at Nicaea, began openly to glory in the name of "Arian." Even a son of Constantine had not disdained the title.

Then, in 361, something far worse happened. Julian, a nephew of Constantine, seized control of the empire and promptly proclaimed himself a pagan. Bold, charismatic and brilliant, the new emperor made a conscious attempt to reverse his uncle's revolution. He restored subsidies to temples. He sought to undermine the Christian monopoly on charitable giving by organising his own. He even grew a beard. Such monstrous actions made it certain, of course, that the Almighty, provoked beyond endurance, would strike the apostate down. Sure enough, when Julian was duly killed on campaign in Mesopotamia just two years after coming to the throne, his death was received with a complacent satisfaction by Christians everywhere. Indisputably, however, they had been given a terrifying jolt. The leaders of the orthodox Church—nervously eyeing heretics on one flank and pagans on the other—lived in perpetual fear that the legacy of Nicaea, and their own authority with it, lay under mortal threat. This dread, over the course of the near century that separated the death of Julian from the appearance of the seven sleepers in Ephesus, saw them press hard for the rout of their many foes. Too much was at stake for them to do otherwise. Not just for the sake of Rome's empire, not just for the sake of humanity even, but for the sake of the heavens themselves, they needed a truly crushing victory—one that would leave the demons, and their mortal agents with them, in full and terminal retreat.

And such a victory, sure enough, was precisely what they had achieved. To the seven sleepers, gazing around them in stupefaction at what their one-time pagan city had become, this would have been most apparent, perhaps, in the sheer physical ubiquity of churches, in the market place, on the main streets, even on the hill overlooking the ruined temple of Artemis. However, much more astounding—and more impregnable by far—was a structure that could not be seen. So novel was it, so revolutionary in its implications, that even the word increasingly used to describe it—*religio*—had quite lost its original meaning. Back in the time of Decius, there had been many different ways for mortals to bind themselves to the gods: for each and every sacrifice, if properly sanctioned by tradition, had ranked as a *religio*. That, however, was not at all what Christians meant by the word.[106] "What binds and ties us to God is piety." Much else inevitably flowed from the presumption. Deep in their souls, Christians knew, as pagans did not, that "it matters not how you worship, but what you worship."[107] Staining an altar with blood was not *religio* but superstition, plain and simple. Demons should be paid no honours, no sacrifices, no dues. There was One God, and One God only—and so there could be only one *religio*.

What the seven sleepers had woken to was a world that accepted such logic as invincible. Emperors, charged as they were with the protection of the Roman people, and desperate for heavenly assistance, now turned instinctively to those men who could most plausibly claim access to the court of heaven: the bishops of the Catholic Church. In turn, the bishops, granted access to the earthly court of Constantinople, had been able to persuade a succession of emperors that there was nothing likelier to boost state security than the proper entrenchment of Nicaean orthodoxy. It was this potent combination of interests that had spelled ruin for the temple of Artemis: for in 391, the great warrior emperor Theodosius I, grandfather of Theodosius II, had officially forbidden all forms of sacrifice, and the veneration of even household idols.

Nor had that been the limit of his efforts in defence of the Catholic Church. Even more gratifying to the bishops, perhaps, had been his harrying of an enemy subtler, less obvious, and much lighter on their feet than the pagans. A decade before the banning of sacrifices, Theodosius had officially defined all those Christians who disputed the

Nicaean settlement as "demented and lunatic."[108] The bishops, then, in their ongoing campaign against heresy, had increasingly been able to take for granted their right of appeal to Caesar. "Help me to destroy the heretics, and I will help you to destroy the Persians."[109] Such was the rallying cry issued to Theodosius II by Nestorius, a brilliant Syrian theologian who in 428 had become Bishop of Constantinople. The bargain struck between emperor and Church could hardly have been spelled out more brutally; and indeed, there were those who thought Nestorius downright vulgar for drawing attention to it. Yet the alliance, in the final reckoning, was founded upon something nobler than mere cynical intolerance. Theodosius, after all, was a man of legendary piety; while Nestorius had been so famed for his holiness in his native Antioch that he had been specially imported to fill the capital's vacant bishopric. Both men yearned to see the pillars of heaven planted on the fallen earth; and each was convinced that God had called upon him, personally, to achieve it. Their great labour it was, emperor and bishop alike, to complete the heroic project initiated by Constantine at Nicaea: to fashion a single Christianity; to shape the first religion.

Granted, tensions always remained. Beyond the limits of the empire, in *Iranshahr*, Christians tended to seize every opportunity they could to demonstrate their independence of Constantinople, since any hint that they might be fifth-columnists would see, "instead of incense, the dust of their demolished churches ascending to the sky."[110] Even within the empire itself, in great cities such as Antioch, the leaders of the Church rarely felt much obligation to kowtow to orders from the capital. If emperors were intimidating figures, then so too were bishops. The aura of God's awful power always encircled them, and Constantinople was far away. The fashion for issuing stentorian pronouncements on the nature of Christ, honed by Nicaea and a host of councils since, was one that any bishop with a strong local power-base, not to mention a fondness for the sound of his own voice, was almost bound to indulge. In 451, a year after the death of Theodosius II, the largest oecumenical council that the Church had ever seen, attended by a full six hundred bishops, was held at Chalcedon, directly across the straits from the imperial palace, in a conscious effort to rein in this tendency. The new regime's aim—just as Constantine's had been at Nicaea—was to muzzle a taste for bickering that had come to threaten, in the opinion of the authorities, not only the unity of the Church but the very security of the Roman people.

At stake for the delegates, however, was no longer the relationship of the Son to the Father, an issue long since triumphantly resolved, but a no less awesome mystery: the identity of the Son Himself. How, Christians wanted to know, had His divine and human natures coexisted? Had they been wholly intermingled, like water and wine in a goblet, to constitute a *mone physis*—a "single nature"? Or had the two natures of Christ in fact co-existed within His earthly body as quite distinct entities, like water and oil? Had both His human and His divine essence experienced birth, suffering and death, or was it the most repugnant blasphemy to declare, as some bishops did, that God Himself "was crucified for us"?[111] Knotty questions—nor easily unpicked. The Council of Chalcedon, nevertheless, did its level best. A determinedly middle road was steered. Due weight was given to both the divine and the human elements of Christ: "the same truly God and truly man." This formula, devised by a bishop of Rome and graced with the approval of the emperor himself, struck the Christians of both the West and Constantinople as eminently reasonable—so much so that never again would they attempt to revise or reverse it.*

Elsewhere, though, there was consternation. By its opponents, Chalcedon was dismissed as—at best—a flaccid equivocation. Across the eastern provinces of the empire, and in Syria and Egypt especially, Christians committed to the belief that Christ's human nature had been blended indivisibly with the divine refused to be bound by the rulings of the council. Chalcedonians, in reciprocal scorn, labelled these

---

* It remains to this day, in the words of Diarmaid MacCulloch, "the standard measure for discussion of the person of Christ, in Churches otherwise as diverse as Greek, Romanian and Slavic Orthodox, Roman Catholics, Anglicans and mainstream Protestants" (p. 226).

dissidents "Monophysites"—a name intended and felt to be profoundly insulting.* Meanwhile, Christians from the opposite wing of the debate—those who believed it monstrous to imagine that God Himself might have been crucified, that God Himself might have died—felt no less bitterly betrayed by all the fine-spun prevarications of Chalcedon than did their Monophysite adversaries. Nestorius himself, had he not died a day before the arrival of his invitation to attend the council, would have been a prominent member of this faction. In an irony typical of the age, however, a couple of decades before Chalcedon, the man who had urged Theodosius to destroy the heretics had himself been convicted of heresy, disgraced and packed off into exile. He and his doctrines still had plenty of followers, though—Christians who felt that the erstwhile Bishop of Constantinople had been the epitome of orthodoxy. Many of them could be found in the famous schools of Edessa; but there were even more in Mesopotamia. In 489, when a Monophysite takeover of the Blessed City forced the closure of its university, the students and teachers simply decamped across the border. As one Mesopotamian bishop smugly put it, "Edessa went dark and Nisibis blazed with light."[112] The Christians of *Iranshahr*—implacable opponents of the Monophysites and contemptuous of Chalcedon—had soon lost any lingering trace of loyalty to Constantinople. In turn, the Christians of the West—Chalcedonians and Monophysites alike—dismissed the Mesopotamians as heretics and labelled them "Nestorians." Chalcedon, far from bringing unity, seemed to have riven the Church for good.

And certainly, as time went on, the rival positions hardened. The Chalcedonians, having seized the commanding heights of the Church's infrastructure and claimed the prized title of "orthodox," were in no mood to surrender their spoils. The Monophysites, never doubting for a moment that it was they who were truly the orthodox, proved equally

---

* Western historians today are much more sensitive to the potential offensiveness of the title than they used to be, but have struggled to come up with a convenient alternative. "Anti-Chalcedonian" is even more of a mouthful than "Monophysite."

intransigent: rather than accept the bishops foisted on them by Constantinople, they simply took to the countryside and preached their doctrines there. A succession of emperors, desperate to heal the breach, veered ineffectually between compromise and repression. When Anastasius daringly permitted a Monophysite phrase to be spoken in the capital's churches, the outraged citizenry responded by toppling statues of the emperor, burning down entire districts of the city, and parading the head of a decapitated Monophysite on a pole, to the catchy refrain of: "A conspirator against the Trinity!"[113] A few years later, when Justin purged the Church hierarchy in Syria of all those with Monophysite leanings, the exiled bishops positively revelled in their misfortunes, and infuriated Constantinople by posing stagily as martyrs.

As for Justinian—an emperor as forceful, energetic and egotistical as any in Roman history—he never doubted for a moment his ability to secure Christian unity. Following in the footsteps of Anastasius, he offered the Monophysites several dramatic concessions; like Julian, he was perfectly happy to depose an obdurate bishop or two and demand their silence if the situation required it. In addition, though, he unleashed a couple of tactics that neither of his predecessors had thought to deploy. The first of these, bred of Justinian's sublime conviction that he had a genius for theology, was to invite Monophysites to Constantinople and grace them personally with his reflections on the mysteries of faith. Although this strategy, to the emperor's own surprise, failed noticeably to shift the convictions of his guests, his self-assurance was barely dented by the disappointment. There lay another means to hand of seducing the Monophysites. Justinian, never a man to squander a potential advantage, and a political operator even when in the throes of his lust, could point to the fact that he had seen fit to take one of their number to his bed.

And not just any Monophysite. Even her bitterest critics—of whom there were many—grudgingly acknowledged that Theodora, consort and beloved of the emperor, was a woman of exceptional abilities. Shrewd, far-sighted and bold, she ranked, in the opinion of Justinian's cattier critics, as more of a man than her husband ever did.

Rumour had it that at the height of the deadly riots of 532, with Constantinople ablaze and Justinian twitchily contemplating flight, she stiffened the imperial backbone by declaring, with a magnificent show of haughtiness, that "purple makes for an excellent shroud."[114] Steel of this order, in a woman, was unsettling enough to the Roman elite; but even more so were the origins of the empress. Theodora, like an exotic bloom sustained by dung, had her roots, so it was darkly whispered, deep in filth. Dancer, actress and stand-up comic, she had also—long before puberty—been honing on slaves and the destitute a career even more scandalous. Her vagina, it was said, might just as well have been in her face; and, indeed, such was the use to which she put all three of her orifices that "she would often complain that she did not have orifices in her nipples as well."[115] The gang-bang had never been held that could wear her out. Most notorious of all had been her trademark floor-show, which had seen her lie on her back, have her genitals sprinkled with grain, and then wait for geese to pick the seeds off one by one with their beaks. Such were the talents, so her critics sneered, that had won for her the besotted devotion of the master of the world.

Yet, this sorely underestimated both husband and wife. Theodora had certainly been a whore: even her admirers admitted as much. What mattered to them, however, and to Justinian as well, was not her record of sin, but rather the radiant glory of her repentance. The one-time prostitute had emerged as a devout Monophysite, a committed student of famous theologians, a woman "more formidable in her understanding and sympathy toward the wronged than any individual ever."[116] Perhaps it was only natural that someone who had endured the pecking of geese at her private parts for public amusement should have empathised with the downtrodden. Whatever had prompted her own personal reformation, though, Theodora undoubtedly provided Justinian with a living, breathing model of all his noblest hopes for the Roman state. Above the gates of the Chalke, the great entrance to the imperial palace, there stretched a magnificent mosaic of Justinian and Theodora together, "both of them appearing to rejoice and celebrate festivals of victory."[117] The message proclaimed by such an image, even if Justinian disdained to spell it out openly, was nevertheless something more than merely subliminal. Stern guardian of orthodoxy though he was, he did not deny to his wife the title of Christian, too. For all the seeming chasm of difference between Chalcedonians and Monophysites, it did not, in the opinion of Justinian himself, threaten the blessings that his empire might expect to receive as its due reward from God. In the ultimate reckoning, what united the Christian people was more significant than what kept them apart.

Most Monophysites—and Nestorians too—shared this view. Despite the festering bitterness of their disputes, none of them truly doubted that they all belonged to the same religion: that there was genuinely such a thing as *Christianismos*. Failure Chalcedon might have been—but not Nicaea. Two hundred years on from the great council, the only Arian churches were in the West: for there they could enjoy the patronage of barbarians who, of course, knew little better. And it was not only Arians who had been largely scoured from the Christian heartlands. The orthodoxies of Nicaea—that God was a Trinity; that the Son was equal to the Father; that Jesus had been more than merely man—were now so entrenched that few Christians were even aware of just how contested these doctrines had once been.

In 367, some four decades after the first formulation of the Nicaean Creed, a famously authoritarian bishop by the name of Athanasius had written to the churches under his jurisdiction. In these letters, he had prescribed the twenty-seven books that henceforward were to be considered as constituting the "New Testament." The list had soon become canonical wherever Nicaea was accepted. Simultaneously, Athanasius had commanded that all gospels not included in his canon, and all letters falsely ascribed to the apostles, should be rooted out and destroyed. On this matter too, his guidelines had been widely followed: in due course, the gospels of Basilides, Marcion and every other Gnostic had been consigned to oblivion. Memories of these other Christians and their doctrines had inevitably faded. By the time of Justinian, a whole new history for the faith had come to be written.

There was simply no recollection, in the history that the Church had succeeded in manufacturing for itself, of its authentic origins and evolution. Right from the beginning, most Christians now took for granted there had only ever been the one Christianity: a religion that was orthodox, catholic and Nicaean.

And it was this same presumption—that the essence of *Christianismos* was something both eternal and unchanging—which gave to Justinian's revolution a distinctive, not to say unsettling, aura of paradox. "This was the commission entrusted to the Emperor by God: to watch over the whole Roman Empire and, so far as was possible, to refashion it."[118] The tone of veiled uncertainty—even nervousness—was telling. Was Justinian properly to be judged as a noble burnisher of ancient verities or as that most disturbing and dangerous of figures, a revolutionary? The question haunted his every move. If his legal reforms, which had served to forge the venerable laws of the Roman people into something novel and intimidating, were palpably shadowed by ambiguity, then so too was an even more awesome project: the modelling of his earthly realm upon the monarchy of the heavens. This, of course, had been the stated goal of a whole succession of emperors since the time of Constantine; but Justinian pursued it with a brutality and literal-mindedness quite without precedent. The emperor was not, by nature, a vicious man; but neither, to put it mildly, was he lacking in self-assurance. Not for him the carefully modulated ambivalence of his predecessors.

"It is our belief," so Theodosius II had declared back in 423, "that pagans no longer exist."[119] The reality, as suggested by the battery of laws that Theodosius himself had continued to promulgate against paganism long after delivering this confident pronouncement, was rather different. "Ask no questions, hear no evil": such had typically been the approach adopted by the imperial authorities towards those who persisted in the worship of the ancient gods. This turning of a blind eye had meant that peasants, even after baptism, could still dance in honour of Artemis and persist in primordial rituals; scholars still base their writings on antique pagan models; and philosophers still pursue a quest for wisdom—*sophia*—that did not have as its ultimate object a knowledge of Christ. Abominations all. Justinian understood, as the pagans in their purblind folly did not, that there existed only the one true wisdom: the "Holy Wisdom"—*Hagia Sophia*—of God. What cult—what philosophy—could remotely compare for timelessness with that? Each one was the merest dust upon the breath of the Holy Spirit. Crushing them for good would allow the world to return to the true, the only, the primal religion. This, in Justinian's devout opinion, was no revolution but the ultimate in renewal.

And so it was, almost two hundred years after a pagan emperor had set himself to uproot the Church, that a Christian Caesar moved to extirpate what remained of paganism, and to rout the demons for good. In the highlands beyond Ephesus, where it was reported that Artemis, a terrifying hag as tall as ten men, still stalked the unwary, missionaries were commissioned to redeem the peasantry from their doltish ignorance of Christ—and with such success that a single bishop reportedly secured a full seventy thousand souls. Meanwhile, in the capital itself, agents were busy sniffing out any hint of demon worship in public life. Ferocious laws were passed against the practice. All Christians found guilty of idolatry were to be put to death, while pagans and heretics were to be granted three months' grace—after which, if they had not converted, they were to be banned from teaching or holding public office, and rendered utterly destitute. Those who sought to escape baptism by committing suicide could expect their corpses to be treated like those of dead dogs. "For killing, in the opinion of Justinian, was hardly to be ranked as murder, if those who died did not share his beliefs."[120]

It did not take long for the ripples of persecution to spread outwards from Constantinople. In 529, news of the emperor's legislation reached the one city that, more than any other, had remained most inveterately addicted to the pagans' damnable teachings and fantasies. To what, after all, did the very name "Athens" bear witness, if not the primordial hold upon her of a demon? The great temple of Pallas Athena, the Parthenon, had long since been emptied of its colossal idol of the goddess, and safely converted into a church; but there remained, in the shadow of the Acropolis, schools where the doctrines of Plato and Pythagoras continued to be taught. Not for long, however. It needed no great training in philosophy to appreciate what Justinian's decrees might mean for even the most eminent of pagan intellectuals. The choices that lay before them could hardly have been any starker: conversion, exile or death. The philosophers—to whom martyrdom appeared no less Christian a fate than baptism—opted for retreat. In 530 or 531,[121] they fled Athens and brought down the curtain on a thousand years of philosophy in the city. Dreading to remain any-where within the reach of Justinian, they threw themselves on the mercy of his only genuine rival: the *Shahanshah*. Khusrow, delighted by the propaganda coup that this represented, duly offered the exiled philosophers an ostentatious welcome. Ctesiphon, however, would prove no second Athens. Barely a year into their exile there, the philosophers—afflicted with crippling homesickness—begged their new patron for permission to leave. Khusrow graciously agreed and even secured an assurance from Justinian that they would be allowed to live in peace back in their homeland, "without being compelled to alter their traditional beliefs or to accept any view which did not coin-cide with them."[122] What happened to the philosophers after that, however, is a mystery. Some have suggested that the philosophers did return to their homeland, where they lived in peaceful obscurity; others claim that they settled in that stronghold of pagan exception-alism, Harran.[123] Wherever they ended up, though, one thing is certain: there was to be no resurrection of philosophy in Athens.

"Has not God made foolish the wisdom of the world?" So Paul, berating the Athenians for their idolatry, had asked.[124] Some five cen-turies later, there were few who could any longer doubt the answer. In 532, even as the Bishop of Athens was preparing to move into a villa recently vacated by the head of the school founded by Plato, Justinian seized the perfect opportunity to ram home the moral.[125] The deadly firestorm of rioting in the heart of Constantinople had left churches as well as bath-houses in ruins. The gravest loss of all had stood just to the north of the Augustaion: the Cathedral of the Holy Wisdom—

Hagia Sophia. Work to replace it began a mere forty-five days after its destruction; but Justinian had in mind something more, very much more, than mere slavish reproduction. The wisdom of God was to be made manifest in the most daring, spectacular, and colossal vaulted interior that had ever been built. A dome, in majesty "like the very firmament that rests upon the air,"[126] would be raised where previously there had been nothing but a gabled roof. Whether viewed from afar—looming vastly above the columns and towers of the Golden City, "so that it seems of a height to match the sky"[127]—or from within—dazzling the eye with the radiance of its fittings, "almost like a second sun"[128]—a new and spectacular edifice was to demonstrate to the Christian people the truth to which Justinian had dedicated his entire life: that heaven could indeed be built on earth.

It took less than six years to complete the Church of Hagia Sophia. When the triumphant Justinian, amid the gusting of incense, the clanging of bells, and the blazing of gold, presided over the dedication on 27 December 537, he knew himself in the presence of an authentic miracle. To stand beneath the great dome of Hagia Sophia was to know that God's wisdom had descended on the fallen earth indeed. The agents of pagan folly had been routed. Order had prevailed over chaos. The empire of the Roman people, once and for all, had been brought to Christ.

But what of those beyond the borders of the empire? Here too, in the minds of Justinian and his advisers, there was cause for optimism. *Religio*—although a Latin word, and a concept that had been refined to a formidable degree of steeliness under the supervision of a whole succession of Caesars—was certainly not for Romans alone. The claims of "religion"—as Christians had come to define it—were global to a degree that far exceeded those of even the most ambitious emperor. Barbarians who had always stood proof against the might of the legions might certainly be brought to Christ. There was nothing, after all, to stop the Gospel from being preached to the outermost limits of the world. Then, that once achieved, the dome of the heavens would serve to make of the entire earth one immense and universal Hagia Sophia.

That, at any rate—in the court of Justinian—was the hope.

4

THE CHILDREN OF ABRAHAM

Making the Desert Bloom

Hagia Sophia was not, nor intended to be, a modest building: "Every structure there has ever been," so one enthusiast gushed, "must cower before it."[1] It was also, of course, the duty of mortals to cower before the god who was glorified there, and whose cross, fashioned out of brilliant gold, blazed from the monumental dome of the cathedral, to the awe and wonder of the worshippers far below. "*Pantokrator*," the Romans of Constantinople termed Christ: "The Ruler of All." In Hagia Sophia, and in churches across the Greek world, He was imagined as presiding over a dominion without limits, surrounded by an exquisitely graded hierarchy of angels and saints, unfathomably distant from the indignities of human existence. Precisely the kind of deity, in short, to appeal to Justinian.

But there were ways too of approaching Christ that did not require the sumptuousness of gold and purple. In 527, five years before work began on Hagia Sophia, a small boy named Simeon had trotted through the bazaars and shanty-towns of Antioch, out through the olive groves that stretched southwards of the city, and up the slopes of a nearby mountain. Its rugged heights were no place for a child, nor for anyone with a care for comfort. The wilderness was a realm of danger: the haunt of bandits, lions and bears. To settle amid its crags was to abandon all that made for civilisation, to become a *monachos*, or "one who lives alone." Yet the fact was, of course, as the Christian people well understood, that no man was ever truly alone—no, nor woman either. Demons, like flies around a butcher's stall, swarmed wherever there rose the stench of sin; angels, serried in fiery ranks, served as the legions of God. Veiled from the gaze of fallen humanity, they blazed no less brilliantly for that. Only a *monachos*—a "monk"—could hope to glimpse them. Those men and women who chose to abandon the perfumed filth of human company, to fix their gaze upon the heavens, to devote themselves exclusively to the service of God, might hope to become suffused with the fire of the Holy Spirit, flesh and bone though they were: "If you will, you can become all flame."[2]

It took more than withdrawal from the world for a man or woman to attain this happy condition, however. One monk, asked how salvation could be attained, promptly stripped stark naked and raised his hands to the sky. "So should the monk be," he declared. "Denuded of all things, and crucified."[3] But in a world where martyrdom was no longer an option, what precisely did it mean to be "crucified"? Here was a question fit to stimulate some truly spectacular feats of self-abnegation. Most monks were content to submit themselves to the communal discipline of a *mone*—a "monastery." They would "strip for the contest, spending their days in physical toil and their nights without sleep in giving praise to the Lord."[4] Some, however, looking to go the extra mile, might make a point of mixing ashes into their gruel, or subsisting entirely on waste scraped off the soles of sandals, or living like cattle, chained to cowsheds, and feeding on grass. One particularly creative act of renunciation saw a woman confine herself to a cell with a spectacular riverside view, and then, for the remainder of her life, refuse even once to look out through the window. It required suffering as well as solitude to become a true athlete of God.

Yet when it came to the training—*ascesis*—required to attain a truly miraculous pinnacle of holiness, there were few who would have denied the palm to the "ascetics" of Syria. Spectacular feats of self-mortification had long been a speciality of the region. One particularly venerable tradition had seen pagans climb pillars—*styloi*—and stay there for a week at a time, "communing with the gods on high."[5] The bathing of Syria in the light of Christ, even though it had scoured the demons from their temples, had not banished the close association between pillars and access to the supernatural. In around AD 430, a whole century before the young Simeon of Antioch abandoned his home town, another Simeon—a shepherd—had climbed a sixty-foot column on the edge of the Syrian desert. There he had remained, precariously balanced, not for a week, but for thirty long years, until in due course his soul had been gathered up to heaven. The challenge aimed at the demons by this unprecedented feat had been quite deliberate. Simeon's prodigious austerities had easily eclipsed anything achieved by the pagans. To a people only recently deprived of their ancient gods, the withered, worm-infested and quite fabulously hairy body of the "stylite" had served as an awesome manifestation of the power of their new deity.* Reports of the miracles achieved by Simeon's prayers had spread as far afield as Ethiopia and Britain. In Rome, his adoring fans had taken to pinning pictures of his pillar to their doorposts. By the time of his death, he had become, quite simply, the most famous man in the world.

The lesson taught by a thoroughbred stylite could hardly have been more emphatic. Sumptuously though great cities might be adorned by monuments to Christ, it was in the wilds that God was likeliest to be heard. Even a child, if sufficiently precocious, might look to part the veil that obscured the realm of the angels and become a vessel for the transfiguring power of the heavens. This was why, almost seven decades on from the death of his illustrious namesake, the young boy named Simeon abandoned his home in Antioch and headed into the wilderness. His aim too was to spend what remained of his life on top of a pillar. Heavenly approval of this youthful ambition was manifest;

---

* Long after Simeon's death, it was his hairiness which particularly enabled people to recognise him when he appeared to them in visions.

only a short while before Simeon's arrival on the mountain, a local monk had been granted a spectacular vision of "a child dressed all in white, and a glowing column, both of them whirling around in the sky."[6] Sure enough, when the boy finally mounted his pillar, after a whole year of heavy-duty training, he was formidably steeled. Not even the demons tugging on his arms, not even the spread of ulcers on his legs, could distract him from his course. Day and night, in rain and blazing sunshine, he kept up his prayers. The infant ascetic was seven years old.

Time passed. As childhood turned to puberty, and puberty to adulthood, and still the demons could not tempt Simeon down from his pillar, his reward was often to see "a great mass of cloud like a carpet of brilliant purple" rolled out before him.[7] This was the dimension of the celestial; and sure enough, angels would often appear to the saint, sometimes flanking Christ Himself, sometimes holding a snow-white parchment on which they would write the names of all those mentioned in Simeon's prayers in blazing letters of gold. As reports of these visions spread, crowds began to mass before his pillar. Many were the miracles performed by the saint, "more numerous than the grains of sand in the sea."[8] The dumb and the blind were healed, as too were a man afflicted by unfeasibly large testicles, "like a pair of clay jars,"[9] and another who suffered from chronic constipation, the consequence of "a demon camped out in his colon."[10] Above all, though, Simeon offered blessings to those who could normally expect to receive none: lepers, whores and children, always children. By contrast, towards the mighty, he was unbendingly stern—as well he might have been, for the rich of Antioch, even by the standards of the time, were notorious for their arrogance and cruelty.

Far from resenting this, however, the local elite took great pride in Simeon. As his fame spread, so a day-trip up the side of the mountain to gawp at him silhouetted on the summit became the height of chic. Simeon, who had fled Antioch for the wilderness, discovered that Antioch had followed him. The opportunity to glimpse the authentic radiance of holiness in the stylite's emaciated and ragged form was simply too precious to waste, even for the very grandest. And perhaps this was just as well: for tourist attractions, after all, did not come cheap. Pilgrims, whether shuffling up the mountainside on leprous stumps or borne in gold-fringed palanquins, needed to be watered, fed, and housed. Inexorably, the longer that Simeon remained on his pillar, the more the rocks that had once surrounded it came to be replaced by impeccably well-dressed marble. The very rage with which the saint berated the rich served only to quicken the flow of gifts to his shrine. This might have appeared a paradox; but it was not. Nothing quite like power, after all, to make the nostrils of the mighty flare; and the power of the divine, the power that made of Simeon a veritable lightning rod of the supernatural, was like nothing else on earth.

Even in far-off Constantinople, where there had always been a tendency to dismiss Syrians as morbid and prone to hysteria, a bona fide stylite had fast become a must-have accessory. As early as 460, a mere year after the death of the original Simeon, one of his disciples had climbed a pillar just outside the capital. There he had remained for the next three decades, lecturing heretics on their duty to submit to the Council of Chalcedon and causing anyone who might jeer at him to explode. A succession of emperors had revelled in his austerities, journeying to the pillar to gawp at his sores "and perpetually boasting of the Saint, and showing him off to all."[11] Nothing but the best for Constantinople; just as Constantine had beautified his capital with the plundered statues of pagan gods, his heirs looked to endow the city with the potent mystique of the Syrian ascetics. Indeed, one emperor's agents had gone so far as to pilfer a few portions of the elder Simeon's corpse from Antioch, where the saint's relics were jealously guarded as the city's most precious treasure. Even those reminders of the stylite that could not be transported to Constantinople had been ostentatiously graced with the marks of an emperor's favour: for the once lonely pillar on which he had stood, halfway to the sky, had ended up flanked by marble hallways and covered by a colossal dome. The precious wellsprings of holiness, even when they existed on the empire's frontiers, right on the margins of the desert, were far too precious not to be stamped as imperial.

Nevertheless, there was, in the acknowledgement by Constantinople that certain locations might rank as hallowed ground, just the hint of defeat. The "New Rome," as its title suggested, had been founded on the presumption that the sacred was readily transferable. Almighty God, who had created the heavens and the entire earth, was not to be pinned down for ever to a single spot. All very well for pagans to imagine that groves, or springs, or rocks might be sacred, and travel on pilgrimage to grovel before them; but Christians were supposed to know better. The charge of the supernatural properly attached itself, not to places but to relics. Of these, Constantinople could boast a quite astounding abundance: for the reach of the emperor was long and grasping, as the guardians of Simeon had discovered to their cost. The heads of prophets, the bodies of apostles, the limbs of martyrs: the capital had bagged them all. Indeed, Constantinople's array of relics was so incomparable that it lent her precisely what her rulers had always most craved for their capital: the authentic aura of a holy city. Yet, as the crowds who continued to cluster around the elder Simeon's empty pillar suggested, there were some things that could not be imported. The same pilgrim who travelled to Constantinople or Antioch to pray before the saint's relics might nevertheless still wish to rub the stone that had once borne the stylite's stinking feet. Foul-smelling though the ascetics of Syria notoriously were, yet in the air that had once been breathed by Simeon there hung, so many Christians believed, a lingering perfume-trace of paradise.

And there were places on the fallen earth that needed no stylites to sanctify them: places that had been touched not by saints but by the presence of God Himself. While human flesh, whether on the tops of pillars or in desert cells, might still become interfused with the Holy Spirit, it had once been possible, back in the mists of time, for men to talk directly with the Almighty. Abraham, of course, was the proof of that: a man graced with the promise that he would become a father of many nations. To his wife, Sarah, though barren and old at the time,

God had granted a son; and that son, Isaac, fathered in turn a son named Jacob. One night, this same Jacob met a mysterious stranger by a ford and wrestled with him "until the breaking of the day." When dawn came and the man asked to be released, Jacob demanded a blessing from him in return; and the stranger, with studied ambiguity, answered, "Your name shall no more be called Jacob, but Israel, for you have striven with God and with men, and have prevailed." And Jacob, who was now called Israel, found himself struck by a sudden realisation: "I have seen God face to face!"[12] Certainly, whoever the stranger might truly have been, his blessing would prove a momentous one. Twelve sons Jacob would father in all—the Children of Israel. These then travelled from Canaan to Egypt, where they and their descendants, gathered into tribes, proved themselves astoundingly fecund, "so that the land was filled with them."[13] Ultimately, so prolifically did the twelve tribes of Israel breed that Pharaoh, the King of Egypt, grew alarmed; and so he ordered them enslaved, "and made their lives bitter with hard service."[14] God, however, had not forgotten His promise to Abraham. As the instrument of His Chosen People's salvation, He selected a man named Moses, a descendant of Israel who had been brought up in high privilege as an Egyptian—the foster-son of Pharaoh's daughter, no less. Then, one day, seeing one of his countrymen under the lash, Moses struck the overseer down dead, and fled into the desert. There, while working as a shepherd, he came across a bush that was on fire: "And he looked, and lo, the bush was burning, yet it was not consumed."[15] The voice of God was in the fire; and it told Moses to return to Egypt and to demand of Pharaoh that he let the Children of Israel go. For, as the Almighty explained, "I have seen the affliction of my people who are in Egypt, and have heard their cry because of their taskmasters; I know their sufferings, and I have come down to deliver them out of the hand of the Egyptians, and to bring them up out of that land to a good and broad land, a land flowing with milk and honey."[16]

Set as this episode was back in the distant reaches of time, and in the wilds of a tenantless desert, it might have been thought hardly the kind to have left much behind in the way of proofs. Christians, however, knew better. The echoes of the voice of God could never truly fade. When, in the fourth century AD, monks ventured into the barren wilderness that stretched to the east of Egypt, they arrived in due course at a narrow valley beneath the granite crags of two steepling mountains. They had not hesitated to identify this spot, from its palpable holiness, as the very place where Moses had seen the burn-ing bush. Not only that, but they even discovered, in a yet further and clinching miracle, the bush itself, "still alive and putting out shoots."[17] The monks, confident that they were walking across rocks trodden by Moses, duly installed themselves in caves at the head of the valley. Over time, they added a small church, complete with a garden in which the bush itself, naturally enough, enjoyed pride of place. Two centuries later, with Justinian on the throne, the renown of the bleak and distant valley was secure across the Christian world. The emperor himself, nobly resisting the temptation to have the holy bush dug up and carted off to Constantinople, opted instead to stamp his mark on the desert by restoring and enlarging the monastery. In addition, at the base of the mountain, he built "a very strong fortress, and estab-lished there a considerable garrison of troops."[18] A touch of Roman power had been brought to the depths of the desert.

The ostensible justification given for this show of strength was the need to intimidate bandits. The walling of the bush served a further purpose, though: no one could see the fortifications and doubt that the hallowed earth enclosed within them was indeed impregnably Christian. This mattered: for Christians were not alone in laying claim to Moses as their own. The Children of Israel, whom the great prophet, in obedience to God's instructions, had redeemed from slav-ery and led from Egypt, amid the thundering of flame-lit wonders, signs and deadly plagues, still had their descendants in the present: none other than the Jews. To the rabbis, Moses was both the foun-tainhead and the model of all their learning: the ultimate rabbi. Great though his achievement had been in securing the *exodus*, or "emigra-tion," of his people, even that had not been his most awesome feat.

Leading the freed slaves through the desert to the east of Egypt, he had arrived at a mountain named Sinai; and "on the morning of the third day there were thunders and lightnings, and a thick cloud upon the mountain, and a very loud trumpet blast, so that all the people who were in the camp trembled."[19] Nothing daunted, Moses had vanished into the fiery depths of the cloud; and there, high on the peak of Sinai, he had spoken again with God, "face to face."[20] The fruit of this conversation was the Torah itself. Portions of it were inscribed on tablets of clay and placed in a transportable chest named an "Ark," which then accompanied and guided the Children of Israel on their journey through the desert. Other portions, though, were not written down, but instead kept hidden by Moses and taught exclusively to Joshua, his favourite pupil. This, at any rate, was what the rabbis taught—and as proof, they could point to the Talmud, which was, in their opinion, nothing less than the final revelation of the Torah that Moses had received on Mount Sinai, and which had been handed down, via assorted elders, prophets and scholars, directly to themselves.

Should Justinian ever have had this notion of a secret Jewish wisdom brought to his attention, he would doubtless have snorted with derision. Yet, he would also surely have been confirmed in his sense of just how urgent was the need to identify Moses, and all the prophets of the Old Testament, with his own faith. Above the valley where God had spoken from the burning bush there rose a particularly barren peak. The monks who lived in its shadow had long since decided that this was none other than Mount Sinai itself. The fort built at its foot ensured that no one could approach its summit without the knowledge of the monks themselves. Just in case there were any who might still miss the implications of this, they could always visit the church built by Justinian and admire a mosaic of the prophet pointing in awe at Christ. "On the mountain of the Father," as an early enthusiast for the monks of Sinai exulted, "there stands a monument to the Son."[21] Moses was best commemorated not as a Jew, let alone as a rabbi, but as a Christian.

It was this that underpinned the monks' claim to the scene of the prophet's greatest triumph; just as it also gave to the universal Church its tenant's stake in an even more precious prize. Moses himself had never made it to Canaan, the land that God had promised to Abraham; but the Children of Israel, after forty years of aimless wandering in the desert, had swept down upon their birthright to take possession of the land itself, and all its milk and honey. It was the story of what had happened next that constituted the greater part of both the Jewish and the Christian scriptures: the "Books"—or *Biblia*, in Greek. Unlike Mount Sinai, which it had required a band of intrepid monks to track down and identify, many locations with a starring role in the "Bible" had never been lost. Take, for example, Jericho, the first Canaanite city to be captured by the Children of Israel, after Joshua, their leader in succession to Moses, had ordered them to blow their trumpets and bring the walls tumbling down. Then there was Bethlehem, the birthplace of David, a shepherd boy who, in addition to rising to rule as king over all the tribes of Israel, had composed some of the most haunting passages in the Bible: songs and poems known as "psalms." Most luminously of all, there stood Jerusalem, a city captured by David to serve him as his capital, and which had remained the stronghold of his dynasty until the calamitous descent upon Judah of the King of Babylon.

Yet all this, so Christians knew, had been only the opening acts of an ongoing drama. The Old Testament had been succeeded by the New, and ground trodden by Abraham, Joshua and David had been hallowed a second time by the footsteps of Christ Himself. In Jericho, He had healed a blind man, and in Bethlehem He had been born in a manger, and in Jerusalem He had been crucified and buried, and after three days had risen from the dead, and then, from the Mount of Olives, just outside the city, ascended to the heavens. Well, then, might Christians have felt proprietorial towards the scene of such cosmos-shaking events. As the self-designated heirs of Abraham and as the followers of Christ, they could feel themselves to have a double claim on it, after all. The land promised to God's people was theirs, triumphantly theirs: a Holy Land.

Admittedly, there were many Christians, anxious about "restricting to a narrow strip of earth Him whom the heavens cannot contain," who remained profoundly uncomfortable with this notion. The presence of God, so they sternly reminded the faithful, might be experienced in even the remotest, the most barbarous of lands: "Access to the courts of heaven is as easy from Britain as it is from Jerusalem."[22] Nevertheless, it is telling that the monk who issued this admonition—a translator of the Bible originally from the Balkans by the name of Jerome—did so from a cell outside Bethlehem. The year was 395, and already, as exemplified by Jerome's own presence in the Holy Land, something unprecedented was afoot. Never before in history had so many pilgrims, from such a wide variety of starting-points, travelled such gruelling distances to the same destinations. Christians, unlike pagans, did not limit themselves to visiting their native shrines. Instead, from the moment when Constantine's conversion had rendered the Holy Land safe for them to visit, a steady stream of Christian tourists had begun to head there from every corner of the Roman world. Pre-eminent among these had been the emperor's own mother, Helena, who had set the trend for later pilgrims by virtue of being female, fabulously wealthy and obsessed with collecting relics. She herself, as befitted her imperial rank, had headed straight for Jerusalem, where she had scooped the most glamorous trophy of all: the very cross and nails used in Jesus's crucifixion. But this sensational find represented only a starting point: for it had not taken locals long to wake up to the opportunities that might be provided them by the sudden arrival in their neighbourhood of a well-heeled Christian lady. Boom time for tour guides; and especially for those who knew where the bones of an Old Testament prophet might be uncovered, or perhaps an exercise book used by the infant Christ, or a robe once worn by the Virgin. The consequence of all this treasure-hunting had been not merely to fill the voracious reliquaries of Constantinople to bursting, but also to provide visitors to the Holy Land with an ever more impressive list of must-see destinations. After all, while a relic could be packed off easily enough to the capital, the same was hardly true of the site of its discovery. Once again, it was Helena who had most trail-blazingly demonstrated the implications of this. Rooting around in the foundations of a pagan temple after the True Cross, she had uncovered the sepulchre of Christ, no less: a thrilling example of just how spectacular the fruits of archaeology in the Holy Land might be. Two centuries later, with the seam of top-grade relics long since exhausted, there was barely an episode in the Bible that had not been identified with some specific pile of stones or patch of dust. It was hardly surprising, then, that pilgrims from every corner of the Christian world should have flocked to tour a landscape so imbued with the numinous. What had once been a trickle of visitors had swollen to become a flood. Their appearance in the Holy Land marked the arrival of a revolutionary new notion—that a specific place might be holy to peoples everywhere, no matter their place of birth.

And there were many Christians who came to the Holy Land not merely as visitors, but as settlers. Even Jerome, despite his occasionally sniffy attitude towards the local tourist industry, rejoiced in the multicultural character of Christian life there, and saw in it the fulfilment of God's primordial promise: "What were His first words to Abraham? Go out, He says, from your land and from your kindred, and go to the land I will show you."[23] While Constantinople, "the second Jerusalem,"[24] was ranked by Christians as the capital of the world, Jerusalem herself was prized as its centre. To walk the winding streets of the Holy City was to see people from every corner of the empire and beyond. In distant Sinai the monastery's leaders were expected to be "learned in Latin, Greek, Syriac, Egyptian and Persian"[25]—but in Jerusalem Gauls, Armenians and Indians might need translators, too. Some of them might be lepers, some aristocrats, some scholars. Even a bona fide empress—Eudocia, the wife of Theodosius II—moved to the Holy City for a couple of decades in the middle of the fifth century. Nowhere else in the empire, with the possible exception of Constantinople itself, was more thoroughgoingly cosmopolitan. Yet if Jerusalem was a city of immigrants, it hardly ranked as multi-faith. Few who lived there were immune to the suggestive power of a place that had witnessed the passion of Christ. A public reading from a gospel might be all it took to reduce them to sudden tears, displays of grief that would then ripple through the crowded streets, filling the colonnades and squares with wails and sobs. Certainly, those who lived in Jerusalem, and especially those who had moved there, had no doubt that they were better Christians for it. The sheer quality of the city's virgins, "like fair flowers or priceless gems,"[26] was proof of that. Some, however, went further. By the sixth century, it had become a popular notion among the monks of Jerusalem, and of the Holy Land generally, that the rest of the faithful owed them a special debt of gratitude. Athletes of Christ, they served Him too as His particular bodyguards: "For, it is we, the inhabitants of this Holy Land, who keep it invulnerable and inviolable."[27]

Perhaps—but not exclusively so. Jerusalem, centre of the world though it may have been, and object of universal Christian devotion, was also, as it had been for five centuries and more, a possession of the Caesars—a city in a province named Palestine. It was hardly to be expected, then, that its Christian rulers would neglect the defences of such an incomparable jewel. Sure enough, a century or so after the conversion of Constantine, a great ring of walls was built to gird the Holy City. Yet the surest defences, it went without saying, were those raised not against mortal adversaries, but against supernatural foes. Jerusalem, which had once been just as pagan a city as Ephesus or Athens, filthy with idols and the smoke of sacrifices, had been systematically scoured clean of the occupying demons. In place of their temples, a great host of churches had risen. The process of renovation seemed a perpetual one. For as long as anyone living in Jerusalem could remember, the blows of hammers and chisels had provided perpetual accompaniments to the clanging of bells and the chanting of hymns. Justinian, predictably, ordered a new church commissioned by Anastasius to be completed in a particularly overweening style: so massive did it end up that entire streets had to be

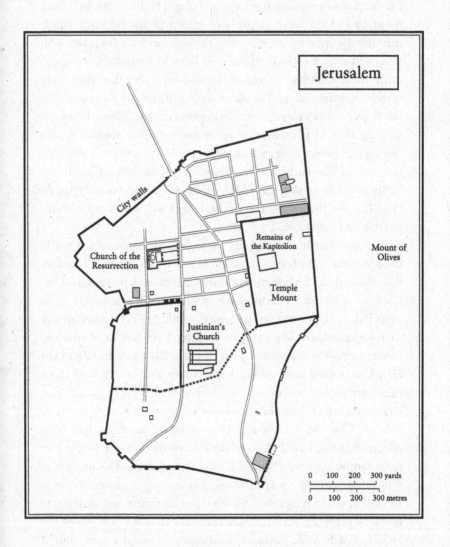

Jerusalem

City walls

Church of the
Resurrection

Remains of
the Kapitolion

Temple
Mount

Mount of
Olives

Justinian's
Church

| 0 | 100 | 200 | 300 yards |
| 0 | 100 | 200 | 300 metres |

demolished before the blocks used in its construction could be transported to the site.

Yet, not even Justinian could hope to rival the holiest and most precious monument founded in Jerusalem by a Christian emperor. Helena, in addition to uncovering the sepulchre of Christ, had excavated the rock of Golgotha—the "Place of the Skull"—where He had suffered death. Although tomb and excavation-ground alike had been buried for centuries beneath a shrine to a particularly noxious demon, there could be no doubting the identification: for Helena had been shown the site by an angel in a dream.* In 326, her son ordered a great domed church to be built over the site of Christ's tomb, and nine years later it was consecrated: the Church of the Resurrection. Next to it, over the site of the crucifixion, another church was built. Together, these two edifices—pairing, as they did, the sites where Christ had died and then risen from the dead—constituted the absolute centre of the centre of the world: a single plot of earth around which the order of the cosmos, and time itself, revolved. Beneath a fissure in the rock of Golgotha, so Christians confidently believed, lay the tomb of Adam—the first man of all to suffer death. Abraham too, in obedience to a command from God that he should sacrifice Isaac, his beloved son, had journeyed to the same identical spot. But it had all been a test; and Abraham, even as he was raising his knife to strike Isaac where he lay bound upon an altar of stone, had been halted by an angel, who had provided him instead with a ram caught in a thicket. An unmistakable foreshadowing of what was to come: for aeons later, of course, it was not a ram that had been slain upon Golgotha, but the

---

* What is today known as the Church of the Holy Sepulchre was rebuilt in the eleventh century after the original was destroyed by a messianic Egyptian Caliph, and it now contains the rock of Golgotha as well as the tomb of Christ. Whether either of these sites is authentically what Christian tradition has for so long presumed them to be is much debated. Ironically, the probability is that Helena's excavations, and her son's subsequent building works, served to obliterate memories that had been preserved by local Christians of the original sites.

Son of God Himself. Who, then, could doubt that there was to be traced, in this awesome patterning of mysteries, the guiding hand of the Almighty? To stand before the rock of Golgotha, and to see there as well the altar on which Abraham had placed Isaac, and the tomb of the first man to die, was to know that there were contained many mirrors in the order of time: a truth that boded well for the future. A Christian Jerusalem at the heart of a Christian empire: here, surely, was the certain evidence of an order destined to endure until the end of things?

No God but One

Such was the sheer number of pilgrims who travelled from across the world to the Holy City that at times it appeared in danger of bursting at the seams. In 516, when a great army of ascetics descended upon Jerusalem, in a particularly rowdy demonstration of support for Chalcedon, ten thousand of them barged into a single church. A few years later, Justinian, looking to raise a monument proportionate to his self-regard, was obliged to extend the ridge on which his new church was being built, so that its foundations ended up "partly on solid rock and partly on air."[28] Space was running out. Jerusalem, which even in the off-season had some eighty thousand inhabitants, was full to overflowing.

Yet, one part of the city—the most prominent of all—remained undeveloped. South of the Church of the Resurrection, beyond the multitude of golden crosses rising triumphantly above the crowded streets, there loomed a great, flat expanse of rubble-strewn and garbage-piled rock. Evidence, perhaps, that the site was of no great significance? Quite the opposite. The rock was the very spot commemorated by ancient prophets as "the mountain of the house," a haunting phrase that Jerome, in his Latin version of the Bible, had chosen to translate as Mons Templi—"Temple Mount."[29] In doing so, he had commemorated the most famous building ever raised in the city: a temple fashioned back in the mists of time by Solomon, the wise and fabulously wealthy son of King David, to serve Almighty God as His earthly house. Here, for anyone with a taste for church-building, was the obvious model to beat: Justinian himself, entering Hagia Sophia, was said to have cried out in triumph, "Solomon, I have vanquished you!"[30] The Temple itself, though, had long since been obliterated: for in 586 BC, after some four hundred years of existence, all its gold and cedar-wood had gone up in flames, together with the rest of Jerusalem, when the King of Babylon had stormed the city. True, the return of the Jews from their exile in Mesopotamia had seen them build a second, and ultimately even more imposing, Temple; but this too, in AD 70, had been put to the torch, after the Jews, resolved to throw off Roman rule, had risen in revolt and been comprehensively flattened for their pains. Roughly sixty years later, another, even more desperate, rebellion had resulted in an even more desperate defeat. The Promised Land was left a charnel-house. The Roman authorities, resolved to abolish the wearying cycle of insurgency and repression once and for all, promulgated a new set of title-deeds. The Jewish homeland became, by imperial fiat, "Palestine"—the name by which it would still be known in the time of Justinian. Furthermore, the Jews were banned from their own ancient capital altogether, so that for them even to glance at Jerusalem from the crest of a far-off hill was accounted a crime. The smoking ruins themselves were renamed "Aelia Capitolina" and rebuilt as a pagan city. This rebranding policy was so successful that by the time of Constantine, when the first Christian tourists began to turn up in the Holy Land and ask for the road to Jerusalem, many of the local officials had no idea where they were talking about, and pointed them vaguely in the direction of Persia.

This ignorance had not lasted for long, of course; but even as the Church set to cleansing the city of demon worship, it showed little enthusiasm for turning back the clock. Just as Christ had superseded the Law of Moses, so did His Holy City glitter all the more brightly for having been raised amid the rubble of the erstwhile capital of the Jews. It was not enough to succeed; others had to fail. Nowhere better served to express this presumption than the Temple Mount. Here, in the wake of repeated Jewish rebellions, a pagan emperor had raised a temple—the Kapitolion—to Jupiter, the king of the Romans' gods. Christian emperors had refined the humiliation. While the Kapitolion was left to crumble into ruins, the Temple Mount was converted into a *sterquilinum*—a refuse dump. What better proof than the reek of shit and pigs' carcasses that the Jews were no longer a Chosen People? It was to ram the point home that the Roman authorities, always suckers for a good procession, allowed the Jews, once every year, on the anniversary of the destruction of the Temple, to star in a humiliating piece of street theatre. A band of Jewish pilgrims—pale, weeping and bedraggled—would climb up the steps of the Temple Mount, reach the perforated rock on the summit, and then start to blow on rams' horns, wail and tear out their hair. It was, for any watching Christians, a most edifying spectacle. "For while the mob of wretches congregates and groans over the ruins of their temple," as Jerome, with palpable relish, had once put it, "the manger of the Lord sparkles, the church of his resurrection glows and the banner of his cross shines forth from the Mount of Olives."[31]

Scorn that was paid back by the Jews themselves with undaunted hatred. Time had not eased the trauma of the ruin that the Romans had wrought on their Holy City. The general whose legions had torched the Temple, so the rabbis taught, now shared a corner of hell with Jesus, where he was destined to be consumed by fire, reassembled and then burned to ashes again for all eternity, as punishment for his unspeakable crime. Four centuries on from the destruction of the Temple, Jewish horror at the sacrilege had, if anything, intensified. The rabbis, struggling to articulate what the Temple itself had once so eloquently expressed, had come to identify its ruins with a novel concept to which they gave the name of "*Shekhinah*": the notion that God Himself might be present on earth. It was not, as the blasphemous and arrogant Christians taught, the rock of Golgotha that stood at the centre of the world, but the Temple Mount. There it was, upon "the foundation-stone of the whole of the universe,"[32] that Abraham had brought Isaac to be sacrificed; that Adam lay buried; and that "the world itself, moulded from its dust, had originally been founded."[33] Reading into the future the patterns cast by such a past, the Jews maintained an invincible confidence, amid all their desolation, that the Temple would one day rise again. Tantalisingly, back in the reign of Julian, they had enjoyed a brief glimpse of how such an eventuality might actually come to pass: for the apostate emperor, ever imaginative when it came to Christian-baiting, had ordered the Temple rebuilt. Only a few months' preparatory excavations had been possible before Julian's untimely death in Mesopotamia, however; and even those had been marked by the eruption on the site of "terrifying balls of fire"[34]—which the Christians, naturally enough, had attributed to divine displeasure, and the Jews to arson. Ever since then, the site had remained barren; but still, three times every day, the Jews would solemnly pray for the restoration of its former glory. Only rebuild the Temple, they knew, and much else as well would be fulfilled: the humbling of Rome; the humiliation of its ruler, who would be forced to eat "dirt like a worm";[35] and the coming of the Messiah.

As things stood, however, many Jews believed that Jerusalem under its Christian rulers was no less polluted than pagan Jerusalem had been: a sump of blood and idols. Ironically enough, those who did journey to the Temple Mount were likely to have been influenced, not by their own teachers, but by the example set by Christian pilgrims. Certainly, in the opinion of most rabbis, energies were better devoted to the study of the Torah, the holiness of which remained inviolably sacrosanct, than in trekking to the nest of heretics that Jerusalem had become. Nor was it necessary to inhabit the schools of Sura and Pumpedita, far from the Holy City, to hold this view: for there were rabbis in Palestine. An entire Talmud too. The scholars responsible for its composition might not have possessed the sheer exhaustive love of nit-picking displayed by their counterparts in the East; but that scarcely dented the growing weight of their authority. Indeed, the rabbis of Palestine were acknowledged to hold the advantage over those of Mesopotamia in several distinctive ways: they were more open to those who were not themselves scholars; they were better able to incinerate those who displeased them with a single glare; and they were more obsessively alert to the menace posed by menstruating women. Valuable though all of these attributes undoubtedly were, however, the Palestinian rabbis' most trend-setting talent was for something more portentous: a rewriting of Jewish tradition so as to give themselves a starring role in it. Control of the past, not for the first time, promised control of the future.

As in Mesopotamia, so in Palestine, the rabbis had long since taken it for granted that they should serve as the leaders of the Jewish people. Needless to say, all of their various writings were designed to offer a ringing endorsement of this view. A version of history in which the Jews of Palestine, disoriented and demoralised by the shattering loss of the Temple, had turned for guidance to the rabbis, whose power and prestige had accordingly known no limits, was promoted with gusto. That the truth had been rather different, and that most Jews had for centuries been in the habit of looking for justice from city councillors, local magnates or even the Roman governor, had inhibited the rabbis not at all. They knew themselves, with a sublime self-confidence, to be the embodiments of God's will—and, sure enough, over the course of the centuries, reality had come to blend with their ideal of what it should be. Their rivals as spokesmen for the Jews of Palestine began to fade from the scene. Their rulings and proscriptions were increasingly accepted. Their understanding of what it meant to be chosen by God started to verge on the definitive. Jewishness, in the Promised Land, had turned decisively rabbinical.

That this was so, however, did not owe everything to the rabbis themselves, and their obdurately learned ambition. A certain debt was owed as well to their bitterest and most inveterate foes. The Jews of Palestine, unlike those of Mesopotamia, were provincials in a Christian empire. As such, they were objects of neurotic fascination to their rulers. Attempts by the imperial elite to spell out precisely what *Christianismos* might be had repeatedly led them to define its presumed opposite: *Ioudaismos*. Even at Nicaea, Arians and Catholics had furiously accused each other of being Jews in Christian clothing. Over the subsequent centuries, the same smear would invariably be applied whenever one faction of the Church wished to charge another with heresy. As a result, Christians increasingly came to cast the Jewish faith in terms of a *religio* that could serve as a mirror of their own: chauvinistic and desiccated where Christianity was universal and fire-touched by the Holy Spirit. The Jews themselves, of course, would hardly have recognised this characterisation, nor the presumption of the Church that they subscribed to and practised a "religion" called *Ioudaismos*. *Religio*, after all, was a Christian concept; and so too, for that reason, was "Judaism."*

Nevertheless, the Church leaders' great labour of ring-fencing their own faith did have far-reaching implications for the faith practised by the Jews. The border between the two was now more firmly patrolled than ever. Bishops and emperors were not the only ones who stood guard over it. Rabbis did as well. This duty, of course, was one that they had always claimed for themselves; but their neighbours were increasingly content, even relieved, to cede to them their role as the watchmen of God's will. The Jews of Palestine, confronted as they were by the monumental and menacing edifice of Christian orthodoxy, had grown increasingly fretful about what their own frameworks of authority, and their own orthodoxy, might be. Rather than have it defined for them by the Christian Church, they preferred to turn to the scholars whose massive achievement in compiling the Talmud had been preparation for precisely such a moment. "Why should a rabbi be hailed as a king? Because it is by virtue of the Torah that kings rule."[36] Hardly the most rib-tickling of jokes, to be sure—but one that bore, by the time of Justinian, an unmistakable hint of truth.

And certainly, among the Jews of Palestine, there was a desperate need of leaders. The tide of affairs was palpably flowing against them. Christian authorities in the Holy Land viewed the continued presence of its previous tenants as both a challenge and an embarrassment.

---

* The word *Ioudaismos* is overwhelmingly confined to Christian texts—most of which date from after the conversion of Constantine. "Judaism," in the sense that it is used in modern English, was a Christian invention.

Although the Roman state, like the Church, recognised Judaism as a distinct and officially sanctioned religion, that hardly implied beneficence. Rather, toleration was the flip-side of a mounting obsession on the part of Constantinople with regulation of the empire's Jews. A people hedged about with legal definitions, after all, were a people who could more readily be targeted with restrictions and indignities. Jewish noses were repeatedly rubbed in the brute fact of their second-class status. They were forbidden to join the army; to serve in the bureaucracy; to buy Christian slaves. Synagogues, although protected by law from being burned down or converted into churches, were permitted only to be renovated, and on no account to be built from scratch. Many Jews, it was true, had felt perfectly free to ignore this prescription—so much so that the ban had coincided with a golden age of synagogue construction. Almost every Jewish village had come to boast one. Even the humblest and most remote might be built out of stone, while the larger, urban synagogues tended to be so sumptuously decorated that it was only their orientation towards Jerusalem that made them readily distinguishable from churches. Nevertheless, even for those wealthy enough to have commissioned all the synagogues' mosaics and gleaming marble, the prosperity these fittings proclaimed was not entirely good news. The boom-time in Palestine owed little to the natives and almost everything to incomers. The mass immigration of Christians into the Holy Land might have generated huge profits for individual Jewish hoteliers and relic-suppliers, but it threatened to swamp the Jews as a people. Those who had not been cowed or seduced into accepting baptism by the triumphant swagger of Christianity were finding themselves obliged to retreat to ever higher ground. By the sixth century, the Jews of Palestine probably numbered no more than 10 per cent of the total population.[37] Even though Christians might fret that the Jews were breeding "like worms,"[38] the reality was that they had long since become a minority in their own land.

And an ever more embattled one at that. Early in the reign of Justinian, that inveterate sponsor of intimidating architectural statements, a team of workmen climbed a mountain named Berenice,

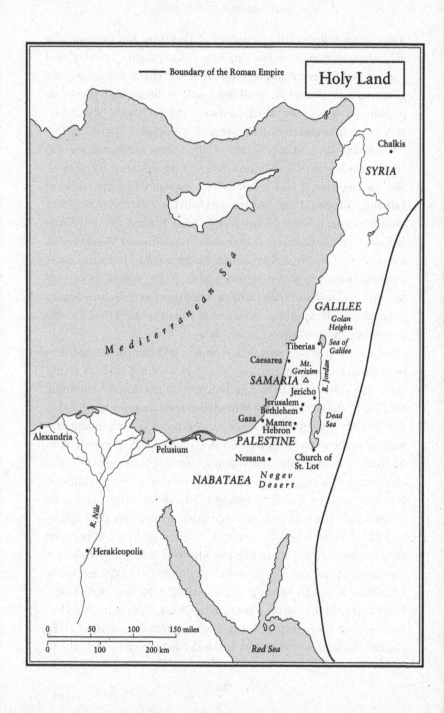

Boundary of the Roman Empire

Holy Land

Chalkis

SYRIA

GALILEE

Golan
Heights

Tiberias · Sea of
Galilee

Caesarea ·

Mt.
Gerizim

SAMARIA △

R. Jordan

Mediterranean Sea

Jericho ·

Jerusalem ·
Bethlehem ·

Dead
Sea

Gaza ·
· Mamre
Hebron ·

Alexandria ·

Pelusium

PALESTINE

Nessana ·

Church of
St. Lot

NABATAEA

Negev
Desert

R. Nile

· Herakleopolis

| 0 | 50 | 100 | 150 miles |

| 0 | 100 | 200 km |

Red Sea

some ninety miles north of Jerusalem.[39] Their view from the summit was spectacular: in the distance rose the Golan Heights, a river-scored plateau that marked Palestine's frontier with Syria; below stretched a glittering lake dotted with fishing boats, so broad that the locals proudly termed it a sea; along its shores, the fields were "a paradise, rich with wheat and fruit, with wine, oil and apples."[40] In fact, so fertile was the land that even the women were renowned for the spectacular bloom of their beauty. The region was known as Galilee—and for centuries it had served as the stronghold of the rabbis of Palestine. Tiberias, a city picturesquely sited on the lower slopes of Mount Berenice, directly beside the lake, boasted the only *batei midrash*—"houses of study"—that could rival those of Mesopotamia for prestige. The city still remained, in the reign of Justinian, overwhelmingly true to its distinguished heritage: its councillors were all Jewish; it had no fewer than thirteen synagogues; even its bath-houses were rabbinically approved. Nowhere in Palestine could rival it as the conscience and watchtower of Jewish life.

Which was precisely why, in the opinion of Justinian, it needed to be reminded of its proper place. The Jews were not alone in laying claim to Galilee: Christians as well revered it as a region hauntingly touched by the sacred. Christ Himself had lived there for much of His life: He had toured its villages, delivered sermons from its mountains, walked on the waters of its lake. Galilee was second only to Jerusalem on the itineraries of Christian tourists. Granted, their behaviour was not always all it might have been: whether carving their names on furniture used by Christ or ogling the famously attractive Jewish women, they had a certain tendency to gaucheness. Yet although, as one Italian visitor ruefully reported, "there is no love lost between the Jews and us,"[41] it was not pilgrims who were chiefly responsible for this mood of tension. As elsewhere in Palestine, so in Galilee: many Christians aimed to be more than tourists. Land was their truest heart's desire—the soil once trodden by Christ. As a result, churches had come to colonise Jewish fields, whole villages of settlers to be planted throughout the region, and walls, bristling emphatically, to gird even the smallest monastery, the most insignificant Christian hamlet. Now, with the arrival of Justinian's workmen on the slopes above Tiberias, the time had come for the rabbis themselves to be issued with a notice of imperial intent. A huge church, designed to glower over the streets below, was to be raised directly on the summit of Mount Berenice. A massive ring of fortifications, complete with the latest fashion in watchtowers, was to be constructed around it. As elsewhere in the empire, so in the very stronghold of Judaism, an emphatic statement was to be made: no defiance of the Christian faith anywhere but the gaze of the emperor, unblinking and all-seeing, would be upon it.

True, there was an element of bluff in this eyeballing of the rabbis. Justinian, who had thought nothing of driving the philosophers of Athens into exile, had no corresponding intention to force the closure of the schools of Tiberias. In fact, to a large degree, they served his purpose. The rabbis offered to the emperor a living assurance that there did authentically exist a religion such as "Judaism," one with authority figures and a clearly defined orthodoxy: the mirror-image of his own. The alternative—to acknowledge that in the great ocean of belief there might still be those who swam untrammelled beyond the twin dragnets of Christianity and Judaism—was infinitely more unsettling. The rabbis themselves would probably not have disagreed. After all, it was hardly unflattering to their pretensions to imagine a world in which there were Jews and Christians, and no one else. It was telling, perhaps, that the watchtowers built on Mount Berenice were not confined to its summit. Although the presence of the great church clearly established where the supremacy lay, Justinian did not neglect to offer his protection to the Jews as well. The fortifications ran right down the slope of the mountain and enclosed the entire city.[42] The Jews may have been second-class subjects—but they were at least within the fold.

There remained others, however, who were harder to sort. Not everyone who trod the sacred dust of the Holy Land could be categorised neatly as a Christian or a Jew. Much though both emperors and rabbis might have wished it otherwise, Palestine was simply too God-haunted, too dream-crowded, too memory-stalked for that. Right in the heart of the province, for instance, there was a people who openly derided both Christian churches and Jewish synagogues as abodes of idolatry, and all those who worshipped in them as upstarts. The Samaritans, inhabitants of a region midway between Jerusalem and Galilee named Samaria, claimed that they, and they alone, had preserved the unadorned wishes of heaven. "There is no God but One,"[43] they declared. "Let us believe in Him and in Moses, His Prophet."[44] From these simple presumptions, so it seemed to the Samaritans, much else inevitably flowed: all the scriptures penned since the time of Moses, whether by Jews or Christians, were mere deluded vanity; the purity of the teachings that God revealed to His Prophet had been corrupted by any number of subsequent accretions; Jerusalem, far from being a holy city, had been promoted as such by David and Solomon for purely political reasons. In truth, it was neither the Temple Mount nor the rock of Golgotha that constituted the centre of the world, but rather a wooded peak in Samaria—Mount Gerizim. It was here—on a flat expanse of rock named the "Eternal Hill" by the Samaritans—that Noah's ark had landed, Abraham had prepared to sacrifice Isaac, and the laws given to Moses had been preserved. To believe any differently, as the Jews and the Christians did, was to distort the primal teachings that God had revealed to the ancient prophets. It was to neglect the principal duty of humanity: due submission to God.[45]

None of which, needless to say, did much for the Samaritans' popularity with their neighbours. Jewish scorn for their pretensions ran particularly deep. For centuries, in a blatantly tit-for-tat manner, the rabbis had accused the Samaritans themselves of being the idolators—this on the supposed grounds that they were descended from pagans and worshipped a dove. As a result, far from embracing them as potential allies, most Jews refused even to sit down with them, let alone consume their wine or food—although the odd rabbi was prepared to grant that it might be legitimate to tuck into one of their boiled eggs.[46] As for Christians, the sanctions they applied would prove, in the long run, to be of an altogether more forceful order of brutality: an exercise in state-sponsored violence bred of wholly predictable tensions. Despite the fact that the Samaritans were permitted to serve in the Roman army, and indeed had long enjoyed an impressive reputation among their commanders for martial savagery, Christian relic-hunters had still ransacked Mount Gerizim, and Christian colonists had still flooded into Samaria. In 484, Samaritan patience had finally snapped. A bishop had been mutilated in his own cathedral; churches had been desecrated; open rebellion had blazed right across central Palestine. The provincial authorities, although initially taken by surprise, had been ruthless in crushing the revolt. Samaria had been left littered with some ten thousand corpses. All Samaritans, unsurprisingly, had been demobbed from imperial service for good. The crowning act of vengeance, however, had been to ban them from the sacred slopes of Mount Gerizim, and to build, on its previously unadorned summit, a church within a fortress. And on the church, as one Samaritan historian would bitterly record, "there was constructed a very high tower which was painted white, and from which lamps were hung to glow in the night, so that all in Constantinople and Rome might see them."[47]

There was, of course—as any Jew could have pointed out—nothing particularly ground-breaking about this display of imperial vindictiveness. The Samaritans, however, had not had four hundred years to adjust to the loss of their holiest sanctuary; nor could they quite bring themselves to believe that God would permit its continued desecration. Desperation and rage duly festered. A few decades on from the great revolt, when a small band of Samaritan insurgents, "prompted by the suggestion of a woman,"[48] sought to seize back the summit of Mount Gezirim from its Christian garrison, the incipient rebellion was quarantined only with difficulty; and in 529, when rioting saw a number of Jews and Christians killed by a mob of Samaritans, the spark proved sufficient to light a second conflagration. For a brief while, it seemed as though not only Palestine but the whole empire might be cut in two: for a warlord who shared with the long-dead pagan emperor the sinister name of Julian, a man variously described as a king, a messiah, or "a bandit chief,"[49] proclaimed the foundation of a Samaritan empire, blocking the roads from the north, and menacing Jerusalem. Adding yet further spice to the rebellion, the insurgents staged a number of highly pointed atrocities, of which the most spectacular was the incineration of a bishop on a bonfire fuelled by the relics of Christian martyrs. Insults such as these, of course, might almost have been calculated to provoke a devastating response. The imperial vengeance, when it finally came, was inevitably a terrible one. The rebel army, brought to battle, was annihilated with such efficiency that twenty thousand Samaritan warriors were left dead, including a summarily decapitated Julian. New, more impregnable fortifications were raised around the summit of the Eternal Hill, and the slopes of Mount Gezirim scoured clean of every last trace of a Samaritan presence. Meanwhile, across the rest of Samaria, the ruin was universal. Land that had once been hailed as "the most fertile in the world"[50] was now a wilderness of carrion, rubble and weeds.

As for the Samaritans themselves, there seemed nothing left to them but despair. Many, abandoning the god who had so transparently failed them, sullenly submitted to baptism; others, slumping into a numb isolationism, hunkered down in remote villages, where they ostentatiously covered any footprints left by visiting Jews or Christians with burning straw. Yet others, however, tried to keep the banner of rebellion flying—not by making a stand in Samaria, but by retreating beyond the border. As many as fifty thousand of them, fleeing the reprisals of Justinian's death-squads, made a break for Mesopotamia, where they threw themselves on the mercy of the aged Kavad. The *Shahanshah*, rather than swallow the assurances of the Samaritans that they could deliver him Palestine, opted instead to put them all in chains and pack them off to toil in a gold mine. Nevertheless, back in Palestine itself, the Roman authorities remained twitchy in the extreme at any prospect of a Samaritan retrenchment just over the border. In the wake of the revolt, when twenty thousand

Samaritan boys and girls were handed over to slavers, it was specifically decreed that they must be sold as far afield as possible—
preferably in Persia or India. The prospect that any of them might
grow up within striking distance of their homeland was altogether
too alarming to be tolerated.

. There was more to this anxiety than mere paranoia. Notwithstanding the milk and honey that flowed through the Holy Land, it
bordered directly onto wilderness—and wilderness, as it had ever
done, spelled danger. Right on the doorstep of Jerusalem, along the
fifteen-mile road that led eastwards to Jericho, menace lurked behind
every barren rock, so that what had long since come to be named the
"Bloody Way"* was as notorious for banditry as anywhere in the
empire. South of Jericho, where steepling cliffs plunged down towards
the aptly named Dead Sea, there was an even more intimidating landscape, formed of nothing but dust, salt and mud. It was here, in the
wake of the burning of the Temple in the first century AD, that an
army of Jewish rebels had made a last, doomed stand. But already,
long, long previously, the region had borne spectacular witness to the
incineration of a sinful people and to the full, devastating horror of
where the angering of God might lead. On the eastern shore of the
Dead Sea, where the mud bubbled at its filthiest and most stinking,
two mighty cities had once stood: Sodom and Gomorrah. Their
inhabitants, so moralists recorded, had been wholly given over to
vice: to rape, to sex with people of their own gender, and to breaking
wind in public.† Provoked beyond endurance by such depravity, the
Almighty had duly decreed the obliteration of the two cities. Fire and
brimstone had rained down upon them. "The smoke of the land went
up like the smoke of a furnace."[51] Of Sodom and Gomorrah, nothing

---

* This is a translation of the biblical "*Adommim.*" According to Jerome, it was on
this road that the traveller in the famous parable of the good Samaritan "fell
among thieves."

† The tradition that the inhabitants of Sodom and Gomorrah were prone to
farting in public was Islamic.

had remained, saving only the odd salt-caked ruin, to serve passers-by as an admonition and a terror.

The lesson was not entirely bleak, though. On the southern shore of the Dead Sea, there stood a church; and inside the church, there was a cave. It was said that Abraham's nephew, Lot, graced by a tip-off from some angels, had sheltered here with his family: the only survivors of the annihilation of Sodom. The implication of this—that a righteous man, such as Lot, might be spared the ruin of a doomed people by fleeing into the wilderness—had not gone unremarked over the centuries. Samaritans were hardly the first refugees to have sought sanctuary beyond the borders of the Promised Land. Back in the days of their own persecution by Rome, Christians had done the self-same thing. Some of them, even after the conversion of Constantine, had refused to return from the desert to the temptations of everyday life: among the cliffs beyond Jerusalem, as on the mountains around Antioch or in the desert of Sinai, ascetics had looked to build for themselves a city of God. In the midst of a drear and bandit-haunted wilderness, the monasteries that dotted the eastern flank of Palestine aimed to blaze like bulwarks of paradise. Manned by warriors of God from across the empire, linked by paths that criss-crossed the wilds like the cords of a far-flung net, and buttressed by imposing stonework that gave them the look of fortresses, these *lavras*, as they were called, served the Church, in its great battle against the demonic, as an awesome first line of defence. Out in the desert, where Christ Himself had been tempted by the Devil, only the spiritual elite could hope to prosper. The weak fell away; the strong grew even stronger. This was why, in the Holy Land, it was the monks who constituted the shock troops of orthodoxy. Forged in the blast furnace of the desert, they brought to the practice of their faith a show of fortitude, of discipline, of steel. They, more than anyone, could be relied upon to embrace martyrdom at the hands of Samaritans; to stage public protests against any hint of concession to Monophysites; to press the imperial authorities to hold their nerve in the battle against every last enemy of God. Vital tasks anywhere—but in the Holy Land especially so.

"Arm yourselves against heresies, against Jews, against Samaritans, against pagans." So had urged Cyril, a golden-tongued Bishop of Jerusalem back in the first century of the city's existence as a Christian capital, warning converts there of the peculiar charge that God had laid upon their shoulders. "Many are your enemies: be sure you have ammunition."[52] Two centuries later, the marks of just how successful Cyril's call to arms had been were everywhere to be seen, stamped on the face of the Holy Land: on the hill above Tiberias, on the summit of Mount Gerizim, in the mouldering shells of abandoned temples. There were, however, few visible traces of perhaps the most telling victory of all. Cyril, in the advice offered to his converts, had lingered on one particularly mortal threat: "If a book is not read in a church, then do not read it yourself, even alone." Specifically, he had cautioned against those seeming-scriptures that "bore the title of 'gospel,' but were false, and full of deceit."[53] Such a warning, of course, would have been valid anywhere; but in the Holy Land, especially so. Not every Christian who flocked there was necessarily orthodox, after all. A yearning to walk in the footsteps of Christ did not necessarily imply obedience to the Council of Nicaea. There were grounds for alarm as well as self-satisfaction in the cosmopolitan character of the Holy Land. Nowhere else in the world, as Cyril had well appreciated, were banned gospels, banned doctrines, banned identities, likelier to be available.

Moreover, immigrants were not the only heretics to be found in Palestine. Camped out on the frontier between Christianity and Judaism, on what had become, since the Council of Nicaea, an ever more brutally patrolled no-man's land, there lingered still a few obdurate squatters. Jews who "honoured Christ as a just man"[54] and Christians who yearned to see the Temple restored: how were these to be categorised? As pestiferous impostors, came the ringing answer of the Church: "for, though they pretend to be both Jews and Christians, yet they are neither."[55] Add to this unsettling mix the Samaritans, who were darkly suspected of having fostered the swarming plague of Gnostics, and it was no wonder that bishops such as Cyril regarded the melting-pot of faiths to be found in Palestine as so potentially toxic. To scholars of his generation, the threat from heresy in the Holy Land seemed as terrifying as ever. After all, if a Jew could be a Christian—and a Christian a Jew—then who was to say what further monstrous fusions of beliefs might be possible?

Answers to that, in the manuscript-littered libraries of the Holy Land, were certainly still there for those with eyes to see. Jerome, ever the assiduous bookworm, had reported in a tone of mingled horror and fascination his perusal of a gospel written in Hebrew that contained the noxious teachings of a sect called the Nazoreans. These, heretics who had the nerve to claim descent from the original Jewish Church that had existed prior to the arrival of Paul upon the scene, taught something truly shocking: that the Holy Spirit was not only female but the heavenly "mother"[56] of Christ. Nor was that the worst, by any means. To true connoisseurs of heresy, the Nazoreans ranked as mere beginners. The Church's leading specialist in such matters, a bishop from Cyprus by the name of Epiphanius, had identified an infinitely more sinister attempt to poison the faithful with the toxin of Jewishness. Explaining to his shocked readers the existence of Christians who denied the Trinity and held Jesus to have been merely a man who obeyed the Law of Moses, and who turned in the direction of Jerusalem when they performed their daily prayers, the learned bishop had fingered a teacher called Ebion: a veritable monster, so Epiphanius claimed, who had blended Judaism with "the repulsiveness of the Samaritans,"[57] not to mention a whole host of other heresies, too. In such a figure, then, could be caught the ultimate glimpse of a world in which Christians and Jews forgot their proper place: a world in which there was nothing to stop some innovative heretic from "taking an item of preaching from every sect, and patterning himself after them all."[58]

No wonder, then, that bishops such as Cyril and Epiphanius, backed up by the militant fervour of the province's monks, and the muscle of the imperial Roman state, should have laboured long and hard to impose an orthodox model of Christianity on the Holy Land. No wonder either that the Jews, menaced as they were by such a project, should have regarded with an increasingly suspicious hatred those of their number who still thought to call upon the name of Christ. People such as the Nazoreans or the Ebionites, squeezed from both sides, duly found themselves pushed ever deeper into the shadows. There was nothing for them to do, in the battleground for rival faiths that Palestine had become, save to retreat into ever deeper oblivion. No-man's land, in the final reckoning, had proved an impossible place to be. Certainly, by the time of Justinian, no bishop thought to bother himself with the Ebionites—nor any rabbi either. Their doctrines and their doings had become things so spectral as to have been almost entirely forgotten. The Christians and the Jews of Palestine, cordially though they might detest one another, could at least agree on one thing: hybrids were beyond the pale.

And perhaps literally so. If indeed the Ebionites and their like did manage to cling on to a precarious existence within the Christian empire, then it could only ever have been on the margins: on the Golan Heights above Galilee, perhaps, or in outposts planted deep in the desert.[59] To those defined by the Church as heretics, as to refugees from Samaria, it was no longer their traditional heartlands that held out the surest prospects of survival, but rather the wilderness. The result was a curious irony: for even as the frontier between Palestine and the desert was being colonised by the shock troops of Christian orthodoxy, by monks and ascetics, so also did it bear a certain ghostly witness to the world as it had been before the establishment of Christianity, when the borders between rival faiths had been less clear-cut, more fissiparous. Just as the massive stonework of a *lavra*, a desert monastery, proclaimed the triumph of the new, so also were there to be glimpsed, faint perhaps, but present all the same for those inspired to track them down, the broken traces of a far more ancient order. In the wilds between Palestine and Sinai, for instance, there stood shrines raised by tribesmen who still worshipped a whole multitude of gods:

"polytheists" as they were contemptuously termed. Meanwhile, in the cliffs above the Dead Sea, it was not unheard of for mysterious scrolls to be excavated from "chambers in the middle of the mountain with many books in them":[60] scrolls that might prove to contain versions of the Jewish scriptures, but fabulously ancient, and with strange and variant readings. Clearly, then, amid the dryness of the sands, prospects for the survival of otherwise long-forgotten manuscripts were not altogether hopeless; and perhaps, that being so, the same was true of long-obsolete doctrines too.

Out in the wilderness, after all, beyond the reach of the Christian empire, and the monks who had colonised its periphery, there was no one greatly to care which gods people might worship, nor which books they might read, nor which obsolete beliefs they might hug to themselves. Out in the wilderness, there was no one to patrol the frontiers of faiths that elsewhere, once and for all, had put up the barricades.

The Wolves of Arabia

Like sand borne on an easterly wind, hints of the strange and aberrant beliefs that simmered in the desert were occasionally still to be found even in the Holy Land itself. Some twenty miles south of Jerusalem, for instance, at a spot set among open fields named Mamre, pagans from beyond the frontiers of Palestine would gather every summer "to keep a brilliant feast."[61] The roots of this festival were quite fabulously ancient: for they had as their focus an oak that was the oldest tree in the world. Neither Jews nor Christians thought to dispute this sensational pedigree. Both were agreed that the tree was "as ancient as creation"[62]—and that it had been a favourite of Abraham's to boot. A well dug by the patriarch still stood beside it, and although the oak itself, thanks to the merciless attentions of Christian souvenir-hunters, had long since been hacked down to a stump, an unmistakable aura of holiness still attached itself to the mutilated trunk. In the first book of

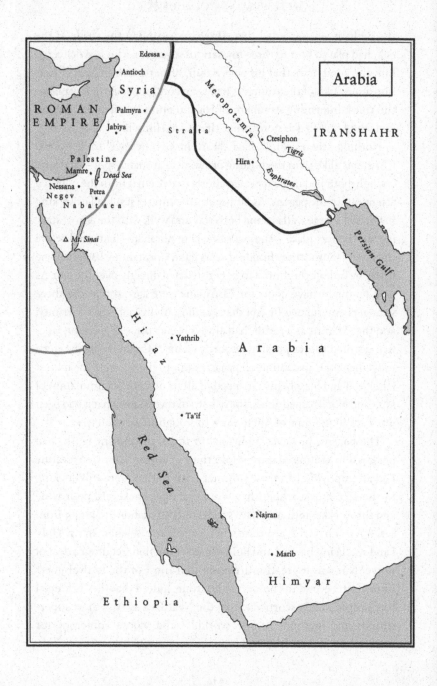

Arabia

ROMAN
EMPIRE

Syria

Edessa
• Antioch

Palmyra •
Jabiya •

Mesopotamia

Strata

IRANSHAHR

Ctesiphon •
Tigris

Hira •
Euphrates

Palestine
Mamre •
Nessana •
Negev
Nabataea

Dead Sea
Petra •

Persian Gulf

△ Mt. Sinai

Hijaz

• Yathrib

Arabia

Red Sea

• Ta'if

• Najran

• Marib

Himyar

Ethiopia

the Bible, it was recorded that Abraham, sitting in the shade of the oak, had played host to three mysterious strangers, who had delivered him the good news that his wife, Sarah, hitherto barren, was to bear him a son: Two of the strangers had then continued on their way; but the third, informing Abraham of His intention to wipe out Sodom, had stood revealed as none other than God Himself.

Nothing, then, could have been more offensive to Jews and Christians alike than the hosting of a festival at such a spot—and sure enough, both had made repeated efforts to redeem it from the polluted attentions of the pagans. As far back as the time of Jesus, a Jewish king had raised a large wall around both tree and well, with the aim of staking out the very place—the *maqom*—where Abraham "had stood before the Lord."[63] Some three hundred years later, Constantine had gone one better by ordering a church to be constructed directly over the oak. As well he might have done: for Christians were agreed that the three strangers entertained by Abraham could only have been the Trinity, and that Mamre, as a result, had always been a place of "pristine sanctity, devoted to the worship of our Saviour."[64] Certainly, in the stern judgement of Constantine, all pagan claims to the site were the merest falsehood and blasphemy. Stripped of all its obscene accumulation of idols and bloodstained altars, the oak stood revealed as what it had been way back in the time of Abraham: a thoroughly Christian tree.

The pagans, however, oblivious to this transcendent truth, had persisted in visiting Mamre. More than a century after Constantine had attempted to ban their summer festival, they were still flocking to the sacred oak, where they would sacrifice cockerels, pour wine and throw cakes into Abraham's well, and ostentatiously abstain from sex. Such behaviour, at a time when paganism elsewhere in the Holy Land was being harried and bullied into extinction, required a deal of nerve. Nor was it greatly surprising that most of the festival-goers came from beyond the borders of Palestine. Indeed that they belonged to a people widely scorned across the Near East as "the most superstitious and ignorant in the world,"[65] and whose contempt for monarchs and their laws had long been notorious.

The Arabs, tribesmen who haunted the interminable wastes that stretched south of the Fertile Crescent, could boast a record of barbarism more venerable than the empires of either Persia or Rome. "Dwelling as they do in the distant desert, they know neither overseers nor officials": a state of affairs so mind-bogglingly unnatural that even a king of Mesopotamia, back in the distant days when Solomon's temple still stood in Jerusalem, had thought to make a note of it.[66] A thousand years on, opinions had barely improved. The Arabs appeared as reluctant as ever to put down roots. They were despised not merely as pagans, but as pagans who lived in tents. To an aristocrat in his palace, as to a peasant in his field, the inveterate shiftlessness of such nomads was both a menace and an affront. That the Arabs, in their disdain for the norms of civilisation, were possessed of an almost timeless quality of ferocity, like that of the deserts where they lurked, was widely taken for granted. Less than human, they were something more than beasts. In battle, it was not unknown for them to drink their victims' blood, while even in their love-making, so it was darkly rumoured, "they were quite explosively violent—women as well as men."[67] Nervous travellers venturing beyond the limits of cities and farms viewed the half-naked Arabs on their horses or camels as a menace no less deadly than the most ferocious desert predator: "For, like rapacious kites, which have only to catch sight of prey from on high to swoop down upon it with outstretched talons, they make off with whatever they can seize."[68]

An insult that would no doubt have delighted the Arabs themselves. To be as free and as feared as a bird of prey was, in many ways, everything they most desired. What other peoples condemned as shiftlessness, they prized as liberty. "I journeyed with a brown whip, its handle bare of its original thonging, with its lash hanging from its loop":[69] to ride like this, alone with the horizon infinite all around, was to know oneself, with a rare and vaunting conviction, the utter opposite of a slave. Wherever Arabs gathered, whether in the shade of an embroidered tent or around a fire beneath the stars, they were sure to sing the praises of wine, slim-waisted women, and warriors who acknowledged no master. The nomads of the desert might have been despised—but they were also feared. When the Persians charged Dahag, the demon king, with having been one of their number, and the Romans condemned them for their slaving and kidnapping as agents of the Devil, the Arabs were being paid a form of tribute. Better a bandit than a dependant, after all. Who were the subjects of the *Shahanshah* or of Caesar to presume otherwise?

In truth, though, the Arabs were not quite the lone wolves of their victims' paranoia. Their realm was an unremittingly harsh one, and no man could possibly survive amid the sand, salt flats and wind-weathered lava beds without others to watch out for him. Even to the hardiest and haughtiest warrior, family was everything. "We follow the ways of our forefathers, those who kindled wars and were faithful to the ties of kinship."[70] This resounding brag expressed the very essence of an Arab's identity. Extended networks of relatives blurred seamlessly into tribe. All men who could claim descent, however implausibly, from a single *imam*—a founding father—were to be reckoned his sons. Bound by a single inheritance of custom and achievement, of *Sunna*, warriors who might otherwise have torn each other to shreds were enabled to unite without loss of face, and turn on all those neighbouring bands of rivals who might have done the same. The great joy of an Arab's life, even more than the pillaging of cara-vans or the slaughtering of camels in honour of some ivory-skinned beauty, was to feud violently with another tribe. Much was bound to derive from it: honour, excitement, maybe even a well or two. That there was an essential pointlessness to such contests, an unvarying and remorseless quality much like that of the desert itself, did not in any way lessen the enjoyment of those who indulged in them. The great deeds performed by a tribe's ancestors, rehearsed as they were in glow-ing, if suspiciously interchangeable, verses by its poets, offered its warriors both backdrop and inspiration. Memories of ancient battles, if gilded with sufficient imagination, might serve to dignify even the most squalid scuffle. As a result, among the Arabs, past and present were barely distinguishable. While it might be possible for one partic-

ularly recent and stirring episode to serve the tribe who commemorated it as a line drawn in the otherwise interminable sands of time, all
it needed was for some new victory to be won, some new livestock or
women to be seized, and the line would promptly be erased and quite
forgotten. Certainly, the lore that every tribe lovingly preserved about
itself was concerned with nothing so tedious as chronology. It was
known quite simply as *ayyam*—"days."

Yet in truth, even in the remotest stretches of the desert, the Arabs
were never wholly immune to the tug of great events in the world
beyond. The ebb and flow of great power politics had even, on occasion, come to alter their entire way of living. Time was, for instance,
when Arab merchants had been famously sweet-smelling: for frankincense, an aromatic spice that had once been burned in near-
industrial quantities on pagan altars, was cultivated exclusively in
Himyar, on the southernmost tip of their peninsula. Back in the age of
Solomon, the queen of this incense-growing land—Sheba, as it had
then been known—had visited the great king in Jerusalem, trailing
perfumed clouds of glory in her wake; while more recently, among
the Romans, its inhabitants had been famed as the happiest and most
prosperous of men. All that, however, had changed with the toppling
of the pagan gods. Christ demanded no incense. The trade between
Rome and the frankincense growers of Himyar had duly withered.
The Arabs, no longer renowned for their perfumes, became notorious
instead for their reek of leather and camel shit. Caravans might still
toil across the desert, but those who rode alongside them now tended
to play the demeaning and insecure role of middle men. That it was
worth the while of camels freighted with all the luxuries of India—
pepper, gemstones and castrated pageboys—to plod their way across
the sands towards Palestine and Syria owed everything to the whims of
distant emperors, to the calculations of bureaucrats. A treaty renego-
tiated here, a customs post closed down there, and everything would
abruptly change. Merchants, camel-drivers, bandits: all might find
themselves ruined overnight.

Prey as they were to such insecurity, there had always been some

Arab tribes eager to set their fortunes on a firmer footing. Some, like the Nabataeans, a people who occupied the southern fringes of Palestine, had exploited their position between the trade routes of the desert and the Mediterranean to create a fabulously wealthy commercial hub, centred on their pink-hued capital of Petra. Others, looking to take a short cut to power, had aimed to infiltrate the cities of other peoples and then to seize their commanding heights: a policy of playing cuckoo in the nest that explained why the kings of Edessa had been of Arab descent. Nevertheless, the independence of such states, menaced as it was by the domineering shadow of Rome, had always been a rickety thing. As early as AD 106, the kingdom of Nabataea had been gobbled up entire, and reconstituted as the province of Arabia—and although Edessa held out against formal assimilation into the empire for a further 150 years, it had never been left in any doubt as to its thoroughly subordinate status. Riches and sophistication: these, it appeared, might certainly be obtained by the Arabs. The price, however, was a high one: the loss of honour, of liberty, of all that made an Arab.

How, then, was this awkward circle to be squared? In 270, just a few decades after the annexation of Edessa, there had arrived a spectacular straw on the wind. Zenobia, the queen of an oasis city named Palmyra, midway between Antioch and Ctesiphon, had made a pitch for nothing less than the whole of the Roman Near East. Syria, Egypt and much of Asia Minor all fell to the sudden onslaught of her armies. Granted, her moment in the sun was fleeting: defeated outside Antioch in 272, she was taken to Rome, and paraded as a living trophy, while her desert capital was abandoned to slow decay and oblivion. The true significance of her comet-like blaze, however, had lain less in its trajectory than in the circumstances that had made it possible. Zenobia's own defeat and humiliation had been paralleled, twelve years previously, by the fate of the Emperor Valerian. His captor, of course, had been a rival monarch, the lord of a dominion no less intimidatingly formidable than Rome's: the recently established empire of *Iranshahr*. By using a Caesar as his mounting block, Shapur had proclaimed—in terms that no Roman emperor would ever again be able to discount—the arrival of an authentic equal upon the global scene. For the Arabs too, the implications of the rise to greatness of the House of Sasan had been momentous. The deserts where they lived had abruptly come to constitute the frontier not of one superpower but of two. Situated as they now were on the world's deadliest geopolitical fault-line, they would never again be able to claim even the most precarious neutrality. Yet the deadly grinding of the twin tectonic plates of Rome and *Iranshahr*, even as it crushed for ever the independence of such cities as Edessa and Palmyra, spelled opportunity as well as calamity for upwardly mobile Arabs. In a war zone, after all, what more precious commodity than bands of seasoned warriors? Rome and Persia alike: both had urgent need of swords. The Arabs found themselves ideally placed to hawk their services to the highest bidder.

To the Romans, of course, there was nothing remotely novel about the employment of barbarians. As along the Rhine prior to the collapse of the western empire, so along the borders of Syria and Palestine, the imperial authorities were well versed in the hiring of tribes as confederates: as *foederati*. Even prior to the emergence of the Persian threat, back in the second century AD, the Romans had successfully bribed and cajoled a number of tribes into serving as a desert police force; and the example of this confederation, the Thamud, would long be commemorated by Arab poets.[71] Understandably so, perhaps: for what it had served to demonstrate was that even the proudly and inveterately fractious tribes of the desert might, under certain circumstances, be forged into a *shirkat*—a "partnership."[72] Such a lesson, against the backdrop of escalating superpower confrontation, had certainly not gone unnoted by ambitious chieftains. Horizons had steadily expanded, wild fantasies taken wing. In 328, for instance, one Arab warlord had been buried beneath a tombstone that grandiloquently proclaimed him to have been "King of all the Arabs." A title no less bogus than it was unprecedented—but most suggestive all the same. As Rome and *Iranshahr* competed ever more vigorously for the services of the desert tribes, so the potential pickings on offer for the tribesmen themselves had indeed grown steadily more lucrative. Although the confederation of the Thamud had long since imploded, having been struck down in sensational fashion, so Arab lore claimed, by a thunderbolt, other *foederati* had fast emerged to take its place.* It is telling that Roman authors, from the fourth century onwards, began to use a new word to designate the Arabs, one that seems ultimately to have derived from *shirkat*: "Saracens."[73] Although the Romans themselves appear to have been wholly ignorant of the original meaning, and although the stereotype they had of the "Saracens" remained the reassuringly traditional one, of nomads, bandits and savages, the use they made of the new name did nevertheless hint at a new and emerging order. In the yawning deserts between Palestine and Mesopotamia, Arab tribesmen were no longer operating merely on a freelance basis. While they still indulged in their traditional pastimes—slaving, cattle rustling, raiding caravans and frontier posts—they increasingly did so as agents of the rival superpowers. "To the Arabs on both sides," so the twitchy inhabitants of the Fertile Crescent began to observe, "war between Persia and Rome is a source of very great profit indeed."[74]

Nowhere better illustrated this than a town famed throughout Arabia as the epitome of power and glamour. Hira stood only a few miles south of Sura, on the southern flank of Mesopotamia; but it might as well have been a world away from the lecture halls of the rabbis. Situated in an oasis between the Euphrates and the desert, it served in every sense as a place of hybrids. Although a linchpin of Sasanian defences, the great bulwark that blocked access from the south to Ctesiphon, it was commanded not by a Persian but by an Arab. The *Banu Lakhm*—"Lakhm's Sons"—had long been based in the region, where they had enjoyed a profitable existence as mercenaries

---

* In the fourth century, some units in both Palestine and Egypt were still described as belonging to the Thamud; but none, so far as we know, beyond the limits of the Roman Empire.

in the service of the *Shahanshah*. Even under Peroz, despite all the tempting convulsions of his reign, they had remained loyal to the Persian crown. The decision had been a thoroughly calculating one—and in due course it had reaped spectacular reward. Kavad, ever innovative, had graced the Lakhmids with an unprecedented promotion when, shortly after the outbreak of war with Rome in 502, he appointed their youthful and brutally able chieftain, Mundhir, to rule as king over all the scattered Arab tribes that were then confederated to *Iranshahr*. Hira—a sprawl of settlements that alternated mud-brick walls with encampments, gardens with desert scrub, and wheat fields with herds of camels—provided the Lakhmid chieftain with the perfect showcase for this trend-setting fusion of royalty and banditry. Not for nothing, in the Lakhmids' own language, did the city's name mean "camp."[75] Mundhir, who spent his time there living alternately in a palace and a tent, aimed to combine the best of Persian sophistication with the noblest traditions of his own people. Profits from plunder were spent not only on beefing up his offensive capabilities but on the manifold glories and pleasures of life as an Arab. From camel-archers to poets, brigands to dancing girls, Hira boasted them all. Even the odd scribe was to be found there: for the city, so it was plausibly claimed, was where the Arabs had first learned to put their language into writing. Unsurprisingly, it attracted a steady stream of migrants from across the desert, all hungry for the patronage that Mundhir could so swaggeringly provide. "A day and a night at Hira," it was said, "are better than a whole year of medicine."[76]

No single place in the Roman sphere of influence could quite rival the dazzle of this appeal. That this was so, however, reflected not any lack of contacts between the Arabs and Rome, but rather their sheer range and antiquity. Along the western fringes of the desert, no particular exoticism attached itself to the notion that the realms of the nomad and the city might be blended. The Nabataeans, and many other tribes too, had been citizens of Rome for centuries. One of their number had even risen to become Caesar: Philip, the same emperor who had presided over the capital's millennial celebrations, had hailed from a city on the frontier, to the east of the Sea of Galilee, and been derisively nicknamed "the Arab." The existence of settlements such as Philip's home town right on the margins of the desert were evidence enough of the whole-hearted relish with which the Arabs, no less than any other people of the empire, might embrace the *pax Romana* and settle down.

Nowhere, however, was this more apparent than in the Negev, the arid wilderness that stretched between the Sinai and Petra, and where, even as Mundhir was establishing his regime in Hira, vines and olives were being conjured from the sand. Take one of the paved roads—the *strata*—that criss-crossed the region, and in due course an entire city would materialise on the horizon, rising like a mirage above the desolation, a paradise of farmland, stone houses and baths. A miracle? Hardly. It was only through the most back-breaking labour that the ceaseless battle against the sands could hope to be won, only with the most exhaustive maintenance of cisterns, aqueducts and dams. Yet the cities of the Negev, for all that the water might sometimes taste brackish, and the scrub-flecked desert stretch away barren in every direction, did truly serve as outposts of the wider world beyond. Even in the most remote, an isolated settlement by the name of Nessana that served pilgrims on the road to Sinai as a final way-stop, there were bureaucrats who wrote in Greek and would-be lawyers who studied Latin. More than two centuries after Constantine had filched the Palladium for his new capital, there was even a copy of the *Aeneid* in the local library. In Nessana, time, as well as distance, might be dissolved: for the myths of which Virgil had sung were older by far than himself, older even than Rome. On frayed papyri in the depths of a lonely desert, the halls of Mount Olympus—where the gods of Greece had reclined on exquisite couches, partnered by ox-eyed goddesses, and served wine by eternally beautiful youths—still preserved a spectral hold.

Given enough time, then, it seemed that even "the wolves of Arabia"[77] might be domesticated into lawyers or literary critics. Certainly, from the perspective of such cities as Nessana—where the prodigious array of hydraulic works was accompanied by a quite striking absence of fortifications—it did genuinely appear as though the desert had been tamed. A comforting reassurance, perhaps—except that, in truth, the imperial authorities had no desire to see every last Saracen de-fanged. Along the limits of the empire, where Mundhir's Lakhmids were conducting ever more audacious raids, there was an urgent need for attack-dogs of their own. Many a Roman base might boast an encampment of Saracens: a *hira*. Other concentrations of Arab *foederati*—entire cities of tents, thronged with a shifting population of warriors, horses and camels—lay under the command of tribal chieftains rather than Roman officers. The reign of Justinian would see the largest of these—a teeming settlement east of the Golan Heights called Jabiya—become to Syria and Palestine what Hira was to Ctesiphon: a key defensive stronghold. The tribesmen who lived there—the *Banu Ghassan*—were recognisably the mirror-image of the Lakhmids: for the "Sons of Ghassan" combined a ferocious loyalty to their imperial patrons with a haughty Arab chauvinism. Certainly, the Latin spoken in Jabiya owed little to the study of Virgil. The phrases familiar to the Arabs of the frontier derived not from poets but from the army. Over the course of the previous centuries, the sheer awesome immensity of Rome's military apparatus had stamped itself indelibly upon the language spoken by the *foederati*. So it was, for instance, that the camps of the frontier-system—the *castra*—had provided the Arabs with their own word for fortress: *qasr*. So it was too that the *strata*, the paved roads built by Roman military engineers to link each camp along the frontier, had bequeathed their name to the entire desert south of Palmyra. Indeed, such was their impact upon the *foederati* that *sirat*—the form that the original Latin word had come to take in Arabic—could signify almost any kind of path.[78] The *strata*, those great gashes of gravel and stone scored in straight lines across even the most unforgiving of landscapes, had become for the Arabs the very quintessence of a highway.

Not that they themselves, of course, had much need of paving stones. What would their record of banditry have been, after all, without a talent for going off-road? In early 529, when Mundhir suddenly appeared in northern Syria, looting and burning almost to the walls of Antioch, the leaden-footed response of the provincial authorities was little different to that of some hapless farmer finding his sheep-pen being cleaned out. "For with such speed did he move, and with such ruthless calculation, that invariably he would be gone with his loot before the military authorities could even discover what was going on, let alone arrive to stop it."[79] Fire of this order could only hope to be fought with fire; and Justinian knew it. A few months after Mundhir's rampage through Syria, he crowned an Arab all of his own. His choice, predictably enough, had fallen upon the chieftain of the *Banu Ghassan*, a youthful but already seasoned warlord by the name of al-Harith—or, as he was known by his patrons, Arethas. Summoned from Jabiya to Constantinople, the Ghassanid prince was splendidly arrayed in the white silken cloak of Roman monarchy and a bejewelled coronet.[80] His promotion bore witness to Justinian's customary eye for talent. Arethas, no less than Mundhir, was a man of boldness, charisma and vision. What was more, he positively revelled in a blood feud. Before long, the two warlords' struggle had come to possess its own furious and deadly rhythm, as relentless as it was personal. To no one's great surprise, the signing in 532 of a treaty between Justinian and Khusrow, for all its ambition to establish "an eternal peace"[81] between the two empires, did little to dampen the mutual hatred of their respective Arab clients. Ghassanid and Lakhmid: both, across the desert sands, continued to eyeball each other.

Nor was it merely their political loyalties, or even their personal vanities, that rendered their mutual hatreds so unblinking. Neither Arethas nor Mundhir had any doubt that they were engaged in a conflict that was more than earthly. If Christians saw in the desert the ultimate arena, where athletes of God might test themselves to the limits of their endurance against entire armies of demonic adversaries, then it certainly needed no baptism for an Arab to recognise in it a realm alive with spirits. Many of these—whether borne on a scorching wind or haunting a bone-littered salt flat—were malevo-lent in the extreme; but not all were, by any means. Some—such as the owls that rose from the heads of men slain in battle—served as the guardians of individual warriors, while others stood watch over particular places. The favour of the divine might be experienced wherever there was water, or shade, or merely a landscape of startling beauty. The Arabs had little need of idols, let alone temples, to alert those who approached a god of his presence. Focus of their awe was much more likely to be a natural feature: if not a tree, as at Mamre, then a spring, or a mountain-peak, or a rock. Always, however, there was only the one certain measure of holiness. A god could be reck-oned no god who did not on occasion keep his sanctuary free of violence. At certain times, in certain places, tribes who might other-wise have slaughtered one another with ferocious abandon would assemble upon ground staked out as hallowed—*haram*—and there join in festivities quite as joyous and peaceable as those staged every summer at Mamre. Of the Arabs' major shrine, which lay surrounded by palm trees somewhere in the desert south of Palestine, and where the local people were reported to gather twice a year for a whole month or more at a time, it was rumoured "that even the wild beasts live in peace with men, and among themselves."[82] Not, however, that pacifism was necessarily on the agenda the whole year round. The gods of the desert, away from their shrines, rarely objected to blood-shed. On occasion, they might positively demand it. At Hira, for instance, there stood two stones sacred to a god named Dushara, which his worshippers would regularly make sticky with gore.[83] A second deity, al-'Uzza—the "Mighty Queen"—was graced with an even more spectacular draught of blood when, in 527, Mundhir sac-rificed no fewer than four hundred Christian virgins in her honour. Such a goddess—one able to consecrate the soil of the Lakhmid cap-ital as *haram* while simultaneously sponsoring the most flamboyant atrocities—could hardly have been better suited to the warlord's needs.

Yet there remained something strangely pallid about her, and

Dushara too, and all the various gods of the desert. Many, to their worshippers, were little more than names. Loyalty, as a result, was rarely a feature of Arab devotions. A deity who failed a tribe in battle, or neglected to keep it in food, or scared away the camels, would be dumped without a moment's hesitation. Many were the oases where there stood altars "old in years, bearing inscriptions in ancient letters of unknown tongues,"[84] raised to gods whose very names had been forgotten. Temples would cheerfully be used to pen goats.[85] To Christian scholars—whose dread of demons such as Artemis was often a form of reluctant tribute paid to their inherent glamour—the Arabs' gods seemed reassuringly dull. Even attempts to condemn them risked making them more interesting than they were. When Epiphanius, the same energetic cataloguer of heresies who had condemned the Ebionites, turned his beady eye on Dushara, he reported that the god's worshippers, in a blasphemous parody of Christian belief, believed the deity to have been born of a virgin—a *ka'iba*. The bishop, however, had misheard: Dushara was not a god of a *ka'iba* but of a *ka'ba*—a "cube." The allusion was to the stone, black and uncarved, that the Nabataeans worshipped as an incarnation of the god, somewhere in a shrine to the south of the Dead Sea.[86] Dushara certainly had nothing so sophisticated as a virgin mother.

Meanwhile, many Arabs were turning to the worship of a god who did. Nabataean cities had grown crowded with churches; and even in the wilds of the desert, beyond the reach of either emperor or bishop, whole tribes were turning to Christ. There was often a fair degree of opportunism in this: for it was well known that the Romans would only ever bestow their patronage upon Arabs who ranked as fellow Christians. Yet, the Ghassanids—and Arethas especially—were the decided opposite of lukewarm. They refused, on principle, to abandon the distinctively Monophysite character of their faith. They built, resplendently solid amid the tents of their encampment at Jabiya, a massive church. They paraded, in their ongoing vendetta against the Lakhmids, a devotion to Christ that was quite as militant as Mundhir's loyalty to al-'Uzza. Granted, the Ghassanids did not think to offer up virgins in sacrifice—but neither did they ever doubt, as they hacked down their pagan adversaries, that their swords were touched by the authentic fire of heaven.

And who was to say that they were wrong? Time was when any notion that the Saracens might have been blessed by the particular favour of God would have been greeted with hilarity—but lately, in the bringing of the desert tribes to Christ, there had been hints, just perhaps, of the workings of some broader, more mysterious providence. Many were the wonders, after all, that had assisted with their conversion. The presence in the desert of so many saints, so many Spirit-charged men of God, had certainly helped to deliver a steady stream of miracles to the Saracens. Their barren had been given children, and their sick had been restored to health: a record of medical achievement that no pagan could begin to rival. Stylites were particularly popular; and many were the tribes who would gather to gawp at them and their austerities in wide-eyed stupefaction. To Christians, most of whom had been brought up to loathe and dread the Saracens, the spectacle of desert nomads smashing idols before the pillar of a saint, pledging themselves loudly to Christ and even, in the ultimate act of renunciation, "vowing to forgo the flesh of donkey and camel,"[87] might be cause for considered reflection. One such, a bishop from Antioch by the name of Theodoret, had been brought to conclude that the Saracens, despite their illiteracy and their taste for slumming it in tents, were "endowed with an intelligence lively and penetrating, and a judgement fully capable of discerning truth and refuting falsehood."[88] He had seen whole crowds of them gathered before the pillar of the original stylite, Saint Simeon the Elder himself—and had marked the effect. To a people wild and free such as the Saracens prided themselves on being, the show of a man prostrating himself before God, as Simeon had done, over and over again, might at first have appeared demeaning; but not after they had watched him persist with it for days and nights at a time. In submission, so the spectacle had taught them, lay the surest path to God. Saracens, even Saracens, might be brought to grasp that truth.

But there was an additional, and more haunting, reason why scholars such as Theodoret should have taken a particular interest in the Saracens: they were the only barbarians who featured in the Bible. Isaac had not been Abraham's sole son; nor Sarah his sole bed-partner. Prior to the dramatic appearance of the Almighty at Mamre, the barrenness of the patriarch's wife had prompted him to take as a concubine her maid, an Egyptian by the name of Hagar. Sure enough, the slave-girl had borne Abraham a son; but Sarah, bitter and jealous, had driven the mother and her newborn baby out into the desert. There an angel had appeared to Hagar and told her that Ishmael, her child, was destined to prove "a wild ass of a man, his hand against every man and every man's hand against him"[89]—and the father of a great people. But which people? The answer to that, the clues being as glaring as they were, was self-evident. The Children of Ishmael, that "wild ass of a man": who were these, if not the Arabs? Certainly, such an identification had long been accepted as fact.[90] And the potential implications of this Hagarene bloodline? They, by and large, had been left to hang. Perhaps, however, they should not have been. Like Isaac, so it was recorded in Holy Scripture, Ishmael had been circumcised by Abraham's own hand; and, like Jacob, he had fathered twelve sons. Suggestive markers of the favour of God, surely? That, at any rate, was what numerous Saracens had begun to ask. Theodoret himself had cited the example of the nomads who roamed the wilds east of Antioch: "for, in that desert live those who are proud to derive their descent from their ancestor Ishmael."[91]

Other Arabs, though, were not so sure. Hagar hardly ranked as the classiest of ancestors, after all. A slave-girl and a brood-mare, she had been a refugee to boot: driven not once but twice into exile by a resentful Sarah. The second occasion had followed the birth of Isaac, when Ishmael and his hapless mother had been obliged to take up residence "in the wilderness of Paran."[92] The location of this particular desert was much debated, with some scholars, including Saint Paul himself, identifying it with the Sinai. The overwhelming consensus, however, was that it could only have been the Negev. No other wilderness stood closer to the sites most associated with Abraham: Mamre, and the Church of Saint Lot, and Hebron, where the patriarch lay buried in a cave with Isaac and Jacob. Certainly, the Arabs of the Negev, when they accepted baptism, appear to have had a particular enthusiasm for naming themselves "Abraham"——as though to remind their fellow Christians that they, unlike other converts, had been blessed by the marks of God's favour long before the time of Christ.[93] Yet this pedigree, even so, was a potentially awkward one for them to flaunt. How, after all, were the Arabs to lay claim to a primal inheritance from Abraham without also acknowledging their descent from a slave-girl? A measure of embarrassment, perhaps, was only natural. So much so, in fact, that it seems to have led one scholar, a contemporary of Theodoret's by the name of Sozomen, to offer a particularly ingenious explanation for the origin of the word "Saracen." "Mortified by the servile character of Hagar," he explained, "the Ishmaelites decided to conceal the opprobrium of their origin by adopting a name which would imply that they were descended instead from Sarah, the wife of Abraham."[94]

An implausible theory——but a telling one all the same. Sozomen came from near Gaza, between the Mediterranean and the Negev, and was an experienced observer of the region. He had travelled to Mamre, for instance, and witnessed the crowds that gathered there: he knew full well that it was not only Christians who reverenced Abraham, but Jews and pagans too. This led him, in contrast to Theodoret, to contemplate a quite hideous possibility. What if the Saracens' knowledge of their ancestry did not necessarily lead them to Christ? What if it led them in a different direction altogether?

> After all, their origin being what it is, they practise circumcision like the Jews, refrain from the use of pork like the Jews, and observe many other Jewish rites and customs. That they deviate at all from the Laws of the Jewish people can only be ascribed to the lapse of time, and to the influence upon them of other, pagan peoples.[95]

It was a devastating insight—and had an obvious corollary. Cleanse the Arabs of their paganism, and it might not be a Christian people at all that emerged from beneath the ordure, but something alarmingly different: whole tribes of Jews. In fact, according to Sozomen, this had already happened: "There are those of them who, by coming into contact with Jews, learn the truth of their origins, and so return to the ways of their kinsmen, and are persuaded to adopt Jewish customs and laws."[96] Who precisely these Jews might be, Sozomen did not think to say; but it certainly suggested that Christianity, beyond the reaches of Roman control, was not the only option available to Arabs embarked on a spiritual quest.

Or indeed to Arabs who wished simply to dig in their heels and defy the superpower. In 524, at a time when Roman ambassadors were closeted with Mundhir, negotiating the release of two prominent prisoners, a delegation of emissaries from the distant kingdom of Himyar arrived unexpectedly at the summit. These ambassadors, to the Romans' horror, brought news of an atrocity fit to put even those of Mundhir in the shade: the wholesale slaughter of the Christians of Najran. Even more terrifyingly, Yusuf, the Himyarite king, had sent a proposal of alliance to his Lakhmid counterpart: one that he suggested be sealed with the blood of the Christians of Hira.

Out of the blue, the ambassadors from Constantinople found themselves confronted by a nightmare of threateningly global proportions. An alliance of pagan and Jewish interests, forged well beyond the reach of Roman arms, was too hellish to be countenanced. With *Iranshahr* in firm control of the Persian Gulf, trade links to India were already being steadily asphyxiated; and now, with a Jewish kingdom established beside the Red Sea straits, there was pressure coming to bear on a second vital windpipe. The menace, however, was more than merely material. The Jewish character of Himyar was no mere pretension or show. Yusuf, although he had seized power by toppling a Christian regime, was not, by any means, the first Jew to rule the kingdom. In fact, there had been Jewish monarchs in Himyar for almost as long as there had been Christian emperors in Rome. In 440, when a massive dam had been repaired at Marib, the ancient capital of Sheba, the king had publicly dedicated it to the God of Israel: *Rahmanan*—"The Merciful."[97] The same identical title, as it happened, was one much bandied about in the Talmud; nor was it surprising that the rabbis of Palestine, resentful as they were of their Christian masters, took a good deal of interest in the Himyarite monarchy. Granted, the enthusiasm of Yusuf and his predecessors for aping King David was hardly one of which they could entirely approve; and it may be that the presence of rabbis from Tiberias at his court reflected a desire on their part to temper some of his more flamboyant excesses. That, however, was not how it appeared to the local Christians, who predictably blamed the holocaust at Najran on the machinations of the rabbis—nor, of course, to the fretful Roman authorities.

To the profound relief of Constantinople, though, no sooner had the danger of an alliance between Hira's pagans and Himyar's Jews flared up than it was successfully being extinguished. Mundhir, far removed from Himyar, was bought off easily enough. Then, even as one Roman embassy returned in triumph from Hira, another set off for the kingdom that lay directly opposite Himyar, and which by great good fortune just happened to be Christian: Ethiopia. Not that the country's king was entirely without his drawbacks. The "Negus," in addition to being a Monophysite, was also quite insufferably conceited: for it was his claim, based as it was on a presumed descent from Solomon and the Queen of Sheba, to rank as the world's pre-eminent Christian monarch. Under normal circumstances, of course, the ambassadors of Caesar would have laughed this pretension to scorn; but the circumstances were hardly normal. A treaty was duly patched up. When the Ethiopians launched their invasion of Himyar, they made the crossing in a borrowed Roman fleet. In the wake of Yusuf's overthrow and death, the conquered kingdom was transformed into an Ethiopian protectorate and Roman merchants were once again free to use its harbours and trading stations. Meanwhile, at Najran, a domed monument named the *Ka'ba*, on account of its cuboid base, was raised above the ruins of the cathedral: a memorial to the priests and virgins left slaughtered by Yusuf.

All of which, back in Constantinople, could be viewed with tremendous satisfaction. Imperial policy towards the Saracens appeared to be in excellent shape. Irrespective of the pestiferous brews of heresy and insurrection that might occasionally bubble up beyond the frontier, the Roman state clearly had the wherewithal—and the reach—to deal with them all. After the successful pacification of Himyar, it was evident that the Roman Empire remained what it had always been: a global superpower.

"Dominion without limit": it seemed that the ancient maxim still held good.

5

COUNTDOWN TO APOCALYPSE

New Wine in Old Bottles

The toppling of Yusuf was a victory for Christ as well as for Caesar. This presumption—that the interests of the two were indistinguishable—came naturally to the Roman people. Even those who journeyed beyond the horizons of the Mediterranean, and could appreciate the true immensity of the world, tended to take for granted that the empire ruled from Constantinople had no rival as a superpower, blessed and protected as it was by God. Even in the far-off island of Taprobane—the land we know today as Sri Lanka—Roman merchants found it easy to put their Persian rivals in the shade. One of them, seeking to demonstrate New Rome's palpable supremacy over *Iranshahr*, placed two gold coins in the local king's palm—one stamped with the image of Caesar and the other with the head of the *Shahanshah*. The Roman currency was magnificently and self-evidently the heavier: a fact that owed much to the watchful financial stewardship of Anastasius, but also, and more transcendently, to the favour of the Almighty. As one merchant, an Egyptian who had visited the markets of Ethiopia and navigated the tides of the Persian Gulf, piously put it: "The empire of the Roman people shares directly in the dignity of the Kingdom of Christ." Its future was therefore assured: "It will never be

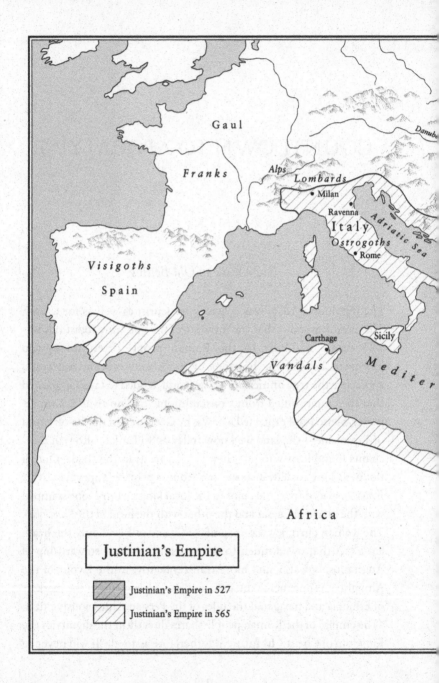

Gaul

Danube

Franks

Alps
Lombards
• Milan
Ravenna
Adriatic Sea

Italy
Ostrogoths
• Rome

Visigoths

Spain

Carthage
Sicily

Vandals

Mediter

Africa

Justinian's Empire

Justinian's Empire in 527

Justinian's Empire in 565

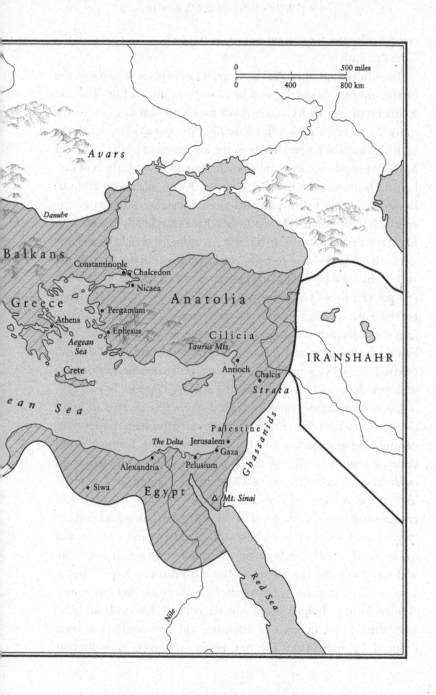

conquered—not for so long as it serves to promote the spread of the Christian faith."[1]

The Church, of course, had been ambitious to plant the cross on the furthermost reaches of the world ever since the time of Paul. That the Roman state had a duty to contribute to this mission was, however, a more radical presumption. Traditionally, "the spread of the Christian faith" beyond the empire had been the achievement of the weak and humble: prisoners of war, and women abducted into the beds of barbarian chieftains. The overthrow of the Jewish regime in Himyar, however, pointed to the potential of an altogether more muscular approach. This lesson, if obvious to merchants, was hardly one likely to have been missed by Justinian himself. Accordingly, even as he set himself to the suppression of paganism and heresy within the limits of the empire, he fixed his unblinking gaze upon the sump that lay beyond. For the first time in Roman history, the conversion of pagan kings became enshrined as a priority of state. Imperially sponsored missionaries were dispatched east, to the mountainous wilds that stretched beyond the Black Sea, and south, past Egypt, to the land of Nubia. Here, bred of Justinian's inimitable blend of piety, restlessness and self-regard, was something fatefully novel: an ethical foreign policy.

Missionaries alone, however, could never be expected to bring everyone to Christ. That much was evident. Fortunately, however, in his ambition to shape the world to his own purposes, Justinian could draw on traditions older by far than the Church. Some sixty years before the emperor's accession, a Roman aristocrat in Gaul, despairing at the collapse of imperial authority all around him, had conjured up from the glories of the vanished past a poignant fantasy: "an armed Caesar, before whose advance both land and sea will quake, until at last, with the renewed power of his war-trumpet, he will serve to rouse the navies of Rome from their sleep."[2] Such a Caesar, of course, had never materialised. Gaul, and the entire Roman West, had slipped from imperial control. The lands administered directly by the heirs to Augustus and Constantine had been reduced by half. That did not mean, however, that Roman pretensions had in any way been diminished. Quite the contrary. If the empire ruled from Constantinople were truly—as Justinian believed it to be—an earthly reflection of the monarchy of God, then its current truncated state was not merely a crisis of geopolitical proportions, but an offence against the heavens. Christians could not be truly Christian unless they were Roman as well.

A presumption with which even some barbarians might concur. In the West, where gangs of one-time *foederati* had been busy carving up the various provinces, the penalty of success had tended to be a certain nagging status anxiety. Naked gangsterdom might win a warlord temporary bragging rights, but it could provide little in the way of either prestige or long-term security. That, however, was precisely where the example of an ancient and ineffably glamorous monarchy had its uses. To any ambitious chieftain, the emperor in Constantinople, who ruled as both the deputy of God and the ultimate in earthly sophistication, was the obvious role-model to hand. This was why, decades after the collapse of imperial authority in the West, the face of power there remained both Roman and Christian. Gewgaws dispatched from Constantinople, rather than being scorned, would invariably be seized upon with delight. Churches and queens alike had an insatiable appetite for the shimmer of silks from the eastern empire. Most prized of all, however, were the antique titles that only Caesar had the power to bestow. In Gaul, when Anastasius appointed the king of a notoriously savage people named the Franks to the consulship—an office that reached back to the earliest days of the republic—the warlord was so delighted by this mark of esteem that he promptly took to sporting a purple tunic and tossing gold coins to passers-by. Another barbarian king, replying to an embassy from Justin, politely assured the emperor that "our homeland is a part of your world, nor does my royal administration in any way reduce your own sovereignty."[3] Total fantasy, of course—but no less mutually flattering for that. Upstart chieftain and distant Caesar: both alike had a stake in pretending that there still existed, in however shadowy a form, a unified empire, Roman and watched over by God.

As a result, the brute realities of regime change in the West might often be veiled behind a certain studied ambivalence. Nowhere served as more of a *trompe-l'oeil* than Italy, that original seat of empire, where the gauze of ambiguity had been woven with a particular brilliance and subtlety. In outward appearance, indeed, it seemed that nothing much had changed since the palmiest days of Roman greatness. In Rome itself, the Senate continued to meet, consuls to be appointed, and chariot races to be run. In Ravenna—the lagoon-girt and therefore readily defensible city on the Adriatic coast that had served the western empire as its final capital—the administration remained in the hands of impeccably Roman bureaucrats. Meanwhile, with a solemn and formal show of legality, Constantinople had entrusted the western empire's defence to a band of some twenty thousand *foederati* diverted specially for the purpose from the Balkans: the so-called Easterly—or "Ostro-"—Goths.[4] Their commander, a one-time hostage in the imperial household by the name of Theoderic, played the part of Caesar's deputy to perfection. Whether addressing crowds in the Forum, slaughtering armies of savages beyond the Alps, or building palaces, aqueducts and baths, he demonstrated to glorious effect just how Roman a king of *foederati* might truly be. By the time of his death in 526, he had ruled as the master of Italy for longer than any Caesar, with the exception of Augustus himself. As a result, it seems barely to have crossed the minds of most Italians that they might not still belong to a Roman empire.

Justinian, however, had not been conned. He knew the sordid truth: a desperate imperial administration had bribed Theoderic and his Ostrogoths with the offer of Italy to remove them from the doorstep of Constantinople. He knew as well that the burnishing of Rome's awesome inheritance, which he had made his life's mission, required the proper ordering of lost provinces as well as of mildewed laws. Barbarian kings, no matter how sedulously they might ape the manners of a Caesar, were self-evidently an affront to God's wishes for the world. Theoderic, for all the sheen of his classical education, had been given to murdering courtiers with his own hands, and sporting a moustache.[5] And even that was not the worst. Monstrously, two whole centuries after the Council of Nicaea, there were churches standing in Ravenna in which it was openly denied that the Son was "of one Being with the Father." Like a ghoul rising from a long-sealed sarcophagus, Theoderic had trailed after him the stench of evils that orthodox Christians had imagined buried for good. Not merely a heretic, he had been that veritable heretic of heretics: an Arian.

There was, in this devotion of Theoderic's to a creed that most Romans had presumed extinct, compelling evidence of just how hospitable to otherwise vanished beliefs a wilderness might be. As in the deserts beyond Palestine, so in the forests beyond the Danube and the Rhine, heresies long since consigned to oblivion within the limits of the empire had demonstrated a striking ability to endure, and even to thrive. The Goths' Arian loyalties had a venerable pedigree. In the late 340s, when a son of Constantine still sat on the throne, and Julian was lurking in the wings, a bishop named Ulfilas, of Gothic extraction and Arian sympathies, had headed north towards the Danube and embarked on a mission to convert his compatriots. If the stories subsequently told about him were something more than fantastical exaggeration, his success had been prodigious. Certainly, within a century of his death, he was being hailed as the Moses of the northern barbarians.[6] This, for people who were all too painfully conscious of Roman snobbery, was a thrilling notion: they too, like the Children of Israel, might have been chosen by God to receive a Promised Land. The consequence was, when a group who called themselves the "Good," or "Visi," Goths, succeeded in winning Spain, they pointedly refused to abandon their Arianism in favour of Catholic orthodoxy. Theoderic too, even after he had won for himself the throne of Italy, clung to his Arian faith with a no less obdurate show of devotion.

Granted, he was careful not to force it down the throats of his Roman subjects. "We cannot impose religion," he solemnly declared, "because no one can be made to believe against his will."[7] A statement of principle, no doubt—but calculating as well. In both Visigothic Spain and Ostrogothic Italy, the invaders constituted a tiny minority.

They certainly had no chance of forcing the natives to renounce Nicaea and embrace the teachings of Arius. As it was, Theoderic was content to leave the Catholics in peace, fattening them up the better to fleece them. Meanwhile, even as he played with dazzling skill and sophistication at being a Roman, his Arian faith helped him to forge an ever more distinctive identity for himself and his followers, recruited as they were from a number of disparate sources. Long hair, an aptitude for running people through with lances while ululating loudly on horseback, and an emphasis on the humanity of Christ: such were the markers of Italy's new elite. "A Goth on the make," so Theoderic had once ruefully observed, "wishes to be like a Roman—but only a poor Roman would wish to be a Goth."[8] This appraisal, however, might have been unduly pessimistic. A few decades into his reign in Ravenna, there was no shortage of high-born Romans eager to master his native tongue. Given time, who knew just how Gothic they might end up?

But time, as events were to prove, was running out. No sooner had Justinian signed up to the optimistically titled "Eternal Peace" with Khusrow in 532 than he was turning his gaze westwards. Most of his advisers—well aware that the war with Persia had emptied the treasury so assiduously filled by Anastasius—were appalled. Justinian imperiously brushed aside all muttered objections. In a dream, an African bishop, martyred a few decades previously on a bonfire, had urged the emperor to conquer Carthage, which for almost a century had been lost to the Roman people. Who could doubt, then, that Christ was all in favour of the emperor's new initiative? Certainly, the bishop's murderers, a gang of unregenerate savages named the Vandals, could hardly have done more to brand themselves as enemies of God. Their theft of the wealthy cities and fertile wheat fields of North Africa had been only the first step in their career of iniquity. Like the Ostrogoths, the Vandals were Arians; unlike the Ostrogoths, they had been prompted by a blend of paranoia, fanaticism and their own force of numbers to strip the Catholic Church of all its privileges, to persecute its leaders, and to proclaim Arianism their state religion. Well, then, might Justinian thunderously denounce them as "the enemies alike of soul and body."⁹ News that the Vandal court had abruptly succumbed to a vicious bout of in-fighting only strengthened his resolve, and his assurance that God was willing him on. Accordingly, it was not Italy but Africa upon which Justinian first set his sights.

In 533, when a great war fleet that had been assembled off the imperial palace weighed anchor and departed the Bosphorus, most of those watching it glide towards the setting of the sun feared the worst. Cavalry and infantry totalled only eighteen thousand men, and although their commander was Belisarius—the general who had so brilliantly defeated the Persians at Dara—the Roman military's record since then did not inspire any great confidence. Before long, though, the people of Constantinople would be thrilling to a catalogue of barely believable accomplishments. The Roman task force, disembarking on African soil after a voyage of two months, briskly marched on Carthage, routed the enemy in a couple of great battles, and forced their surrender. The churches and cathedrals of North Africa, cleansed of all traces of Arianism, were lovingly restored to Catholic worship. Meanwhile, the defeated Vandal king, transported to Constantinople along with all his treasure, was paraded in chains before the cheering crowds of the Hippodrome. "Vanity of vanities," he was heard to mutter wistfully, "all is vanity."¹⁰

Hardly, of course, a message for which Justinian had much time; and sure enough, buoyed by his stunning victory, he did not hesitate to press for further conquests. In 535, Belisarius duly swept down with a fresh war fleet upon Sicily, where the garrison of Ostrogoths was routed with promising ease. A year later, and the long-awaited invasion of Italy itself was launched. By the early winter of 536, Belisarius was advancing upon Rome; and on 9 December, at the prompting of the city's bishop, the ancient capital opened its gates to the imperial forces. "So it was," as an aide to Belisarius exulted, "that Rome once again, after a period of sixty years, became subject to the Romans."¹¹

Which was, of course, to overlook the awkward fact that Italy—officially, at any rate—had never ceased to be subject to the Romans.

Certainly, to the Italians themselves, the news that they were being liberated came as something of a surprise. If there were many who welcomed with open arms what Justinian grandly termed a "renewal" of the Roman world, then there were many more who despaired of the slaughter and impoverishment that this "renewal" seemed to mean in practice. The Ostrogoths, unlike the Vandals, displayed an infuriating reluctance to crumple. Only a few weeks after the fall of Rome to Belisarius, they were back, camped out in such prodigious numbers before the walls of the city that "the people of Rome, who were entirely unacquainted with the evils of war and siege,"[12] hurried to their liberator and begged him to capitulate. Belisarius, playing the role of an antique hero from the city's distant past to perfection, sternly refused. One year and nine days later, after an immensely creative and obdurate defence, it was the Ostrogoths who were obliged to retreat. By then, though, the one-time "Head of the World" had effectively been decapitated. Rome's aqueducts, which for centuries had provided the city with its life-blood of water, had been ruined beyond repair; its baths emptied; its harbours destroyed; its water-mills clogged with corpses; its senators, those who had not been captured and executed by the indignant Ostrogoths, reduced to beggary. Even worse was to follow. By 538, famine was rife across central Italy. Food shortages were so severe that innkeepers, so it was credibly reported, were reduced to spit-roasting the occasional guest, just to get by. The following year, the Ostrogoths, signalling as brutally as they could their determination to continue the fight, wiped out the city of Milan. Here, even to someone as supremely self-confident as Justinian, was unmistakable evidence that not everything was going according to plan.

Visionary the emperor might have been—but not to the point of pig-headed impracticality. The gamble that he had taken, in overriding the instinctive caution of his treasurers, and launching his western wars, had already brought him impressive winnings. The gold of the Vandals, the taxes busily being screwed out of the new provincials: these, if the situation in Italy could only be stabilised, would surely enable him to pause for breath, and reckon himself still well ahead. Accordingly, in 539, Justinian made his barbarian foes a shrewdly calibrated offer of peace: the rump of northern Italy, and half of Theoderic's treasure. The cornered Ostrogoths were minded to sign— and so perhaps they would have done, had not Belisarius, convinced that total victory lay within his grasp, exploited the swirl of negotiations to seize Ravenna. A pyrrhic triumph: for much would be lost by his act of treachery. Justinian's offer of peace, unsurprisingly, was rejected out of hand; the Ostrogoths picked up their lances once again; the murderous conflict ground on. As for Belisarius, his star was left much diminished. Recalled to Constantinople, he was greeted by his master with a notable *froideur*. Although permitted to show off the riches captured in Ravenna in the Senate, the great general was pointedly refused a second chance to grandstand in the Hippodrome. To the general's admirers, this appeared the rankest ingratitude; but Justinian, scanning not merely the western front, but the entire sweep of his empire, could appreciate better than anyone the opportunity that Belisarius had lost him.

That the emperor was a man of terrifying appetites, a megalomaniac "who has tried to seize the whole earth, and been captured by the desire to take for himself each and every realm," appeared self-evident to his opponents: fit reflection of his demonic-seeming energy and ambitions.[13] Yet Justinian, even as he laboured to reshape the world in the image of the heavens, had learned the hard way that the affairs of a mortal monarchy might always, if pushed too far, abruptly reach a breaking point. Back in 534, as he had sat in state to watch the parading of the Vandal king, neither he nor any of the cheering crowds would have been able to forget that only two years previously the Hippodrome had been piled high with corpses. A grim but not, perhaps, unprofitable lesson: unpleasant surprises might be lurking around the corner even for the most God-blessed of emperors.

Justinian was certainly not oblivious to the danger that his window of opportunity in Italy might close at any moment. What had been risked by the opening of a western front, after all, was the same prospect as had haunted Roman policy-makers ever since the time of Valerian, and which threatened the eastern provinces with a stench of smoke and blood more terrible by far than any that Constantinople had known. Sat in the hurriedly renovated Hippodrome in 534, watching through no doubt narrowed eyes the strut and glitter of Belisarius's triumph, had been the ambassadors of Khusrow. Their master, *Shahanshah* for a mere three years, had been much preoccupied at the time with stamping his authority on both his realm and his own household. Even as Justinian's armies were sweeping westwards, the young King of Kings had been fighting for his life against a coup led by his uncle. Aspebedes, whose treachery was compounded by the fact that he was also the father of Khusrow's beloved queen, had been a peculiarly menacing adversary. The death struggle had convulsed the royal household as well as the empire at large. By the time Khusrow finally emerged victorious, he did not have much in the way of male relatives left. Uncles, brothers and nephews: all had been ruthlessly culled. A brutal expedient—but one that had left the *Shahanshah* free to turn his attention to other, more profitable, matters. In 539, when two undercover Gothic agents crossed the border into *Iranshahr* and appealed to Khusrow for help, he listened to their urgings with great attention. The supposed eternity of his peace with Constantinople did not blind him to the potential advantages of stabbing the old enemy in the back. Envy of Justinian's feats; anxiety as to what they might bode for *Iranshahr*; quiet confidence that the Roman military might be ill-prepared to fight simultaneously on two fronts: here were incentives aplenty. Only the one problem intervened: how was Khusrow, "the divine, virtuous and peace-loving Khusrow,"[14] to get away with such flagrant treachery?

It was his ever-dependable attack-dog, Mundhir, who provided him with the solution. To the plunder-hungry Lakhmids, the Eternal Peace had only ever been a minor inconvenience. Low-level skirmishes with the Ghassanids had continued unabated throughout the decade, and by 539 Mundhir and Arethas were busy amusing themselves by scrapping over the desert of Strata. Even though the Ghassanids, with perfect justification, could point to the fact that the region had a Latin name and was therefore self-evidently Roman, Khusrow gave his full backing to the Lakhmids. As orders went out across *Iranshahr* to prepare for war, he shamelessly escalated the crisis. By the spring of 540, he had worked himself up into a fury so self-righteous that he could feel himself perfectly justified in breaking the Eternal Peace with the Romans. Riding at the head of a mighty strike force, the King of Kings headed west out of Ctesiphon, along the Euphrates, towards the border. Unlike his father four decades previously, though, Khusrow did not intend to waste his energies battering the defences of the frontier itself. Rather, he planned to bypass them. Beyond him and his army, rich, fat and tantalising, lay the cities of Syria. Khusrow, by striking hard and deep at the very vitals of the province, aimed to put his great adversary to a searching test. Just how much of a distraction had Justinian's wars in the West been to his level of preparedness at the opposite end of the empire?

The grim truth was that few of the cities now in the path of "the wind of the East"[15] boasted walls to compare with those that girded Dara. Fortifications built centuries earlier were in a state of crumbling disrepair. Nor was that the limit of dilapidation in the province. Cities across Syria appeared to have been swamped with squatters. Buildings that once lent them an aura of sumptuous monumentality had increasingly been converted into public quarries, so that in the centre of many a city, one-time splendid temples or arenas were now nothing but vagrant-filled shells. Elsewhere too, contours were similarly being lost, whether in statue-lined squares or along grand processional avenues, as public space after public space vanished beneath a sprawl of makeshift stores and workshops. What had originally been broad, marble-paved thoroughfares were becoming ever narrower, meandering, donkey-crowded lanes. Every so often, it was true, attempts might be made to impose at least a measure of regulation, "by clearing away the stalls which had been built by tradesmen in the colonnades and streets"[16]—but all in vain. The city authorities, however, were not fighting decline, but something no less awkward to keep in check: success. Syria was rich, exceedingly rich; and the spirit of commerce in the province had simply grown too flourishing to be pruned back.

Everyone knew that Syrians were "natural businessmen, and the greediest of mortals."[17] It was hardly surprising, then, that disapproving moralists were inclined to see in the chaos and clamour of their cities monstrous infernos of worldliness. Such a perspective, though, was not entirely proportionate. The Syrians, for all their love of money, were much given to the contempt of it as well. The same people whose "devotion to profit takes them across the whole world"[18] were also celebrated for their stylites. While they no longer lavished their wealth on beautifying cities, they did not merely squander or hoard it, either. "If you would be perfect, go, sell what you possess and give to the poor." Here were words that pious Syrians—wealthy ones included—had engraved on their hearts. If the giving of alms to the poor lacked the ready visual impact that the construction of a theatre, say, or a bath-house would have done, then the poor most likely did not much care. Not all the decay of a city's pagan monuments could disguise the emergence, obtruding through the shabbiness of the old, of an entirely new cityscape: one characterised by hospitals, orphanages and homes for the aged. Blithely indifferent to the miseries of the poor though many Syrian plutocrats remained, enough of them were not to have made some kind of a difference. Public welfare, in a Christian city, had become the surest mark of wealth.

And Khusrow knew it. Leading his army deep into Syria, finding city after city effectively defenceless, Khusrow soon discovered that those who were in the habit of giving to charity were quite prepared to cough up danger money, too. Bishops, frantic to protect their flocks from annihilation, had only to catch a rumour of the *Shahanshah*'s approach and they would scrabble to meet his demands for gold, no matter how outrageous. But Khusrow, even as he swaggered and plundered his way across Syria, had more in mind than mere extortion: he wanted to stage a spectacular. Accordingly, he aimed directly for the richest prize of all, "the fair crown of the East,"[19] a city so globally celebrated that scholars in the far-off land of China invariably muddled it with Constantinople: Antioch.

News of the Persian advance, in Antioch itself, threw the citizens into a state of disbelieving panic. Rich their city might have been—but it was also, even by Syrian standards, quite exceptionally run-down. Over the course of several decades, its wretched inhabitants had suffered a whole succession of calamities: riots, fires, earthquakes. The vast circuit of walls was so cracked and pockmarked that the city was, to all intents and purposes, without defences. Frantically, however, the people of Antioch did all they could to prepare for the looming onslaught: by sending to Palmyra and Damascus for reinforcements, and to Simeon on his pillar for a miracle. The news brought back from the stylite, however, could hardly have been any bleaker. God Himself, speaking to Simeon in a vision, had revealed His plans for Antioch—and they were terrible. "I will fill her with her enemies," so the Almighty had declared, "and I will abandon the greater part of her population to the sword, and those who survive to captivity."[20]

And so it came to pass. Although Simeon himself, courtesy of a divinely dispatched mist, managed to avoid capture by the Persians, the people of Antioch were not so fortunate. Despite a valiant initial defence, their city was soon overrun, put to the torch, and left in ruins. Khusrow, pausing only to have a celebratory dip in the Mediterranean, then turned on his heels and returned to *Iranshahr* in triumph. He took with him long wagon-trains of gold and the survivors from Antioch—some thirty thousand people. Back in Mesopotamia, the *Shahanshah* settled these captives in a new city, built from scratch just outside Ctesiphon: a crowing statement of triumph, inscribed emphatically in fresh mud-brick. Its name was *Veh-Antioch-Khusrow*—"Khusrow-Made-This-City-Better-Than-Antioch."

To the Romans, and to Justinian in particular, the rape of Syria—and the flattening of its famous capital—was a bitter humiliation. Four years earlier, shortly before the invasion of Italy, the emperor had proclaimed his hopes that "God will consent to our establishing our dominion over all of those whom in former times the Roman people ruled, from the boundaries of the one ocean to the other, but lost by their negligence."[21] Now, so it began to be whispered, Justinian's own negligence had turned Italy into a wilderness and Antioch into a desert. In the space of only a year, so it seemed, all his triumphs had turned to dust. Was it possible, some began to wonder, that the very attempt to repair the world had only worsened its fractures?

Justinian himself had no patience with such pessimism. Amid all the sudden calamities that had engulfed him and his dream of fashioning a globe-spanning Christian order, he still maintained his invincible confidence that he was serving the will of God. But disaster was not done with him yet. As the calamitous year of Antioch's sack drew to a close, a horror of barely comprehensible proportions was drawing near to the southernmost borders of his empire.

It threatened not merely the fracture but the annihilation of the world.

The Earth Shall Sit in Mourning

Late summer, 541, and the Egyptian sun was at its most broiling. Those who lived along the shoreline might well have turned their faces to the sea, for the blessed relief that a breeze on the cheeks could bring. That August, however, there was something eerie to be seen out on the water—a sight fit, not to cool, but to chill the blood. Phantasms were sailing the sea. As the sun set and twilight thickened to darkness, dozens of spectral bronze ships, glowing like fire, grew more distinct on the horizon. Sitting on their decks were men with bronze staffs: "And those who travelled in these glittering boats, moving at an unearthly speed across the sea, were black—and they had no heads."[22] Soon enough, it became clear that these ghostly apparitions were not appearing merely at random, but were tracking along the coast; by the end of the month, one fleet of the bronze ships had left Egyptian waters altogether and were observed off Gaza. Meanwhile, a second fleet was heading westwards. Past the various mouths of the Nile it glided until, as August turned into September, it had almost left the delta behind. Ahead stood the greatest port in the entire Mediterranean, where the sight of red and orange light flickering on night-time waves was hardly a novelty: for its harbours boasted a watchtower of such stupefying height that the beacon which blazed from the summit of the structure could be seen up to fifty miles out at sea. Wonders, certainly, were nothing new at Alexandria.

The very name of the city bore witness to its glamorous pedigree. Not even Constantinople could boast a founder to compare with Alexander the Great. Planted on the Mediterranean coast, fashioned out of the marble which had long served as the badge of cosmopolitan chic, and with the Pharos, its astounding lighthouse, to illumine the international shipping-lanes, the city had always defined itself as haughtily, indeed defiantly, Greek. Its inhabitants liked to call it "Alexandria-by-Egypt"—as though to do otherwise might risk their being submerged beneath the peasant-worked mud of the Nile. Geography could not be totally denied, though. Right from the beginning, Alexandria had been touched by schizophrenia. Alexander, travelling to the spit of land on which he would found his great city, had journeyed from Siwa, an oracle in the depths of the western desert, where Amun, the ram-headed king of the Egyptian gods, had revealed to him the secrets of his destiny—and instructed him, it may be, to found Alexandria.[23] This was why, on coins minted by his successors, the great conqueror had often been shown sporting the two curling horns of Amun: an image that had perfectly fused traditions of Greek portraiture with those of the ancient and mysterious land that Alexander had brought beneath his rule. In similar manner, the greatest temple in Alexandria—a massive complex of shrines, libraries and lecture halls named the Serapeum—had been raised in honour of Serapis, a deity who combined a thoroughly Greek beard and robe with a primordially Egyptian lineage.* Artificially multicultural the

---

* "Serapis" was the Greek form of "Osiris-Apis": Osiris being the Egyptian god of the dead, and Apis a sacred bull who manifested himself at regular intervals in Egypt. There was a massive Serapeum at Saqqara, to which Alexander made offerings, and it was this that inspired the cult of Serapis in Alexandria.

god may have been—but that was precisely what had rendered him the perfect patron for a city such as Alexandria, created as it had been from nothing, and poised between two very different worlds.

Yet if gods could be created, then so too, of course, could they be killed. Eight centuries had passed since the founding of Alexandria, and in that time the cults that had once dominated the city had passed into oblivion. It was hardly to be wondered at, perhaps, in a place that had played host to the gods of both Olympus and the Nile for so long, that certain marks of paganism should still have lingered—but as memorials now to a toppled order. Sail into the easternmost of Alexandria's harbours, for instance, and there, dominating the water-front, the traveller would see a massive temple precinct, originally built by a Greek queen, and fronted by plundered obelisks—but which had served the city's bishop for more than a century now as his cathe-dral. Not that the birth pangs of a Christian Alexandria had been easy, though. The Alexandrians were notorious for their "rebellion and riot-ing,"[24] and the convulsions that had accompanied the overthrow of paganism had been predictably bruising. In 391, when a mob of Christians had attempted to storm the Serapeum, the pagans had fought back. They had barricaded the gates of the temple and, so it was plausibly reported, nailed Christian prisoners to crosses on its walls. Such resistance, of course, had only made the eventual capture of the temple all the sweeter. Its 750-year-old statue of Serapis had been hacked to pieces, the contents of its libraries destroyed,* and its various buildings either converted to Christian worship or left as mouldering shells. Alexandria, once the intellectual powerhouse of paganism, had been reconsecrated as something new: as "the most glorious and Christ-loving city of the Alexandrians."[25]

Christ-loving or not, though, it still maintained, in the opinion of a long succession of Christian emperors, its reputation as a nest of

---

* No source explicitly states that the scrolls stored in the Serapeum were destroyed by the triumphant Christians, but it is hard to imagine what else might have happened to them.

troublemakers. It had not gone unnoted, for instance, that Arius had originally been from Alexandria. In point of fact, however, the city's tradition of enquiry into the nature of God—a uniquely brilliant and searching one—had always preferred to stress the opposite extreme to that of Arianism: downplaying the human nature of the Saviour, and emphasising the divine. Any hint of a counter-argument, any suggestion that Christ might after all have had two natures rather than one, would invariably prompt in the Alexandrians an explosion of mingled scorn and fury that was inimitably their own. One inheritance from their pagan forebears that they had most certainly not discarded was an unshakeable conviction that they were, quite simply, the cleverest people in the world. The Patriarch of Alexandria, with imperious immodesty, had even taken to calling himself the "Judge of the Universe." Others, less flatteringly, labelled him "a new Pharaoh."[26] Certainly, the patriarchs had more than intellectual firepower at their fingertips. Intimidation might come physical as well. The trend-setter here was Athanasius, the bishop who had first definitively catalogued the books of the New Testament. Back in the fourth century, he had ruled Alexandria with a rod of iron, not hesitating to have his opponents beaten up or kidnapped if the situation demanded it. A century later, and it had been the turn of another patriarch, Dioscorus, to blend rarefied theology with the tactics of a gangland boss. Travelling to Ephesus in 449 for a showdown with the Nestorians of Antioch, he took with him an escort of paramilitaries so rowdy and intimidating that his fellow bishops, shocked to find themselves howled down every time they opened their mouths, termed the summit in outrage the "Robber Council." *Parabalani*, these thugs of Dioscorus had been called: black-robed enforcers who worked ostensibly as hospital attendants, but who, whenever summoned by the patriarch, would cheerfully demonstrate their devotion to Christ through often spectacular displays of violence. Pagans, Jews, heretics: all felt their fists.

By introducing the *Parabalani* onto the international stage, however, Dioscorus had fatefully over-reached himself. The Council of

Chalcedon, summoned two years after the debacle of Ephesus, pointedly refused to legitimise the Monophysite doctrines that had been so subtly honed in Alexandria. The result was a stand-off. As self-confident in the superiority of their own intellects as they had ever been, most Alexandrians dismissed Chalcedon's resolutions with predictable contempt. The threat of violence continued to smoulder—and occasionally to burst into flames. In 457, for instance, after the distant emperor had ousted the disgraced Dioscorus and foisted a replacement on the Alexandrians, an indignant mob hacked down the wretched new patriarch in one of his own churches and paraded his mangled corpse in triumph through the streets. No mob like an Alexandrian mob for combining intellectual snobbery with a taste for atrocities. Nevertheless, in the sheer scale of hostility to Chalcedon, there was something new. Rarefied debates about the nature of the universe were no longer, as they had been in pagan times, the sole preserve of the metropolis. Across the whole, vast expanse of Egypt—whether in the churches of obscure provincial towns or in monasteries out in the desert—few were those who doubted that Christ had only the single nature. Indeed, the province was so teeming with Monophysites that they increasingly came to be known simply as "Copts," an abbreviation of the Greek word for Egyptians. At last, after centuries of scorning and exploiting its hinterland, Alexandria had come to speak for the whole of Egypt.

The result was a display of mass disobedience fit to give even Justinian pause. Only in 536, buoyed by his successes in Italy, had he finally presumed to reprise the measure first attempted in 457, and impose his own choice of patriarch upon the recalcitrant Alexandrians: a step greeted by the Alexandrians themselves as "the opening up of the pit of the abyss."[27] Such hysteria was hardly surprising: for Justinian's nominee, a monk from the Delta by the name of Paul, had known better than to take for granted the obedience of his new flock. Rather than risk the fate of his hapless predecessor, he had opted instead to get his own blows in first: a policy that had served to confirm for the Alexandrians all their darkest suspicions of the

Chalcedonian Church. Their new patriarch, even by the autocratic standards of his predecessors, verged on the psychopathic: corrupt, brutal and with "a taste for spilling blood."[28] So uninhibited was his thuggery that Justinian, after a couple of years, was prepared to acknowledge something startling: that he might perhaps have made a mistake. Paul was duly sacked; a new patriarch, a Syrian by the name of Zoilus, was dispatched from Constantinople as his replacement; the Alexandrians, scorning their new leader as both a foreigner and a Chalcedonian, but finding him otherwise inoffensive, opted simply to ignore him. So ended Justinian's project to reunite Egypt with the imperial Church: amid inglorious compromise.

As, perhaps, had always been inevitable. The Copts were simply too numerous, too distant and too Monophysite to be brought to heel. Nor were these the only considerations weighing on Justinian's mind. It was no coincidence, surely, that the squalid episode of Paul's tenure in Alexandria coincided with a far more crowd-pleasing initiative: the closure, in an isolated Libyan oasis, of the very last functioning temple of Amun. This step, although clearly taken in accordance with the wishes of the heavens, was not wholly devoid of earthly calculation: for Justinian was keen to remind the Copts that he and they, despite their disagreements, were all of them lovers of Christ. Urgent though it clearly was to secure the unity of the Church, it was no less urgent to ensure the continued loyalty of Egypt—and thereby to secure for the vast population of Constantinople, and the soldiers of the eastern front, the incomparable harvests sprung from the flood-plains of the Nile. Every year, gliding downriver to Alexandria, great fleets of barges would bring hundreds upon thousands of tons of grain; and every year, giant ships would then transport the precious cargo onwards to the capital. Alexandria might have been a marble-clad cosmopolis of lecture halls and churches; but she was no less an entrepôt of warehouses, docks and silos. Had she not been, the New Rome would long since have found the flesh shrinking off her bones: "For Constantinople and all the region around it are fed, in the main, by Alexandria."[29]

Yet, in the summer of 541, as the ghostly fleet of bronze ships appeared along the Mediterranean coast, it was becoming terrifyingly clear that death too, as well as life, might be had from Egypt. In July, reports had reached Alexandria of an epidemic in the port of Pelusium, on the far eastern side of the Nile Delta, that had left the city a charnel house. Panic at this news, however, was unlikely to have been immediate: for sudden flare-ups of disease were common, and usually, "by the grace of God which protects us, do not last long."[30] The outbreak in Pelusium, however, had not abated. Instead, from coastal town to coastal town, it had begun to spread with lethal speed. Every time a bronze ship was spotted out on the night-time waters, people on the shore would abruptly find themselves struck down by a fever, and then, touching their groins, or their armpits, or behind their ears, discover painful black swellings—*boubones*, as they were called in Greek—until finally, it might be, staggering out into the streets, they would fall, and "become a terrible and shocking spectacle for those who saw them, as their bellies were swollen and their mouths wide open, throwing up pus like torrents, their eyes inflamed and their hands stretched out upward, and over the corpses that lay rotting on corners, and in the porches of courtyards, and in churches, and everywhere, with no one to bury them."[31] And so the pestilence raged; and as it raged, it drew ever closer to Alexandria.

By September, the first headaches, the first buboes, the first rattling expectorations of blood, were being reported in the docks. Within days, the plague was general over the city, and far beyond. Alexandria, ever the intellectual powerhouse, boasted the most prestigious medical schools in the world; but even the city's famous teaching specialists found themselves helpless before the spread of the mysterious pestilence, unable to diagnose it, still less prescribe any cure. The death rate rose inexorably, until "many houses became completely destitute of human inhabitants."[32] So putrid were the streets with piles of the dead, so thick with flies, so slippery underfoot with blood and melted flesh, that it was impossible to clear them. Those who dared to venture out into the fetid heat—whether to loot or simply to scavenge food—

wore tags, so that their families could be alerted to come and bury them should they too be overwhelmed by the plague while abroad. Unless, of course, as was entirely probable, their families had themselves been struck down in the meanwhile. Nor, the observant noted, was it only humans who were perishing of the epidemic. Animals too were succumbing. "Why, even rats, swollen with buboes, were to be seen, infected and dying."[33]

Week after week, the pestilence continued its scything progress. Then finally it began to subside; until at last, four months after its first appearance on the streets of Alexandria, the dying was largely done. Yet the plague, "always moving forward and travelling at times favourable to it,"[34] was still far from spent. Traders from Egypt might sail as far afield as Britain—and those who had survived the pestilence still needed to make a living. In the spring of 542, as the storms of winter died down, the ships of Alexandria started to put out to sea, bearing with them their freights of merchandise: papyrus and linen, spices and medicines, glassware and exotic sweets. Pet birds too, and even camels, were sometimes transported; and then, of course, travelling as stowaways, there were always rats. On the rats were fleas; and in the fleas was *Yersinia pestis*, the deadly pathogen that, unknown to anyone, was spreading the plague.[35] The science of bacteriology, it went without saying, lay immeasurably beyond the orbit of the scholarship of the age. Even the most brilliant of Alexandria's doctors did not think to associate the spread of a pandemic so lethal and unprecedented with anything so commonplace as a flea bite. The result was, as ships fanned out across the Mediterranean, that the pestilence too, invisible and unsuspected, continued on its deadly way. Sometimes it happened, in the midst of a voyage, that a vessel would be attacked so suddenly "by the wrath of God,"[36] and to such devastating effect, that it would be left to drift aimlessly on the currents, manned by nothing but corpses, until it sank or ran aground. More commonly, a ship would dock in some distant port and then, a day or two later, the first buboes would start to appear on the groins and armpits of the locals. "And always, after beginning on the coast, the disease would then head on inland."[37]

In Constantinople, rumours of doom had been sweeping the city for months. Back in the autumn of 541, as Alexandria had been twisting upon the rack, a woman had fallen into a rapture and cried out to the Byzantines that death was arriving from the sea to swallow up the world. The following spring, with the first grain ships of the year looming off the Golden Horn, and granaries along the harbour front busily being filled, so mysterious apparitions began to be glimpsed. Whoever was touched by one of these phantoms would immediately fall sick. Within days, across the whole of Constantinople, thousands upon thousands were dying. At first, only the poor perished; but soon even the most exclusive quarters of the city were succumbing. Such was the lethal effect of the plague's spread that entire palaces might be transformed into sepulchres, their mosaic floors littered with corpses, senators and servants alike left as pus-streaked food for worms. Even in the imperial palace, in the bedchamber of the emperor himself, the burning mark of the plague was felt; for Justinian too fell ill. That he went on to recover was proof that the pestilence, though virulent, was not necessarily fatal: for there were some, a small minority, who did survive infection. Whether this was necessarily a blessing, however, was debatable: for what pleasure could there be in life if spouse and children, friends and kin, were all of them dead? Certainly, to those who lived through that summer in Constantinople, the entire city appeared condemned. The streets were empty of the living; no business of any kind was undertaken, save for the burying of corpses; the butchers' shops stood empty, the markets deserted, the bakers' kilns unlit. "So it was, in a city prodigiously full of good things to eat, that starvation ran riot."[38] The pestilence, adding to all the manifold sufferings that it had already dealt, now trailed famine in its wake.

To many of those who survived its passage, the plague appeared a calamity "by which the whole of humanity came close to annihilation."[39] An exaggeration? Perhaps—but then again, accurate figures were hard to come by. The imperial statisticians had tried to keep track of the death rate in the capital, but had fast been overwhelmed. In due course, confronted by the mounds of corpses in the streets, Justinian gave orders for them to be dumped at sea, and then, as the water turned into a soup of decomposing flesh, for vast pits to be dug on the far side of the Golden Horn. Within these, rows of bodies were laid and then "trodden upon by feet and trampled like spoiled grapes,"[40] so that further corpses, when they were hurled down from the rim of the pit, would sometimes vanish into the mulch. To those haunted by such a hellish vision the entire world seemed to have become a winepress, in which countless multitudes were being crushed by the wrath of God. Even though the plague, by August 542, had finally spent itself in Constantinople, reports of its onward sweep across the rest of the empire, and beyond, did not diminish in horror. Asia Minor too, it was reported, had been visited by the pestilence, and Jerusalem, and the rubble-strewn shanty town that was Antioch. By December, it was endemic in Sicily, and by 543 across much of Italy, Spain and Gaul. That the West could boast no cities on the scale of those to be found in the East did not serve to spare it. In the most remote village, no less than in the darkest urban slum, the pestilence stalked down the living. "The world seemed returned to its primordial silence, for no voices rose in the fields, no whistling was heard of shepherds." So it was reported of the Italian countryside. "Places where men once lived had become lairs for savage beasts."[41]

Meanwhile, along the eastern frontier of Justinian's empire, where Khusrow had frantically constructed a *cordon sanitaire*, the plague was briefly halted in its tracks. One outbreak of buboes, in the ranks of the *Shahanshah*'s own army, had been effectively quarantined, and another in Media. But the pestilence could not be kept at bay for ever. By 545, it had breached the bulwarks of *Iranshahr* and was sweeping eastwards with a violence even more terrible, if anything, than it had displayed on its westward course. Across Mesopotamia, in particular, it raged for longer than it had ever done in Alexandria or Constantinople, so that all was "famine, madness and fury."[42] Nothing was proof against it. Time would see it spread as far afield as China. Never before in history had so much of humanity been united by a common experience of suffering. If some communities were wiped out utterly by the plague, and some were mysteriously spared, then most, if reports are collated, and the evidence carefully sifted, appear to have suffered a mortality rate of something around a third.[43] Not annihilation, then, by any means; but a culling, nevertheless, on a wholly shattering scale.

Always, however, after every visitation, the time would come when even "the evil stench"[44] of the rotting corpses would lift, and people, rubbing their eyes, would emerge on to weed-covered streets or fields. Many of them—artisans, tradesmen, peasants—found the world they were returning to ripe with unanticipated opportunity. The ready supplies of labour that the wealthy had hitherto always taken for granted were suddenly at a premium. Demands that previously, before the coming of the plague, the poor would never have dared to push were now increasingly theirs to make. Inflation, as a result, began to gallop. By 545, just three years after the departure of the plague from Constantinople, Justinian was appalled to discover that wages in the capital had more than doubled. The emperor's response to this unsettling state of affairs was his habitual one: he passed a law. By its terms, it was declared illegal for any labourer to be paid more than he would have received prior to the plague. The effect of this legislation, to Justinian's bafflement and indignation, was minimal. Wages continued to spiral upwards. The world, it seemed, was not to be restored to its former condition simply on the say-so of an edict.

And in truth there was barely a sinew, barely a muscle of the great machine of imperial administration that had not been left enfeebled by the pestilence. Physicians noted with interest that those who had contracted the plague and survived would invariably bear the stamp of their brush with death. Some were left bald; others with a lisp; others with a staggering, lurching gait. Almost all suffered a terrible lassitude, often for years. To this rule, it was true, Justinian himself stood as a notable exception; but he knew, none better, that what might be true of individuals was true as well of his entire dominion. Infinitely more than the feckless tribes of the barbarians, more even than the kingdom of Khusrow, the empire of the Roman people had always depended on a sizeable population for its healthy functioning. Civilian state that it essentially was, it could not hope to prosper without a hefty tax base. Now, in the wake of the plague, that tax base had suffered perhaps irreparable damage. Nor was that the limit of the danger. In provinces that only a few years previously had provided ready supplies of recruits for the imperial armies, whole villages, whole regions now stood denuded. This, at the best of times, would have posed a formidable challenge. At a moment when Roman forces were engaged in a number of debilitating conflicts, from Italy to Syria, it threatened catastrophe.

As for Justinian himself, so devastating and unexpected had been the blow to all his ambitions that he might well have been expected to buckle under it. But he did not. Instead, grimly, doggedly, heroically, he set to shoring up his battered empire against utter ruin. From the summer of 548 onwards, he would be forced to do so without the woman who for over twenty years had been the companion both of his bed and of his councils: for in June that year, Theodora died. Justinian, who for the rest of his life would never cease to light candles before the mausoleum which he had built to serve the pair of them as their final resting place, could not endure to take another wife: henceforward, he would be married to his work. Day and night—"for he had little need of sleep"[45]—he devoted himself to the thankless task of compensating for the most precipitous drop in revenue that any emperor had ever faced. Ruthless austerity measures were imposed: courier services slashed, road maintenance abandoned, the civil service streamlined. Tax-collection was overtly professionalised, so as to throttle any prospect of evasion. Even the manufacture of silk was nationalised. Such measures won for Justinian, against all the odds, funding sufficient to bring his many wars to a seemingly satisfactory close. By the time of his death in 565, he had stabilised the eastern frontier by signing yet another "Eternal Peace" with Khusrow, and decisively defeated the Ostrogoths in the West. He had even acquired a whole new province in southern Spain. Only fitting, then, it might have been thought, that the body of the great emperor, as it lay in state, had been covered by a pall on which he was shown trampling down a barbarian king, of the kind that it had always been the traditional prerogative of the Roman people to crush. Happy days, so the image proclaimed, were come again.

But the pall told only part of the story. Its portrait of the emperor as the youthful and Christ-favoured visionary who, in the joyous year of 534, had sat in triumph over the Vandals, veiled the withered corpse of an eighty-three-year-old man. Between the image of an empire restored to its ancient supremacy over most of the Mediterranean and the grim reality there stretched a similarly yawning chasm. In the opinion of Justinian's critics—of whom, behind closed doors, there were many—the emperor's cure had proved quite as deadly as the disease. In Italy, for instance, no matter how shrilly his propagandists might seek to deny it, "victory" had left the peninsula immeasurably less Roman than it had ever been under Theoderic. Over the course of two decades, the bloody and wearisome slog to overthrow the Ostrogoths had witnessed the abolition of the consulship, the flight to Constantinople of almost every senator, and even, during the winter months of 550, the most shocking of all the breaks with the past: the complete, albeit temporary, depopulation of Rome itself. Not since the time of Romulus had the Eternal City stood so empty, so abandoned to grass and swamps. Victory of such an order seemed scarcely different from defeat. Why, then, had Justinian waded through a whole mire of destruction to secure it? "Because he was bloodthirsty and murderous by nature,"[46] some thought to whisper. That his reign had seen "the entire world drenched with human blood"[47] was due, not to his desperate struggle against evil circumstance, but to the startling fact that he had literally been an agent of hell. Even his tireless burning of the midnight oil might be interpreted as evidence, not of his devotion to the Roman people, but of his diabolic nature. One servant had reported seeing Justinian late at night without his head; another that the emperor's face had suddenly metamorphosed into a hideous and shapeless lump of flesh. "How, then, could this man have been anything other than a demon?"[48]

Admittedly, those who pushed this particular theory did tend to have axes to grind.[49] Justinian, never popular with the traditional elite at the best of times, had hardly risen in their estimation by taking such strenuous measures, in the years before his death, to slash the budget deficit. Nothing about him quite so infernal, in the opinion of stymied tax-dodgers, as what they bitterly dismissed as his "avarice." Nevertheless, it was hardly necessary to believe that the imperial throne had genuinely been occupied by "the Lord of Demons"[50] to dread that the gates of hell might be yawning increasingly wide. Zoroastrian priests were not alone in warning their flocks that time itself was destined to come to an end, amid a titanic death-struggle between good and evil. The same mood of mingled terror and hope that had inspired Mazdak to declare that the horizon was not far off, that the great climax of things was drawing near, had repeatedly haunted the imaginings of the Christian people, too. Christ Himself had warned His disciples what to expect: His own return, like lightning that "comes from the east and shines as far as the west";[51] His sitting in judgement over the living and the dead; His delivery of the wicked to eternal punishment, and of the righteous to eternal life. And the day and hour of these events? Not even the angels themselves, so Christ had declared, could be sure of that. Nevertheless, certain clues, certain signs, would herald for the faithful the coming of the Day of Judgement: "For nation will rise against nation, and kingdom against kingdom, and there will be famines, and pestilences, and earthquakes in various places."[52]

In the wake of Justinian's reign, this was a message as unsettling as any in scripture. The plague, after its initial devastating eruption, had still not abated. By striking seemingly at random, at different times and in different places, it cast a perpetual shadow of menace. "Its recurrence," so a lawyer in Antioch recorded in numb despair, "has seen me lose, at various times, several of my children, my wife, and many of my kin, not to mention numerous servants, both in town and in the country."[53] Time would see him lose a grandson as well: a pattern of bereavement repeated across the empire and far beyond. Yet pestilence was only one of the harbingers of the End Days to have afflicted the Roman people. Prior to the plague's appearance, back in 536, a mysterious dust cloud had cast the world into darkness for months.[54] Then, in December 557, a terrible earthquake had shaken Constantinople, rocking it so severely that the dome of Hagia Sophia had collapsed the following spring, necessitating years of repairs. Most ominous of all, in 559, an army of barbarians had crossed the frozen Danube and struck so far south as to menace Greece and the capital itself. Constantinople had been preserved from seemingly inevitable ruin only by the desperate summoning of Belisarius out of retirement: for the aged general, frail though he had become, had lost none of his aptitude for winning victories. Elsewhere, however, the rising tempo of barbarian assaults had proved less easy to repulse. Bands of migratory peasants known as Slavs had been infiltrating the Balkans since the 540s, when the plague had first harrowed the region. Then, from beyond the Danube, a tribe of peculiarly brutal savages, steppe-land nomads named the Avars, had started to make alarming demands for danger money. Most demoralising of all, perhaps, was the descent upon Italy in 568 of a shaven-headed, long-bearded people called the Lombards, who in next to no time had succeeded in dismembering Constantinople's hard-won mastery of the peninsula for good. Less than a decade after the death of Justinian, and imperial control had been pegged back to a corridor of land between Ravenna and Rome. So much blood, so much destruction—and all in vain.

How were these catastrophic eruptions to be explained? On one level, the answer was very simple. Nomads, by and large, had proved immune to the reach of the plague. As a result, whether descending across the Danube or from the Alps, they usually vastly outnumbered the local garrisons. Even Belisarius, in his last-ditch defence of Constantinople, had been able to muster only a few hundred veterans, and had depended largely for his victory on a rag-bag of peasants, and plenty of bluff. Elsewhere, for all the conscientiousness with which Justinian had devoted his tax revenues to the construction of fortresses along the empire's frontiers, not even the most bristling of walls could be made serviceable without soldiers to man them. Time and again, as barbarian horsemen advanced into Roman territory, they would find themselves passing fields that stood overgrown, and villages that lay abandoned. Whole stretches of the empire, to all intents and purposes, were now "deserted."[55]

All of this had long been foretold. Christ had not been alone in warning of how the world was destined to end. Jewish prophets and Christian saints alike had predicted that fearsome and savage hordes would descend on God's people "like a cloud covering the land"[56] in the run-up to the End Days: hordes to whom, in the Bible, had been given the sinister names "Gog" and "Magog." The hint of dark mystery in all this had been sufficient, as the world had become increasingly Christian, and barbarians ever more of a threat, to prompt much heated speculation. Who were Gog and Magog? Where were they lurking? Why would they not materialise until the end of time? The answers to these questions had been found, somewhat unexpectedly, in the biography of Alexander the Great. Historians had long known that the famous conqueror, in the course of his global travels, had discovered a mountain pass on the edge of the world, which he had sealed with "iron gates."[57] Over the centuries, this story had been much improved. By the time of Justinian, it was known for a fact that the gates had been faced with bronze; that the peoples they had served to imprison had been none other than Gog and Magog; and that Alexander, upon whom "the Spirit of the Lord rested,"[58] had built them with the direct encouragement of an angel.

To the Christian people of Alexandria, this was not wholly bad news, perhaps. It provided a welcome reassurance: that the founder of their city, despite his regrettable taste for sporting the horns of a pagan demon, had all along been a self-proclaimed servant of God.[59] By and large, however, the implications were unnerving in the extreme. It was hard, with barbarians gathering outside the walls of Constantinople and the whole world seemingly on the move, to avoid the obvious conclusion: that yet another portent of the End Days had arrived upon the scene. The bolts set on Alexander's gates, so many dreaded, were starting to crumple, and buckle, and give. Beyond them, straining to be released upon the world, were waiting Gog and Magog—fiends so terrible that they thought nothing of drinking the blood of babies and snacking on kittens. Before the onset of such invaders, then, who could say what the fate of the world would be?

No wonder, in the final years of the sixth Christian century, that many in the empire of the Romans should have looked to the future with a peculiar foreboding: "Calamities are approaching, such as the current generation cannot imagine."[60] A sobering reflection: that the worst might be yet to come.

The Great War

Around Easter, AD 600, the plague returned to Galilee. So virulently did the outbreak rage that it had soon spread beyond the Golan Heights and into the wilderness of scrub and sand that bordered Palestine. Prominent among the frontier settlements devastated by its coming was Jabiya, the great tent city of the Ghassanids. There, the horror of the pestilence would long be remembered. "Like whirlwinds," wrote one of their poets, "it left the smoke of its blazing passage."[61]

Arabs who lived beyond the frontiers of the empire had previously been spared the worst of the plague. Infection stalked the desert less readily than it did streets or fields. More than half a century had passed since the first appearance of the pestilence, and still the Arabs took for granted that it was a disease of "the land of the Romans."[62] To the Ghassanids, and to the Lakhmids as well, the culling of peoples along the entire sweep of the Fertile Crescent had spelled considerable opportunity: for the exhaustion and impoverishment of both their respective sponsors had inevitably resulted in a certain loosening of leashes. Back in the 540s, for instance, at the height of the devastation wrought by the pestilence, Arethas and Mundhir had been free to escalate their vendetta "without reference to either the Romans or the Persians."[63] Superpower patronage, amid the swirl of their own venomous hatred, became almost an irrelevance. The two sides increasingly battled in the names of heavenly, rather than earthly, sponsors. Mundhir, following his capture of one of Arethas's sons, did not hesitate to top his earlier sacrifice of four hundred virgins to al-'Uzza by offering up the Ghassanid prince to the goddess al-'Uzza. Other Christian captives, so it was claimed, were tortured by the Lakhmid king until they agreed to join in her worship. News of these atrocities, brought to Saint Simeon on his pillar, so appalled the stylite that he promptly lent his prayers to the Ghassanids. Sure enough, in 554, Arethas had been graced with a stunning and climactic triumph. In a great battle fought at Chalcis, in Syria, a Lakhmid invasion force was annihilated. Simeon, borne from his pillar by the agency of the heavens to a hill overlooking the action, made his own personal contribution to the victory by asking the Holy Spirit to strike down Mundhir with a fireball—a request which the Holy Spirit obligingly met. Arethas hailed the Ghassanid dead, among them his own eldest son, not merely as heroes but as martyrs in the cause of Christ.

Here, in this notion—that killing might be done as a service to the heavens as well as to secure plunder—was an intoxicating new possibility for the Arabs to contemplate. To the Ghassanids, in particular, it had fast become something more: the irreducible core of their identity. By 600, there could be no doubting their commitment to the image they had of themselves: as the shields of a Christian empire. Not even a host of insults from the increasingly twitchy Roman establishment—including, in 582, the exiling of their king to Sicily and a brief, disastrous attempt to dissolve their federation altogether—could shake their loyalty. In their own opinion, they were warriors of God or they were nothing. It was a potent conceit. Other Arab tribes, rather than dismissing the Ghassanids as Roman stoolpigeons, increasingly viewed them as they had previously viewed the Lakhmids: as cynosures of chivalry. So open was the table at the Ghassanid court, poets claimed, that Jabiya's watchdogs had quite fallen out of the habit of barking at strangers. Even their recipes were of a quality appropriate to favourites of the heavens. No higher compliment could possibly be paid to a woman, for instance, than to compare her excellence to that of the local speciality, the *tharidat Ghassan*—a stew of brains and gravy.*

The Ghassanids' influence ran far deeper than haute cuisine, though. Their aura of glamour and invincibility served as invaluable marketing for their celestial patron, too. By 600, even the king of the Lakhmids had become a Christian. In Hira, as in Jabiya, stone churches were erected amid the tents. From the north to the distant south— where Najran's *Ka'ba* preserved the glorious memory of the city's martyrs—the margins of Arabia increasingly bore the physical signs of the Christian faith. To ambitious warlords, these promised not merely heavenly salvation in the hereafter, but ready access within their life-times to the dimension of the angelic. The conviction that a man of exceptional holiness, by virtue of his sufferings, might come to see through the veil of his tears the blaze of the heavenly hosts, their drawn swords flickering with fire, was held by many Arabs with a wolfish literalness. The military potential of a saint, after all, had been amply demonstrated by the fireball that had incinerated Mundhir. Many warriors, in the wake of their great victory at Chalcis, had duly flocked to Saint Simeon's pillar, as though to be touched themselves with something of his power. Decades later, the Ghassanids continued to see in their own Christian piety a weapon more prodigious by far than any other in their armoury.

A perspective fit to awe even those tribes that had not submitted to baptism. Between the belief of Christians in an unseen realm of spir-its, and that of the Arabs, there was considerable overlap. Pagans as well as monks might claim to see angels. Dushara, for instance, was said by his worshippers to employ a particularly potent one as his

---

* Muhammad himself agreed. A celebrated *hadith* recorded the Prophet's praise of his favourite wife. "Allah's Apostle said, 'The superiority of Aisha over other women is like the superiority of Tharid to other meals.'" (*Sahih al-Bukhari*: Vol. 5, Book 57, 114).

lieutenant; while at Mamre, according to Sozomen, the draw for pagan pilgrims was precisely that "angels had appeared there to men."[64] All this, though, to fretful Christians, was anything but reassuring. That a pagan might be familiar with angels implied that some of them, at the very least, must in truth have derived from hell. The full, alarming implications of this were best illustrated by what had happened in a city on the edge of Palestine, where, at the height of the plague, demons in the form of angels had appeared to the terrified inhabitants and told them that they would be spared only if they worshipped a bronze idol. Clearly, then, when dealing with supernatural messengers, it was essential to be alert to the possibility of disinformation. Yet this in turn, ironically enough, was nothing with which the pagans of the desert would have disagreed. Just as it was possible for them to accept the existence of angels, so also did they dread the malignity of *jinn*, invisible spirits bred of fire, many of whom took an active pleasure in the sufferings of mortals. Even the Ghassanids had blamed the onset of the plague on their "stinging."[65] A Christian Arab, picturing combatants engaged upon a celestial battlefield, would doubtless have imagined very little to perplex his pagan counterpart. Between *jinn* and demons, it appeared, the boundaries were easily blurred. And between goddesses and angels too? Very possibly. Messengers from heaven appeared to have a definite preference for matching image to audience. Angels who manifested themselves in a Roman province, for instance, were as like as not to sport the medallions and "bright crimson belts"[66] of imperial bureaucrats. Perhaps, then, in those reaches of Arabia as yet only semi-illumined by the blaze of Christ, it was only to be expected that they would adopt the look, and sometimes even the names, of pagan deities.[67] Suspended as a goddess such as al-'Uzza was in an eerie, distorting half-light, midway between the past and the future, between paganism and the worship of a single god, who was to say what her future would be: whether as demon or as angel, or to be forgotten altogether?

Certainly, in the decades that followed the onset of the plague, there could be little doubt that the border zone beyond the Holy Land was indeed extending ever further south, into Arabia. That this was so reflected not the strength of the Christian empire, however, but its debilitation. A pronounced shift had occurred in the balance of power, not just in the region of the Fertile Crescent, but along the entire southern frontier. In Carthage, for instance, fretful commentators noted that, while the empire's "once countless military units had dwindled in number, the plague, that ally of war, had not so much as touched the rancorous tribes."[68] It was as a consequence of this that the Berbers, natives of North Africa who lurked in the mountains beyond the reach of any imperial strike force, had begun to change from a nuisance to a threat. In Arabia, too, the desert nomads, spared the devastation of the pestilence, scented opportunity in the Romans' agony. They may have lacked the teeming numbers of the Slavs or the Avars, but they too were increasingly on the move. By 600, entire populations of emigrants—*muhajirun*, in Arabic—had settled between Palestine and the Hijaz, the region of Arabia that abuts the upper half of the Red Sea. Tribes completely unknown to the imperial authorities only a few decades earlier—the Judham, the Amila and the Bali—now joined the roster of *foederati*. Whether they were truly to be reckoned as friends of the Roman people, however, or as troublesome intruders bought off with danger money, was not altogether clear. Bluff, even at the best of times, worked best without an excess of scrutiny.

Indisputable, however, was the fact that the authorities in Palestine did need allies to patrol a buffer zone for them. The same collapse in manpower and revenues as had afflicted the northern and western fronts had resulted in particularly devastating cuts along the frontier of the Holy Land. Indeed, ever since the arrival of the plague, it had effectively been demobilised. Forts stood abandoned to weeds, jackals and the odd ascetic. A radical streamlining—but informed, nevertheless, by a certain brutal logic. Predatory nomads might be a nuisance—but they scarcely compared in terms of menace with the House of Sasan. Sixty years after Khusrow had plundered the cities of Syria, the frontier with *Iranshahr* remained Roman strategists' supreme priority, and the source of all their nightmares. Such resources as the empire could muster continued to be lavished on its garrisons. The consequence was, at a time when even the previously booming cities of Syria were afflicted by contraction and impoverishment, that the border zone with *Iranshahr* alone defied recession.[69]

And here, for those Arabs beyond the frontier keen to better themselves, was yet further scope for battening onto Roman gold. Not since the collapse of the spice trade had business conditions been more in their favour. It was not only Syria's cities but its countryside that had been devastated by the plague. Repeated outbreaks had crippled agricultural production.[70] Passers-by, observing the overgrown fields, the rotting apples and grapes, the feral cattle, sheep and goats, were moved to quote the words of the prophet Isaiah: "the earth shall be laid utterly waste and be utterly despoiled."[71] Yet garrisons, of course, still needed food for their messes, provender for their horses and pack animals, leather for their armour, shields and tents. Under normal circumstances, the costs of overland transport would hardly have made it worth the while of Arab merchants to trade in such basic commodities; but circumstances, in the wake of the plague, were very far from normal. The Arabs, for the first time in many centuries, found themselves major players in a sellers' market.

Nor was it only the Romans who offered them ripe opportunity for doing business. The same pestilence that had so devastated Syria had brought ruin to Mesopotamia as well. Formidable though the Persians continued to appear when viewed from the watchtowers of Dara, the truth was that they too, no less than their western rivals, had found the legacy of the plague a devastating one. Khusrow's successes—no less than Justinian's—appeared to have left his empire only the more exposed. In 557, in the greatest triumph of his reign, he had succeeded in annihilating the Hephthalites once and for all, so that of the people who had once brought such ruin and humiliation upon *Iranshahr* nothing had remained but the memory of their name. Yet that victory had come at high cost. The battle had been won in alliance with the Turks: "an ugly, insolent, broad-faced, eyelashless mob."[72] These new arrivals, gorging themselves on their winnings, had soon established themselves as a presence on *Iranshahr*'s northern frontier no less menacing than the Hephthalites had ever been. Nomadic, and therefore largely unaffected by the plague, they were even more numerous than the Avars, whose khan they imperiously dismissed as a runaway slave. Khusrow, pressured from the north by the Turks and along the western front, as ever, by the Romans, had duly found himself locked into a struggle to defend his borders no less desperate than the one faced by Justinian. Still, into his ninth decade, he had been obliged to remain upon the campaign trail. By the time that he finally died, in 579, he had, so it was reliably reported, "lost his appetite for war."[73]

The challenge of how to cope with the escalating crisis was inherited by his son, Hormizd. The solution attempted by the new *Shahanshah*—who would long be remembered for his "benevolence toward the weak and destitute"[74]—was to accuse the Parthian nobility of hoarding wealth that could better be spent by himself on succouring his needy people, and to aim, as not even Khusrow had dared to do, at the permanent breaking of their power. There was, of course, in this attempt at increased centralisation, more than an echo of the policies adopted by Justinian in the wake of the plague; but the Parthian nobility, unlike their Roman counterparts, had never been content merely to snipe and moan from the sidelines. In 590, the leader of the Mihran, a renowned general by the name of Bahram Chobin, suffered a minor reverse at the hands of the Romans, and was sent an outfit of women's clothes to wear by a contemptuous Hormizd. Such, at any rate, was the story later told; and whether true or not, it is certain that the onset of the campaigning season saw Bahram Chobin marching, not against the Romans, but directly on Ctesiphon. The news of his approach was sufficient to inspire two other Parthian dynasts in the capital to stage a coup. Hormizd was toppled, blinded and put to death, all in brisk succession. His young son was thrust on to the throne and proclaimed Khusrow II. Not since the dark days following the death of Peroz, a hundred years previously, had the House of Sasan appeared more beleaguered.

And worse was to come. Bahram Chobin went further than even his most audacious ancestors had done. Rather than rest content with the toppling of Hormizd, he took the ultimate, the blasphemous step: he declared himself king. Here, for the Zoroastrian Church as much as for the House of Sasan, was a manoeuvre that threatened the breaking of the universe itself: for how could the one hope to survive without the other? Bahram Chobin, it seems, did not shrink from answering this question in the boldest terms imaginable. He was, so he declared, the living embodiment of the Fire of Mihr is Great. If it were true, as seemed entirely probable, that the End Days were approaching, then clearly *Iranshahr* needed not so much a king as a saviour. This, mimicking the strategy of Mazdak, was precisely what Bahram Chobin claimed to be. Far from ducking the *mowbeds'* charge that his rebellion threatened the end of the world, he seems openly to have revelled in the fact.[75]

In the event, his occupation of the throne of Ardashir lasted no more than a year. Khusrow II, with the inevitable backing of the Mihran's rival Parthian dynasts and the far more unexpected support of the new Caesar, Maurice, defeated the rebel *Shahanshah*, who promptly fled to the Turks. There, soon afterwards, he was assassinated by Sasanian agents. Order, it appeared, had been restored to heaven and earth. Yet this would prove to be a spectacular delusion. In truth, the presentiment of Bahram Chobin that the framework of things stood upon the brink of dissolution was to prove all too justified. Like the plague, the contagion of violence initiated by his rebellion was destined to spread far and wide. As in Ctesiphon, so in Constantinople—its effects would be cataclysmic.

Maurice, in his decision to override the advice of the Senate, and lend his backing to the House of Sasan, had been influenced by one prime consideration: the urgent need to save money. The gambit had initially appeared a great success: the restoration of a grateful Khusrow II to his throne had indeed resulted in a peace dividend. Fatefully, though, this had encouraged in Maurice a terminal delusion: that he could now afford to stint on the pay of his soldiers. Back in 588, the Army of the East, used as it was to lavish subsidy, had already mutinied over this issue. When the high command had sought to intimidate the fractious soldiery into submission by unveiling before their gaze the self-portrait of Christ from Edessa, "the mob, far from being brought to its senses, had gone so far as to pelt the ineffable object with stones."[76] More than a decade later, in 602, it was the turn of the soldiers in the Balkans to explode into open insurrection. Phocas, their leader, and a man quite as contemptuous of proprieties as Bahram Chobin had been, opted to do what no Roman commander had ever done before: he marched on Constantinople. The proud boast of the Christian empire—that for centuries "no emperor had perished by the hands of either domestic or foreign foes"[77]—was trampled brutally into the dirt. Maurice, apprehended in Chalcedon as he sought to escape the Balkan rebels, was beheaded, and his corpse exposed to the jeers of the Hippodrome. His replacement as Caesar, inevitably, was Phocas. Eight years later, the usurper too had been overthrown. His genitals were hacked off, his body skinned, and his head paraded through the streets of the capital on a pole. The toxin of something murderous, it appeared, was now well and truly loose in the New Rome.

Yet, if any man was fitted to the finding of an antidote, then it was, ironically enough, the same faction-leader who had toppled Phocas: an Armenian by the name of Heraclius. "Handsome, tall, brave, and a born fighter,"[78] the new emperor had already more than demonstrated his capabilities by seizing power in the wake of an almost unfeasibly ambitious operation: a naval assault from Carthage, where his father had been governor-general. Certainly, situated as he now was in the eye of a storm as violent as any in all of Rome's long history, Heraclius faced the most searing test imaginable of his many talents. The cracking of the ages that Bahram Chobin had sensed in *Iranshahr* was increasingly being experienced in Constantinople, too. When crosses in the city began to shake and jump about, few doubted that it portended a truly cosmic evil. In the opinion of Theodore—the empire's most celebrated living saint, and a man of such awesome holiness that he wore a fifty-pound metal corset and subsisted entirely on lettuce—the arrival of the Devil on earth was near: "There will be inroads of many barbarous peoples, and the shedding of much blood, and destruction and captivity throughout the world, and the desolation of holy churches." Then, stated with a terrifying finality, the most shocking forecast of all: "The empire itself will fall."[79]

Such an eventuality, of course, could only herald the End Times—and yet astoundingly, within a mere decade of the ascent of Heraclius to the throne, it had become not merely a possibility, but a terrifying likelihood. The descent of Constantinople into factionalism had not gone unnoted in Ctesiphon. There, eager to escape the shadow of the great Parthian dynasts, and to give some colour to his still pallid authority, Khusrow II had recognised in the deposition of Maurice the perfect opportunity to busy giddy minds with foreign quarrels. Never before had *Iranshahr* witnessed such florid mourning for a Caesar. Khusrow—despite describing himself as "the king who hates war"[80]—posed, with a great show of indignant piety, as his murdered benefactor's avenger. As was traditional, he launched his campaign by settling down before the walls of Dara. Abandoned to its fate by the distracted authorities in Constantinople, the great fortress duly surrendered, albeit after a three-year siege. Three years after that, in 609, Amida fell, too. Then, in 610, the supposedly Christ-protected city of Edessa opened its gates to the Persians. Suddenly, not only Syria but Anatolia and Palestine lay naked and defenceless before the armies of the *Shahanshah*. Not since the time of Cyrus had a Persian king been presented with such a deliriously tempting opportunity for westward conquest. Khusrow, scarcely believing his luck, decided to go for broke.

One army, plundering, slaving and killing as it went, struck so deep into Anatolia that in 614 even Ephesus, on the shores of the Aegean, was put to the torch.[81] Meanwhile, a second task force, under the command of a Mihranid warlord by the name of Shahrbaraz, swung southwards.[82] Its mission: not merely to loot but to annex. Its success was beyond Khusrow's wildest hopes. By 615, the whole of Syria and Palestine belonged to the *Shahanshah*, with even hippodromes converted into polo pitches. Four years later, he ruled as the lord of Egypt, too.

The dream that had haunted every King of Kings since the time of Ardashir—of an authentically universal, world-spanning monarchy—appeared close to realisation at last. The empire of the Romans, meanwhile, stood on the brink of annihilation.

"As for the fourth beast, there shall be a fourth kingdom on earth, which shall be different from all the kingdoms, and it shall devour the whole earth, and trample it down, and break it to pieces."[83] Such had been the dream of Daniel; and an angel, explaining the vision, had foretold that the time was destined to come when the beast would be destroyed, "and given over to be burned with fire,"[84] and that the people of God would then inherit the earth. This, in the time-sanctioned opinion of the Church, had been a prophecy of the fate of Rome's pagan order; but perhaps it was only to be expected that the Jews, tracking in amazed astonishment the implosion of the New Rome's Christian empire, should have interpreted it rather differently. Surely now, many of them dared to hope, the coming of the Messiah could not be long delayed? Surely, with Gog and Magog "clashing mightily" and terror filling "the hearts of the nations," the time had come at last when "Israel will be cleansed of her sins"?[85]

Focus of all these expectations, only naturally, was Jerusalem. Here, when Shahrbaraz appeared before its walls in the early summer of 614, the patriarch flatly refused to countenance the appalling possibility that the Holy City might actually fall to pagans. Rather than negotiate terms with the invaders—as most other urban authorities, remembering the fate of Antioch, had hurried to do—he insisted on trusting to the protection of Christ.[86] Three weeks later, the Persian army stormed the city. The slaughter was something prodigious: some fifty thousand corpses were said to have been left piled up in the streets. A further thirty-five thousand Christians, including the patriarch himself, were hauled off into captivity. With them, exhumed from a vegetable patch where it had been buried upon news of the Persian approach, went the single most precious object in the entire Christian empire: the True Cross. A shudder at the humiliation of this had naturally run deep across the Roman world. No less naturally, it was taken for granted by most Christians that a calamity of such an order could only ever have been the fault of the Jews. Indignant rumour-mongers insisted that it was they who had acted as spies for the Persians, had opened the city's gates, and had led the slaughter of Jerusalem's virgins. Most terrible of all, it was claimed that in the aftermath of the siege, Jews had rounded up some 4500 Christian captives, had ordered them at sword-point to change their religion, and then, upon their refusal, had slaughtered every last one. True or not, such allegations were universally believed— and were only fuelled by the naked euphoria of the Jews themselves. No sooner had Jerusalem passed into Persian hands than a mysterious figure, "Nehemiah the son of Hushiel,"* stepped forward to lead the city's Jews up on to the Temple Mount, where they constructed an altar. Sacrifices, for the first time in five hundred years, were offered on the sacred rock in accordance with the Law of Moses. The opportunity had come at last, it appeared, "to found a temple of holiness."[87]

Yet, all these ecstatic expectations were soon cruelly dashed. The Persians, no less tolerant of Jewish pretensions than the Romans had been, did not have the slightest intention of permitting the construction of a new Temple, or allowing some upstart Jew to proclaim himself the Messiah. Only a few months into their occupation of Jerusalem, they arrested Nehemiah, accused him of sedition, and executed him. Whether in fact he had claimed to be the Messiah or not, it was clear that he could not, after all, have been the "son of man" foretold by Daniel, who was destined, after the burning of the fourth beast, to achieve "dominion and glory and kingdom."[88]

Meanwhile, far to the north, Heraclius was preparing to hammer a further nail into the coffin of Jewish hopes. Perilous though his circumstances certainly were, yet he had not despaired of them, nor of

---

* Almost certainly not his real name. The original Nehemiah had served as a governor of Jerusalem back in the fifth century BC, under the original Persian Empire. A book in the Bible is named after him.

his empire. The decade that Khusrow had spent in making extravagant conquests, Heraclius had spent in firming up his power base. By 624, he was finally in a position to go on the offensive, confident that he would not be stabbed in the back. This, for his prospects of success, could hardly have been more critical: for the emperor's campaigning plans were the height of ambition. Just as he had toppled Phocas by striking directly at him from across a prodigious expanse of sea, so now did he aim to repeat the trick by crossing the mountains of Armenia and "cutting out at its roots the very source of the evil—Persia."[89] The gamble was a prodigious one: for Heraclius, straining every financial and logistical muscle to the limit, had mustered a task force that was effectively his empire's last line of defence. Teetering on the edge of such peril, he too, just as the Jews had done, looked to scripture for reassurance: "And Heraclius, taking the book of Daniel, discovered in it written thus: 'The goat of the west will come forth, and he will destroy the horns of the ram of the east.' Then the emperor rejoiced, and was convinced that everything would succeed for him against the Persians."[90]

And so it did. Four long years Heraclius would be gone from Constantinople: a period of absence that would culminate in one of the most stunning comebacks ever recorded in military history. Relentless though the fighting was, and doomed though the Roman cause would certainly have been had the emperor and his tiny army ever been wiped out, yet the greatest aspect of this astonishing campaign was the one that pitched faith directly against faith. In Palestine, shortly before the sack of Jerusalem, heavenly armies had been seen clashing in the sky; and now, on the fallen earth, a battle no less celestial in its character was due to be fought. Heraclius, taking a leaf out of the Ghassanid book, did not hesitate to proclaim himself a warrior of Christ. In doing so, he put on the line not merely his own life and his empire's survival, but the entire authority of the Christian god. As a stake, he wagered the most precious thing he had: Constantinople itself. In 626, when Khusrow ordered Shahrbaraz to advance directly to the shores of the Bosphorus, Heraclius did not waver in his conviction that the Christian people of his capital lay secure beneath the watch of the heavens. Not even the fact that the Avars were simultaneously descending from the north, complete with the very latest fashion in siege-towers and catapults, could persuade him to abandon his plan of campaign, and retreat from *Iranshahr*. His confidence, in the event, was to be richly rewarded. The Virgin Mary—whose silhouette, "a woman alone in decorous dress,"[91] was said to have been glimpsed by the Avar Khan himself upon the battlements—stood directly on guard over the capital. It helped as well that the Byzantine navy, sallying out into the Bosphorus, succeeded in sinking the entire Persian transport fleet. The great siege lasted only a couple of weeks before both Shahrbaraz's army and the Avars withdrew. The citizens of Constantinople, steeled by such an ultimate test, could know themselves truly the people of God.

Meanwhile, far distant in *Iranshahr*, Heraclius was busy demonstrating to the fire-worshipping subjects of "the destructive and ruinous Khusrow"[92] that their own lord was heaven-cursed. Rather than aim at direct, immediate military conquest—an objective that was well beyond his resources—he made it his goal instead to demolish every conceivable underpinning of the prestige of the House of Sasan. This was why he chose to open his campaigning by sweeping down upon the Fire of the Stallion, storming the summit of the lonely mountain on which it stood, wasting the temple, and stamping out the sacred embers. Then, emboldened by a whole string of victories, he descended from the mountains of Media, and scythed a bloody course across the open mudflats of Mesopotamia, leaving canals, roads and villages polluted with corpses. Finally, in December 627, he began to target Khusrow's own palaces. Their overseers were taken captive; the animals in the royal parks, from ostriches to tigers, barbecued and fed to his soldiers; the silks, and carpets, and bags of spices in the treasuries put to the torch. "Let us quench the fire before it consumes everything,"[93] Heraclius wrote to his great rival—but already, even as he sent the letter, the flames lit by his soldiers were to be seen from the walls of a terrified Ctesiphon.

Meanwhile, Heraclius had more than likely been in secret communication with Shahrbaraz.[94] The Parthian general, his troops stationed in ostentatious inactivity in Syria, had been in deep disgrace with Khusrow ever since the failure of the assault on Constantinople. Now, with the *Shahanshah* in headlong flight before Heraclius' outriders, the Mihranid warlord prepared to add to his dynasty's long record of treachery towards the House of Sasan, and stab Khusrow in the back. On 23 February 628, two of Shahrbaraz's sons arrested the bedraggled monarch, who was suffering from chronic dysentery at the time, and imprisoned him in one of his own palaces. There, they set before him "a great heap of gold, and silver, and precious stones"[95]—but no food. The wretched Khusrow was left to starve, and literally shit himself, for five days. On the sixth day, his captors shot him to death with arrows. With that, the great war—which had raged for twenty-five years and had spread destruction to the furthest limits of East and West—was over at last.

The victory belonged, decisively, to Heraclius. His insight, that in a world rendered a living hell by plague and war what mattered most was to have a convincing claim upon the favour of the heavens, had been proved correct in the most resounding fashion imaginable. Khusrow had not been defeated militarily: the walls of his capital would certainly have stood proof against the tiny Roman invasion force, and his western conquests were still staked out by Persian garrisons. Yet so meticulously had his prestige been shredded that all his authority had simply melted away—leaving his subjects to ponder the unthinkable, and ask themselves whether the House of Sasan itself might have been abandoned by its *farr*. Certainly, by the summer of 629, when Heraclius negotiated the treaty that officially concluded the great war, the key player was not the seven-year-old grandson of Khusrow who now sat perched precariously on the Persian throne, but Shahrbaraz. Ignoring the infant *Shahanshah* with high-handed disdain, the emperor and the Parthian dynast "agreed among themselves that all Roman territory occupied by the Persians should be restored to the Romans."[96] Then, quietly, tipping his fellow negotiator the wink,

Heraclius agreed to back Shahrbaraz, should the Mihranid chief wish to pursue his own royal ambitions. To no one's great surprise, in April 630, Shahrbaraz duly made his power grab, murdered the child-king and proclaimed himself *Shahanshah*. A mere forty days later, he himself was dead—toppled in yet another coup. Assorted Sasanian wraiths, backed by assorted Parthian sponsors, now set to clawing one another to pieces. Heraclius could feel well content. Like a fish, *Iranshahr* was patently rotting from its head.

Yet, even as the House of Sasan snatched desperately after its disintegrating authority and prestige, Heraclius knew that there was an urgent need to preserve his own empire from suffering a similar fate. Even in Constantinople, that victorious and Christ-guarded city, a mood of exhaustion was manifest: in the suburbs left wasted by the Avars, and in the churches stripped bare to fund the war effort. Elsewhere, in the provinces only just evacuated by their Persian occupiers, marks of ruin were even more omnipresent: in the forts now blackened and gate-less; in the fields overrun by bandits; in the weed-choked streets of ravaged cities. Burned, looted, depopulated—entire swaths of the empire lay mouldering in a state of the most gangrenous misery. Clearly, then, urgent as it was to restore to the redeemed provincials the long-atrophied habits of obedience to Roman rule, more urgent still was the need to reassure them that the victory won by Heraclius had indeed been a victory won by God. This was why, in his negotiations with Shahrbaraz, no more urgent demand had been pressed by the emperor than the return from its ignominious captivity of the True Cross. On 21 March 630, stripped of all his imperial regalia and walking humbly on foot, as Christ Himself had done on his way to Golgotha, Heraclius entered Jerusalem, bearing with him the precious relic. Men reported that the manner of his arrival had been the result of advice given him by an angel, who had personally instructed him to take off his diadem, and to dismount from his horse. A supreme honour for Heraclius to receive: orders direct from the heavens to imitate the last journey of his Saviour.

The restoration of the True Cross to Jerusalem was the profoundest demonstration imaginable of the great victory that had been won in the cause of Christ. It also served as a ringing statement of Heraclius's intent: never again would he permit the Christian empire to be pushed by its enemies to the edge of oblivion. On his approach to Jerusalem, he had made a point of stopping off in Tiberias, where he had been hosted by a wealthy Jew notorious, under the Persian occupation, for his persecution of the city's churches. Asked by Heraclius why he had so mistreated the local Christians, the Jew had answered disingenuously, "Why, because they are the enemies of my faith."[97] Heraclius, grim-faced, had advised his host to accept baptism on the spot—which the Jew had prudently done. Two years later, this order was repeated on a far more universal scale. From Africa to distant Gaul, leaders across the Christian world received news of a startling imperial decision: all Jews and Samaritans were to be brought compulsorily to baptism. Heraclius, conscious of how close he had come to defeat, and of the debt he owed to Christ, was not prepared to take any second chances. From now on, the Roman Empire would be undilutedly, and therefore impregnably, Christian.

But what of those who lay beyond the reach of the empire? In 632, the same year that saw Heraclius issue his decree on the forcible conversion of the Jews, barbarian horsemen, "harsh and strange,"[98] descended upon Palestine, ravaging the undefended margins of the province and then disappearing as suddenly as they had arrived. Who were they, and what did they portend? No one could be entirely certain. There were some Christians, however, notwithstanding the triumphant return to Jerusalem of the True Cross, who feared the worst. Dread that the end of time might be at hand had not entirely been abated by the great victory of Heraclius. "To see a savage people emerge from the desert and run through land that is not theirs, as if it were their own, laying waste our sweet and organised country with their wild and tamed beasts"[99]—what could be more ominous than that?

Perhaps, then, indeed, when the End Times arrived, it would be upon the winding shadows of the indignant desert birds.

III

HIJRA

Once the world of ideas has been
transformed, reality cannot hold out for
long.

> Georg Wilhelm Friedrich Hegel

6

MORE QUESTIONS THAN ANSWERS

When?

Those who anticipated that Heraclius's triumph would provide only a temporary lull in the surge and swirl of great events were to be proved quite spectacularly correct. A bare three decades after the conclusion of the terrible war between *Iranshahr* and the New Rome, the balance of power that for centuries had divided the Fertile Crescent into two rival spheres of influence was no more. In the East, Persian rule had collapsed utterly. All the glory of the House of Sasan had been trampled into the dust. The *Shahanshah* himself had perished squalidly in the wilds of Khorasan, murdered, so it was said, by a local miller for his gold. His son, the heir of Ardashir and Khusrow the Great, was now a fugitive in China. Such an outcome, it might have been thought, was all that generations of Caesars had ever dreamed of achieving; and yet the overthrow of *Iranshahr* had certainly not been due to any triumph of Roman arms. A new people had risen to greatness; and these conquerors aimed at the conquest of Constantinople no less than they had Ctesiphon. The Roman Empire, unlike that of the Persians, still stood defiant; but only just. As in the darkest days of the war against

Iranshahr, so now, nothing but a rump remained to the New Rome of her dominions. Syria, Palestine and Egypt had all been lost. Even in Anatolia, the front line was being held only through desperate and blood-sodden effort.

Stupefied onlookers, in their attempts to make sense of these astounding convulsions, naturally turned to scripture for elucidation. Was it possible, they began to ask themselves, that the fourth beast seen by Daniel was not, as had long been presumed, the empire of the Romans, after all? It had certainly never been more manifest that God, for His own inscrutable reasons, was redrawing the affairs of men in a wholly startling manner. Global rule had passed into the hands of those previously scorned descendants of Ishmael, the bastard offspring of Abraham, the children of the slave-girl Hagar: the Arabs. "And behold, a fourth beast, terrible and dreadful and exceedingly strong; and it had great iron teeth; it devoured and broke in pieces, and stamped the residue with its feet."[1] Already, by the 660s, there were many prepared to revise their understanding of what Daniel had meant by this vision. "He is saying," so a chronicler in Armenia suggested, "that this fourth beast, which arises from the south, is the kingdom of the sons of Ishmael."[2]

As the decades and then the centuries passed, and still the empire won by the Arabs endured, this reading became ever more accepted among Christians and Jews alike. The Arabs themselves, of course, would have bristled at any notion that they were something bestial; but they too, as they surveyed with pride the awesome sweep of their dominions, never doubted for a moment that their conquests were indeed the expression of the will of the heavens. How else to explain their astonishing dismemberment of what had once been the two greatest empires in the world? "We went to meet them with small abilities and weak forces, and God made us triumph, and gave us possession of their territories."[3] By the tenth Christian century, when this self-satisfied assertion was penned, the defeat of the Persians and the Romans had come to be interpreted as something even more epochal than the replacement of two superpowers by a third. The lands won by "the sons of Ishmael" were no longer defined as an Arab empire but as the *Dar al-Islam*—the "House of Islam." The first generation of conquerors, even though they had called themselves "believers" or "emigrants"—Muhajirun—had come to be designated by a quite different word: "Muslims."[4] The collapse of Persian and Roman power was attributed, not to the agonies of plague and war that had racked the Near East for decades, but to the revelation of the word of God to His Prophet in far-off Mecca. "When you encounter the unbelievers, blows to necks it shall be until, once you have routed them, you are to tighten their fetters." So Muhammad, serving as the mouthpiece of God, had informed his followers. "Thereafter, it is either gracious bestowal of freedom or holding them to ransom, until war has laid down its burdens."[5]

The notion that a people might be entrusted by the heavens with a charge to spare the vanquished and to overthrow the haughty was hardly original to the Qur'an, of course. Back in the heyday of Roman greatness, Virgil had articulated a very similar sense of mission. What had changed, however, and to seismic effect, was people's understanding of what the sanction of the heavens might actually mean. Just as Constantine had discovered in Christ an infinitely more potent patron than Athena or Artemis had ever been, so those who turned to the pages of the Qur'an found revealed there a celestial monarch of such limitless and terrifying power that there could certainly be no question of portraying Him—as the Christians did with their own god—in human form. Nothing, literally nothing, was beyond Him. "If He wishes, O mankind, He can make you disappear and bring others in your stead."[6] To a deity capable of such a prodigious feat of annihilation, what was the overthrow of an empire or two? Remarkable though it certainly was that the *Dar al-Islam* had been raised upon the rubble of Persian and Roman power, no explanation was needed for this, so Muslim scholars taught, that did not derive from an even more awesome and heart-stopping miracle: the revelation to the Prophet of the Qur'an. What surprise that a fire lit far beyond the reach of the ancient superpowers should have spread to illumine the entire world, when that fire was the Word of God?

And it is here, of course, in any interpretation of Islam's origins as an intrusion of the divine into the sweep of earthly events—as a lightning strike from heaven, owing nothing to what had gone before—that history must needs meet and merge with faith. Almost fourteen centuries on from the lifetime of Muhammad, the conviction that he was truly a prophet of God continues to move and inspire millions upon millions of people around the globe. As a solution to the mystery of what might actually have taken place in the early seventh-century Near East, however, it is unlikely to strike those historians raised in the traditions of secular scholarship as entirely satisfactory. By explaining everything, it runs the risk of explaining nothing much at all. Nevertheless, it is a measure of how potently an aura of the supernatural has always clung to the Qur'an, and to the story of its genesis, that historians have found it so difficult to rationalise its origins. Mecca, so the biographies of the Prophet teach us, was an inveterately pagan city, devoid of any Jewish or Christian presence, situated in the midst of a vast, untenanted desert: how else, then, are we to account for the sudden appearance there of a fully fledged monotheism, complete with references to Abraham, Moses and Jesus, if not as a miracle? In a sense, the entire history of secular enquiry into the origins of Islam has been an attempt to arrive at a plausible answer to this question. Muslims, understandably sensitive to any hint that the Prophet might have been a plagiarist, have always tended to resent the inevitable implications of such a project; and yet, once God is discounted as an informant, it is surely not unreasonable to wonder just how it came to be that so many characters from the Bible feature in the Qur'an. Perhaps, so it has been suggested, Muhammad absorbed Jewish and Christian influences during his business trips to Syria.[7] Or perhaps, despite what the Muslim sources tell us, there were in fact thriving colonies of Jews, Christians, or both in Mecca.[8] Or perhaps there was a crisis of capitalism among the Quraysh, one that saw successful merchants and financiers growing ever more obscenely rich, even as those on the breadline were left "searching for a new spiritual and political solution to the malaise and disquiet in the city,"[9] and finding it—somehow, in some unspecified manner, in the spirit of the age.

Yet all these explanations run up against a familiar stumbling block. Given that the Prophet's earliest biographers were writing almost two centuries after his death, how far can we legitimately accept their presumption that seventh-century Mecca was genuinely a place of great significance and wealth—the "Mother of Cities"?[10] It is plausible enough that it might have been a centre of pilgrimage for the local pagans, but that it ranked as the Dubai of its day, a prosperous and cosmopolitan trading hub brought to flourish in the depths of the desert, is most certainly not. What incentive could there possibly have been for anyone with an eye for a profit to base himself in a barren valley many hundreds of miles from the nearest consumerist fleshpot? Even the few camel-trains that still plodded northwards from Himyar, heading for a Roman market that had long since lost its appetite for incense, went by a road that bypassed Mecca altogether.[11] A merchant from Alexandria might cheerfully discourse about the trading opportunities in entrepôts as far afield as India, and never even so much as allude to Mecca—on his doorstep though it effectively was.[12] In gazetteers written by Muhammad's contemporaries—whether diplomats, geographers or historians—mentions of it are notable by their glaring absence.[13] Even in the Qur'an itself, the word appears just once. "In the belly of Mecca, it was God who held their hands back from you"[14]—an allusion that might as well be to a valley as to a city. Otherwise, in all the vast corpus of ancient literature, there is not a single reference to Mecca—not one.[15] Only in 741, more than a hundred years after the Prophet's death, does it finally crop up on the pages of a foreign text—and even then the author locates it in Mesopotamia, "midway between Ur and Harran."[16] Clearly, then, whatever else Mecca might have been in the early seventh century, it was no multicultural boom-town.

So how is it, in a book supposedly composed there in Muhammad's lifetime, that the monotheisms of the far-distant Fertile Crescent should have been given such a starring role? It is all very mysterious; and made even more so by the fact that Mecca is not alone in seeming to have had a spectrally low profile in the early decades of the Arab Empire. So too did the Qur'an itself. As with the reputed birthplace of the Prophet, so with the compendium of his revelations: there is not a single mention of it in writings of the period. In the first flush of the Ishmaelite takeover, the Patriarch of Antioch assumed that his new masters' holy book was the Torah.[17] Such a presumption, of course, might well have reflected nothing more than wilful blindness—except that it was far from being confined to bishops. More than a century after the death of Muhammad, Muslims—as they were now starting to call themselves—might betray a very similar ignorance. Even as Christian bureaucrats, tracking the peculiar beliefs of their Arab over-lords, began to note the existence of various "frivolous tales"[18] composed by Muhammad, Muslim scholars, in their concern to iden-tify precisely what the Prophet might have taught, were still perfectly capable of overlooking the Qur'an altogether. How, for instance, did God wish adulterers to be punished? To this question, *hadith* after *hadith* provided the same unyielding answer as was to be found in the Torah: He wished them to be stoned. Yet this was not at all what was taught in the Qur'an. There, it could be read that God, "ever-compassionate," merely wished adulterers to be given "a hundred lashes."[19] How to explain such a discrepancy? If the Qur'an truly originated in the lifetime of Muhammad, and had been preserved and cherished by his followers ever since as the unchanging word of God, why was it that so many Muslim jurists—and prominent ones at that—had disregarded it as a source for their rulings? The mystery seems only compounded by the complete absence of any commentaries on the Qur'an prior to the ninth Christian century, and by the fact that even then different com-munities of the faithful preserved different versions of the holy text.*

---

* A Muslim scholar of the tenth century, Ibn Mujahid, established what sub-sequently became the orthodoxy: that there were seven, equally valid *qira'at*—"readings"—of the Qur'an. The modern, widely held notion that there is one single text was established only in 1924, with the publication in Cairo of an edition of the Qur'an that went on to become the global standard.

Perhaps it is hardly surprising, then, that many a scholar today, confronted by the dogma which teaches that the Qur'an derives unaltered and immaculate from the lifetime of Muhammad, should be tempted to raise an eyebrow, at the very least.

How far is such scepticism justified? Much, of course, hangs on the answer. Nothing better illustrates the extreme sensitivity of the issues at stake than the fate of a cache of Qur'ans that were found some forty years ago in Sana'a—capital of what was once the Jewish Kingdom of Himyar and is now the Muslim Republic of Yemen. Uncovered by workmen in the ceiling of the city's oldest mosque, stuffed into seventeen rough hessian sacks and preserved from oblivion only by the sharp eyes of the Yemeni antiquities chief, the great mass of parchment contained fragments of what are almost certainly the oldest Qur'ans in existence. Four decades on from their discovery, however, these precious manuscripts remain shrouded in mystery. Only two researchers, both German, have been permitted to study them. When one of these, an expert in Arabic palaeography by the name of Gerd-Rüdiger Puin, publicly asserted that the fragments demonstrated that the Qur'an, no less than the Bible, had evolved over time and was a veritable "cocktail of texts,"[20] the Yemeni authorities reacted with fury. To this day, the Qur'anic fragments in Sana'a remain unpublished—nor have any further Western scholars been permitted to study them. As a result, their true significance remains opaque.

But not wholly so. Granted that Puin's researches do indeed seem to suggest that words, spellings and even the order of verses in the Qur'an were perfectly capable of being misread and miscopied, it is apparent as well that these alterations were only ever involuntary errors. There is not a hint of deliberate fabrication in any of the Sana'a fragments. Phrases may vary substantially from manuscript to manuscript, but entire passages never do. At no point, it seems, was the Qur'an ever the equivalent of a collection of *hadiths*—something to be added to upon the whim of some Caliph or scholar. In fact, nothing better testifies to the dread and reverence with which every last word of it, every last letter, was patently regarded than the fact that jurists were prepared to swallow even a glaring embarrassment such as its ruling on adultery. Wriggle though they might—with some claiming that stoning was actually prescribed in the Qur'an as the original penalty for the offence, but that the relevant verse had been devoured by a hungry goat—no attempt was ever made to improvise something new. Even the earliest Sana'a fragments reveal an awed sense on the part of those responsible for them that something of profound and terrible holiness was being put to paper, far transcending human invention. If, as both Puin and his colleague have argued, these earliest fragments are to be dated to the beginning of the eighth century, it would suggest that their ultimate origins must lie well before that time.[21] The daring thesis floated some decades back, by a few venturesome scholars, that the Qur'an might have been the product of protracted evolution, and that it arrived at something like its current state only at the end of the eighth Christian century, seems to have been conclusively disproved.[22] Irrespective of all the revisions and variations Puin has traced in the Sana'a fragments, the bedrock of the Qur'an appears hewn out of solid granite.

This, however, begs any number of questions in turn. How was it that a book so revered should simultaneously have been neglected for so long by so many Muslim jurists? What, precisely, was the prehistory of the Qur'an prior to its first appearance in the written record in the early eighth century? Does the fact that every man who ever copied it appears to have done so in the unshakable conviction that he was transcribing words of unparalleled holiness mean that we can trust the Muslim traditions that explain how it came into being, after all? Perhaps. But a familiar problem, like a nagging headache, persists. It remains the case, and disconcertingly so, that the earliest surviving biographies of the Prophet were written whole generations after his death—and that their accounts of the origins of the Qur'an are such as cannot possibly be taken for granted. Just how yawning, then, just how much of a rupture, might the gap between the traditional date of the holy book's composition and the first commentaries on it actually have been? The Qur'an, as it disarmingly acknowledges in one of its own verses, contains no lack of "ambiguous"[23] material: there are contradictions, abrupt shifts in voice, topic and tone, and baffling allusions. That brilliant intellects, from the ninth century onwards, should have devoted themselves to the immense task of clarifying these same ambiguities does not necessarily mean that they had inherited authentic information as to what the holy text had originally meant.

In fact, it might mean just the opposite. Long before the coming of Islam, scholars labouring over other works of scripture had inadvertently demonstrated an unsettling truth: the greater the sense of awe with which a text was regarded, the more complete might be the amnesia as to the original circumstances of its composition. Back in the *Iranshahr* of Peroz, the Zoroastrian priests, resolved as they were to adapt their inheritance of ancient scriptures to the political requirements of their Church, had shown not the slightest hesitation in shifting the birthplace of Zoroaster to Media. The Talmud, of course, was nothing if not a project to demonstrate that Moses would have been perfectly at home in the *yeshivas* of Sura and Tiberias. Christian scholars, keen to establish the primal antiquity of their own faith, wrote whole reams of commentaries on the Tanakh, proving that what they termed the "Old Testament" was in fact a foreshadowing of Christ. If adherents of the evolving religion of Islam, confronted by a scripture of indubitable holiness, but rife all the same with passages that they could barely understand, did set themselves to the elucidation of its mysteries, not as historians but rather as men concerned to comprehend the workings of God, then they would have been doing nothing that *mowbeds*, or rabbis, or bishops had not already set themselves to achieve.

To establish when the Qur'an might have been composed, therefore, and whether it does indeed provide us with an authentic source for the Prophet's life and times, it is essential first to strip away the great cladding of commentary that has been woven tightly around the holy text since the early ninth century, and make an attempt, at the very least, to see it naked and unadorned. This is no easy task, however. The same ambiguities that prompted Muslim scholars to compose their immense array of commentaries and biographies of the Prophet still render it challenging, to put it mildly, to read the Qur'an in the light of the Qur'an alone. Unlike the Bible, which name-checks any number of conveniently datable rulers—from Cyrus to Augustus—the Qur'an betrays what is, to any historian, a most regrettable lack of interest in geopolitics. Those who are named in its pages tend to be angels, demons or prophets. There are the four mentions of Muhammad himself, of course. Then there is an enigmatic figure called Zayd, who seems to be both the ex-husband of one of the Prophet's wives and his adopted son: tradition would subsequently identify him as a one-time slave who died in battle as an early martyr for Islam. Finally, there is an unbeliever by the name of Abu Lahab, who appears in the biographies of the Prophet as his uncle, and who is condemned, together with his wife, to "burn in the Flaming Fire."[24] No other contemporaries of Muhammad are mentioned by name in the holy text. The focus of the Qur'an is fixed implacably, not on the personal, but on the divine. Before the awful dimension of such a radiance, in which God's omnipotence can be experienced as something both intimate and cosmic, as a presence that is simultaneously closer to the believer than his own "jugular vein"[25] and more remote than the most distant star in the universe, what is any mere mortal? The voices that feature in the Qur'an are those of God Himself and His prophet: no one else gets much of a hearing.

Which is not to say that there is no sense of dialogue in the Qur'an—for in truth it is a most disputatious book. Always, however, those who are being variously scorned, chided and refuted by the Prophet lurk off-stage—their voices unheard, their beliefs unaired. *Mushrikun*, they are called—"those who are guilty of *shirk*." Such an offence—the belief that supernatural beings might be partnered with God as fit objects of worship—would end up enshrined by Islam as the most unforgivable of sins, of course; and so perhaps it is no surprise that the presumption should have grown up among Muslim scholars that the *Mushrikun* had been rank idolators and pagans, worshippers of stock and stone. This, however, is not at all what the Qur'an itself implies.[26] Indeed, based purely on the evidence contained in the holy text, the *Mushrikun* seem to have shared a whole range of beliefs with Jews and Christians— not to mention the Prophet himself. That the world was created by a single god; that this god would listen to those who approached him, whether through prayer or pilgrimage; that he ruled as lord of the angels: all this, it is clear enough, was common ground between Muhammad and his opponents. So too was familiarity with characters from the Bible—something taken wholly for granted in the Qur'an. Where the *Mushrikun* erred, however, according to the Prophet, was in their adherence to a truly shocking notion: that God had fathered the angels, and would listen to any prayers that might be raised to Him through their agency. Even worse, in a world where no man ever doubted his superiority over women, the *Mushrikun* actually presumed "to turn the angels, servants of the All-Merciful, into females"![27]

Whether this was actually what the *Mushrikun* had done is, of course, a rather different matter. "They follow nothing, those who worship partners apart from God—they follow nothing but conjecture; they utter nothing but lies."[28] Hardly, it is fair to say, the most nuanced cataloguing of what the *Mushrikun* might actually have believed. The Prophet was clearly no encyclopedist: he lacked the insatiable passion of an Epiphanius for cataloguing the precise details of his opponents' follies. Whoever or whatever the *Mushrikun* may have been, it is impossible to glimpse them save through a swirling fog-bank of polemic. Certainly, there is nothing in the mere fact of their existence that helps us to pinpoint when they flourished.

It is fortunate, then, that the Qur'an does not float entirely free of history's moorings. Among its 114 chapters—or "suras"—there are just a few scattered clues to its likeliest date of composition. Of one thing, at least, we can be certain: its final form long post-dates the implosion of the Thamud, that large confederation of Arab tribes employed by the Romans, and who are commemorated by the Prophet as the exemplification of worldly greatness brought low. Time was, he reminds their ghosts, when God "granted you mastery over the earth, when you seized its plains to build your mansions, and carved houses from the mountains"[29]—until, as payback for straying off the straight and narrow, they were dispatched by a scream so terrible that it left them withered, like dry straw. If this name-checking of the Thamud appears to imply a certain familiarity on the part of the Prophet with the workings of Roman imperialism, then it is dramatically confirmed by another verse—the only one in the entire Qur'an to name a contemporary power. "The Romans," it is reported, "have been defeated in a nearby land, and yet, after their defeat, they shall be victorious—in a few years."[30] It is hard to know to what this might conceivably be alluding, if not the loss of Palestine to Khusrow II. The prophecy might appear brief, and almost throwaway—but its implications are momentous. So terrible was the great war between Persia and the New Rome, and so devastating its impact, that even in the very throne-room of the heavens its reverberations were being felt. No other earthly conflict, after all, had served to prompt a long-range forecast from the Lord of Worlds Himself.

All of which, for the historian, suggests a most welcome and promising conclusion. Compared to the bogs and quicksand of other sources for the life of the Prophet, the book of his revelations does authentically appear to offer us something precious: something almost like solid ground. Unlike the witness provided by the *hadiths*, or the biographies of Muhammad, or the commentaries on the Qur'an, the text of the Qur'an itself does seem to derive authentically from the Prophet's lifetime. That makes it, a few other brief and enigmatic documents aside, our only primary source for his career. Such a resource is, in consequence, beyond compare: one that positively demands to be sifted for clues to the Prophet's career and background. Identify these, and it may then be possible to find reflected in the Qur'an glimpses, not merely of the Prophet's personal circumstances but of something even more suggestive: the broader context of the age.

Take, for instance, the verse that prophesies which of the two great imperial peoples will emerge victorious from their terrible war. In its presumption that God favours the cause of the Romans, and that their fate has been graced with a literally cosmic significance, there is nothing incompatible with the Romans' own perennial self-conceit. Elsewhere in the Qur'an, too, there can be detected just the faintest echo of Heraclius's blowing on the embattled empire's war-trumpet. "They ask you," God tells Muhammad, "about 'The Two-Horned One'"[31]—Dhu'l Qarnayn, in Arabic. This, so the Qur'an goes on to reveal, was the title of a great ruler who journeyed to the ends of the earth, where he built gates of iron faced with bronze, and thereby imprisoned the surging hordes of Gog and Magog. To the apocalypse-haunted Roman people, this biography would have suggested only one man—and during the reign of Heraclius, especially so. Alexander the Great, conqueror of the Persians, and gaoler of Gog and Magog, had lately become the name on every Christian's lips. Amid the humiliations and triumphs of the great war against *Iranshahr*, Roman propagandists repeatedly invoked his memory. Then, in 630, with Khusrow finally toppled and Heraclius about to enter Jerusalem, a fabulous story had begun to circulate in Syria, clearly written in honour of the moment, and featuring Alexander.[32] The great conqueror, it appeared, had not only reached the setting of the sun and walled up Gog and Magog—he had also delivered a prophecy, foretelling how, at the end of days, the sway of the Christian empire would be extended to the limits of the world. Reassuring news for Heraclius—and sure enough, just to ensure that no one missed the point, Alexander was shown in the story vowing to head for Jerusalem, and to take with him a silver throne, "so that when the Messiah comes from heaven, He may sit upon this kingly throne, for His kingdom lasts for ever."[33] Not the most subtle parallel with Heraclius's own shouldering of the True Cross, perhaps—but ringing enough, to be sure. In fact, it is a measure of just how effective the story was as a celebration of the emperor's entry into Jerusalem that the tale of Dhu'l Qarnayn in the Qur'an appears to have been modelled directly upon it. Plot, imagery, even the hero's distinctive horns—all are identical.[34] Here, then, if anywhere, it is possible to pin a precise date upon a segment of the Qur'an. And yet, despite this, the tale told of Dhu'l Qarnayn betrays barely a trace-element of its genesis in the Roman propaganda

of mankind before an omnipotence that can convert the entire world into dust, is no less of its time for having a perspective that disdains to focus on specific events—whether a plague that had recently wiped out a third of the population of the Near East or a war that had been raging for decades.

"For every nation there is an appointed span of time; when their time arrives, they can neither delay it nor bring it forward, even for an instant."[37] Viewed from this perspective, the calamities that were even then convulsing the empires of Persia and the New Rome were nothing exceptional. The gaze that Muhammad brought to the agonies of his own generation was one that distinguished in the rise and fall of great powers merely the ceaseless gusting of grains of sand upon desert winds. Ever since the moment of creation, what had mattered to humanity was not the vagaries of history but rather a question as eternal as it was urgent: how best to choose between good and evil. This is why, in the pages of the Qur'an, it is not kings or emperors who feature, but prophets. Muhammad was, of course, only one in a long succession of messengers sent by God to summon people to repentance. What need, then, when the truths that they revealed were unchanging, to specify where or when they might have lived? To God, and to God alone, belongs "the knowledge of all that is hidden in the heavens and earth."[38] Figures from even the recent past were of interest to Muhammad only once they had been bleached of all context, all individuality. So, for instance, when the seven sleepers of Ephesus are introduced into the Prophet's revelations, to be praised by him as "youths who believed in their Lord,"[39] he does not mention Ephesus, nor that there were seven of them, nor even that they were Christians. As with "the Two-Horned One," so with "the People of the Cave," threads drawn from the rich tapestry of Roman fantasy have been woven into a very different pattern.

Not, of course, that every filament drawn from the past could be reworked in such a manner. The world, as Muhammad well knew, was a various and error-ravaged place. It behoved the Believers to stand on their guard. A stern and awful warning—and one that the

IN THE SHADOW OF THE SWORD

Prophet would never tire of issuing. Here, in the fretful consciousness that there existed only the One True God, but that many different faiths claimed to understand Him, was the authentic neuralgia of the age. No less than a rabbi fretting over the *minim*, or a bishop sniffing anxiously after heretics, Muhammad was both appalled and transfixed by the sheer variety of peoples with different beliefs who filled the world. The adherents of some of these—such as the *Mushrikun* and the fire-worshipping devotees of Zoroaster—clearly lay beyond the pale.[40] But what of the Jews, say, or the Christians? "Who so disbelieves in God, His angels, His Books, His messengers and the Last Day has strayed far in error."[41] By this measure—as Muhammad himself seems to have been uncomfortably aware—there was precious little to separate a rabbi or a monk from a *mu'min*: a "believer." Indeed, to some extent, all the Prophet's many pronouncements on the Jews and the Christians, scattered throughout the pages of the Qur'an, resemble nothing so much as a protracted twisting in the wind. At times, the Torah and the Gospel might be hailed as "Guidance to mankind,"[42] sent down from heaven, and those who reverence them as the *Ahl al-Kitab*—the "People of the Book." At other times, the Jews might be damned with blood-curdling ferocity for their treachery, and the Christians for ascribing a son to God. Such tension was nothing new: it echoed the same mingling of fascination and loathing that had characterised Jewish and Christian attitudes to one another in the first few centuries after Christ. Perhaps, had a Christian written a book that gave a voice to Ebionites and Marionites in the years before the Council of Nicaea, it would have spanned the same extremes of tolerance and hostility towards the Jews that are found in the Qur'an. Muhammad, in his struggle to decide where precisely to draw the frontier between his own teachings and those of the "People of the Book," and how high to raise the barriers and watchtowers, was wrestling with a problem many centuries older than himself.

Nor, it seems, was he wholly oblivious to the fact. On one level, it is true, the Qur'an records a very specific moment in history: a moment that internal evidence, as well as tradition, identifies with the early decades of the seventh Christian century. Muhammad, in his concern to define for the Believers the troublesome border zone that separated them from the Jews and the Christians, was perfectly capable of doing so in a manner that any pious Caesar would have recognised. Just as Justinian had prescribed swingeing financial penalties for "all those who do not rightly worship God,"[43] so was it decreed in the Qur'an that Jews and Christians should pay a special tithe, the *jizya*—and in such a manner as to render their inferiority manifest to all.[44] Taxation combined with triumphalism: here was bullying in the grand tradition of the Roman state. That it was Christians who now faced fiscal penalties for belonging to a superseded faith, rather than imposing the fines themselves, only compounded the irony, of course. The Prophet, insofar as he did care to offer specific policy recommendations to his followers on the patrolling of religious diversity, was very much a man of his age.

And yet, in truth, his gaze was only partially fixed upon the present. In the Qur'an, the pretensions of the Jews and Christians are presumed to be something timeless. As with great empires, so with great religions: the precise parabola of their evolution was as nothing to the Prophet. The stirring events that had shaped the imperial Church no more intruded upon his consciousness than did the wars of the Caesars. Of the great councils, of the anguished disagreements between Chalcedonians and Monophysites, of all those emperors, bishops and saints who, over the centuries, had struggled with such passion and such earnestness to arrive at a consensus as to the nature of Christ—of these, in the Qur'an, there is not so much as a hint. In fact, there are no Christians at all in its pages that the contemporary Church would have acknowledged as its own, save for the monks of the desert—and even these are so shadowy a presence that the Prophet can never quite decide whether to laud them as models of humility or condemn them as monsters of greed.[45] So, when Muhammad spoke of Christians, whom did he have in mind? A clue, perhaps, lies in the unexpected word he uses to describe them: *Nasara*. The name would have meant very little to the vast majority of seventh-century Christians. Only the learned—scholars familiar with the works of Jerome and Epiphanius, perhaps—might have pricked up their ears. The Nazoreans—those curious heretics who held to the Law of Moses and believed that the Holy Spirit was Christ's mother—had long since vanished from their ancient Palestinian heartland. Yet, in the Qur'an—composed a full two centuries after Jerome had noted the Nazoreans as a mere fading curiosity—not only is their name used by the Prophet as shorthand for all the "People of the Gospel,"[46] but their doctrines provoke some of his bitterest contempt. " 'Did you really say to people,' " God is shown asking of Jesus, " 'Take me and my mother as two gods, instead of God?' "[47] An indignant Jesus volubly protests his innocence. As well he might have done—for the charge being laid against him was the mortal charge of *shirk*.

Now, it is true, of course, that the Qur'an was labouring here under an almost grotesque misapprehension: orthodox Christians, despite what the Nazoreans may have believed, had absolutely no notion of any "God the Mother." Nevertheless, the Prophet had not wholly got the wrong end of the stick. By accusing the Christians of *shirk*, he had ripped the bandage off a very ancient sore. For six hundred years, the issue of how the relationship between God and Jesus was properly to be defined had been an itch that few Christians had been able to leave alone. For half of this span, admittedly, ever since the Council of Nicaea, it had pleased the leaders of the Catholic Church to imagine that there did exist a definitive answer to the problem, approved by Caesar, and sanctioned by the heavens. In reality, of course, as the Arian loyalties of the Ostrogoths and Vandals had shockingly served to demonstrate, the garden of Christian orthodoxy had never been totally cleared of weeds. A heresy, if it could manage to put down roots beyond the reach of the imperial Church, might still enjoy a certain, late-flourishing bloom. What, then, to make of the references in the Qur'an to the mysterious *Nasara*? That Arianism had long been able to prosper amid the bogs and forests of the North suggests that the Nazoreans might very plausibly have endured in the deserts of the

South. The implications of this, nevertheless, are more than a little disorienting. The origins of the Nazoreans, after all, stretched far beyond the time of Jerome—right back to the origins of the Christian Church. The questions posed by their doctrines struck at the heart of what Christianity, in the wake of Nicaea, had evolved to become. What, precisely, did it mean to say that Jesus was the Son of God? How might the Trinity best be defined and explained? Were Jews and Christians doomed to eternal mutual hatred, or were they better regarded as children of the same book?

Certainly, if the *Nasara* are indeed to be equated with the Nazoreans, then it might help to explain why the Qur'an, despite clearly having attained something like its final form early in the seventh Christian century, should seem haunted as well by the whispers of some very ancient ghosts. The one-sided debate to be found in its pages on the nature of Christ—one which firmly rejects the Trinity and affirms that Jesus himself was only ever a man—has a breath about it that seems to rise from an eerily distant age. Older than Nicaea, let alone Chalcedon, it had raged most bitterly back when there was no single Church, merely a multiplicity of sects. "They killed him not," the Prophet declares, "nor did they crucify him, but so it was made to appear to them."[48] Such a notion had not been heard for many centuries. What was it, after all, if not the very argument of the long-scotched Gospel of Basilides?

The voice we hear is not necessarily that of Basilides himself, of course. Nevertheless, the echoes of long-muted Christian heretics— of Gnostics and Nazoreans—are sufficiently loud in the Qur'an to make one wonder from where, if not from God, they might possibly have come. This issue is rendered all the more haunting because vanished gospels are not the only traces of an often fabulously distant past to be found in the verses of the holy text. Like a mighty cliff-face compounded of different layers of sediment, in which, just occasionally, fossils are to be glimpsed, exposed by rock-falls and weathering, the Qur'an hints at entire aeons that have been and gone, and yet endure contained within itself. Many of these same hints, not surprisingly, have always been regarded by commentators as somewhat of a puzzle. Just as fossils, prior to a proper understanding of the earth's geology, provoked many a furrowed brow among those who found them, there are phrases and even entire passages in the Qur'an that have always perplexed the learned. What, for instance, might one make of a short sura that takes as its theme the punishment of wrongdoers known as "the People of the Trench"?[49] Over the course of the centuries, numerous attempts have been made to explain this enigmatic phrase. Perhaps, so one early scholar suggested, it referred to the servants of a king who fired Abraham into a burning trench by means of a catapult. Or perhaps it related to the atrocities perpetrated by Yusuf against the Christians of Najran.[50] But what if it were not original to the Qur'an at all, but derived instead from another written source—specifically, one of those mysterious, ancient Jewish texts that occasionally cropped up in the wilds of the desert beyond Jerusalem in late antiquity? The discovery in more recent times of an entire cache of such manuscripts—the so-called "Dead Sea Scrolls"—has led a number of scholars to suspect a link between their teachings and those of the Qur'an.[51] What should be a designation for hell in the Dead Sea Scrolls, for instance, if not "the Trench"? And what should be the fate of the damned on the Day of Judgement if not to be consigned to that Trench's fires? Could this, then, be a possible source for the mysterious and much-debated phrase in the Qur'an—a vision of the End Days preserved from a distant Jewish past?

Certainly, it is notable, throughout the course of his revelations, that the Prophet returns again and again to a notion that few of his contemporaries in either synagogue or monastery would have thought to dispute: that the will of God can indeed be fathomed through the written word.

> With Him are the keys of the Unseen; none but He has knowledge thereof.
> He knows all that is on land and on sea;
> Not a leaf falls but He knows it.

Not a seed in the darkness of earth,
Not anything, fresh or dried,
But it is inscribed in a Manifest Book.[52]

This, rather in the manner of the Talmud, is to cast the whole of creation as a scripture; but elsewhere, the Prophet is more explicit in his praise of the truths to be found in "ancient scrolls." By these, he hurriedly goes on to specify, he means "the scrolls of Abraham and Moses"[53]—and yet the sheer wealth of allusions, echoes and remembrances in the Qur'an, enriching it and yet never overwhelming it, drawn from a bewilderingly eclectic array of sources, and yet made triumphantly, inimitably its own, serves to suggest that Abraham and Moses were not, perhaps, alone in having influenced the Prophet. From the propaganda of Roman emperors to tales of Christian saints, from long-vanished Gnostic gospels to ancient Jewish tracts: traces of all these writings have been convincingly identified in the Qur'an. Just as Muhammad claimed to be the Seal of the Prophets, so did his revelations contain within themselves, as a revenant and spectral presence, hints of how other peoples, back in the often distant past, had similarly had experience of the divine. Even gods that were ancient when Alexander was born are not wholly absent from its pages: for what are the horns that Dhu'l Qarnayn sports, after all, if not the ram horns of Amun? Some would go further yet, and claim that the very visions of paradise contained within the Qur'an, complete with eternally boyish cup-bearers, handsome "like hidden pearls,"[54] who are bestowed upon the Believers when they ascend to heaven, and beauteous, "wide-eyed maidens,"[55] shimmer with the primordial glamour of the banished gods of Greece and Rome. Certainly, it would seem a striking coincidence otherwise that Zeus, the pagan Lord of Olympus, should have had as his cup-bearer an exquisitely pearl-like youth and that his queen, Hera, the goddess of marital bliss, should have been famed for her seductively large eyes. Muslim scholars would certainly find themselves both perplexed and unsettled by the Prophet's insistence that celestial maidens had "wide eyes," believing it a description better

319

suited to cows. Their twitchiness would hardly have been improved if they had known that Hera, in the poetry of the pagan Greeks, was invariably hailed as "ox-eyed."[56] The Olympians might have been long toppled from their thrones—and yet, in the pages of the Qur'an, the golden halls of their palace still blaze with a brilliant after-glow.

Yet if this is the case, and if the revelations of the Prophet do draw for at least some of their power upon visions of the sacred that else-where, in the Christian empire of the Romans, had long since been driven underground, then the mystery of their origins seems only to deepen. Even more far-fetched than the portrait of Mecca as a bustling city of merchant princes, after all, is any likelihood that it might once have been teeming with Gnostics, Roman propagandists and enthusiasts for Homer and Virgil. Yet if the Qur'an, with all its rich and haunting sophistication, did not originate in Mecca, then from where did it come?

If we are to attempt an answer to that question, there is only one place to look: within the pages of the Qur'an itself.

Where?

Muhammad is most unlikely to have realised it, but his claim to be set-ting a seal on the revelations of earlier prophets was not, in fact, original to him.[57] "Wisdom and deeds have always from time to time been brought to mankind by the messengers of God."[58] So it had been declared, some three and a half centuries prior to the composition of the Qur'an, by a man who had aspired, and with great self-consciousness, to write the ultimate in holy books.

Mani, more than anyone before him, positively revelled in the blending of rival faiths. Born near Ctesiphon in 216, shortly before the city fell to Ardashir, he grew up within a Christian sect that, just like the Nazoreans, practised circumcision, held the Holy Spirit to be female, and prayed in the direction of Jerusalem. Such an upbringing clearly imbued in Mani a pronounced taste for the multicultural by

240, when he appeared before the newly crowned Shapur I, he had already successfully fused Jewish, Christian and Zoroastrian teachings into a spectacular new whole, while also claiming, just for good measure, to be the heir of the Buddha. Although Shapur himself, while intrigued by Mani's teachings, had failed to be converted by them, the self-proclaimed prophet's disciples spread to the limits of West and East and fashioned out of their master's teachings an authentically global faith. From Carthage to China, there had come to exist cells of Manichaeans "in every country and in every language."[59] They were even to be found, it may be, in Arabia: for the "Sabaeans," a mysterious people who feature in the Qur'an alongside the Jews and Christians as one of the three "Peoples of the Book," were, so it has plausibly been argued, none other than Manichaeans.[60]

If that identification is correct, though, they were, at most, a tiny and beleaguered sect. Manichaeism, despite the best efforts of Mani himself, never managed to capture the loyalty of a *Shahanshah*, let alone a Caesar. As a result, by the lifetime of Muhammad, the two great empires of the age had forced its adherents into a desperate and bloody retreat. In *Iranshahr*, the prophet himself had ended up martyred on the personal orders of Shapur's heir. Meanwhile, the Roman authorities, even prior to Constantine's conversion, regarded his teachings with the utmost suspicion—as a perfidious Persian attempt to corrupt their "innocent and modest"[61] citizens. The Christian empire, naturally enough, had inherited and refined this hostility, so that Manichaeism, by the time of Justinian's death, had effectively been extirpated from the entire sweep of Constantinople's dominions. The most bitter and implacable opposition to Mani's doctrines had come, however, not from monarchs but from the leaders of rival faiths: bishops, *mowbed*s and rabbis. To them, the upstart prophet's claims were doubly monstrous. It was not simply that Mani had cast their own scriptures as superseded revelations—although that, of course, was offensive enough. Even more loathsome, in their opinion, was the manner in which he had served as bawd to any number of rival faiths, forever mating and cross-breeding them, until, brought to life out of all the endless miscegenation, there had emerged the deformed hybrid that was his own sinister compound of teachings. Steeled by this perspective, both the Roman and the Persian authorities were confirmed in a fundamental presumption. The blurring and merging of beliefs, such as once had been common across the Fertile Crescent, was an offence that stank to the highest heavens. The no-man's land that stretched between the various faiths was on no account to be trespassed upon. What the faithful needed, as a synod of Nestorian bishops expressed it in 554, were "high walls, impregnable fortresses, protecting their guardians against danger."[62] Divided though Christians, and Zoroastrians, and Jews might be, yet on one thing they could all agree: the prospect of a second Mani was a horror not to be borne.

War served only to deepen this conviction. Across the mangled provinces of *Iranshahr* and the New Rome, the horrors of the age saw an increasingly violent and desperate scrabbling by rival communities of monotheists for the patronage of God. Whether it was by Christians lamenting the rape of Jerusalem, or by Zoroastrians mourning the extinguished Fire of the Stallion, or by Jews bewailing the rumours of forced conversions, barricades were being raised, and trenches dug, on an ever more formidable scale. In such a world, where the borders of faith had come to be trammelled and patrolled as never before, what best enabled a religion to thrive was reach, and organisation, and scale: much the same advantages, in short, as made for military muscle. Any sect unable to command such resources was doomed to suffer a lethal rate of attrition.

By the start of the seventh century, monotheism's triumph throughout the two rival empires was almost total. Of the ancient habits of pagan worship that had once been so universal, only a few scattered outposts still held out. In Khorasan, for instance, all the empire-building efforts of the Zoroastrian priesthood had failed to topple Mihr—that awful and sleepless avenger of injustice—from his mountainous and dawn-illumined throne. In Harran, too, which had long relied on its position midway between Rome and *Iranshahr* to perpetuate its venerable cult of Sin, the majority of the inhabitants still persisted in defying their nominal lord in Constantinople and refused to worship Christ. Nevertheless, the future for the Lord of the Moon looked bleak. Under Maurice, a particularly officious bishop had been appointed to the city's see, charged with scouring it clean of demon worship once and for all. Secret pagans in high places had been exposed, put to death, and gibbeted in the high street. For the worshippers of the Moon, then, occupation by Khusrow II's forces had come in the nick of time. The Persians had been far too preoccupied with their conquest of the world to concern themselves with the cult of Sin. By 629, however, with the conclusion of peace and the evacuation of the Persians from Harran, a restoration to Roman control was imminent. The writing now really did seem to be on the wall for the city's idols.

Pagans and Manichaeans, Jewish Christians and Christian Jews: persecution had been the common fate of all. There was no secure refuge from the imperial authorities to be found anywhere in the Fertile Crescent, save where it had always been: along its margins. For centuries, whether as a sanctuary or as a place of exile, the immense wilderness to the south of the two great empires had played host to beliefs that elsewhere had faded away, like ink on a crumbling scroll. To cross the frontier and head into the desert was therefore to step back in time. Only in Arabia, beyond the reach of monarch, bishop or *mowbed*, did the ancient promiscuity of cults endure. That Jews and Christians were to be found among the Arabs was certainly true—but not so that either could be confident of dominating the other. Even in Himyar, where first a Jewish king and then a Christian invader had seized power, neither regime had done much to dispel Arabia's ancient reputation as a breeding ground for heresy. By posing as the heir of David, Yusuf had indulged in precisely the kind of showmanship fit to appal most rabbis, while in Najran, the name given to the great shrine raised in honour of those martyred for Christ—the *Ka'ba*—bore unmistakable witness to the relish of the pagan Arabs for reverencing cubes. Nor, indeed, had Himyar ever been securely fire-proofed as a Christian realm. In the last years of Khusrow I's reign, a Persian-sponsored coup had terminated the Ethiopian occupation, and within a couple of decades Ctesiphon had established direct rule over the kingdom. The merchant from *Iranshahr*, "adorned with ear-rings, and with a Persian twang to his speech,"[63] had become an ever more familiar figure to the Arabs; and with him, in his wake, he had brought the worship of Ohrmazd. One more religion added to all the others in the teeming seedbed.

Meanwhile, far to the north of Himyar, on the margins of the Fertile Crescent—and especially along the margins of Palestine—there was even greater scope for cross-pollination. Nowhere else in the entire Near East had so many varieties and shades of faith survived intact. There were Jews, whose appeal to the Arabs of the desert had been noted long previously by Sozomen; and monks, those unyielding defenders of Chalcedonian orthodoxy; and the Monophysite warriors of the *Banu Ghassan*. Samaritans too, despite the calamitous failure of their revolt against Justinian, had continued to dash themselves against the rock of Roman power, and then, in the wake of the inevitable defeat and repression that followed, to stream in broken misery out into the neighbouring deserts. By abandoning the Holy Land, they were merely following paths already well-trodden by others: by Ebionites, by Nazoreans, by any number of Christian heretics. Not, it went without saying, that every pattern in the mosaic of belief to be found in northern Arabia was fashioned out of materials that were brought across the Roman frontier. The pagan traditions that had prompted Mundhir to wet al-'Uzza's altar stones with the blood of four hundred virgins and the Nabataeans to worship the black *Ka'ba* of Dushara had never—in contrast to those of the Fertile Crescent—suffered active repression. If even the Christians of Najran had preserved, in the name they gave to their great shrine, evidence of their ancestors' reverence for worshipping rocks, then it suggests that elsewhere too in Arabia, wherever the faiths and customs of outsiders met with those native to the Arabs themselves, the scope existed not merely for conflict but for that ultimate nightmare of the imperial authorities: the cross-breeding of rival beliefs.

And this, by the time of the great war, was a nightmare becoming reality. Mutant habits of worship were indeed being spawned in Arabia. In these hybrid cults was provided alarming evidence of what might emerge in consequence of a free market in faiths. What, for instance, were rabbis or monks to make of a community that acknowledged a single god to be the creator of the world, freely confessed his omnipotence, and had a thoroughgoing knowledge of Moses and Jesus—yet offered up prayers to al-'Uzza? Here, so its bitterest critic fulminated, was nothing but the filthiest and most degraded example of *shirk*. But the man levelling this accusation was no Jew or Christian. To Muhammad, the *Mushrikun* were not unfathomable aliens but something altogether more unsettling: men and women forged in the identical crucible that had steeled his own message. The Prophet, although implacably contemptuous of his adversaries' reverence towards al-'Uzza—and to other names summoned from the shadows of Arabian idol worship, those of al-Lat "and the third one, Manat"—never actually accuses the *Mushrikun* of worshipping this trinity of "females."[64] The word "goddess" does not appear once in the Qur'an; nor does the Prophet so much as mention the existence of pagan sanctuaries or shrines. Idols too, despite all the triumphant smashing of images that the Prophet is supposed to have got up to at Mecca, are notable by their absence from his revelations—as also they are from the archaeological record.[65] So, if the *Mushrikun* did not think of al-'Uzza as a deity, what did they believe her to be? No sooner has the Prophet name-checked her than he makes sure to provide the answer: "Those who deny the life to come give the angels female names."[66] Here was the record of a signal demotion. No longer a goddess, al-'Uzza had become merely a daughter of God: one of those many messengers of the Almighty whose beating wings, a brilliant gold amid the darkness of the age, were being heard in increasing numbers across the span of an anguished and desperate world.

Muhammad was hardly the first to insist that those who, like the *Mushrikun*, claimed to be monotheists, and yet directed prayers to angels, were hardly to be reckoned monotheists at all. Christians, ever since the time of Paul, had done exactly the same.[67] "To call upon the angels by name, and to organise their worship, is strictly forbidden." Such was the stern admonition of a Church Council held shortly after the death of Julian, at a time when bishops had particular reason to warn the faithful off practices that might smack of the pagan. "Anyone who is apprehended devoting himself to this concealed idolatry, let him be cursed."[68] Muhammad himself could hardly have put it any better. How easy it was for human beings, even those who devoutly believed themselves to be servants of the One True God, to remain in thrall to *shirk*. Time and again, it was the dread of a veiled paganism—a pretended monotheism—that most unsettled and outraged the Prophet. The offences of the *Mushrikun* were not only rank but insidious. Just as bishops in the time of Justinian, touring the hinterlands of their dioceses, had been appalled to discover the abiding relish of Christian peasants for the rituals that had been practised by their unbaptised forefathers, so was the Prophet no less obsessed by what one eminent scholar has termed "minor malpractices regarding the use of farm animals."[69] It was not only by the worship of angels, he charged, that the *Mushrikun* insulted the Almighty. They did it as well by slitting the ears of their livestock, by exempting certain cattle from ever having to pull a plough or carry a load, and by sometimes refusing to utter the name of God in an abattoir.[70] Offences as heinous as these, the Prophet sternly warned, would see the guilty "consigned to Hell."[71]

None of which, it is fair to say, would come to feature prominently in his biographies. If a concern to regulate the behaviour of agriculturalists seems to square awkwardly with the far more dramatic and crowd-pleasing accounts told centuries later of his activities at Mecca, then that is because it so plainly does. It is hard to know which is the more perplexing: the complete lack of evidence in the Qur'an for any idol smashing on the part of Muhammad, or its portrait of the *Mushrikun* as owners of great herds of oxen, cows and sheep. Mecca, a place notoriously dry and barren, is not, most agronomists would agree, an obvious spot for cattle ranching—just as the volcanic dust that constitutes its soil is signally unsuited to making "grain grow, and vines, fresh vegetation, olive trees, date palms, luscious gardens, fruit and fodder."* Yet God, according to the Prophet, had furnished the *Mushrikun* with all of these blessings. Nothing, of course, is impossible for the Almighty—but it would indeed have been a miracle had Mecca truly been adorned with spreading "gardens of vines, olives, and pomegranates."[72] These, if they were to be found in seventh-century Arabia at all, would have been confined to oases, or else to Nabataea and the Negev, where the desert, by the lifetime of the Prophet, had been made to bloom, and agriculture was flourishing as never before amid the desolate bleakness of the sands.† Such a redemption of the wilderness, secured as it had been only on the back of quite astounding ingenuity and effort, was, of course, an achievement fit to give any community a certain thrill of pride. Perhaps, then, it is telling that the Prophet, amid all the other charges he levelled against the *Mushrikun*, accused them of both ingratitude and conceit: of believing that it was they, and not the Almighty, who had made the dead land come to life. "Consider the seeds you sow in the ground— is it you who make them grow, or We?"[73]

Here, then, is one yet further puzzle, to add to all the many others. No less than the report to be found in the Qur'an of a Roman defeat in "a nearby land," or its precise echoing of a tale told in Syria about Alexander the Great, or its fascination with the Thamud, the extensive details revealed by the Prophet as to how his opponents made their living would appear to suggest something rather unexpected: a

---

* Qur'an: 80.27–31. The traditional accounts of Mecca's rise to greatness also imply that the city, as a teeming hub of international trade, must have had a substantial agricultural hinterland. The patent impossibility of this has led some historians to propose that grain was imported from Syria and Egypt: a case of the mountain coming to Muhammad, if there ever was one.

† Although vines and pomegranates would have been grown in oases such as Yathrib, the cultivated olive would not. In late antiquity, it was indigenous to the Mediterranean region.

context for Muhammad's revelations well to the north of Mecca. A far-fetched notion, perhaps—were it not for a striking fact. As with politics, so with topography: the gaze of the Prophet was fixed on horizons infinitely beyond the local. That is why, in the entire Qur'an, there are only nine places actually named. Of these, in turn, only two can be securely identified from the records of the time: Mount Sinai and Yathrib, the oasis settlement that would subsequently become known as Medina. It is true that a third location, Badr, where the Qur'an indicates a battle was fought, had been mentioned a hundred years previously by a poet praising a particularly nifty camel—but the only clue he had given to its location was that it stood somewhere in the middle of an enormous desert.[74] Another five places, including Mecca itself, appear for the first time in the Qur'an, and might as well have been anywhere, for all the detail about them that the holy book provides.* Most enigmatic of all, though, is the final site to be name-checked in the Qur'an: a "House" at a place called Bakka. Muslim scholars, puzzled by this allusion, and with a show of some considerable ingenuity, sought to demonstrate that here was merely an alternative name for Mecca—as well they might have done, for Bakka, in the Qur'an, is identified as a site of primal and incomparable holiness.† "Pilgrimage to the House," so the Prophet declares, "is a duty owed to God."[75] No wonder, then, that the attempt to establish the precise location of this awesome site should have inspired commentators to pile speculation upon speculation. That Bakka was Mecca, and that Mecca stood in the Hijaz, were propositions taken

---

* Hunayn—which, like Badr, is clearly identified in the Qur'an as the site of a battle—features in biographies of the Prophet as the location of a decisive Muslim victory. Safa and Marwa are identified by Muslim tradition as small hills in the immediate vicinity of the Ka'ba, while Arafat is equated to a mountain that lies some twelve miles outside Mecca.

† Most scholars distinguished Bakka from Mecca by identifying the former specifically with the Ka'ba and the latter with the surrounding area, although some suggested the opposite.

wholly for granted by Ibn Ishaq and his heirs. Yet the unsettling fact remains that not a shred of backing for either exists within the pages of the Qur'an itself. Moreover, the texts in which they first appeared were separated from the lifetime of Muhammad by several generations. The suspicion must be, then, that they are no more likely to reflect authentic tradition than did the nose of Palestinian landowners for previously forgotten biblical landmarks, back in the first flush of Christian tourism to the Holy Land.

A murk such as this spreads impenetrably. Where precisely Muhammad believed Bakka to have stood it is surely now impossible to say. Such evidence as might once have existed has long since been lost. Clues remain, but they are all of them ambiguous and fragmentary in the extreme. The ancient Greeks told the story of a robber named Procrustes, who would tie his victims to a bed, and then either stretch or mutilate them until they had been made to fit it: a methodology that the historian of early Islam often has little choice but to follow. Speculation as to where Bakka may originally have stood must perforce be procrustean—but since this caveat applies as surely to theories that would identify it with modern-day Mecca as to those that would not, there seems no need to apologise for it. Some mysteries are doomed forever to defy solution.

That said, it is possible to hazard a speculation. It is surely significant, at the very least, that Arabs in the wilds beyond Palestine had a pronounced taste for the appropriation of biblical settings. No less than Jews or Christians, they had long flocked to the sanctuary at Mamre: the very place—or *maqom*—where Abraham "had stood before the Lord." Furthermore, they had achieved what no other people beyond the limits of the Christian empire had even thought to obtain: a convincing claim upon the authentic bloodline of Abraham. The right of the Arabs to the title of "Ishmaelites," by virtue of their descent from Hagar, Abraham's concubine and Ishmael's mother, was freely acknowledged across the Fertile Crescent; and if the faintest hint of a sneer might occasionally linger when someone from beyond the deserts brought up the name, then the Arabs themselves were perfectly capable of a matching snobbery all of their own. Far from feeling embarrassed at having had a slave-girl in the family, those who were aware of their Hagarene lineage had come to revel in it. In the 660s, some two centuries after Theodoret had first reported the Ishmaelites' pride in their ancestry, a Nestorian chronicler on the Persian border with Mesopotamia alluded to the existence of a mysterious domed sanctuary, supposedly founded by Abraham and sacred to the Arabs. "Indeed," the chronicler added, "it is nothing new for the Arabs to worship there—for, from the beginning, from their earliest days, they have shown reverence to the father of the head of their nation."[76] A most arresting detail—for this is almost identical to what is reported in the Qur'an. There, in the passage on the House at Bakka, the Prophet identified the man who founded it as having been none other than Abraham himself. Is it possible, then, that the sanctuary praised in the Qur'an as the primal, the "blessed place,"[77] was the same identical one known as far afield as Persia as "the Dome of Abraham"?

Muslim scholars, in their understandable efforts to identify Bakka with Mecca, went to great and often fantastical lengths to explain how a patriarch who, according to venerable tradition, had been promised Canaan by God, and not Arabia, might conceivably have ended up in Mecca. Some had him abandoning Hagar and Ishmael there during the course of an extended road-trip; others, rather startlingly, described him as being guided by the *Shekhinah*—the name applied by the rabbis to the divine presence on earth. Such theories—floated in contradiction to both the Bible and an entire millennium of obsessive elaboration upon the story of Abraham and his bloodline—seem to have been wholly original to the Muslim scholars themselves.* Certainly, if any contemporaries of Muhammad believed that Abraham had been active in Mecca, there is no record of it. That

---

* The composition of Genesis, the book of the Bible in which Abraham appears, is generally dated to the seventh or sixth century BC. The implications of this for the historicity of Abraham are, of course, not themselves without significance.

Abraham had settled in Canaan, and that Hagar and Ishmael had taken refuge in one of the various stretches of wilderness that neighboured it, remained in the Prophet's lifetime what it had always been: something that everyone took utterly for granted.

Nor, in fact, is there anything in the Qur'an itself that would serve to contradict this universal presumption. Just the opposite, in fact. The Bakka described by the Prophet shimmers with the same numinous aura that had long attached itself to another sanctuary: Mamre. "It is the place where Abraham stood to pray":[78] so the Prophet describes Bakka. Of what, then, can this conceivably be an echo, if not the *maqom*? Certainly, between the Hebrew word for "place" and its Arabic equivalent, there was a manifest resonance. "Take as your place of prayer," it is recorded in the Qur'an, "the place where Abraham stood"[79]—the *Maqam Ibrahim*. In time to come, with Mecca enshrined once and for all as the site of Islam's holiest sanctuary, Muslim scholars would identify this *Maqam Ibrahim* with a stone that stood just to the north of the *Ka'ba*—an explanation that gives little hint as to its far more likely origins, many hundreds of miles to the north.[80]

That the Prophet repeatedly echoes the traditions associated with Mamre in his accounts of how the House at Bakka came to be built does not mean, of course, that the two shrines were one and the same thing—but it does suggest, to haunting and potent effect, a very particular context for his revelations. The Qur'an is a work manifest with distinctive habits of worship. Again and again, throughout its pages, the Prophet is insistent that these derive, not from his own invention but from the deepest wellsprings of monotheism. The ground he treads, he and the *Mushrikun* both, is stamped with the footprints of Abraham, and of Ishmael, the patriarch's son, and of Lot, his nephew, as well. Why, then, the Prophet demands, do his opponents not read the lessons that are written for them in such a landscape? "Lot too was a messenger," he reminds the *Mushrikun*:

Remember when We delivered him and all his household,
Except for an old woman, who was left behind.

Then We destroyed the others.

You pass by them morning and night; will you not understand?[81]

The allusion is to the petrified remains of the Sodomites—and it could hardly be any clearer in its implications. Wherever the Prophet's audience may have been settled, it was evidently at no great remove from what the Arabs themselves called the *Bahr Lut*, the "Sea of Lot"—what we know today as the Dead Sea.

And if the Qur'an is to be trusted, and if Muhammad's opponents did indeed live within an easy journey of the ruins of Sodom and Gomorrah, then the significance of the sanctuary at Bakka would hardly have been confined to the dimension of the heavenly alone. Back in the reign of Justinian, when a Roman ambassador had reported on the great desert shrine where "even the wild beasts live in peace with men," he had included another intriguing detail: that it was sacred to "a majority of the Saracens."[82] Could this desert shrine have been Bakka? The ambassador's description is so vague that it is impossible to say for sure. Nevertheless, a particularly intriguing detail among the Prophet's many revelations does seem to echo the Roman report. The Qur'an reveals that Abraham and Ishmael raised a prayer to God as they laboured to build the House at Bakka: "Make our descendants into a community devoted to you."[83] Which was, of course, to cast those descendants, the Ishmaelites, as something rather more than the sum of their parts. Fragmented into various tribes they might have been, and yet they were to be regarded, so it would seem from the Qur'an, as a single people—a "community." Bound by a unity of purpose, and joined by a common ancestry, what would they therefore share in, if not a God-sanctioned partnership—a *shirkat*?

Except that God, in the wilds beyond Palestine, was not the only patron of such partnerships. Behind the Thamud—and every confederation of Arab tribes since—had lurked Roman interests and Roman influence. It was only to be expected—in an age when proxy-fighting between the two superpowers cast a longer shadow over Arabia than ever before, extending as far south as distant Himyar—that the provincial authorities in Palestine should have shown themselves grimly determined not to drop their guard an inch. It was this, in the decades prior to the great war with Persia, that had encouraged a major recruitment drive on the part of Roman strategists, as they sought to compensate for their relative lack of manpower along the frontier by hiring Arabs to patrol it in depth. This, in turn, encouraged mass emigration from all over Arabia, with entire tribes drifting steadily northwards from the Hijaz towards Palestine. The concern of the provincial authorities to control and regulate this movement was evident in the care with which they sought to catalogue the newcomers. Exotic names duly flourished on the roster of *foederati*. Not an ethnic grouping between Palestine and the Hijaz, but the provincial authorities had sought to sponsor it. Never before, perhaps, had the tribal make-up of Arabia quite so pressingly held the interest of Roman strategists.

And yet, in every register of the age, there is one intriguing absence. As with Mecca, the city in which the Prophet supposedly grew up, so with the Quraysh, the tribe to which Muhammad supposedly belonged—all is deafening silence. Once again, it is not until a century and more after the Prophet's death that the name makes its first, fleeting appearance in a datable text—and even then it is not entirely clear what is meant by the allusion.[84] This is doubly puzzling: for not only were the Quraysh, according to Muslim tradition, the dominant power in the Hijaz, renowned far and wide across Arabia, but Muhammad's own ancestor, an adventurer named Qusayy, is supposed to have seized power in Mecca only after *Qaysar*—"Caesar"— "had extended him aid."[85] Why, then, should the Romans appear never to have heard of the Quraysh? Such a group of people certainly did exist: they are described in four tantalising verses of the Qur'an as embarking on winter and summer journeys, and receiving both provisions and security from God. Yet, even eminent Muslim scholars might confess themselves puzzled by the precise meaning of the word "Quraysh." Perhaps, they mused, it derived from the name of a prominent travel guide, or else a breed of camel, or perhaps a type of shark? The truth was, however, that no one—not two centuries on from the

Prophet's death—really knew any more. The derivation of "Quraysh" had long since been forgotten.

There was nothing particularly unusual about this. Back in the fourth century, when the Romans had started to refer to the Arabs as "Saracens," few of them had appreciated that the name might well have derived from a word in the Arabs' own incomprehensible tongue: *shirkat*. So perhaps it is not a total coincidence that Quraysh itself should seem to echo the same identical concept of "partnership"—but in Syriac. *Qarisha*, in the language that had increasingly come to be the Fertile Crescent's readiest lingua franca, meant "collected together"—"confederated."[86] Is this, then, to what "Quraysh" had originally referred—those tribes brought together in a common partnership, as *foederati* of the New Rome? It is telling, certainly, that the Ghassanid kings—and doubtless other Arab commanders—spoke at least a smattering of Syriac as a matter of course.[87] The word *qarisha*, duly Arabised, might well then have been used far beyond the imperial frontier: a convenient shorthand for all those tribes that had grown fat on Roman patronage.

All of this is speculation, of course. Nevertheless, it would imply, if true, that the mention of "Quraysh" in the Qur'an does not refer to a specific people in a specific place, but rather to an entire confederation of peoples; that the lands where they were to be found ranged from the Negev to the northern Hijaz; and that the sustenance and security provided them by God was mediated by Caesar. If so, then it would certainly explain why tidings of Roman defeat "in the nearby land" should have been broadcast even in the Qur'an itself. After all, the Arabs beyond the frontier were not far distant from the earthquake that convulsed the lands of the Fertile Crescent; rather, they were directly and intimately affected by it. By shattering the Roman hold on Syria and Palestine, the Persian onslaught severed for good what the Arab *foederati* had always previously taken for granted: the supply of gold from their imperial sponsors. Not, perhaps, that this would necessarily have spelled total disaster: for the Persian occupiers would have been desperate for the same leather, provisions and provender that Arab merchants had previously supplied to the Romans. Moreover, on the evidence of the Qur'an, the *Mushrikun* could provide these items to order. It is telling that trade, no less than agriculture, appears to have obsessed the Prophet, with even God being cast by him as a merchant: one who accepts the souls of mortals as pledges for their debts and remorselessly keeps track of their deeds in "an unblotted ledger-book."[88] Telling as well, no doubt, is the Prophet's evident familiarity with what appear to have been lengthy business trips—across the sea as well as the land. Perhaps here, then, in the need to travel by ship during the summer, and with pack animals during the winter, is an explanation for the two ventures made annually by the Quraysh.[89] As for the Prophet himself, more than a century before Ibn Hisham's biography, in the 690s, and it was already being recorded by a Christian chronicler in Edessa that "Muhammad travelled for the purposes of trade to the lands of Palestine, Arabia and Syria."[90] A tantalising snippet of detail—and if authentic, one that would suggest a record of business dealings at the height of the Persian occupation. "No offence," as the Qur'an itself puts it, "to seek some bounty from your Lord."[91] War, after all, will often provide scope for those on its margins to coin a profit.

But also for much more: reflections upon the mutability of all things, and the evils of the age, and the pettiness of human doings when compared to the omnipotence of God. "Have they not travelled the world," the Prophet asked the unbelievers, "and seen how those before them met their end?"[92] All that is human can totter: a lesson fit for the age. The Prophet's revelations may have been haunted by ancient cities abandoned to encroaching sands, but they also contained hints of other, more recent monuments to human vanity. Traces of the decaying imperial frontier are manifest in the very language of the Qur'an: the words for roads, forts and even legionaries' painted shields—transliterated from the original Greek and Latin—all have spectral presences in the Prophet's revelations.[93] When, for instance, in the opening sura of the Qur'an, the prayer was raised to God, "Guide us to the straight path,"[94] it represented a dazzlingly audacious act of appropriation. The great military roads—the *strata*—that for centuries had girded the eastern frontier, and served as both emblems and tools of Roman might, were being brought to fade before the radiance of a celestial *sirat*—a road eternally straight.

This vision, of a truth so blinding that earthly empires were as nothing before it but shadows, was hardly novel, of course. Even the candlelit golds of Hagia Sophia, even the fires in the three holiest temples of *Iranshahr*, blazed as the merest reflections of the effulgence of God. This, in the barren desert beyond Palestine, far from the cockpits of worldly power, was a truth that had long been appreciated. Not only in the souls of the fugitive and the penitent, but as words inscribed on manuscripts, many of them centuries old, the experience of the divine had taken many forms and left many marks. Whether they were otherwise forgotten gospels, or ancient Jewish writings discovered in caves, or copies of pagan epics that had been stashed in libraries for would-be lawyers to use, books as well as people might speak of the yearning to understand heaven. "Those who disbelieve say: 'This is nothing but fables of the ancients.'"[95] That the Prophet was sensitive to this particular accusation is evident enough from his repeated efforts, made throughout the Qur'an, to rebut it.[96] Yet, never did he veer to the opposite extreme, and proclaim the novelty of his message. "It is indeed a revelation from the Lord of the Worlds, brought down by the Trustworthy Spirit, upon your heart, so that you may be a warner, in manifest Arabic speech—but it is also in the Books of the ancients." Just as Jews might cast the Talmud as a record of eternity, and Christians see an image of the immutable order of the heavens in the Church, so did the Prophet—ever a man of his time—insist upon the timelessness of his message. Well might he have proclaimed "the straight path" to God with such boldness and conviction. When set against such a highway, what were the rutted and weed-covered *strata*, long since left in a state of chronic disrepair by Justinian's budget cuts? One was eternal; the others were already returning to the desert sands.

And just as roads might crumble, so might confederations. Compared with a community of believers faithful only to God, what

This niche at Petra once held an image of the goddess al-'Uzza – the "Mighty Queen" of the Arabs. In 527, an Arab king sacrificed four hundred Christian virgins in her honour. (Tom Holland)

From Petra in the north of Arabia – where this photograph was taken – to Najran in the south, the cube, or "*ka'ba*," seems to have been a shape held in peculiar reverence by the Arabs. (Tom Holland)

Theodoric, viceroy of the Roman emperor in Italy, and King of the Ostrogoths. He poses like a Caesar, and sports a thoroughly Germanic moustache. (akg-images)

Under Khusrow I, the image of the Persian monarchy attained an unprecedented magnificence. Khusrow himself was hailed by his subjects as "divine and virtuous, peace-loving and powerful, a giant among giants, the favourite of the heavens." (Ullstein Bild)

Saint Mark, who was believed by Christians to have founded the Church of Alexandria, is shown surrounded by his successors as bishop, with the balconies and rooftops of the great city rising behind them. (akg-images/ Erich Lessing)

The tomb of a plague victim in Avdat, a predominantly Arab city in the Negev Desert. Although the plague tended not to penetrate deep into the desert, those who lived on its margins were always susceptible to its visitations. (Tom Holland)

Heraclius. His reign witnessed some of the greatest triumphs and most calamitous defeats in all Roman history. (Dumbarton Oaks Collection, Washington, DC)

The skulls of monks slain by the invading Persians – and preserved to this day in the monastery of Mar Saba, in the Judaean desert. (Tom Holland)

Heraclius, before leaving Constantinople for *Iranshahr*, made sure to reinforce the already massive walls that surrounded his capital. This stretch buttressed the approach to the Golden Horn – from where, in 626, the Byzantine navy sallied out to sink the transport fleet of the invading Persians. (Tom Holland)

A page from one of the Qur'ans found stuffed into the ceiling of the oldest mosque in Sana'a, in Yemen. It has been provisionally dated to the end of the first Islamic century – making it one of the oldest Qur'ans in existence.

Alexander the Great, shown on a coin wearing the horns of Amun. In the Qur'an, Alexander appears as Dhu'l Qarnayn – "The Two-Horned One." (Bibliothèque Nationale, Paris/ Giraudon/Bridgeman Art Library)

Mecca. Despite the starring role that the city is given by Muslim tradition, no source prior to the Qur'an so much as mentions it. The first dateable reference to it in any foreign text appears in 741 – more than a century after the death of Muhammad – and locates it in a desert south of Iraq. (AFP/Getty Images)

A church built in the sixth century to commemorate the cave beside the Dead Sea where Lot was believed to have taken shelter after the destruction of Sodom. The episode is first mentioned in the Bible, but is also alluded to in the Qur'an. One verse implies something puzzling: that the Prophet and his audience lived within easy reach of the petrified remains of the Sodomites. "You pass by them morning and night; will you not understand?" (Tom Holland)

The outline of an early mosque found at Be'er Ora, in the Negev Desert. It has two semi-circular architectural features that indicate the direction – the *qibla* – in which the faithful should pray. The oldest, pointing directly ahead, is oriented towards the east; the later, on the right of the photograph, points towards Mecca. (Tom Holland)

The river Yarmuk, with the Golan Heights in the background. Nowadays, the river constitutes the border between Syria and Jordan; back in the seventh century, it was the site of a stunning and decisive Arab victory over the Romans. (Tom Holland)

A coin issued in 685 or 686. It is stamped with the first dateable inscription on any coin or building to mention a Muhammad who is also "the Messenger of God."

The Dome of the Rock. (Tom Holland)

Abd al-Malik, the Deputy of God, girt with a whip. (The Art Archive/Ashmolean Museum)

The marker of a revolution. For a thousand years, the Greek and Roman rulers of the Near East had been issuing coins stamped with the human image – but in 696, Abd al-Malik brought an end to that tradition by issuing coins that featured nothing but writing.

The Great Mosque in Damascus, like the Dome of the Rock, made something novel and stunningly beautiful out of the inheritance of the past. (Tom Holland)

Faded and damaged as it is, this painting on the wall of a caliphal palace in the desert beyond Syria demonstrates just how vibrant and enduring classical traditions might be, even a whole century after the Arab conquests.
(Tom Holland)

The Caliphs – and the Arab conquerors generally – were great connoisseurs of female flesh. This particular statue comes from the exquisite palace built at Jericho by Hisham, the last of Abd al-Malik's sons to rule as Caliph. "He who wishes to take a slave girl for pleasure," so Abd al-Malik himself had advised, "let him take a Berber." (Tom Holland)

The failure of the great Arab siege of Constantinople in 716 owed much to the devastating Roman weapon of *hygron pyr* – liquid fire. (Bridgeman Art Library)

Iraq under the Abbasids remained what it had been under the Sasanians: a prodigiously wealthy land of rivers and canals. The Tigris is on the right-hand side of the map and flows southwards from the bottom of the page towards Baghdad, the greatest and most cultured city in the world.
(Bridgeman/Egyptian National Library, Cairo)

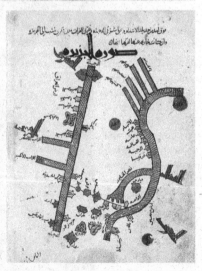

was a ragbag of mercenaries in hock to a foreign power? The Thamud had long since fallen, and so too, God willing, would their heirs. "We conferred guidance upon them—but they chose blindness over guidance."[97] The Prophet's opponents were doubly Mushrikun: for not only did they partner angels with God as fit objects of worship, but they themselves were bound in a shared subservience as associates in a Roman-sponsored *shirkat*. They were not only blasphemers but collaborators. Naturally, it was the offence against God that stank most noxiously to the heavens—but there were hints as well, in the Qur'an, of more earthly crimes and follies. Remorselessly, the Prophet casts his followers as the mirror-image of the *foederati*. Just as whole tribes had long been emigrating northwards, eager for Caesar's bounty, so in a similar manner, but now in the cause of God, were the Believers to rank as emigrants—as the Muhajirun. A manoeuvre of genius. Service was being offered to a monarch infinitely greater than either Caesar or *Shahanshah*. An entire pattern of mass-movement was being reconfigured and set in spectacular reverse. "Whoso leaves his home as an emigrant to God and His Messenger and is overtaken by death, his reward falls upon God, and God is All-Forgiving, Compassionate to each."[98]

Not that one necessarily had to die before being rewarded for joining the Muhajirun. If it was the pleasures of heaven—the ox-eyed maidens and the pearl-like cup-bearers—that shimmered most deliciously before the gaze of the Believers, then earthly profits as well were far from being disdained. "They ask you about booty." So begins one sura, in bald and ringing terms. "Say: 'Booty belongs to God and His Messenger.'"[99] Here, at a time of global calamity, was a message calculated to appeal to anyone feeling the economic pinch. Well and good as were the profits to be had from flogging leather to the Persians, these were hardly likely to compensate, even in small part, for the loss of subsidies from Caesar's agents. The Arab tribes who had emigrated northwards on the scent of Roman gold—and who had relied on their paymasters' lucre for decades—had grown much impoverished. Well, then, might the message proclaimed by the Prophet—that he had a licence from God to plunder unbelievers—have met with an enthusiastic up-take. "Remember a time when you were few in number and held to be weak on earth, when you feared men would tear you to pieces. He gave you refuge and aided you with His victory; and He bestowed His bounties upon you."[100] Bounties that once, perhaps, Muhammad's followers would have been content to receive from the Roman authorities—but not anymore. A wellspring that had run dry was no longer a wellspring at all.

Here, then, was a crisis, and an attempt to resolve it, bred thoroughly of its time. The arc of its parabola can still just about be traced, discernible despite all the thick overlay applied centuries later by pious biographers and commentators. The Qur'an, far from standing at some fantastical remove from the currents and convulsions of the age, is the supreme monument to them. It is the record of a man living through an unprecedented period of upheaval, alert, in every way he can be, to the word of God, and betraying a sensibility, even as he contemplates the ruin of the universe itself, that is decidedly bookish. "That will be the Day," so God says at one point, in a description of the looming End Times, "when We roll up the sky, as a writer rolls up his scrolls." Such images, which occur throughout the Qur'an, suggest a man who was the polar opposite of illiterate, and who, even as he laid claim to traditions of divine inspiration that were immeasurably venerable, knew full well what he was doing. Such it was to be the Seal of the Prophets: "a herald of good tidings, a bearer of warning."[101] The good tidings provided a solution to humanity's troubles that did not depend upon mortal agency; the warning explained what would happen to those who closed their ears to it.

But it was not enough for the Prophet's message to be inscribed simply upon the souls of his audience. The evils of the time were as political as they were spiritual, and as economic as they were moral. Like the rabbis of Mesopotamia and Tiberias, like Justinian and his great team of jurists, the Prophet appreciated that not only individuals but society itself required moulding to the purposes of God. This was why, it seems, he set himself to the founding of a state—first among the *Mushrikun*, and then, in the wake of their rejection, among the

Muhajirun. And its capital? Here, at any rate, there is no contradiction between the Qur'an and the great spider's web of subsequent Islamic tradition. A battle fought against overwhelming odds, "a violent wind and invisible forces"[102] sent by God against the Prophet's enemies, a glorious victory snatched from the jaws of defeat: all this, so the Qur'an records, occurred at a place that, for once, it actually names. Yathrib, that fertile oasis in the northern Hijaz, was indeed, it would appear, *'Madinat an-Nabi*—the "City of the Prophet." Medina, just as tradition records, ranked as the very first bridgehead of the heavenly established by Muhammad on earth.

Does that mean, then, that the story told of a single, dramatic flight there, a *hijra*, is similarly based on fact? It is notable, certainly, that the word itself does not appear anywhere in the Qur'an; and, as with so many details of his biography, all references to the Prophet's escape to Yathrib are frustratingly late in origin.[103] Reason enough, then, perhaps, to be suspicious—and to wonder whether the whole notion of "emigration" might possibly have had a significance for the Prophet and his followers that subsequent tradition has obscured. Memorable the story of the *hijra* may be—and yet there seems to lurk behind it the hint of something much more seismic. In the Qur'an, emigration is cast as a duty incumbent upon all believers—no matter their circumstances, no matter their location. Far from alluding to a single journey into exile— whether to Yathrib or to anywhere else—it seems to imply a call to arms that is all-embracing, universal and unbounded by time or place. "Anyone who migrates for God's cause will find many a refuge and great plenty in the earth."[104] Nothing could conceivably have sounded more radical or terrifying to the Prophet's audience. Abandoning family and tribe was the most stomach-churning prospect imaginable for any Arab. And yet, if the Qur'an is to be trusted, this was precisely the commitment that the Prophet was demanding—and not just of his own people but of all the various descendants of Ishmael, wherever they might live, across the entire sweep of Arabia. The successful planting of his banner in Yathrib, set against the backdrop of the apparent breaking of the world, was to be only the start. All those with the courage—or perhaps the sheer desperation—to accept the Prophet's challenge and embark on a new beginning were invited to join him on a journey that might lead God alone knew where.

And to be sure—whether they were tempted by heaven, plunder, or both—there was clearly no lack of Arabs who were prepared to answer the summons. "You are the best community ever brought forth among mankind, commanding virtue and forbidding vice, and believing in God." So the Prophet hailed the Muhajirun: as a band of warriors who had it within them not only to found a whole new order of society but to inherit, as their reward for doing so, the earth itself.

A claim that was to be proved, and in short order, quite spectacularly correct.

Why?

Early in AD 634, alarming news reached Caesarea, the handsome city on the coast of Palestine that had long served as the hinterland's capital. A war band of Saracens, trespassing directly on Roman territory, had crossed into the Negev, and was now aiming northwards for the rich fields and villages of Samaria. A most tiresome intrusion—and one that the provincial authorities were naturally anxious to nip in the bud. No matter that the Roman military, in the wake of plague and war, remained extremely stretched: a task force of infantry, summoned hurriedly to arms, marched out into the open, and swung briskly south.[105] At their head, resplendent in the white uniform that marked him out as a personal favourite of the emperor, rode a patrician by the name of Sergius.[106] He had particular cause to relish the challenge ahead. Already, he had been looking to replenish the finances of the exhausted province by restricting the profits that Saracen merchants were permitted to take back across the frontier. Now, with the barbarians seemingly provoked to open larceny by this measure, it was time to reacquaint them with the brute facts of Roman might. The region's ancient mistress, after her temporary absence, was back.

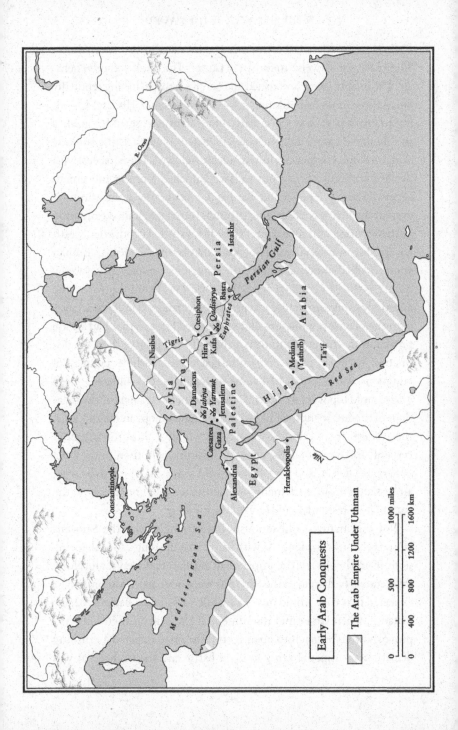

Early Arab Conquests

The Arab Empire Under Uthman

Sergius and his small army met the invaders in the afternoon of 4 February, some twelve miles east of Gaza.[107] The result was utter debacle. The infantry were ambushed and Sergius himself, having reputedly fallen three times from his horse, was taken prisoner. His fate, according to one report, was a peculiarly unpleasant one: sewn up inside a freshly flayed camel hide, he was suffocated to death as the stinking skin dried out. Further calamities quickly followed. The Saracens, with devilish cunning, turned out to have launched a pincer movement against Palestine. The second war band, crossing the eastern frontier even as the first was rampaging through the Negev, joined exultantly in the scouring of the province. Over fields thick with thistles, weed-covered highways and crumbling walls they swept. "Saracens," Roman strategists had always asserted with imperious complacency, "are by nature unable to conduct sieges"[108]—but now, to the horror of the authorities, this reassurance was proving a worthless one. If it was cities, with their dense populations and rat-infested byways, that had always proved most vulnerable to the scythings of the plague, then the distinction between town and countryside, after whole decades of visitations, was one that had come increasingly to be blurred. Sheep grazed amid toppled pillars, while cattle, tethered against the depredations of bandits, spent their nights in abandoned shops and foundries. If the average city of Palestine was not yet wholly a ghost town, then it certainly had one foot in the grave.[109] Unsurprisingly, then, in the wake of Sergius's defeat, and with Roman field armies nowhere to be seen, ambassadors from settlement after settlement sought to follow the path of least resistance, and buy off the invaders.

Not that many could seriously have thought that the Saracens would be around for long. As with Samaritan uprisings, so with incursions from the desert: the imperial authorities had seen it all before. Inveterately barbarian as the Saracens were, perhaps it was only to be expected that they would once in a while turn rogue. Back in 582, for instance, when Ghassanid resentment at the exile of their king had provoked the *foederati* into open revolt, they had inflicted a crushing defeat on an imperial army in open battle and then ranged at will across Syria. A couple of centuries before that, an Arab queen named Mavia, "long celebrated in song by the Saracens,"[110] had launched a series of devastating raids that had taken her all the way to Egypt. The Roman response, on both occasions, had been the time-honoured one of dazzling the barbarians with bribes. Both Mavia and the Ghassanids, despite the undoubted scares that they had given the provincial authorities, had been successfully pacified with a whole range of exotic gewgaws. Golden furnishings and fancy titles had, as ever, proved their worth. No reason, then, for Heraclius to feel particularly perturbed by the defeat outside Gaza. Alarming though the swift return of warfare to Palestine clearly was, the Saracens hardly rivalled the Persians as foes. After all, if history had taught Roman officials anything, it was that the wolves of Arabia, no matter how much of a passing threat they might be on occasion, could always be muzzled in the end.

This latest invasion would prove very different, though. The Saracens did not content themselves with the extortion of subsidies and silken cloaks. Rather than wait to be graced with treasure from the hands of Caesar, they aimed instead to rip it brutally from his grasp. With Palestine effectively secured, they immediately flung themselves against the defences of Syria. Fifty years later, a monk writing in Sinai would record what ensued: two terrible battles, one at the Ghassanid camp city of Jabiya, and the other a few miles to the west, on the Golan Heights above the River Yarmuk.[111] The details are slight—and it is the measure of how impossible it has proved for historians to agree on the actual progress of the Arab invasion, and the struggle of the Romans to resist it, that not a single earlier reference to these fateful clashes exists in either Arabic or Greek.* The dates, the details and the course of the

---

* A few lines scribbled in Syriac on the fly-leaf of a gospel allude to a battle fought at Jabiya. From internal evidence, this source seems to be almost contemporaneous with the battle, but its date cannot be definitively established. Fredegar, a chronicler writing in Gaul some twenty years after the Arab invasion of Syria, refers to Heraclius's army being "smitten by the sword of God: 52,000 of his men died where they slept"—valuable evidence for the probable scale of the Roman defeat.

Syrian campaign—all are veiled by contradiction and confusion.[112] Nevertheless, if the particulars of what happened during the campaigning have defied repeated attempts to arrive at a consensus, then not so the result. "For the Roman army," as the monk in Sinai would note with bleak finality, "it proved a defeat as fatal as it was terrible."[113] By late 636, with the campaigning season drawing to a close, Heraclius seems to have bowed to the inevitable. Burning villages and fields as he withdrew, he abandoned the very provinces that he had moved heaven and earth to retake just a few years previously. "Peace be upon you, Syria!" he is said to have cried, as he paused for one last yearning look back. "What a rich country is this for the enemy!"[114]

Yet others were richer still. Across the desert from Syria, where the humiliating collapse of the House of Sasan into debilitation and factionalism had brought a beardless king by the name of Yazdegird to the throne, *Iranshahr* itself was no less exhausted and divided than its royal family. The marks of the Roman invasion still scarred the landscape. The River Tigris, having burst its banks in AD 629, had swept away an immense swath of irrigation works and left Kavad's great canal silted up. Parthian warlords, snarling and snapping as ever, now threatened the entire fabric of the imperial high command with disintegration. Never—not even in the dark days following the death of Peroz—had the empire been so enfeebled; and the Arabs, alert as they were to the scents of weakness, well knew it. Either a few weeks or a few years after the Roman defeat at the Yarmuk—the sources, as usual, are at sixes and sevens—a similarly decisive battle was fought on *Iranshahr*'s desert flank.[115] Qadisiyya was a small, palm-fringed town just to the south of the one-time Lakhmid capital of Hira. Now, it would be the scene of an epically terminal disaster for *Iranshahr*. After fighting that spanned several days, and the failure of elephants as well as the Persian heavy cavalry to turn the tide, the Arabs emerged triumphant. Their women, stalking the palm groves, were said to have busied themselves slitting the throats of those of the enemy still left there alive. Meanwhile, the exultant Arab army, pursuing the remnants of their defeated foes across canals and pontoon bridges, caught up with the fugitives amid the ruins of Babylon and briskly wiped them out. *Iranshahr* had been decapitated, "for all the leading nobles were killed."[116] Ctesiphon, a bare hundred miles to the north, now lay directly in the Arabs' path. Its fall, with the flower of the empire's chivalry left blackened and rotting in the killing fields of the south, was only a matter of time. Sure enough, despite bitter resistance that seems to have lasted almost a year, the great city was duly stormed. Yazdegird himself, amid much confusion, managed to escape his doomed capital, zigzagging across the mudflats in a desperate effort to evade his pursuers. He finally reached the relative security of the Iranian uplands and his ancestral hometown of Istakhr, from which Ardashir, five centuries previously, had embarked on his own great project of conquest; but the royal regalia and the imperial treasury, all were lost. So too was Mesopotamia—which the invaders, in imitation of the Persians, knew by the name of "Iraq."

That Arab fingers could prod at the crown worn by Khusrow the Great; that Arab feet could tread on carpets from the royal palace woven with gold and adorned with precious stones; that Arab prayers could be heard in the great throne room of Ctesiphon, from the sides of which statues of Yazdegird's ancestors gazed out stern and impassive, oblivious to the ruin that had engulfed the House of Sasan: all this, in the opinion of the Arabs themselves, taught a lesson so edifying that they would never tire of repeating it. The coin of contempt dealt them for so long by Caesar and *Shahanshah* alike had been richly, deliciously, repaid. Two and a half centuries on from Qadisiyya, by which time the Muslims ruled an empire even vaster than Khusrow the Great's, their pride in having scorned superpower dazzle could still rank for them as the surest measure of their dignity. "In the past, those of us who came to you were obedient to you, they humbled themselves before you, they sought what was in your hands." So one Arab, as pious as he was lacking in personal hygiene, was supposed to have told the silken Persians on the eve of the great battle. "But now we no longer come to you looking for the things of this world. Our desire and aspiration is for paradise."[117]

Hairy, badly dressed, and stinking of camel as he was, this ambassador to the perfumed tents of the Persian high command would be commemorated in histories of the conquest as the heroic embodiment of Muslim brotherhood. "God loves not the swaggering and the conceited."[118] So the Prophet had taught. Even though, if tradition is to be trusted, Muhammad died in 632, two whole years before the first rubbing of a superpower nose in the dirt, it was his revelations, of a God who humbles the proud, and slaughters them in battle, and permits them to be despoiled of all their goods, that had given the Arabs the courage and sheer self-confidence to go eyeball to eyeball with their former masters.[119] Riding in to meet Roman or Persian officials, their ambassadors were said to have made a point of trampling down their cushions and stabbing with spears at their carpets. The conquest of the world, and the scorning of its seductions: such, it seemed to Muslim historians writing centuries later, had been the supreme achievement of the generation that had known Muhammad.

It had one supreme exemplar. Umar bin al-Khattab had ranked as the most formidable and domineering of all the Prophet's companions, the leader under whose guidance both Syria and Iraq had been won, the veritable sword arm of the Prophet. Tradition would commemorate him not merely as a great *Amir*—"commander"—but as something very much more: as a Muslim so flame-lit by his knowledge of God's will that several Qur'anic verses were said to have been revealed purely to provide his opinions with some heavenly back-up. Even Muhammad, according to certain traditions, had acknowledged that Umar was the better Muslim of the two. "When people differ on any issue," one celebrated ruling declared, "look for Umar's doing and abide by it."[120] Like the Qur'an itself, then, the character of the second Caliph was a book in which might be read the lessons of God's will. Mighty warrior and mighty ascetic; quick to draw his sword and no less quick to trample down in righteous scorn the luxuries won by that same sword; a man who from his mud-brick home in Medina could direct the overthrow of mighty empires, and yet who, if he saw his lieutenants dressed in silks and brocade, would leap down from his saddle and pelt them with stones: such, in the opinion of Muslim scholars, was the man who had secured the world for Islam.

A plausible characterisation? Certainly, as with Muhammad, so with Umar—his historicity is beyond dispute. An Armenian bishop, writing a decade or so after Qadisiyya, described Umar in a brief, throwaway sentence much as Muslim historians would subsequently do: as a mighty potentate coordinating the advance of "the sons of Ishmael" from the depths of the desert.[121] Nor is that all. There do indeed seem to be found, preserved in the traditions that Muslims would record of the *Sahabah*, the "Companions," of Muhammad, authentic echoes of the God-haunted and strife-torn age that had witnessed the *Futuh*—the "Conquest." If there seems no reason to doubt that Umar, that model of ferocious piety, was directly inspired by the awesome thunder of the Prophet's revelations, then so too is it evident that the Prophet himself, in his summoning of the Arabs to holy war, was perfectly in accord with the spirit of the times. "In truth," he informed his followers, "the punishment of those who make war against God and His Messenger, and roam the earth corrupting it, is that they be killed, or crucified, or have their hands and feet amputated, alternately, or be exiled from the land."[122] Such a message was all the more resonant, no doubt, for being delivered direct from the Almighty Himself; and yet, the sentiments informing it would have been instantly recognisable to anyone familiar with the workings of Roman power. Whether it was Justinian breaking the rebellious Samaritans, or Saint Simeon incinerating Mundhir with a fireball, or Heraclius bringing ruin to the fire-temples of the Persians, examples were hardly lacking of spectacular violence committed in the cause of God. Umar, turning the pretensions of the Christian empire back upon itself, seemed to those he conquered, as well as to those he commanded, a warlord of a thoroughly recognisable kind. What added incomparably to his prestige, however, and did truly suggest something novel, was that his earth-shaking qualities as a generalissimo were combined with a most distinctive cast of virtue. Rather than ape the manners of a Caesar, as the Ghassanid kings had done, he drew on the example of a quite different kind of Christian. Umar's threadbare robes, his diet of bread, salt and water, and his rejection of worldly riches would have reminded anyone from the desert reaches beyond Palestine of a very particular kind of person. Monks out in the Judaean desert had long been casting themselves as warriors of God. The achievement of Umar was to take such language to a literal, and previously unimagined, extreme.

Just like the Qur'an itself, then, the heroic stories that were told of the second Caliph seem to reach back to a specific place and moment: to the fringes of Palestine, and that terrifying period of superpower conflict when it appeared that the world itself stood in the shadow of the End Days. That war might be waged in the name of God, and that a contempt for earthly pleasures too was a form of warfare: these twin presumptions, which Umar embodied in a supremely radical way, were nevertheless far from being original to him. Naturally, the truth of this cannot help but be obscured by histories that locate his beginnings, like those of the Prophet himself, in a desert backwater many hundreds of miles from the Fertile Crescent. Composed centuries later, by men of intense piety who could feel God nearer to them than their jugular veins, it is no wonder that such narratives, like sandstone shaped by ceaseless weathering, should have been transformed out of recognition over the course of the generations. Hence, in trying to explain how a state came to be forged in the depths of Arabia formidable enough to subdue the Fertile Crescent, the perennial frustration. The aftermath of the conquests masterminded by Umar could hardly be more manifest—but not so the course, and still less the cause, of the original eruption.

Which said, despair need not be total. There has been preserved, embedded within the vast corpus of subsequent writings on the Prophet, at least a single lump of magma sufficiently calcified to have stood proof against all erosion. The "Constitution of Medina," it has been termed: a series of eight brief treaties concluded between the Muhajirun and the natives of Yathrib, and which—not least because they refer to the emigrants as "Believers" rather than "Muslims"—are accepted by even the most suspicious of scholars as deriving from the time of Muhammad. Here, in these precious documents, it is possible to glimpse the authentic beginnings of a movement that would succeed, in barely two decades, in prostrating both the New Rome and *Iranshahr*. That the Prophet consciously aimed at state-building; that it was his ambition to forge his own people and the local Arab tribes into a single *Umma*; that this confederation was to fight "in the path of God":[123] these brief details, the veritable building blocks out of which all the much later stories of Muhammad's life would be constructed, do authentically seem rock solid. What the Constitution of Medina does not tell us, however, is where the Muhajirun had originally come from; nor does it reveal precisely whom they felt called upon by God to fight. Most regrettably of all, it sheds no light on how an alliance stitched together in a remote oasis might conceivably have expanded to embrace the whole of Arabia, and then to take on the world. Nevertheless, its very existence would seem to suggest that the hard core of Muslim tradition may truly derive from the time of Muhammad, and have stood proof, after all, against the weathering effects of time. Conflict between the upstart *Umma* and the Quraysh; eventual compromise on both sides, and the agreement between them of a treaty; a brutal crushing by the new confederation of any Arab tribes bold enough to stand in its way: such a process of state-building seems, at the very least, plausible.

And if accurate, then it would imply that there may perhaps be other clues, preserved in the stories told centuries later of the Prophet's career, as to how and why, as if from the blue, the imperial authorities in both Syria and Iraq were overwhelmed by precisely the kind of Arab federation that hitherto had always been theirs to sway. Even though Muslim tradition would cast the conflict between Muhammad and the Quraysh as a struggle for control of Mecca, this tradition itself contains hints of a suggestively alternative one. Particularly striking, for instance, is the number of leading Qurayshi dynasts who, despite supposedly being based in Mecca, are said to have purchased estates in Syria during the Prophet's lifetime: an example of long-distance property speculation which, if genuinely conducted from the Hijaz, would have had no precedent in the entire span of Roman history. Previously, whether along the Rhine or in Armenia, the only barbarians who owned land on either side of the imperial frontier were those who directly bordered it.[124] All of which would seem to imply a rather awkward conundrum. Either the Quraysh truly came from Mecca, in which case they could not have owned property in Roman territory—or else they owned property in Roman territory, in which case they are most unlikely to have come from Mecca.

Of these two alternatives, it is clear that the second is the likelier. Even on the evidence of Muslim tradition itself, the obsession of the Prophet with securing the border zone south of Palestine is manifest. With the single exception of Mecca itself, all the targets of his campaigning, all the objects of his military ambitions, are said to have lain in this region: the stretches of desert that the Romans' Arab allies had always traditionally patrolled. If the Quraysh did go from attempting to strangle the Prophet's infant confederation in its cradle to allying themselves with it—and there seems no reason to doubt it—they would obviously have been putting their stake in any imperially sanctioned order in serious jeopardy. This, however, at a time when the supply of gold from Caesar had long since dried up, seems to have struck them as a gamble well worth taking. The winnings on offer, after all, were potentially dazzling. It was not only the plunder promised them by Muhammad's terrifyingly omnipotent god that would have glimmered in the imaginings of the Qurayshi leaders. So too would something even more seductive: the prospect of toppling the Ghassanids, of laying claim to the heritage of the Lakhmids, of fashioning a whole new *shirkat*, with themselves as the region's top dogs. What the new confederation of Muhajirun and Quraysh appears initially to have aimed at, as their primary strategic goal, was the mastery of the Syrian desert. That it ended up conquering Syria itself, and Mesopotamia too, may well, then, have come as big a surprise to its leaders as it did to the Romans and Persians themselves.

It certainly seems no coincidence that the invaders' two most decisive victories were won on the doorsteps of two places that had long featured prominently in Arab dreams. For generations, the tales told of the courts of Jabiya and Hira, and the songs sung of their splendours, had haunted the imaginings of the desert tribes. Now, with the defeat of the Romans at the Yarmuk, calamity had overwhelmed their Ghassanid clients as well—just as the shattering of the Persian monarchy at Qadisiyya had spelled doom for all those local desert chieftains with fantasies of sitting on the vacant throne of the Lakhmids. The likelihood is, in fact, that both imperial armies, as they sought to stem the Saracen onslaught, consisted themselves in large part of Arab tribesmen. Muslim historians, not surprisingly, would take an exultant delight in emphasising the immensity of the manpower available to the toppled empires: of how their troops numbered in the hundreds of thousands, and of how their blood, when it was spilled, had flowed in such prodigious quantities as to turn the wheels of local watermills.[125] Contemporaries knew better, though. They understood the true condition of anaemia that had afflicted both superpowers. Heraclius, as one bishop bluntly put it, "could raise no more troops to oppose the Ishmaelites."[126] Given the absence of regular troops, he had no alternative but to rely on *foederati* to defend Roman territory. The Ghassanids, and all the other tribes allied to them, repaid Heraclius's trust with fierce loyalty; but it ensured, when the Muhajirun first appeared across the Syrian desert, that the Roman military itself was reduced to something of a sideshow.[127] Almost a century of pestilence, and whole decades of war: these, in their combined effects, had left the emperor with no clothes.

So it was that Syria and Palestine slipped away a second time from the grasp of the New Rome, and those Qurayshis who had previously held estates under the sufferance of the imperial authorities now took possession of entire provinces. But they were not alone, of course, in claiming title deeds to the Holy Land—as the defeated Christians, in their bewilderment and demoralisation, were all too bitterly aware. Torn between blaming the calamities that had overwhelmed them on either their own sinfulness or the machinations of the Jews, many, not surprisingly, plumped for the latter option. Was it any coincidence, they wondered, that "the horror of the invasion of the Ishmaelites"[128] should have followed so fast upon Heraclius's campaign of forced baptisms? Dark rumours began to swirl: of how Jewish refugees from this decree had fled to Arabia; of how, upon their arrival in the desert, they had turned the head of the Saracens with honeyed talk of their shared descent from Abraham; of how Muhammad, looking to claim their birthright, had duly set off at their head to conquer Palestine. Stories such as these, of course, were prone only to grow wilder with the telling; and yet the wildest rumours of all, perhaps, were the very earliest. Back in 634, with Sergius freshly entombed in his shroud of camel skin, fabulous reports of a Saracen prophet had swept through Caesarea. By Christians, of course, he had been scorned as the rankest impostor—"for since when did prophets come armed with a sword?" Among the Jews of the city, however, the reaction had been very different. Delight, no doubt, would have been their response to any Roman defeat; but their joy, in that spring of 634, had been blended with a fierce and familiar hope. "People were saying that the prophet had appeared, coming with the Saracens." And his message? "They say that he is proclaiming the advent of the Anointed One—the Christ who is to come."[129]

It was exactly twenty years since Nehemiah, amid a similar groundswell of excitement, had sought to rebuild Jerusalem's Temple, and promptly been impaled for his pains. To the Jews of Palestine, though, the Ishmaelites must have seemed altogether more promising agents of deliverance than the Persians had ever been. They might have been wild asses among men—but they were at least distant cousins. Then there was the fact that the Prophet himself, or so it would seem, had chosen Moses as his particular role model. "O people, enter the holy land which God has marked out for you, and do not go back to your old ways, only to end up as losers."[130] Any Jews, hearing Muhammad attribute this exhortation to their greatest prophet—the original rabbi, the man who had led them out of bondage and back to the Promised Land—might well have pricked up their ears. Indeed, some might well have done a good deal more than that. Such, at any rate, is the evidence of the Constitution of Medina. Muhajirun and local Arabs, it seems, were not alone in having ranked as original members of the *Umma*. Also listed as Believers, and graced with a starring role in the founding document of their state, had been some other, perhaps rather more unexpected enthusiasts for the Prophet: whole quantities of Jews.

Later Muslim historians, clearly discombobulated by this, would attempt to explain them away as members of three Jewish clans supposedly native to Medina, who were said initially to have given their backing to the Prophet, and then, after turning fractious, to have been variously driven into exile or massacred and dumped into pits. Yet there are serious difficulties in accepting this tradition as true. It is not simply that the three Jewish clans mentioned by the historians do not feature anywhere in the Constitution of Medina. There is also another, and familiar, problem: that our only sources for the annihilation of these Jews are all suspiciously late. Not only that, but they date from the heyday of Muslim greatness: a period when the authors would have had every interest in fabricating the sanction of the Prophet for the brusque slapping down of uppity infidels.[131] Certainly, if it were truly the case that entire communities of Jews had been expelled into the desert or else wiped out by Ishmaelites in a bloodbath, then no contemporary seems to have noted it. This, at a time when Jews, just like Christians, had never been more alert to the propaganda value of martyrs, is most peculiar. So peculiar, in fact, as to appear downright implausible. Far likelier, it would seem, is that the compact recorded in the Constitution of Medina, between the Muhajirun and assorted bands of Jewish warriors, had held firm—and that it had culminated in the conquest of Palestine. Christians, when they fingered their old enemies as the tutors of Muhammad, were undoubtedly indulging themselves in a familiar paranoia—but less so, perhaps, when they accused "the sons of Israel" of joining with the Arabs "to form a large army."[132] Venerable the scorn of the Jews for the Ishmaelites may have been; but it was nothing like so savage as their loathing for the Romans. "Do not fear, son of man": So an angel was supposed to have reassured a twitchy rabbi. "The Almighty only brings the kingdom of Ishmael in order to deliver you from the wicked ones."[133]

In the first disorienting flush of the Ishmaelite occupation, such a reassurance might well have seemed a perfectly convincing one. How else, after all, was the humiliation of Heraclius to be interpreted, if not as a deliverance ordained of God? Unsurprisingly, then, in the wake of the Jews' redemption from the threat of forced baptism, their enthusiasm for the new order seems to have flared with some flamboyance—and to have had a familiar focus. Jerusalem, that perennial object of Jewish longing, had been lost to the Romans along with the rest of the Holy Land. The Arabs—who, in a curious show of antiquarianism, insisted on calling it Iliy'a, after its old pagan name of Aelia Capitolina—were quick to mark it with their own stamp. To Christian horror, the ancient ban on Jews entering the city's sacred limits—which dated back to the heyday of the pagan empire and which Heraclius had pointedly renewed—was revoked. Work also began on clearing rubble and refuse from the holiest Jewish spot of all—the Temple Mount. No surprise, then, that Umar, "the second king who arises from Ishmael," and the man who had given the order, should have been hailed in breathless tones by one rabbi as "a lover of Israel."[134] As the work continued, first with the levelling of the bedrock, and then with the cannibalisation of the Kapitolion, the temple of Jupiter, there were some Jews who dared to go even further and dream that it was the Temple itself being rebuilt. No prospect could possibly have been more dazzling. With the Temple restored, after all, there would arise a new Israel. Inevitably, then, the excited rumours prompted by the defeat of Sergius at Gaza, of the Messiah's imminent arrival, continued to swirl.

Time, it was true, would prove this optimism sorely misplaced. The more extravagant hopes of the Jews were destined, as ever, to be disappointed. The Temple was not restored. The Messiah did not appear hot on the heels of the Ishmaelites' prophet. Nevertheless, there was, in the febrile speculations of the Jews, something more than mere wishful thinking. Those who sensed in the Ishmaelites a particular obsession with the Promised Land were surely not mistaken. Just as Jabiya and Hira had been the initial objects of the conquerors' strategic ambitions, Palestine had clearly blazed in their imaginings as a prize that transcended mere earthly considerations. Although it had been a simple matter for them to cross the undefended frontier into what the Prophet had termed the "Holy Land," ease of access had hardly been the primary consideration. God had promised Palestine to the descendants of Abraham—and so it had come to pass. No wonder, then, in the immediate wake of the conquest, that Muhajirun as well as Jews appear to have indulged in any number of wild surmises. Indeed, on occasion, it might be hard to tell them apart. Amid the general fracturing of the times, old identities and old certainties had the potential to warp very quickly. When Jews, praising Umar for his scouring of the Romans from Jerusalem, and his cleansing of the Temple Mount, hailed him as the Messiah, there were certain Muhajirun who did not think to scorn the notion. Instead, caught up in the mood of excitement, they surrendered to it. Umar, so it was boldly proclaimed, ranked as none other than *al-Faruq*—"the Redeemer."[135] Such, it appeared, was the true potency of the Temple Mount: that it could persuade Arabs to share in the fantasies of Jews.

And perhaps, had the Muhajirun rested content with their conquest of the Holy Land, and not set their horizons far wider, then their faith might ultimately have mutated into something truly messianic—a Jerusalem-haunted blurring of Jewish beliefs and the Prophet's revelations. Yet already, even as Umar's workmen set to work on clearing the rubbish from the Temple Mount, it was apparent that Palestine, no matter how awesome a prize, provided far too small a stage for the evolving pretensions of the conquerors. What value the Promised Land, after all, when God had graced the Muhajirun with so much more besides? A question fit, perhaps, to perplex the conquerors themselves. Certainly, there had been nothing in the Prophet's revelations to forewarn them that they might end up the masters of the world. Muhammad himself, when reporting God's assurance that He would settle the Muhajirun "in a good abode," had seemed to take for granted that this same "good abode" was merely their inheritance from Abraham.[136] The limits of his ambitions, it would appear, had been Arabia and Palestine. Yet both, in the event, had provided merely stepping-stones. As too, in due course, would the entire glittering sweep of Syria and Iraq. Fabulous a prize though the Fertile Crescent was, infinitely beyond the dreams of previous generations of Arabs, it ultimately served only to whet the appetite of the Muhajirun for more. The world lay all before them—and God, it seemed, intended them to take it.

So it was, in late 639, that a tiny war band of Arabs, following the high road that led south from Gaza, crossed into Egypt. The bread-basket of Constantinople, most precious of all the various territories retrieved by Heraclius from Persian occupation, the province had been back under imperial rule for a decade—but not contentedly so. The return of Roman administrators had seen the return as well to the determinedly Monophysite province of a Chalcedonian patriarch. Heraclius, no less determined than Justinian had been to secure the unity of the Church, had sponsored a programme of increasingly repressive bullying. The Copts, digging in their heels, had responded by embracing every opportunity to pose as martyrs. The brother of the Monophysite patriarch, for instance, despite having his flanks griddled over a fire and his teeth pulled out, proved so obdurate in his defiance that the Chalcedonians, giving up on their attempts to convert him, had him dumped out at sea. Or so the story went. Certainly, the fact that so many Monophysites could swap such a rumour, and believe it to be true, reflected a groundswell of hostility to Constantinople that would ultimately prove fatal to Roman rule. Imperial exhaustion, Arab self-confidence and the studied neutrality of the vast majority of the native population all contributed to the Muhajirun winning their most glittering prize yet. In September 642, after the expiration of an eleven-month armistice and a wholesale evacuation of the province by the Roman forces, the new lords of the Nile entered Alexandria. The disaster, so a Monophysite bishop piously declared, had been entirely due "to the wickedness of the emperor Heraclius, and his persecutions."[137] If so, then God had exacted a high price. There were to be no more grain ships sailing from Alexandria to Constantinople.

Meanwhile, the demand slapped on the city fathers of Herakleopolis for sixty-five sheep was an early indication of what the toppling of Roman rule might mean for those Christian officials left behind in Egypt. The *Magaritai*—the Muhajirun—still thought instinctively, as their ancestors had ever done, in terms of plunder and rustled livestock. Even when clattering down marble-paved high streets, past palaces and cathedrals, they retained instincts bred of the desert. Great cities such as Alexandria and Ctesiphon, for all the fabulous wealth that they promised, were viewed with dark suspicion—as breeding grounds of pestilence and black magic. Just as their forefathers had done when making their own *hijra* northwards from the depths of Arabia to serve Caesar or *Shahanshah*, the Muhajirun preferred to settle amid open fields, where they could live among their own kind and graze their sheep. Above all, they aimed to revel in the pleasures and the profits that war, by venerable tradition, had most honourably provided the Arabs. No wonder, then, that the settlements in which they congregated should fast have developed the character of garrison towns.

In Iraq, where the unconquered uplands of Iran beckoned tantalisingly, two particularly large cities of tents and reed huts were soon sprouting among the mudflats. One, Basra, lay in the far south, near where the Tigris and Euphrates met with the sea. The other, Kufa, stood across the palm groves from the God-blessed site of Qadisiyya. Regularly, in the decade that followed the fall of Alexandria, Muhajirun from these two bases would ride out eastwards, embarked upon a fresh, and far more challenging, project of conquest. Persia, in marked contrast to Egypt, was a land of mountains and defiant citadels. Unremitting in a way that none of the previous campaigns of the Muhajirun had been, the subjugation of the Sasanian heartlands was to prove a brutal one. Although certainly marked by some lucrative gains—including the capture of yet more royal treasure and the body of the prophet Daniel, no less—it was only in 650, after a grinding, five-year campaign, that Istakhr was finally stormed. Although Yazdegird, once again, made good his escape, the rest of the population were not so lucky. Forty thousand in all were put to the sword, and the monuments and fire temples of Ardashir's city left as smoking rubble. No such calamity had been visited upon Persia since the time of Alexander, and the burning of Persepolis.

And in truth, with triumphs everywhere being recorded for Arab arms, the prospect shimmered before the victors of winning an empire even more vast than Alexander's. Yet greatness, for all the plunder and the glory that it had brought the Muhajirun, was not without its challenges. That God had favoured them, and humbled their enemies, was obvious enough to everyone—conquerors and conquered alike. That God fully intended the Muhajirun to enjoy the profits of their victories was also—to the Muhajirun themselves, at any rate—no less self-evident. Even as the tide of warfare and ready plunder rolled ever onwards, to the limits of East and West, the extortion of tribute ensured that the already-subjugated lands would continue to turn a profit. It was true, of course, that such a pension scheme was bound to depend upon skills that were not readily associated with warriors on camels; but bureaucrats, as the town fathers of Herakleopolis had efficiently demonstrated, were hardly lacking in the conquered territories. Indeed, so remorseless had been the tax machines of both the New Rome and *Iranshahr* that despairing Christians had long taken for granted that it would take the return of Christ to ease their exactions. By that reckoning, at any rate, the arrival of the Ishmaelites did not presage the End Days. Officials of the two decapitated superpowers, seasoned as they were in the arts of extortion, and eager to maintain their positions of authority, had every incentive to work hard for their new masters. Vast and implacable, like a kraken of the deep undisturbed by storms raging across the ocean surface, the apparatus of empire still coiled its prodigious tentacles, ready to flex and squeeze its victims tightly, as it had ever done.

Such was the beast that had served Justinian, the beast that had served Khusrow the Great. What more awesome proof of God's power and mercy, then, than that He should have delivered it up into the hands of a leader such as Umar—a man so contemptuous of worldly rank that on inscriptions he might very well be name-checked without any title at all?[138] Naturally, as *Amir* of the Faithful—their "Commander"—he was due their obedience; but hardly their grovelling. The stern message of the Prophet, that all his followers were brothers, made a mockery of any notion, such as the people of the conquered territories were prone to take for granted, that Umar might rank as their king. His right to all the prodigious wealth won by the Muhajirun lay precisely in the fact that he so palpably scorned it. What is virtue? So the Prophet had insistently demanded. Umar, conqueror of the known world though he might be, never disdained to illustrate the answer.

> Who dispenses money, though dear, to kinsmen, orphans, the
>   needy, the traveller, the beggars and for ransom;
> Who performs the prayer and pays the alms;
> Who fulfil their contracts when they contract;
> Who are steadfast in hardship, calamity and danger;
> These are the true believers.
> These are truly pious.[139]

Yet, as the years passed, and the expanse of sword-won lands continued to increase, so memories of the Prophet, inevitably, grew less immediate, and the value of his example more problematic. In 644, ten years into the great adventure of the Arab conquests, Umar was murdered by a deranged Persian slave, and the Faithful, in their search for a new commander, found themselves torn two ways. Their eventual choice, a man named Uthman, might have seemed the perfect continuity candidate: for tradition—and there seems no reason to doubt it—identifies him as one of the Prophet's earliest and most pious companions. Yet, he also had the unmistakable whiff of a dynast: a man sprung from a family that was perfectly at ease with power and wealth. The Umayyads, according to Muslim historians, were Qurayshis who had made a fortune trading with the Romans, and had then invested it in Syrian real estate: a tradition that would seem to indicate an origin, not in the depths of Arabia, but somewhere along the imperial frontier. Certainly, they had enjoyed a track record of success during the conquest of the region that might well have suggested local knowledge: one brother, Yazid, is said to have ranged with a war band far and wide across the province, while another, Mu'awiya, had captured Caesarea, and been appointed governor of Syria by Umar. Uthman not only confirmed him in this role but also, in a blatant display of nepotism, made sure to promote other members of his family to similarly lucrative posts.

Understandably, then, the Umayyads fast gained a reputation for quite spectacular greed. One nephew, a smooth opportunist by the name of Marwan, developed a particular name for insatiability: no sooner had he been graced with a hundred thousand silver coins by Uthman than he was off to North Africa, where he proved as effective at screwing the natives out of their wealth as he was shameless in monopolising the plunder. A second Umar he most decidedly was not.

None of which, it went without saying, reflected well on the new *Amir* himself. Yet there was worse. Uthman, unlike Umar, was not content to divide up the loot of empires in the time-honoured manner of a bandit chieftain sharing out plunder after a successful raid. The Arabs, so it seemed to the new *Amir*, had moved on from that. The conquerors, if they were to make best use of the defeated superpowers' bureaucracies, would themselves have to accept certain disciplines: a centralised administration, not least, and a clear-cut chain of command. Precisely the marks of slavery, in short, that the desert Arabs had always derided. No wonder, then, as Uthman sat in Medina and struggled to fashion his immense agglomeration of provinces into a properly imperial administration, that God, in the words of an Armenian bishop, "should have sent a disturbance among the armies of the sons of Ishmael, so that their unity was split."[140] In 656, a band of Muhajirun in Egypt, resentful of a newly appointed place-man, travelled back to Arabia to complain to the *Amir* in person. Uthman, taken by surprise, pretended to meet their grievances, but was then caught red-handed going back on his assurances. The Egyptians, outraged by his double-dealing, laid siege to his house, stormed it, and hacked him to death.

Here, after all the noble talk of brotherhood that had animated the Muhajirun since their first emigration to Medina, was an abrupt reversion to a far more primordial way of conducting affairs. Uthman's widow, so tradition had it, dispatched her husband's bloodstained robe to Mu'awiya in Syria, together with a pointed quotation from the Prophet: "Fight the oppressors until they submit to God's command."[141] In truth, though, it needed no divine revelation to prompt the Umayyads to seek vengeance. Nothing, to an Arab warlord, came more instinctively than a blood feud. That the Prophet had sternly warned against precisely such brawling seems to have inhibited Mu'awiya not in the slightest. In Syria, the sense of community that had supposedly obliterated all distinctions between the Quraysh and the Muhajirun was glaring by its absence. There, in contrast to Iraq and Egypt, there had been no great influx of settlers, no sudden rash of garrison towns. Even Jabiya, the original tent city, had been left largely abandoned after a particularly devastating visitation of the plague in 639. Mu'awiya, and other Qurayshi warlords like him, had not the slightest intention of sharing what they regarded as their patrimony with ragged newcomers from the desert. Syria was theirs: a private fiefdom to be ruled in the manner less of the Prophet than of a Ghassanid.

That is not to say that Muhammad's teachings were wholly cast aside. Back in Medina, his original capital, leaders of the state that he had founded were desperately struggling to hold together his legacy. Even as the empire palpably began to fragment—with banners of revolt raised in Iran as well as Syria, and a host of Arabs in Egypt rumoured to have accepted "belief in Christ"[142]—a new *Amir* was succeeding the murdered Uthman. Ali ibn Abi Talib could hardly have been more intimately associated with golden memories of the Prophet. At once both the cousin and the son-in-law of Muhammad—or so tradition reports—he also had a fierce commitment to the primal values of the *Umma*: of egalitarianism and brotherhood. As a result, to his admirers, he ranked as a veritable *imam*: a father to his people, and a Lion of God. Far from disdaining emigrants from the desert, Ali regarded them—no matter how hairy or stinking—as his natural constituency. Determined that the Muhajirun should retain their grip on the empire, he opted to abandon Medina and make Kufa his new capital. From there, with the energy of the seasoned general that he was, Ali set himself to stamping his authority on all the *Umma*. In order to secure his rear, he first routed an army of rebels outside Basra. Buoyed by this success, he then led the Muhajirun of Kufa up the line of the Euphrates, with the aim of taming Syria. A great battle was fought, Mu'awiya brought to peace negotiations, and victory claimed. Ali, returning to Kufa, naturally made sure to trumpet the news as loudly as he could. The unity of the *Umma*, so his propaganda ran, had been triumphantly restored. The *fitna*—the "time of trial"—was at an end.

Except that it was not. Mu'awiya, withdrawing from the Euphrates, coolly began to proclaim a message of victory identical to that of his rival. Even more threatening to Ali's position, however, there were many now in his own ranks who likewise refused to accept him as *Amir*. His opening of negotiations with Mu'awiya, and his patching together of a treaty, was behaviour that smacked, in their opinion, less of an "*imam*" than of some arrogant and self-serving monarch. A true Believer, so they argued, would have trusted his fate, not to diplomacy, but to ongoing warfare and the will of God. The charge was a crippling one. All very well for the Umayyads to pose as the heirs of the Ghassanid kings; but Ali was a blood relative of Muhammad. Nothing, then, could have been more damaging to his prestige than to be dismissed as merely a latter-day Lakhmid—"the *Amir* of Hira."[143]

As Ali made his way back to Kufa, many of his soldiers seem

simply to have melted away. *Kharijites*, these deserters were called—
"those who go out." What they were decidedly not, however, were
deserters from the teachings of the Prophet. Instead, it was Ali whom
the Kharijites condemned as the unbeliever, as the man who had
strayed from the Straight Path. The fact that he was Muhammad's
nephew only confirmed them in the militancy of their egalitarianism: that the true aristocracy was one of piety, and not of blood.
Even a Companion of the Prophet, if he did not pray until he developed marks on his forehead "comparable to the calluses of a
camel,"[144] if he did not look pale and haggard from regular fasting, if
he did not live like a lion by day and a monk by night, ranked, in the
opinion of the Kharijites, as no better than an apostate. "Those who
reject God after believing in Him," so the Prophet had warned, "and
open their hearts to disbelief, will have the wrath of God upon them,
and a grievous punishment awaiting them."[145] Here was a ruling that
the Kharijites were more than willing to help enforce. So it was, for
instance, that a band of them, meeting an aged Companion of the
Prophet outside Basra, were said to have demanded that he renounce
his loyalty to Ali; and when the Companion refused, they butchered
him over the carcass of a pig, slit open the belly of his pregnant concubine, and murdered her three attendants. Other Kharijites, so it
was reported, might "go out with their swords into the markets
while people would stand around not realising what was happening;
they would shout 'no judgement except God!' and plunge their
blades into whomever they could reach, and go on killing until they
themselves were killed."[146] A militant devotion to the Prophet's
teachings indeed; and fit for that reason, in the opinion of many of
their fellow Muhajirun, profoundly to be admired. But not in the
opinion of Ali. Abandoning his attempt to bring Mu'awiya to heel,
he made it his priority instead to extirpate the Kharijites. In 658, he
won a victory over them as crushing as it was to prove pyrrhic:
for all he had done, in effect, was to fertilise the soil of Iraq with
the blood of their martyrs. Three years later, and there came the
inevitable blowback: a Kharijite assassin struck him down while he

was praying in Kufa.* The Prophet's dream of brotherhood, of a shared community of believers, seemed dealt a fatal blow, too.

Into the breach, with great smoothness, stepped Mu'awiya. With Ali gone, no one in Iraq now had the resources to oppose him. Even Hasan, Ali's eldest son and his obvious heir as *imam*, was persuaded to retract his claim and retire on a pension to Medina. With him too went his younger brother, Husayn—who as a boy, so it was said, had been a particular favourite of the Prophet, and been dangled lovingly on his knee. True, the removal from Kufa of the two grandsons of Muhammad did not neutralise all opposition to Mu'awiya. The Kharijites, on principle, remained obdurately opposed to Umayyad rule. So too did many Kufans, who preserved a ferocious loyalty to their murdered *Amir*. Yet Mu'awiya, who had not the slightest intention of basing himself in Kufa, could afford to ignore both the Kharijites and the *Shi'a*—or "Party"—of Ali. Annoyances they might be—but only in the manner of distantly buzzing wasps. The gaze of Mu'awiya was fixed, not upon a scurvy ragbag of desert Arabs, but upon altogether worthier opponents.

Even though the last hint of resistance from the House of Sasan had been crushed back in 651, with the murder of Yazdegird in that great eastern stronghold of his dynasty, Merv, the Romans, despite all their losses, still stood defiant. Mu'awiya, looking to keep the Muhajirun busy, duly renewed the onslaught against the Christian empire with a vengeance. In 674, he even sponsored a siege of Constantinople itself. In the event, after a blockade of four years, the effort to capture the New Rome had to be abandoned; yet what was striking, perhaps, was not its failure but how close it had come to success. Certainly, there could be no denying that Mu'awiya—in the scope and sweep of his achievements, in the awesome scale of his authority, and in the radiant splendour of his name—was patently a favourite of God.

---

* The date of Ali's assassination derives from Muslim historians, but it is typical of the general murk of the sources for the period that a near-contemporaneous Christian chronicle, written in Syria, dates it to 658.

But which God, precisely? Shrewd and calculating as he was in all his dealings with mortal powers, Mu'awiya seems to have practised a certain opportunism in his dealings with the heavens, too. Although he termed himself "Commander of the Faithful," in succession to Umar and Uthman, his definition of who actually ranked as members of the "Faithful" was altogether more subtle and ambiguous than theirs had been. Rather than gathering to hail his accession at Medina, the Arabs had assembled in the shadow of the Temple Mount: for Mu'awiya had "refused to go to the seat of Muhammad."[147] Not even Umar, the *Amir* whose attentions to the sacred rock had seen him hailed by Jews as their "redeemer," had thought to demonstrate to quite such flamboyant effect the abiding status of Jerusalem as the holiest city in the world. Mu'awiya, however, in providing this reassurance, was concerned principally to woo, not his Jewish but his Christian subjects. That the Arabs, in their original assault upon Palestine, had fought in alliance with Jews was now, to the new "King of the Holy Land," something of an embarrassment. Both his tax base and his bureaucracy, after all, were composed primarily of Christians. The Jews could hardly compare. So it was, in addition to receiving the submission of the Arabs, that he had made sure to mark his investiture as Commander of the Faithful by going on pilgrimage around Jerusalem in the footsteps of Christ—"and he went up and sat down on Golgotha, and prayed there."[148] Evidently, that the Prophet had declared the crucifixion a fraud bothered Mu'awiya not a bit.

In fact, there is precious little evidence that Mu'awiya paid much attention to the Prophet at all. Nowhere in his inscriptions, nor on his coins, nor in any of the documents preserved from his reign, is there so much as a single mention of Muhammad. Nor, despite the much later tradition that would attribute the compilation of the Prophet's revelations to Uthman, are there any Qur'ans—or even fragments of Qur'ans—datable to Mu'awiya's lifetime either. Records of the words spoken by Muhammad—"twigs of the burning bush, aflame with God"[149]—must surely have been preserved by those who still tended the light of his memory: the Muhajirun of Kufa, the *Shi'a* of Ali, the

365

7

THE FORGING OF ISLAM

God's Deputy

In 679, almost twenty years after Mu'awiya had sat and prayed at Golgotha, a Frankish bishop named Arculf arrived in Jerusalem for his own tour of the city's sites. The stresses and convulsions of the age had failed to fracture one of Christianity's most innovative presumptions: that pilgrimage to its holy places was as much for those who lived on the edge of the world as it was for locals. Even though Jerusalem's tourist trade was greatly diminished from what it had been in its heyday, the city still seemed to the wide-eyed bishop to be positively heaving with "crowds of all different peoples." With beasts of burden too—and in such numbers that Arculf found himself clutching his nose, and sloshing uncomfortably through "the filth from their discharges, which spreads everywhere across the streets."[1] Not, of course, that a pilgrim hardened by a gruelling journey from Gaul was likely to be thrown off his stride by a few droppings—and sure enough, Arculf proved himself a tireless enthusiast for the city's many wonders. The highlight, inevitably, was the Church of the Resurrection: a shrine unimpaired in its magnificence, the bishop was delighted to discover, since the time of Constantine. Indeed, to an out-of-towner such as Arculf, it might have seemed that Roman rule had never ended. The travel documents issued to him were written in Greek. The coins in his purse were weighted according to standards set by the mints of Constantinople. Many of them were even stamped with that ultimate symbol of the Christian empire—a cross. Power, in the Holy Land, still sported a decidedly Roman look.

Naturally, Arculf was not oblivious to the recent changing of the guard. News of the calamities afflicting the New Rome had circulated to sensational effect in Gaul. It was widely reported that the Saracens had laid waste entire provinces, "as was their habit."[2] Even Jerusalem, that incomparable city of churches, was branded with the stamp of their rule: "In the celebrated place where once the Temple arose in its magnificence," Arculf noted, "the Saracens now have a quadrangular prayer house."[3] He was almost certainly describing the building begun by Umar, and still unfinished in the early years of Mu'awiya's reign: a *mosque*—or "place of prostration"—as the Arabs termed it. That they might apply this designation to any place of worship had certainly done little to lower Christian hackles: for it was clear enough, whatever else the "prayer house" might be, that it was no church. The supreme blasphemy of its location, of course, only heightened Christian anxiety—as did the fact that there were still Jews, ever optimistic, who clung to the hope that the Arabs were actually restoring "the walls of the Temple."[4] An infernal project, then, it seemed to most Christians—and sure enough, one monk, taking a peek at the building site, reported seeing the workforce accompanied in their labours by a whole crack squad of demons.[5]

Notwithstanding this supernatural assistance, however, the end result did seem rather jerry-built. That, at any rate, was the verdict of Arculf himself. Despite being large enough to accommodate some three thousand worshippers, the building did not impress the bishop: "They put it up roughly," he complained, "by erecting upright boards and great beams on some ruined remains."[6] Perhaps, however, it took a Frank to notice such things. The barbarians of the West had certainly had a good deal of practice in the art of cannibalising Roman monuments. Indeed, as Theoderic had demonstrated to notable effect, the entire labour of state-building amid the wreckage of the crumbled empire might easily rank as precisely such a project writ large. Perhaps, then, that is why Arculf, although dismissive of the Saracens' mosque, seems not to have been greatly startled by it—nor by their presence in Jerusalem. Although Mu'awiya had risen to become incomparably mighty, yet the difference between him and Arculf's own king, back in Gaul, was one of quality, not of kind. Saracens and Franks both lived like squatters amid the splendours of a vanished greatness. No matter that this inheritance from the past was immeasurably richer and more imposing in the East than in the West—the helplessness of the Saracens to improve upon it seemed no less than that of the Franks. Patched together as it was out of brick and wood, Mu'awiya's palace inspired eye-rolling paroxysms of condescension in Roman ambassadors. "The ceiling will do for birds," one sniffed, "and the walls will do for rats."[7] Even the great ambition of Mu'awiya's life—the capture of Constantinople—spoke of cultural cringe. Fuelling it was an unspoken acknowledgement of the Romans' own perennial conceit—that a man could truly rule the world only from the city of Constantine.

Yet in one sense, despite the failure of Mu'awiya's assault on *al-Qustantiniyya*, his pretensions had already surpassed those of the Caesars. Not even Justinian at his most megalomaniacal had presumed to pose as an intercessor between the great toiling mass of humanity and God Himself. Clearly, then, in Mu'awiya's precocious conception of monarchy, there were influences coming to bear that owed nothing to Roman example. Was it mere coincidence, for instance, that he should have cast himself in a relationship to God so similar to that played by angels in the prayers of the *Mushrikun*? Assuredly, a ready supply of building materials was far from the limit of what the Fertile Crescent had to offer invaders. Richer as well than anything to be found in the West was its immense array of faiths. Theodoric—keen to distinguish himself from the emperor in Constantinople and from his own Roman subjects—had lived and died an Arian. Mu'awiya—the lord of Chalcedonian and Monophysite Christians, of Jews and Samaritans, of Zoroastrians and Manichaeans—had far more options available to him. Above all, in the swirl of beliefs that was his inheritance as an Arab, he possessed something formidably precious: an assurance of God's favour that owed nothing to Rome or to any other earthly power. That he was perfectly content to pray at the site of the crucifixion, or to restore Edessa's cathedral after it had been toppled by an earthquake, or to have the odd public inscription on a bath-house adorned with a cross, implied, not that he was a Christian, but rather that he shared in that respect for Jesus, and for the Jewish prophets too, which had once united Muhammad and the *Mushrikun*.[8] Whatever the precise doctrines in which Mu'awiya put his trust, though, they were certainly not supported by anything that could compare with the massive buttressing that rabbis, bishops and *mowbeds*, over the course of the centuries, had erected around their faiths. Nothing as yet had been fashioned out of the various teachings and traditions held sacred by the Arab conquerors that a Christian would have recognised as a *religio*: a "religion." Instead, like blazing points of fire scattered by a starburst, there was a whole shimmering flamescape of sects. For a global monarch such as Mu'awiya, this was opportunity on a scale that not even Constantine had enjoyed. In his determination to understand why God had graced him with the rule of the world—and what best might be done to ensure that rule's perpetuation—he could toy with beliefs and doctrines that were still very much up for grabs.

Mu'awiya, nevertheless, was not alone in seeking to capitalise on this opportunity. In Iraq, at a safe distance from both his direct authority and the gravitational pull of the Holy Land, the urgent question of what, precisely, God wanted from His people had prompted a quite bewildering array of responses. The Kharijites, as militant as ever in their loathing for anything that smacked of monarchy, had retreated from Kufa to the deserts around the Persian Gulf, where they had founded a series of tiny, terrorist republics. Meanwhile, their old adversaries, the *Shi'a* of Ali, still clung to their own passionately held convictions. There were some partisans of Muhammad's murdered cousin, taking a leaf out of the Sasanian book, who had even begun to claim that only under the command of a leader who shared directly in his bloodline could the world of men hope to know true order, and be assured of the favour of God. Others went further still and proclaimed themselves prophets. One of these, an illiterate tailor who claimed to be the heir of both Jesus and Muhammad, and to have a book from heaven that proved it, was eventually cornered by an imperial task force and vanished into a hole that mysteriously opened in the side of a mountain. Finally, aged but hedged about still by the numinous, there were the last remaining *Sahabah*: the Companions of Muhammad. The most celebrated of these, a Qurayshi aristocrat by the name of Abdullah ibn al-Zubayr, had been just eight years old when the Prophet had died, but his admirers still revered him as a living link to a more heroic and God-touched age. Certainly, his disdain for the Umayyads knew no bounds. For some twenty years, his response to the blasphemy of Mu'awiya's reign had been to remain in Medina, in a pious and ostentatious sulk, and lovingly tend the flame of the Prophet's memory.

Among people who believed themselves graced by the most sensational revelation imaginable, of a direct intrusion into the fabric of human history by God Himself, such rivalries were only to be expected, perhaps. The struggle to make sense of such a mystery, as the prodigious appetite for factionalism of the early Christians had shown, was bound to be a gruelling one. Unlike the Church, however, the Muhajirun had not had to wait three long centuries before seizing the commanding heights of a mighty empire. They had captured theirs in a matter of decades. As a result, disagreements between the Umayyads and their opponents—although no less fixated on the purposes of God than the conflicts between Marcion and the Ebionites had been—had an extra, and ominously geopolitical, dimension. When Mu'awiya, corpulent and near death, proclaimed that his son—a notorious playboy by the name of Yazid—was God's choice as his successor, the result was not merely widespread shock at the blasphemy but a jolting lurch towards civil war. It was bad enough, in the opinion of the pious, that Yazid himself was "a sinner in respect of his belly and his private parts"[9] and kept a monkey as a pet; more truly shocking was any notion that all the upheavals of the previous sixty years, all the struggles and the stupefying triumphs, might have had as their only object the installation of a dynasty such as the Umayyads upon the throne of the world.

As news travelled in April 680 of Mu'awiya's death, something else was abroad as well. The baleful spectre of *fitna* had returned to stalk the Arabian Empire. Syria, unsurprisingly, held firm for Yazid—but Arabia and Iraq did not. First to raise the banner of rebellion was Husayn, the youngest and by now only surviving grandson of the Prophet. Middle-aged and long since retired from the bear pit of the Fertile Crescent, he made for an improbable warrior. Sure enough, when he led his small band of followers on a sudden dash from Medina to Kufa, the local Umayyad agent found it a simple matter to block their approach. Holed up in a flea-bitten village called Karbala, frustrated in his expectation of support from the Muhajirun of Kufa, and increasingly tormented by thirst, Husayn decided to trust his fate to the will of God. Charging the large army that had boxed him in, he and his pathetic retinue were hacked down amid the unforgiving sands. A squalid end for a grandson beloved of the Prophet; and although in the long run his death at the hands of Umayyad heavies would do wonders for his standing as a martyr, in the short term it ensured that Iraq, however precariously, remained under Yazid's control.

Meanwhile, back in Medina, an altogether more dangerous adversary had been biding his time. Ibn al-Zubayr, as grim and austere as ever, had very publicly refused to take the oath of allegiance to the new *Amir*. As a result, he, rather than any relative of Ali, had emerged as the most prominent opponent of the Umayyads. Tempers in Medina were not helped by the fact that Yazid's representative in the oasis was none other than the fabulously venal and slippery Marwan. The locals' mistrust of their new governor ran particularly deep. Rumours abounded that it was he, back in the last calamitous days of Uthman's rule, who had advised his uncle to double-cross the Egyptian war band that had come to visit the *Amir*, and thereby goaded it into becoming a lynch-mob. Nothing Marwan had done since, during all the years of his tenure as governor of the Hijaz, had helped to improve his reputation for double-dealing. Negotiations between

Ibn al-Zubayr and the Umayyads grew increasingly fractious. By 683 they had broken down for good. Ibn al-Zubayr damned the new *Amir* as a usurper. As Marwan fled Medina for Syria, Yazid sent a task force in the opposite direction. The rebels made frantic efforts to gird their oasis with fortifications, but their defiance was doomed to prove no more effective than had been that of Husayn at Karbala. Despite some brave resistance, Yazid's army stormed the makeshift ditches and ramparts, wiped out the defenders, and seized the city. The stories of what happened next grew ever more blood-bolstered with the telling. The City of the Prophet, it is said, was put to the sword for three days; and nine months on from the sack, over a thousand babies were born.

Ibn al-Zubayr, however, was not among the dead. Implacable in his piety, and "full of threats against the Syrians, whom he claimed were transgressors of the law,"[10] he had resolved to make a stand that would truly challenge his opponents to do their worst. Accordingly, rather than wait in Medina to confront Yazid's strike-force, he had headed for a spot that was even more redolent of holiness: the "House of God."[11] Muslim historians, writing more than a century after the fact, would take for granted, of course, that such a sanctuary was to be identified with Mecca; but nowhere in the writings of contemporaries is this actually said. Instead, all is studied indeterminacy. "He came to a certain locality in the South where their sanctuary was, and lived there."[12] So wrote one Christian chronicler about Ibn al-Zubayr. Evidently, then, the precise location of the Arabs' desert shrine remained as much a puzzle to outsiders as it had ever been. Nevertheless, there were certain suggestive clues. It was noted by one bishop, for instance, that the Muhajirun of Iraq, when they bowed to pray, did so towards the West— "towards the *Ka'ba*, the primordial wellspring of their race"—while those in Alexandria turned to the East.[13] Muslim tradition too, rather startlingly, recorded something very similar. The founder of the first mosque in Kufa, so it was said, had fired an arrow to determine the *qibla*—the direction of prayer—and it had landed not to the south of the mosque, in a line with Mecca, but somewhere to its west. So, although no contemporary tells us explicitly where Ibn al-Zubayr took refuge, the weight of evidence would suggest a location to the north of the Hijaz, midway between Kufa and Alexandria. Since this is precisely the region with which Muhammad himself appears to have been most familiar, and since Ibn al-Zubayr was consciously aiming to defend the Prophet's legacy, the likelihood must surely be that the House of God in which he barricaded himself stood not in Mecca but between Medina and Palestine: in that "blessed place" named by the Prophet himself as Bakka.

Yet whether all the Arabs, a full half-century on from his death, would necessarily have revered it is another matter. The notion inherited from Jews and Christians—that a single shrine might be possessed of a holiness so awesome as to merit pilgrimage from every corner of the world—competed in their minds with a radically opposed tradition. All very helpful of a bishop to identify the sanctuary of the Muhajirun as "the Ka'ba"—except, of course, that there were Ka'bas reaching from Nabataea to Najran. To glimpse the sacred in a feature even as relatively mundane as a spring, or a well, or an oddly coloured stone was a time-hallowed instinct among the Arabs; and yet, while this indisputably spoke of a sensitivity to the numinous, it also betrayed a certain cavalier attitude towards the status of specific shrines. Over the course of the generations, sanctuaries had repeatedly been staked out as hallowed—haram—and then just as abruptly been abandoned. Even the Prophet, while trying to define the direction in which his followers should pray, had been capable of the occasional volte-face: "The foolish people will say, 'What has turned them away from the prayer direction they used to face?'"[14] What the original qibla might have been, and what its replacement, the Prophet had not thought to specify—but that one sanctuary had been promoted, and at the expense of another, was clear enough.* No wonder then, descending upon the House of God, that Ibn al-Zubayr should have been concerned to make "his voice heard from a distance."[15] After all, with time passing by, with those who could

---

* Muslim scholars would identify this verse as referring to a change in the direction of prayer from Jerusalem to Mecca—a tradition for which, of course, there is absolutely no evidence within the Qur'an itself.

remember the Prophet slipping into oblivion, and with the double-dealing Umayyads preening themselves amid the magnificent and seductive monuments of Christian Jerusalem, who was to say how long the memory—let alone the primacy—of Bakka could be kept alive?

In the event, two accidents would serve to boost Ibn al-Zubayr in his ambitions for the site. The first of these, paradoxically, might have seemed to spell its doom. In the summer of 683, with Yazid's army camped out before the House of God, the *Ka'ba*, it is said, caught fire and burned to the ground. Some blamed this calamity on torches hurled by the Syrians, others on Ibn al-Zubayr's own clumsiness; but all are agreed on the ruinous extent of the damage. And so, perhaps, the sanctuary might well have been left, as nothing but blackened rubble—had not the second accident then intervened. Yazid, back in Syria, keeled over and died. The news, when it reached the task force, left them abruptly shiftless. With Yazid's death, they felt themselves doubly bereft: not only of their *imam* but of the favour of God. Not so Ibn al-Zubayr, of course. He, with his great enemy dead, could now feel even more soaringly justified in all his pretensions. When Yazid's army, scouting around for a new *Amir*, promised him their loyalty if he would only accompany them to Syria, Ibn al-Zubayr indignantly refused. He had higher things by far on his mind.

As the Syrians drifted aimlessly away from their siege, Ibn al-Zubayr set about constructing a sanctuary that could serve, without any further compromise or ambiguity, as a fit object for the veneration of all the Faithful. Taking a pick in his own hands, it is said, he levelled what remained of the incinerated shrine and raised an entirely new one in its place. The whiff of paradox in this was palpable, even by the standards of the Arabs—a people who traditionally had always been perfectly content to abandon sanctuaries with barely a second thought. A question as obvious as it was unsettling shadowed Ibn al-Zubayr's labours: how precisely could his new House of God be reckoned timeless when it had only just been erected? His propagandists, it would appear, had not stinted in providing answers. Centuries on from Ibn al-Zubayr's great building project, fantastical stories of the discoveries that were made during the course of the excavations would still be lovingly repeated. It was said that the original foundations, laid down by Abraham, had been miraculously brought to light. A mysterious text had been found, guaranteeing divine favour for all who visited the sanctuary. Most sensationally of all, when a black stone had been dug up, the whole sanctuary had begun to tremble. On this stone, so some reported, had been stamped the very name and title of God: "I am Allah, the Lord of Bakka."[16]

And as with the House of God, so with the great empire beyond: Ibn al-Zubayr aimed to set it on new foundations. Just as fire had left the *Ka'ba* a crumbling ruin, *fitna* had come to ravage the world. In Syria, Yazid had been succeeded by his son—an infant so sickly that he had died after only a couple of months on the throne. Amid the resulting power vacuum, the Arabs had once again begun to turn upon themselves. Partisans of Ali, in mourning for Husayn, vented their sense of mingled grief and shame upon the garrisons of the hated Umayyads. Kharijite war bands, fanning out across southern Iraq, renewed their campaign of shadowy and calculated terror. In Kufa, a charismatic figure whom posterity would damn as "Mukhtar the Deceiver" seized the city's treasury, distributed its entire reserve of nine million coins to the poor, and urged a revolution in which all men were to be equal, "claiming he was a prophet."[17] He provoked particular excitement by parading a brocade-draped chair, which his enemies ridiculed as a piece of junk looted from Ali's attic, but which enthusiasts, taking a leaf out of a thoroughly Jewish book, hailed as a manifestation of the presence of God Himself: the *Shekhinah*. The presence of this fabulous totem on campaign, either carried on a grey donkey or borne aloft into battle by litter-bearers, proved, not surprisingly, a potent boost to Mukhtar's record as both a general and a prophet. It helped as well that Mukhtar himself, whenever he charged his enemies, was said to be accompanied by a bodyguard of angels mounted on horses of flame.

In the face of such wild and competing enthusiasms, the frameworks of governance just lately restored by Mu'awiya began once again to buckle. The antagonisms unleashed by the *fitna* proved relentless, the hatreds bewildering, the violence exhausting and savage. Much, after all, was at stake. To the venerable thrill of tribal rivalries—still potent as these were among the various Arab emigrants—had been added whole new dimensions of chauvinism. Factionalists, when they chose an *imam* or a prophet to follow, were choosing as well what their fate in the next world was to be—and so it was, when they fought, that they would invariably do so to the death. Once again, as in the time of the great war between Heraclius and Khusrow, or that of the first coming of the Arabs, the sense was palpable of a conflict in which more, very much more, was at stake than mere earthly ambitions.

Even those whose fate it was to cower as impotent bystanders before the agonies of the age were alert to this. War was far from being the only expression of God's anger. Plague too had returned to Iraq, strewing roads with the dead and polluting the canals and rivers with corpses. Pestilence, in turn, led to famine: children with limbs "like dry sticks of wood" would graze on withered grass, while mothers, it was darkly rumoured, might feed on their own babies. "Worst of all were the looters, from whom no one could escape—for they wandered about everywhere, following their prey like gleaners, hauling them out of hidden places and stripping them of their belongings, and leaving them naked."[18] It could be hard to tell the difference between such bandits, the Kharijites and Mukhtar's "cudgel-bearers."[19] Humanity, like monsters of the deep, was preying on itself. Events, once again, appeared to be portending the end of days.

Certainly, whether such an eventuality were imminent or not, it was the divinely appointed duty of Ibn al-Zubayr, as Commander of the Faithful, to prepare the world for it. "Nearer to mankind their reckoning draws, and yet in heedlessness they turn away."[20] So the Prophet had lamented. Ibn al-Zubayr, in harkening to this ominous warning, made sure to take decisive steps. Doing as Umar and Uthman had done, and directing the affairs of the world from the depths of the desert, he sent his brother, Mus'ab, to bring order to Iraq. Mus'ab undertook this seemingly thankless commission with efficiency and relish. Mukhtar, that preacher of an unsettlingly radical egalitarianism, was briskly defeated, cornered in the governor's palace, and put to death. His severed hand, a trophy for the faithful to admire on their way to prayers, was nailed to the side of Kufa's mosque, while his holy chair was consigned to a bonfire. Simultaneously, across the south of Iraq, the far bloodier and more exhausting task of suppressing the Kharijites inspired Mus'ab to launch a troop surge that reached as far as the Persian uplands.

It was not only through a counter-insurgency campaign, however, that Ibn al-Zubayr aimed to bring order to a tottering world. Not every message was to be delivered on the point of a sword. "Judgement," so the Kharijite slogan ran, "belongs to God alone."[21] Ibn al-Zubayr and his lieutenants, while certainly not disputing this message, aimed to refine it: by stating with the utmost clarity just how and when it was that the judgement of God had been made known. So it was, in either 685 or 686, as the *fitna* continued to rage in Iraq, that one of his lieutenants minted a coin in Persia with a novel and fateful message. "*Bismallah Muhammad rasul Allah*," it ran—"In the name of God, Muhammad is the Messenger of God."[22]

The potency of this slogan, amid the carnage and confusion of the times, was self-evident. Ibn al-Zubayr's genius was to recognise, as Constantine had recognised long before him, that any lord of a great empire who claimed God's favour must ensure that the basis of that favour stood rock solid. Military action alone would never serve to bring the *fitna* to an end. Only a framework of doctrines that all the combatants could accept as authentic and bestowed of God had any hope of achieving that. Hence the supreme value of the example of the Prophet. Whereas Constantine at Nicaea had been obliged to depend upon fractious and fallible bishops to stamp a particular brand of his chosen faith as orthodox, Ibn al-Zubayr had identified a far less troublesome sanction: for not only had Muhammad claimed to be a medium for divine revelation, but he was also safely dead. Ram home the point that he had authentically been a Messenger of God, and anything that could be attributed to him would perforce have to be accepted by the faithful as a truth descended from heaven. "Those who offend the Prophet," so it had been revealed to Muhammad, "are cursed by God in this life and in the hereafter."[23] Here, for any warlord looking to damn his enemies, was a literal godsend. This was why, with Ibn al-Zubayr and his henchmen increasingly alert to its potential, they made ever more play with their new message: that Muhammad had truly been the Prophet of God. Far more effectively than any troop surge in Iraq, it seemed to promise them the rule of the world.

There was, however, a problem. Ibn al-Zubayr was not the only self-proclaimed Commander of the Faithful to have spotted the uses to which such a slogan might be put. Widely though he had established his authority, across Arabia, Iraq and Persia, Syria still stood defiant. There, the Umayyad cause, though scotched, had not been killed. Conditions in the wake of Yazid's death, chaotic as they were, had been ideally suited to the talents of a schemer such as Marwan. At a tribal assembly convened at the old Ghassanid capital of Jabiya in the summer of 684, held to debate whether Ibn al-Zubayr should be acknowledged as *Amir*, he proposed putting the whole issue to a vote—and so finessed the proceedings that, to much astonishment, "it was his own name that came up."[24] Marwan, a man grown old in his pursuit of power, would have only nine months to enjoy his triumph; but already, by the time he died in the spring of 685, he had done enough to ensure that Syria, at any rate, would remain Umayyad. His successor, hailed enthusiastically by the Syrians as *Amir*, was also his son: a man in his forties, notorious for his golden dentures and the foul quality of his halitosis, named Abd al-Malik.

The new *Amir* had talents that extended far beyond an ability to slay flies with a single breath. Abd al-Malik was very much a chip off the Umayyad block. Brutality was seamlessly fused in him with ambition, intelligence and vision. The same man who could leash a political rival, lead him around like a dog and then straddle his chest to hack off his head was also a man who could swallow his own pride sufficiently to pay tribute to the Romans in an effort to secure his northern border, and lurk patiently in Syria, leaving it to Mus'ab to crush the Kharijites and the *Shi'a*. Only in 689, four years after he had succeeded his father as *Amir*, did Abd al-Malik finally go on the offensive, doing as Julian had done long before him, and snatching after global empire by invading northern Iraq. Unlike Julian, however, he was to secure fabulous success. In early 691, beneath fluttering banners and swirling dust, he succeeded in bringing Mus'ab to defeat and death:

> The tribesman saw clearly
> the error of their ways,
> And he straightened out the smirk
> upon their faces.[25]

Yet Abd al-Malik, even as he trampled down the corpse of his rival, did not neglect to heed the lessons of Mus'ab's earlier triumphs in Iraq. Smirks had to be straightened out—but so too, if the conquerors of the far-flung empire were ever to be unified as a single people, did their sense of what they owed to God. Abd al-Malik, having wrenched Iraq from Ibn al-Zubayr's grasp, did not hesitate to purloin his slogan as well. Even as the last embers of opposition to Umayyad rule were being stamped out in Basra, new coins were starting to circulate in the city: "In the name of God," they proclaimed, "Muhammad is the Messenger of God."

The assertion was no less potent for appearing on the coins of an Umayyad. Startling though the sudden emphasis on the Prophet's role must have appeared to those in the markets and counting-houses of Basra, there is no reason to doubt Abd al-Malik's personal sincerity. Not only had he grown up in Medina—where memories of Muhammad were uniquely vivid and cherished—but his reputation for austere godliness rivalled that of Ibn al-Zubayr. Nevertheless, it is clear as well that his abrupt parading of Muhammad's name—something that no other member of his dynasty had ever thought to do—was prompted by self-interest as well as piety. Concerned as Abd al-Malik was to spike Ibn al-Zubayr's pretensions, he also had an eye fixed on a second adversary. Despite the expediency of the tribute that he had paid to Constantinople, it still rankled as a bitter humiliation, and one that he aimed to wipe clean. What better way, then, than by striking directly at the heart of Roman conceit? Mu'awiya, despite his unwearying appetite for dyeing the Christian empire with blood, had never thought to dispute with his adversaries the truth of their faith. Abd al-Malik, however, suffered from no such inhibition. Not for him a respectful pilgrimage to Golgotha. Rather than soothing Christian sensibilities by professing a vague brand of monotheism, he sought to rub Roman noses in the obvious inferiority of their superstitions. As surely as Mu'awiya had sought the annihilation of Constantinople's worldly power, Abd al-Malik aimed to shred her claim to a special relationship with God. A radical—and far from easy—step to take. Just as the strategy of challenging the Romans by sea had required the building of entire fleets from scratch, disputing the highway to heaven with them would demand truly formidable feats of innovation. Out of the scattered flotsam and jetsam of beliefs left scattered by the great floodtide of Arab conquests, something coherent—something manifestly God-stamped—would have to be fashioned: in short, a religion.

And if the enshrining of Muhammad as its founder was a start, then it was only that—a start. No better way to appreciate the full scale of what remained to be done than to visit the city where Abd al-Malik, like Mu'awiya before him, had first been saluted as *Amir*: Jerusalem. There, where the radiance of candles in the churches burned so bright that, by night, the entire city and the hills that surrounded it appeared as one great dazzling blaze of light, the splendour of Christianity, and the heft of its antiquity, remained intimidating things. Well might Abd al-Malik, "noting the scale of the dome of the Church of the Resurrection and its magnificence, have been moved lest it dazzle the minds of the Faithful."[26] Yet the possession of Jerusalem, although certainly a challenge, presented an opportunity, too. Even as Abd al-Malik was leading his armies to victory in Iraq, workmen on the Temple Mount were busy labouring to secure him an equally brilliant triumph. The ramshackle mosque sniffed at so disdainfully by Arculf had been demolished, and was now being replaced in sumptuous style. A wall was being built around the limits of the rock, to mark it out as *haram*, and gates set in the wall opened on to upgraded roads. Most stupefying of all, however, and most wondrously beautiful too, was an octagonal building of such prominence as to put even the Church of the Resurrection in the shade. That this was a deliberate ploy could hardly have been made any more emphatic. Not only did the dimensions of the new structure exactly replicate those of Constantine's great church, but its piers were to be surmounted, when completed, by a vast gilded cupola. Yet, what really served to fling back in the teeth of Christians all their arrogance and their pretensions was the deliberate positioning of this same "Dome of the Rock." Enclosed within it, its surface unadorned and bare, was the perforated expanse of stone over which the Roman authorities had permitted a ragbag of sobbing Jews to blow their rams' horns each year. Just as the rabbis had identified this spot with the *Shekhinah*—the immanence of the divine on earth—Abd al-Malik and his architects attributed to it a no less awesome role. At the beginning of time, they believed, with the universe just completed, God had stood upon the rock and then ascended into heaven—leaving behind an imprint of His foot.* The end of time too would see the rock transfigured: for on the Day of Judgement all the faithful, and all the mosques across the world, and even the *Ka'ba* itself, were destined to travel to Jerusalem, "so that the people will cry, 'Hail to you, who come as pilgrims, and hail to her to whom the pilgrimage is made.'"[27]

Perhaps, given the seeming imminence of the End Days, it was only to be expected that Abd al-Malik should have wished to raise a monument appropriate to the climactic role in them that the Rock was destined to play. Only to be expected as well—with the "House of God" still in the hands of Ibn al-Zubayr—that he should have been reluctant to wait for

---

* In due course, this tradition would become an embarrassment to Muslim theologians, since it implied that God had a body. In the eleventh century, an alternative explanation for the construction of the Dome of the Rock was enshrined: that it commemorated the ascension into heaven not of God but of Muhammad, who was supposedly transported from Mecca to Jerusalem specifically for the purpose.

the Day of Judgement before promoting it as a site of pilgrimage. He even went so far as to furnish it with souvenirs of Abraham. As a result, the local Muhajirun had no need to travel into the desert to wonder at relics of their august forefather. Instead, they could journey to the Dome of the Rock and see hanging there the desiccated horns of the ram that Abraham had supposedly offered up in sacrifice on the very spot. Sure enough, among his immediate subjects, Abd al-Malik's *grand projet* proved a quite stunning success. "All the rough Arabs of Syria," so a Kharijite sneered, "go to it on pilgrimage."[28] What was the Dome of the Rock, so locals might boast, if not "the holiest spot on earth"?[29]

Yet there was in this same vaunt a nagging irony. Flattering to Abd al-Malik it may have been—but it also had the potential to be lethal to the broader sweep of his ambitions. It was all very well for inscriptions repeated across the Dome of the Rock to echo the slogan on his coins and proclaim that Muhammad was the "Messenger of God"—but it begged a most awkward question. Since the Prophet had never stepped foot in Jerusalem, how could any notion of the Temple Mount as "the holiest spot on earth" be squared with Abd al-Malik's simultaneous promotion of Muhammad as the founder of his infant religion? Inexorably though the years had slipped by, and hazy though memories of the Prophet had become, yet there could be no forgetting that he had dwelt beyond the limits of Palestine. Clearly, then, Abd al-Malik could not afford to do as the Roman and Persian authorities had done, and simply leave the depths of the desert well alone. He had no option but to go after Ibn al-Zubayr. His rival's continued hold upon the holy places where the Prophet had received his revelations affronted not only Abd al-Malik's authority but that of the heavens themselves. Jerusalem on its own would never be adequate to the full purposes of his mission. He urgently needed Arabia as well. Otherwise, without it, what prospect of fashioning what Abd al-Malik devoutly believed himself set on earth to complete: the authentic "Religion of Truth"?[30]

In the autumn of 691, an army of some two thousand men duly set off from Kufa into the desert. Abd al-Malik, whose eye for talent was not a whit inferior to all his many other capabilities, had appointed his most trusted servant as its commander: a youthful former schoolteacher by the name of Al-Hajjaj. Not for nothing was this brilliantly able young man known as "Little Dog"; ugly and diminutive he may have been, but his nose for a scent was outstanding, and his teeth were razor sharp. By the spring of 692, he had cornered his quarry. Once again, Ibn al-Zubayr found himself holed up inside a "house of worship."[31] This time, though, there was to be no reprieve. Al-Hajjaj blockaded the old man for six months, pulverising his defences with catapults to such lethal effect that by autumn the entire sanctuary had once again been reduced to rubble and left littered with corpses—one of which was Ibn al-Zubayr's. The whole of Arabia was finally Abd al-Malik's.

Two years later, the *Amir* himself journeyed through the desert on an ostentatious pilgrimage. Already lord of the Temple Mount, where the Dome of the Rock had been completed in the same year as the defeat of Ibn al-Zubayr, he now also claimed dominion over a site equally awesome and sacred. "To us," as a court poet wrote in celebration of his glittering achievement, "belong two Houses: the House of God, of which we are the governors, and the revered House on the mount of Jerusalem."[32]

Yet here, once again, was a telling ambiguity. No mystery as to the location of the Dome of the Rock, of course—but where precisely was the enigmatic "House of God"? The poet did not think to specify. Nor did any of his contemporaries. Perhaps, however, this was only to be expected. Literate people, after all, did not tend to live in the desert—or visit it either. Even if the habit of going on pilgrimage to Arabia had become well established before the time of Abd al-Malik—and there is no evidence that it had—then the mounting anarchy of the times would surely have halted the practice. As a result, among those believers sufficiently educated to put pen to parchment, the precise details of the distant desert sanctuary, even down to its very name, appear to have been a blur. The surest pointers to its location were to be found, not in poetry, or in chronicles, or in gazetteers, but in stone. The years that followed Abd al-Malik's pilgrimage to Arabia saw workmen tinkering with the layout of numerous mosques. From the busiest stretch of the Nile to the loneliest corner of the Negev, *qiblas* that had previously pointed east were painstakingly reoriented to the south. Meanwhile, in Kufa, the west-facing *qibla* was carefully angled in an identical direction.[33] The House of God no longer seemed to stand where it had previously—between Medina and Palestine. Rather, if the calculations of the mosque renovators were to be trusted, it lay much further to the south, at a site in the depths of the Hijaz. A site that can only have been the one place: Mecca.

Naturally, such a change did not go unnoted. There were opponents of Abd al-Malik, a full sixty years on, who still damned him as the man who had "destroyed the sacred House of God."[34] Already, however, even in the immediate aftermath of his conquest of Arabia, confusion as to what might actually have happened, and what constituted "the sacred House of God," was rife, and escalating. Umayyad propagandists, while not denying the destruction wrought by Al-Hajjaj, insisted that the true vandal had been Ibn al-Zubayr, and that Abd al-Malik had merely restored the *Ka'ba* to its original, pristine condition. Few Arabs thought to dispute this claim: the conviction that a sanctuary might be demolished and reconstructed, not once but several times, and still somehow remain numinously the same, was widely held. In due course, Abd al-Malik and Ibn al-Zubayr would take their places on a long list of people who had supposedly either repaired the House of God or rebuilt it from scratch: luminaries as heavyweight as Muhammad, Abraham and Adam. The future of the *Ka'ba* was one that would see it enshrined as both a marker of Adam's tomb and the pivot of the cosmos itself. If there was an echo, in this sensational array of attributes, of the traditions that Christians, in the wake of Helena's discovery of the True Cross, had attributed to the rock of Golgotha, then that was surely no coincidence. Just as it had taken Constantine to establish, once and for all, the site of Jesus's crucifixion, so likewise, perhaps, had it needed a ruler such as Abd al-Malik—an autocrat no less visionary, self-confident or domineering—to define for his own religion the eternal heartbeat of the world.

None of which, of course, solves the mystery of why an obscure and barren spot a thousand miles from the centre of Umayyad power should have been chosen for such an honour. Clearly, though, Abd al-Malik must have had reasons that far transcended the merely opportunistic. Just as he would never have promoted Muhammad as the founder of his religion without truly believing that the Prophet had been an authentic medium for the words of God, so would he never have gone on pilgrimage to a site that lacked any aura of the sacred. Long before his arrival there, a *Ka'ba* must surely have stood on the spot. Perhaps, like the one at Bakka, it also had some association with Muhammad. If not, then the Umayyads would certainly have had both motive and opportunity for promoting it as the shrine named in the Prophet's revelations as Mecca. Mu'awiya, based as he had been throughout his reign in Syria, had made a conscious effort to tighten his grip on Arabia. Any plot of land capable of supporting crops had been ruthlessly appropriated; its water supplies diverted; its settlements commandeered. In Medina, the intrusion of Umayyad henchmen into the oasis had only compounded the family's unpopularity and precipitated Ibn al-Zubayr's coup. But further south, in the Hijaz, the policy had reaped notably greater success. Indeed, Mu'awiya's investment in the region had been so substantial that its summer capital, a flourishing oasis named Ta'if, was said to have migrated there from Palestine. Abd al-Malik's links to the town were probably even closer. Not only had his father, Marwan, served as its governor, but his most trusted lieutenant, Al-Hajjaj, had grown up in the oasis. Both, then, would surely have been intimately familiar with the shrine that stood a mere sixty miles to the north-west, behind a wall of wind-scoured, black-baked mountain, and which Abd al-Malik himself, in 694, made a point of honouring as the House of God: the shrine that posterity would commemorate as the *Ka'ba* of Mecca.

So it was that a second sanctuary—paired with the Dome of the Rock—came to be enshrined once and for all as a fit object of pilgrimage for the faithful. This much seems clear enough. Beyond that, however, everything is obscurity and murk. Was Abd al-Malik the first *Amir* to renovate the site, or did he follow in the footsteps of Ibn al-Zubayr? Where had the sanctuary demolished by Al-Hajjaj stood—

at Bakka or at Mecca? What had it been more important for the victor to establish—continuity with the past or a clean break? Certainly, more than a century after the time of Abd al-Malik, a vague sense still lingered that the House of God might not always have stood rooted to the spot in Mecca. "At the time of the Prophet, may God save him and give him peace, our faces were all turned in one direction—but after the death of the Prophet, we turned ourselves hither and thither."[35] So one Muslim scholar would recall. Others, in the reports given of Mecca itself, might betray similar anxieties. It was not only the *Ka'ba*, in these stories, that was forever being demolished and rebuilt—so too was the mosque that enclosed it. A sacred well was lost and then miraculously rediscovered on no less than two separate occasions. Most bewildering of all, perhaps, was the sheer range of sacred stones associated with the holy site, and which were forever being shifted or discovered. There was the *Maqam Ibrahim*, for instance, which had been carried along by a flood. Then there was the rock uncovered by Ibn al-Zubayr, and which had been stamped with the name of God. Finally, and perhaps most enigmatically of all, there was the much-venerated "Black Stone," which enjoyed a prominent position in the wall of the *Ka'ba*. Some claimed that Adam had found it, whereupon it had gobbled up the parchment on which was written his contract with God. Others insisted that it was Abraham who had excavated it, and that he and Ishmael had then lugged it all the way to Mecca. Still others claimed that Ibn al-Zubayr had placed it in an ark, of the kind used by Moses to transport the Torah around the desert. The Black Stone, it seemed, was not only fabulously ancient—it was surprisingly mobile as well.

And as such, hardly unique. For any ruler who wished to veil the parvenu status of a recent foundation behind a sheen of class, a talisman like the Black Stone had long been an essential prerequisite. Antiquity, after all, spelled class. This was why Constantine—if the story that had him pilfering the Palladium from Rome were to be trusted—had brought to his upstart capital a touch of antique Troy. It was also why the *mowbeds*, back in the reign of Peroz, had no sooner lit the Fire of the Stallion amid the desolate peaks of Media, than they were insisting that its flames were, in fact, eternal and had originally roamed the world. The claim, within a mere couple of generations, had worked a spectacular magic. Zoroastrians appalled by Heraclius's destruction of the Temple had certainly had no idea that it might have been in existence for a mere century and a half. The past attributed to a sanctuary, especially if a lonely one, might bear witness, not to the preservation of authentic customs, of authentic traditions, of authentic memories, but to the polar opposite: bold innovation.

And certainly, in his determination to shape the world as he saw fit, Abd al-Malik was nothing if not a revolutionary. Even before his final victory over Ibn al-Zubayr, he had been plotting how to stamp his vast empire as he had already stamped Jerusalem: as hallowed by the authentic religion of God. In 691, the coins that had given Arculf the reassuring delusion that Palestine still belonged to a Christian order had been re-minted with images that owed nothing to Constantinople: a spear in a prayer niche, Abd al-Malik himself girt with a whip. Meanwhile, in Iraq, a matching programme of reform saw the erasure from the coinage of every last trace of the House of Sasan. Nothing or no one was permitted to obstruct this policy. All the coins were to be standardised, and all were to promote the authority of Abd al-Malik's new religion. "Long have you pursued a course of faction and followed the path of waywardness—but now, by God, I will beat you as one does a camel not of the herd at the watering-hole."[36] So thundered Al-Hajjaj, following his appointment to the governorship of Iraq in 694. The warning was issued to a crowd of rebellious Basrans, but it might as well have been delivered to the Greek- and Persian-speaking elites. Unsettling though they had found Abd al-Malik's initial reforms, far worse was brewing. An even more outright declaration of war against the past was about to be delivered. In 696, a radically new style of coin began to be minted, one that featured no images at all, but only writing—and Arabic writing, at that. Nothing, to bureaucrats long accustomed to regard the language as a marker of barbarism, could possibly have been more shocking. The world, however, as Abd al-Malik did not stint in emphasising, had been turned upside down. Coins were not the only expression of the new linguistic dispensation. So too were passports, and tax returns, and contracts, and laws, and receipts: everything, in short, that made for the running of a global empire.

To functionaries who suddenly found themselves with no prospect of employment unless they spoke or wrote in their master's language, this was an upheaval that shook the foundations of their entire world. To Abd al-Malik himself, of course, it was something much more. Arabic, in his devout opinion, was the proper language of empire because it was also the language of God. Adorning the walls of the Dome of the Rock, fashioned out of cubes of brilliant gold, inscriptions proclaimed the core tenets of the *Amir*'s faith: the prophethood of Muhammad, and the sheer folly of believing, as did the Christians in their blindness, that God might conceivably be Three. Much of what was written consisted of excerpts patched together from the Prophet's own revelations: the earliest surviving examples of phrases from the Qur'an. Posterity would claim that it was Uthman, decades previously, who had first collected and pieced these together, to compile what was from that moment on a fully formed scripture—but the snatches of verse patched together by Abd al-Malik on the Dome of the Rock suggest something rather different. So too, of course, does the resounding lack of even a single Qur'anic inscription dating from the reigns of his predecessors; and so too do the scattered hints from contemporaries. Christian scholars, noting for the first time the existence of writings attributed to Muhammad, described them not as a single book but rather as a jumble of fragments with such titles as "The Cow," "The Woman" and "God's She-Camel."* If true, then

---

* A monk in Iraq, writing in the early eighth century, alludes to a "Qur'an" but also to other writings by Muhammad, including a "Book of the Cow." John of Damascus, a high-ranking civil servant in the last years of Abd al-Malik's reign who took a deep interest in his master's faith, also refers to a "Book" composed by Muhammad, together with various other texts that had supposedly been written by him. "The Cow" ended up as the title of a sura in the Qur'an; "The Woman" seems to be the same text as the sura that appears under the title "Women" in the Qur'an; "God's She-Camel," despite scattered references throughout the holy book to such a beast, bears no resemblance to any existing Qur'anic sura.

who might have been tracking down these various scraps of text, and piecing them together? Certainly, that Abd al-Malik's reign had indeed seen the Qur'an subjected to a state-sponsored makeover was something that no Muslim scholar would subsequently think to deny. In the vanguard of this editing process, as of so much else, was Al-Hajjaj. Peerless warrior, formidable governor, he would also enjoy a splendid posthumous reputation as a proof-reader of the Qur'an. Some traditions, however, would ascribe to him a role infinitely more intriguing. Rejecting the presumption that God, in the wake of Muhammad's death, no longer permitted His purposes to be known through the agency of mortals, Al-Hajjaj is said to have retorted, "I work only by inspiration!"[37] Ever the loyal servant, though, he always emphasised that his own role in collecting, collating and distributing the revelations of Muhammad—heaven-sanctioned though it might be—was as nothing compared to that of Abd al-Malik. In fact, so Al-Hajjaj declared flatly, his master "stood higher in God's view than did the angels and prophets."[38]

An opinion that the Commander of the Faithful himself, never a great one for modesty, did not think to dispute. The age of the prophets might have ended—but that did not mean, in the opinion of Abd al-Malik, that God had no further need of a chosen agent on earth. Deploying his favourite medium of coinage, he made sure to broadcast to the world precisely how he saw his role: as the *Khalifat Allah*, or "Deputy of God." Just as Muhammad had been chosen to reveal the divine word, Abd al-Malik had been appointed to interpret it and broadcast it to humanity—and who was to say which one had been allotted the graver responsibility? Certainly, the title of "Caliph"—introduced to the public gaze for the first time by Abd al-Malik's agents in the imperial mints—implied a dominance over realms that were no less supernatural than earthly. If it was upon the command of Abd al-Malik that roads were built and dams constructed, then it was also through his person that people might "pray for rain."[39] Formidably though his warriors stood guard upon the frontiers of the empire, yet they were not so formidable as the Caliph himself, who stood guard upon the highway that led to heaven. A "beater of skulls," he was also the ultimate "*imam* of guidance."[40]

These vaunting claims were not mere idle propaganda. The breathtaking scope of Abd al-Malik's ambition was matched only by the sheer drive and creative brilliance with which he sought to fulfil it. By the time of his death in 705, a ramshackle patchwork of conquests that only two decades previously had been on the verge of utter disintegration had been reconstituted as a state no less brutally efficient than had been its toppled predecessors. Even more awesomely, it had been consecrated to a vision of the due owed by humanity to the divine that brooked very little contradiction. "Religion, in God's eyes, is submission."[41] So Muhammad had declared. Featured on the Dome of the Rock, however, the meaning of the verse had been subtly altered. The "submission" demanded by God had come almost to serve as a proper noun. The faith proclaimed by Abd al-Malik, lord of an empire that reached from the rising to the setting of the sun, had been given a name. The slogan stamped on the Dome of the Rock had become one fit for the entire world.

"Religion, in God's eyes," so it declared, "is *Islam*."

Sunna-*Side up*

An ancient city, like a battle-scarred veteran, might often wear the marks of long-concluded wars. In Syria, no city was more ancient than Damascus. Indeed, the fame of its delights—from its climate to its plums—reached so far back in time that there were some rabbis prepared to rank it as a gateway to paradise. A whole century after its conquest by the Arabs, and four centuries after the reign of Constantine, Damascus had still not sloughed off every last mark of its pagan past. High and massive above the sprawl of the teeming markets, there loomed the walls of what might have seemed, to the first-time visitor, a particularly brooding citadel, but was in truth the outer shell of what had once been the city's most domineering temple.

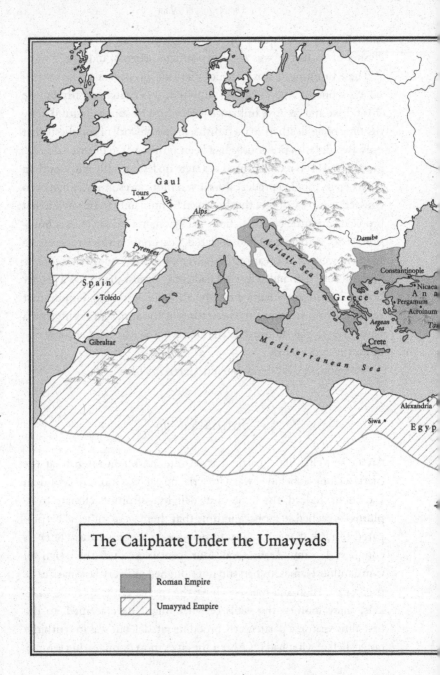

The Caliphate Under the Umayyads

Roman Empire

Umayyad Empire

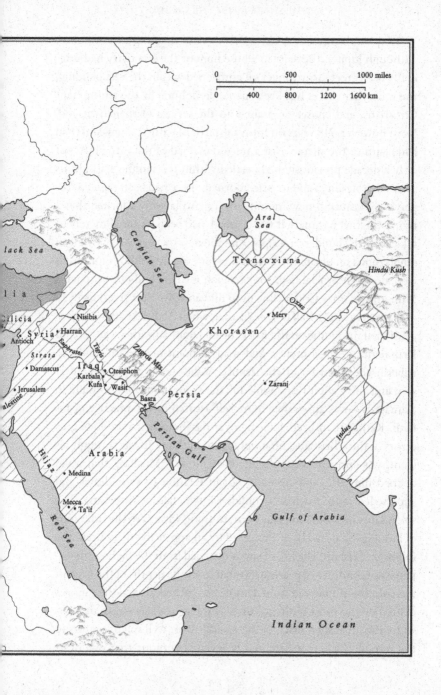

Black Sea

Caspian Sea

Aral Sea

Transoxiana

Hindu Kush

lia

ilicia

Nisibis

Syria

Harran

Antioch

Strata

Damascus

Euphrates

Tigris

Zagros Mts.

Khorasan

Merv

Oxus

Iraq

Ctesiphon

Karbala

Kufa

Wasit

Jerusalem

alestine

Basra

Persia

Zaranj

Indus

Persian Gulf

Hijaz

Arabia

Medina

Red Sea

Mecca

Ta'if

Gulf of Arabia

Indian Ocean

0   500   1000 miles

0   400   800   1200   1600 km

Worship on the site was as old as Damascus itself—and as continuous. Although Jupiter, the deity in whose honour the sanctuary had originally been erected, no longer sat enthroned within the vast building, the walls themselves had been spared demolition by the triumphant Christians, and consecrated anew to the service of their own god. Now, however, 715 years on from the birth of Christ, a new faith had laid claim to the shrine. Not a trace remained of the cathedral that only a decade previously had nestled within the temple walls. In its place, marble-lined and mosaic-adorned, there had been raised a stupefyingly beautiful new monument: one so lavishly adorned that a train of eighteen camels, it was claimed, had been required merely to take away the builders' receipts. And the new owners? An inscription emblazoned on one of the walls left no one in any doubt. "Our lord is God alone," it proclaimed, "our religion is Islam, and our prophet is Muhammad, may God incline unto him and give him greeting."[42]

A bare two and a half decades earlier, when Abd al-Malik had commissioned the Dome on the Rock, he had done so with a wary eye on Jerusalem's great churches, and made a point of using its walls to rubbish the doctrine of the Trinity. Walid—Abd al-Malik's eldest son, and the Caliph responsible for the sumptuous new mosque in Damascus—was altogether more self-assured in the practice of his faith. Rather than keep glancing over his shoulder at the ludicrous errors of the Christians, he simply ignored them. It was through his identity as someone who submitted to God, as a "Muslim," that Walid defined himself—and certainly not in relation to some lesser and superseded faith. Such self-confidence was hardly surprising. The splendours of Walid's mosque bore stunning witness to the full range of blessings that had been showered by an approving deity upon the followers of Islam. The fire of jewels quarried from the highest mountains, the shimmer of pearls harvested from the depths of the oceans, the columns plundered from demolished cathedrals and the mosaics crafted by the most brilliant artists of the age: all served to demonstrate the unrivalled reach of the *Khalifat Allah*. Well might visitors to the mosque have reported, and believed, a rumour that one of its pillars had been fashioned out of the "magnificent throne"[43] of the Queen of Sheba. Just as Islam contained within itself all that was best and most noble in other faiths, the great mosque of Damascus enclosed within its towering walls any number of treasures garnered from vanished dominions: detritus reconfigured in the cause of a new and universal empire.

"There is hardly a tree or a notable town that has not been pictured on those walls."[44] So wrote one admirer, in the assurance that the images he could see portrayed on them, from winged plants to hippodromes, were nothing if not a reflection of the many lands—extending infinitely beyond Damascus—that had been brought beneath the sway of Islam. By 715, when Walid declared his great mosque open, Arab armies had long since swept far beyond the limits of the crumbled empires ruled from Ctesiphon and the New Rome. In the East, they had advanced into the one-time kingdom of the Hephthalites, passing not only the abandoned red wall of Gurgan but an even mightier barrier, the River Oxus: a natural frontier so immense and fast flowing that the Arabs would come to define the whole vastness of Central Asia simply as "Transoxania." Meanwhile, in the West, with Carthage and the long coastal strip of North Africa already subdued, they had crossed the sea in pursuit of fresh conquests. In 711, a tiny Arab raiding party had landed on Gibraltar. Within the course of only a few months, this venturesome war band had succeeded in defeating the Visigoths in battle, killing their king and seizing their capital of Toledo, deep in the vitals of Spain. An achievement such as this, secured on the outermost edge of the world, appeared so astounding to the Arabs as to verge on the fantastical. Stories of the conquest, told back in Damascus, cast Spain as a land of mysteries and wonders, where statues spoke, locked rooms contained miraculous visions of the future, and cities were made of bronze. So astounding had the scope of Arab triumphs become that they no longer seemed wholly real.

Which said, the proofs of Muslim conquests were a simple enough matter for anyone in Damascus to track down. Leave behind the courtyard of Walid's mosque, with its gleaming marble and delicately ornamented fountains, and there in the city's markets, penned amid their own filth and misery, were to be found human cattle corralled from every corner of the world. The stories told of Spain might have been conjured from a realm of fantasy—but not so the coffle of thirty thousand prisoners brought back to Syria by the conquerors of the Visigoths. Nothing had served more violently to rub the noses of the vanquished in the brute fact of the Arabs' might than the depredations of their slavers. "Annually," one monk recorded, "their robber bands went to distant parts and to the islands, bringing back captives from all the peoples under the heavens."[45] Of course, there was nothing particularly novel about this expression of superpower status. The Romans had never shown the slightest hesitation in selling off inveterate rebels such as the Samaritans, while the presumptions governing the Persians' treatment of their prisoners-of-war had been evident in the fact that *ansahrig*—their word for "slave"—had originally meant "foreigner." Now, though, the boot was very much on the other foot. Wretches harvested from the former provinces of the Christian empire toiled on the estates or in the mines of great Arab landowners—and although it was not unknown for the odd prayer to be heard, and the occasional slave-driver to be felled by some miraculous act of the Virgin Mary, most could only lament that they had been abandoned by the heavens. "Why does God allow this to happen?":[46] such was the cry that had gone up back in the time of Umar, when a band of Arab slavers had raided a festival held in the hills outside Antioch in celebration of Saint Simeon's sojourn on his pillar. It was not only Christians who might ask the question. The terrible violence that marked the conquest of the Sasanian heartlands had seen the markets of Kufa and Basra flooded with a quite staggering number of Persian captives, while even on the easternmost frontiers of Iran— where Arab control was altogether more precarious—a tribute of slaves was the very least that might be demanded by the conquerors. Typical was the fate of Zaranj, a great fortress that commanded the approaches to the Hindu Kush, whose inhabitants had agreed as a term of their surrender to deliver annually a thousand of their most beautiful boys, each one holding in his hands a golden cup: a delicious foretaste for pious Muslims of the delights of paradise.

Like the blades of a giant plough, then, the Arab armies sliced apart families, scattered communities far and wide, churned up and mingled peoples who might otherwise never have met. Not since the first coming of Rome to the Near East eight hundred years earlier, when the conquest of the region by the legions had reputedly seen ten thousand slaves sold daily in a single entrepôt, had there been transplantation of human livestock on anything like such a scale. Naturally, for the Arabs themselves, there was peril as well as profit in this trade. Just as Italy, back in the distant days of the Roman Republic, had repeatedly been racked by slave revolts, so too, in times of *fitna*, had the heartlands of the Caliphate. Amid the chaos that followed the death of Mu'awiya, for instance, an army of prisoners-of-war had broken free and made a stronghold of Nisibis, so that "dread came upon all the Arabs."[47] Nor dread alone—spluttering indignation as well. "Our slaves are rebelling against us!" So the warlords of Kufa had exclaimed in outrage. "But they are our booty—granted us by God!"[48]

To the rebels themselves, however, it was far from self-evident that God did intend them to rank as booty. Presumptions that had underpinned the Roman slave trade back in its heyday were not all they once had been. Over the course of the centuries, callousness had grown ever less innocent. Among Christians, for instance, in an empire that had learned to take seriously Saint Paul's injunction that there was neither slave nor free in Christ, the habit of regarding human chattels as mere walking machines had become increasingly problematic. "If God does not enslave what is free," as one bishop sternly enquired of his slave-owning flock, "then who is he that sets his own power above God's?"[49] In *Iranshahr* too, the communism preached by Mazdak had anticipated a golden age of universal brotherhood, when every class, so it was trusted, would be as one. It was true, of course, that Mazdak's followers had ended up buried head-first in Khusrow's flower-beds, and true as well that most Christian scholars, although they certainly regarded slavery as a damnable thing, tended to presume that it would endure until the end of days. Nevertheless, the logic of a faith that claimed all human beings, without exception, to have been created by a loving God ensured that increasingly, in pious Christian circles, the freeing of slaves was regarded less as charity than as a pressing obligation. Similarly, dutiful Muslims—if they only paid close attention to the awesome conception of their responsibilities as articulated by the Prophet—could hardly dispute that even the very lowest of the low might be a brother. "What will explain to you what the steep path is?" So Muhammad—slave-owner though he reputedly was himself—had demanded of his followers, before supplying his own answer. "It is to free a slave, to feed at a time of hunger an orphaned relative or a poor person in distress, and to be one of those who believe and urge one another to steadfastness and compassion."[50]

Which was all very well—except that there were plenty of Arabs who had not the slightest intention of sharing their god with foreigners. Right from the earliest days of their empire, they had been all too painfully aware of the danger of being swallowed up by the vast, amorphous mass of their subjects. This was why, in Iraq, they had founded entirely new cities on the margins of the desert, and it was why, in Syria and Palestine—where the Arabs had opted to settle directly among the natives—they had introduced a whole host of petty regulations in order to establish clear water between themselves and their inferiors. Christians, to their horror, found themselves subjected to laws originally designed by the Roman authorities to keep Jews in their place. Forbidden as they were to dress or speak like Arabs, to sit in the presence of an Arab, to wear swords or to ride on a saddle, the chasm of difference that separated them from their overlords could hardly have been more humiliatingly emphasised.[51] "It was God who made you inherit their lands, their homes and their wealth."[52] So Muhammad had assured his followers. Well, then, might the Arabs, living off the fat of their conquests and revelling in their possession of a God-granted empire, have been protective of their winnings. Much, after all, was potentially on offer to those who could legitimately claim a descent from Ishmael. A couple of generations on from the defeat of the perfumed Romans and Persians, the taste for luxury of some Arabs would have given Umar apoplexy. Anxious though they were to differentiate themselves from the common run of their subject peoples, they did not have the slightest hesitation in aping the manners of the toppled ruling classes. In Syria, the furnishings of high-end properties owed nothing to Medina and everything to the Roman relish for wine, nude sculptures and mosaics. In Iraq, the peacock tastes of the Persian aristocracy were enthusiastically adopted by wealthy Arab warlords, who delighted in parading through the streets of Kufa or Basra arrayed in silken flares and shimmering robes of many colours, with their beards dyed a startling shade of yellow or red. Who, then, were the foreign slaves who escorted them on such processions, or kept their golden goblets polished back in their palaces, or toiled in chains on their fields, to imagine that they too might have a stake in such an inheritance?

Yet, in truth, any prospect of fashioning for the Arabs a religion comparable to that of the Jews—a legacy of faith borne on the bloodline of Abraham—had already long since been dissolved upon the swirl and clamour of their dazzling conquests. When Al-Hajjaj, in 702, founded a new city named Wasit to stand sentinel between Kufa and Basra, and posted guards upon its gates, to ensure that only Arabs could settle there, he was closing the doors of a stable from which the horse had long since bolted. How could there be any prospect of affirming the purity of an Ishmaelite descent when the streets of Wasit, and of every other garrison city too, were filled with slaves uprooted from every corner of the world, deprived of their families, their homes, their native lands, and with no consolation save the glimpse of heaven provided them by the faith of their masters? These captives were not only to be found in the streets: they were in the conquerors' bedrooms, too. The right to sleep with "such slaves as God has assigned to you as war-booty"[53] was one that Muslims could enjoy on the say-so of the Prophet himself—and plenty of them had duly capitalised upon it with relish. The slave markets of the Caliphate were so glutted with female flesh that wealthy Arabs might debate the various merits of the merchandise as though evaluating the pedigree of bloodstock. Abd al-Malik himself was a noted connoisseur. "He who wishes to take a slave girl for pleasure," the great Caliph sagely advised, "let him take a Berber; he who wishes to take one as a domestic servant, let him take a Roman; and he who wishes to take one to produce a child, let him take a Persian."[54] In Iraq, however, where the markets were particularly well stocked with women plundered from Iran, Persian girls' value was boosted by more than mere fecundity. Daughters from Zoroastrian families, each of whom was expected to kneel three times a day before her husband and humbly beg of him his desires, were famously well conditioned to obedience. At the absolute top end of this market were princesses of the House of Sasan: one raised the fabulous sum of fifty thousand gold pieces, while another, a granddaughter of Khusrow II himself, was installed in a specially built palace in Basra that supposedly had a thousand gates. The children of such mothers, it went without saying, were hardly likely to rest content with a status as the inferiors of anyone.

Nor, when slaves and their offspring looked around them at the insolent pride and squandered riches of their masters, could they fail to prick up their ears at the teachings of the Prophet:

You do not honour the orphan,
Nor urge one another to feed the poor.
You consume an inheritance to the last mouthful,
And you love wealth with a love inordinate.[55]

Here was a vision fit to inspire even the most downtrodden. Slaves might resent their masters, after all, and yet find fuel for that same resentment in the fecund range of their masters' beliefs. The rebels who seized control of Nisibis, for instance, had claimed to be followers of Mukhtar—and they were duly massacred as such. Others sought inspiration in the relish of the *Shi'a* for tyrant-hatred. Then—with the ending of the *fitna* and the great labour of forging performed by Abd al-Malik upon the half-fashioned doctrines and recollections of the Arabs—fresh opportunities for damning those who would scorn the wretched began to present themselves. Inadvertently, by their very public promotion of Muhammad as a Messenger of God, the Umayyads provided those dismissed by the Arab warrior elite with a potent means of opposing their own continued subordination. With the likes of Al-Hajjaj enthroned behind gates and towers like latter-day *Shahanshahs*, those consigned to the stinking slums of Kufa or Basra might ponder the scorn of the Prophet for the arrogant and the over-mighty, and fashion a very different understanding of Islam to that of the Caliph and his lieutenants.

Meanwhile, beyond the ramparts of the great garrison cities of Iraq, others had also begun to observe the religion of the Arabs with a mixture of envy and fascination. After all, the Caliphate's subjects hardly needed to be sold into slavery to feel the sting of their own inferiority. As Arab rule increasingly came to be identified with Abd al-Malik's vision of Islam, so natives eager to join the society of their masters rushed to embrace the embryonic religion. Predictably, the Arabs, far from welcoming these converts as brothers, placed as many roadblocks as they could on the "straight path." Those who wished to convert faced a whole host of indignities. It was not enough to submit to God. Only by submitting to an Arab patron as well might a Persian, or an Iraqi, or a Syrian come to be ranked as a Muslim. Here, for those with so much as a trace of snobbery, was a humiliation, perhaps, too far. Even for those habituated to tutelage, the path to Islam was rarely straightforward. During the reign of Abd al-Malik, for instance, when bands of Iraqi peasants converted *en masse* and took themselves off to the fleshpots of Basra, Al-Hajjaj's response was iron-fisted. Far from delighting in a victory secured for Islam, he rounded up the renegades and returned them to the estates of their masters. Arab rule, as it had ever done, depended on the vanquished knowing their place.

By the time of Walid and his successors, conversions to Islam were coming to threaten not merely the exclusivity of the conquerors but the stability of the tax base. Abd al-Malik's reforms, by transforming the toppled empires' bureaucracies into something more acceptably Arabic, had given their extortions a tone that was increasingly Islamic, too. Taxes were coming to be demanded, not as dues of the kind that conquerors had always levied as a matter of course, but as something subtly different: a fine on unbelief. The Prophet might not have anticipated that his followers would subdue the whole world, but he had still given them helpful tips on how Jews and Christians should properly be exploited. That God wished infidels to pay a poll-tax—the *jizya*—to their Muslim masters, and to feel humiliated while doing so, was recorded in the Qur'an itself, after all. Granted, the precise form that this humiliation should take was something much disputed by commentators. Indeed, it was a mark of just how profoundly the chasm yawned between the compilation of the Prophet's revelations into a single book and the original revelations themselves that the meaning of the Arabic phrase that specified how the *jizya* should be paid had ended up quite forgotten.[56] Fortunately, though, despite the inadequacy of all the frantic efforts to make good this embarrassing amnesia, the underlying message of the verse remained clear enough: Jews and Christians, if they wanted the right to live unmolested, would have to pay for it. Tolerance might be theirs—but only at a price.

Yet in truth, what made this protection racket viable was less the say-so of the Qur'an than presumptions forged over many centuries among Jews and Christians themselves. That the "Peoples of the Book" might be defined as such for taxation purposes was ringing and climactic affirmation of just how successful had been generations of rabbis and bishops in the construction of impregnable barriers around their respective faiths. In Iraq, certainly—where the Sasanian authorities had long categorised their subjects in religious, rather than ethnic, terms—Jews and Christians saw nothing remotely untoward in the weight-throwing of their new Muslim masters. Not, of course, that this made them any the keener to cough up taxes—and Christians, in particular, were often adept at evading them. One bishop in northern Iraq, for instance, managed to secure a tax exemption for his clergy by the dramatic expedient of casting out demons from the local governor's daughters. Meanwhile, a second governor granted rebates to a monastery in the Zagros Mountains after a hermit living there had healed his horse. No Christians, however, nor Jews, ever thought to dispute the right of the Muslim authorities to tax them. Protection, in a world that had repeatedly been trampled down by contending war bands, was usually held to be well worth the price. In general, then, to the Jews and Christians of Iraq, the coming of Islam had represented less a dramatic upheaval than the final institutionalising of what they had always rather assumed was simply the way of the world.

The followers of Zoroaster, however, saw the convulsions of the age in a quite different light. To pious worshippers of Ohrmazd, the collapse of Sasanian power—and the conquest of *Iranshahr*—was a calamity beyond their darkest nightmares. "The faith was ruined and the *Shahanshah* slain like a dog." So, in numbed terms, the catastrophe would always be commemorated by the *mowbed*s. "The world passes from us."[57] Toppled as it had been into the dust from its former position of privilege and power, the Zoroastrian Church would never again enjoy the ear of kings. Instead, denied by the Qur'an even the pallid status enjoyed by rabbis or monks as "Peoples of the Book," the *mowbed*s found their beloved religion of truth and light being treated with brutal contempt.* In the eastern reaches of Iran—where Arab rule was most sketchy and dependent for such authority as it possessed upon treaties signed with still formidable Parthian dynasties such as the Karin—fire temples might continue to blaze as they had ever done; but elsewhere, only payment of extortionate bribes could stave off their demolition. In Iraq, they had fast been obliterated altogether. Their scorched ruins were abandoned to weeds and black ravens: birds of ill-omen that everyone knew were really demons.

Many worshippers of Ohrmazd, witnessing fire temples lost to such

---

* In the long run, a majority of Muslim jurists would decide that Zoroastrians were in fact a "People of the Book."

darkness, found their faith in the Lord of Light mortally shaken. Under the House of Sasan, such apostasy would have been punishable by death; but no longer. Instead, where previously all had been checks and restrictions, Iraq had come to provide, in the first decades following the implosion of Sasanian authority, something that it had not done for centuries: a free market in faiths. So where were the orphaned of Ohrmazd to go? Most, seeking shelter behind the most solid ramparts they could find, had turned in their misery to the Nestorian Church. As a result, Christians, far from being diminished by the Arab conquest of Iraq, rapidly became the majority. Under the strong and paternalistic rule of the Umayyads, they would enjoy a golden age. Across the northern reaches of Iraq, now far removed from the front line with the Romans, churches flourished as never before. Nisibis, especially, blazed with a particular brilliance. The city's scholars, who were as familiar with the classics of Greek philosophy as they were with those of their own faith, soon re-established it as the foremost centre of learning in the entire Fertile Crescent, and far beyond. Meanwhile, outpacing even the advance of the Arab armies, Christian missionaries had begun to fan out from Iraq, treading the roads that stretched eastwards to the fabulous kingdoms of India and China. In time, the head of the Nestorian Church would plan a bishopric "for the peoples of Tibet,"[58] and the nomads of Mongolia adopt a version of the Syriac script. To many Christians, then, it appeared self-evident that the future of Asia belonged to them.

Except that there lay open as well, for bewildered refugees from the Zoroastrian Church, the pathway to a very different faith: one as newly-sprung and as yet unformed as Christianity was venerable and massy of structure. A hundred years on from the Arab conquest, it was a common complaint among the ruling elite of the Caliphate that Zoroastrian converts to Islam "have not become Muslims seriously, but only to escape the poll-tax."[59] But this was sorely to underestimate the appeal of their prophet's revelations. Tax-dodge though conversion certainly provided, yet it might represent as well something very much more. To the troubled, to the heaven-shadowed, to the seeker after truth, the awesome proofs that God had spoken to Muhammad were often irresistible. "Guide us to the straight path: the path of those You have blessed, those who incur no anger and who have not gone astray."[60] How could the one-time *mowbed* who for the first time spoke these words, words that had supposedly proceeded from God Himself, not feel redeemed from the many errors to which his previous faith had been prey? Yet he could know as well, even as he set off along the straight path, that the road ahead still had to be cleared and mapped. The revelations of Muhammad, unlike those of Zoroaster, had been in circulation for barely a century. Among the followers of Islam, there was nothing to compare with the ancient legacy of hymns, commentaries and laws that had descended down the millennia to the Zoroastrian Church. Rather, in the great project of clarifying what precisely the Prophet's message might have been, and the full scope of his intentions, there were roles a-plenty for those, like former *mowbeds*, with an aptitude for scholarship. As a result, in mosques and courtyards across Iraq, converts from the Zoroastrian Church began to join the descendants of the Arabs' slaves, and meet with them in their urgent striving to define what a properly Muslim society should be.

Observing this process with some interest was a rabbi named Rav Yehudai. Living just a short distance from Kufa, in the great Talmudic school of Sura, he was well placed to note an intriguing development. The hearts of those *mowbeds* who had "converted to the religion of the Ishmaelites," so he reported, were still not entirely clear of the trace of their former beliefs, even down to the third generation: "for part of their original religion still remains within them."[61] What evidence might the rabbi have had for making such a claim? Converts from the Zoroastrian Church did often, it was true, bring with them into Islam notions that might have seemed distinctively their own: that apostates should be executed, for instance, or that prayers should be offered up five times a day, or that it was a singular mark of piety to use a toothbrush.* Certainly, there was no direct support in the

---

* The toothbrush was called a *siwak* and comprised a twig of the arak tree.

Qur'an for any of these presumptions: hell, not execution, was the fate that it prescribed for apostates; prayers were mandated, not at five, but "at three times of day";[62] while of toothbrushes there was no mention at all. How strange it might have seemed, then, and how striking a coincidence, that Muslims, when dictating what the penalty for apostasy should be, or how many times a day they should pray, should increasingly have opted to side with Zoroastrian proscriptions and ignore the Qur'an altogether. What was more, they had developed a positive craze for dental hygiene.

"Whenever the Prophet got up at night, he used to clean his mouth with a toothbrush."[63] A most intimate detail—and one fit to gladden the heart of any former *mowbed*, certainly. But how, when some other Zoroastrian convert might simply have made it up, could he, and the Muslim people as a whole, be sure that it was actually true? Such a question was more than mere idle nit-picking. The subjects of Abd al-Malik—who almost overnight had found themselves being informed every time they pulled out a coin or received an official document that Muhammad was the Prophet of God—had not been slow to grasp the implications. Only establish that an opinion had truly been voiced by this same Prophet of God, and it would immediately come to possess the full terrifying force of eternal law. Here, for the restless and ever-growing number of Muslims who were unable to trace their origins back to the first generation of the conquest, who were resentful of the haughty Arab elite and who yearned to fathom the true purposes of God, was a truly golden opportunity. Nevertheless, their way ahead was challenging. Unlike the Caliph, they could hardly claim to be God's deputies, graced by the heavens with a direct responsibility for defining and regulating the Muslim realm. Only by compiling the sayings of the Prophet could they possibly hope to trump the forbidding authority of the *Khalifat Allah*. If a *Sunna*—a body of law capable of taming the extravagances and injustices of the age—were indeed to be fashioned without reference to the Caliph, then its origins would need to be grounded, and very publicly so, in the life and times of the Prophet himself. No other source, no other wellspring, would possibly do. But how to authenticate Muhammad's sayings? Such was the question, a century on from the death of the Prophet, that confronted the first generation of a whole new class of scholars: legal experts whom Muslims would come to know as the *ulama*.

Fortunately for them, just across the mudflats from Kufa—where the yearning to forge a new understanding of Islam was at its most turbulent and intense—the perfect role models were ready to hand. The rabbis of Sura, after all, had been labouring for many centuries to solve precisely the sort of problem that now confronted the *ulama*. The secret Torah, so it was recorded in the Talmud, "had been received at Sinai by Moses, who communicated it to Joshua, who communicated it to the elders, who communicated it to the prophets"[64]—who, in turn, had communicated it to a long line of rabbis, right down to the present. Nowhere in the world, in consequence, were there scholars better qualified to trace the chains of transmission that might link a lawyer and the sayings of a prophet than in the *yeshivas* of Iraq. Was it merely coincidence, then, that the earliest and most influential school of Islamic law should have been founded barely thirty miles from Sura? It was in Kufa, at around the same time as Walid, far distant in Damascus, was building his great mosque, that Muslim scholars first began to explore a momentous proposition: that there existed, alongside the Prophet's written revelations, other, equally binding revelations that had never before been written down. Initially, in the manner of rabbis citing their own masters, members of the *ulama* were content to attribute these hitherto unrecorded doctrines to prominent local experts; then, as time went by, they began to link them to the Prophet's companions; finally, as the ultimate in authorities, they fell to quoting the Prophet himself directly. Always, however, by bringing these previously unrecorded snatches of the past—these *hadiths*—to light, Muslim scholars were following a trail that had been blazed long before. Islamic though the *isnads* were, they were also more than a little Jewish.

The rabbis of Sura and Pumpedita, immured within their famous *yeshiva*s, had spoken of their ambition to "build a fence around the Torah."[65] And so they had done—a thoroughly impregnable one. Yet some of them, hearing as a faint roar the tumult of debate and enquiry that was filling the streets of nearby Kufa, might just have felt a touch of claustrophobia—and even envy. The mosques of Iraq were coming to offer what no synagogue, or church, or fire temple had done for centuries: a venue for enquiry into the nature of God where the terms of debate had not already long since been set in stone. More than that—in the teeming warrens of Kufa and Basra, people from various religious backgrounds were free to meet, and collaborate, and merge their perspectives in a way that had never previously been possible. There were the conquerors: the Arab elite, with their language, their venerable traditions and their burnished memories of the age of Muhammad. Then there were the slaves and the descendants of slaves: all impatient to apply to the wrongs of an unjust society the austere and chilling message of the Prophet. Finally, there were ever-increasing numbers of converts. "Part of their original religion still remains within them." So Rav Yehudai, the rabbi of Sura, had observed of those *mowbed*s who turned to Islam. But what of those Muslims who had once been rabbis—was the same to be observed of them? If so, that would certainly help to explain why the *Sunna*—just like the Torah—aimed to regulate every dimension and aspect of human existence; why it should have forged for itself chains of transmission such as rabbis, and only rabbis, had ever previously deployed; and why, in direct contradiction of the Qur'an, it prescribed death as the punishment for adultery rather than whipping. As it had been written in the Torah by Moses himself: "They shall bring out the young woman to the door of her father's house, and the men of her city shall stone her to death with stones, because she has wrought folly in Israel by playing the harlot in her father's house."*

---

* Deuteronomy: 22–21. In fact, as was invariably their way, the rabbis appended so many qualifications to the biblical proscriptions that they effectively abolished

Such a ruling, once it had been reworked by Muslim lawyers, was no less authoritative for having been garnered from another—and infinitely more ancient—source. Rather, like Walid's great mosque, the *Sunna* was a monument to just what could be achieved by fashioning old fragments into something new and extraordinary. Shards gleaned from the Torah, and from Zoroastrian ritual, and from Persian custom: all featured in the edifice pieced together by the *ulama*. The consequence of their labours, taking on an ever more clearly delineated form as the decades of Umayyad rule slipped by, was a guide to the wishes of God of quite astounding potency: one that even the most chauvinistic governor might learn to ignore at his peril.

Indeed, as a check upon the appetites and arrogance of an imperial elite, it was perhaps the most remarkable that a defeated people has ever devised. The *ulama*, whether descended from prisoners-of-war, or Zoroastrians, or Jews, were overwhelmingly comprised of the victims of the conquest. Yet they had won for themselves, by their collective efforts, a rare and impregnable dignity. It was they, not their ostensible masters, who had become the arbiters of the will of God. The jumble of beliefs and doctrines carried by bands of overwhelmingly illiterate warriors from the desert had been transformed, over the course of barely a century, into a religion of lawyers. Such an achievement, secured in the face of such odds, was a truly astounding one.

Yet it was an achievement as well, by its very nature, that could never be acknowledged. Although the *Sunna* was recognisably a product of its place of birth—a world where legally minded intellectuals, of whatever faith, had long endeavoured to frame God's purposes—it could only ever hope to flourish by denying its roots in such a seedbed. Not a *hadith*, but there was a pressing obligation to derive it from the innermost bowels of Arabia. As a result, there could be no question of doing as the rabbis of the *yeshivas* had done, or the jurists at the court

the death penalty in Jewish society. For instance, it could be enforced only if the adultery had been committed before two valid witnesses, and even then only after multiple warnings had been delivered.

of Justinian, and revelling in the antiquity of the laws that it was their ambition to marshal. Quite the contrary: no matter how venerable a snatch of legal opinion might be, it could never have the force of law unless it had first been demonstrated to have emerged from the lifetime of Muhammad. Consequently, the *Sunna* was founded upon a paradox: the more the *ulama* of Iraq, in their eagerness to fashion a just society, drew upon the incomparable legacy of those who had laboured in a similar cause for millennia, the more did they identify the source of that wisdom with a barren and peripheral desert. Experience of the perfect society, so they taught, had been granted to one single place, and to one single period of history: Medina, in the lifetime of the Prophet. The role of the *Sunna*, and its supreme glory, was to serve the Muslim people as a signpost: one that could point them the way—the *shariah*—back to paradise lost.

And yet the way to paradise already had its guardians, of course. To the Umayyads the pretensions of the *ulama* constituted something altogether more menacing than a simple affront. What role, if the Prophet were to end up enshrined as the ultimate authority for the Muslim people, did this conceivably leave for the rival claims of the Caliph? Much, of course, was at stake. It was not merely the right of Abd al-Malik and his heirs to their privileged status as "deputies of God" that risked being undermined. The entire legitimacy of their regime was grievously threatened too. Cast the Prophet as the only acceptable wellspring for Islam, after all, and everything that had followed him was bound to seem a decline and fall. Indeed, how could the empire ruled from Damascus, when compared to the seductive vision of a primal and unspotted Islamic state, not appear a tyranny? The Umayyads risked appearing, not as the bulwarks and sponsors of Islam but as the opposite: deviants and usurpers, blotting the purity of the *Sunna*.

The Caliph and the lawyers, then, for all that they might not initially have realised it, were locked in mortal conflict. At stake was not merely the shape of the future but how the past would come to look as well. In the great and ongoing struggle between autocrats and clerics for God's favour, one that long pre-dated both Caliphate and *ulama*, a new and potentially decisive battle had been joined.

The nature of Islam itself, and much more besides, would hang upon its outcome.

The House of Islam

If the Umayyads found it hard to take the pretensions of uppity scholars seriously, then this was in part at least because a succession of Caliphs had their gaze fixed on an adversary that appeared altogether worthier of their attentions. Although Damascus stood at the heart of a mighty empire, it was only a few days' ride from what Muslims termed *al-dawahi*—"the outer realm." Venturing north from the Syrian heartlands, which by now had grown fat and prosperous under Umayyad rule, the road might seem to be leading the traveller back in time, to an age when Muhammad's followers had ranked not as citified civilians, but as tireless warriors—Muhajirun. In Antioch, emigrants from across the Caliphate might still be seen riding on wiry ponies past the crumbling remains of great palaces and churches, embarked for the murderous badlands that marked the frontier with the empire of *Qaysar*—Caesar.

It was the Romans themselves who had first put the region to the torch. The ruin inflicted by Heraclius on his retreat north-westwards from Antioch had been ruthless and desperate in equal measure. Hunkering down behind a particularly forbidding range of mountains, the Taurus, the defeated emperor had made a deliberate effort to establish a *cordon sanitaire* between himself and the Syrian frontier. Almost a hundred years on, and the once-prosperous province of Cilicia—as the coastal lowlands were known—was a weed-choked and corpse-littered wilderness: the most dangerous place on earth. The very wildlife had turned carnivorous. Lions, descending from their customary haunts in the mountains, had taken to lying in ambush for human prey in overgrown marshes and fields. Not even an innovative attempt by Walid to trample down such hideaways through the introduction of Indian water buffalo had served to neutralise the menace. Bad news for the harried locals, to be sure—but not for visiting ascetics. To any Muslim scornful of idle pleasures, and with an appetite for hardship, the killing fields of Cilicia were close to paradise. *Zuhhad*, the Arabs termed such warriors: men who aimed to glimpse the dimension of the heavenly through a renunciation of the world.

A venerable ambition, of course. The *Zuhhad* themselves tended to look back to the heroic figure of Umar for their readiest role model— but in truth the wellsprings of their inspiration rose much further back in time, in the spectacular feats of self-mortification practised by those warriors of Christ, the monks. Between the stylite who consecrated his gangrenous flesh to worms and the Mujahid who willingly courted frostbite by raiding the villages of the Taurus throughout the bitter depths of winter, the differences were less of quality than of kind. That this was so might be perfectly evident to both monks and Muslims themselves. One traveller, happening to meet with a Christian hermit, and marking how his eyes were puffy from weeping, asked him the reason for his tears. "Because the hour of my death is fast approaching," the monk replied, "and I still have far to go." Some time later, when the traveller passed the monk's cell again and saw that it was empty, he asked where the monk had gone. "He had become a Muslim," came the answer, "and gone raiding, and been killed in the lands of the Romans."[66]

A telling anecdote—and all the more so for having been founded upon an astounding reversal of fortunes. Back in the heyday of the Christian empire, it was the desert, the realm of the Arabs, that had provided ascetics with the wilderness most appropriate to their ambitions—but now, in the age of the Caliphate, it was the Christian empire itself. That Cilicia had become a nightmarish realm of abandoned cities, blackened fields and mosquito-clouded swamps went without saying; but even beyond the Taurus, across the rump of what had once been the universal empire of the Romans, decay and impoverishment were rife. Muslim war bands, whenever they succeeded in breaking through the mountain passes, would make a point of plundering and destroying all they could—but found themselves hamstrung, as they would often grumble, by the lack of portable wealth. "Rich cities are few in their kingdom and country, despite its situation, size, and the antiquity of their rule." So one Muslim, anatomising the Romans, sniffed. "This is because most of it consists of mountains, castles, fortresses, cave dwellings and villages dug out of the rock or buried under the earth."[67] The world had been turned upside down. A people who had once disdained the Arabs as wolves were now, thanks to Muslim prowess, reduced themselves to living like hunted beasts—whether by clinging to the tops of mountains, or else by burrowing deep underground.

Yet it did not do to scorn the "*Rum*" out of hand. Dread of their power remained something visceral in many Arabs: a foreboding that the Romans, given even the sniff of a chance, might descend upon Kufa and "flatten it like a leather skin."[68] Stretched almost to breaking point though they were, and despite almost a century of unrelenting pressure, they had refused to give way. Still, albeit with bleeding fingertips, they clung on to their empire's status as a great power. Such an achievement, secured with such indomitability, and in the face of such odds, had owed much to the Romans' own courage and resolve—but even more to their inheritance from the past. There were officers stationed in the wilds of the Taurus who still bore Latin titles and commanded regiments that could trace their origins back to the time of Constantine. There were engineers, and architects, and shipwrights, trained in the skills that had been honed when the New Rome had stood at the pinnacle of her power, who could still provide her with a technological edge. Above all, across the span of the shrunken empire, there were Christians everywhere, from the heights of the imperial palace down to the most flea-bitten hamlet, who took for granted that they remained a people chosen of God. The loss of the southern provinces, calamitous though it had been, had at least served to shear the New Rome of any number of troublesome heretics: Monophysites, and Samaritans, and Jews. At long last, in the teeth of all its troubles, the empire had become precisely what Justinian had always dreamed that it might be: impregnably orthodox.

Roman and Arab alike, then, were united in the one conviction: that the future of the world would be decided by the fate of Constantinople. And very possibly of the entire universe as well. Although certainly an incomparable strategic prize—the key to all the former and present lands of Rome's ancient empire—the city's ultimate significance was as the stage for an altogether more cosmic drama. Among Christians, the inevitable failure of a great Ishmaelite assault upon the Roman capital was confidently expected to herald the coming of the last and greatest Caesar of them all: a conqueror who would triumph over the Arabs even more heroically than Heraclius had done over Khusrow, recapture Jerusalem and usher in the return of Christ. Among Muslims, it was the capture of Constantinople that was expected to presage the End Days. Nevertheless, they could not help but be haunted by a dread that time might be running out for them. Just like the Romans, they anticipated the coming of a mighty Caesar; but as a nightmare. A prince would be born in Constantinople who would grow as fast in one day as a normal child grows in a year; when he was twelve, he would launch a devastating war of reconquest: his fleets and armies would spread ruin across the Caliphate. The more that *hadiths* expressing this alarming prospect spread, the more urgent it seemed to foreclose it once and for all. The continued existence of a Christian empire was a menace patently not to be borne. The gaze of the Umayyads, as it had not done since the time of Mu'awiya, began to turn upon *al-Qustantiniyya* itself.

By 715, when Walid was succeeded as Caliph by his brother, Suleiman, it was evident that the hammer blow would not be long in falling. In Cilicia, brutal campaigning temporarily cleared the Taurus of Roman garrisons, while in Syria, freshly minted *hadiths* proclaimed "the name of the Caliph destined to take Constantinople to be the name of a prophet."[69] Not that Suleiman, despite sharing his name with the fabled king who had built the Temple in Jerusalem and married the Queen of Sheba, intended to lead the campaign in person. In

716, when a mighty task force smashed its way through the mountain passes and advanced towards the Aegean, its commander was yet another of Abd al-Malik's sons: a seasoned *Rum*-fighter by the name of Maslama. Effective generalship and sheer weight of numbers combined to devastating effect. The Roman high command proved helpless in the face of the invasion. Those in the path of the Arab juggernaut found themselves with no recourse save for appeals to the supernatural. Most raised their prayers to heaven; but some, in their desperation, turned to hell. At Pergamum, an ancient city just north of Ephesus, the sight of Maslama's army camped outside the walls reduced the citizens to such terror that a necromancer was able to persuade them to slice open the belly of a pregnant woman, boil her foetus, and then dip their sleeves in the resulting casserole. The spell proved signally ineffective. Maslama stormed Pergamum, ransacked it, and converted it into winter quarters for his army. Then, with the coming of spring, the invaders continued their advance. When they reached the straits directly opposite Europe, the Arab fleet, freshly arrived from Cilicia for the purpose, ferried them to the far shore. Nothing now stood between Maslama and the Roman capital, that abiding object of all his dynasty's fondest dreams. In mid-summer, guards on the walls of Constantinople were able to mark a haze of darkness spreading towards them from the western horizon, as fields and villages were burned, and dusty roads were trampled by a great multitude of marching feet. Then Arab outriders began to appear, approaching the landward bulwarks of the New Rome, and ships from Maslama's fleet, churning the waters directly below the great palace of the Caesars. By 15 August, the encirclement was complete: Constantinople was besieged, enclosed in a ring of foes.

Well might her citizens have offered up desperate prayers. Almost a century had passed since the Persians and the Avars had appeared before the city's walls, and in that time the calamities that had afflicted the empire had hardly spared the capital itself. Her former greatness now seemed to hang loose about her, like a giant's robe on a dwarfish thief. Harbours once crowded with colossal grain ships had contracted to a quarter of their former size; beneath the triumphal column where ambassadors had once been greeted with splendid and awful ceremonial a pig market now stood; entire stretches of the city consisted of nothing but farmland interspersed with ruins, from which masonry would periodically crash. Yet even if much in the great city had crumbled, so equally much had not. The Hippodrome, the imperial palace and Hagia Sophia: all endured. Above all, monuments to an age when the New Rome's resources had truly matched her pretensions, there loomed the giant walls of Theodosius, and which now, once again, proved their impregnable worth. Nor, as the Arab sea captains would soon find out to their horror, had the Romans permitted their primordial habits of attack to atrophy either. The sheer scale of Maslama's navy, its vast expanse of timbers, rendered it mortally vulnerable to a counter-strike. In the still of late summer, with the Bosphorus glassy calm, the Arab war fleet sought to force the city's sea walls: a fatal error. The Romans, launching their own ships from the Golden Horn, unleashed the deadliest weapon at their command: fire. Blazing hulks crashed into the Arab fleet and sent flames dancing across the great forest of masts, while smaller ships, armed with siphons, sprayed viscous oil so miraculous and terrifying in its effects that sailors continued to burn from its touch even as they screamed and tore at themselves on the boiling waves. *Hygron pyr*, this devastating invention was called: "liquid fire." That the secret had been brought to Constantinople a few decades earlier by an architect called Callinicos did not obscure for the city's defenders, as they watched the blazing Arab ships sink, or else drift helplessly into one another or out to sea, its ultimate derivation. Clearly, it was God who had shattered all the invaders' plans—"at the intercession of His wholly chaste Mother."[70]

Nor was the Virgin done yet. Calamity after calamity struck at the besiegers. Some of these—the thick snow that covered the Arab camp during the winter, the famine and plague that afflicted it during the summer—clearly derived from the prayers of the Christian people; but so too, they knew in their souls, did the many triumphs of their agents. When Coptic squadrons from the Arab fleet were persuaded to desert, or when barbarians from the north were bribed to attack Maslama's land forces, the dramatic success of these various gambits seemed to the defenders to bear striking witness to the favour of the heavens. By the summer of 717, after a siege of almost a year, it was evident that the Arab attempt on Constantinople had failed. In Syria, Suleiman was already dead, and the new Caliph, cutting his losses, ordered the expedition to withdraw. Maslama, even though his missives home had been growing ever more cheery as the situation worsened, was left with no choice but to obey. The retreat, afflicted as it was by devastating storms at sea, proved brutal. "Many terrible things happened to them," as a monk piously gloated, "so that from their own efforts they realised that God and His all-holy maiden Mother watched over the City and the Empire of the Christians."[71]

Naturally, this was not remotely the Muslim perspective. Although the great siege had certainly been a calamity, the debacle could have been far worse: no sinister, twelve-year-old Caesar had materialised, for instance, nor had Kufa been squashed flat. In the decade that followed the failure to take Constantinople, the raids launched by the vengeful Muslims were as savage and remorseless as they had ever been, slicing so deep into Roman territory that in 727 an Arab army even managed briefly to put Nicaea under siege. Yet there was, in the sheer frenzied quality of these assaults, something of a raging against the dying of the light. The blaze of a dream that the Umayyads had long nurtured, that the entire world might be brought beneath their sway, was coming to gutter badly. Victory, which God had previously been pleased to bestow upon their armies whenever they met with unbelievers, could no longer, it seemed, be taken entirely for granted. In 732, for instance, in the distant wilds of Gaul, a Muslim raid on the Franks' wealthiest and most cherished shrine, a great church in a town named Tours, was met by a phalanx of outraged locals, and murderously put to flight. Eight years later, near the town of Acroinum, beyond the Taurus Mountains, it was the turn of the Romans to corner an Arab war band, and inflict on it a decisive defeat. Thirteen thousand were killed, and many more taken prisoner: a serious loss of manpower. This, the first victory ever won by the hated *Rum* in pitched battle against a Muslim army, seemed to confirm that God, in His ineffable wisdom, did indeed intend to leave entire swaths of His creation in the darkness of unbelief. For the first time, the devout dared to contemplate a chilling possibility: that humanity, rather than being brought into a single "House of Islam," was destined to remain forever divided in two. Increasingly, when pious Muhajirun in the shadow of the Taurus gazed out at the grim mountainscape before them, they did not see a gateway to fresh conquests but rather the ramparts of a perpetual "House of War." The fall of Constantinople—and the End Days—no longer seemed imminent. Instead, Muslims were coming to see in their war with the Romans only a grinding stalemate: one that might well endure for numberless generations. "They are people of sea and rock." So the Prophet himself was said to have lamented. "Alas, they are your associates to the end of time."[72]

Against the backdrop of such prophecies, defenders of the House of Islam came to cast the empire of Constantinople, and all the Christian realms beyond it, as a ghoul-like *doppelgänger*: hellish, predatory, undead. Against such an adversary, it was not only warriors who were needed, but lawyers: men who could advise the faithful on how best to secure and maintain the favour of God. By 740, the year of the disastrous defeat at Acroinum, men whose truest proficiency lay in a library rather than on the battlefield were becoming a common sight on the Roman front.[73] Such scholars, it was true, hardly lacked for martial courage: one, Ali ibn Bakkar, when slashed across his belly, cheerfully used his turban to stop his entrails from spilling out and then went on to kill no fewer than thirteen enemy soldiers, while his idea of relaxation, when away from the battlefield, was to make pets out of the dreaded lions of Cilicia. Yet the true value to the Muslim cause of these scholars lay neither on the battlefield nor in the field of pest control. Rather, what they contributed to the great death-struggle with the House of War was something even more precious: an assurance to the faithful that they were indeed, by taking up arms against the unbelievers, performing the will of God.

Standing in the shadow of the Taurus Mountains, it was not enough for the frontier guards of the Caliphate merely to construct fortifications out of the plundered rubble of abandoned Roman cities. Far more urgent was the need to fashion, along the border with the House of War, a dimension that could rank as authentically, purely and impregnably Islamic. This was why the frontiersmen's word for a fortified stronghold—*ribat*—was also applied to the particular brand of pious activity associated with the *ulama*: a determination to permit nothing to the faithful that did not derive directly from the Prophet. "He was the one who taught the inhabitants of the frontier region how to behave." So it was recorded of one lawyer, a Kufan by the name of Abu Ishaq. "He instructed them in the Sunna and used to command and prohibit. Whenever a man inclined to innovation entered the frontier region, Abu Ishaq would throw him out."[74]

Yet there was, in the presence of such figures amid all the dangers and deprivations of Cilicia, an awkward paradox. When Abu Ishaq risked a whipping to upbraid a local commandant, when Ali ibn Bakkar wept until he went blind, when other scholars fasted, or ate dust, or wore rags, or refused to wash, they were not following the example of Muhammad. Rather, they were aping Syria's famously ascetic monks. This, in the context of the interminable war with the Christians, could hardly help but appear a mounting embarrassment. How could Islam ever hope to scour the world of unbelief, when there still lurked in the souls of its own shock troops a lingering taint bred of their foes? Fortunately for the *ulama*, however, the solution to this problem—an increasingly tried and tested one—lay ready to hand. "The words of our Prophet have reached us—a correct and truthful statement."[75] So declared Ibn al-Mubarak, a Turk whose relish for fighting the *Rum* had led him to travel to the Taurus all the way from far distant Khorasan, and who would come to rank as perhaps the most formidable of all the warrior-scholars. The "*imam* of the Muslims," as he was admiringly hailed, he possessed not only a rare

419

aptitude for defeating Romans in single combat, but a familiarity with *hadiths* so detailed and passionate that he was known to discourse on them even in the heat of battle. Who better, then, to reassure the Muhajirun that the mortifications required of them on the frontier had in fact been authentically Islamic all along, and owed nothing to the example of infidels? Why, the Prophet himself, so it suddenly appeared from a flurry of *hadiths* brandished to triumphant effect by Ibn al-Mubarak, had given Muslims explicit instructions not to copy monks. "Every community has its monasticism—and the monasticism of my comunity is *jihad*."[76]

Quite what was being suggested by this word remained, however, in Ibn al-Mubarak's own lifetime, something very much up for grabs. Its literal meaning was "struggle," and in the Qur'an reference to the *jihad* required of believers was as likely to imply a good argument with the *Mushrikun*, or the giving of alms, or perhaps the freeing of a slave, as it was any commitment to pious violence. With warrior-scholars such as Ibn al-Mubarak desperate to claim the Prophet as their exemplar, however, the word came increasingly to take on a much narrower connotation: warfare in the cause of God. Riding to the frontiers of the embattled House of Islam and slaughtering stiff-necked Christians was cast not merely as an option for dutiful Muslims, but as a positive obligation. To one battle-shy friend who had boasted of his pilgrimages to Mecca and Medina, Ibn al-Mubarak gave a blistering retort. "Were you to see us," he lectured, "you would realise your worship is mere play. For you the fragrance of spices, but for us the fragrance of dust, and dirt, and blood flowing down our necks—which is altogether more pleasant."[77]

And certainly, a hundred years and more after the death of the Prophet, evidence for this robust approach to the essentials of Islamic worship was coming to be marshalled in impressive quantities. Ibn al-Mubarak himself compiled an entire book of *hadiths* devoted to the single topic: *jihad*. Other scholars, turning to the Qur'an and finding themselves puzzled by the alternation of passages that urged perpetual warfare with others that seemed to urge the precise opposite, sought to organise the verses in what they trusted was a chronological manner—with one in particular, targeted originally at treaty-breaking *Mushrikun*, being placed right at the end of the Prophet's life. "Kill them, seize them, besiege them, wait for them at every lookout post"[78]— maxims with an obvious value for those with a taste for fighting Romans. It was therefore crucial for such scholars to establish that the verse was indeed revealed to the Prophet late in his career: for only so could it plausibly be demonstrated to have superseded other, less bellicose passages. As a result, it was not only *hadith* collections that were starting to be shaped by the martial enthusiasms of the *ulama*, but details of the Prophet's biography. For scholars such as Ibn al-Mubarak, the stakes could hardly have been higher. Fail to demonstrate that they were following Muhammad's example, and not only their increasingly complex doctrine of *jihad* but all their suffering amid the killing fields of Cilicia would effectively rank as worthless. Render the Prophet satisfyingly in their own image, however, and the prize would be a truly fabulous one. Not only would the past of Islam be theirs— its future would as well.

A prospect fit to give the Umayyads apoplexy, of course. It was bad enough that jumped-up pen-pushers—Turks, and Persians, and who knew what—should presume to dispute with the *Khalifat Allah* his right to determine the law of Islam; but it was beyond insufferable to have them prescribe for him the correct way to "fight in the way of God."[79] No dynasty in history had presided over a more staggering array of conquests than the Umayyads. It was under their rule that the faithful had witnessed the fall of Carthage and Merv, the conquest of Spain and Transoxiana, the reaching of the Loire and the Hindu Kush. Clearly, then, the approval of God for their rule was something beyond dispute. And yet, like rodents burrowing and gnawing their way beneath some particularly glorious citadel, the *ulama* did dispute it. In their portrayal of Muhammad as the archetype of what they themselves felt a warrior of Islam should be, there was a peculiarly insidious threat to Umayyad authority. Any failure on the part of a Caliph to measure up to it could immediately be cast by them as a sinister deviation from true Islam—as defined, of course, by themselves. Even the proud assertion first made by Abd al-Malik—that to rule the Muslim people was to serve as the "Deputy of God"—might be turned against his dynasty. The earliest Commanders of the Faithful, so the *ulama* began to point out, had never thought to arrogate to themselves such a haughty title. Any notion of posing as God's deputy, to a man as austere and devout as Umar, would surely have been beyond the pale. Accordingly, in the version of history written by the *ulama*, he came to be endowed with a far more modest title: not "Deputy of God" but "Deputy of the Prophet of God." The Umayyads, when set against such a paragon, could hardly help but appear a gang of impious upstarts: arrogant gate-crashers squatting in the House of Islam.

Propaganda both brilliant and black. Indeed, such a travesty was it of all the many achievements wrought by the dynasty of Abd al-Malik on behalf of the Muslim people that the Umayyads, under more favourable circumstances, might well have laughed it to scorn. Circumstances, however, during the lengthy reign of the last of Abd al-Malik's sons to ascend the caliphal throne—a squinting skinflint by the name of Hisham—were anything but favourable. Able and innovative a statesman though Hisham was, and especially when screwing his subjects out of their money, the seeming brilliance of his administration was in truth possessed of a mere surface glitter. His own personal lack of courage, which saw him palpitate violently whenever he received news of some reverse, did not prevent him from being guided by one fundamental conviction: that it was the prime and proper responsibility of a Caliph to secure the expansion of the House of Islam. Neither defeats at the hands of the Franks and the Romans nor a widespread revolt in North Africa in 739 could persuade him to reconsider this core presumption. As a result, by the time of his death in 743, his coffers were seriously depleted, and the Syrian army, which had served as the cutting edge of Umayyad power ever since the time of Mu'awiya, had been perilously blunted. Worn down by endless campaigning, the professionals who constituted its units were now scattered far and wide—from the Pyrenees to the Indus. In Syria itself, almost none remained.

And this, for Hisham's successors, was to spell mortal danger. Even prior to his death, unrest was spreading fast. In Syria, it took the form of increasingly tribal-based factionalism; but in Iraq, it had an even more ominous source. Ghosts still unexorcised despite almost a century of Umayyad rule were re-emerging from the often blood-boltered mists of the past. In 740, the *Shi'a* demonstrated that they had lost none of their appetite for doomed uprisings when some two hundred Kufans, rallying in support of one of Ali's great-grandsons and confident that they still enjoyed the favour of God, hurled themselves against an Umayyad attack squad ten times their size. The rebels were duly wiped out beneath a hail of arrows, and the headless trunk of Ali's heir was nailed to a cross. At the same time, less flamboyantly but more effectively, agents for another family with a claim on the name of the Prophet were also at work, damning the Umayyads as false Muslims and usurpers. Despite their seeming obscurity, the Abbasids—a Qurayshi dynasty based in a remote farmstead in Nabataea—could lay claim to a truly priceless ancestor: none other than Abbas, the uncle of Muhammad. In the years that followed Hisham's death, this was enough to pique the interest of a growing number of Muslims—and not only among those inveterate malcontents, the *ulama*. With the times seemingly fractured, speculation over the possible cause of God's anger was rife. The answers given were rarely favourable to the *ancien régime*. Consequently, as Abbasid propagandists murmured their honeyed promises of a new dawn, the faithful began to listen to such whisperings with ever more attention. Perhaps, at such an excruciating moment of crisis, the appearance on the political scene of such living links with the Prophet might indeed be a part of God's plan?

Umayyad loyalists were hardly alone in snorting at this notion. It was almost inevitable, with factionalism rife across the Caliphate, that Islam's most fanatical insurgents would seize the opportunity to launch an uprising of their own; and sure enough, in 745, it was the turn of the Kharijites to raise the banner of revolt. Rather than martyr themselves needlessly—as the *Shi'a* had such a taste for doing—they brought to the business of revolution their customary attributes of ruthless efficiency and savagery. A few weeks after proclaiming their own Caliph, they had already gnawed off a major chunk of Iraq. Yet in truth, the Kharijites would never have had the opportunity to establish this breakaway state had it not been provided them by the most lethal of all the various outbreaks of *fitna*: a faction fight among the Umayyads themselves. In 744, Hisham's heir, a dashing poseur by the name of Walid, had been assassinated in one of his desert pleasure palaces—a murder that had served to unleash an unparalleled bout of blood-letting among his relatives. The man who eventually emerged victorious from this carnivorous feuding was a grizzled but curly-headed warlord ostensibly well suited to power: a nephew of Abd al-Malik's named Marwan. By 747, he had decisively trampled down his Umayyad and Kharijite rivals, and amply demonstrated both the kick and the stubbornness of the beast to which he was most often compared: a mule. Yet his triumph had come at a terrible cost. Iraq and Syria both lay in ruins, and Marwan was so despised in Damascus that he decamped from Syria altogether and established his court in Harran. An astounding development, to be sure: even with the Caliphate in a state of near collapse, a city still "ulcerous with idolatry"[80] had come to be established as the capital of the Deputy of God.

Many Muslims would doubtless have been shocked to learn that the moon continued to be worshipped anywhere in the House of Islam. The cult of Sin might almost have been designed to provoke their horror. Yet the pagans of Harran—who had suffered brutal persecution in the final years of Roman rule—had found their new masters, if not exactly more tolerant, then more *laissez-faire*, at least. Christians would snidely attribute this to the gullibility of the Muslim authorities, who were supposed to have been tricked into accepting that the moon worshippers were in fact the enigmatic "Sabaeans" mentioned in the Qur'an—and therefore, according to the Prophet, one of the three "Peoples of the Book."[81] Whatever the truth of such a tall-sounding story, Harranians were certainly still studying the future by sacrificing animals and then "examining their livers,"[82] directly under Marwan's nose. The persistence of such ancient practices within a capital of the Caliphate serves as a vivid reminder that Muslims were not alone, amid the evils of the age, in attempting to fathom the purposes of the heavens. In 745, for instance, during Marwan's devastating campaign in Syria, a stylite had presumed to warn the passing warlord that he would be dealt with by God even as he had dealt with his subjects. "When Marwan heard this, he commanded that the pillar should be overthrown; and he brought down the old man, and burned him alive in the fire."[83] Caliphs, of course, might treat Christian saints with a brutality and dismissiveness that would have appalled a Caesar—and yet even as Marwan hunkered down in Harran, he neglected the sensibilities of his non-Muslim subjects at his peril. Floodtides were swirling around him older by far than Islam. These were rising, however, not in the traditional heartlands of the Caliphate, in Syria or Iraq, but far to the east: in Khorasan.

Almost three centuries had passed since Peroz, in his war against the Hephthalites, had set the seal on a disastrous reign with one final, calamitous battle. Much had changed since then, and yet the miseries suffered by Khorasan under Hisham and his successors had come to wear a very familiar look. As resentments and frustrations bred of heavy taxation gnawed at an oppressed population, so had Muslim armies beyond the Oxus suffered a series of humiliating reverses. Not even the ultimate stabilisation of Transoxiana could erase the notorious reputations of a succession of incompetent Umayyad governors. "You abandoned us like pieces of a slaughtered beast, cut up for a round-breasted girl,"[84] the Arabs of the eastern front sang of one particularly epicene appointee from Damascus. Yet Umayyad authority was threatened by more than the resentments of Muslim settlers; it was in peril as well from the same traditions that had once blackened the name of Peroz. In Khorasan—where great Parthian dynasts such as the Karin still jealously guarded their prerogatives against the upstart Muslim elite, and where most towns and villages remained wholly untouched by Islam—it often seemed as though *Iranshahr* had never fallen. That the world was divided into rival spheres of good and evil; that a great monarch was either a defender of truth or he was nothing; that the wickedness of an oath-breaker would bring ruin to his realm: here were presumptions still widely taken for granted along the eastern marches of Iran. The result was, as Umayyad rule began to implode, that the stirrings of rebellion could be felt well beyond the Fertile Crescent. In 745, even as the Kharijites were launching their latest insurgency, a mysterious prophet appeared in Khorasan. Dressed all in green—the colour of Mihr—brandishing a book of revelations written in Persian, and proclaiming himself familiar with the byways of heaven, Bihafarid was a revolutionary conjured, it seemed, from the most haunting mists of the Iranian past. Having died and then risen again—or so his disciples proclaimed—he announced his mission in terms that nakedly scorned all the pretensions of Muhammad: "O people, I am Bihafarid, the Messenger of God!"[85]

Of course, it could not possibly last. Muslim rule, whatever the hopes of the great multitudes of peasants who flocked in excitement to Bihafarid's banner, was not so easily overthrown. Sure enough, in 749, the self-proclaimed prophet was arrested, put in chains and hanged in a nearby mosque. Yet his executioners, for all that it would have appalled them to contemplate it, were not, perhaps, wholly dissimilar to the man they had put to death. Bihafarid's murderers were themselves followers of an insurrectionist who had emerged abruptly on the fringes of the former *Iranshahr*, and combined charisma with a dramatic claim to be an agent of God. "Father of a Muslim," he called himself: a name so obviously a pseudonym as to give away nothing at all. His glamour, in part at least, was that of a man in a mask. "The knowledge of my deeds," as he put it with a calculated show of mystery, "is better for you than the knowledge of my pedigree."[86] Yet whether an Arab or an Iranian, an aristocrat or a former slave, one thing, at least, is certain: he was powerfully assisted in his preachings by the same identical swirl of yearnings and expectations as had inspired Bihafarid. Along the easternmost fringes of the Caliphate, faiths were not easily patrolled. So it had ever been, of course, in border zones. No wonder, then, far distant as they were from all the efforts of the *ulama* to raise barriers around the practice of their religion, that the Muslims of Khorasan should have betrayed the influence of beliefs older by far than the *Sunna*. What helped to give Abu Muslim his prestige among them was that he dared, as once the critics of Peroz had done, to damn their ruler as a man condemned by God. Although he did not, like Bihafarid, clothe himself in green, yet in the summer of 747, when he declared open rebellion against Marwan, he unfurled a banner dyed a single colour: black. That he did this in a village outside Merv, where the fugitive Yazdegird had been murdered, was hardly suggestive, of course, of any nostalgia on Abu Muslim's part for the House of Sasan; and yet, to Iranians, his preachings might well have stirred memories of the toppled monarchy. The cause proclaimed by Abu Muslim was that of a single family, appointed by God to the rule of the world; and if the mark of their claim to this awesome status was the possession, not of a *farr* but rather of a bloodline traceable back to the uncle of the Prophet, then that, in an Islamic empire, promised qualification enough. Abu Muslim, like so many other rebels trained in subterfuge and insurrection, was an agent of the Abbasids; and by raising the East in their cause, he had succeeded in fusing the past with the future, the Iranian with the Arab, the Sasanian with the Islamic. It was to prove a quite staggeringly potent combination—and the ruin of the Umayyads.

The flames of rebellion swept westwards from Khorasan so fast and so ferociously that Marwan was caught out fatally short. Already, as the spring of 749 turned to summer, Abbasid forces had secured complete control of Iran. By August, they were across the Euphrates; by September, they were inside Kufa. On 28 November, in the very mosque where Ali had been murdered, an Abbasid was publicly hailed as Caliph. Marwan now had no option but to meet the provocation head on. Rather than wait for the full roster of his veterans to assemble, he opted instead to cobble together such units as were already available to him in Harran and lead them against the pretender. On 25 January 750, on the bank of a tributary of the Tigris called the Greater Zab, he spotted the black banners of the Abbasids, advanced, and fell upon the rebels. The result was calamity. His army was obliterated. As unyielding as ever, even in the face of such a disaster, the tireless Marwan fled the battlefield and desperately struggled to marshal further troops—but there were none to be found. Galloping past both Damascus—the capital he had abandoned—and Jerusalem— the city that now mocked his dynasty's crumbled greatness more than any other—he made his way into Egypt. Here, in the heat of the summer, he was finally cornered by his pursuers. His head, topped by the frizz of his curly hair, was dispatched to his replacement upon the throne of the Caliphs. His tongue was fed to a cat.

Marwan's relatives too were systematically tracked down. The death squads were grimly efficient. Of the entire Umayyad brood, the only one who managed to evade capture was a grandson of the miserly Hisham, who fled to Spain, where he set himself up as *Amir*. Otherwise, Islam's founding dynasty was finished. The last wretched gaggle of survivors, hauled before the Abbasid Caliph, were butchered, laid side by side, covered by a carpet, and used as a banqueting table by honoured guests: "And those who were present at the scene," it is said, "ate while the death-rattle still sounded in the throats of the expiring victims."

An atrocity fit to stand as a gruesome coda to a revolution beyond compare, manifest in pages of divine revelations, and capacious systems of law, and incomparably beautiful buildings, and whole new cities, and would-be global empires, and entire habits of thought transformed. In the most literal and bloody way imaginable, the slaughter of the Umayyads served to illustrate what had been—for half a millennium or more—the supreme theme of the age: the raising of a new order upon the ruins of the old.

ENVOI

PLUS ÇA CHANGE?

Dinner parties hosted on corpses were hardly the limit of Abbasid achievement. In 762, on the banks of the Tigris, where the Garden of Eden had once stood, the construction began of a capital designed to serve as an image of paradise. Baghdad, "the City of Peace," would certainly prove to be, if not a vision of heaven, then a place of superlatives. A mere couple of generations on from its founding, it was already the largest, the richest and the most beautiful city in the world. Damascus, that abandoned showcase for Umayyad power, was decisively eclipsed. So too was everywhere else. The universe, as even ambassadors from Constantinople might reluctantly acknowledge, had a whole new crossroads.

No denying, then, the talent of the Abbasids for clearing decks. Their founding from scratch of a city as incomparable as Baghdad was on a par with their incineration of the exhumed corpses of the Umayyad Caliphs, or their murder in 755 of Abu Muslim, the over-mighty subject who had first helped them to the Caliphate: a demonstration that rivals were on no account to be brooked. Yet nowhere as dazzling and sophisticated as the Abbasids' new capital could possibly have shimmered as hypnotically as it did by merely repudiating the past. "The people of every age and era acquire fresh experiences, and have knowledge renewed for them, in accordance with the decree of the stars."[1] So wrote the court astrologer, in the earliest days of Baghdad's splendour. What he could see, mirage-like beyond the palaces and spreading suburbs of the freshly minted capital, were the phantoms of other global cities that had also once glittered amid the mudflats: Ctesiphon, and Seleucia, and Babylon. It was certainly no diminution of Baghdad's own glory to see the new city as the culmination of such a line of descent. The Abbasids, by restoring the capital of the world to Iraq, were consciously laying claim to traditions that would burnish, not diminish, their own prestige. If there was in this more than a hint of how Ardashir, arriving in Mesopotamia from Iran, had established a capital beside the Tigris while still retaining the name of a Persian, then it did not go unnoted by shrewd observers.[2] Despite the descent claimed by the Abbasids, the family they most closely resembled was not that of the Prophet but the House of Sasan. Increasingly, the comparison of a Caliph to a *Shahanshah* was no blasphemy, but a statement of the obvious. When the Commander of the Faithful sat in majestic inaccessibility upon his throne, or staggered in his silken robes beneath the weight of his jewels, or strolled through his gardens past cooling fountains and leopards, he was no less the lord of a Persian empire for claiming descent from an Arab.

It might have seemed, then, when Haroun al-Rashid—the Abbasid immortalised in *The Arabian Nights* as the cynosure of Caliphs—rode out to war against the Romans, that very little in the world had actually changed. In 806, while heading for the frontier, he and his troops clattered along almost the identical road that Kavad, some three centuries before, had followed when embarking on his own campaign against the *Rum*. Anyone emulating the seven sleepers of Ephesus, and jolting awake after a three-hundred-year-long snooze, would have experienced a palpable sense of *déjà vu*. Just as the *Shahanshah* had ended up bogged down in a protracted siege of Amida, so now, in his own attempt to force the frontier, did the Commander of the Faithful find himself camped out for weeks around a Roman stronghold—and not all the wild scenes of rejoicing when the fortress finally fell could alter the fact that it might just as well have been left well alone. The Romans barely noticed the loss. The Caliph certainly won no long-term advantage. The face-off between the great empires of East and

West—those "twin eyes of the world"—continued much the same as it had ever done. It was as though entire centuries had never been.

And yet, in truth, of course, all was changed—changed utterly. If history might sometimes appear to be repeating itself on the banks of the Tigris, it was also—literally—being made. Ibn Ishaq, whose biography of the Prophet would go on to be reworked by Ibn Hisham, was only one of numerous scholars to be attracted, moth-like, to the bright lights of the Abbasids' infant capital. Over the succeeding decades, the work done by the *ulama* of Baghdad would set the seal on how pious Muslims, from that time forward, would understand the origins of their religion. Even as Haroun al-Rashid was squandering gold and men in the wilds of the Taurus, so scholars were compiling the first biographies of the Prophet to have survived into the present, the first commentaries on the Qur'an, and the first collections of *hadith*s. The impact of their labours would prove to be infinitely more enduring than the capture of a few border forts. Over the centuries, they would serve to neutralise the pretensions of the Caliphs themselves. The compilers of the *Sunna*—who regarded the Abbasids with scarcely more enthusiasm than they had the Umayyads—remained implacable in their determination to geld the *Khalifat Allah*. What served to complete this protracted operation was the acceptance by everyone, even the Caliph himself, of a version of Islam's beginnings that gave no scope for anyone to rule as a Deputy of God. The *ulama*, by tightly controlling what went into the history books, were able to propagate an understanding of their own dazzlingly rich and complex civilisation that attributed almost every single thing of value within it to the Prophet, and the Prophet alone. There was no question of acknowledging the momentous roles played in the forging of Islam by countless others—be they autocrats such as Abd al-Malik or scholars such as themselves. Submission to God was definitively cast as submission to the *Sunna*. By 1258, when Baghdad was flattened by the Mongols, and the heir of Haroun al-Rashid, wrapped up in a carpet, was trampled to death by horses, the victory of the *ulama* had long since been secured. For centuries, Caliphs had played no more than an ornamental role. The death of the last Abbasid to rule in Baghdad had no effect whatsoever on the fortunes of the *ulama*. Just as Christianity had survived the collapse of Roman power, so Islam, it appeared, could flourish perfectly well without a Caliphate.

The peoples of late antiquity, then, when they imagined themselves to be living through the End Days foretold by the prophet Daniel, had been mistaken. Not the empire of the pagan Romans, nor that of their Christian successors, nor that of the Ishmaelites had proved to be the Fourth Beast. Nevertheless, those who saw in the convulsions of the age a process of transformation unlike any other, by means of which a kingdom would end up established on earth "which shall be different from all the kingdoms," were not so far wrong. Caesars, *Shahanshahs* and Caliphs, none of them remain—but the words of the rabbis who taught in Sura, the bishops who met in Nicaea and the *ulama* who studied in Kufa still shape the world as living things today. There could be no more conclusive testimony to the impact of the revolution witnessed by late antiquity than the existence, in the twenty-first century, of billions upon billions of people who profess belief in a single god and lead their lives in accordance with that belief.

The pen, it seems, is indeed mightier than the sword.

Timeline

Italicised dates are either approximate or traditional.

753 BC	The foundation of Rome.
586	The Babylonians' sack of Jerusalem.
539	Cyrus captures Babylon.
330	Alexander the Great burns Persepolis.
29	Virgil starts work on the *Aeneid*.
AD 33	The crucifixion of Jesus.
70	The Romans' sack of Jerusalem.
220	The death of Tertullian.
224	Ardashir establishes the Sasanian Empire.
226	Ardashir conquers Mesopotamia.
250	The seven sleepers of Ephesus take refuge from persecution in a cave.
260	Defeat and capture of Valerian by Shapur I.
301	The conversion of Tiridates, King of Armenia, to Christianity.
312	The conversion of Constantine to Christianity.
324	The foundation of Constantinople.
325	The Council of Nicaea.
326	Helena discovers the True Cross in Jerusalem.
363	Death of Julian on campaign in Mesopotamia; Rome cedes Nisibis to Persia.
428	Nestorius becomes Bishop of Constantinople.
430	Simeon the Elder climbs his pillar.
451	The Council of Chalcedon.

476   The deposition of the last Roman emperor of the West; Italy comes under the rule of the Ostrogoths.

484   The Hephthalites defeat Peroz.

496   The forced abdication of Kavad.

498   The return of Kavad to the Persian throne.

502   Kavad crowns Mundhir as King of Hira.

503   Kavad captures Amida.

505   The foundation of Dara.

524   The martyrdom of the Christians of Najran.

525   The defeat and death of Yusuf of Himyar; Justinian marries Theodora.

527   Justinian becomes emperor; Simeon the Younger leaves Antioch.

528   The execution of Mazdak.

529   The closure of the philosophical schools of Athens; the Samaritan revolt; Arethas is crowned King of the Ghassanids.

531   Kavad is succeeded as *Shahanshah* by Khusrow I.

532   Mass rioting in Constantinople almost topples Justinian; Justinian and Khusrow sign the "Eternal Peace."

533   Justinian's commissioners publish their Digest of Roman Law; Belisarius invades North Africa.

535   Belisarius invades Sicily.

536   Belisarius captures Rome.

537   The dedication of Hagia Sophia.

540   Khusrow sacks Antioch.

541   The plague spreads from Egypt.

554   Arethas defeats Mundhir at the Battle of Chalcis.

557   The collapse of the Hephthalite Empire.

565   The death of Justinian.

570   The birth of Muhammad.

579   The death of Khusrow I.

590   The coup and usurpation of Bahram Chobin.

591   The defeat of Bahram Chobin and accession of Khusrow II.

602	The murder of Maurice and usurpation of Phocas.
610	The overthrow of Phocas by Heraclius
610	Muhammad receives his first divine revelation.
614	The Persians burn Ephesus and storm Jerusalem.
619	The Persians capture Alexandria.
622	The emigration, or *hijra*, of Muhammad from Mecca to Medina.
626	The Persians and Avars lay siege to Constantinople.
627	Heraclius invades Mesopotamia.
628	The death of Khusrow II; Heraclius and Shahrbaraz sign peace treaty.
630	Heraclius returns the True Cross to Jerusalem.
632	The death of Muhammad.
634	The Arabs invade Palestine; the Battle of Gaza.
636	The Romans are defeated at the Yarmuk, and withdraw from Syria.
637	The Battle of Qadisiyya.
638	The Arabs capture Jerusalem.
639	The Arabs invade Egypt.
642	Alexandria falls to the Arabs.
644	The assassination of Umar.
650	The Arabs cross the River Oxus for the first time.
651	The murder of Yazdegird III.
656	The assassination of Uthman.
657	Ali and Mu'awiya fight an inconclusive battle on the banks of the Euphrates.
658	Ali defeats the Kharijites.
661	The assassination of Ali; Mu'awiya is hailed as "Commander of the Faithful" in Jerusalem.
674	The first Arab siege of Constantinople.
680	Yazid succeeds Mu'awiya; the Battle of Karbala; the rebellion of Ibn al-Zubayr.
683	The Umayyad sack of Medina; the burning of the *Ka'ba*; the death of Yazid.

684	Marwan is hailed as "Commander of the Faithful" in Syria.
685	Marwan is succeeded by Abd al-Malik; Mukhtar rebels against Ibn al-Zubayr.
686	The first mention of Muhammad on an Arab coin.
689	Work begins on the Dome of the Rock.
692	The defeat and death of Ibn al-Zubayr.
694	Al-Hajjaj appointed governor of Iraq.
702	Al-Hajjaj founds Wasit.
705	Abd al-Malik is succeeded by Walid; the final Arab conquest of Khorasan.
711	The Arabs invade Spain.
715	Walid inaugurates the great mosque of Damascus.
716–17	The second Arab siege of Constantinople.
732	The Franks defeat the Arabs outside Tours.
740	The Romans defeat the Arabs at Acroinum; Iraq is convulsed by an anti-Umayyad uprising.
747	Marwan II emerges from civil war as the new Umayyad Caliph; Abu Muslim declares open rebellion against Marwan in Khorasan.
750	The Abbasids defeat and overthrow Marwan.
755	The murder of Abu Muslim.
762	The founding of Baghdad.

Dramatis Personae

Iranshahr

Ardashir I (ruled AD 224–41) Founder of the Sasanian Empire.

Shapur I (241–70) The great warrior *Shahanshah* who captured the Roman emperor Valerian.

Peroz (459–84) Hephthalite-fighter, Jew-persecutor, oath-breaker.

Raham The head of the Mihrans, a Parthian aristocratic family; and the early power behind Peroz's throne.

Kavad (488–96/498–531) Son of Peroz, and a royal enthusiast for communism.

Sukhra The head of the Karin, a Parthian aristocratic family, and a classic over-mighty subject.

Mazdak A mysterious Persian prophet who appears to have preached communism and to have been sponsored by Kavad.

Zamasp (496–98) Kavad's brother and briefly installed on the throne as his replacement.

Aspebedes A Parthian general, and brother-in-law of Kavad.

Kavus Kavad's eldest son, and a committed Mazdakite.

Khusrow I (531–79) The son of Kavad and Aspebedes's sister. Known to posterity as *Anushirvan*—"Immortal Soul."

Hormizd IV (579–90) The son of Khusrow I.

Bahram Chobin (590–1) A Mihranid general, and the first Parthian dynast to usurp the Sasanian throne.

Khusrow II (590–628) The son of Hormizd IV. Restored to the throne with Roman help, his reign witnessed the near destruction of the Roman Empire.

Shahrbaraz (630) Mihranid general who conquered Syria and Palestine for Khusrow II.

Yazdegird III (633–51) The last Sasanian *Shahanshah*.

Rome

Posidonius Greek philosopher and enthusiast for globalisation.

Augustus (27 BC–AD 14) First of the Roman emperors.

Virgil Author of the *Aeneid*, the great epic of the Roman people.

Nero (54–68) Psychotic Roman emperor whom rabbis claimed became a Jew.

Philip (244–9) Nicknamed the "Arab." Presided over Rome's millennial celebrations.

Decius (249–51) Killer of Philip, killed by Goths. A persecutor of Christians.

Valerian (253–60) Captured by Shapur I.

New Rome

Constantine (306–37) The founder of Constantinople, and the first Christian Caesar.

Helena Constantine's mother, and the discoverer of the True Cross.

Julian (361–3) The last pagan Caesar.

Theodosius I (379–92) The last Caesar to rule both halves of the Roman Empire.

Theodosius II (408–50) The grandson of Theodosius I. Renowned for his piety, and for the walls around Constantinople that were built during his reign.

Anastasius (491–518) A bureaucrat turned bean-counting emperor.

Justin (518–27) A Balkan peasant who rose through the ranks to the imperial throne.

Justinian (527–65) Justin's nephew. A worthy rival to Khusrow I.

Theodora A one-time actress, whore and comedian who became Justinian's wife.

Belisarius Justinian's best general.

Maurice (582–602) Sponsor of Khusrow II. Deposed by Phocas.

Phocas (602–10) Deposed and killed by Heraclius.

Heraclius (610–41) A proto-crusader whose reign witnessed extraordinary highs and lows.

Sergius Defeated and killed by the Arabs outside Gaza.

The Christian Church

Peter Chief of Christ's disciples.

Paul Early Christian apostle who argued that Gentiles, if they converted to Christ, were not obliged to follow the Jewish Law.

Ignatius Supposedly appointed Bishop of Antioch by Peter himself, he was the first Christian to deploy the word *Christianismos*—"Christianity."

Basilides The second-century author of a heretical gospel that claimed Christ had not died on the cross.

Marcion Another second-century heretic. He viewed the deity of the Old Testament as inferior to the True God, the Father of Christ, and dismissed the entire Old Testament itself as worthless.

Tertullian Born in Carthage in the mid-second century, he was the first Christian to define the Trinity. He died around 220.

Arius A priest from Alexandria who argued that God the Father had existed before God the Son. His teachings were condemned as heretical at the Council of Nicaea in 325.

Athanasius Bishop of Alexandria who took a leading role against Arius at the Council of Nicaea, and was the first to prescribe the contents of what is still the Christian New Testament.

Cyril Bishop of Jerusalem in the fourth century.

Epiphanius A bishop from Cyprus who compiled an exhaustive encyclopedia of heresies in the fourth century.

Jerome A translator of the Bible into Latin who settled permanently in Bethlehem in 388.

Nestorius Bishop of Constantinople who was condemned as a heretic in 431 for arguing that the relationship between the human and the divine in Christ had been one of coexistence rather than union.

Dioscorus Thuggish Bishop of Alexandria who helped to provoke the summoning of the Council of Chalcedon.

Theodoret A Syrian bishop in the first half of the fifth century who took a keen interest in the Arabs.

Sozomen A historian from Gaza who in around 440 published a history of the Church that repeatedly touched on Arab affairs.

Simeon the Elder The first and most famous of the pillar-topping saints known as stylites.

Simeon the Younger The most celebrated stylite of the sixth century.

Paul An Egyptian monk appointed by Justinian to be Bishop of Alexandria.

Zoilus A Syrian sent by Justinian to replace Paul as Bishop of Alexandria.

Barbarians, Mercenaries and Rebels

Zenobia Queen of Palmyra and—briefly, following Shapur I's capture of Valerian—much of the Roman East.

Mavia Fourth-century Arab queen who briefly emulated Zenobia's conquests.

Mundhir Persian attack-dog and King of the Lakhmids.

Arethas Roman attack-dog and King of the Ghassanids.

Julian Leader of the Samaritan revolt against Justinian.

Yusuf As'ar Yath'ar Jewish king of Himyar.

Theoderic Mustachioed Ostrogothic king of Italy.

Nehemiah Jewish leader who attempted, after the capture of
Jerusalem by the Persians, to rebuild the Temple.

Arculf A Frankish pilgrim to Jerusalem in the reign of Mu'awiya.

The Arab Empire

Muhammad The Prophet of Islam.

Abu Bakr (632–4) According to Muslim tradition, the first of the
Rashidun—the "rightly guided" Caliphs.

Umar I (634–44) Warrior leader and mighty ascetic.

Uthman (644–56) Heir to Umar as leader of the Arab Empire, and
the man responsible, according to Islamic tradition, for the
compilation of Muhammad's revelations into a single book. An
Umayyad.

Ali (656–61) Muhammad's cousin and son-in-law.

Yazid Umayyad general who took a leading role in the conquest of
Syria.

Mu'awiya (661–80) Brother of Yazid, governor of Syria, and rival of
Ali for control of the Arab Empire.

Yazid I (680–3) The son and heir of Mu'awiya. Alternately
idolised as a man of the people and loathed as a drunken
playboy.

Husayn Muhammad's youngest and favourite grandson.

Marwan I (684–5) Uthman's half-brother: a smooth operator.

Abd al-Malik (685–705) Marwan's son: the Arab Empire's
equivalent of Constantine.

Abdullah ibn al-Zubayr Venerable Companion of Muhammad,
and Abd al-Malik's principal rival in the second civil war for
control of the Arab Empire.

Mus'ab Brother of Ibn al-Zubayr, who entrusted him with the
pacification of Iraq.

Mukhtar Nicknamed the "Deceiver" by his enemies, he led a
revolutionary movement in Iraq against the regime of Ibn
al-Zubayr. He owned a holy chair.

Al-Hajjaj Nicknamed "Little Dog." Abd al-Malik's principal and
most brilliant lieutenant.

Walid I (705–15) Son and heir of Abd al-Malik who built the great
mosque of Damascus.

Suleiman (715–17) Son of Abd al-Malik and heir of Walid who
sponsored the second siege of Constantinople.

Maslama Son of Abd al-Malik and commander in charge of the
expedition against Constantinople.

Ali ibn Bakkar Warrior-scholar.

Abu Ishaq Warrior-scholar.

Abdullah ibn al-Mubarak Warrior-scholar.

Umar II (717–20) Nephew of Abd al-Malik and sufficiently pious to
be recognised by subsequent Islamic tradition as an authentic
Caliph—the only Umayyad to be granted that honour.

Hisham (724–43) Last of Abd al-Malik's sons to become Caliph.

Walid II (743–4) Abd al-Malik's great-nephew, and a renowned
playboy, whose murder precipitated a third bout of civil war.

Marwan II (744–50) Last of the Umayyad Caliphs.

Abu Muslim An enigmatic Abbasid-sponsored rebel who led a
revolt in the far east of the Caliphate that culminated in the
overthrow of the Umayyads.

Glossary

Abbasids The second dynasty to rule the Caliphate, after the
   toppling of the Umayyads in 750.

Ahriman The evil spirit in Zoroastrianism, opposed to Ohrmazd.

Al-'Uzza An Arab goddess who served as patron of the Lakhmids
   and is mentioned dismissively in the Qur'an.

Amir Arabic for "Commander."

Anahita An Iranian warrior goddess with a major shrine at
   Istakhr in Persia. She was cast by Zoroastrians as a lieutenant
   of Ohrmazd, the supreme benevolent deity of
   Zoroastrianism.

Arian A supporter of the Christian priest Arius, who argued in the
   early fourth century that God the Father had existed before
   God the Son. His teachings were condemned as heretical at the
   Council of Nicaea in 325.

Ascetic A word that derived from the Greek for "training" and
   referred originally to Christian hermits who practised
   spectacular feats of self-mortification.

Asha The Zoroastrian principle of Truth and Order.

Byzantine A word used after the foundation of Constantinople to
   describe a citizen of the city. Many modern historians—
   although not me—refer to the late Roman Empire as
   "Byzantine."

Caliph Anglicisation of the Arabic *khalifa*—a word that appears
   twice in the Qur'an, where it seems to have meant "man."
   Subsequently, it came to mean "deputy." When Abd al-Malik
   laid claim to the title of *Khalifat Allah*, he was describing himself

as the "Deputy of God." Confusingly, the word can also mean "successor": the title of *Khalifat Rasul Allah*—"Successor of the Prophet of God"—was retrospectively applied to all the early leaders of the Arab Empire.

Caliphate The Arab—and then Muslim—Empire.

Catholic From the Greek word for "universal." It was used, like "Orthodox," as a self-description by supporters of the Council of Chalcedon—which served, in turn, to cast those opposed to it as mere factionalists.

Chalcedonian Someone who subscribes to the doctrinal formulations of the Council of Chalcedon, held in 451. It is a measure of the triumph of the Chalcedonians over their various rivals in the Christian Church that they succeeded in appropriating the adjectives "Catholic" and "Orthodox." Today's Roman Catholic, Greek Orthodox and Protestant Churches are all Chalcedonian.

Dar-al-Islam Literally, the "House of Islam"—the lands where Muslims are in authority.

Drug "The Lie"—in Zoroastrianism, the principle opposed to *Asha*.

Dushara A god widely worshipped by the pagan Arabs as their principal deity.

Ebionites A sect of Christians who claimed descent from the original Jewish Church.

Ecclesia Greek for "church." Originally, it referred to an assembly of citizens.

Farr The supernatural mark of a Persian king's majesty.

Fitna Arabic for "time of trial"—shorthand for civil war.

Foederati A Latin word used to designate barbarian troops employed by the Romans as mercenaries, generally beyond the frontiers of the empire.

Gentile A non-Jew.

Ghassanids An Arab warrior dynasty employed by the Romans against the *Shahanshah*.

Gnostics Intellectual mystics who believed that *gnosis*—the Greek word for "knowledge"—would provide them with salvation from the material world.

Gog and Magog Kitten-eating savages imprisoned by Alexander the Great behind gates of brass, and destined to be set free at the end of time.

Hadith The report of a saying or an action of Muhammad—or, in the early years of Islam, of a Companion of Muhammad. In Islam, *hadith*s are second in authority only to the Qur'an.

Haram Arabic for "hallowed space."

Hijra The Arabic equivalent of "exodus"—a migration. In Muslim tradition, Muhammad's *hijra* from Mecca to Medina in 622 is the event that brought the Islamic order of time into being.

Imam In pre-Islamic Arabia, the "founding father" of a tribe or people; but under Islam, the word increasingly came to signify a religious leader.

Iranshahr "The Dominion of the Aryans": the name given by the Sasanian kings to their empire.

Isnad The chain of informants stretching back to the time of Muhammad that serves to validate his sayings.

Ius Latin for "law."

Jahiliyya A word that derives from the Arabic for ignorance—*jahl*—and refers, in Muslim tradition, to the "Age of Ignorance" that existed before Islam.

Jinn Supernatural creatures bred of fire that haunt the mythology of both pre-Islamic and Islamic Arabia.

Jizya The poll-tax imposed on Jews and Christians by order of the Qur'an.

Ka'ba Arabic for "cube"—a shape that the pre-Islamic Arabs seem to have associated strongly with the sacred. Not to be confused with *ka'iba*, meaning "virgin," and certainly not with *ku'ba*, meaning "breasts." The most celebrated *ka'ba* stands to this day in the centre of the sanctuary of Mecca.

Kai An ancient Persian title, meaning "king."

Karin A Parthian aristocratic dynasty.

Kayanids A legendary dynasty from Persian mythology, celebrated for their wondrous exploits and heroic record as fighters of barbarians.

Khalifat Allah See "Caliph."

Kharijites An early Muslim sect celebrated equally for their piety and ferocity.

Lakhmids An Arab warrior dynasty employed by the *Shahanshah* against the Romans.

Magaritai The Greek form of the Arab word *muhajirun*.

Manichaeism A religion that fused Jewish, Christian, Zoroastrian and Buddhist teachings, first taught in the third century AD by a prophet from near Ctesiphon named Mani, and savagely persecuted almost everywhere.

Maqom Hebrew for "place." The Arabic equivalent is *maqam*.

Mathran An ancient Persian word meaning "prophet."

Mazdakite A follower of Mazdak, a Persian prophet who preached a radical religious message of communism in the early sixth century AD.

Mihr An ancient Iranian god with special responsibility for the punishment of oath-breakers. His home was the Alburz Mountains in northern Iran, and his sacred colour was green. Zoroastrians regarded him as being, like Anahita, a lieutenant of Ohrmazd; but there were many, in the remoter reaches of *Iranshahr*, who worshipped him as a great god in his own right.

Mihran A Parthian aristocratic dynasty.

Minim A Hebrew word that the rabbis applied to heretics; sometimes used as shorthand for "Christians."

Monophysite An insulting term that Chalcedonians applied to their opponents in the Christian Church who held that the divine and human natures of Christ had been so interfused as to constitute a *mone physis*—Greek for "single nature."

Mowbed A Zoroastrian priest.

Muhajirun An Arab word meaning "those who go on a *hijra*"— therefore, "emigrants." In the early years of the Arab Empire, religiously motivated conquerors seem to have used it in preference to "Muslims" as a self-designation.

Mushrikun "Those who are guilty of *shirk*": the opponents of the Prophet in the Qur'an.

Nazoreans A sect of Christians, like the Ebionites, who claimed descent from the original Jewish Church.

Nestorians A word applied by their opponents to those Christians who believed that the two natures of Christ, the divine and the human, had existed distinct within his earthly body. Nestorius, a Bishop of Constantinople, was condemned for heresy in the first half of the fifth century.

Ohrmazd The supreme God of Truth and Light in Zoroastrianism.

Orthodox From the Greek words for "correct belief."

Palladium The image of the goddess Pallas Athena supposedly taken from Troy to Rome, and from Rome to Constantinople.

Parthians An Iranian people who lived mainly in the north of Iran. The dynasty overthrown by the Sasanians was Parthian, but so were other aristocratic dynasties that flourished well into the Islamic period.

Qibla The direction of prayer. In mosques, it is generally indicated by a niche in a wall called a *mihrab*.

Quraysh The tribe into which, according to Muslim tradition, Muhammad was born.

Rashidun "Rightly guided." An adjective used, from the third Muslim century (ninth century AD) onwards, to describe the first four Caliphs: Abu Bakr, Umar, Uthman and Ali.

Sabaeans A mysterious people who are mentioned in the Qur'an alongside Jews and Christians as one of the three "Peoples of the Book." The most widely supported theory is that they were Manichaeans.

Sahabah The personal associates and followers of Muhammad—literally, his "companions."

Shahanshah The title of the Sasanian kings: "King of Kings."

Shekhinah A Hebrew word that refers to God's dwelling place on earth.

Shi'a An Arab word—literally "party"—that came to be applied to the followers of Ali and his descendants.

Shirk Associating gods or other supernatural beings with the One True God—in Islam, the ultimate crime.

Shirkat Arabic for "partnership."

Sira An Arab word—literally "exemplary behaviour"—used for a biography of Muhammad.

Stylites Christian hermits who spent lengthy periods of time—often years—on top of pillars.

Sunna An Arab word meaning "custom" or "achievement." In Islam, it refers to the collection of *hadiths* that constitutes the body of sacred law.

Syriac Prior to its replacement by Arabic, the most widely spoken common language in the Middle East.

Tafsir A commentary on the Qur'an.

Talmud The written record of rabbinical learning, composed in Palestine and Mesopotamia during late antiquity.

Tanakh Hebrew for the body of scriptures known by Christians as the "Old Testament."

Theotokos A Greek title—meaning "the one who gives birth to God"—bestowed by many, although not all, eastern Christians on the Virgin Mary.

Torah From the Hebrew for "instruction," the shorthand term for the sacred law of the Jews.

Ulama Muslim scholars and lawyers.

Umayyads The first dynasty to rule the Caliphate.

Umma A word used in the Qur'an to mean "community" or "people."

Yeshiva A rabbinical school. The most famous *yeshivas* were in Sura and Pumpedita, in Mesopotamia, and Tiberias, in Galilee.

Zuhhad Muslim ascetics.

Notes

1 Known Unknowns

1 From a letter of Simeon of Beth Arsham, discovered and quoted by Shahid (1971), p. 47.

2 Ibid., p. 57.

3 *Chronicon ad Annum Christi 1234 Pertinens*: 1.237.

4 From a poem written in the Hijaz, the region of Arabia where Mecca is situated: quoted by Hoyland (2001), p. 69.

5 Theophylact Simocatta: 4.2.2.

6 Eusebius: *History of the Church*, 1.4.10.

7 Eusebius: *Life of Constantine*, 1.6.

8 Ibn Hisham, p. 629

9 Ibid., p. 105.

10 Qur'an: 96.1–5.

11 Ibn Hisham, p. 106.

12 Qur'an: 6.102.

13 Ibid.: 15.94. Or perhaps "Do what you have been commanded to do."

14 Qur'an: 1.1.

15 Ibid.: 33.40.

16 Ibn Hisham, p. 155.

17 The "Quraysh" are often referred to in English simply as "Quraysh," without a definite article, reflecting the Arabic, which never refers to them as "al-Quraysh."

18 Qur'an: 89.20.

19 Ibid.: 42.42–3.

20 Ibn Hisham, p. 303.

21 Waqidi:*Kitab al-Maghazi*, quoted by Hawting (1999), p. 69.

22 Ibn Hisham, p. 555.

23 From a West Syrian Christian text which records a disputation between a monk and "a man of the Arabs." Although the monk—hardly surprisingly, considering its authorship—ends up decisively winning the argument, the suggestion that God's approval of Islam had manifested itself in the sheer scale of the Arab conquests was a difficult one for Christians to rebut. The

date of the text is unknown, but Hoyland, who quotes it (1997, p. 467), suggests that it is unlikely to be earlier than the mid-eighth century.

24 Al-Jahiz, quoted by Robinson, p. 88.

25 Qur'an: 33.21.

26 Ibn Qutayba, p. 217.

27 *Al-Adab al-Mufrad al-Bukhari* 6.112.

28 Qur'an: 16.89.

29 Ibid.: 29.51.

30 Ibid.: 16.88.

31 Or five, if a verse that alludes to a Messenger called "Ahmad" is counted (61.6).

32 Qur'an: 3.164.

33 Al-Tahawi, quoted by Watt (1994), p. 48.

34 Gibbon, ch. 37, n. 17. The saint whose biographies of other saints are being dismissed is Jerome.

35 Quoted by Wilson, p. 174.

36 The great German theologian of the first half of the nineteenth century, Wilhelm M. L. de Wette, quoted by Friedman, p. 25.

37 Or, as it is more commonly phrased by scholars of Islamic law, "the gate of *ijtihad*"—*ijtihad* being, according to the definition of Hallaq, "the exertion of mental energy in the search for a legal opinion to the extent that the faculties of the jurist become incapable of further effort" (p. 3). As Hallaq has convincingly demonstrated, the conventional attribution of the phrase to the tenth century is mistaken.

38 Gibbon: Vol. 3, p. 230.

39 Quoted by Gilliot, p. 4.

40 Gibbon: Vol. 3, p. 190.

41 Schacht (1977), p. 142.

42 Ibid. (1950), p. 149.

43 Ibid. (1949), p. 147.

44 Rahman (1965), p. 70.

45 Qur'an: 8.9.

46 Ibn Hisham: p. 303.

47 Rahman (1965), pp. 70–1.

48 See, for instance, Gabriel, p. 94.

49 Wansbrough (1978), p. 25.

50 See Crone (1987a), pp. 226–30: a typically brilliant piece of detective work. The papyrus fragment is Text 71 in Grohmann (1963).

51 Qur'an: 8.41. It refers to the nameless battle as having been fought on "the day of the *furqan*," or "deliverance," which we know from 2.181 was in Ramadan.

52 The single name-check is Qur'an: 3.123.

53 Ibn Ishaq is just one of many writers whom we know only through later authors' reworkings of their texts. Another is Malik ibn Anas, a jurist who was known, somewhat optimistically, as "The Proof of the Community."

54 Robinson (2003), p. 51.

55 Although see Nevo and Koren.

56 *Doctrina Iacobi*: 5.16.

57 Of more than four hundred private inscriptions from the Negev Desert in southern Palestine, carved in the eighth century AD, a mere eleven mention Muhammad by name. See Donner (1998), p. 88.

58 Ibn Hisham, p. 691.

59 Peters (1991), p. 292.

60 For these theories, see books by, respectively, Wansbrough, Luxenberg and Ohlig.

61 The paradigmatic example of the problems that can be faced by Muslim revisionists is the series of misfortunes that were suffered by an Egyptian academic, Nasr Abu Zayd, when he published a reading of the Qur'an as a work of literature that had evolved over the course of time. His book provoked a storm of outrage, and led to him being condemned as an apostate, having his wife declared divorced from him by virtue of his offence, and ultimately fleeing into exile. For a brief but suggestive account of how Abu Zayd himself views his intellectual pedigree, see his book, *Reformation of Islamic Thought*, pp. 53–9. At least, though, he was not defenestrated: the fate suffered by the unfortunate Palestinian historian Suliman Bashear.

62 Muhammad Sven Kalisch. See http://www.qantara.de/webcom/show_article.php/_c-478/_nr-812/i.html

63 Manzoor, p. 34.

64 al-Azami (2003), p. 341. Interestingly, when it is the Bible which finds itself in the sights of revisionist scholars, the good professor suddenly becomes a great enthusiast for sceptical enquiry. He certainly never doubts the right of Muslims to deconstruct Jewish and Christian writings.

65 The biography most widely read by non-Muslims is probably the one by Karen Armstrong, which in turn is a redaction of earlier biographies by Rodinson and Watt. Remarkably, for a book written by someone who has written extensively about the grand tradition of biblical scholarship, it does not so much as mention the problematic nature of the sources for the life of Muhammad. Among eminent scholars who still hold the Muslim tradition to be acceptable as historical evidence, by far the most readable is Hugh Kennedy.

66 Donner (1998), p. 2.

67 Neuwirth, p. 1. See also Donner's frank admission that, "Those of us who study Islam's origins have to admit collectively that we simply do not know some very basic things about the Qur'an—things so basic that the knowledge of them is usually taken for granted by scholars dealing with other texts" (in Reynolds, p. 29).

68 For a taster of the range of opinions on offer, the interested reader could try sampling the mind-boggling perspectives on *isnad* authenticity to be

found in al-Azami (1985), Motzki (2002) and Cook (1981). For a survey of all three studies, and many more, see Berg (2000), whose analysis of the entire "*isnad* debate" was particularly helpful in the writing of this chapter. Although Berg does not actually use the word "schism," he sees academic opinion on early Islam as being riven down the middle. "Whether motivated by the need for positive results or the desire for methodological and theoretical sophistication, we are left with two very different, mutually exclusive, and to the outsider, almost equally plausible models of Islamic origins," he writes. "Any conclusion drawn therefore will be a product of these underlying assumptions" (p. 226).

69 Berg (2000), p. 219.

70 Crone (1980), p. 7.

71 There are three mentions of Gabriel in the Qur'an, two of which appear in Qur'an: 2.97–8. The warning to two gossiping wives that Gabriel is ready to intervene on the Prophet's side appears in Qur'an: 66.4.

72 John: 1.1.

73 *Sahih Bukhari* 1.1.2. The *hadith* is attributed to Aisha, Muhammad's favourite wife. The Prophet is remembered in it as describing the experience of revelation as being "like the ringing of bell. This form of inspiration is the hardest of all."

74 See, for instance, *Gospel of Pseudo-Matthew*, ch. 20. There are strong parallels generally between the Qur'anic account of Mary's life and various Christian apocryphal writings. For more detail, see Horn. Suleiman Mourad, in a stimulating essay, has convincingly argued that the Christian legend of the palm tree that fed the pregnant Mary itself derives from the Greek myth of Apollo and Artemis, whose mother Leto was similarly nourished by a palm tree.

75 The word itself derived from the Qur'an—although the use to which Muslim scholars put it probably did not.

76 PERF 558—"PERF" being the standard abbreviation of the "Archduke Rainer Collection." See Grohmann and Jones (1998). A full transcript of PERF 558 can be found at http://www.islamic-awareness.org/History/Islam/Papyri/PERF558.html. A second document, P Berol 15002, also gives us the date "Twenty-Two," but it is fragmentary.

77 One partial exception is the treatment by Muslim historians of Persia, which does seem to preserve authentic native traditions. See Noth (1994), p. 39.

78 Averil Cameron, in Bowersock, Brown and Grabar, p. 16.

2 Iranshahr

1 *Letter of Tansar*, p. 64.

2 Ibid.

3 Ibid., p. 27.

4 Procopius: *History of the Wars*, 1.3.

5 Procopius (*History of the Wars*, 1.3) records that the Hephthalite capital was named "Gorgo," and that it lay not far beyond the Persian frontier. The likeliest location of the city, and therefore of the Persian invasion, is somewhere in the region of Gonbad-e Kavus, site of the magnificent eleventh-century AD tower so admired by Robert Byron. It is true that later sources have Peroz crossing the Oxus, a river much further to the north, but scholars are generally agreed that Procopius's account must derive from a contemporary Persian source, and is therefore much to be preferred.

6 Ammianus: 19.1.2.

7 Theophylact Simocatta: 4.4.8.

8 Procopius: *History of the Wars*, 1.4. Based on the evidence of his coins, Peroz also had earrings comprised of three pearls.

9 Ammianus: 26.6.80.

10 Ibid.: 26.6.77

11 Tabari: Vol. 5, p. 112. Scholars have long recognised that some authentic Sasanian material was preserved by Persian historians and poets following the Arab conquest of their country; but how much precisely is a question that has become increasingly controversial. As with the Muslim sources for Arab history, so with those for the Sasanian period: no methodology exists for distinguishing authentic material from that which has been mangled or simply fabricated from scratch. The stern admonition of a leading historian of the period is worth bearing in mind: "none of the information which [Tabari] presents should be accepted unless it receives some corroboration from independent sources of provable worth" (Howard-Johnston (2006), p. 172).

12 This process began under Peroz's father, Yazdegird II.

13 This is the so-called "Alexander's Wall." In fact, as recent archaeological surveys have demonstrated, it had nothing to do with Alexander. Dated as it has been to a period in the fifth century or early sixth century, its association with Peroz appears, if not certain, then highly probable. See Rekavandi *et al.*

14 Agathias: 4.27.3.

15 *Letter of Tansar*, p. 64.

16 In point of fact, only three of the "Seven Houses"—including the Karin—are attested to in pre-Sasanian sources, but others are mentioned in inscriptions dating from the early Sasanian period, implying that they must have held prominent positions under the previous regime. It is always possible, of course, that some of the families may have fabricated the antiquity of their lineages. See Christensen (1944), pp. 98–103.

17 Theophylact Simocatta: 3.18.7.

18 Elishe, p. 167.

19 For a detailed explication of the relationship between the Persian monarchy and the dynasts of Parthia, see the ground-breaking work of Parvaneh Pourshariati. Whereas once the Sasanian state was seen as the very model of a centralised autocracy, scholars now increasingly emphasise its character as a confederacy: yet another paradigm shift, to go along with all the others that are currently revolutionising the study of late antiquity.

20 Elishe, p. 242.

21 According to Procopius, this was "Gorgo," "located just beyond the Persian frontier, and frequently fought over as a result" (1.3.2). No archaeological traces of such a city have been found, and it seems improbable that the region could have supported any major settlement. Presumably, then, "Gorgo" was a tent city, of the kind common on the steppes. I am grateful to Eberhard Sauer, the excavator of the Gurgan Wall, for a discussion on this point.

22 Heliodorus: 9.15.1.

23 Ibid.: 9.15.5.

24 Ibid.: 9.15.3.

25 Procopius: *History of the Wars*, 1.4.

26 Joshua the Stylite, p. 11.

27 It is suggested in the *Cambridge History of Iran* (p. 403) that the details preserved by later Iranian historians of raids on the mythical Kayanid realm were modelled on actual events that took place in the aftermath of Peroz's defeat: yet another example of how late antiquity can sometimes resemble a hall of mirrors.

28 Strabo: 15.3.15. The description dates from the first century BC, but corresponds to the physical remains of fire temples from the Sasanian period: a reflection of the ancient roots of Zoroastrian practice.

29 Lazar P'arpec'i, p. 213.

30 An alternative theory places this fire temple even further north. See Boyce, "Adur Burzen-Mihr."

31 *Greater Bundahishn*: 18.8.

32 *Yasna*: 30.3.

33 Ibid.: 29.8.

34 Agathias: 2.26.3.

35 Ibn Miskawayh, p. 102. The phrase is attributed to the supposed will of Ardashir, a document faked in the fifth or sixth century, and then preserved in Arabic.

36 *Letter of Tansar*, pp. 33–4. The realisation that such a statement was an aspiration rather than a statement of fact has been one of the great breakthroughs in contemporary Sasanian studies. As Pourshariati (2008, p. 326) has aptly warned, "In assessing church–state relations, it is prudent to remember that the history of the Zoroastrian church as a

monarchy-independent, hierarchically organised church dates only to the 5th C AD."

37   From the *Denkard*, a Zoroastrian text that dates from a few decades after the reign of Peroz. Quoted in the *Cambridge History of Iran*, p. 894.

38   The exact date is uncertain, but it was some time in the late fifth or early sixth century—precisely the period when the Zoroastrian Church was coming into being. See Kellens, p. 1.

39   *Yasht*: 13.100.

40   Lazar P'arpec'i, p. 213.

41   *Mihr Yasht*: 102–3.

42   Ibid.: 7.

43   Ibid.: 23.

44   Ibid.: 2.

45   Joshua the Stylite, p. 11.

46   Christensen (1925), p. 93, argues that Kavad was in his thirties when he ascended the throne, but the majority of sources contradict this. The likelihood is that he was either fifteen or twelve when he became king. See Crone (1991), p. 41.

47   Tabari: Vol. 5, p. 117. The stories of Sukhra's heroism that have been preserved in Arab histories must ultimately derive from traditions propagated by the Karin.

48   See Pourshariati, p. 380.

49   Did this mean that the Parthian traditions of Mihr worship were so unacceptable to the standards of Zoroastrian orthodoxy as to constitute a rival school of religion? The question has provoked intense disagreement among Iranists. The late Mary Boyce, doyenne of Zoroastrian studies, argued that Mihr always ranked as a god subordinate to Ohrmazd, even in Parthia; but more recent scholarship has questioned this. See Pourshariati, pp. 350–68.

50   For the history, and the rewriting of the history, of the three sacred fires, see the respective essays by Boyce. The likelihood that the Median temple, the Fire of the Stallion, was built as late as the fifth century is particularly striking. As Boyce points out, "no clearly datable objects have been found in the ruins earlier than the reign of Peroz."

51   Tabari: Vol. 5, p. 132.

52   *Letter of Tansar*, p. 40.

53   Quoted from a multiplicity of sources by Crone (1991), p. 23.

54   Ibid.

55   For the apocalyptic strain in fifth-century Iran, see Yarshater, p. 996.

56   Tabari: Vol. 5, p.132.

57   The best introduction to Mazdakism is Yarshater's essay in the *Cambridge History of Iran*. He traces the origin of the movement all the way back to the third century AD. Crone (1991), in a typically bracing article, argues that

the dating of Mazdak's career to the reign of Kavad, which all the sources agree upon, is wrong, and should be placed several decades later. For criticisms of this theory, see Zeev Rubin (1995), p. 230, n. 11. For the argument that Mazdak never so much as existed, see Gaube.

58 Procopius: *History of the Wars*, 1.6.

59 Ibid.: 1.5.

60 Procopius: *On Buildings*, 1.1.12.

61 From *The Book of the Deeds of Ardashir*, quoted by Stoneman, p. 41.

62 Ibid.: p. 42.

63 Herodian: 6.2.2.

64 Ammianus: 22.12.2.

65 See Robert Adams, pp. 179–83, who estimates that the population of Mesopotamia grew by 37 per cent over the course of the Sasanian period.

66 Ammianus: 24.8.3.

67 Procopius: *On Buildings*, 3.3.10.

68 Joshua the Stylite: p. 1.

69 "Aspebedes" was almost certainly not his proper name, but a transliteration into Greek of his official title: the *Spahbed*, or "Generalissimo," of the West. If this is the same *Spahbed* who took part in Kavad's attack on Amida in 503, then "Aspebedes" was actually called Bawi. (See Joshua the Stylite, p. 76.)

70 Procopius: *History of the Wars*, 1.11.

71 *Letter of Tansar*, p. 43. Although ostensibly written during the reign of Ardashir, the identification of the events described with the Mazdakite revolt is almost universally accepted.

72 Ibid.: p. 38.

73 Ammianus: 24.6.3.

74 Theophanes, p. 26. The description is of Khusrow II's gardens at Dastagerd, but would certainly have been applicable to the great park of Ctesiphon.

75 Ibid.

76 Genesis: 2.8.

77 Daniel: 7.3. The Book of Daniel is conventionally dated to the mid-second century BC, some four hundred years after Daniel himself is supposed to have lived.

78 Ibid.: 7.18.

79 Cassius Dio: 68.30.

80 Jeremiah: 51.7.

81 Ibid.: 51.37.

82 Procopius: *History of the Wars*, 2.13.13.

83 For the identification of the Harranian rituals as described by Christian and Muslim sources with the *akitu* festival, see Green, pp. 156–7.

84 *Letter of Jeremiah*: 72.

85 Berosus, pp. 20–1.

86 Ammianus: 23.6.25.

87 Genesis: 11.28. Muslim and some Jewish traditions identify Ur with Urfa, the ancient city of Edessa, not far from Harran. There seems to be some support for this attribution in the fact that Abraham received his first revelation from God not in Ur but in "Haran"—which was almost certainly Harran. However, most scholars agree that the Ur mentioned in Genesis was the ancient city of the same name in Chaldaea, in the south of Mesopotamia. This had its final flourishing as a major cultural centre during the first half of the sixth century BC, under the Babylonian monarchy—precisely the period when the Judaeans were in exile in Babylon and the Book of Genesis was reaching its final form. Therefore, the exiles' desire to link their ancestor to a sophisticated place of origin probably explains the association of Abraham with a city that is specifically described in Genesis (11.28) as "Ur of the Chaldaeans." Of course, this strongly implies that Abraham himself was a mythical, rather than a historical, figure—which, by and large, is the current scholarly consensus. It is perhaps not entirely coincidental that doubts about the historicity of Abraham entered the academic mainstream in the 1970s—precisely when scepticism about what Muslim tradition had to say about the origins of Islam was also gaining currency in scholarly circles.

88 Ibid.: 12.1–2.

89 Ibid.: 17.8.

90 Ibid.: 17.5.

91 *Letter of Tansar*, p. 64. The reference is to Persia itself, but the market place of Persia lay in Ctesiphon, not Iran.

92 Genesis: 17. 9–10.

93 Exodus: 20.4.

94 *b. Berachoth* 8b. Quotations from the Talmud are often prefaced by one of two letters—"b" and "y"—which indicate whether they derive from the "Bavli," or Babylonian Talmud, or the "Yerushalmi," or Palestinian Talmud.

95 *b. Avodah Zarah* 16a.

96 *Denkard*: 3.229. Though composed in the early ninth century, the material that this source incorporates mostly dates from the Sasanian period.

97 Elishe: p. 63.

98 Elishe: p. 63.

99 There is a late and fantastical tradition that narrates the rise to power of one last exilarch—Mar Zutra. He supposedly exploited the chaos unleashed by the Mazdakite revolt to carve out an independent Jewish state before being toppled by Kavad and crucified on a bridge in Ctesiphon. For a long time, there was an "uncritical acceptance of the fabulous stories as literally true, factual historical accounts, though with the exclusion of the more miraculous of the miracles" (Neusner [1986], p. 98). As the

leading contemporary historian of the Mesopotamian Jews has conclusively demonstrated, however, the evidence is patently "inadequate, indeed incredible" (ibid., p. 104).

100   *b. Hullin* 62b.

101   Nowhere are we specifically told this, but the enthusiasm with which Jews flocked to serve in Kavad's armies is inexplicable unless we presume as much.

102   Eusebius: *Preparation for the Gospel*: 9.18. The phrase is a quotation from an otherwise largely vanished book named *Concerning the Jews of Assyria*, by a second-century BC Jewish historian named Eupolemus.

103   Such, at least, is the overwhelming scholarly consensus, which dates the start of the transcription of the Talmud to around AD 500.

104   *Exodus Rabbah* 15.21.

105   *b. Sanhedrin* 98a.

106   *Genesis Rabbah* 42.4.

107   *b. Sanhedrin* 36a. The rabbi was Jehuda ha-Nasi, who lived in the late second century AD.

108   *b. Yevamot* 20a.

109   *b. Berakhot* 58a.

110   *b. Kethuboth* 111b.

111   *b. Shabbat* 30b.

112   *Numeri Rabbah* 14.10.

113   See Marcel Simon, p. 196.

114   *b. Gittin 57a.* The references to Jesus in the Talmud are notoriously elliptical and enigmatic, and have traditionally—for understandable reasons—been skated over by both Christian and Jewish scholars. For a fascinating and persuasive survey, see the recent book by Peter Schäfer, who demonstrates how the "[mainly] Babylonian stories about Jesus and his family are deliberate and highly sophisticated counternarratives to the stories about Jesus's life and death in the Gospels" (p. 8).

115   *Numeri Rabbah* 14.10.

116   *Abodah Zara* 2a.

3 New Rome

1   Propertius: 3.22.21.

2   The quotation comes from Athenaeus, 6.273A–275A.

3   Plutarch, *Roman Questions*: 61.

4   This process had begun long before the formal absorption of Greece into the Roman Empire, and seems initially to have drawn upon contacts between Rome and the Greek settlements in Italy. "The Greeks imposed the Trojan legend upon the West as a form of Hellenic cultural imperialism, only to see it appropriated by the westerner to define and convey a Roman cultural identity" (Gruen, p. 31).

5   Livy: 26.27.
6   Virgil: 6.852–3.
7   Aristides: 26.59 and 99.
8   Virgil: 6.792–3
9   Ibid.: 1.279.
10 Such, at any rate, is the claim made by our admittedly hostile Christian sources. It is possible that their accounts of the humiliations inflicted upon Valerian reflect a measure of wishful thinking.
11 Cicero: 17.
12 Optatianus Porphyrius, *Carmen*: 4, line 6. The poem was composed to celebrate the founding of Constantinople, and clearly suggests that the new city's status as a rival to Rome was manifest from the very beginning.
13 Eusebius, *Life of Constantine*: 3.54.
14 The earliest reference to this tradition can be dated to the fifth century AD. See Sozomen: 2.3.2.
15 See Fowden (1991) for a much earlier source which implies that the porphyry actually came from Rome.
16 *Chronicon Paschale*, p. 16.
17 Zosimus: 1.58.4.
18 Procopius: *History of the Wars*, 1.11.9.
19 Procopius: *On Buildings*, 1.5.10.
20 Zosimus: 2.35.2.
21 Corippus: 3.244.
22 *The Oracle of Baalbek*, line 166.
23 Procopius: *The Secret History*, 14.2.
24 Ibid.: *On Buildings*, 2.6.6.
25 This derives from Procopius (*The Secret History*, 30.21–3), who was admittedly almost rabid in his undercover hostility to Justinian. Nevertheless, even if some of the details of the changes to court ceremonial may have been exaggerated, the drift towards ever-greater formality is irrefutable.
26 Procopius: *The Secret History*, 8.27.
27 Ibid.: 8.24.
28 *Novels* 43, prologue.
29 *Novels* 98: 16 December 539.
30 Cicero, *On the Orator*: 1.197.
31 *Novels* 111.
32 *CJ Constt. Summa*, preface.
33 The notion that the emperor constituted the law dated back at least to the fourth century AD.
34 John Lydus: 3.44.
35 A decree of Theodosius II (r. 408–50), quoted by Kelly, p. 187.
36 Procopius: *The Secret History*, 7.10.
37 Even the lowest figure we have, Procopius's estimate of thirty thousand, is

staggering. All ancient historians exaggerated battle casualties, but the massacre in the Hippodrome undoubtedly resulted in a prodigious death toll.

38 John Lydus: 3.70.
39 *Novels* 72: 538.
40 Procopius: 1.14.52.
41 Ibid.: *On Buildings*, 2.1.11.
42 Whether Procopius exaggerated the scale of Justinian's contributions to the fortifications of Dara is a moot point. See Croke and Crow.
43 Isaiah: 40.15.
44 Ibid.: 40.17.
45 Genesis: 22.18.
46 *Tractate Paschale* 8. The rabbi himself, Eleazar ben Pedat, was born in the Holy Land.
47 "Ambrosiaster," a commentator on St. Paul's letters who was long mistaken for St. Ambrose. Quoted by Cohen, p. 159.
48 I am indebted to Shahrokh Razmjou for alerting me to this.
49 *b. Kiddushin* 70b.
50 Galatians: 3.28.
51 Ibid.: 3.25–6.
52 The first known use of the phrase "Old Testament" occurred in the writings of Melito of Sardis (c. AD 180), and that of the "New Testament" in Irenaeus's *Against Heresies* (4.91), from around the same time.
53 Gospel of St. John: 14.6.
54 Gospel of St. Matthew: 28.19. See also 2 Corinthians: 13.13.
55 Acts: 2.2.
56 1 Corinthians: 12.13.
57 "Letter to Diognetus" (a): 5.
58 Ignatius, "Letter to the Ephesians": 6.
59 Gospel of St. Matthew: 19.21.
60 Ibid.: 7.15.
61 Tertullian, *The Prescription Against the Heretics*: 21.
62 Ibid.
63 Romans: 15.19.
64 Gospel of St. Matthew: 5.18.
65 Tertullian, *Against Praxeas*: 2.
66 Irenaeus, *Against Heresies*: 1.8.1.
67 For the value placed on eyewitness accounts by both early Christian writers and classical historians, and the concurrent suspicion of written evidence, see Alexander (1990) and Byrskog. Unfortunately, the question of whether the canonical gospels do indeed preserve eyewitness accounts is not one that can be tackled in a single footnote.
68 See, for instance, the Gospel of Thomas, a number of Infancy Gospels, and

the Gospel of Pseudo-Matthew—the same text which features Christ's conversation with His mother from the womb. In some of these gospels, Christ makes the birds come to life, not to amuse His friends, but to demonstrate to a killjoy Jew that it is permissible to work clay on the Sabbath.

69 See Origen: 1.1. No trace of the Gospel of Basilides has survived, however, so we are entirely dependent upon the reports of his enemies for a sense of what might have been contained within it.

70 Irenaeus, *Against Heresies*: 1.24.4.

71 Origen: 1.1.

72 Clement of Alexandria: *Stromateis* 7.106.4.

73 Justin Martyr: 47.

74 *t. Hul.* 2.24.

75 Gospel of St. John: 3.7.

76 Alan Segal (p. 1) gives the metaphor a more biblical colouring: "Like Jacob and Esau, the twin sons of Isaac and Rebecca, the two religions fought in the womb." See also, for a more radical phrasing of the same metaphor, Boyarin (2004, p. 5): "Judaism is not the 'mother' of Christianity; they are twins, joined at the hip." As with so many other aspects of the history of ancient religion, the question of when Judaism and Christianity "parted ways" has been revolutionised over the past few decades. In the words of Carleton Paget, this constitutes "the most significant recent development in the discussion of Jewish–Christian relations" (p. 18). Carleton Paget's is the best, most nuanced overview of recent scholarship (pp. 1–39).

77 Bardaisan, p. 49.

78 Evidence for this can be adduced from a site such as Sardis, in what is now western Turkey, where a synagogue built around AD 400 adjoined a colonnade that contained shops owned by a healthy mix of Christians and Jews. If this was the state of affairs in what was, by then, a Christian empire, then something similar almost certainly prevailed in third- and fourth-century Mesopotamia. See the essay by Rutgers.

79 See Becker, p. 380.

80 See Rouwhorst, pp. 81–2.

81 See Weitzman. Others argue that the translation was made by Jews who had already been baptised.

82 Eusebius, *History of the Church*: 3.27. Paul did not, in fact, advocate the abandonment of the Torah by Jewish converts, but that was rarely appreciated, either by the Gentile Christians who so admired him or by the Jewish Christians who often regarded him with deep suspicion.

83 From an inscription on a Persian curse bowl, quoted by Levene, p. 290.

84 Ignatius, "The Letter to the Magnesians": 10.3.

85 The city was briefly lost to Ardashir in 241, but it was recaptured a couple of years later.

86   *b. Gittin* 55b. The rabbi was Rabbi Meir.
87   *Kohelet Rabba* 10.5.
88   Acts: 19.26.
89   Such, at any rate, is the tradition. It is probably true.
90   Eusebius, *History of the Church*: 5.1.
91   An alternative theory derived the word *religio* from *relegere*—"to write or reflect upon over and over again." Whatever the derivation, *religio* itself signified practice, rather than belief.
92   The emperor was Galerius, in a decree of 311, quoted by Lactantius: 34.1.
93   From an inscription by one Demeas, who, in his own words, tore down "the deceitful likeness of the demon Artemis." Quoted by Foss (1979), p. 32.
94   Jacob of Serugh, quoted by Griffith (2008), p. 123.
95   Daniel: 7.7.
96   Ibid.: 7.19.
97   Lactantius: 44.5.
98   Daniel: 7.11.
99   Isidore of Pelusium, p. 217.
100 *Theodosian Code*: 16.2.16.
101 Eusebius, *Life of Constantine*: 1.28.
102 Ibid.: 2.12.
103 Ignatius, "The Letter to the Magnesians": 10.1. See also "The Letter to the Philadelphians," 6.1.
104 From a letter written by Constantine jointly to Arius and his bishop. It is quoted by Eusebius in his *Life of Constantine*: 2.71.
105 Eusebius, *Life of Constantine*: 3.10.
106 As so often with Christian neologisms, Tertullian seems to have been the first to use the word *religio* in a way analogous to our word "religion." See Sachot, pp. 111–16.
107 Lactantius, *Divine Institutes*: 4.28.
108 *Theodosian Code*: 16.10.12.
109 Socrates Scholasticus: 7.29.
110 *Acta Martyrum et Sanctorum*: Vol. 2, p. 149.
111 The phrase was added in the 470s, by the Patriarch of Antioch, to the formula "Holy Powerful One, Holy Deathless One." See Brown (2003), p. 119.
112 Barhadbeshabba of Holwan, p. 605.
113 John Malalas, p. 228.
114 Procopius: *History of the Wars*, 1.24. Opinions on the veracity of the episode vary widely.
115 Procopius: *Secret History*, 2.9.
116 John Lydus: 3.69.
117 Procopius: *On Buildings*, 1.10. The mosaic was part of the renovations to the Chalke that were required after the Hippodrome riots.

118   Ibid.: 2.6.
119   *Theodosian Code*: 16.10.22.
120   Procopius: *Secret History*, 2.13.
121   The exact chronology is obscure. See Watts, pp. 128–39.
122   Agathias: 2.31.4.
123   For the theory that the philosophers may have settled in Harran, see
       Athanassiadi (1993). As she has subsequently acknowledged, however, the
       theory remains controversial (1999, pp. 51–3).
124   1 Corinthians: 1.20.
125   It is Athanassiadi (1999, pp. 342–7) who argues (convincingly) that a bishop
       took up residence in this villa.
126   Paul the Silentiary: 489.
127   Procopius: *On Buildings*, 1.27.
128   Ibid.: 1.30.

4 The Children of Abraham

1   Paul the Silentiary: 144.
2   *Sayings of the Desert Fathers*: Joseph of Panephysis, p. 103.
3   *Wisdom of the Desert Fathers*, p. 3.
4   *Life of Sabbas*: 8.92, in *Three Byzantine Saints*.
5   Lucian, *De Dea Syria*: 28, quoted by Frankfurter, p. 178.
6   *Life of Symeon the Younger*: 11.
7   Ibid.: 40.
8   Ibid.: Prologue.
9   Ibid.: 199.
10   Ibid.: 115.
11   *Life of Daniel Stylites*: 54, in *Three Byzantine Saints*.
12   Genesis: 32.24–30.
13   Exodus: 1.7.
14   Ibid.: 1.14.
15   Ibid.: 3.2.
16   Ibid.: 3.7–8.
17   Egeria, p. 8.
18   Procopius: *On Buildings*, 8.9.
19   Exodus: 19.16.
20   Deuteronomy: 34.10.
21   Quoted by Sivan (2008), p. 68.
22   Jerome, *Letters*: 58.3.
23   Ibid.: 46.2.
24   *Life of Daniel Stylites*: 10, in *Three Byzantine Saints*.
25   A sixth-century pilgrim, quoted by Sivan (2008), p. 70.
26   Jerome, *Letters*: 46.13.

27 From a letter written by two monks to the Emperor Anastasius, quoted by Wilken, pp. 168–9.

28 Procopius: *On Buildings*, 5.6.

29 Micah: 3.12. For the evolution of the phrase "Temple Mount," see Goodblatt, pp. 193–203.

30 Although the anecdote is suspiciously late: from the eighth or ninth century.

31 Jerome, *On Zephaniah*: 1.16.

32 *Tanhuma to Leviticus* (*Qedoshim* 10).

33 *b. Yoma*, 54b.

34 Ammianus Marcellinus: 23.1.

35 From a sixth-century Jewish hymn, quoted by Weinberger, p. 34.

36 *b. Gittin* 62a.

37 The estimate is Avi-Yonah's, p. 241. Others regard the figure as over-optimistic.

38 Jerome, *On Isaiah*: 48.17.

39 A combination of carbon-dating and circumstantial evidence points to the first decade of Justinian's reign.

40 Quoted by Meyers, p. 353.

41 Ibid.: 5.

42 Procopius: *On Buildings*, 5.9. Procopius does not mention the church: for evidence of that, we are dependent exclusively upon archaeology.

43 See Ab Isda of Tyre (quoted in Crown, p. 457), for the classic formulation. The phrase is at least as old as the fourth century AD: archaeologists on Mount Gerizim have found it on a large number of inscriptions. See Sivan (2008), p. 119.

44 Quoted in Crown, Pummer and Tal, p. 161.

45 For the possible influence of Samaritan notions of "submission" to God on early Islam, see Crone and Cook, p. 19 and Crown, Pummer and Tal, p. 21.

46 Specifically, Rabbis Judah bar Pazzi and Rabbi Ammi. See p. *Abodah Zarah* 5.4. (III.a).

47 Abu l-Fath, p. 241.

48 Procopius: *On Buildings*, 5.7.

49 John Malalas: 446.

50 Procopius: *Secret History*, 11.

51 Genesis: 19.28.

52 Cyril of Jerusalem, "Prologue to the Catechetical Letters": 10. At the time he delivered this lecture, Cyril was still two or three years away from becoming bishop.

53 Ibid., "Catechetical Lecture": 4.36.

54 Theodoret, *Compendium of Heretical Fables*: p. 390.

55. Jerome, *Letters*: 112.12. It is only fair to point out that no rabbi would have disagreed.

56 Jerome, *In Esaiam*: 40.9, quoted by de Blois (2002), p. 15.

57 Epiphanius: 30.1.3.

58 Ibid.: 30.1.2.

59 For the strong likelihood that there were villages of Christian Jews on the Golan, see Joan Taylor, pp. 39–41. A broader issue is the degree to which we can trust the evidence for the survival of a recognisably Jewish form of Christianity into the sixth and seventh centuries. A seminal essay by Pines in 1968, arguing that there was evidence from as late as the tenth century, generated much controversy, but in the words of Gager (p. 365), it has been "largely vindicated, though with certain modifications."

60 Quoted by Strugnell, p. 258, from a letter written by the Nestorian patriarch Timothy I in 786. As the remainder of Strugnell's article demonstrates, there is incontrovertible evidence from Syriac manuscripts of even earlier discoveries of what have become known as the Dead Sea Scrolls. That Jews in the Middle Ages were also familiar with one of them, at least—the so-called "Damascus Document"—is evident from the discovery in the late nineteenth century of two copies of the "Damascus Document" in the Jewish quarter of Cairo.

61 Sozomen: 2.4.

62 Josephus: 4.533.

63 Genesis: 19.27.

64 From a letter of Constantine to the bishops of Palestine, quoted by Eusebius in his *Life of Constantine*: 3.53. The identification of the three angels who visited Abraham with the constituent parts of the Trinity had first been made in the second century.

65 The opinion of a late sixth-century Christian who lived in Mesopotamia. Quoted by Hoyland (1997), p. 25.

66 Sargon II, the King of Assyria. Quoted by Hoyland (2001), p. 96.

67 Ammianus: 14.4.4. For the blood-drinking, see Ammianus: 31.16.5–7. Greek and Roman writers never missed an opportunity to cast barbarians as cannibals.

68 Ibid.: 14.4.1.

69 From "*al-Murqqish al-Akbar*," in Alan Jones (1996, Vol. 1), p. 112.

70 Abid ibn al-Abras, quoted by Hoyland (2001), pp. 121–2.

71 For the argument that the Thamud were indeed a confederation, and not, as is sometimes assumed, merely a tribe, see Bowersock (1983), pp. 97–8, and Graf and O'Connor, pp. 65–6.

72 The word features on a second-century AD temple at Ruwwafa, a remote site in western Arabia, where there is an inscription written in both Greek and Nabataean. See Milik for the translation of *shirkat* as "confederation."

73 The derivation has only recently been recognised, courtesy of new epigraphic evidence. See Graf and O'Connor.

74 Joshua the Stylite, p. 79.

75 Or at least it is "practically certain" this is what it meant. See Shahid (1989), p. 213.
76 Quoted in the *Cambridge History of Iran*, p. 597.
77 Cyril of Scythopolis: 24.
78 The Arabic word seems to have derived from a Greek form of the original Latin. See Jeffrey, p. 196.
79 Procopius: *History of the Wars*, 1.17.
80 It is possible that the visit to Constantinople took place after the formal appointment of Arethas as king. See Shahid (1989), pp. 103–9.
81 Procopius: *History of the Wars*, 1.22.
82 From a report by Nonnosus, a Roman diplomat whose father and grandfather had both served as ambassadors to various Arab chieftains, and who himself was sent by Justinian on a mission to Ethiopia and the central and southern reaches of Arabia. What Gibbon describes as "a curious extract" from his memoirs was preserved by Photius, a ninth-century Patriarch of Constantinople, in his *Biblioteka*. The precise location of the shrine mentioned by Nonnosus is unknown, but the specifications that he does give, although frustratingly vague, make it clear enough that it was not Mecca, but somewhere in northern Arabia. See Crone (1987a), p. 197, n. 127.
83 Dushara was the Greek form of the god who was known by the Nabataeans as Dhu l-Shara and by the Lakhmids as Ashara. See Ryckmans, p. 246.
84 Diodorus Siculus: 3.42.
85 A temple in the Jabal Qatuta, near Marib, is the best example of this.
86 For Epiphanius's confusion over *ka'iba* and *ka'ba*, see Sourdel, p. 67.
87 Theodoret, *Ecclesiastical History*: 26.13.
88 From ibid., *The Cure of Greek Maladies*: Vol. 1, p. 250.
89 Genesis: 16.12.
90 However, the Bible does not equate the Children of Ishmael with the Arabs. For an account of how the two came to be seen as synonymous, see the essays by Eph'al and Millar.
91 From *The Life of Simeon Priscus*, quoted by Shahid (1989), p. 154.
92 Genesis: 21.21.
93 For the "highly unusual frequency of occurrence of the name Abraham in the sixth-century Negev," see Nevo and Koren, p. 189.
94 Sozomen: 6.38.
95 Ibid.
96 Ibid. For the evidence of a Jewish presence in north Arabia during the Roman period, see Hoyland (1995), p. 93.
97 The title was also applied to the Christian God in the wake of Yusuf's defeat. See Nebes, pp. 37–8.

5 Countdown to Apocalypse

1 Cosmas Indicopleustes, p. 113.
2 Sidonius Apollinaris: Vol. 1, p. 41.
3 Sigismund of Burgundy, quoted by Harris, p. 33.
4 For the likely derivation of the word "Ostrogoth," see Wolfram, p. 25.
5 As Ward-Perkins (p. 73) points out, "there is not even a word in the Latin language for 'moustache.'"
6 For the commemoration of Ulfilas as Moses, see Amory, p. 241.
7 Quoted by O'Donnell (2008), p. 131.
8 Quoted by Brown (2003), p. 103.
9 *Codex Justinianus*: 27.1.1.
10 Procopius: *History of the Wars*, 4.9.12.
11 Ibid.: 5.14.14.
12 Ibid.: 6.
13 Ibid.: 2.2.6.
14 Menander the Guardsman: fragment 6.1.
15 John of Ephesus (as he is known, although in fact he was called Yuhannan, and came from Amida, not Ephesus), p. 83.
16 Joshua the Stylite, p. 29.
17 Jerome: *Letters*, 130.7.
18 Ibid., *Commentary on Ezekiel*: 8.225.
19 Ammianus Marcellinus: 22.9.14.
20 *Life of Symeon the Younger*: 57.
21 *Novella* 30.11.2.
22 John of Ephesus, p. 77.
23 Although only one source, and a late one at that, explicitly states that Alexander was instructed by the oracle to found Alexandria, the circumstantial evidence is strong. See Welles.
24 Ammianus Marcellinus: 16.15.
25 A formula often used by Christians in Alexandria. Cited by Haas, p. 130.
26 Isidore of Pelusium, quoted by Haas, p. 10.
27 Stephen of Herakleopolis: 10–11.
28 John of Nikiu: 92.7.
29 *Expositio Totius Mundi et Gentium*: lines 229–30.
30 Joshua the Stylite: 26.
31 John of Ephesus, pp. 74–5.
32 Procopius: *History of the Wars*, 2.23.4.
33 John of Ephesus, p. 87.
34 Procopius: *History of the Wars*, 2.22.7.
35 A 2005 DNA study of two skeletons found in Germany conclusively proved that the pestilence of the 540s was caused by *Yersinia pestis*. In the words of the scientists who conducted it: "The identification of *Y. pestis*–specific DNA sequences in these two skeletons, buried in the second half

of the 6th century AD, constitutes molecularly supported evidence for the presence of *Y. pestis*, the causative agent of plague, during the first pandemic recorded" (Wiechmann and Grupe, p. 48). It is worth noting that the prevalence of plague during the winter as well as the summer months and the description in contemporary accounts of some of the symptoms suggest that one of the strains might have been pneumonic, the most deadly and infectious of all.

36 John of Ephesus, p. 75.
37 Procopius: *History of the Wars*, 2.22.9.
38 Ibid.: 2.23.18.
39 Ibid.: 2.22.1.
40 John of Ephesus, p. 95.
41 Paul the Deacon: 2.4. This passage refers to an outbreak of plague in Italy in 565.
42 John of Ephesus, p. 102.
43 Michael Morony (in Little, p. 73) suggests that a mortality rate of a third is "realistic and believable." Following an influential article by Jean Durliat, estimates of the total death toll were reduced downwards throughout the nineties, but recent DNA studies have reversed that trend. We now know that the sixth-century pestilence was humanity's first experience of bubonic plague, so it is probable—indeed, almost certain—that its impact (upon a population that had no immunity whatsoever) was even greater than that of the Black Death in the fourteenth century. Historians are still in the process of making their calculations in light of this.
44 Procopius: *History of the Wars*, 2.23.10.
45 Procopius: *The Secret History*, 13.28.
46 Ibid.: 18.29.
47 Ibid.: 18.30.
48 Ibid.: 12.27.
49 For a fascinating analysis of how admirers and opponents of Justinian both put their spin on the selfsame policies of the emperor, see Scott.
50 Procopius: *The Secret History*, 12.26.
51 Gospel of St. Matthew: 24.27.
52 Ibid.: 24.7. Some versions omit the Greek word *loimoi*—"pestilences"—but this seems to have been due to confusion because of its proximity to the very similar word for "famines"—*lomoi*. The similarity of Matthew 24.7 to Luke 21.11 makes it clear that "pestilences" were always on the agenda.
53 Evagrius Scholasticus: 4.29.
54 See Keys for the argument that the proximity of this event to the first coming of the plague to Egypt may not have been coincidental.
55 Agathias: 5.11.6.
56 Ezekiel: 38.16.
57 Josephus: 7.7.4.

58 Jacob of Serugh, "Metrical Discourse upon Alexander": line 544, in *The History of Alexander the Great*. The attribution of the poem to Jacob, who died in 521, is no longer generally accepted. The likeliest date of the poem is the early seventh century. See Stoneman, p. 177.

59 Ibid.: line 322.

60 *Life of Theodore of Sykeon*: 119, in *Three Byzantine Saints*.

61 Hassan ibn Thabit, quoted by Conrad (1994), p. 18, who argues convincingly for its authenticity.

62 Ibid., p. 18.

63 Procopius: *History of the Wars*, 2.27.12.

64 Sozomen: 2.4.

65 Quoted by Conrad (1994), p. 18.

66 From the vision of a monk in Egypt. Quoted by Kelly, p. 232.

67 This phenomenon was not unique to Arabia. As early as the second century AD, pagans across the Roman Empire were interpreting the gods of their various pantheons as the angels of one supreme deity, and by late antiquity this process had become near universal. For a useful survey, see Crone (2010), pp. 185–8.

68 Corippus, p. 108.

69 Hugh Kennedy, in a valuable essay on the impact of the plague on Syria, demonstrates that "the expansion of settlement that had characterised much of rural and urban Syria in the fifth and early sixth centuries came to an abrupt end after the middle of the sixth century" (Little, p. 95).

70 For the impact of the plague on agriculture in central and southern Syria, see Conrad (1994), p. 54.

71 John of Ephesus: p. 81, quoting Isaiah: 24.3.

72 Moses Dasxuranci: 2.11.

73 Menander: 16.1.13.

74 Tabari: Vol. 5, p. 295.

75 The sources for Bahram Chobin's reign are mostly late and heavily mythologised, yet it appears that his rebellion did indeed embody messianic expectations. See the ground-breaking essay by Czeglédy, and further analysis of the episode by Pourshariati (2008), pp. 397–414.

76 Theophylact Simocatta: 3.1.10.

77 Evagrius Scholasticus: 3.41.

78 Fredegarius: 4.65.

79 *The Life of Saint Theodore of Sykeon*: 134, in *Three Byzantine Saints*.

80 Theophylact Simocatta: 4.8.

81 For the devastation caused across Anatolia by the Persians, see Foss (1975).

82 For the Mihranid ancestry of Shahrbaraz, see Gyselen, p. 11.

83 Daniel: 7.23.

84 Ibid.: 7.26.

85 From a *piyyut*, or liturgical poem, convincingly dated by Hagith Sivan (2000)

to the period of the Persian occupation of Jerusalem, and quoted by her on p. 295.

86 According to one—later—source (Sebeos, p. 72), the authorities in Jerusalem did negotiate a surrender, but this was followed by rioting, a revolt and then the siege. Eyewitness accounts, however, insist that the city refused to submit from the start.

87 From a second *piyyut*, quoted by Sivan (2000), p. 289.

88 Daniel: 7.13–14.

89 George of Pisidia: 2.106–7.

90 *The History of King Vaxt'ang Gorgasali*, p. 234. The biblical passage paraphrases Daniel: 8.5–7.

91 *Chronicon Paschale*: 725.

92 Sebeos, 72.

93 Theophanes, p. 324.

94 See Kaegi (2003), p. 174.

95 Nikephoros: 15.

96 Ibid.: 17.

97 Theophanes, p. 328.

98 Maximos the Confessor, quoted by Laga, p. 187

99 Ibid., p. 186.

6 More Questions Than Answers

1 Daniel: 7.7.

2 Sebeos: 142.

3 From an anonymous anti-Christian pamphlet. Quoted by Sizgorich (2009), pp. 1–2.

4 For the evolution of the word "Muslim" from its original Qur'anic usage, see Donner (2010), pp. 57–8 and 71–2.

5 Qur'an: 47.4.

6 Ibid.: 4.133.

7 This suggestion has its roots in traditions that are even older than the first Muslim biographies of the Prophet. A Christian chronicler, Jacob of Edessa, for instance, writing at the end of the seventh century, referred to him as going "for trade to the lands of Palestine, Arabia and Syrian Phoenicia" (quoted by Hoyland (1997), p. 165).

8 This has been most radically argued by Günter Lüling, who proposes that the Meccans were largely Christian, and that the original core of the Qur'an consisted of Christian hymns. For the suggestion that Jews had settled in Mecca, and powerfully influenced Muhammad, see Torrey.

9 Armstrong, p. 68. The thesis derives, via Montgomery Watt, from the Jesuit—and scabrously Islamophobic—scholar Henri Lammens.

10 Qur'an: 6.92. Muslim tradition takes for granted that the phrase refers to

Mecca, but there is nothing in the Qur'an itself that would justify such a presumption. Adding to the general fog of mystery enveloping it is the fact that the phrase literally means the "Mother of Settlements."

11 See Crone (1987a), p. 6, and for the implausibility of Mecca as a great trading hub, the entire book.

12 See Cosmas Indicopleustes.

13 Most striking of all is the absence of any mention of Mecca in Procopius, since in one passage of *The History of the Wars* (1.19), the historian provides a remarkably detailed survey of the western coast of Arabia. This is testimony to the range and depth of Roman knowledge of the peninsula, and to the seeming lack of any Meccan sphere of influence.

14 Qur'an: 48.24.

15 As Crone (1987a, p. 134) points out, the silence "is so striking that attempts have been made to remedy it." For the forced nature of these attempts, see ibid., pp. 134–6.

16 *The Byzantine-Arab Chronicle*: 34. The dating of the *Chronicle* to 741 is based on its latest references, but Hoyland (1997, p. 426) suggests that it may well be truncated, and floats the possibility that it may actually date from 750.

17 See "The Letter of John of Sedreh," the record of a discussion about holy texts held in 644 between the patriarch and an Arab emir, a full translation of which appears in Saadi. Although Saadi himself dates the document to the mid-seventh century, others place its composition in the early eighth century. If correct, the later dating makes the absence of any reference to the Qur'an even more striking. See Reinink (1993).

18 John of Damascus: 769B.

19 Qur'an: 24.2.

20 Quoted by Lester, p. 283.

21 A useful list of the earliest-known Qur'ans in existence—not all of which were found in Sana'a—is at http://www.islamic-awareness.org/Quran/Text/Mss/.

22 Admittedly, Wansbrough—one of the principal proponents of this thesis—was typically tentative when he suggested that the Qur'an reached its final form only towards the end of the eighth century. Scholars of the calibre of Gerald Hawting and Andrew Rippin still argue that it took decades, at least, for the holy text to reach anything like its final form.

23 Qur'an: 3.7.

24 Ibid.: 111.3. The punishment is a pun on Abu Lahab's name, which means "Man of Flame" in Arabic.

25 Ibid.: 50.16.

26 For a detailed and intellectually thrilling exposition of this point, see *The Idea of Idolatry and the Emergence of Islam* by Gerald Hawting: a ground-breaking work that has resulted in a paradigm shift in the way that scholars understand the role of the *Mushrikun* in the Qur'an.

27 Qur'an: 43.19.
28 Ibid.: 10.66.
29 Ibid.: 7.74.
30 Ibid.: 30.1.
31 Ibid.: 18.83.
32 For the dating and political context of the Syriac story of Alexander, see Reinink (1985 and 2002).
33 "A Christian Legend Concerning Alexander": 146, in *The History of Alexander the Great*.
34 For a detailed analysis of the strikingly precise correspondences between the two stories, see Van Bladel, pp. 180–3. As he conclusively demonstrates, "they relate the same story in precisely the same order of events using many of the same particular details" (p. 182).
35 Qur'an: 82.1–5.
36 Ibid.: 30.56. It is telling, perhaps, that the phrase appears as the conclusion to the sura which opens with God's prophecy that the Romans will emerge victorious in their war against the Persians.
37 Ibid.: 7.34.
38 Ibid.: 18.26.
39 Ibid.: 18.13.
40 The Qur'an refers to them as *al-Majus*, or Magians (22.17): the word applied by the Greeks to Persian priests since the time of Cyrus.
41 Qur'an: 4.136.
42 Ibid.: 3.3.
43 Justinian Code: 1.5.12 (summer 527).
44 Qur'an: 9.29. The precise meaning of this verse is notoriously problematic. For a sample of the various attempts to make sense of it, see Ibn Warraq (2002), pp. 319–86.
45 Qur'an: 5.82 and 9.34.
46 Ibid.: 5.47.
47 Ibid.: 5.116.
48 Ibid.: 4.157.
49 Ibid.: 85.4.
50 Irfan Shahid, the leading expert on the martyrs of Najran, is studiedly agnostic about the possibility: see (1971), p. 193.
51 See, for instance, Bishop and especially Philonenko.
52 Qur'an: 6.59.
53 Ibid.: 87.18–19.
54 Ibid.: 52.24. Not surprisingly, this verse has always featured prominently in the Muslim homoerotic tradition.
55 Ibid.: 44.54.
56 For more on this, and other parallels between the Greek and Qur'anic notions of paradise, see the brilliant online article by Saleh. As he points out

(p. 54)—albeit possibly with tongue in cheek—the very word used in the Qur'an to signify the heavenly maidens—*hur*—has an echo of Hera's name.

57 According to much later Muslim sources, Mani's followers actually termed him "the Seal of the Prophets"—but this is most likely to have been a backward projection. Manichaeans did use the word "seal" to refer to Mani—but implying "confirmation" rather than "terminus." See Stroumsa (1986b).

58 Quoted by Lieu, p. 86.

59 The words are supposedly those of Mani himself. Quoted by Boyce (1975b), p. 29. Manichaeism had reached North Africa within a few decades of Mani's death, and China by the mid-sixth century.

60 See de Blois (1995).

61 From an imperial edict of either 297 or 302. Quoted by Dignas and Winter, p. 217

62 *Synodicon Orientale*, p. 255.

63 Al-Aswad bin Ya'fur, in Alan Jones (1996, Vol. 1), p. 148.

64 Qur'an: 53.19–21.

65 All but one of the mentions of idols in the Qur'an feature in the context of its retelling of biblical stories. The one allusion to contemporary "idolatrous beliefs" (22.30) seems to refer to blood spilled on sacrificial altars, rather than idols *per se*. See Crone (2010), pp. 170–2.

66 Qur'an: 53.27.

67 See, for instance, his letter to the Colossians: 2.18.

68 Canon 35 of the Council of Laodicea.

69 Crone (2010), p. 171.

70 Qur'an: 4.119, 6.138 and 6.121, respectively.

71 Ibid.: 4.121.

72 Qur'an: 6.99. Mecca, in the laconic phrase of Donner (1981), "is located in an area ill suited to agriculture" (p. 15).

73 Ibid.: 56.63–4.

74 The poem is exceedingly obscure. A commentary by a later Muslim commentator sought to explain its meaning: "Badr and Kutayfah are two places, the distance between which is vast. It is as though they have come together due to the speed of this camel." Poem and commentary alike appear in *Six Early Arab Poets*, p. 95. My thanks to Salam Rassi for the translation.

75 Qur'an: 3.97.

76 *Khuzistan Chronicle*: 38 (translation by Salam Rassi). The authorship is dated to the 660s.

77 Qur'an: 3.96.

78 Qur'an: 3.97. The Arabic for "place" in this verse is *maqam*.

79 Ibid.: 2.125.

80 For the difficulty of squaring the Qur'anic accounts of the *Maqam Ibrahim*

with the stone of the same name in Mecca, see Hawting (1982)—an essay to which this chapter is hugely indebted. Although Hawting himself does not allude to the sanctuary at Mamre, he cites an intriguing Muslim tradition in which Abraham is guided to the House at Bakka by three heavenly beings. As Hawting points out (p. 41), "this is reminiscent of Abraham's three visitors in the Genesis story, one of whom could be identified with the Lord before whom Abraham ministered in the *maqom*"—which took place, of course, at Mamre.

81 Qur'an: 37.133–8.

82 See Chapter 4, n. 90, above.

83 Qur'an: 2.128.

84 The Quraysh, along with Mecca, Muhammad and someone called Majid, are mentioned in the final line of the papyrus fragment that also name-checks the Battle of Badr for the first time. Its editor dated this fragment to the mid-eighth century (Grohmann (1963), text 71). A group of people called the Qrshtn are mentioned in a south Arabian inscription dating from the AD 270s, and some scholars have interpreted this as a possible allusion to Qurayshi women. However, that theory is most implausible, because the Qrshtn seem to be ambassadors on a trade mission.

85 This is mentioned by a ninth-century historian named Ibn Qutayba, and is quoted by Shahid (1989), p. 356. It is indicative of an enduring ambiguity in the Muslim sources that Qusayy, although supposedly born in Mecca, is described as having been settled on the Palestinian frontier.

86 See Margoliouth, p. 313. It is telling that a theory floated by Muslim commentators suggests that "Quraysh" derived from the Arabic word *taqarrush*—"gathering"—another word that powerfully conveys a sense of *foederati*. The great scholar al-Azraqi wrote, "It is said that the Quraysh were so named on account of [their] gathering (*tajammu*) around Quṣay ... For in some dialects of the Arabs, *tajammu* (= meeting/gathering) is referred to as *taqarrush*" (p. 108; translation by Salam Rassi, to whom I am also indebted for the reference from Margoliouth).

87 See, for instance, Shahid (1995), p. 788, for the strong likelihood that Arethas could speak Syriac.

88 Qur'an: 10.61.

89 By and large, commentators on the Qur'an explained the summer and winter trips as being to Syria and Yemen, respectively. However, there was a raft of alternative explanations, too. See Crone (1987b), pp. 205–11.

90 Jacob of Edessa: 326.

91 Qur'an: 2.198.

92 Ibid.: 47.10.

93 *Zukhruf*, a word that is used to mean "ornamentation" in the Qur'an, has been plausibly derived from *zograpsos*—a Greek word meaning a "painter of shields." See Shahid (1989), p. 507.

94 Qur'an: 1.6.

95 Ibid.: 6.25.

96 Ibid.: 8.31, 25.5 and 46.17, for instance.

97 Ibid.: 41.17.

98 Ibid.: 4.100.

99 Ibid.: 8.1–2.

100 Ibid.: 8.26.

101 Ibid.: 2.119.

102 Ibid.: 33.9.

103 For a tracing of its likely evolution, see Crone (1994).

104 Qur'an: 4.99.

105 As with virtually every aspect of the Arab invasions, precision is impossible. One source claims that the task force numbered three hundred, another that it amounted to five thousand.

106 It is typical of the murk of the sources for the Arab invasions that in one account he is named "Bryrdn."

107 The unusually specific time and date derive from a notice in a Syrian chronicle written some time around the year 640, and which in turn seems to draw on a near-contemporary record. See Palmer, Brock and Hoyland, pp. 18–19.

108 Procopius: *On Buildings*, 2.9.4.

109 For the decayed state of towns in Syria and Palestine in the wake of the plague, see Kennedy (1985).

110 Sozomen: 6.38.

111 Anastasius of Sinai: 1156C.

112 As with the origins of the Qur'an, so with the course of the Arab conquests: the range of scholarly opinion is dizzying. Christian sources are contemporary, but too patchy to provide anything like a coherent narrative; Arabic sources are plentiful, but frustratingly late. The contradictory nature of the evidence from Arab historians for the Battle of the Yarmuk is best set out in Donner's magisterial survey of the Islamic conquests (1981, pp. 133–48). However, even he comes across as a model of guarded optimism when compared to Lawrence Conrad, whose ground-breaking essay on the conquest of the obscure Levantine island of Arwad served as a landmine beneath the entire project of reconstructing the Arab invasions from Muslim sources. For the most recent attempt to clear up the mess, see Howard-Johnston (2010), who locates the decisive Roman defeat not at the Yarmuk but near Damascus.

113 Anastasius of Sinai: 1156C.

114 Baladhuri, p. 210.

115 Given, as Donner (1981) wistfully comments, "the chronologically ambiguous nature of many of the accounts about the conquest, it is impossible to do more than guess at the true dates involved" (p. 212).

116 Sebeos, 137.

117 Tabari: Vol. 12, p. 64.

118 Qur'an: 4.36.

119 Contemporaneous reports on the battle outside Gaza seem to imply that Muḥammad was still alive at the time. The first text to mention the existence of an Arabian prophet, and which has been most plausibly dated to the summer of 634, refers to "the prophet who *has* appeared to the Saracens" (*Teachings of Jacob*: 5.16) Another, dated to around 640, and the first to mention him by name, describes the battle as having been won by "the Arabs of Muhammad" (quoted by Hoyland (1997), p. 120.) For a survey of later Christian and Samaritan sources that presume the survival of Muhammad into 634, see Crone and Cook, pp. 152–3, n. 7. As they point out, "The convergence is impressive"—and proof of just how slippery is our evidence for the Prophet's life.

120 The saying is attributed to an early eighth-century scholar, Mujahid bin Jabr (quoted by Hakim, p. 161). Muslim opinion on the virtues—or otherwise—of Umar covers a broad spectrum.

121 Sebeos, 139.

122 Qur'an: 5.33.

123 Constitution of Medina: Document A.9, as reproduced in Serjeant (1978), p. 19.

124 My thanks to Michael Kulikowski for this.

125 It is only fair to point out that Christian authors, looking to explain the defeat of the Romans, cast the Saracen armies as no less teeming. In fact, as Donner (1981) has pointed out, "perhaps the most striking fact about the armies that carried out the Islamic conquest of the Fertile Crescent was their small size" (p. 231).

126 Sebeos, 136.

127 According to the best estimate, Arab *foederati* "may have numbered two to five times the size of the available regular and garrison troops" (Kaegi (1992), p. 43).

128 Sebeos: p. 141.

129 *Teachings of Jacob*: 5.16.

130 Qur'an: 5.20.

131 Hans Jansen has suggested, very plausibly, that "these stories about Jews who had entered into talks with the enemies of Islam and were killed as a consequence had as their primary aim the cowing of the Christians of the Middle East" (p. 134). (My gratitude to Liz Waters for the translation.)

132 Sebeos, 135.

133 From the so-called "Secrets of Rabbi Simon ben Yohai," quoted by Hoyland (1997), p. 309. The rabbi had lived back in the second century AD, but the vision of the Arab conquests attributed to him seems to have been contemporaneous with the events it describes.

134 Ibid., p. 311.
135 Subsequent Islamic tradition would explain this as a title bestowed on
     Umar by Muhammad. However, it is clear—from both contemporaneous
     Jewish records and later Muslim histories—that the title actually derived
     from the Jews of Jerusalem and was prompted by Umar's activities on the
     Temple Mount. See Bashear (1990).
136 Qur'an: 16.41.
137 John of Nikiu, p. 200.
138 A recently discovered inscription in the Arabian desert south of Palestine
     reads simply, "In the name of God, I, Zuhayr, wrote [this] at the time
     Umar died in the year twenty-four." Quoted by Hoyland (2006), p. 411.
139 Qur'an: 2.177.
140 Sebeos, 175.
141 Qur'an: 49.9.
142 Sebeos, 176.
143 From a Christian tract written around 680 and quoted by Hoyland (1997),
     p. 141. Although the author was a Syrian, Hoyland convincingly argues
     that his informant was an Arab.
144 Dhu al-Thafinat, quoted by Sizgorich (2009), p. 206.
145 Qur'an: 16.106.
146 Muhamad b. Ahmad al-Malati, quoted by Sizgorich (2009), p. 215.
147 From the Christian chronicle mentioned above, and quoted by Hoyland
     (1997), p. 136.
148 Ibid.
149 Padwick, p. 119.
150 From an inscription on a dam near Ta'if, in Arabia, quoted by Hoyland
     (1997), p. 692.
151 John bar Penkâye, p. 61.

7 The Forging of Islam

1 Arculf, p. 41.
2 Fredegarius: 154.
3 Arculf, p. 43.
4 "A Jewish Apocalypse on the Umayyads," quoted by Hoyland (1997), p. 317.
5 The monk was Anastasius of Sinai. See Flusin, pp. 25–6.
6 Arculf, p. 43.
7 Quoted by Humphreys, p. 11.
8 Mu'awiya is hailed as "Commander of the Faithful" on an inscription in
   the main hall of the bath-house of Hammat Gader, a few miles from
   Tiberias, which was one of the *Amir*'s favourite winter resorts.
   Accompanying this very public articulation of Umayyad legitimacy is a
   cross—which, inevitably, has always deeply puzzled scholars committed

to the notion that Mu'awiya was a Muslim. In the words of Clive Foss (2008), "the further implications of this phenomenon remain to be explored" (p. 118).

9 Abu Hamza, quoted by Crone and Hinds, p. 131.

10 John bar Penkâye, p. 61.

11 Ibid.

12 Ibid.

13 Jacob of Edessa, quoted by Hoyland (1997), p. 566.

14 Qur'an: 2.142.

15 John bar Penkâye, p. 61.

16 Quoted by Hawting (1982a), p. 44.

17 *Syriac Common Source*, in Hoyland (1997), p. 647.

18 John bar Penkâye, pp. 68–9.

19 Ibid., p. 66.

20 Qur'an: 21.1.

21 From a coin issued in 688–9, quoted by Hoyland (1997), p. 695.

22 Quoted by Hoyland (1997), p. 694.

23 Qur'an: 33.57.

24 *Syriac Common Source*, in Hoyland (1997), p. 647.

25 Al-Akhtal, 19, in Stetkevych, p. 92.

26 Al-Muqqadasi, quoted by Rabbat, p. 16.

27 Al-Muqqadasi, quoted by Rosen-Ayalon, p. 69.

28 From a sermon preached towards the end of the Umayyad Caliphate. Quoted by Elad (1992), p. 50.

29 This phrase dates from the twelfth century: evidence for the fact that Syrians continued to regard Jerusalem, rather than Mecca, as Islam's holiest shrine for several centuries. Quoted by Van Ess, p. 89.

30 Qur'an: 61.9.

31 *Syriac Common Source*, in Hoyland (1997), p. 648.

32 Farazdaq, quoted by Kister (1969), p. 182. The literal translation of "the mount of Jerusalem" is "the upper part of Iliy'a."

33 The mosque in Egypt was at Fustat, a garrison city that would ultimately evolve into Cairo. Its *qibla* was reoriented in 710–11; see Bashear (1989), p. 268. The mosque in the Negev was at Be'er Ora. For a description and illustration of the change in the orientation of its *qibla*, see Sharon (1988), pp. 230–2. For the change to Kufa's *qibla*, see Hoyland (1997), p. 562.

34 From the Kharijite sermon quoted by Elad (1992), p. 50.

35 Nu'aym b. Hammad al-Marwazi, in the *Kitab al-Fitan*, quoted by Sharon (1988), p. 234, fn. 7.

36 Tabari: Vol. 22, p. 14.

37 Ibn Asakir, quoted by de Prémare, p. 209.

38 Quoted by Crone and Hinds, p. 28.

39 Al-Akhtal, 19, in Stetkevych, p. 91.

40   Farazdaq, quoted by Crone and Hinds, p. 43.
41   Qur'an: 3.19.
42   Quoted by Hoyland (1997), p. 702.
43   Qur'an: 27.23.
44   Al-Muqqadasi, quoted by Ettinghausen, p. 28.
45   John bar Penkâye, p. 61.
46   Michael the Syrian, in Palmer, Brock and Hoyland, p. 152, n. 363.
47   John bar Penkâye, p. 67.
48   Tabari, quoted by Hoyland, p. 198.
49   Gregory of Nyssa, p. 74. Gregory's fourth homily on Ecclesiastes is
     exceptional for being the only document from antiquity—as far as I am
     aware—specifically and unequivocally to condemn slavery as an institution.
50   Qur'an: 90.12–17.
51   These restrictions are conventionally attributed to a pact signed between
     the Christians of Syria and Umar, but Western scholars have tended to date
     them to the end of the eighth century, a hundred and fifty years after the
     time of Umar. Recently, though, it has been convincingly argued that the
     so-called "Pact of Umar" may indeed date—in its essentials if not its final
     form—from the period of the early conquests. See Noth (1987).
52   Qur'an: 33.27.
53   Ibid.: 33.50.
54   Al-Suyuti, quoted by Robinson (2005), p. 20.
55   Qur'an: 89.17–20.
56   For a sample of the various attempts to make proper sense of it, see Ibn
     Warraq (2002), pp. 319–86.
57   A Zoroastrian text anticipating the End Days, from the eighth or ninth
     century, quoted by Minorsky, p. 257.
58   Quoted by Brown (2003), p. 314.
59   The complaint of an eighth-century Muslim governor in eastern Iran,
     quoted by Dennett, p. 120.
60   Qur'an: 1.6–7.
61   *Sefer ha-Eshkol*: Vol. 2, pp. 73–4.
62   Qur'an: 24.58. The three prayers specified by the Qur'an are the Dawn
     Prayer, the Noon Prayer and the Night Prayer.
63   *Sahih al-Bukhari*: 1.4.245.
64   *The Talmud*, p. 553.
65   Ibid.
66   Ibn Qutayba, quoted by Sizgorich (2009), p. 160.
67   Ibn Hawqal, quoted by Haldon and Kennedy, p. 97.
68   Artat b. al-Mundhir, quoted by Bashear (1991a), p. 178.
69   Tabari, quoted by Brooks (1899), p. 20.
70   Theophanes, p. 396.
71   Theophanes, pp. 397–8.

72 Quoted by Bashear (1991a), p. 191.
73 The first scholars to be recorded on the front line joined Maslama's expedition against Constantinople in 716. Therefore, although the two examples mentioned here by name were active after the fall of the Umayyads, they can be taken as representative of a trend that spanned most of the eighth century.
74 Ibn Asakir, quoted by Bonner (2004), p. 409.
75 Ibn al-Mubarak, quoted by Yahya, p. 33.
76 Ibn al-Mubarak, quoted by Sizgorich (2009), p. 161.
77 Ibn al-Mubarak, quoted by Yahya, pp. 32–3.
78 Qur'an: 9.5.
79 Ibid.: 2.190.
80 The words of a Christian scholar of the eighth century, quoted by J. B. Segal (1963), p. 125.
81 The story dates from the mid-tenth century, and is attributed to the reign of a Caliph who lived some eighty years after Marwan's Caliphate. The link between the Harranians and the Sabaeans appears to have been made much earlier than that, however. It also seems to date to around the time that Marwan was present in Harran. See Green, p. 106.
82 Bar Hebraeus: p. 110. The liver inspection recorded by Bar Hebraeus took place in 737.
83 *History of the Patriarchs of the Coptic Church of Alexandria*: 18.156.
84 Tabari, quoted by Kennedy (2007), p. 288.
85 Tha'alibi, quoted by Pourshariati (2008), p. 431.
86 Baladhuri, quoted by Sharon (1983), p. 203.

Envoi

1 Abu-Sahl, quoted by Gutas, p. 46.
2 See Gutas, p. 80.

Bibliography

Primary Sources

Abu l-Fath: *The Kitab al-Tarikh of Abu l-Fath*, trans. P. Stenhouse (Sydney, 1985)

Acta Martyrum et Sanctorum, ed. Paul Bedjan (7 vols) (Paris, 1890–7)

Agathias: *The Histories*, trans. Joseph D. Frendo (New York, 1975)

al-Azraqi: *Kitab Akhbar Makkah*, in *Der Chroniken der Stadt Mekka*, ed. Ferdinand Wilstenfeld (Leipzig, 1857–61)

Ammianus Marcellinus: *The Later Roman Empire: A. D. 354–378*, trans. Walter Hamilton (London, 1986)

Anastasius of Sinai: *Sermo* 3, in *Patrologia Graeca [PG* from hereon] 89 (1152–80)

Arculf: *Adamnan's De Locis Sanctis*, ed. D. Meehan (Dublin, 1958)

Aristides: *Aristides in Four Volumes*, ed. C. A. Behr (Cambridge, 1973)

Athenaeus: *Deipnosophistae*, ed. Charles Burton Gulick (7 vols) (Cambridge, Mass., 1927–41)

Augustine: *The City of God*, trans. Henry Bettenson (London, 1972)

Avodah Zarah: http://www.jewishvirtuallibrary.org/jsource/Talmud/avodazara1.html

Baladhuri: *The Origins of the Islamic State*, trans. Hitti and F. Murgotten (2 vols) (New York, 1916–24)

Bar Hebraeus: *The Chronography of Bar Hebraeus*, trans. E. A. Wallis Budge (Oxford, 1932)

Bardaisan of Edessa: *The Book of the Laws of Countries: Dialogue on Fate of Bardaisan of Edessa*, ed. H. J. W. Drijvers (Piscataway, 2007)

Barhadbeshabba of Holwan: *Histoire ecclésiastique*, ed. F. Nau, in *Patrologia Orientalis* 9

Berosus: *The Babyloniaca of Berosus*, trans. Stanley Mayer Burstein (Malibu, 1978)

Bukhari: *Al-Adab al-Mufrad al-Bukhari*, trans. Ustadha Aisha Bewley (www.sunnipath.com/library/Hadith/H0003P0006.aspx)

The Byzantine-Arab Chronicle, trans. Robert Hoyland, in Hoyland (1997), pp. 612–27

Cassius Dio: *Roman History*, trans. Earnest Cary (9 volumes) (Cambridge, Mass., 1914–27)

481

Chronicon ad Annum Christi 1234 Pertinens, ed. J.-B. Chabot and A. Abouna (2 vols)
    (Paris, 1937 and 1974)

Chronicon Paschale: 284–628 AD, trans. Michael Whitby and Mary Whitby
    (Liverpool, 1989)

Cicero: http://classics.mit.edu/Cicero/cic.man.html

Clement of Alexandria: *Stromata*, in *Clemens Alexandrinus*, ed. Otto Stählin,
    Ludwig Fruchtel and Ursula Treu (Vol. 3) (Berlin, 1970)

Corippus: *Flavius Cresconius Corippus: In Laudem Iustini Augusti Minoris Libri IV*, ed.
    Averil Cameron (London, 1976)

—— *The Iohannis or de Bellis Libycis of Flavius Cresconius Corippus*, trans. George W.
    Shea (Lewiston, 1998)

Cosmas Indicopleustes: *Topographia*, in *PG* 88

Cyril of Jerusalem: http://www.newadvent.org/fathers/3101.htm

Cyril of Scythopolis: *Vita Euthymii*, in *Kyrillos von Skythopolis*, ed. Eduard Schwartz
    (Leipzig, 1939)

Denkard: http://www.avesta.org/denkard/dk3s229.html

Diodorus Siculus: *Library of History*, (12 vols), ed. C. H. Oldfather (Cambridge,
    Mass., 1933–67)

Egeria: *The Pilgrimage of Etheria*, trans. M. L. McClure and C. L. Feltoe (London, 1919)

Elishe: *History of Vardan and the Armenian War*, trans. Robert W. Thomson
    (Cambridge, Mass., 1982)

Epiphanius: *The Panarion of St. Epiphanius, Bishop of Salamis*, trans. Philip R. Amidon
    (Oxford, 1990)

Eusebius: *Preparation for the Gospel*, trans. E. H. Gifford (5 vols) (London, 1903)

—— *The History of the Church*, trans. G. A. Williamson (London, 1989)

—— *Life of Constantine*, trans. Averil Cameron and S. G. Hall (Oxford, 1999)

Evagrius Scholasticus: *The Ecclesiastical History of Evagrius Scholasticus*, trans. M.
    Whitby (Liverpool, 2000)

Expositio Totius Mundi et Gentium, ed. Jean Rougé (Paris, 1966)

Fredegarius: *Chronicon Fredegarii*, in *Monumenta Germaniae Historica: Scriptores Rerum
    Merovingicarum* (Hannover, 1888)

George of Pisidia: *Heraclias*, in *PG* 92

Gospel of Pseudo-Matthew: http://www.gnosis.org/library/pseudomat.htm

Greater Bundahishn: http://www.avesta.org/pahlavi/grb1.htm

Gregory of Nyssa: *Homilies on Ecclesiastes*, ed. Stuart George Hall (Berlin, 1993)

Heliodorus: *Aethiopica*, ed. A. Colonna (Rome, 1938)

Herodian: *History of the Empire*, trans. C. R. Whittaker (2 vols) (Cambridge,
    Mass., 1969–70)

The History of Alexander the Great Being the Syriac Version of the Pseudo-Callisthenes, ed.
    E. A. W. Budge (Cambridge, 1889)

The History of King Vaxt'ang Gorgasali: Rewriting Caucasian History: The Medieval

Bibliography

Armenian Adaptation of the Georgian Chronicles, trans. Robert W. Thomson (Oxford, 1996)

History of the Patriarchs of the Coptic Church of Alexandria: trans. B. Evetts (4 vols) (Paris, 1906–15)

Ibn Hisham: *The Life of Muhammad: A Translation of Ishaq's Sirat Rasul Allah*, trans. A. Guillaume (Oxford, 1955)

Ibn Miskawayh: *Tagarib al-umam (The Book of Deeds of Xusro I Anosarvan)*, ed. L. Caetani (Leyden, 1909)

Ibn Qutayba: *La Traité des Divergences du Hadit d'Ibn Qutayba (mort en 276/889)*, trans. Gérard Lecomte (Damascus, 1962)

Ignatius of Antioch:
http://web.archive.org/web/20060813114040/www.ccel.org/fathers2/ANF-01/anf01-17.htm

Irenaeus: http://www.newadvent.org/fathers/0103.htm

Isidore of Pelusium: *Letters*, in *PG* 78

Jerome: http://www.newadvent.org/fathers/3001.htm

John bar Penkâye: "Northern Mesopotamia in the Late Seventh Century: Book XV of John bar Penkâye's *Rish Mellê*" (*Jerusalem Studies in Arabic and Islam* 9, 1987)

John of Damascus: *De Haeresibus*, in *PG* 94: 677–780

John of Ephesus: *Pseudo-Dionysius of El-Mahre: Chronicle, Part III*, trans. Witold Witakowski (Liverpool, 1996)

John Malalas: *The Chronicle of John Malalas*, trans. Elizabeth Jeffreys, Michael Jeffreys and Roger Scott (Melbourne, 1986)

John of Nikiu: *The Chronicle of John (c. 690 AD) Coptic Bishop of Nikiu*, trans. Robert Henry Charles (London, 1916)

Josephus: *The Antiquities of the Jews*, in *The Complete Works of Josephus*, trans. William Whiston (Peabody, 1987)

Joshua the Stylite: *The Chronicle of Pseudo-Joshua the Stylite*, trans. Frank R. Trombley and John W. Watt (Liverpool, 2000)

Justin Martyr: *Iustini Martyris Dialogus cum Tryphone*, ed. Miroslav Marcovich (New York, 1997)

Khuzistan Chronicle, ed. I. Guidi (Louvain, 1960)

Lactantius: *De Mortibus Persecutorum*, ed. and trans. J. L. Creed (Oxford, 1984)
—— http://www.newadvent.org/fathers/0701.htm

Lazar P'arpec'i: *The History of Lazar P'arpec'i*, trans. Robert W. Thomson (Atlanta, 1991)

Letter of Tansar, trans. Mary Boyce (Rome, 1968)

"Letter to Diognetus": (a) http://www.ccel.org/ccel/richardson/fathers.x.i.ii.html
—— (b) http://www.ccel.org/l/lake/fathers/diognetus.htm

Life of Symeon the Younger: La Vie Ancienne de S. Syméon le Jeune, ed. P. Van den Ven (Brussels, 1970)

Livy: *The War with Hannibal*, trans. Aubrey de Sélincourt (London, 1965)

Menander the Guardsman: *The History of Menander the Guardsman*, trans. R. C. Blockley (Liverpool, 1985)

Mihr Yasht: http://www.avesta.org/ka/yt10sbe.htm

Moses Dasxuranci: *History of the Caucasian Albanians*, trans. Charles Dowsett (Oxford, 1961)

Nikephoros: *Short History*, trans. Cyril Mango (Dumbarton Oaks, 1990)

Novels: http://uwacadweb.uwyo.edu/blume&justinian/novels2.asp

Origen: *Homilies on Luke* (http://www.bible-researcher.com/origen.html)

Paul the Deacon: *Historia Langobardorum*, in *Monumenta Germaniae Historica: Scriptores Rerum Langobardicarum* (Hannover, 1878)

Plutarch: *Roman Questions*, ed. Frank Cole Battitt (Cambridge, Mass., 1936)

—— *The Rise and Fall of Athens*, trans. Ian Scott-Kilvert (London, 1960)

Porphyrius: *Carmina* (http://www.thelatinlibrary.com/porphyrius.html)

Procopius: *History of the Wars*, trans. H. B. Dewing (5 vols) (Cambridge, Mass., 1914–28)

—— *On Buildings*, trans. H. B. Dewing and Glanville Downey (Cambridge, Mass., 1940)

—— *The Secret History*, trans. G. A. Williamson (London, 2007)

Propertius: *Elegies*, ed. G. P. Goold (Cambridge, Mass., 1990)

Sahih Bukhari: http://www.quranenglish.com/hadith/Sahih_bukhari.htm

The Sayings of the Desert Fathers, trans. Benedicta Ward (Collegeville, 2005)

Sebeos: *The Armenian History Attributed to Sebeos*, trans. R. W. Thomson, with commentary by J. Howard-Johnston (2 vols) (Liverpool, 1999)

Sefer ha-Eshkol, ed. Abraham ben Isaac (4 vols) (Halberstadt, 1868)

Sidonius Apollinaris: *Poems and Letters*, ed. W. B. Anderson (2 vols) (Harvard, 1936–65)

Six Early Arab Poets: New Edition and Concordance, ed. Albert Arazi and Salman Masalha (Jerusalem, 1999)

Socrates Scholasticus: http://www.newadvent.org/fathers/2601.htm

Sozomen: *Ecclesiastical History*, trans. Edward Walford (London, 1846)

Stephen of Herakleopolis: *A Panegyric on Apollo Archimandrite of the Monastery of Isaac by Stephen Bishop of Heracleopolis Magna*, ed. K. H. Kuhn (Louvain, 1978)

Strabo: *The Geography of Strabo*, ed. H. L. Jones (8 vols) (Cambridge, Mass., 1917–32)

Synodicon Orientale: ed. and trans. J.-B. Chabot (3 vols) (Paris, 1902)

Tabari: *The Marwanid Restoration: The Caliphate of Abd al-Malik* (vol. 22), trans. Everrett K. Rowson (Albany, 1989)

—— *The Battle of al-Qadisiyyah and the Conquest of Syria and Palestine* (vol. 12), trans. Yohanan Friedmann (Albany, 1992)

—— *The Sasanids, the Byzantines, the Lakhmids, and Yemen* (vol. 5 of *The History of Tabari*), trans. C. E. Bosworth (Albany, 1999)

The Talmud: The Soncino Talmud, ed. I. Epstein (18 vols) (London, 1935–48)

Teachings of Jacob: "Doctrina Iacobi Nuper Baptizati," ed. N. Bonwetsch (Berlin, 1910)

Tertullian: http://www.tertullian.org/

Tha'alibi: *Ghurar Akhbar Muluk al-Fars*, trans. H. Zotenberg (Paris, 2000)

Theodoret: *Ecclesiastical History* (London, 1844)

—— *The Cure of Greek Maladies (Thérapeutique des Maladies Helléniques)*, ed. P. Canivet (Paris, 1958)

—— *The Ecclesiastical History, Dialogues, and Letters of Theodoret*, trans. B. Jackson (Grand Rapids, 1979)

—— *Life of Saint Simeon Stylites*, in *The Lives of Saint Simeon Stylites*, trans. Robert Doran (Kalamazoo, 1992)

—— *Compendium of Heretical Fables*, in *PG* 83, pp. 335–555

Theodosian Code: http://ancientrome.ru/ius/library/codex/theod/tituli.htm

Theophanes: *The Chronicle of Theophanes*, trans. Harry Turtledove (Philadelphia, 1982)

Theophylact Simocatta: *The History of Theophylact Simocatta*, trans. Michael Whitby and Mary Whitby (Oxford, 1986)

Three Byzantine Saints, trans. Elizabeth Dawes and Norman H. Baynes (Crestwood, 1977)

Virgil: *The Aeneid*, trans. C. Day Lewis (Oxford, 1952)

Wisdom of the Desert Fathers: trans. Benedicta Ward (Oxford 1979)

Yasna: http://www.avesta.org/yasna/yasna.htm

Zonaras: *The History of Zonaras: From Alexander Severus to the Death of Theodosius the Great*, trans. Thomas M. Banchich and Eugene N. Lane (Abingdon, 2009)

Zosimus: *New History*, trans. Ronald T. Ridley (Sydney, 1982)

Secondary Sources

Abu Zayd, Nasr: *Reformation of Islamic Thought: A Critical Historical Analysis* (Amsterdam, 2006)

Adams, Charles: "Reflections on the Work of John Wansbrough," in Berg 1997

Adams, Robert McCormick: *Heartland of Cities: Surveys of Ancient Settlement and Land Use on the Central Floodplain of the Euphrates* (Chicago, 1981)

Afsaruddin, Asma: *The First Muslims: History and Memory* (Oxford, 2008)

Alexander, L. A: "The Living Voice: Scepticism towards the Written Word in Early Christian and in Graeco-Roman Texts," in *The Bible in Three Dimensions*, ed. D. J. A. Clines, S. E. Fowl and S. E. Porter (Sheffield, 1990)

Bibliography

Alexander, Paul J.: *The Byzantine Apocalyptic Tradition* (Berkeley and Los Angeles, 1985)

Alexander, Philip S.: "Jewish Believers in Early Rabbinic Literature (2nd to 5th Centuries)," in Skarsaune and Hvalvik

Amory, Patrick: *People and Identity in Ostrogothic Italy, 489–554* (Cambridge, 2003)

Anderson, Andrew Runni: "Alexander's Horns" (*Transactions and Proceedings of the American Philological Association* 58, 1927)

Ando, Clifford: "The Palladium and the Pentateuch: Towards a Sacred Topography of the Later Roman Empire" (*Phoenix* 55, 2001)

Andrae, Tor: *Les Origines de l'Islam et le Christianisme*, trans. Jules Roche (Paris, 1955)

—— *In the Garden of Myrtles: Studies in Early Islamic Mysticism*, trans. Birgitta Sharpe (Albany, 1987)

Angold, Michael: "Procopius' Portrait of Theodora," in *Studies in Honour of Robert Browning*, ed. C. N. Constantinides, N. M. Panagiotakes, E. Jeffreys and A. D. Angelou (Venice, 1996)

Armstrong, Karen: *Muhammad: A Western Attempt to Understand Islam* (London, 1992)

Aslan, Reza: *No god but God: The Origins, Evolution and Future of Islam* (London, 2005)

Athamina, Khalil: "The Pre-Islamic Roots of the Early Muslim Caliphate: The Emergence of Abu Bakr" (*Der Islam* 76, 1999)

Athanassiadi, Polymnia: "Persecution and Response in Late Paganism" (*Journal of Hellenic Studies* 113, 1993)

—— *Damascus: The Philosophical History* (Athens, 1999)

Avi-Yonah, M.: *The Jews of Palestine: A Political History from the Bar Kokhba War to the Arab Conquest* (Oxford, 1976)

Ayoub, M.: *The Qur'an and its Interpreters*, vol. 1 (Albany, 1984)

al-Azami, Mohammad Mustafa: *On Schacht's Origins of Muhammadan Jurisprudence* (Riyadh, 1985)

—— *The History of the Qur'anic Text, from Revelation to Compilation: A Comparative Study with the Old and New Testaments* (Leicester, 2003)

Bagnall, Roger S. (ed.): *Egypt in the Byzantine World, 300–700* (Cambridge, 2007)

Bamberger, Bernard J.: *Proselytism in the Talmudic Period* (New York, 1968)

Bashear, Sulayman: "Qur'an 2.114 and Jerusalem" (*Bulletin of the School of Oriental and African Studies* 52, 1989)

—— "The Title '*Faruq*' and its Association with 'Umar I" (*Studia Islamica* 72, 1990)

—— "Apocalyptic and Other Materials on Early Muslim–Byzantine Wars: A Review of Arabic Sources" (*Journal of the Royal Asiatic Society* 1, 1991a)

—— "Qibla Musharriqa and Early Muslim Prayer in Churches" (*Muslim World* 81, 1991b)

—— *Studies in Early Islamic Tradition* (Jerusalem, 2004)

Bassett, Sarah: *The Urban Image of Late Antique Constantinople* (Cambridge, 2004)

Bauer, Walter: *Orthodoxy and Heresy in Earliest Christianity*, ed. Robert A. Kraft and
　　Gerhard Krodel (Philadelphia, 1971)

Bausani, Alessandro: *Religion in Iran: From Zoroaster to Baha'ullah*, trans. J. M.
　　Marchesi (New York, 2000)

Beard, Mary, North, John A. and Price, S. R. F: *Religions of Rome* (Cambridge,
　　1998)

Becker, Adam H.: "Beyond the Spatial and Temporal *Limes*: Questioning the
　　"Parting of the Ways" outside the Roman Empire," in Becker and Reed

Becker, Adam H. and Reed, Annette Yoshiko: *The Ways That Never Parted: Jews and
　　Christians in Late Antiquity and the Early Middle Ages* (Tübingen, 2003)

Berg, Herbert (ed.): *Islamic Origins Reconsidered: John Wansbrough and the Study of
　　Early Islam* (special issue of *Method and Theory in the Study of Religion* 9 (1),
　　1997)

—— *The Development of Exegesis in Early Islam* (Richmond, 2000)

—— (ed.): *Method and Theory in the Study of Islamic Origins* (Leiden, 2003)

Bier, Lionel: "Sasanian Palaces and their Influence in Early Islamic
　　Architecture" (http://www.cais-soas.com/CAIS/Architecture/
　　sasanian_palaces_islam.htm)

Bishop, Eric R.: "The Qumran Scrolls and the Qur'an" (*Muslim World* 48, 1958)

Bivar, A. D. H.: "Hayatila," in *Encyclopaedia of Islam*

—— "Gorgan: Pre-Islamic History," in *Encyclopedia Iranica*

Blankinship, Khalid Yahya: *The End of the Jihad State: The Reign of Hisham Ibn Abd al-
　　Malik and the Collapse of the Umayyads* (Albany, 1994)

Blockley, R. C.: *The Fragmentary Classicising Historians of the Later Roman Empire:
　　Eunapius, Olympiodorus, Priscus and Malchus* (2 vols) (Liverpool, 1981–3)

Bobzin, Hartmut: "A Treasury of Heresies: Christian Polemics against the
　　Koran," in Wild

Bonner, Michael (ed.): *Arab–Byzantine Relations in Early Islamic Times* (Aldershot,
　　2004)

—— *Jihad in Islamic History: Doctrines and Practice* (Princeton, 2006)

Bowersock, Glen W.: *Roman Arabia* (Cambridge, Mass., 1983)

—— *Martyrdom and Rome* (Cambridge, 1995)

Bowersock, G. W., Brown, Peter and Grabar, Oleg: *Late Antiquity: A Guide to the
　　Postclassical World* (Cambridge, Mass., 1999)

Boyarin, Daniel: *Dying for God: Martyrdom and the Making of Christianity and Judaism*
　　(Stanford, 1999)

—— "Semantic Differences; or 'Judaism'/'Christianity,'" in *The Partition of
　　Judaeo-Christianity*, ed. Adam H. Becker and Annette Yoshiko Reed:
　　(Philadelphia, 2004)

Boyce, Mary: "On the Sacred Fires of the Zoroastrians" (*Bulletin of the School of
　　Oriental and African Studies* 31, 1968)

—— "On Mithra's Part in Zoroastrianism" (*Bulletin of the School of Oriental and African Studies* 32, 1969)

—— *A History of Zoroastrianism*, vols 1 and 2 (Leiden, 1975a)

—— *A Reader in Manichaean Middle Persian and Parthian* (Leiden, 1975b)

—— *Zoroastrians: Their Religious Beliefs and Practices* (London and New York, 1979)

—— "Adhur Burzen-Mihr," in *Encyclopedia Iranica*

—— "Adhur Gusnasp," in *Encyclopedia Iranica*

—— "Adhur Farnbag," in *Encyclopedia Iranica*

Brague, Rémi: *The Law of God: The Philosophical History of an Idea*, trans. Lydia G. Cochrane (Chicago, 2007)

Brock, S. P.: "The Conversations with the Syrian Orthodox under Justinian" (*Orientala Christiana Periodica* 47, 1981)

—— "Christians in the Sasanid Empire: A Case of Divided Loyalties," in *Church History* 18, ed. Stuart Mews (Oxford, 1982)

—— "Syriac Views of Emergent Islam," in Juynboll

—— *Syriac Perspectives on Late Antiquity* (London, 1984)

—— "North Mesopotamia in the Late Seventh Century: Book XV of John bar Penkaye's *Ris Melle*" (*Jerusalem Studies in Arabic and Islam* 9, 1987)

Brooks, E. W.: "The Arabs in Asia Minor (641–750), from Arabic Sources" (*Journal of Hellenic Studies* 18, 1898)

—— "The Campaign of 716–718, from Arabic Sources" (*Journal of Hellenic Studies* 19, 1899)

Brown, Peter: *The World of Late Antiquity* (London, 1971)

—— "Understanding Islam" (*New York Review of Books*, 22 February 1979)

—— *Power and Persuasion in Late Antiquity: Towards a Christian Empire* (Madison, 1992)

—— *Authority and the Sacred: Aspects of the Christianisation of the Roman World* (Cambridge, 1995)

—— *The Rise of Western Christendom: Triumph and Diversity*, AD 200–1000 (Oxford, 2003)

Browning, Robert: *Justinian and Theodora* (London, 1971)

Bulliet, Richard W.: *Conversion to Islam in the Medieval Period: An Essay in Quantitative History* (Cambridge, Mass., 1979)

Burton, John: *The Collection of the Qur'an* (Cambridge, 1977)

—— Review of *The History of al-Tabari, Vol. VI* (*Bulletin of the School of Oriental and African Studies* 53, 1990)

—— "Rewriting the Timetable of Early Islam" (*Journal of the American Oriental Society* 115, 1995)

Busse, Heribert: "Omar's Image as the Conqueror of Jerusalem" (*Jerusalem Studies in Arabic and Islam* 8, 1986)

—— "Antioch and its Prophet Habib al-Najjar" (*Jerusalem Studies in Arabic and Islam* 24, 2000)

Bibliography

Byrskog, Samuel: *Story as History, History as Story: The Gospel Tradition in the Context of Ancient Oral History* (Leiden, 2002)

Calder, Norman: *Studies in Early Muslim Jurisprudence* (Oxford, 1993)

Cambridge Ancient History, Vol. 14: Late Antiquity: Empire and Successors, AD 425–600, ed. Averil Cameron, Bryan Ward-Perkins and Michael Whitby (Cambridge, 2000)

Cambridge History of Iran, Vol. 3. The Seleucid, Parthian and Sassanian Periods, ed. Ehsan Yarshater (Cambridge, 1983)

Cameron, Averil: *Procopius and the Sixth Century* (Berkeley, 1985)

—— *The Mediterranean World in Late Antiquity, AD 395–600* (London, 1993)

—— (ed.): *The Byzantine and Early Islamic Near East III: States, Resources and Armies* (Princeton, 1995)

Cameron, Averil and Conrad, Lawrence I. (eds): *The Byzantine and Early Islamic Near East: Problems in the Literary Source Material* (Princeton, 1992)

Carleton Paget, James: *Jews, Christians and Jewish Christians in Antiquity* (Cambridge, 2010)

Christensen, A: *Le Règne de Kawadh I et le Communisme Mazdakite* (Copenhagen, 1925)

—— *L'Iran sous les Sassanides* (Copenhagen, 1944)

Cohen, Mark R.: "What Was the Pact of 'Umar? A Literary-Historical Study" (*Jerusalem Studies in Arabic and Islam* 23, 1999)

Cohen, Shaye J. D.: *The Beginnings of Jewishness: Boundaries, Varieties, Uncertainties* (Berkeley and Los Angeles, 1999)

Conrad, Lawrence I.: "Al-Azdi's History of the Arab Conquests in Bilad-al-Sham: Some Historiographical Observations" (*Bilad al-Sham Proceedings* 1, 1985)

—— "Abraha and Muhammad: Some Observations Apropos of Chronology and Literary 'Topoi' in the Early Arabic Historical Tradition" (*Bulletin of the School of Oriental and African Studies* 50, 1987)

—— "Theophanes and the Arabic Historical Tradition: Some Indications of Intercultural Transmission" (*Byzantinische Forschungen* 15, 1988)

—— "Historical Evidence and the Archaeology of Early Islam," in *Quest for Understanding: Arabic and Islamic Studies in Memory of Malcolm H. Kerr* (Beirut, 1991)

—— "The Conquest of Arwad: A Source Critical Study in the Historiography of the Early Medieval Near East," in Cameron and Conrad

—— "Epidemic Disease in Central Syria in the Late Sixth Century: Some New Insights from the Verse of Hassan ibn Thabit" (*Byzantine and Modern Greek Studies* 18, 1994)

Cook, Michael: *Early Muslim Dogma* (Cambridge, 1981)

—— *Muhammad* (Oxford, 1983)

—— "Eschatology and the Dating of Traditions" (*Princeton Papers in Near Eastern Studies* 1, 1992)

—— "The Opponents of the Writing of Tradition in Early Islam" (*Arabica* 44, 1997)

—— *The Koran: A Very Short Introduction* (Oxford, 2000)

—— *Commanding Right and Forbidding Wrong in Islamic Thought* (Cambridge, 2000)

—— *Studies in the Origins of Early Islamic Culture and Tradition* (Aldershot, 2004)

Costa, Paolo M.: *Studies in Arabian Architecture* (Aldershot, 1994)

Croke, Brian and Crow, James: "Procopius and Dara" (*Journal of Roman Studies* 73, 1983)

Crone, Patricia: *Slaves on Horses: The Evolution of the Islamic Polity* (Cambridge, 1980)

—— *Meccan Trade and the Rise of Islam* (Oxford, 1987a)

—— *Roman, Provincial and Islamic Law: The Origins of the Islamic Patronate* (Cambridge, 1987b)

—— "Kavad's Heresy and Mazdak's Revolt" (*Iran* 29, 1991)

—— "Serjeant and Meccan Trade" (*Arabica* 39, 1992)

—— "The First-Century Concept of *Higra*" (*Arabica* 41, 1994)

—— *From Kavad to al-Ghazali: Religion, Law and Political Thought in the Near East, c. 60 –c. 1100* (Aldershot, 2005a)

—— "How did the Quranic Pagans Make a Living?" (*Bulletin of the School of Oriental and African Studies* 68, 2005b)

—— "Quraysh and the Roman Army: Making Sense of the Meccan Leather Trade" (*Bulletin of the School of Oriental and African Studies* 70, 2007)

—— *From Arabian Tribes to Islamic Empire: Army, State and Society in the Near East c. 600–850* (Aldershot, 2008)

—— "The Religion of the Qur'anic Pagans: God and the Lesser Deities" (*Arabica* 57, 2010)

Crone, Patricia and Cook, Michael: *Hagarism: The Making of the Islamic World* (Cambridge, 1977)

Crone, Patricia and Hinds, Martin: *God's Caliph: Religious Authority in the First Centuries of Islam* (Cambridge, 1986)

Crown, Alan D. (ed.): *The Samaritans* (Tübingen, 1989)

Crown, Alan D., Pummer, Reinhard and Tal, Abraham (eds): *A Companion to Samaritan Studies* (Tübingen, 1993)

Czeglédy, Károly: "Bahram Cobin and the Persian Apocalyptic Literature" (*Acta Orientalia Hungarica* 8, 1958)

Dabrowa, E. (ed.): *The Roman and Byzantine Army in the East* (Krakow, 1994)

Dagron, Gilbert: *Constantinople Imaginaire* (Paris, 1984)

Dagron, Gilbert and Déroche, Vincent: "Juifs et Chrétiens dans l'Orient du VIIe Siècle" (*Travaux et Mémoires* 11, 1991)

Daryaee, Touraj: "National History or Keyanid History? The Nature of Sasanid Zoroastrian Historiography" (*Iranian Studies* 28, 1995)

Bibliography

—— "Apocalypse Now: Zoroastrian Reflection on the Early Islamic Centuries" (*Medieval Encounters* 4, 1998)

—— "Memory and History: The Construction of the Past in Late Antique Persia" (*Name-ye Iran-e Bastan* 1–2, 2001–2)

—— *Sasanian Persia: The Rise and Fall of an Empire* (London, 2009)

Dauphin, C.: *La Palestine Byzance* (3 vols) (Oxford, 1998)

De Blois, François: "The 'Sabians' [sâbi'ûn] in Pre-Islamic Arabia" (*Acta Orientalia* 56, 1995)

—— "*Nasrani* (*Nazoraios*) and *Hanif* (*ethnikos*): Studies on the Religious Vocabulary of Christianity and Islam" (*Bulletin of the School of Oriental and African Studies* 65, 2002)

De Jong, Albert: "*Sub Specie Maiestatis*: Reflections on Sasanian Court Rituals," in *Zoroastrian Rituals in Context*, ed. Michael Stausberg (Leiden, 2004)

De Maigret, Alessandro: *Arabia Felix*, trans. Rebecca Thompson (London, 2002)

De Prémare, Alfred-Louis: *Aux Origines du Coran: Questions d'Hier, Approches d'Aujourd'hui* (Paris, 2007)

Dennett, D. C.: *Conversion and the Poll-Tax in Early Islam* (Cambridge, Mass., 1950)

Dignas, Beate, and Winter, Engelbert: *Rome and Persia in Late Antiquity* (Cambridge, 2007)

Dixon, Abd al-Ameer Abd: *The Umayyad Caliphate: 65–86/684–705* (London, 1971)

Dols, Michael: *The Black Death in the Middle East* (Princeton, 1977)

Donner, Fred M.: "Mecca's Food Supplies and Muhammad's Boycott" (*Journal of the Economic and Social History of the Orient* 20, 1977)

—— *The Early Islamic Conquests* (Princeton, 1981)

—— "Sources of Islamic Conceptions of War," in *Just War and Jihad*, ed. J. M. Kelsay and J. T. Johnson (New York, 1991)

—— *Narratives of Islamic Origins: The Beginnings of Islamic Historical Writing* (Princeton, 1998)

—— Review of *The Idea of Idolatry and the Emergence of Islam: From Polemic to History*, by G. R. Hawting (*Journal of the American Oriental Society* 121, 2001)

—— *Muhammad and the Believers at the Origins of Islam* (Cambridge, Mass., 2010)

Donner, Herbert: *The Mosaic Map of Madaba* (Kampen, 1992)

Downey, Glanville: *Constantinople in the Age of Justinian* (Norman, 1960)

—— *Ancient Antioch* (Princeton, 1963)

Drake, H. A.: *Constantine and the Bishops: The Politics of Intolerance* (Baltimore, 2000)

Drijvers, H. J. W.: "Jews and Christians at Edessa" (*Journal of Jewish Studies* 36, 1985)

Duffy, John: "Byzantine Medicine in the Sixth and Seventh Centuries: Aspects of Teaching and Practice" (*Dumbarton Oaks Papers* 38, 1984)

Duri, A. A.: *The Rise of Historical Writing Among the Arabs*, trans. Lawrence I. Conrad (Princeton, 1983)

Durliat, Jean: "La Peste du VIe siècle: Pour un nouvel examen des sources byzantines," in *Hommes et richesses dans l'empire Byzantin*, ed. V. Kravari, C. Morrison and J. Lefort (2 vols) (Paris, 1989–91)

Ehrman, Bart: *The Orthodox Corruption of Scripture: The Effect of Early Christological Controversies on the Text of the New Testament* (Oxford, 1993)

—— *Lost Christianities: The Battles for Scripture and the Faiths We Never Knew* (Oxford, 2003)

Elad, Amikam: "Why Did 'Abd al-Malik Build the Dome of the Rock? A Re-examination of the Muslim Sources," in Raby and Johns

—— "The Southern Golan in the Early Muslim Period: The Significance of Two Newly Discovered Milestones of 'Abd al-Malik" (*Der Islam* 76, 1999)

El Cheikh, Nadia Maria: *Byzantium Viewed by the Arabs* (Cambridge, Mass., 2004)

Encyclopaedia of Islam, ed. P. J. Bearman, Th. Bianquis, C. E. Bosworth, E. van Donzel and W. P. Heinrichs *et al.* (2nd edn) (Leiden, 1960–2005)

Encyclopedia Iranica, ed. Ehsan Yarshater (London and New York, 1996–)

Eph'al, I.: "'Ishmael' and 'Arab(s)': A Transformation of Ethnological Terms" (*Journal of Near Eastern Studies* 35, 1976)

Esmonde Cleary, A. S.: *The Ending of Roman Britain* (London, 1989)

Ettinghausen, Richard: *Arab Painting* (Geneva, 1962)

Evans, J. A. S.: *The Age of Justinian: The Circumstances of Imperial Power* (London, 1996)

Farrokh, Kaveh: *Sassanian Elite Cavalry, AD 224–642* (Oxford, 2005)

—— *Shadows in the Desert: Ancient Persia at War* (Oxford, 2007)

Flood, Finbarr Barry: *The Great Mosque of Damascus: Studies on the Makings of an Umayyad Visual Culture* (Leiden, 2001)

Flusin, Bernard: "L'Esplanade du Temple à l'arrivée des Arabes, d'après deux récits byzantins," in Raby and Johns.

Fonrobert, Charlotte Elisheva, and Jaffee, Martin S. (eds): *The Cambridge Companion to the Talmud and Rabbinic Literature* (Cambridge, 2007)

Forsyth, George H. and Weitzmann, Kurt: *The Monastery of Saint Catherine at Mount Sinai* (Ann Arbor, 1974)

Foss, Clive: "The Persians in Asia Minor and the End of Antiquity" (*English Historical Review* 90, 1975)

—— *Ephesus after Antiquity: A Late Antique, Byzantine and Turkish City* (Cambridge, 1979)

Fowden, Garth: "Constantine's Porphyry Column: the Earliest Literary Allusion" (*Journal of Roman Studies* 81, 1991)

—— *Empire to Commonwealth: Consequences of Monotheism in Late Antiquity* (Princeton, 1993)

Frankfurter, David T. M.: "Stylites and *Phallobates*: Pillar Religions in Late Antique Syria" (*Vigiliae Christianae* 44, 1990)

French, D. H. and Lightfoot, C. S. (eds): *The Eastern Frontier of the Roman Empire* (2 vols) (Oxford, 1989)

Friedman, Richard Elliott: *Who Wrote the Bible?* (New York, 1987)

Frye, Richard N.: *The Golden Age of Persia: The Arabs in the East* (London, 1975)

—— *The History of Ancient Iran* (Munich, 1984)

Gabriel, Richard A.: *Muhammad: Islam's First Great General* (Norman, 2007)

Gager, John G.: "Did Jewish Christians See the Rise of Islam?" in Becker and Reed

Garnsey, P. D. A. and Whittaker, C. R. (eds): *Imperialism in the Ancient World* (Cambridge, 1978)

Gaspar, C.: "The King of Kings and the Holy Men: Royal Authority and Sacred Power in the Early Byzantine World," in *Monotheistic Kingship: The Medieval Variants*, ed. Aziz Al-Azmeh and Janos M. Bak (Budapest, 2004)

Gaube, Heinz: "Mazdak: Historical Reality or Invention?" (*Studia Iranica* 11, 1982)

Ghirshman, R.: *Les Chionites-Hephthalites* (Cairo, 1948)

—— *Persian Art: The Parthian and Sasanian Dynasties* (London, 1962)

—— *Persia: From the Origins to Alexander*, trans. Stuart Gilbert and James Emmons (London, 1964)

Gibbon, Edward: *The History of the Decline and Fall of the Roman Empire* (3 vols) (London, 1994)

Gilliot, Claude: "Muhammad, le Coran et les 'Contraintes de l'Histoire,' " in Wild

Gnoli, Gherardo: *Zoroaster's Time and Homeland: A Study on the Origins of Mazdeism and Related Problems* (Naples, 1980)

—— *The Idea of Iran: An Essay on Its Origin* (Rome, 1989)

Goldziher, Ignaz: *Muslim Studies*, trans. Barber and Stern (2 vols) (London, 1967–71)

—— *Introduction to Islamic Theology and Law*, trans. Andras Hamori and Ruth Hamori (Princeton, 1981)

Gonen, Rivka: *Contested Holiness: Jewish, Muslim and Christian Perspectives on the Temple Mount in Jerusalem* (Jersey City, 2003)

Goodblatt, David M.: *Elements of Ancient Jewish Nationalism* (Cambridge, 2006)

Grabar, Oleg: *The Formation of Islamic Art* (New Haven, 1973)

—— *The Dome of the Rock* (Cambridge, Mass., 2006)

Graf, David F.: *Rome and the Arabian Frontier: From the Nabataeans to the Saracens* (Aldershot, 1997)

Graf, D. F., and O'Connor, M.: "The Origin of the Term Saracen and the Rawwafa Inscriptions" (*Byzantine Studies* 4, 1977)

Green, Tamara M.: *The City of the Moon God: Religious Traditions of Harran* (Leiden, 1992)

Gregory, Timothy E.: *A History of Byzantium* (Oxford, 2005)

Grierson, Philip: "The Monetary Reforms of 'Abd al-Malik" (*Journal of the Economic and Social History of the Orient* 3, 1960)

Griffith, S. H.: " 'Syriacisms' in the Arabic Qur'an: Who Were 'Those who said that Allah is third of three, according to *al-Ma'idah* 73'?" in *A Word Fitly Spoken: Studies in Mediaeval Exegesis of the Hebrew Bible and the Qur'an*, ed. Meir M. Bar-Asher, Simon Hopkins, Sarah Stroumsa and Bruno Chiesa (Jerusalem, 2007)

—— "Christian Lord and the Arabic Qur'an: The 'Companions of the Cave' in *Surat al-Kahf* and in Syriac Christian Tradition," in Reynolds

Grohmann, A.: "Aperçu de papyrologie arabe" (*Études de Papyrologie* 1, 1932)

—— *Arabic Papyri from Hirbet el-Mird* (Louvain, 1963)

Gruen, Erich S.: *Culture and National Identity in Republican Rome* (Ithaca, 1992)

Grunebaum, G. E. von: *Classical Islam: A History, 600 AD to 1258 AD*, trans. Katherine Wilson (New Brunswick, 2005)

Guidi, M.: "Mazdak," in *Encyclopaedia of Islam*

Guilland, Rodolphe: "L'Expédition de Maslama contre Constantinople" (*Études Byzantines* 1, 1959)

Gutas, Dimitri: *Greek Thought, Arabic Culture* (London, 1998)

Gyselen, Rika: *The Four Generals of the Sasanian Empire: Some Sigillographic Evidence* (Rome, 2001)

Haas, Christopher: *Alexandria in Late Antiquity: Topography and Social Conflict* (Baltimore, 1997)

Hakim, Avraham: "Conflicting Images of Lawgivers: The Caliph and the Prophet," in Berg 2003

Haldon, J. F.: *Byzantium in the Seventh Century: The Transformation of a Culture* (Cambridge, 1990)

Haldon J. F., and Kennedy, H.: "The Arab–Byzantine Frontier in the Eighth and Ninth Centuries: Military Organisation and Society in the Borderlands" (*Zbornik Radova* 19, 1980)

Hallaq, Wael B.: "Was the Gate of Ijtihad Closed?" (*International Journal of Middle East Studies* 16, 1984)

Hardy, Edward R.: "The Egyptian Policy of Justinian" (*Dumbarton Oaks Papers* 22, 1968)

Harris, Anthea: *Byzantium, Britain and the West: The Archaeology of Cultural Identity, AD 400–650* (Stroud, 2003)

Harvey, Susan Ashbrook and Hunter, David G. (eds): *The Oxford Handbook of Early Christian Studies* (Oxford, 2008)

Hawting, G. R.: "The Disappearance and Rediscovery of Zamzam and the 'Well of the Ka'ba'" (*Bulletin of the School of Oriental and African Studies* 43, 1980)

—— "The Origins of the Muslim Sanctuary at Mecca," in Juynboll

—— Review of *Die Widerentdeckung des Propheten Muhammad*, by G. Lüling (*Journal of Semitic Studies* 27, 1982b)

—— Review of *The Early Islamic Conquests*, by Fred M. Donner (*Bulletin of the School of Oriental and African Studies* 47, 1984)

—— "Al-Hudaybiya and the Conquest of Mecca: A Reconsideration of the Tradition about the Muslim Takeover of the Sanctuary" (*Jerusalem Studies in Arabic and Islam* 8, 1986)

—— "The 'Sacred Offices' of Mecca from Jahiliyya to Islam" (*Jerusalem Studies in Arabic and Islam* 13, 1990)

—— "The *Hajj* in the Second Civil War," in *Golden Roads: Migration, Pilgrimage and Travel in Mediaeval and Modern Islam*, ed. Ian Richard Netton (Richmond, 1993)

—— *The Idea of Idolatry and the Emergence of Islam* (Cambridge, 1999)

—— *The First Dynasty of Islam: The Umayyad Caliphate, AD 661–750* (Abingdon, 2000)

Hawting, G. R., and Sharee, Abdul-Kader A.: *Approaches to the Qur'an* (London and New York, 1993)

Heather, Peter: *Empires and Barbarians: Migration, Development and the Birth of Europe* (London, 2009)

Heck, Gene W.: "'Arabia without Spices': An Alternate Hypothesis: The Issue of 'Makkan Trade and the Rise of Islam'" (*Journal of the American Oriental Society* 123, 2003)

Herrmann, G.: *The Iranian Revival* (London, 1977)

Hirschfeld, Yizhar: *A Guide to Antiquity Sites in Tiberias*, trans. Edward Levin and Inna Pommerantiz (Jerusalem, 1992a)

—— *The Judean Desert Monasteries in the Byzantine Period* (New Haven, 1992b)

Hopkins, Keith: "Christian Number and its Implications" (*Journal of Early Christian Studies* 6, 1998)

Horn, Cornelia: "Intersections: The Reception History of the *Protoevangelium of James* in Sources from the Christian East and in the *Qur'an*" (*Apocrypha* 17, 2006)

—— "Mary Between Bible and Qur'ān: Soundings into the Transmission and Reception History of the *Protoevangelium of James* on the Basis of Selected Literary Sources in Coptic and Copto-Arabic and of Art Historical Evidence Pertaining to Egypt" (*Islam and Muslim–Christian Relations* 18, 2007)

Howard-Johnston, James: *East Rome, Sasanian Persia and the End of Antiquity* (Aldershot, 2006)

—— *Witnesses to a World in Crisis: Historians and Histories of the Middle East in the Seventh Century* (Oxford, 2010)

Hoyland, Robert G.: "Sebeos, the Jews and the Rise of Islam," in *Medieval and Modern Perspectives on Muslim–Jewish Relations*, ed. Ronald L. Nettler (Luxembourg, 1995)

—— *Seeing Islam as Others Saw It: A Survey and Evaluation of Christian, Jewish and Zoroastrian Writings on Early Islam* (Princeton, 1997)

—— "Earliest Christian Writings on Muhammad," in Motzki 2000

—— *Arabia and the Arabs: From the Bronze Age to the Coming of Islam* (London, 2001)

—— "New Documentary Texts and the Early Islamic State" (*Bulletin of the School of Oriental and African Studies* 69, 2006)

Huft, Dietrich: "The Functional Layout of the Fire Sanctuary at Takht-i Sulaiman," in Kennet and Luft

Humphreys, R. Stephen: *Mu'awiya ibn Abi Sufyan: From Arabia to Empire* (Oxford, 2006)

Huyse, P.: "La Revendications de Territoires Achéménides par les Sassanides: Une Réalité Historique?" (*Studia Iranica Cahier* 25, 2002)

Ibn Warraq (ed.): *The Origins of the Koran: Classic Essays on Islam's Holy Book* (New York, 1998)

—— (ed.): *The Quest for the Historical Muhammad* (New York, 2000)

—— (ed.): *What the Koran Really Says: Language, Text, and Commentary* (New York, 2002)

Irwin, Robert: *For Lust of Knowing: The Orientalists and Their Enemies* (London, 2006)

Isaac, Benjamin: *The Limits of Empire: The Roman Army in the East* (Oxford, 1990)

Janin, R.: *Constantinople Byzantine: Développement urbain et répertoire topographique* (Paris, 1950)

Jansen, Hans: *De Historische Mohammed: De Verhalen uit Medina* (Amsterdam, 2007)

Jeffrey, Arthur: *The Foreign Vocabulary of the Qur'an* (Leiden, 1937)

—— *The Foreign Vocabulary of the Qur'an* (Baroda, 1938)

Jenkins, Philip: *The Lost History of Christianity* (New York, 2008)

—— *Jesus Wars: How Four Patriarchs, Three Queens, and Two Emperors Decided What Christians Would Believe for the Next 1,500 Years* (New York, 2010)

Johns, Jeremy (ed.): *Bayt al-Maqdis: Jerusalem and Early Islam* (Oxford, 1999)

—— "Archaeology and the History of Early Islam: The First Seventy Years" (*Journal of the Economic and Social History of the Orient* 46, 2003)

Jones, A. H. M.: *The Later Roman Empire 284–602* (3 vols) (Oxford, 1964)

Jones, Alan: *Early Arabic Poetry* (2 vols) (Oxford, 1996)

—— "The Dotting of a Script and the Dating of an Era: The Strange Neglect of PERF 558" (*Islamic Culture* 72, 1998)

Juynboll, G. H. A.: *Studies on the First Century of Islamic Society* (Carbondale and Edwardsville, 1982)

Kaegi, Walter Emil: *Byzantium and the Decline of Rome* (Princeton, 1968)

—— "Initial Byzantine Reactions to the Arab Conquest" (*Church History* 38, 1969)

—— *Byzantium and the Early Islamic Conquests* (Cambridge, 1992)

—— *Heraclius: Emperor of Byzantium* (Cambridge, 2003)

Kaldellis, Anthony: "The Literature of Plague and the Anxieties of Piety in Sixth-Century Byzantium," in *Piety and Plague: From Byzantium to the Baroque*, ed. Franco Mormando and Thomas Worcester (Kirskville, 2007)

—— *The Christian Parthenon: Classicism and Pilgrimage in Byzantine Athens* (Cambridge, 2009)

Kalisch, Muhammad S.: "Islamische Theologie ohne historischen Muhammad—Anmerkungen zu den Herausforderungen der historisch-kritischen Methode für das islamische Denken" (http://www.unimuenster.de/imperia)

Kalmin, Richard: "Christians and Heretics in Rabbinic Literature of Late Antiquity" (*Harvard Theological Review* 87, 1994)

—— *The Sage in Jewish Society of Late Antiquity* (London, 1999)

—— *Jewish Babylonia Between Persia and Roman Palestine* (Oxford, 2006)

Karsh, Efraim: *Islamic Imperialism: A History* (New Haven, 2006)

Kellens, Jean: *Essays on Zarathustra and Zoroastrianism*, trans. Prods Oktor Skjaervo (Costa Mesa, 2000)

Kelly, Christopher: *Ruling the Later Roman Empire* (Cambridge, Mass., 2004)

Kennedy, Hugh: "From *Polis* to *Madina*: Urban Change in Late Antique and Early Islamic Syria" (*Past and Present* 106, 1985)

—— *The Prophet and the Age of the Caliphates: The Islamic Near East From the Sixth to the Eleventh Century* (London, 1986)

—— *The Armies of the Caliphs: Military and Society in the Early Islamic State* (London, 2001)

—— *The Byzantine and Early Islamic Near East* (Aldershot, 2006)

—— *The Great Arab Conquests: How the Spread of Islam Changed the World We Live In* (London, 2007)

Kennet, Derek and Luft, Paul: *Current Research in Sasanian Archaeology, Art and History* (Oxford, 2008)

Keys, D.: *Catastrophe: An Investigation into the Modern World* (London, 1999)

Kiani, Mohammad Yusuf: *Parthian Sites in Hyrcania: The Gurgan Plain* (Berlin, 1982)

King, G. R. D. and Cameron, Averil (eds): *The Byzantine and Early Islamic Near East: Land Use and Settlement Patterns* (Princeton, 1994)

Kister, M. J.: " 'You Shall Only Set out for Three Mosques': A Study of an Early Tradition" (*Le Muséon* 82, 1969)

—— "*Maqam Ibrahim*: A Stone with an Inscription" (*Le Museon* 84, 1971)

—— *Studies in Jahiliyya and Early Islam* (London, 1980)

—— "Social and Religious Concepts of Authority in Islam" (*Jerusalem Studies in Arabic and Islam* 18, 1994)

Klijn, A. F. J.: *Jewish–Christian Gospel Tradition* (Leiden, 1992)

Klijn, A. F. J. and Reinink, G. J.: *Patristic Evidence for Jewish–Christian Sects* (Leiden, 1973)

Laga, Carl: "Judaism and Jews in Maximus Confessor's Works: Theoretical Controversy and Practical Attitude" (*Byzantioslavica* 51, 1990)

Lammens, Henri: *Études sur le Règne du Calife Omaiyade Mo'awia Ier* (Paris, 1908)

—— *Fatima et les Filles de Mahomet* (Rome, 1912)

—— *La Mecque à la Veille de l'Hégire* (Beirut, 1924)

Bibliography

Leaman, Oliver (ed.): *The Qur'an: An Encyclopedia* (London, 2006)

Leites, Adrien: "*Sira* and the Question of Tradition," in Motzki 2000

Lester, Toby: "What is the Koran?" (*Atlantic Monthly*, January 1999)

Levene, Dan: "'. . . and by the Name of Jesus . . .': An Unpublished Magic Bowl in Jewish Aramaic" (*Jewish Studies Quarterly* 6, 1999)

Lieu, Samuel N. C: *Manicheism in the Later Roman Empire and Medieval China* (Tübingen, 1992)

Lings, Martin: *Muhammad: His Life Based on the Earliest Sources* (London, 1983)

Little, Lester K.: *Plague and the End of Antiquity: The Pandemic of 541–750* (Cambridge, 2007)

Lüling, Günter: *A Challenge to Islam for Reformation: The Rediscovery and Reliable Reconstruction of a Comprehensive Pre-Islamic Christian Hymnal Hidden in the Koran Under Earliest Islamic Reinterpretations* (Delhi, 2003)

Luttwak, Edward N.: *The Grand Strategy of the Byzantine Empire* (Cambridge, Mass., 2009)

Luxenberg, Christoph: *The Syro-Aramaic Reading of the Koran: A Contribution to the Decoding of the Language of the Koran* (Berlin, 2007)

Maas, Michael: *John Lydus and the Roman Past: Antiquarianism and Politics in the Age of Justinian* (London, 1992)

—— *The Cambridge Companion to the Age of Justinian* (Cambridge, 2005)

MacCulloch, Diarmaid: *A History of Christianity* (London, 2009)

MacMullen, Ramsay: *Christianity and Paganism in the Fourth to Eighth Centuries* (New Haven, 1997)

Mango, Cyril: *Byzantium: The Empire of New Rome* (London, 1980)

—— *Studies on Constantinople* (Aldershot, 1993)

—— *Le Développement urbain de Constantinople (IV–VII Siècles)* (Paris, 2004)

Manzoor, Pervez S.: "Method Against Truth: Orientalism and Qur'anic Studies" (*Muslim World Book Review* 7, 1987)

Margoliouth, J. P: *Supplement to the Thesaurus Syriacus of R. Payne Smith, S.T.P.* (Oxford, 1927)

Markus, R. A.: *The End of Ancient Christianity* (Cambridge, 1990)

Marsham, Andrew: *Rituals of Islamic Monarchy: Accession and Succession in the First Muslim Empire* (Edinburgh, 2009)

Mason, Steve: "Jews, Judeans, Judaizing, Judaism: Problems of Categorization in Ancient History" (*Journal for the Study of Judaism* 38, 2007)

Mathisen, Ralph W.: "*Peregrini, Barbari,* and *Cives Romani*: Concepts of Citizenship and the Legal Identity of Barbarians in the Later Roman Empire" (*American Historical Review* 111, 2006)

Mathisen, Ralph W., and Sivan, Hagith S.: *Shifting Frontiers in Late Antiquity* (Aldershot, 1996)

Matthews, John: *The Roman Empire of Ammianus* (London, 1989)

McAuliffe, Jane Dammen (ed.): *Encyclopaedia of the Qur'an* (5 vols) (Leiden, 2001–6)

—— (ed.): *The Cambridge Companion to the Qur'an* (Cambridge, 2006)

McCormick, Michael: *Eternal Victory: Triumphal Rulership in Late Antiquity, Byzantium, and the Early Medieval West* (Cambridge, 1986)

—— "Bateaux de vie, bateaux de mort: Maladie, commerce, transports annonaires et le passage économique du Bas-Empire au Moyen Âge," in *Morfologie Sociali e Culturali in Europa fra Tarda Antichita e Alto Medioevo*, ed. Centro Italiano di Studi Sull'Alto Medioevo (Spoleto, 1998)

—— *Origins of the European Economy: Communications and Commerce, AD 300–900* (Cambridge, 2001)

Meyers, Eric M (ed.): *Galilee Through the Centuries: Confluence of Cultures* (Winona Lake, 1999)

Milik, J. T.: "Inscriptions Grecques et Nabatéennes de Rawwfah" (*Bulletin of the Institute of Archaeology* 10, 1971)

Millar, Fergus: "Hagar, Ishmael, Josephus and the Origins of Islam" (*Journal of Jewish Studies* 44, 1993)

Minorsky, V.: *Iranica* (Hartford, 1964)

Misaka, T. (ed.): *Monarchies and Socio-Religious Traditions in the Ancient Near East* (Wiesbaden, 1984)

Moorhead, John: *Theodoric in Italy* (Oxford, 1973)

Morimoto, Kosei: *The Fiscal Administration of Egypt in the Early Islamic Period* (Dohosha, 1981)

Morony, Michael G.: *Iraq After the Muslim Conquest* (Princeton, 1984)

—— "'For Whom Does the Writer Write?': The First Bubonic Plague Pandemic According to Syriac Sources," in Little

Mottahedeh, Roy Parviz, and al-Sayyid, Ridwan: "The Idea of the *Jihad* in Islam Before the Crusades," in *The Crusades from the Perspective of Byzantium and the Muslim World*, ed. Angeliki E. Laiou and Roy Parviz Mottahedeh (Washington, 2001)

Motzki, Harald: "The Prophet and the Cat: On Dating Malik's *Muwatta* and Legal Traditions" (*Jerusalem Studies in Arabic and Islam* 22, 1998)

—— (ed.): *The Biography of Muhammad: The Issue of the Sources* (Leiden, 2000)

—— *The Origins of Islamic Jurisprudence: Meccan Fiqh before the Classical Schools*, trans. Marion H. Katz (Leiden, 2002)

—— (ed.): *Hadith: Origins and Developments* (Trowbridge, 2008)

Mourad, Suleiman A.: "From Hellenism to Christianity and Islam: The Origin of the Palm Tree Story Concerning Mary and Jesus in the Gospel of Pseudo-Matthew and the Qur'an" (*Oriens Christianus* 86, 2002)

Myers, Eric M. (ed.): *Galilee Through the Centuries: Confluence of Cultures* (Winona Lake, 1999)

Nebes, Norbert: "The Martyrs of Najran and the End of the Himyar: On the

Political History of South Arabia in the Early Sixth Century," in Neuwirth, Sinai and Marx

Nees, Lawrence: *Early Medieval Art* (Oxford, 2002)

Neusner, Jacob: *A History of the Jews in Babylonia* (5 vols) (Leiden, 1960–70)

—— *Talmudic Judaism in Sasanian Babylonia: Essays and Studies* (Leiden, 1976)

—— *Israel's Politics in Sasanian Iran: Jewish Self-Government in Talmudic Times* (Lanham, 1986)

—— *Judaism, Christianity, and Zoroastrianism in Talmudic Babylonia* (Lanham, 1986)

—— *In the Aftermath of Catastrophe: Founding Judaism, 70 to 640* (Montreal, 2009)

Neuwirth, Angelika: "Qur'an and History—a Disputed Relationship: Some Reflections on Qur'anic History and History in the Qur'an" (*Journal of Qur'anic Studies* 5, 2003)

Neuwirth, Angelika, Sinai, Nicolai and Marx, Michael (eds): *The Qur'an in Context: Historical and Literary Investigations into the Qur'anic Milieu* (Leiden, 2010)

Nevo, Yehuda D.: "Towards a Prehistory of Islam" (*Jerusalem Studies in Arabic and Islam* 17, 1994)

Nevo, Yehuda D. and Koren, Judith: *Crossroads to Islam: The Origins of the Arab Religion and the Arab State* (New York, 2003)

Newby, Gordon Darnell: *The Making of the Last Prophet: A Reconstruction of the Earliest Biography of Muhammad* (Columbia, 1989)

Noth, Albrecht: "Abgrenzungsprobleme zwischen Muslimen und Nicht-Muslimen: Die 'Bedingungen 'Umars (*as-surut al-'umariyya*)' unter einem anderen Aspekt gelesen" (*Jerusalem Studies in Arabic and Islam* 9, 1987)

—— *The Early Arabic Historical Tradition*, trans. Michael Bonner (Princeton, 1994)

O'Donnell, James: "Late Antiquity: Before and After" (*Transactions of the American Philological Association* 134, 2004)

—— *The Ruin of the Roman Empire: A New History* (New York, 2008)

Ohlig, Karl-Heinz and Puin, Gerd-R.: *The Hidden Origins of Islam: New Research into Its Early History* (New York, 2010)

The Oracle of Baalbek: in Alexander, Paul J.: *The Oracle of Baalbek: The Tiburtine Sibyl in Greek Dress* (Washington D. C., 1967)

Ory, S.: "Aspects religieux des textes epigraphiques du début de l'Islam" (*Revue du Monde Musulman et de la Méditerranée* 58, 1990)

Padwick, C.: *Muslim Devotions* (London, 1961)

Palmer, Andrew; Brock, Sebastian P.; Hoyland, Robert G.: *The Seventh Century in the West-Syrian Chronicles* (Liverpool, 1993)

Parker, Philips: *The Empire Stops Here: A Journey Along the Frontiers of the Roman World* (London, 2009)

Parker, S. T.: *Romans and Saracens: A History of the Arabian Frontier* (Winona Lake, 1986)

Parkes, James: *The Conflict of the Church and Synagogue: A Study in the Origins of Anti-Semitism* (London, 1934)

Parsons, Peter: *City of the Sharp-Nosed Fish: Greek Lives in Roman Egypt* (London, 2007)

Patai, Raphael: *Ignaz Goldziher and His Oriental Diary: A Translation and Psychological Portrait* (Detroit, 1987)

Pazdernik, C.: "Our Most Pious Consort Given us by God: Dissident Reactions to the Partnership of Justinian and Theodora, AD 525–548" (*Classical Antiquity* 13, 1994)

Peters, F. E.: "Who Built the Dome of the Rock?" (*Graeco Arabica* 1, 1982)

—— "The Commerce of Mecca before Islam," in *A Way Prepared: Essays on Islamic Culture in Honor of Richard Bayly Winder* (New York and London, 1988)

—— "The Quest of the Historical Muhammad" (*International Journal of Middle East Studies* 23, 1991)

—— *Muhammad and the Origins of Islam* (New York, 1994a)

—— *The Hajj: the Muslim Pilgrimage to Mecca and the Holy Places* (Princeton, 1994b)

—— *The Arabs and Arabia on the Eve of Islam* (Aldershot, 1999)

Petersen, Erling Ladewig: *'Ali and Mu'awiya in Early Arabic Tradition: Studies on the Genesis and Growth of Islamic Historical Writing Until the End of the Ninth Century* (Copenhagen, 1964)

Philonenko, Marc: "Une Tradition essénienne dans le Coran" (*Revue de l'Histoire des Religions* 170, 1966)

Pigulevskaja, Nina: *Les Villes de l'état Iranien aux Époques Parthe et Sassanide* (Paris, 1963)

Pines, Shlomo: "The Jewish Christians of the Early Centuries of Christianity According to a New Source" (*Proceedings of the Israel Academy of Sciences and Humanities* 2, 1968)

Potter, David S.: *The Roman Empire at Bay, AD 180–395* (London, 2004)

Pourshariati, Parvaneh: "Local Histories of Khurasan and the Pattern of Arab Settlement" (*Studia Iranica* 27, 1998)

—— *Decline and Fall of the Sasanian Empire: The Sasanian–Parthian Confederacy and the Arab Conquest of Iran* (London, 2008)

Prémare, Alfred-Louis de: "'Abd al-Malik b. Marwan and the Process of the Qur'an's Composition," in Ohlig and Puin

Pummer, Reinhard: *Early Christian Authors on Samaritans and Samaritanism* (Tübingen, 2002)

Rabbat, Nasser: "The Meaning of the Umayyad Dome of the Rock" (*Muqarnas* 6, 1989)

Raby, Julian and Johns, Jeremy (eds): *Bayt Al-Maqdis: 'Abd al-Malik's Jerusalem* (Oxford, 1992)

Rahman, Fazlur: *Islamic Methodology in History* (Karachi, 1965)

—— *Major Themes of the Qur'an* (Chicago, 1980)

—— "Some Recent Books on the Qur'an by Western Authors" (*Journal of Religion* 61, 1984)

Ramadan, Tariq: *The Messenger: The Meanings of the Life of Muhammad* (Oxford, 2007)

Rautman, Marcus: *Daily Life in the Byzantine Empire* (Westport, 2006)

Regnier, A.: "Quelques Énigmes littéraires de l'Inspiration coranique" (*Le Muséon* 52, 1939)

Reinink, Gerrit J.: "Die Enstehung der syrischen Alexanderlegende als politisch-religiöse Propagandaschrift für Herkleios' Kirchenpolitik," in *After Chalcedon: Studies in Theology and Church History*, ed. C. Laga, J. A. Munitiz and L. Van Rompay (Leuven, 1985)

—— "The Beginnings of Syriac Apologetic Literature in Response to Islam" (*Oriens Christianus* 77, 1993)

—— "Heraclius, the New Alexander: Apocalyptic Prophecies," in Reinink and Stolte

Reinink, Gerrit J. and Stolte, Bernard H.: *The Reign of Heraclius (610–641): Crisis and Confrontation* (Leuven, 2002)

Rekavandi, Hamid Omrani, Sauer, Eberhard, Wilkinson, Tony and Nokandeh, Jebrael: "The Enigma of the Red Snake: Revealing One of the World's Greatest Frontier Walls" (*Current World Archaeology* 27, 2008)

Reynolds, Gabriel Said (ed.): *The Qur'an in Its Historical Context* (Abingdon, 2008)

Rippin, Andrew: "Literary Analysis of Qur'an, Tafsir and Sira: The Methodologies of John Wansbrough," in *Approaches to Islam in Religious Studies*, ed. Richard C. Martin (Tucson, 1985)

—— (ed.): *Approaches to the History of the Interpretation of the Qur'an* (Oxford, 1988)

—— *Muslims, Their Religious Beliefs and Practices* (London, 1991)

—— "Muhammad in the Qur'an: Reading Scripture in the 21st Century," in Motzki 2000

—— *The Qur'an and its Interpretative Tradition* (Aldershot, 2001)

—— (ed.): *The Blackwell Companion to the Qur'an* (Oxford, 2009)

Robinson, Chase F.: *Islamic Historiography* (Cambridge, 2003)

—— "The Conquest of Khuzistan: A Historiographical Reassessment" (*Bulletin of the School of Oriental and African Studies* 67, 2004)

—— *Abd al-Malik* (Oxford, 2005)

Rodinson, Maxime: *Mohammed*, trans. Anne Carter (New York, 1971)

Rogerson, Barnaby: *The Prophet Muhammad: A Biography* (London, 2003)

Rosen, William: *Justinian's Flea: Plague, Empire, and the Birth of Europe* (New York, 2007)

Rosen-Ayalon, Myriam: *The Early Islamic Monuments of Al-Haram Al-Sharif: An Iconographic Study* (Jerusalem, 1989)

Rostovzeff, M. I.: *The Social and Economic History of the Roman Empire* (Oxford, 1957)

Rouwhorst, Gerard: "Jewish Liturgical Traditions in Early Syriac Christianity" (*Vigiliae Christianae* 51, 1997)

Roziewicz, M.: "Graeco-Islamic Elements at Kom el Dikka in the Light of New

Discoveries: Remarks on Early Mediaeval Alexandria" (*Graeco Arabica* 1, 1982)

Rubin, Uri: "The 'Constitution of Medina': Some Notes" (*Studia Islamica* 62, 1985)

—— "Hanifiyya and Ka'ba. An Inquiry into the Arabian Pre-Islamic Background of Din Ibrahim" (*Jerusalem Studies in Arabic and Islam* 13, 1990)

—— *The Eye of the Beholder: The Life of Muhammad as Viewed by the Early Muslims* (Princeton, 1995)

—— (ed.): *The Life of Muhammad* (Aldershot, 1998)

Rubin, Zeev: "The Mediterranean and the Dilemma of the Roman Empire in Late Antiquity" (*Mediterranean Historical Review* 1, 1986)

—— "The Reforms of Khusro Anushirwan," in Cameron 1995

Ruether, Rosemary Radford: "Judaism and Christianity: Two Fourth-Century Religions" (*Sciences Religieuses/Studies in Religion* 2, 1972)

Russell, James C.: *The Germanization of Early Medieval Christianity: A Sociohistorical Approach to Religious Transformation* (Oxford, 1994)

Russell, Josiah C.: "That Earlier Plague" (*Demography* 5, 1968)

Rutgers, L. V.: "Archaeological Evidence for the Interaction of Jews and Non-Jews in Antiquity" (*American Journal of Archeology* 96, 1992)

Ryckmans, G.: "Dhu 'l-Shara," in *Encyclopaedia of Islam*

Saadi, Abdul-Massih: "The Letter of John of Sedreh: A New Perspective on Nascent Islam" (*Karmo* 1, 1999)

Sachot, Maurice: "Comment le Christianisme est-il devenu religio?" (*Revues des Sciences Religieuses* 59, 1985)

Saleh, Walid: "In Search of a Comprehensible Qur'an: A Survey of Some Recent Scholarly Works" (*Royal Institute for Inter-Faith Studies* 5, 2003)

—— "The Etymological Fallacy and Quranic Studies: Muhammad, Paradise and Late Antiquity" (http://www.safarmer.com/Indo-Eurasian/Walid_Saleh.pdf)

Sand, Shlomo: *The Invention of the Jewish People* (London, 2009)

Sarris, Peter: *Economy and Society in the Age of Justinian* (Cambridge, 2006)

Schacht, Joseph: "A Reevaluation of Islamic Tradition" (*Journal of the Royal Asiatic Society of Great Britain and Ireland*, 1949)

—— *The Origins of Muhammadan Jurisprudence* (Oxford, 1950)

—— "Classicisme, Traditionalisme et Ankylose dans la Loi Religieuse de l'Islam," in *Classicisme et Déclin Culturel dans l'Histoire de l'Islam*, ed. Robert Brunschvig and Gustave E. von Grunebaum (Paris, 1977)

Schäfer, Peter: *Jesus in the Talmud* (Princeton, 2007)

Schwartz, Seth: *Imperialism and Jewish Society from 200 BCE to 640 CE* (Princeton, 2001)

Scott, Roger D.: "Malalas, the Secret History, and Justinian's Propaganda" (*Dumbarton Oaks Papers* 39, 1985)

Segal, Alan F.: *Rebecca's Children: Judaism and Christianity in the Roman World* (Cambridge, Mass., 1986)

Segal, J. B.: "Mesopotamian Communities from Julian to the Rise of Islam" (*Proceedings of the British Academy* 41, 1955)

—— *Edessa and Harran* (London, 1963)

—— *Edessa 'the Blessed City'* (Oxford, 1970)

Sells, Michael: *Approaching the Qur'an: The Early Revelations* (Ashland, 1999)

Serjeant, R. B.: "The *Sunnah Jami'ah*, Pacts with the Yathrib Jews, and the *Tahrim* of Yathrib: Analysis and Translation of the Documents Comprised in the So-called 'Constitution of Medina'" (*Bulletin of the School of Oriental and African Studies* 41, 1978)

—— "Meccan Trade and the Rise of Islam: Misconceptions and Flawed Polemics" (*Journal of the American Oriental Society* 110, 1990)

Shahid, Irfan: *The Martyrs of Najran: New Documents* (Brussels, 1971)

—— *Rome and the Arabs: A Prolegomenon to the Study of Byzantium and the Arabs* (Washington, 1984)

—— *Byzantium and the Semitic Orient Before the Rise of Islam* (London, 1988)

—— *Byzantium and the Arabs in the Fifth Century* (Washington, 1989)

—— *Byzantium and the Arabs in the Sixth Century* (2 vols) (Washington, 1995)

Shaki, Mansour: "The Cosmogonical and Cosmological Teachings of Mazdak," in *Papers in Honour of Professor Mary Boyce* (*Acta Iranica* 24, 1985)

Shani, Raya: "The Iconography of the Dome of the Rock" (*Jerusalem Studies in Arabic and Islam* 23, 1999)

Sharon, Moshe: *Black Banners from the East: The Establishment of the Abbasid State* (Jerusalem, 1983)

—— (ed.): *Pillars of Smoke and Fire: The Holy Land in History and Thought* (Johannesburg, 1988)

Shoufani, Elias: *Al-Riddah and the Muslim Conquest of Arabia* (Toronto, 1973)

Simon, Marcel: *Verus Israel: A Study of the Relations Between Christians and Jews in the Roman Empire (133–425)*, trans. H. McKeating (Oxford, 1986)

Simon, Róbert: *Ignác Goldziher: His Life and Scholarship as Reflected in his Works and Correspondence* (Leiden, 1986)

Sivan, Hagith: "From Byzantine to Persian Jerusalem: Jewish Perspectives and Jewish/Christian Polemics" (*Greek, Roman and Byzantine Studies* 41, 2000)

—— *Palestine in Late Antiquity* (Oxford, 2008)

Sivers, Peter von: "The Islamic Origins Debate Goes Public" (http://www.blackwellpublishing.com/pdf/compass/hico_058.pdf)

Sizgorich, Thomas: "Narrative and Community in Islamic Late Antiquity" (*Past and Present* 185, 2004)

—— "'Do Prophets Come with a Sword?' Conquest, Empire and Historical Narrative in the Early Islamic World" (*American Historical Review* 112, 2007)

—— *Violence and Belief in Late Antiquity: Militant Devotion in Christianity and Islam* (Philadelphia, 2009)

Skarsaune, Oskar and Hvalvik, Reidar (eds): *Jewish Believers in Jesus: The Early Centuries* (Peabody, 2007)

Skjærvø, P. O.: "Azdaha: In Old and Middle Iranian," in *Encyclopedia Iranica*

Sourdel, D.: *Les Cultes du Hauran* (Paris, 1952)

Stathakopolous, Dionysius: "The Justinianic Plague Revisited" (*Byzantine and Modern Greek Studies* 24, 2000)

—— *Famine and Pestilence in the Late Roman and Early Byzantine Empire: A Systematic Survey of Subsistence Crises and Epidemics* (Aldershot, 2004)

Stemberger, Günter: *Jews and Christians in the Holy Land: Palestine in the Fourth Century*, trans. R. Tuschling (Edinburgh, 2000)

Stetkevych, Suzanne Pinckney: *The Poetics of Islamic Legitimacy: Myth, Gender, and Ceremony in the Classical Arabic Ode* (Bloomington, 2002)

Stoneman, Richard: *Alexander the Great: A Life in Legend* (New Haven, 2008)

Stroumsa, Guy: "Old Wines and New Bottles: On Patristic Soteriology and Rabbinic Judaism," in *The Origins and Diversity of Axial Age Civilizations*, ed. S. N. Eisenstadt (Albany, 1986a)

—— "'Seal of the Prophets': The Nature of a Manichaean Metaphor" (*Jerusalem Studies in Arabic and Islam* 7, 1986b)

—— "The Body of Truth and Its Measures: New Testament Canonization in Context," in *Festschrift Kurt Rudolph*, ed. H. Preissler and H. Seiwert (Marburg, 1995)

Stroumsa, Rachel: *People and Identities in Nessana* (Ph.D. thesis, Duke University, 2008)

Strugnell, John: "Notes on the Text and Transmission of the Apocryphal Psalms 151, 154 (= Syr. II) and 155 (= Syr. III)" (*Harvard Theological Review* 59, 1966)

Taylor, Joan E.: *Christians and the Holy Places: The Myth of Jewish–Christian Origins* (Oxford, 1993)

Taylor, Miriam S.: *Anti-Judaism and Early Christian Identity: A Critique of the Scholarly Consensus* (Leiden, 1995)

Teall, John L.: "The Barbarians in Justinian's Armies" (*Speculum* 40, 1965)

Teixidor, Javier: *The Pagan God: Popular Religion in the Greco-Roman Near East* (Princeton, 1977)

Thieme, P.: "The Concept of Mitra in Aryan Belief," in *Mithraic Studies: Proceedings of the First International Congress of Mithraic Studies*, vol. 1 (Manchester, 1975)

Torrey, Charles Cutler: *The Jewish Foundation of Islam* (New York, 1933)

Traina, Giusto: *428 AD: An Ordinary Year at the End of the Roman Empire*, trans. Allan Cameron (Princeton, 2009)

Trimingham, J. Spencer: *Christianity Among the Arabs in Pre-Islamic Times* (London, 1979)

Van Bekkum, Wout Jac: "Jewish Messianic Expectations in the Age of Heraclius," in Reinink and Stolte

Van Bladel, Kevin: "The *Alexander Legend* in the Qur'an 18:83–102," in Reynolds

Van Ess, J.: "Abd al-Malik and the Dome of the Rock: An Analysis of Some Texts," in Raby and Johns

Wansbrough, John: *Quranic Studies: Sources and Methods of Scriptural Interpretation* (Oxford, 1977)

—— *The Sectarian Milieu: Content and Composition of Islamic Salvation History* (Oxford, 1978)

—— *Res Ipsa Loquitur: History and Mimesis* (Jerusalem, 1987)

Ward-Perkins, Brian: *The Fall of Rome and the End of Civilization* (Oxford, 2005)

Watt, William Montgomery: *Muhammad at Mecca* (Oxford, 1953)

—— *Muhammad at Medina* (Oxford, 1956)

—— *Islamic Creeds: A Selection* (Edinburgh, 1994)

Watts, E.: *City and School in Late Antique Athens and Alexandria* (Berkeley, 2006)

Weinberger, Leon J.: *Jewish Hymnography: A Literary History* (London, 1998)

Weitzman, M. P.: *The Syriac Version of the Old Testament: An Introduction* (Cambridge, 1999)

Welles, C. B.: "The Discovery of Serapis and the Foundation of Alexandria" (*Historia* 11, 1962)

Wellhausen, J.: *The Arab Kingdom and its Fall*, trans. M. G. Weir (Calcutta, 1927)

Wheeler, Brannon M.: "Imagining the Sasanian Capture of Jerusalem" (*Orientalia Christiana Periodica* 57, 1991)

—— *Moses in the Quran and Islamic Exegesis* (Chippenham, 2002)

Whitby, M.: "The Persian King at War," in Dabrowa

—— "Recruitment in Roman Armies from Justinian to Heraclius (*ca.* 565–615)," in Cameron 1995

Whittow, Mark: *The Making of Orthodox Byzantium, 600–1025* (Basingstoke, 1996)

Wickham, Chris: *The Inheritance of Rome: A History of Europe from 400 to 1000* (London, 2009)

Wiechmann, Ingrid and Grupe, Gisela: "Detection of *Yersinia Pestis* DNA in Two Early Medieval Skeletal Finds from Aschheim (Upper Bavaria, 6th Century AD)" (*American Journal of Physical Anthropology* 126, 2005)

Wiesehöfer, Josef: *Ancient Persia*, trans. Azizeh Azodi (London, 2001)

Wild, Stefan (ed.): *The Qur'an as Text* (Leiden, 1996)

Wilken, Robert L.: *The Land Called Holy: Palestine in Christian History and Thought* (New Haven, 1992)

Wilson, A. N.: *God's Funeral* (London, 1999)

Wolfram, Herwig: *History of the Goths*, trans. Thomas J. Dunlap (Berkeley, 1988)

Yahya, Farhia: "The Life of 'Abdullah Ibn al-Mubarak: The Scholar of the East and the Scholar of the West"

(http://fajr.files.wordpress.com/2010/08/biography-abdullah-ibn-al-mubarak.pdf)

Yarshater, Ehsan: "Mazdakism," in *Cambridge History of Iran*

—— "The Persian Presence in the Islamic World," in *The Persian Presence in the Islamic World*, ed. Richard G. Hovannisian and Georges Sabagh (Cambridge, 1998)

Young, William G.: *Patriarch, Shah and Caliph: A Study of the Relationships of the Church of the East with the Sassanid Empire and the Early Caliphates up to 820 AD* (Rawalpindi, 1974)

Zaehner, R. C.: *The Dawn and Twilight of Zoroastrianism* (London, 1961)

Index